D0385933

100
GREAT LIVES

This edition edited by
JOHN CANNING

A CENTURY BOOK
Published by
SOUVENIR PRESS

ISBN 0 285 62040 1

SOUVENIR PRESS EDITION: 1975
Second Impression: 1978
Reprinted 1982
Reprinted 1984

Printed photolitho in Great Britain by
J. W. ARROWSMITH LTD., BRISTOL

CONTENTS

SCIENTISTS AND INVENTORS

WRITERS AND POETS

PAGE

SOLDIERS AND STATESMEN

LIST OF ILLUSTRATIONS

FACING PAGE

ARCHIMEDES OF SYRACUSE

(*c.* 287–212 B.C.)

The ancients, although their speculations and their theories have influenced the world in many ways through the centuries, did not, for the most part, bequeath to posterity many practical contributions to science. Archimedes, the Greek mathematician who lived in Sicily in the third century B.C., *was a brilliant exception to this dictum. His work in geometry, hydrostatics and mechanics was of a pioneer nature, and the principles he laid down have been of paramount and lasting importance.*

THE heat of the Mediterranean day had gone. A well-dressed crowd thronged the busy main street of the Sicilian town. Men sat at the open cafés gossiping and sipping their wines or syrups. Sailors from the ships in the harbour swaggered along. Ox-carts rattled over the cobble-stones to the accompaniment of the drivers' shouts. A quiet gaiety pervaded the place, for war had not yet come, and peace and prosperity reigned. It was too early in the evening for any excitement or untoward happening such as might take place when the sailors' roll would become more pronounced, and the pickets would land from the ships.

But suddenly the smiling calm was disturbed. The carters' shouts were stilled. The rattle of the carts was stopped. The drinkers at the cafés placed their beakers on the tables, and rose to their feet. They gazed up the street towards the public baths where the sailors' guffaws and the ribald shouts of the commoner folk betokened something out of the ordinary. Questions leapt from mouth to mouth. Soon no explanation was needed, for to the unconcealed joy of the idlers and the horror of the few ladies who were taking the air, a man was seen running down the middle of the road, blindly, taking no account of obstacles—stark naked! He was shouting something—one word—one word which he repeated over and over again.

Foreheads were tapped. A madman, obviously, suffering from the effects of the day's sun. The man was recognized by somebody among the well-dressed idlers. His name passed from lip to lip. It was a well-known name—the name of the greatest mathematician and mechanical engineer of his time, the greatest then known to the civilized world.

Long after he had passed busy tongues speculated on the happening, but the true explanation of the great man's eccentric behaviour did not leak out till the following day. Then the story of the greatest feat of absent-mindedness known to history was told. It has been told many times since throughout the twenty-two centuries which separate us from the event, but it remains always worth telling.

The naked runner was Archimedes, Greek mathematician and pioneer in the domain of mechanics, who was born in the Sicilian town of Syracuse about two hundred and eighty-seven years before the birth of Christ. Here is the tale of why a venerable philosopher ran in the roadway without his clothes.

Hiero, King of Syracuse, had commissioned from a goldsmith of the town a crown of pure gold, but, having taken delivery of the finished article, he was suspicious. There was reason to believe that the craftsman had mixed with the gold a certain amount of other metal of inferior value. But how to find out? There was no direct evidence, and it was therefore obviously a case for the learned men of the city. And who more learned than Archimedes?

The mathematician was therefore charged with the task which would nowadays be considered a simple one, but was then a matter for serious thought. Nothing known to science could be brought forward to prove fraud or otherwise on the part of the goldsmith.

It is more than probable that the human side of the problem interested Archimedes not at all, but the scientific puzzle worried him intensely. This worry pursued him everywhere he went for days, and persisted through the routine acts of his daily round.

In the normal course of that routine, he went to the public baths. We can imagine him standing at the edge of the bath tub as he prepares to enter it, absently allowing the water to flow until he cannot help noticing it. We may watch him lowering himself into the tub, then rising from it, studying with an interest and preoccupation which seems childish the changing level of the liquid, and all the while keeping his gold problem at the back of his mind, ever ready to push its way to the front.

Suddenly he splashed out of his tub, shouting at the top of his voice: "*Eureka! Eureka!*" (I have found it! I have found it!). Without waiting, or even thinking of such a detail as clothes, he tore out of the building and rushed through the streets of Syracuse, still shouting: "*Eureka! Eureka!*"

Arrived at his house, the mathematician put his newly found discovery to a practical test, and found indeed that a body plunged in a fluid loses an amount of its weight which is equal to the weight of the fluid displaced by it. With this as a starting point—as it was to prove the starting point of many subsequent discoveries of importance—Archimedes was able to tell his king how much pure gold was in his crown.

Thus was the first fundamental law in hydrostatics enunciated more than two thousand years ago.

Archimedes was by this time well known to his fellow townsmen, and his sometimes strange appearance and unusual actions probably met with indulgent smiles. He came from a good family; his father Pheidias was an astronomer; he was on intimate terms with, and—according to some—was even a kinsman of King Hiero himself.

In his youth and early manhood he had studied at Alexandria, where, no doubt, seeing the pressing need for the irrigation of the Egyptian soil, he invented the Archimedean screw, one of the fundamental discoveries in mechanics, an inspiration of genius. It is also said that this contrivance for raising water—which is the basis of many types of grain conveyors today—was invented for King Hiero in order to empty of water the hold of a large ship built by him. The principle of the Archimedean screw is well known. In its simplest form it is a flexible tube bent spirally round a solid cylinder the ends of which are furnished with pivots so as to admit of the whole turning round on its axis. When the cylinder is inclined towards the horizon with its lower end in the water to be raised, the revolution of the contrivance lifts the water gradually from one turn of the spiral to the next.

This was only one of many machines invented by Archimedes. During his late manhood, the entire Mediterranean seaboard was in an almost continual state of war. Carthaginians, Romans, Greeks, were fighting one another; towns were being besieged and sacked; armies deserted from one side to another in a wholesale manner. King Hiero, though the greater part of his reign had been peaceful, was farseeing enough to take precautions. He prevailed upon the famous mathematician, therefore, to construct weapons of offence and defence which were far more potent and ingenious than any as yet known.

It may seem strange that an absent-minded mathematician with his head in the clouds should have been charged with such a practical task, but it was Archimedes himself who had said to the king one day: "Give me a lever and a place on which to rest it, and I will move the world." Only a foolish king in the circumstances would refuse to give the opportunity to put such an assertion to at least a partial test, and accordingly we have an account by Plutarch of a demonstration of the scholar's ability to move unwieldy objects by new and apparently simple means. A galley was beached, loaded up with cargo, and fully manned with a complete crew. Then Archimedes, standing at a distance, "without any pains, only moving with his hand the end of the machine which consisted of a variety of ropes and pulleys, . . . drew her to him in as smooth and gentle a manner as if she had been under sail."

There is sufficient testimony to the fact that when the Roman general, Marcellus, laid siege to Syracuse, he found the garrison ready for him. On the seaward side of the town Archimedes had seen to the erection of enormous machines with the necessary tackle which shot out over the walls huge beams of sufficient power to sink any galley which they might hit. In addition, enemy ships found themselves suddenly hoisted up by the bows by iron grapples or hooks "like the beaks of cranes," and then, being set on their stern ends, plunged to the bottom of the sea. Other ships were pulled to the shore by ropes, and dashed on the rocks, and in some cases ships were lifted high in the air above the sea, and hung there swinging to and fro.

Marcellus, it can be well imagined, called many a conference of his engineer officers in order to devise means of countering these machines. Many contrivances were tried, culminating in a machine mounted on eight galleys, which, owing to its resemblance to a giant musical instrument, the soldiery called a "Sambuca." The Romans ran this up towards the walls of Syracuse, but before it had moved far, Archimedes used one of his apparently simple engines and disabled the formidable floating attacker as easily as if it had been an ordinary galley.

It was during this siege that Archimedes is sometimes credited with having set the Roman fleet on fire by means of an arrangement of mirrors and lenses, but as neither Plutarch, nor Livy, nor Polybius mention the incident, it can probably be regarded as legendary. Things, however, came to such a pass that the Romans became terrified of the Greek mathematician. They had only to see a stick or a rope projected out over a wall for them to cry out that Archimedes was levelling some terrible machine at them, and they promptly took to their heels. Finally, Marcellus realized with natural chagrin, mixed with no little admiration for his enemy, that his engineers could not cope with the Syracusan, and decided to turn the siege into a blockade.

"Why fight with this mathematical Briareus?" he said, "who sits on the beach and baffles all our naval assaults as if they were a huge joke!"

Plutarch says of Archimedes at this period of his life: "In truth all the rest of the Syracusans were no more than the body in the batteries of Archimedes, while he himself was the soul which animated them. All other weapons lay idle and useless; his were the only offensive and defensive arms of the city."

A curious sidelight is thrown on the mentality of the inventor of all those deadly weapons by the fact that although his reputation had spread far and wide through his organization of the defence of Syracuse, he actually despised the ingenious mechanical contrivances which had made him famous. He carried this contempt so far that with one exception he refused to commit any record of them to writing. The solitary exception was far from being a warlike weapon, for it was a sphere which he made to imitate the motions of the sun, the moon, and the five planets in the heavens. Even the record of this is now lost, but Cicero more than a century later saw the apparatus and describes it.

The refusal of Archimedes to attach any value to his mechanical inventions does not seem to be due to any antimilitaristic or pacifist tendencies, but rather to the fact that he regarded them as beneath the dignity of pure science. Perhaps Plutarch's explanation is another way of expressing the same thing: "He considered all attention to *mechanics* and every art that ministers to common uses as mean and sordid, and placed his whole delight in those intellectual speculations which, without any relation to the necessities of life, have an intrinsic excellence arising from truth and demonstration alone."

That his work on these inventions was no more than a sideline dictated by the public needs of the moment, is evident from the list of those learned works from his hand of which existence is known to us. Who is the modern wrangler who would not be proud to put his name to a tithe of the following highly technical and abstruse essays, to which modern science owes so much:

1.—*On the Sphere and Cylinder*. (A work in two books dealing with the dimensions of spheres, cones, solid rhombi, and cylinders, all demonstrated in the purely geometrical method.)

2.—*The Measurement of the Circle.* (One book of three propositions.)

3.—*On Conoids and Spheroids.* (One book containing thirty-two propositions.)

4.—*On Spirals.* (One book containing twenty-eight propositions.)

5.—*On the Equilibrium of Planes or Centres of Gravity of Planes.* (Two books.) This is the foundation of theoretical mechanics, Aristotle's previous contributions being relatively vague and hardly scientific. In the first book there are fifteen propositions with seven postulates. The second book has ten propositions. Demonstrations are given, *practically identical with those employed at the present day,* of the centres of gravity of (1) any two weights; (2) any parallelogram; (3) any triangle; (4) any trapezium.

6.—*The Quadrature of the Parabola.* This is a book of twenty-four propositions containing two demonstrations that the area of any segment of a parabola (i.e., a curve or conic section formed by cutting a cone with a plane parallel to its slope) is four-fifths of the area of the triangle which has the same base and equal height as the segment.

7.—*On Floating Bodies.* A treatise in two books.

8.—*The Psammites.* (Sand Reckoner.) A work dealing with the nomenclature of numbers.

9.—*The Method.* An important treatise, discovered in 1906, in which Archimedes explains the mechanical methods whereby he arrived at many of his conclusions.

10.—A collection of *Lemmas* or propositions in plane geometry. This was probably not written by Archimedes in the form in which it survives, for it is a Latin version of an Arabic manuscript.

In addition to these, we know from quotations from contemporaries and later writers that Archimedes wrote a number of other books, now lost. The subjects of these were, naturally, mainly geometrical, but some treated of such matters as balances and levers, one dealt with astronomy, while yet another was an optical work, for a later author has quoted from it a remark on refraction.

It is difficult to estimate justly and accurately the merits of Archimedes as a mathematician without a more complete knowledge than is available to us of the state of science as he found it. Certain it is, however, that he made discoveries on which modern mathematicians have based their methods of measuring solids and curved surfaces. He is, in fact, the only one of the ancients who has contributed anything of real value to the theory of mechanics and hydrostatics. This long-dead thinker did, indeed, play no small part in the making of our present-day mechanical civilization.

Like many another great man, his reputation with the populace was based on work by which he himself set no great store, but the cultured men of his own time and of later ages have been unanimous in considering him a pioneer and a genius. Their admiration for him was increased rather than diminished by the fact that by his works he made difficult things so easy that men wondered why they had not thought of those things themselves. "In fact," says Plutarch, "it is almost impossible for a man of himself to find out the demonstration of his propositions, but as soon as he has learned it from him [Archimedes] he will think that he could have done it without assistance—such a ready and easy way does he lead us to what he wants to prove."

Of Archimedes the man little is known. That he was sometimes strange in his manner is beyond doubt, and it is equally certain that he was often so absorbed by his scientific problems that he neglected his person and had even to be taken to the baths by force. It is recorded that during his ablutions he drew geometrical designs in the soapsuds on his body.

He was, as has been seen in the case of his discovery of the principle which bears his name, childishly elated by each new discovery, but he was at the same time modest and unassuming. Before publishing his work to the world, he invariably submitted it to his friend, Conon of Samos, whom he had probably met as a student at Alexandria, and whom he admired greatly as a mathematician.

Archimedes, the inspired engineer, had kept the Roman Marcellus at bay for nearly three years. In the end, it was weapons of treachery that succeeded where engines had failed, and Syracuse fell in 212 B.C. Its fall involved the death of its chief defender, but yet it was not the brilliant inventor of arms of war who was killed on that day; it was the absent-minded dreamer who on another occasion, years before, had run naked through the streets of his native town in the joy of a new discovery.

We do not know what problem it was which so engrossed him on the fatal day, for even the accounts of his death do not agree in details. We do know, however, that the victorious Marcellus had for his great opponent an unbounded admiration, and that he wished to meet him—not to crow over him, but to express the esteem in which he held him.

It is not difficult to imagine the final scenes. Marcellus, in the midst of his other preoccupations, must have wondered why the great Archimedes was not among those who submitted to him. It could not have occurred to him that the man who had immobilized the Roman army and navy for three years was even then seated on the floor of his house, entirely forgetful of events outside, even unaware that the city had been captured. We can see that Roman as he gives an order to a member of his staff:

"See if you can find Archimedes for me! I should like to see him!"

We can hear the repetition of that order as it is passed on to subordinates in true military fashion:

"Find Archimedes! The general wants him!"

A soldier finds him. He sees an old gentleman seated on the floor, drawing funny lines on the tiles.

"Come on, you!" he orders. "The general wants you!"

The elderly gentleman pays no attention—has not even heard. The order is repeated.

"Eh? What? Oh, go away. I'm busy!" That is all the soldier gets for an answer.

And so he takes a pace forward. He has his orders, and he will execute them. Archimedes is to be taken to the general. Is a silly game of noughts and crosses to interfere with military duty? Not so! He catches hold of the old man's arm. Archimedes shakes him off, mildly but firmly.

"I really cannot go until I have finished my problem."

This is insolence. There is only one way to deal with it. An angry flush mounts to the Roman's cheek. A last warning. It is unheeded. A thrust of the short, broad sword, and Archimedes falls on top of his unfinished problem—dead through absent-mindedness. And the life-blood that fed one of the world's most marvellous brains poured itself away.

Marcellus, whose orders had been thus tragically interpreted, was grieved to the heart at the death of Archimedes. "He turned his face away from the murderer as from an impious and execrable person," and seeking out the great man's relations, he bestowed special favours on them. The sage was given an honourable burial, and at his own request, expressed long before, his tomb was marked by the figure of a sphere inscribed in a cylinder, as he regarded his discovery of the relation between the volumes of a sphere and its circumscribing cylinder as his most valuable achievement.

After the death of Archimedes, his reputation was kept alive in the memory of men of science and letters, but his native city of Syracuse fell upon evil days, and it was more than a hundred and thirty years later—in 75 B.C.—that Cicero, then Quaestor in Sicily, found the tomb of Archimedes near the Agrigentine gate, overgrown with briars and thorns.

"Thus," the great Roman orator says, sadly, "would this most famous and once most learned city of Greece have remained a stranger to the tomb of one of its most ingenious citizens, had it not been discovered by a man of Arpinum."

WILLIAM CAXTON

(*c.* 1422–1491)

Not by virtue of the craft he fathered, nor for the practical success of the enterprise he boldly began, is the name of William Caxton honoured by his countrymen. He was a great and successful merchant who carried and upheld the good name of England abroad, and he was the man who brought the new art of printing from the Continent into England in the fifteenth century. But he was also a patriotic, pious and cultured Englishman, and he printed by the same ideals as those by which he lived. He was not only England's first printer, but one of her first educators, a moulder of taste, and an establisher of literary tradition.

WITH a national genius for giving people misleading tags, the British have dubbed Caxton "the first English printer," and let him go at that. The Englishman who loved his native language, and did more for it than all its patrons and hundreds of its writers, has been lost in the printer. Caxton was no mere introducer of a new trade; he was a pioneer and a creator, a man of letters and an educationist who strove all his life for the benefit of his country's culture as expressed in its literature. England owes Caxton a debt of gratitude as her first printer, it is true, but she owes him a thousand times more for the spirit in which he printed. As a craftsman he was not exceptionally good, being far inferior to some of the Continental printers. "But . . . Caxton had a noble conception of his duty as a printer," writes Mr. H. R. Plomer. "To him the mere mechanical process was a secondary consideration. His aim was to perpetuate such books, for preference those of English authors, or translators, who had the highest moral or literary value, and so long as the paper was strong and durable, the type clear and readable, and the press-work correct, nothing else mattered. The road he set out to make was none other than to educate and brighten the lives of his countrymen by circulating hundreds of copies of the best literature at a low price where only half a dozen had been obtainable before, and those only by the rich."

William Caxton was born in Kent about the year 1422. The exact date of his birth is unknown, nor is there any record of his early years and education, until on June 24, 1438, his name was entered in the books of the Mercers' Company as an apprentice to Robert Large, mercer, of London.

That fact gives us two others: that he was born about 1422-4, for he would hardly be less than fourteen nor more than sixteen when he was apprenticed; and that his family was influential, for the Mercers' Company was one of the most exclusive and powerful of the London Guilds, and Robert Large was an important member of it; he was elected Lord Mayor of London the year after Caxton had joined him.

For three years, Caxton lived with Large in Old Jewry, working and playing and leading the normal life of an apprentice. Then, on April 24, 1441, Robert Large died, leaving Caxton twenty marks* in his will.

Presumably Caxton was transferred to a new master, and certainly in the same year he left England for the Continent. In 1471 he wrote that he had "continued by the space of xxx yere, for the most parte in the contres of Braband, Flandres, Holand, and Zeland."

We have few glimpses of the man during his rise to wealth and consequence. We know that he was pious and industrious, and he probably applied to his trade the enthusiasm he later brought to publishing. Within nine years he was a man of substance and credit, for in 1450 it is recorded that he and another mercer were sued for a sum of £110, equal to about £3,000 today.

Three years later Caxton visited London, and was admitted to the Livery of the Mercers' Company. He returned to Bruges and worked steadily, becoming eminent among the merchants of that town.

In 1462 Edward IV renewed the charter of the Company of Merchant Adventurers, a powerful guild that looked after the interests of English merchants trading abroad, and he gave permission to the Company to appoint a Governor at Bruges. A year later Caxton was fulfilling the duties of the governor, and soon he was officially appointed Governor of the English Nation at Bruges. His duties consisted of adjudicating in disputes among the merchants, supervising the importation and exportation of goods, and protecting the commercial interests of England.

In 1464 he took part in negotiations with Philip the Good, Duke of Burgundy, for the renewal of the trade treaty between England and Flanders. But the treaty was allowed to lapse and the English merchants in Bruges sought to overcome the difficulties by

* Worth about £300 in present-day money.

smuggling. Caxton received a letter from the Earl of Warwick telling him to stop this illegal trading. So it is evident that Caxton was kept busy with public business as well as his own trading. Nevertheless he found time to travel, and more important, to read.

The hostility between Flanders and England ended with the death of Philip in 1467. A year later his successor, Charles the Bold, married Edward IV's sister Margaret at Bruges, and in 1469 Caxton resigned his position as Governor of the English Nation and entered the service of the new Duchess of Burgundy.

A little while before this important change Caxton read a French manuscript by Raoul le Fevre, *Le Recueil des Histoires de Troyes*. The book gave him "great pleasyr and delyte," and he had the immediate inspiration to translate it into English. He began straightway, but after working hard through a score or so of pages became weary and disheartened and put the unfinished work away.

But his new patroness, the Duchess, became an inspiration and a patron when she heard what he had been doing. She asked to see the work that had been done.

> " and whan she had seen hem, anone she fonde defaute in myn Englisshe whiche she comanded me to amende and more ouer commanded me straytly to continue and make an ende of the resydue than not translated, whos dredfull comandement y durst in no wyse disobey becase y am a servant unto her sayd grace and resseive of her yerly fee and other many goode and grete benefets, and also hope many moo to resseyve of her highnes, but forthwith wente and labouryde in the said translacion aftyr my simple and poor conning also nygh as I can followyng myn auctour. . . ."

The translation which he had begun at Bruges he now continued at Ghent, and eventually finished at Cologne. Then at Cologne, in 1472, he learned the new and wonderful craft of printing. Two years later he set up a press at Bruges with Colard Mansion, who was a calligrapher and illuminator of manuscripts, and from that press issued the first book ever printed in the English language—his own translation of the *Recuyel of the Historyes of Troy*. In the Prologue he wrote:

> "And for as moche as in the wrytyng of the same my penne is worn, myn hand wery and not stedfast, myn eyen dimed with ouermoche lokyng on the whit paper, and my corage not so prone and redy to laboure as hit hath been, and that age creepeth on me dayly and feebleth all the bodye, and also because I have

promysed to dyuerce gentilmen and to my frendes to addresse to hem as hastely as I myght this sayd book. Therefore I have practysed and lerned at my grete charge and dispense to ordeyne this said book in printe after the maner and forme as ye may here see."

Caxton worked with Colard Mansion for two years. In 1476 they printed *The Game and Play of Chess Moralised* which Caxton himself translated from the French. Thus the first two books printed in the English language were not the fruits of chance, but were deliberately chosen by their scholarly printer as being worthy to entertain and elevate his fellow countrymen. Caxton realized that printing had opened the golden gates of literature to all, and he was determined to produce work worthy of that wonderful opportunity.

Before the end of that year Caxton had left Mansion and the press at Bruges, and had set up at the sign of the Red Pale at the Almonry in the precincts of the Abbey of Westminster in London.

He began work at once, printing "small storyes and pamflets" and preparing to produce larger works. The first book which bears a date was the *Dictes or Sayengis of the Philosophres*, published at Westminster in 1477. The translation was made from the French by Earl Rivers, who asked Caxton to revise it before printing.

Earl Rivers became one of Caxton's constant patrons; among the most notable of these were Margaret, Countess of Richmond, Henry Bourchier, Earl of Essex, and William Fitzallan, Earl of Arundel, while many rich city merchants were his friends and helpers. Above all, Edward IV and his successors, Richard III and Henry VII, gave Caxton patronage and encouragement.

On June 15, 1479, Edward IV gave Caxton £20 for "certain causes and matters performed." To Richard III was dedicated the *Order of Chivalry*, while Henry VII himself commanded Caxton to translate and print *The Faytte of Arms*.

Soon after his arrival at Westminster, Caxton gave another proof of his desire to give Englishmen the best of English literature. By 1478 he had printed for the first time Chaucer's *Canterbury Tales* —a heavy task for his small press. He was in such a hurry to get this great work out that he chose a bad manuscript and issued a corrupt text. When he discovered this he was greatly distressed, but some years later he procured a better manuscript from which he printed a second edition.

And now books flowed fast from the tiny printing press.

Caxton's energy was amazing. He laboured at editing and translating, probably leaving most of the presswork to his foreman, Wynkyn de Worde, who carried on the shop after Caxton's death.

While he worked at the books he loved and at those works which he thought were fittest to publish for the general good, he also turned out Church service books and psalters. In connection with one Church service guide, Caxton published the first broadside and book advertisement to appear in England:

> "If it plese ony man spiritual or temporal to bye ony pyes of two and three comemoracions of salisburie use, enprynted after the forme of this present lettre, whiche ben wel and truly correct, late hym come to westmonester in to the almonetrye at the reed pale and he shal have them good chepe."

Caxton's success in England soon attracted others to the trade. Oxford had a printer by 1478, and a year later another appeared in St. Albans. Then came a close rival to Caxton in John Lettou, a Lithuanian, who set up a press in the City of London.

Lettou's work was technically superior to Caxton's, and the competition led the Englishman to make improvements in his types and formats. In 1479 he began to use a new type, the Black Letter, and also the type known as Caxton No. 4. He also resorted to the use of signatures and spaced his lines out to even lengths. In 1481 he published the *Mirrour of the World,* the first of his books to be illustrated. The illustrations were woodcuts and were of poor quality. None of Caxton's books were printed with title pages; some had no punctuation at all; some were only punctuated with the long comma, which consisted of a straight thin line between the words; some were punctuated with full stops and colons only; and he never numbered the pages.

But Caxton was always more interested in the matter than in the appearance of his productions. Piety, moral value, and literary worth were the chief criteria he employed in choosing books to print; but he did not neglect any work which would expound knowledge of any kind, nor did he despise good stories. Some idea of his tireless energy may be gathered from the fact that his tiny press at Westminster turned out over eighty books, of which twenty-one were translations made by Caxton himself! That his judgment and taste were popular is proved by the fact that many of the volumes he issued ran into two and three editions.

Besides those books already mentioned, these are the most interesting of Caxton's publications: *The Chronicles of England,* which was a work called the *Chronicles of Brute* brought up to within a few years of the date of publication (1480) by Caxton; this came to be known as *Caxton's Chronicle*. Cicero's essays on *Old Age and Friendship* in English together with the *Declamation of Noblesse* in one volume (1481). His own translation of *Reynard the Fox*, a clever German satire. Higden's *Polychronicon*, brought up to the accession of Edward IV by Caxton (1482). The *Golden Legend*, one of the most important and influential books printed in England at that time. Chaucer's *Hous of Fame* and *Troilus and Cressida*, *Æsop's Fables*, and Malory's *Morte d'Arthur*. He also published the works of the English poets, Gower and Lydgate. That short list is evidence enough of Caxton's taste and care for literature.

In 1491 Caxton was engaged on translating the *Lives of the Fathers*. At last he reached the end of the long task and concluded his version with these words:

> "God thenne give us his grace to find in us such an house that it may please him to lodge therein to the end that in this world he keep us from adversity spiritual. And in the end of our days he bring us with him in to his Royame of heaven for to be partyners of the glorye eternal, the which grant to us the holy trynyte. Amen."

With that he laid down his pen—and his life; for Wynkyn de Worde tells us that his translation of the *Vitae Patrum* was finished by Caxton "at the last daye of his lyff."

He died in harness, with a prayer on his pen. And all who love literature should pray for William Caxton, not for the mechanical invention he brought to England, but for the ideals which he set steadfastly before him.

GALILEO GALILEI

(1564–1642)

Galileo Galilei was one of the greatest of scientific pioneers. His name lives as that of an astronomer who perfected the refracting telescope and showed men the new worlds of the heavens. But his support of the Copernican theory that the earth moved round the sun brought him under the ban of the Church and darkened his life and achievement. His achievements in the studies of mechanics and dynamics were even greater than his astronomical discoveries: he had a happy method of applying mathematical analysis to physical problems and in his work on the laws of motion he paved the way for Newton.

On the morning of June 22 in the year 1633, an old man stood in a room in the Convent of Minerva at Rome, and faced the Inquisition. Clothed in the sackcloth of a penitent, his face pale, his limbs trembling, he gazed timidly upon the grave faces of the assembled cardinals, as if in an attempt to read there the nature of his sentence. At length, amid an oppressive silence, a figure rose from the ranks of the examiners, and in flat, colourless tones, began to speak:—

". . . But from all these consequences he is to be held absolved, provided that, with a sincere heart and a faith unfeigned, he abjures and curses the heresies he has cherished, as well as every other heresy against the Church . . . and that he shall be condemned to the prison of the Inquisition during its pleasure . . ."

The droning voice ceased. The venerable penitent fell on his knees before the assembly, and invoked the Divine aid in vowing never again to teach his heretical doctrines. These he enumerated, but the principal one which his trial had emphasized was the droll idea that the earth revolved round the sun. Then, with shaking hand, he signed a paper, setting out his wrong-doing. The assembled cardinals rose, and the penitent was taken from the room. As he walked away he is said to have muttered defiantly, "*Eppur si muove*" ("But it moves, just the same!"). The man was Galileo, a man of science, an astronomer, one of the world's greatest leaders in scientific discovery.

Galileo was born at Pisa in Italy, in February, 1564, of a nobly-born father who himself was a philosopher of some attainments. The first picture we have of him is as a boy spending his leisure hours in the construction of little instruments and pieces of machinery, which greatly amused and stimulated his schoolfellows and himself. His father had already perceived in him the signs of latent genius and, though by no means able to afford it, enrolled him as a student of arts at the University of Pisa. This was in 1581.

The young student was intended to devote his time to medicine, but a study of the works of Euclid turned his mind into other channels. Enraptured with the new truths which burst upon him, Galileo renounced medicine and, from the elementary works of geometry, passed on to the writings of Archimedes. His brain assimilated quickly and his observation was quick also. He investigated the reigning philosophy, the philosophy of Aristotle, and, with the enthusiasm and exultation of a youth of eighteen, he regarded its errors and absurdities, even then apparent to him, as his lawful, intellectual prey. He attacked the followers of Aristotle with a zeal that bordered on indiscretion, and when he found that they would not see his reasonings against their axioms, he appealed to direct experiment.

In 1583 he discovered, by watching the oscillation of a lamp suspended from the cathedral roof, the value of the pendulum for the exact measurement of time, for he noted that each swing was equal in time whatever its scope. From this time, too, dated his work on the hydrostatic balance. But his chief interest was in mathematics, and by 1588 he had become professor in that subject in the university. It was then that he performed his famous experiment at the leaning tower of Pisa.

One of the axioms in the Aristotelian doctrine of mechanics was that the heavier of two falling bodies would reach the ground before the other, and that their velocities would be in proportion to their weights. The fiery young philosopher derided this. He maintained that all bodies will fall through the same height in the same time if they are not unequally retarded by the resistance of the atmosphere. He gathered together some of the leading followers of Aristotelian philosophy, and showed them what he meant. With scorn written on his face, he ascended to the top of the leaning tower of Pisa, and let fall two objects of unequal weight. His assembled enemies saw with their own eyes the two bodies strike the ground at the same time. Galileo, triumphant, descended and, with unutterable disgust, he heard the verdict. The Aristotelians coolly ascribed the effect to some unknown cause, and remained unshaken in their allegiance. Yet he had discovered an important principle in physics. They forced him to resign and retire to Florence, but in 1592 Galileo was appointed to a professorship at Padua. He was becoming famous all over Europe. Then, in 1604, he turned his attention to astronomy. A new star had appeared, which was exciting the attention of the astronomers. Some said it was a meteor, while others were frankly puzzled.

To crowded lecture rooms Galileo proved that it was not a meteor and that, like the fixed stars, it was situated far beyond the bounds of the known solar system. The subject attracted thousands to hear him. The benches were packed, and people jammed against each other, almost unable to breathe, in their determination to hear him. High and low were there, ruffles and swords, jerkins and cudgels, motionless, listening with bated breath. And still newcomers arrived and fought to force their way in, so that Galileo was obliged to adjourn to the open air.

It is a striking picture. The sun beats down on the parched ground, and on the great crowd of people. On a mound the great philosopher stands. He is about the middle height, with a burly but well-proportioned frame. His hair is almost red, his eyes penetrating. He is decidedly not handsome, for his nose is broad and almost flat, but his face is relieved by the animated expressions that flash over it as he talks. His audience hang on his words, and at the end he has the boldness to reproach them for showing so much enthusiasm over a transient phenomenon while they forget the great wonders which are continually presented to their view.

Galileo was now publishing his theories. He wrote works on mechanics, on motion, on the system of the universe, on sound and speech, on light and colour. But it was in 1609 that the great sensation came.

In that year Galileo heard of a curious optical instrument which possessed the singular property of causing distant objects to appear nearer. He experimented, destroyed what he had made, and tried again. At last he hit upon an idea. He procured two glasses, one convex on one side and the other concave. These he placed one at each end of a leaden tube. He looked through it . . . Eureka! the thing was done. He had made a telescope and opened a new and marvellous window through which to read the great book of the heavens.

He carried the new instrument to Venice in triumph, and presented it to the Senate, who rewarded him by conferring on him for life the professorship at Padua, and raising his salary from five hundred and twenty to one thousand florins.

For months the telescope was a tremendous sensation. The excitement of the citizens amounted to frenzy. Hundreds flocked to his house to see the magic instrument. One day a friend of his ascended the tower of St. Mark's, where he could use the new device without interference. But he was recognized by a crowd in the street, and such was the excitement that they took possession of the wonderful little tube and detained the impatient experimenter for more than six hours, until all had seen its effects.

And now, with an improved telescope, Galileo began to make the discoveries which were to astonish the world, change the science of astronomy, and bring all the troubles of his life in their train.

He found, with " incredible delight," the ranges of mountains and deep hollows on the surface of the moon. In the dark silence of his little room at the top of the house, with the vastness of the heavens to explore, he discovered the number of the stars in the Pleiades, picked out the four secondary planets revolving round Jupiter, and received the first glimmerings of the position of Saturn and its rings.

His discoveries, which he published immediately, raised a storm of protest, and Galileo found himself surrounded with enemies. Some struck at him by professing to have made the discoveries before him, others hastened to cry that his doctrines were heretical.

In 1611 Galileo went to Rome, where he was received with honour. Enmity had not yet accomplished its aim, for princes, cardinals and prelates hastened to meet the intellectual giant of the age. He had with him his best telescope, and he showed these distinguished people his latest discovery, the spots on the sun's surface.

Still, the ardour of the man's mind, his clear perception and fanatical love of the truth exasperated his enemies; and Galileo did nothing to soften them. On the contrary, his character was such that, with almost reckless boldness, he sought to make proselytes of his enemies. It was a common sight to see him arguing and contesting—almost in the manner of the Renaissance disputes—with twenty or more people, most of them secretly hating him all the while. He let them talk, listened to them gravely, heard what they had to say one by one, and then, in a few simple words, he struck back. His enemies could do nothing but look at each other in confusion, or bite their lips, so foolish did he make them and their ideas appear.

But now the Church was beginning to disapprove of Galileo's theories. A Dominican, Caccini, rose in his pulpit in his high, vaulted, Gothic church, and reviled and ridiculed the astronomer and his followers in such terms that his hearers first listened in amazement, and then began to titter. This attack was not approved by the Church, and the General of the Dominicans made a personal apology to Galileo. But Galileo refused to be warned by the signs of the coming storm. He went on.

The whole conflict between Galileo and the Church arose out of Galileo's defence and teaching of the heliocentric theory, which sets out that the sun is fixed and the earth in motion. The accepted theory in those days was that of Ptolemy, who taught a fixed earth with everything revolving round it in cycles and epicycles. The heliocentric theory had been proposed before by Copernicus, but without much proof, and it was not until Galileo saw the satellites of Jupiter and the movements of sunspots across the face of the sun that he was able to defend the theory.

He raised a storm of protest. The defenders of the Ptolemaic system declared that his theory was contrary to Holy Scripture, and quoted, among other texts, Joshua x, 13, "And the sun stood still . . . in the midst of heaven," and Ecclesiastes i, 4, ". . . the earth abideth for ever. The sun also ariseth, and the sun goeth down, and hasteth to his place where he arose."

The discussion became more and more acute until, in 1615, Pope Paul V conveyed a semi-official warning to Galileo. In the following year the theologians of the Holy Office decided that the theory that the sun is immovable in the centre of the world and that the earth has a diurnal motion about it, was heretical, and Galileo was admonished not to "hold, teach or defend" the forbidden theory.

For a long time the astronomer made his observations and worked in silence. And then in 1632 he published his great work, *The Dialogue of the Two Principal Systems of the World*. It made a tremendous stir, for it combined an animated and elegant style with lucid and strong scientific exposition. But it was clearly written in defiance of the ban of 1616 and, moreover, it was believed to contain a caricature of Pope Urban VIII.

The sequel was inevitable. Galileo was summoned to appear before the Inquisition in Rome. In answer to the charges, he declared flatly that he had never "maintained or defended that the earth moves and that the sun is stationary, but had demonstrated the opposite, and shown that the arguments of Copernicus are weak and inconclusive." Three days after this evasive plea, at a second examination, Galileo changed round, and, under advice, acknowledged that he had defended the heliocentric theory, and admitted his fault. He was found guilty and sentenced to imprisonment; but instead, he was allowed to depart to Siena and eventually to retire, in strict seclusion, to his own villa at Arcetri.

There is no doubt that, in spite of its obscurantist attitude, the Inquisition treated Galileo with unusual leniency. In fact, the enlightened Cardinal Bellarmine, who took a prominent part in the whole affair, wrote afterwards: "I say that if real proof be found that the sun is fixed and does not revolve around the earth, but the earth around the sun, then it will be necessary, very carefully, to proceed to the explanation of the passages of Scripture which appear to the contrary, and we should rather say that we have misunderstood these than to pronounce that to be false which is demonstrated."

From the end of the trial onwards the life of Galileo was a life of tragedy. He knew that he was free, but soon after he had joined his family under his own roof, his favourite daughter was seized with a sudden illness and died. This blow worked deeply upon the philosopher, whose frame had been undermined for years by a malady contracted while young.

Yet he went on working. In 1636 he wrote his *Dialogue on the New Science,* which contained accounts of his early experiments and mature meditations on mechanics. In 1637 he made his last astronomical discovery, of those curious appearances in the lunar circle known as the moon's librations; a few months later he was blind.

A sad, shrunken figure, nearly overwhelmed with the calamity but courageous still, he laboriously wrote a letter to a friend: "I am totally and irreparably blind. These heavens, this earth, this universe, which by wonderful observation I had enlarged a thousand times beyond the belief of past ages, are henceforth dwindled into the narrow space which I myself occupy. So it pleases God; it shall, therefore, please me also."

His friend, a priest, Father Castelli, wrote soon after: "The noblest eye which nature ever made is darkened . . ."

And still he went on. He applied himself to his scientific correspondence. He thought out the means of using the pendulum to regulate clockwork, a scheme which Huygens brought to fruition fifteen years afterwards.

He was dictating his latest theories on impact of matter to his pupils, Viviani and Torricelli, when the end came. He had become a shell of a man, yet he was still grappling with the mysteries of the universe when he contracted a slow fever and died on January 8, 1642, in his seventy-eighth year.

Galileo's chief discoveries were such as to revolutionize the study of the sciences. His early essay on the hydrostatical balance, in which he described the construction of the instrument, and the method by which Archimedes detected the fraud committed by the jeweller in the composition of Hiero's crown, led men to experiment for themselves. It turned them towards the purely practical. His work on the centre of gravity in solid bodies and his experiments in magnetism, were new, and were received with astonishment.

He revolutionized the world of thought with his discovery of the mountains in the moon, of the stars in the Pleiades, of Jupiter's satellites, the crescent of Venus, the ring of Saturn and the spots on the sun. All these, like his theory of floating bodies, involved him in controversy over and over again. Today we regard him as a pioneer, as a man who gave the lead for enthusiasm and research in astronomy.

WILLIAM HARVEY

(1578–1657)

There are some scientific phenomena with which we are so familiar, that it seems impossible that their truth could ever be doubted. It appears incredible that only a few centuries divide us from the discoveries of the principle of gravity, of solar motion . . . and of the circulation of the blood. When William Harvey put forward his theory, or rather his observation, of the circulation of blood in the body, he shattered the medical beliefs of a thousand years and opened a new era of medical science.

OF how many books can it be said that their publication directly affected the personal well-being of every person alive, or yet to be born?

Many books have been written which have altered the outlook of millions, changed social institutions, and even deflected the course of history, but of few can it be said that their contents concerned the health not only of contemporaries but of all posterity, that they expounded a discovery vital to the whole of mankind. Yet such a claim may justly be made for a book published three centuries ago. At that time only a few read it and not all believed it. Today still fewer people read it, but none would dream of doubting it.

The book was William Harvey's work on blood circulation, published in 1628 in Latin under the title of *Exercitatio Anatomica de Motu Cordis et Sanguinis in Animalibus*. It overthrew the accepted doctrine of fifteen centuries. It proved that what men had thought about the movement of the blood in the human body was utterly wrong.

William Harvey, the man who discovered the circulation of the blood—a discovery that has been described as "an almost faultless solution of the most fundamental and most difficult problem in physiology"—was born at Folkestone on April 1, 1578.

His father was a prosperous merchant and William was sent to King's School, Canterbury, and afterwards to Cambridge. Whilst his work at the university was good, it was not sufficiently distinguished for the most prophetic of professors to suggest that the hard-working undergraduate was likely to gain immortality as the elucidator of one of the most important truths known to medical science.

In 1597 Harvey travelled to Padua, at that time the most famous school of medicine in the world. There, in the candle-lit lecture hall of the university, he listened to Fabricius of Aquapendente, the great anatomist. From him he learned something that was later to prove the starting point of his great discovery. Fabricius had found that the veins in the human body had valves, and while he imparted this information to his students he was altogether unable to offer a suggestion as to the function of the organs. It remained for Harvey to realize that the valves prevented the flow of blood from any direction except towards the heart.

After becoming a Doctor of Medicine at Padua he returned to Cambridge, where he took a similar degree, after which he set up in practice in London. It was about this time that he fell in love with Elizabeth Browne, the daughter of Launcelot Browne, who had been physician to Queen Elizabeth. The marriage proved of great use in helping him to gain initial entry to Court.

In 1609 Harvey was appointed physician at St. Bartholomew's Hospital. His task was to "attend the hospital one day in the weeke at the leaste through the year, or oftener as neede shall requye." He was to "give the poore full benefit of his knowledge," and to prescribe only medicines that would do the poor good "without regard to the profit of the apothecary." This last was a reference to the practice of the apothecaries, the chemists of the day, who used to buy up doctor's prescriptions to sell to their customers. Harvey apparently was not regarded as much of a doctor by the apothecaries, for none of them would give more than threepence for his prescriptions.

At the hospital Harvey would sit at a table, his patients seated before him on a settle. The physicians did not attend to patients in the wards, that being the surgeons' duty. Harvey would go into the wards only to treat a patient who was unable to walk to him.

His experience at the hospital was of the utmost value. He was able to collect a mass of data from the cases he attended and some of it made him ponder on what was soon to become the main idea in his mind. For it had begun to dawn upon him that the age-long theories on the subject of the movement of the blood in the human body were unreliable. He did not immediately realize where the errors lay, but that there were errors, and fundamental ones, he was becoming more and more convinced.

To Harvey, whose well-balanced, scientific mind valued truth above all else, it mattered not that the notions he wished to upset were hoary with age and hallowed by tradition. To put forward new ideas might even suggest heresy, but Harvey pursued his experiments. For years he had been dissecting everything he could lay hand on—the bodies of men, animals, birds, frogs, snakes, rabbits, everything that might help him to solve his problem. The more he studied the more certain he became that his colleagues' ideas on blood movement were wrong.

The human heart consists of four chambers, the right and left auricles and the right and left ventricles. Dividing the heart vertically is the septum. In Harvey's time there had been almost no change in the theory of blood movement since Galen in the first century A.D. had made a few improvements on Aristotle. Fabricius and Sylvius, another sixteenth century anatomist, had made other minor discoveries but the main body of opinion had remained substantially unchanged. This was that the blood originated from the liver and was of two different kinds. One kind, it was held, came from the right ventricle of the heart and travelled through the body by way of the veins. The other came from the left ventricle and travelled to the body through the arteries. Both streams were believed to be slow and irregular and quite distinct.

Now Harvey had learnt from Fabricius that the veins had valves, and subsequent investigation confirmed this. These valves meant that blood could only flow through the veins in one direction, and that direction, Harvey found, was towards the heart. Therefore the idea that blood travelled through the veins from the right ventricle was erroneous.

Further, where was the blood coming from? He worked out the amount of blood that was entering the arteries. It was far too much for it to come from the stomach. The whole thing seemed unsatisfactory. Harvey continued his experiments, studied every available word that had been written on the subject and obtained a thorough knowledge of the anatomy of the body.

Then the solution came to him. There were not two different kinds of blood in the body. There was only one kind, the same in the veins as in the arteries. There was but one mass of blood that passed round and round, being driven on its journey by the heart, the body's motor. The blood was pumped from the heart, passed through the body in a "kind of circle," and returned once more to its source. The blood stream was a continuous circulation.

Not without the fullest possible research, not until he had viewed the matter from every angle, was Harvey satisfied that he had found the truth. Even then he did not rush into print. In 1616, twelve years before his book was published, he began to expound the theory in lectures delivered at the Royal College of Physicians. No one took much notice.

The volume was issued in 1628, and created a tremendous sensation in medical circles. Such a revolutionary theory could not be accepted without careful investigation. For a while Harvey's practice fell off. We are told that "'twas believed by the vulgar that he was crackbrained and all the physicians were against him."

Yet in England opposition soon died down. After due inquiry the theory was accepted. Once it had been examined it was seen to be indisputably true. The doctor's practice not only recovered but grew considerably, for on his death he left a large fortune. On the Continent the theory met with more opposition. Much paper was wasted in attempts to refute it, and it was many years before due credit was given it.

Harvey was now in high favour at Court. He was physician to Charles I, who displayed great interest in his work and gave him the use of his parks at Windsor and Hampton Court to aid him in his researches. Harvey had dedicated his book to the king, saying that the monarch was to his kingdom what the heart was to the body.

In 1636 Charles commanded him to accompany the Earl of Arundel on his embassy to the Emperor Ferdinand II. The man of science caused his noble colleague great anxiety by wandering off to look for specimens for dissection. Germany at that time was infested by robbers in consequence of the Thirty Years War, but it required more than thieves and vagabonds to prevent Harvey from searching for new specimens. He seems to have been disappointed by the poverty of material. "By the way," he wrote home, "we could scarce see a dogg, crow, kite, raven or any bird, or anything to anatomise, only sum few miserable people, the reliques of the war and the plague, whom famine had made anatomies before I came."

Then came the Civil War. Harvey himself cared little for politics. He had one serious interest in life and that was medicine, but his sympathies were Royalist and he was the king's physician, so he left London with his master. Even while attending on his Majesty his thoughts were with his work. While the king's forces were gathering Harvey went to Derby to visit his friend, Percival Willoughby, in order to discuss with him the problem of uterine diseases.

He was present at the Battle of Edgehill. His immediate task was to take care of the Prince of Wales and the Duke of York, then lads of twelve and ten respectively. Harvey sought the shelter of a hedge not far from the fight and drew forth a book from his pocket. His study was rudely interrupted by a cannon-ball dropping nearby, and he thought it well to remove his royal charges to a safer spot.

Harvey was delighted when the king went to Oxford in the following year. He was then able to continue his work on anatomy, and incidentally was made a Doctor of Medicine of the university. It was during this period that his home in Whitehall was raided and searched. Invaluable manuscripts and anatomical preparations were taken away, and the loss was a serious one. His Royalist sympathies also nearly cost him his post at St. Bartholomew's, for the hospital raised the question of appointing a successor because Harvey "had withdrawn himself from his charge and retired to a party in arms against the Parliament."

At Oxford, Harvey did considerable research on the question of generation, and from the conclusions he reached there is little doubt that, given the necessary apparatus, he would have made startling and revolutionary discoveries. But he was in advance of his times. The use of a microscope was essential, and it had not yet been invented. Nevertheless, so important were the discoveries considered to be that when Harvey was persuaded by a friend to give him the manuscript for publication he said he felt like a second Jason with another Golden Fleece.

After Fairfax had captured Oxford the doctor returned to London to live in honourable retirement with his brothers, all of whom were prosperous merchants. He was sixty-eight years of age and much troubled with gout, which he sought to ease by putting his feet in cold water.

His theory of the circulation of the blood was now known and accepted everywhere. Even the European medical pundits had been forced to admit its truth. In 1654 the Royal College of Physicians wished to confer upon him the highest honour in the profession, that of president of the college. Harvey declined on account of his age, satisfying his desire to serve the institution by erecting a new building and equipping it with a well-filled library, a museum and a conversation room.

Harvey's busy life was now drawing to a close. His health was poor, though almost to the last he maintained his clarity of mind. On June 3, 1657, he was struck down by paralysis. Unable to speak, he managed to distribute some of his personal belongings to his nephews and then died. He was buried at Hempstead, in Essex.

His wife having died childless some years previously, Harvey made a gift of his estate at Burmarsh, Kent, to the Royal College of Physicians, together with a fund for an annual lecture to be delivered at the college. In making this bequest Harvey urged the Fellows "to search out and study the secrets of nature by way of experiment, and also for the honour of the profession to continue mutual love and affection among themselves." The Harvey Oration is still delivered annually.

In 1883 the Fellows of the College had the remains of the great investigator removed to a white marble sarcophagus in the Harvey Chapel erected in Hempstead Church. In it they placed a copy of the large edition of his works.

Harvey's life was actuated by one great motive—to perfect mankind's knowledge of the human body so as to battle the more successfully against disease and pain. His own discovery stands out as one of the greatest, made all the more glorious by the circumstances in which he worked. Without even the most elementary devices now used in research he was able to divine a truth that remains the greatest and most fundamental in the realm of physiology.

JOHN FLAMSTEED

(1646–1719)

"A prophet is not without honour, save in his own country," and truly, few Englishmen today know or honour the name of John Flamsteed. Yet he was the father of modern astronomy, the first Astronomer Royal, who corrected all the astronomical tables in use in the seventeenth century, who provided Newton with the observations that made that great man's own discoveries possible. Racked with pain, handicapped by poverty, cramped and thwarted by his contemporaries, even by Newton himself, John Flamsteed gave to the world in his life's work one of the greatest contributions to practical astronomy ever made by one man.

In the summer of 1660, the year of Charles II's restoration, a fourteen-year-old boy went for a bathe, and caught a cold. That cold gave Britain her first Astronomer Royal, Greenwich Observatory, and all that these names stand for. The boy's name was John Flamsteed; and he was a scholar at the Derby Free School. His father, Stephen Flamsteed, was a maltster. The boy had been born at Denby, five miles away, on August 19, 1646, and three years later his mother had died.

The cold brought other ailments in its wake. The chief of them was a rheumatic affliction of the joints. Young John Flamsteed became very ill; rheumatism crippled him; he grew unable to walk to school, and left in May, 1662.

From his fourteenth year to his death Flamsteed struggled against illness and physical agony, but the illness gave him opportunity. He could not go to school, so he began to teach himself. He picked up a copy of Sacrobosco's *De Sphaera,* and read it between the agonizing bouts of his illness. The book interested him and attracted him to astronomy. He read other works on the same subject, and at once began to practise. He observed a partial solar eclipse in September, 1662. He made himself a rough quadrant. He compiled a table of the sun's altitudes. Already, the sick, crippled boy was an astronomer. He tells us how he worked away "under the discouragement of friends, the want of health, and all other instructors except his better genius."

Stephen Flamsteed tried all kinds of treatments to get his son cured, but there was little help in medicine. In 1664 he sent John to a man named Cromwell, who was "cried up for cures by the nonconformist party." But Cromwell could do no better than the physicians, and in the next year John Flamsteed went to Ireland to be "stroked" by Valentine Greatrakes, who had acquired a tremendous reputation as a faith healer. He "stroked" Flamsteed in September, 1665, but the young astronomer "found not his disease to stir." When Greatrakes visited Worcester in the following February, Flamsteed went to him again, also with no result, "though several there were cured." So Flamsteed gave himself up to a life of illness and work.

It was not long before his talents attracted notice. Friends lent him books, and he repaid them by writing papers. His first published observation was of the solar eclipse of October, 1668. He accompanied it with the statement "that the tables differed very much from the heavens." The correction of the tables became his chief object and the greatest work of his life.

Towards the end of the year 1669, John Flamsteed sent a paper to the Royal Society on some calculations of appulses of the moon to fixed stars. The paper was published in *Philosophical Transactions,* and brought Flamsteed immediate correspondence. The principal writers were Oldenburg, the natural philosopher, and John Collins, the mathematician. Collins, who from that time corresponded regularly with Flamsteed, did him a great service. The astronomer tells how, in the spring of 1670, he made "a voyage to London. Visited Mr. Oldenburg and Mr. Collins; and was by the last carried to see the Tower and Sir Jonas Moore (Master of the Ordnance), who presented me with Mr. Townley's micrometer and undertook to procure me glasses for a telescope to fit it." Sir Jonas Moore, kind at this first interview with the astronomer, was to prove a still kindlier patron.

From London Flamsteed journeyed to Cambridge, where he made the acquaintance of Isaac Newton, and entered his name at Jesus College. Next year, in October, 1671, Flamsteed began his systematic observations, and "by the assistance of Mr. Townley's curious mensurator they attained to the preciseness of 5″." He soon found out that the varying dimensions of the moon completely contradicted all the theories of lunar motion except those of Horrocks, the brilliant English astronomer who had died some thirty years before. Flamsteed's observations proved the validity of Horrocks's theory and, at the request of Newton and Oldenburg, he prepared it, with additional explanations, for publication.

His next work was even more important, and had a wider effect. He wrote, in 1673, a tract on the real and apparent diameters of the planets, which gave Newton the data for the subject of the third book of his *Principia*.

A year later Flamsteed took the degree of M.A. by letters patent, intending to take orders and settle down in a small living near Derby. But a greater destiny was in store.

In the summer of 1674, he was the guest of Sir Jonas Moore at the Tower. Acting on Sir Jonas's advice, he compiled a table of tides for the king's use. He also supplied the king and the Duke of York each with a barometer and a thermometer made from his own models, and a copy of his rules for forecasting the weather by them. Early in the next year, a "bold and indigent Frenchman," styled the Sieur de St. Pierre, put forward a scheme for finding the longitude at sea. Through the patronage of the Duchess of Portsmouth, Charles the Second's mistress, he obtained a royal commission to consider the proposal. Sir Jonas Moore got Flamsteed nominated as a member, and the astronomer at once showed that the Frenchman's plan was hopeless, until they had far more accurate knowledge of the moon's course and of the places of fixed stars. Whereat Charles II cried: "I must have them anew observed, examined, and corrected for the use of my seamen."

So, by a royal warrant of March 4, 1675, Flamsteed was made "Astronomical Observator," with directions "forthwith to apply himself with the most exact care and diligence to the rectifying of the tables of the motions of the heavens, and the places of the fixed stars, so as to find out the so much desired longitude of places for the perfecting the art of navigation."

A sale of spoilt gunpowder raised £520, and this miserable sum was applied to the cost of the observatory. Sir Christopher Wren chose the site in Greenwich Park, and the building was hastily run up, from second-hand materials, to his design. Thus was founded the Royal Observatory at Greenwich, the most important and most famous astronomical observatory in the world.

When Flamsteed entered the observatory as its first Astronomer Royal, on July 10, 1676, he found it destitute of any instrument provided by the government!

While the observatory was being built Flamsteed was ordained, and he filled his time, when waiting to enter his new domain, by observing at the Tower and at the Queen's House at Greenwich. His first problem, as Astronomer Royal, was to procure accurate instruments and expert help. Sir Jonas Moore once again came to his rescue by presenting him with an iron sextant of seven-feet radius, and two clocks by Tompion. Flamsteed himself brought a three-foot quadrant and two telescopes from Derby.

His salary was the magnificent sum of £100 a year, cut by taxation to £90. For this he was expected to reform astronomy and even instruct two boys from Christ's Hospital. His official assistant was a "surly, silly labourer," available for moving the sextant. In order to buy instruments Flamsteed was obliged to take private pupils, and between 1676 and 1709 no less than 140 sat under him.

In spite of all these handicaps, in spite, too, of his continued ill health, John Flamsteed, first Astronomer Royal, achieved amazing results. All the astronomical theories and tables in use were wrong. Flamsteed set himself the colossal task of correcting them single handed. His first observation for this purpose was made in September, 1676: by 1689 he had made twenty thousand.

He could measure only intermutual distances and fix the relative places of stars, for as yet he had no instrument to determine the position of the equinox. It was not until he had been presented to the living of Burstow, Surrey, in 1684, and had inherited money from his father in 1688, that he was able, with the aid of Abraham Sharp, to construct the mural arc with which his most valuable work was done. His original method, by which he determined the position of the equinox, has been called the basis of modern astronomy.

His observations on the great comet, during the early months of 1681, were transmitted to Newton, who used them in the *Principia*. The comet caused the first breach between the two scientists. Flamsteed said that it was one which had appeared in November, 1680, but Newton held that there were two comets and cast "magisterial ridicule" on Flamsteed's theory. But Flamsteed was right, and four years later Newton acknowledged his mistake.

Newton was now urging Flamsteed to publish a catalogue of leading stars; but Flamsteed had large schemes in view and was not interested in partial publication. This tended to widen the breach between Flamsteed and Newton, but in 1694 and 1695 Flamsteed was supplying Newton with lunar observations. Here again was a source of mutual irritation. Flamsteed was often ill and kept Newton waiting, and often he was annoyed, and kept him waiting for that reason too. Newton offered him money for his help but the offer was brusquely rejected.

In 1704 Newton dined at the Royal Observatory: his aim was to find out about the catalogue which Flamsteed, to " obviate clamour," had said was nearly ready for printing. It was about half finished, and Newton offered to recommend its publication to Prince George of Denmark. Flamsteed " civilly refused." " Plainly," he remarked afterwards, " his design was to get the honour of all my pains to himself."

But in spite of Flamsteed, a committee of the Royal Society, consisting of Newton, Wren, Arbuthnot and Gregory, was appointed by Prince George to supervise the work, and arrangements were made for publication. The Prince was to pay. The result was deadlock, delay and exasperation, but at last, in 1707, the first volume, containing the sextant observations for 1676-1689 was published. The second volume caused still more bitterness and quarrelling. The committee went ahead without Flamsteed, the editor being his *bête noir,* Edmund Halley, who was to succeed him as Astronomer Royal.

In 1711 Flamsteed was summoned to meet the president (Newton) and other members of the board at the Royal Society rooms in Crane Court. He was asked the condition of his instruments, and replied that they were his own, and that he would suffer no one to concern himself with them. Newton burst out: "As good have no observatory as no instruments!"

" I proceeded from this to tell Sir Isaac (who was fired)," writes Flamsteed, " that I thought it the business of the Society to encourage my labours, and not to make me uneasy for them, and that by their clandestine proceedings I was robbed of the fruits of my labours; that I had expended above £2,000 in instruments and assistance. At this the impetuous man grew outrageous, and said: ' We are, then, the robbers of your labours.' I answered I was sorry they acknowledged themselves to be so. After this, all he said was in a rage. He called me many hard names—*puppy* was the most innocent of them. I only told him to keep his temper, restrain his passion, and thanked him as often as he gave me ill names."

Such was the state of affairs between England's two greatest scientists.

In the next year the *Historia Coelestis* was published. Flamsteed's observations were incompletely and inaccurately given; Halley's preface was offensive. Halley boasted in Child's Coffee House of the care he had taken in correcting the faults. Flamsteed called him " a lazy and malicious thief, who has very effectually spoiled my work."

Flamsteed's aim now was to publish, independently, a complete and proper account of his work. He was racked by gout, by headaches and painful disease, but nothing could curb his energy. "Though I grow daily feebler," he wrote, "yet I have strength enough to carry on my business strenuously."

Newton acted meanly towards him; but Flamsteed had some slight revenge when, in 1714, he obtained three hundred copies out of the edition of four hundred of the *Historia Coelestis* and burned them.

He was still working and observing when he was taken ill on December 27, 1719; on the last day of the year he was dead.

Joseph Crosthwait, his assistant, and Abraham Sharp edited his works. The *Historia Coelestis Britannica,* published in 1725, contained the British Catalogue of 2,935 stars observed at Greenwich, "one of the proudest productions of the Royal Observatory."

For John Flamsteed, the chuckling, rheumatic, crippled, suffering, irritable old man, who first studied the heavens from a bed of pain, had made one of the richest contributions to practical astronomy that the world has seen.

As for the man, he lived in his work. But he was no cold, dry-as-dust mathematician. He was a "humourist and of warm passions." He loved a joke, practical or otherwise. But he was irritable, a pardonable fault considering his almost constant pain, and his quick temper did not aid his relations with his fellow scientists. He was jealous, too, of his professional reputation, and did not like criticism or rivalry.

Against these blemishes set the facts that he was patient in suffering, pious and conscientious, abstemious and straightforward, and—more important than them all—that his wife, his assistants, and his servants loved him and were devoted to him even after death.

SIR ISAAC NEWTON

(1642–1727)

Our knowledge of the law of gravity, of the principle by which the whole universe of sun, moon, earth and stars exist and move, is due in the main to one man—Isaac Newton. To call him the greatest English mathematician is poor praise for one of his achievement. At the age of twenty-four he had discovered the binomial theorem and the principles of integral calculus—and ten years before he had been a farm boy with two years at a grammar school to his credit! The invention of a reflecting telescope brought him to the notice of the Royal Society and later he was annually elected president of the society for the last twenty-five years of his life. That and knighthood were the only tangible rewards given to one whose genius established for mankind "Nature and Nature's laws."

ROUNDHEADS and Cavaliers, poor men and gentry, farmers and townsmen all over England were up in arms, but it is doubtful if the inhabitants of Woolsthorpe, in the county of Lincolnshire, were greatly disturbed by the war and rumours of wars. The Christmas of 1642 was approaching and they were equally indifferent to an event which was to take place in their hamlet—an event which was to have perhaps as much effect on the lives of posterity as the civil war then raging.

For the year was remarkable, not only in English history for the beginning of a fratricidal civil war, but also in the history of science by the fact that on Christmas Day, Hannah Newton of Woolsthorpe, gave birth to a son, Isaac.

Three years later, Mrs. Newton married again, her second husband being one Barnabas Smith, rector of North Witham, Lincolnshire, and the boy was left in charge of his grandmother, Mrs. Ayscough, at Woolsthorpe. There, no doubt, he received the spoiling which all grandmothers are reputed to give to their children's children, for in 1654, when she sent him to the Grammar School at Grantham, he seems to have taken little interest in his books, and to have felt himself inferior in the physical domain to the majority of his class mates.

One day, however, a sudden change takes place. At Mr. Stokes's Grammar School, as at every other, there is a bully on the look-out for a suitable victim. Young Newton, an only child, brought up by an old woman who doted upon him, deprived by the circumstances of his environment of the companionship of other boys, is the obvious choice. So Master Bully lets his hand fall a little more heavily than usual on the quiet lad from Woolsthorpe and, to his surprise, and probably to the surprise of the prospective victim as well, it is the bigger lad who is laid low.

From that moment, Isaac Newton knew himself and, having gained that knowledge, gained also self-confidence. A few short weeks were sufficient for him to catch up with his comrades in class work; one more term made him head of the school.

His triumph was short-lived. In 1656 Barnabas Smith, the stepfather whom he had hardly known, died, and his mother was left alone with the cares and worries of a farm. The help of the boy of fourteen was required to keep things going, and she withdrew Isaac from the grammar school.

The experiment was not a success. The boy had gained just enough knowledge of mathematics to whet his appetite for more, and instead of the simpler operations of ploughing parallel furrows or counting heads of cattle or sheep, his every interest and thought was centred in acquiring the knowledge which his withdrawal from school had apparently placed beyond his reach.

Hannah Smith may have had difficulty in appreciating her son's point of view, but, fortunately for the boy, there was one who sympathized. His uncle, William Ayscough, Rector of Burton Coggles, Lincolnshire, was a member of Trinity College, Cambridge. His fellow-feeling for the youth's thirst for learning led him to prevail upon his sister Hannah to send Isaac back to school in 1660, that he might prepare for college. If Isaac Newton, farmer boy, had been wasting his time in that capacity, it is certain that the student cannot have allowed his faculties to rust, for already, on June 5, 1661, we see him admitted as a sub-sizar at Trinity College, Cambridge.

Nothing much is known of his life as an undergraduate, beyond the fact that he must have applied himself with diligence to his studies. On July 8, 1661, he matriculated as sizar of Trinity. On April 28, 1664, he was elected scholar, and he took his degree of Bachelor of Arts in January, 1665. During the three years that intervened between his matriculation and the taking of his degree, he must have made himself master of most of the existing mathematical works of any value. In the two years after his graduation, his mental activity was phenomenal, for already, in 1665, he discovered what is now known as the binomial theorem, and shortly afterwards what he called fluxions, now known as the principles of the integral calculus and the method for calculating the area of curves or the volume of solids.

He writes in May, 1666: "I had entrance into the inverse method of fluxions, and in the same year I began to think of gravity extending to the orb of the moon. . . . All this was in the two years 1665 and 1666, for in those years I was in the prime of my age."

According to Voltaire's *Lettres sur les Anglais,* it was while walking in the garden at Woolsthorpe that the fall of an apple suggested to him the greatest and most famous of all his later discoveries—the law of universal gravitation. Matter-of-fact people of today are inclined to doubt the simple story, but Newton's step-niece, Mrs. Conduitt, who told it to the great Frenchman, can hardly have invented it.

His first attempt, however, about this time, to explain the motions of the moon and the planets by means of the law thus suggested to his mind, was not a complete success, for the current estimate of the length of a degree of latitude with which Newton used to calculate the radius of the earth was so far in error as to produce a considerable discrepancy between the theoretical and the real forces of gravity.

Newton returned to Cambridge in 1667 and was elected in that year to a Fellowship of Trinity. For the next few years he devoted himself entirely to optical work, mainly consisting of investigations into the nature of light and the construction of telescopes. In 1668 he made his first reflecting telescope, an instrument six inches long, with an aperture of about an inch. With this he was able to see the satellites of Jupiter. The form of telescope thus devised is the same as that which at much later periods reached such a height of perfection as the result of the work of Sir William Herschel and Lord Rosse.

In 1669, Barrow, Lucasian Professor of Mathematics at Trinity, resigned, and Newton was elected to his post. In January, 1671, he was elected a member of the Royal Society, to which he had become known through his reflecting telescopes. His first Royal Society paper dealt with optics, and especially with experiments which he had made with a prism bought by him at Stourbridge Fair in 1666. This paper led to considerable controversy at the time, especially in the matter of the dispersion and the separation of the colours of the spectrum—the colours that we see in the rainbow. Newton thought that the length of the band of colours (spectrum), produced at a given distance from the prisms, was identical for prisms of any substance, provided that their angles were such that the deviation for the mean ray of the band was the same in all. (In this belief, which he held throughout his life, Newton was wrong, but the very error helped him in his work. As a result of his prism theory, Newton decided that astigmatic, or colourless images could not be produced with lenses, so he despaired of making an astigmatic refracting telescope and turned instead to the reflecting type which brought him to the notice of the Royal Society.)

"Light," wrote Newton in this important paper, "consists of rays differently refrangible . . . Colours are not qualifications of light derived from refractions of natural bodies, as is generally believed, but original and connate properties, which in divers rays are divers . . . to the same degree of refrangibility ever belongs the same colour and to the same colour ever belongs the same degree of refrangibility."

The paper was reported on to the Royal Society by Robert Hooke, who accepted Newton's observations but not his conclusions. Publication of the paper aroused considerable scientific interest throughout Europe, and the discussions lasted until 1675—until Newton was tired of them. "I was so persecuted," he writes, "with discussions arising out of my theory of light, that I blamed my own imprudence for parting with so substantial a blessing as my quiet, to run after my shadow."

The dispute, however, was not unprofitable, for it led him to investigate the question of light in greater detail. "I suppose," he wrote in 1675, "light is neither aether nor its vibrating motion, but something of a different kind produced from lucid bodies . . . it is to be supposed that light and aether mutually act upon one another." Was this already an insight into those matters which have been the subject of so much research in our own time?

Newton was the founder of the emission theory of light. That is to say, he attributed the origin of light to the emission, by a luminous body, of a multitude of minute particles travelling at a hundred and ninety thousand miles per second in empty space. This theory held sway until 1801, when Thomas Young, by establishing the principle of interference, confirmed Hooke's vague surmises that light travelled in waves.

During these years Newton's financial position was not particularly good, for he had been obliged to ask the Royal Society to excuse him the subscription of one shilling per week. In February, 1675, he was admitted Fellow of the Society.

It is not clear when, precisely, Newton resumed his calculations on gravitation, leading finally to those discoveries which make his name secure to fame for all time. Since his first attempt, many years earlier, he had advanced piecemeal, but it was not until 1684 that Halley, discovering that Newton was in possession of the entire theory and its demonstration, induced him to write a systematic treatise on the matter. This was called *De Motu Corporum,* but the discoveries therein described were more fully explained in a work entitled *Philosophiae Naturalis Principia Mathematica* (Mathematical Principles of Natural Philosophy), published in 1687.

The steps by which Newton reached his all-important law of gravitation are briefly these: —

In 1666, as we have already seen, Newton had his first conception of gravitation and made his first rough calculations. He knew, even then, by making a simple deduction from Kepler's third law, that if the moon were kept in a circular orbit by a force directed to the centre of the earth, that force must be inversely proportionate to the square of the distance between the moon and the earth.

In 1679, while in correspondence with Hooke, Newton discovered how to calculate the orbit of a body moving under a central force; and he showed that if the force varied as the inverse square, the orbit would be an ellipse, with the centre of the force in one focus.

And then, in 1684, he overcame what had been the chief obstacle to the establishment of the theory of gravitation—the impossibility of calculating the size of the sun and moon owing to their immense distance from the earth. Newton now demonstrated that every particle attracts every other with a force which is inversely proportional to the square of the distance between them. In fact, therefore, the force of attraction between two spheres is the same as it would be if each sphere were reduced to the size of its central point. Calculations, then, no longer became approximate but could be made accurately, and Newton, this time using Picard's exact calculation of the length of a degree of latitude, brought his workings to a triumphant conclusion.

He had established the law of gravitation: he had discovered the principle which governs the existence and movement of the universe.

It is to Halley that the world owes the *Principia*: Halley prevailed on Newton to write it, and when that was done, with amazing speed, in the years 1685–1686, Halley undertook publication at his own expense and smoothed out the difficulties made by Hooke, who claimed to have forestalled Newton in many of his discoveries.

Shortly before this work appeared, Newton had taken an active part in defending what was then regarded as an essential prerogative of the University against James II. The king wished the University to admit as Master of Arts a Benedictine monk, Father Alban Francis, without requiring from him the oath of supremacy. Newton's share in the affair led to his election to a university seat in the Convention Parliament in 1689. He kept the seat until the dissolution in 1690.

From 1692 to 1694 Newton's work was interrupted by an extremely serious illness, during which he suffered from insomnia and from a nervous disorder so severe that it was rumoured, not only in England but in scientific circles abroad, that he had gone out of his mind and had been interned in a mental hospital.

Meanwhile, his friends had been busy on his behalf, and in 1695 he was offered, and accepted, the office of Warden of the Mint. Four years later he became Master of the Mint. He was afterwards elected one of the eight foreign associates of the French Academy of Sciences.

In 1701 he was again elected to Parliament for the University. Now, his parliamentary and other duties took up so much of his time that there was little left for scientific study. On being appointed Master of the Mint, he had nominated a deputy for his work as Lucasian professor, but in 1701 he resigned both the Fellowship and the professorship.

He was a most efficient Master of the Mint from the beginning, and he held the post until his death. He did not, however, entirely abandon his interest in matters scientific. In 1703 he was elected President of the Royal Society, and was re-elected every year after that for twenty-five years. During his presidency he superintended personally the publication of Flamsteed's *Greenwich Observations,* though this task involved a considerable amount of controversy and bitterness between the astronomer and himself.

In 1705 Queen Anne visited Cambridge as the guest of the Master of Trinity, and the occasion was chosen for the bestowal of a knighthood upon Newton.

About the same time there began a controversy with the Continental mathematician, Leibniz, with regard to the priority of discovery of the differential calculus. The beginning of the discussions is to be found in an anonymous review of Newton's tract on quadrature, where the writer, who was Leibniz himself, accused Newton of having borrowed his ideas on fluxions. The controversy went on for years, and even after the death of Leibniz there were partisans of either philosopher in every school in Europe. Even today it is difficult to pronounce a verdict, though the impartial historian is inclined to the opinion that the methods in question were invented independently, and that, although Newton was the first, Leibniz's method was the easier and the more complete.

Early in 1727 Newton again fell seriously ill. His health had been failing for some time, and he died of stone in Kensington on March 20, 1727. He was buried in Westminster Abbey on March 28, where a monument was erected to his memory in 1731.

There are several portraits of Newton in existence. One by Kneller and another by Thornhill are in the possession of Lord Portsmouth, while another by Kneller is at Petworth. The Royal Society has three portraits of him, one of which, that by Jervas, was presented by Newton himself and hangs over the president's chair. Trinity College has several others. Roubilliac's magnificent full-length statue of Newton was presented to Trinity by the master, Dr. Smith, in 1750, and erected in the ante-chapel of the college in 1755. It is to this that Wordsworth's noble lines refer:—

"The marble index of a mind for ever
Voyaging through strange seas of thought alone."

The best tribute, however, to the memory of the world's greatest natural philosopher is perhaps the epitaph written by Pope, which is inscribed on a tablet in the room where Newton was born:—

"Nature and Nature's laws lay hid in night;
God said: 'Let Newton be' and all was light."

LUIGI GALVANI

(1737–1798)

AND THE PIONEERS OF ELECTRICITY

From the earliest times scientists have been trying to grasp, understand, harness, and control that mysterious force which we call electricity. The patient research, the untiring work, the brilliant discoveries, that have led the world to our present age of electrical wonders, have been the work of a continuous chain of seekers, carefully piecing their knowledge together to build a foundation for the seekers who came after. And so through the years, from the days of Thales, we reap the fruits of the great minds, of Galvani, who showed the way, of Volta, of Franklin, Coulomb, Oersted, Henry, Davy, until we come to the mighty Faraday, who switched on the power for the modern world.

WHO is not familiar with the theory of Galvanism and with the galvanic battery? The word "galvanize" has become a semi-correct colloquialism, and we regularly speak of a lethargic person, or body of persons, being galvanized into activity. Yet thousands use the word without thinking at all of Professor Luigi Galvani, of Bologna University, who first discovered the principle of animal electricity, and was the father of galvanism. He was one of the pioneers of electrical science as we know it today.

It is, of course, idle to pretend that the powers and properties of electricity were first seriously noticed in the eighteenth century, when Galvani lived. Thales of Miletus, who lived before the Christian era, spoke of experiments in rubbing a piece of amber with silk and thus causing it to attract other objects. In fact, the very word electricity comes from the Greek word *electron,* meaning amber. Theophrastus and Pliny mention the experiments with amber; but the actual word "electricity" did not appear in print until 1650, when an Englishman, Walter Charleton used it in his *Ternary of Paradoxes.* Yet the two Italians, Volta of Pavia and Galvani of Bologna, who were contemporaries, did more in their day to advance electrical science than had been done in all the preceding centuries.

In saying this we are not forgetting the pioneer work done by Stephen Iraq in 1729, by Desaguliers in 1736, by de Fay in 1733, and by others, such as Hanskbea, who in 1709 made the first machine from which sparks were obtained.

Luigi Galvani was born at Bologna in 1737. He was of a deeply religious cast of mind, and wished to enter the Church; but his parents stifled this boyish ambition, and had him educated as a physician. He made anatomy his special study, and in due time was appointed lecturer in that subject at the University of Bologna, one of the oldest and most famous seats of learning in Europe.

Galvani married the daughter of a physician named Galeazzi; and the story goes that it was mainly to this lady's observant eyes and sound sense that we owe the discovery of galvanism. She noticed that the legs of a dissected frog lying on her husband's table were violently convulsed when they touched a scalpel which had been in contact with an electrical machine. This she mentioned to her husband when he returned to his experiments and he at once set to work to make further tests. He transfixed a dead frog with a brass wire through the spinal marrow, and allowed its feet to touch an iron plate. He found that when the wire was connected with the plate, the frog's legs gave convulsive movements. Another story of the discovery leaves out Signora Galvani altogether; and says that Galvani had hung a bundle of frogs' legs fastened with a copper wire on an iron window-rail. The twitchings of the frogs' legs were produced by the contact of the two metals. From these experiments came the galvanic battery, named after its inventor.

Volta, professor of physics at Pavia, investigated Galvani's experiments, and his own efforts along those lines resulted in the voltaic pile. He had discovered, along with Galvani, the great truth that powerful electricity could be produced by metallic pairs.

He placed a disk of copper and one of zinc alternately, each pair being separated from the next by a disk of moist cloth. One end of the pile terminated in a zinc disk and the other in a copper disk, and a continuous current of electricity was produced as soon as the two were connected by a wire or other conductor. There was a long dispute over the cause of electricity produced by the pile. Volta himself attributed it to the mere contact of differing metals, but another school of thought ascribed it to chemical action.

The lives of these two men, Galvani and Volta, so closely allied in science, present great contrasts. Galvani seldom stirred out of his native city, never out of his native land. Volta travelled in Switzerland, Holland, Germany, France and England, when the

Royal Society presented him with the coveted Copley medal. Galvani was deprived of his professorship. Volta was not only honoured in Italy, but summoned to Paris by Napoleon himself, and made director of the physical faculty at Padua by the Emperor of Austria.

At the time of the investigations of Galvani and Volta, other scientists of various nationalities were labouring in the same field. Von Kleist and Musshenbrock, of Leyden, simultaneously invented the Leyden jar. Other useful work was being done by Coulomb, Poisson, William Watson, and Joseph Priestley of Birmingham. Benjamin Franklin, afterwards one of the framers of the Constitution of the United States, had engaged in important experiments. The story has often been told of how he excited the ridicule of his neighbours by flying a boy's kite during a thunderstorm. Their descendants, and millions of other American citizens, do not ridicule the lightning conductor which was the result of those experiments. Franklin's kite had a pointed piece of wire at the top, and at the lower end of the string a key, insulated by a piece of silk ribbon. After flying his kite, Franklin found that he could extract a spark from the key with his knuckle. He then charged a Leyden jar from the key, and thus established the fact that lightning was in truth an electric fluid.

The experiments of Franklin were made in 1752, and it was some years afterwards that Galvani discovered what he called "animal electricity." He had jumped to the conclusion that the phenomena connected with the frog's legs was produced in some mysterious way by electricity in the reptile's tissues.

In the first quarter of the nineteenth century, one Seebeck was experimenting with Voltaic pairs, when he found that current could be produced in a complete metallic circuit consisting of several metals joined together, by keeping those joinings at different temperatures. Later, Peltia found that if a current were passed over a junction of two different metals, the junction was either heated or cooled, according to the direction of the flow of the current. In these ways and others the original discoveries of Galvani and Volta were illuminated and improved upon.

Years afterwards, Gaston Planté was to make the first accumulator of any practical use, and after Fauré had improved upon Planté's construction, other inventors were led into making further modifications, and so the accumulator as we know it came into being. The practical applications of accumulators are many and various. We should be badly off for power and light if it were not for Planté, Fauré, and their successors.

Galvani published a treatise on his discoveries, which became celebrated and was reprinted several times. He continued to teach and lecture as well as experiment, and generally led the quiet uneventful life of a respected university professor. But this calm existence was not to continue. Politics invaded the realm of science; and the result was disaster to Luigi Galvani.

To understand this situation, we must consider the state of the continent of Europe in Galvani's times. "United Italy" was still nearly a century away; and the country consisted of many states, some large, some petty, but all jealous of each other. Bologna was, and had been for centuries, part of the temporal domains of the Popes, but a successful revolution resulted in the end of Papal rule and the foundation of a new Cisalpine republic.

All citizens were required to take the oath of allegiance to the young republic. Here Galvani's religious scruples came into conflict with his worldly interests. Mention has already been made of his early desire to enter the Church, and the event proves that he had never wavered in his devotion to the Papacy. In his view, the Pope had been almost feloniously despoiled. So he refused to swear allegiance to the new form of government.

Luigi Galvani was quite prepared to suffer for his fidelity to the Papacy. Deprived of his post at the university of Bologna, he retired into private life, taking refuge with his brothers. This disastrous end to his career affected his bodily health; and through grief and mortification he fell into a "decline," as it used to be called. He took no more interest in life, and, though the authorities, recognizing his gifts were less doubtful than his loyalty, offered to reinstate him in his post, the offer came too late, for he died in Bologna in 1798. Volta was to survive him for thirty years and to invent, among other things, the electrophorus—an instrument for obtaining electricity by induction.

In direct descent from Galvani and Volta—as regards electrical knowledge—come such men as Hans Oersted, whose research work did much to help forward the invention of the electric telegraph, and Michael Faraday. The latter was seven years old when Galvani died. He grew up with a distinct bent towards electricity, and carrying on the traditions of the older men, invented the first dynamo.

The machine which Faraday invented was inefficient beside any of our powerful modern dynamos, but the idea was there. It consisted of a plate of copper rotated between the poles of a horseshoe magnet. There is a tale of Faraday and his dynamo which ought to be true even if it is not. A lady admitted that his discovery was very interesting, but went on to ask what the good of it all was. "Madam, what is the use of a baby?" replied Faraday.

The lady's remark shows the opinion of the general public towards electrical science in those days. People believed that it was of very little practical value. Now the pendulum has swung the other way; electricity has not only become an essential of modern life, it is a source of power for a huge range of functions which affect every aspect of our lives.

The Voltaic battery, derived from Galvani through Volta, became in 1802 the subject of some very interesting experiments by Sir Humphry Davy, one of the greatest English scientists. As lecturer on chemistry to the Royal Institution he was provided with a large battery composed of 2,000 cells. He found that if a rod of carbon were attached to each terminal a brilliant light resulted. This was the beginning of lighting by electricity. Many years were to pass before a certain operetta house in the Strand could boast that it was the only electrically lighted theatre in London; but now, everyone takes this light for granted.

It is to Galvani and Volta also that we owe the immensely important electric telegraph. The voltaic battery stimulated inventiveness in this direction. Little progress was made until the appearance of the Daniell cell in 1836. The earlier forms of cell so quickly polarized that it was difficult to obtain from them a constant current, but the non-polarizing Daniell cell removed this difficulty. Wheatstone and Cooke were the English scientists who contrived the first electric telegraph ever seen in the British Isles, and at approximately the same time as Morse in the United States, and Steinheil in Germany, were perfecting their similar inventions.

The next step on the way was the invention of the submarine cable, the story of which is in itself an epic of struggle, disaster, and ultimate triumph.

Another heir of Galvani was Lord Kelvin, who introduced the dynamical theory of heat. And so Galvani's legacy has come down to us, ever increasing through the years, until we arrive at our own age where such phenomena as radio, television and space travel seem commonplace.

JOSEPH-MICHEL AND JACQUES-ETIENNE MONTGOLFIER

(1740–1810, 1745–1799)

The history of mankind is the history of his conquest of the elements; the climax of the struggle is his mastery of the air. For many centuries men had tried to solve the problem of flight: individual pioneers had made daring and reckless attempts to rise into the air or to maintain themselves by wings; Leonardo da Vinci had actually designed an aeroplane, but he had no fuel or driving power which could make his plan a practical proposition: it was not until the end of the eighteenth century that the ingenuity of the two Montgolfiers produced the balloon. They enabled man to make his first flight, and by their practical success kindled a universal enthusiasm for aeronautics which will never be quenched.

It is June 5, 1783. The French town of Annonay, near Lyons, is thronged by vast crowds. Powdered and bewigged aristocrats, silk-clad immaculates, elaborately-gowned beauties mingle with the russet burghers and the peasantry, for the States General of Vivarais is assembled in the town, and all its members are abroad in Annonay.

But on this summer day the gaily filled streets present a holiday air. There is no anxious movement to and fro, no hustle of daily business. The crowds are all moving in one direction, until at length a vast concourse gathers in a large open space. The members of the States General, guests of honour, are to the fore: behind them and around them are packed thousands of excited men and women.

In the centre of the space is a strange object, a huge sheet of linen cut out and shaped to form a globe. The crowds stare at this extraordinary sight, as well they might, for the great globe is over a hundred feet in circumference; its linen is lined with paper, and the whole is poised over a giant brazier. The spherical envelope is open at the bottom, and the brazier is immediately beneath this opening. A fire of damped fuel smoulders, throwing up dense clouds of smoke into the linen globe. Attendants feed the fire with bundles of chopped straw, and as the heat increases, and the smoke belches upwards, the great globe, dignified by the name of aerostat by its inventors, begins to swell.

Suddenly the mighty crowd gives a shout. The aerostat is moving! It is leaving the ground! Then, like a live thing, the great globe bounds upward into the air. Higher and higher it goes. The people stare in breathless wonder, straining their eyes as the aerostat becomes a tiny dot a mile above the earth.

The glorious flight lasts but a brief ten minutes. Then the linen globe comes rushing down and falls to land a mile and a half away. The crowd disperses. The experiment is over. But the first balloon has risen from the earth. Man has begun the conquest of the air.

The men whose knowledge and ingenuity made the aerostat rise into the air at Annonay, were two brothers, Joseph-Michel and Jacques-Etienne Montgolfier, the sons of a paper manufacturer of Vidalon-les-Annonay. Joseph was born in 1740 and Etienne in 1745.

Their father derived a comfortable income from his paper mill, and he was able to maintain his nine children in easy circumstances. All the children showed a taste for science, and for mechanics; but it was for Joseph and Etienne to turn that taste to the world's benefit.

Joseph Montgolfier was a gentle and modest young man, but he was independent. His temperament was mercurial, and he was capable of sudden and tremendous enthusiasms. He went to the college at Annonay, where he showed himself to be but a mediocre scholar, and was then taken into his father's business.

Joseph was full of ideas and saw possibilities of introducing improvements in every department of the mill. But his suggestions were not well received by his father, who kept a curb on his son's ingenuity. Impatient of this restraint, and anxious for complete liberty, Joseph left the paternal business and founded a paper mill at Voiron, which he ran with his brother Augustin.

Joseph unfortunately never experimented fully nor gave his projects a proper trial. Athirst for novelty, he turned from one scheme to another. Such conduct could have only one result. His paper mill was a failure and Joseph ran into debt. But he was still full of schemes, and his wit was of more value than his mechanical ingenuity, for none of his creditors could bring him to justice.

In 1770, Joseph pulled himself together, married, and settled down. He was able to set his business affairs in order, and then, leaving the management of his household to his wife, devoted himself to production and salesmanship. His long foot journeys, as a traveller, gave him much time for thought and scientific speculation.

Joseph Montgolfier's inventive genius had not been entirely a failure; he had already translated some of the fruits of his mechanical brain into actuality. He had found a way of printing from stereotype plates, and had planned a new kind of fire-fighting pump. He had made valuable excursions into hydraulics, which were later to yield important results. Now he turned his attention to aeronautics, and here he found common ground of interest with his brother Etienne.

Etienne had started life as an architect. He studied under Soufflot, and then practised for some time, but eventually abandoned architecture and took over the management of his father's paper mills. He quickly showed himself at home at his new task. He improved the plant, perfected the process for manufacturing vellum-finished paper, and kept the business on a prosperous basis, for Etienne combined with his mechanical ingenuity a level head.

The two brothers began their researches into the new science of aeronautics from the very beginning. They had observed the suspension of clouds in the atmosphere, and it struck them that if they were able to enclose some vapour, such as that of which a cloud is composed, in a large and very light bag, the bag would rise into the air. But before they made an experiment of this nature, Joseph tried out some parachute descents, probably to find out the capacity of air to sustain, under pressure, an extended surface. In 1779 he made a sort of parasol some seven feet in diameter, and attached a basket to it. He put a sheep in the basket and let the contraption fall from a high tower in Avignon. Later he himself made a parachute descent from a housetop at Annonay. Then the brothers began the series of experiments which led to the invention of the balloon.

A shirt inspired Joseph Montgolfier with the principle which made possible the first balloon. He was idly watching a shirt airing over an open fire, when suddenly it began to swell and inflate, and then to rise in the air.

He and Etienne were quick to put their new discovery to a practical test. They made an air-filled parallelepiped of taffeta and heated it. It rose! Then they made little paper bags, and put fire beneath them. They rose! Now they made a little balloon and inflated it over a brazier. It rose! And in 1783 they constructed the great aerostat of Annonay, and before the assembled multitude sent the first man-made machine bounding to the skies.

The effect of the Annonay experiment was immediate and

tremendous. The news spread across Europe, and even reached America. Like wildfire the success of the Montgolfiers flashed over the western world; like wildfire a dozen experimenters tried to emulate them.

In August, 1783, the brothers Robert made a balloon under the supervision of the physicist, J. A. C. Charles, the most able of the followers of the Montgolfiers. He suggested filling the bag with hydrogen gas, invented the valve for release of the gas, and first thought of netting and a hoop for suspension of the basket. The cover was of silk varnished with a solution of elastic gum, and it was thirteen feet in diameter. The balloon took three days to inflate, and when it was ready it ascended rapidly to a height of some three thousand feet. A large crowd witnessed the ascent, which was made from the Champ de Mars, Paris, in a downpour of rain. The rain had no effect on the crowd, or on the balloon, which remained in the air for three-quarters of an hour. It eventually fell in a field thirteen miles away, where it so terrified the peasants that they set upon it and tore it to shreds.

The example of the Montgolfiers produced a crop of balloon experiments in every country. Members of the Philadelphia Philosophic Society were soon sending up gas balloons, and the first flight in England was made in November, 1783, by an Italian, Count Francesco Zambecarri, who rose from the Artillery Ground, London, and landed forty-eight miles away in Sussex, after a voyage of two hours and a half.

Within two years of that first ascent at Annonay, balloonists had crossed the English Channel! Jean Pierre Blanchard, and an American physician, Dr. J. Jeffries, made a flight from England to France on January 7, 1785.

Such was the ingenuity and daring stimulated by the experiment of Annonay.

There is another and more curious tribute to the influence of the Montgolfier experiments and to the world-wide interest they aroused. Some of the incredible adventures of the great "Baron Munchausen" were based on the then fantastic ventures of the two Frenchmen. Raspe published his collection of travellers' tales about 1785, and there is no doubt that, like Verne and Wells in a later age, he made use of the marvels of the new world which the physicists and scientists of the late eighteenth century were then creating.

But to return to the Montgolfiers. As soon as the news of the Annonay ascent reached Paris, the brothers were summoned by the Academy of Science. Etienne complied with the summons and gave to the academicians an account of the methods which he and his brother had employed. On August 20, 1783, the academy put the two Montgolfiers on its list of correspondents and awarded them six hundred livres " as to scientists to whom we owe a new art, and one which marks an epoch in the history of human science."

Louis XVI decorated Etienne with the ribbon of St. Michel, and bestowed a title upon his father. Joseph received a pension and an award of forty thousand livres. Thus, unlike many of the benefactors of humanity, the Montgolfiers received immediate and abundant reward for their great work.

On September 19, Joseph Montgolfier repeated the Annonay experiment at Versailles in the presence of the king and queen, the court, and an immense crowd of spectators. The balloon was painted in ornamental designs with oil colours, and it presented a gay sight. A cage was hung beneath it, in which were placed a sheep, a cock and a duck. The inflation began at 1 p.m. and was finished in eleven minutes. The balloon rose rapidly to a height of fifteen hundred feet, remained in the air for eight minutes and descended two miles away in the wood of Vaucresson. The birds and animal were uninjured, save that the cock's right wing had been injured by a kick from the sheep; but this had occurred before the balloon went up.

Although they had made two extremely successful pioneer flights of balloons, the Montgolfier brothers did not realize that the balloons rose through the expansion of the air by heat. They thought that the smoke, or some vapour given off by the burning straw, enabled the balloons to rise.

On October 15, 1783, in a captive fire balloon made by the Montgolfiers, Jean Francois Pilâtre de Rozier made the first human ascent into the air. A month later this intrepid young man made the first free flight in the company of the Marquis d'Arlandes. The balloonists took up a brazier with them to maintain the flight, and the fabric caught alight; but the blaze was extinguished by the cool-headed de Rozier, who had provided himself with a sponge for such an emergency.

The Montgolfiers went on building balloons, and each one they made was larger than its predecessor. In June, 1784, the greatest of all, a monster christened La Gustave, took up seven passengers. They included Joseph Montgolfier, who was making his first flight, Pilâtre de Rozier, and the first woman to rise in the air, a Mme. Tible.

From this time the Montgolfiers fade from the history of ballooning. The disadvantages of their type of balloon were obvious:

they were exposed to constant danger through carrying an open fire, and their flight was of limited endurance. But they had been the pioneers. Their balloons, crude as they may have been, had shown the way.

Their subsequent history is brief. Etienne, the business man of the partnership, died in 1799.

Joseph turned his attention once more to hydraulics. His inventiveness had not been exhausted by his aeronautical experiments, and soon he invented an hydraulic ram which attracted wide attention. We have a few glimpses of his later years. In the terror of 1792 we find him using all the influence he could command on behalf of some of his friends who had been proscribed, and he was successful in saving their lives.

The Revolution apparently ruined his business, and he went to Paris, where he was appointed to a consulting bureau of art and manufacture. Later he became an administrator of the Conservatoire des Arts et Metiers, and in 1807 was elected a member of the Academy of Science. His writings include three works on ballooning, two of which were written in collaboration with Etienne, and a paper on his hydraulic ram. He died of apoplexy in 1810.

Today the name of Montgolfier means little to the man in the street. But it is to these two brothers that we owe our first step in our ever-increasing domination of the air, of the stratosphere, and of limitless space beyond.

JAMES WATT

(1736–1819)

AND THE PIONEERS OF STEAM

The harnessing of steam power has been one of the scientific romances of the last two hundred years. Men had knowledge of the power of steam nearly two thousand years ago, but it was not until the beginning of the eighteenth century that practical means were devised for its use. Then Captain Savery invented his pump, and Thomas Newcomen followed it up with the atmospheric steam engine. Newcomen was the pioneer, but James Watt was the perfecter, and, in fact, the inventor of the modern steam engine. Watt is the central figure in the romance of steam, which boasts also the names of Trevethick, Stephenson, and Fulton, and, later, those of Parsons and de Laval.

IT is generally supposed that James Watt was the inventor of the steam engine. He was nothing of the kind. The properties of steam had aroused the curiosity of scientists and inventors for the nine centuries preceding him. Watt was actually an improver who worked out in detail the practical application of the theories of these pioneers of steam power.

In the first century before Christ, Hero, a Greek philosopher living in Alexandria, harnessed steam by means of a curious toy he called the Æoliphile or Ball of Æolus. This machine consisted of a hollow globe of metal, moving on its own axis and communicating with a cauldron of water underneath. The globe was provided with several tubes projecting at right angles to it. The ends of the tubes were closed, but had slits in the sides. When the fire was lit under the cauldron, the steam filled the globe and the impact of the steam against the air coming through the openings in the tubes caused the globe to spin on its own axis.

This toy, probably the first machine driven by steam power, aroused in the sixteenth century the wonder of scholars who saw plans of it in Italy. Throughout the next two centuries, speculation on the properties of steam preoccupied scientists throughout Europe. Philosophers would often discuss at their gatherings the properties of the vapours of boiling water. They noted that steam forced within a confined space on to the surface of water would drive the fluid up a pipe to a height which was dependent on the pressure of the atmosphere above. Another peculiarity which aroused curiosity was that steam condensed in a vessel caused a vacuum, thus making it possible for water to be raised from one level to another, owing to the atmospheric pressure, which forced the water to replace the vacuum so produced.

Solomon de Caus applied the first principle to making a steam pressure fountain. His apparatus consisted of a spherical vessel with two pipes; the first to fill the metal globe with water, the other to serve as a vent or jet for the water forced upwards by the pressure of the steam resultant from heating the vessel. Captain Thomas Savery, an English military engineer, contrived to use the second principle for a pump in order to empty the water out of Cornish tin mines.

The story goes that Savery, having drunk a flask of Florence wine (Chianti) at a tavern, threw the empty flask into the fire and called for a basin of water in which to wash his hands. He noted that the dregs of the wine in the discarded flask were turned to steam. Thereupon, he took the flask out of the fire and plunged it neck-first into the basin. To his astonishment, after the steam was condensed, a partial vacuum was formed and the water was driven into the flask by the pressure of the atmosphere.

His pump was a more elaborate version of the inverted Chianti bottle. It consisted of two cylindrical vessels, filled alternately with steam from an adjoining boiler and water from the mine to be emptied. When either vessel was filled with water, steam was turned on, and the liquid was forced out by another pipe. The process then started all over again in the other cylinder. Thus the steam served both to cause suction, by the vacuum it caused when condensed, and exerted pressure to expel the water. In practice Savery's pump was too slow to be of much service to the Cornish miners, who found that the water came in faster than he could pump it out. Like many of his predecessors he did not realize that the great future of steam power lay in its being harnessed to machinery. The early pioneers thought of steam as something as finite as a primary force.

The first man to employ steam in the sense we understand it was Thomas Newcomen (1663–1729). By the agency of steam he caused certain portions of machinery to move, and applied their motion to work other machines, which in his case were pumps.

Newcomen's engine comprised a vertical cylinder, with a piston working within it. The steam was generated in a separate boiler, from which it was conveyed to the underside of the piston. The piston was attached to a beam, moving on an axis, at whose other end was attached a rod operating the pump. In this way when the piston was depressed, the pump-rod at the other end was raised, and vice versa. The operation of the engine was as follows: the steam, admitted at a little over atmospheric pressure, pushed up the cylinder. The steam, as soon as the piston reached the top of its stroke, was then shut off by hand, and a jet of cold water was turned on to the walls of the cylinder. This last operation caused the steam to condense and a partial vacuum to be formed in the chamber below the piston; atmospheric pressure did the rest, by depressing the piston. Thus, by this slow method, work was done, and the pump was raised and lowered midst much coughing and spurting of steam and water. The engine made twelve strokes per minute and could raise fifty gallons of water from a depth of one hundred and fifty-six feet.

To keep the engine at work, one man was required to attend to the fire and another, usually a boy, to turn alternately two cocks, one to admit steam into the chamber under the cylinder, the other to admit a jet of cold water to condense it. The turning of these cocks proved monotonous work for a boy named Humphrey Potter, who hit on the idea of applying the "up and down" motion of the beam to opening and shutting the cocks. His device, called, picturesquely, the "scoggan," which in north country dialect meant "skulking work," consisted of a catch worked by strings from the beam.

Of Newcomen, who may be said to be the real father of steam power, surprisingly little is known. In those days inventors were frowned upon as schemers, and more the objects of suspicion than of respect. The biographer, therefore, had too little scope to make it worth his while to study closely the background and intimate details of the life of such social benefactors.

Newcomen's early interest in the rise and fall of the lid of steaming kettles has been attributed, as was the case in later years, with James Watt, as the cause of his life-long study of steam-driven machines. Most authorities believe this story to have been invented to add colour to the life of a man whose romance was his achievement. Newcomen was a blacksmith who lived in Dartmouth. At some period he was consulted by Savery, who wanted certain parts of his pump made by a skilled workman. Later, Newcomen took an interest in the work of his employer and it is assumed that he took over the latter's patents at his death. The commercial exploitation of the engine followed under the supervision of a glazier friend of his named Colley. Certain it is that for the next seventy-five years his "fire engine" was used for keeping the mines free of water.

The work Newcomen did has been too little recognized. Much of the credit for the discovery of the steam engine has fallen to James Watt (1736–1819). In part this claim has been justified, because Watt converted the steam engine from an inefficient machine with but limited uses into a producer of power which could be applied to an infinite number of different purposes. It was used, after he had perfected his design, to pump mines, drive machinery in factories, work flour mills, dig tunnels, build houses, empty ships or mines, and haul masses of goods over ocean, mountain or desert. But at best Watt was no more than an improver of Newcomen's designs.

The exaggerated reputation which has been given to Watt is to no small extent due to a popular story. As a child he showed no promise, and his indolence much exasperated his parents. At the tea table his aunt saw fit to reprove him. "James Watt," said the worthy lady, "I never saw such an idle boy as you are: take a book or employ yourself usefully; for the last hour you have not spoken one word, but taken off the lid of that kettle and put it on again, holding now a cup and now a silver spoon over the steam, watching how it rises from the spout, catching and counting the drops it falls into."

Later commentators, on what is unquestionably an apocryphal story, have tried to prove that while he watched intently that kettle he was working out the theories of thermodynamics. Actually, his interest in steam was probably a pure accident. He became an instrument maker, and by good fortune was allowed to ply his craft within the precincts of Glasgow University. It so happened that a model of Newcomen's engine in the college laboratory was given him to repair. Although mechanically the engine appeared to be in perfect condition, he found that the engine would not function for more than a few turns. Puzzled, he consulted some of his friends on the properties of steam. One Sunday morning, while he was taking his constitutional after church, he hit on the idea which was to make him the father of the Industrial Revolution. The boiler was too small to operate the engine, therefore the engine was too wasteful in its consumption of steam. The solution was to produce an engine consuming less steam.

Watt found that two necessary conditions for an economical

consumption of steam were for the temperature of the condensation chamber to be kept low and the temperature of the cylinder to remain high. He brought this about by removing the condensation process from the cylinder of Newcomen's engine to another vessel, which although it communicated with the cylinder was not a part of it. Steam was exhausted into this neighbouring chamber, which was kept cool with a constant flow of cold water, and there condensed; a partial vacuum was formed by this process without the temperature of the cylinder being lowered. In order to maintain the vacuum and to remove the condensed steam and any air which might have leaked in, Watt added an air pump.

This engine was able to do no more than Newcomen's because it was designed solely as a pumping machine for use in the Cornish tin mines, but it brought about a saving of three-quarters in fuel consumption. Watt's firm claimed as a royalty one-third of the saving effected. The efficiency of the engine was such that at Peacewater, in Cornwall, where the first engine was set up, the mine was emptied in seventeen days, a task which the old engine would have taken months to do.

It was the improved engine Watt produced in later years which made possible the full development of steam power. In order to make the steam engine capable of driving machinery it was necessary for his engine to be converted from a reciprocating into a rotating device. The simplest way of bringing this about was by the use of a crank and flywheel on the same principle as the treadle lathe. Unfortunately, indiscretion on the part of one of his workmen over his beer, at the Soho "Coach and Horses," led to his patent being stolen by an eavesdropper.

Balked by theft of his plan, Watt evolved another method of converting the power generated by his engine, by what he called the "sun and planet" motion. This consisted in a cogged wheel attached to the crank connected with the piston. This wheel was enmeshed with another, in its turn fixed to a large wheel which transmitted the power to the machines it drove. Other important refinements of design were the incorporation of the double-acting principle by means of which the power and the speed of the engine were much increased, owing to both ends of the cylinder being kept in communication with the boiler; the use of "parallel motion," an arrangement of links by which the top of the piston-rod is connected to the beam so that it may either pull or push, and is at the same time guided to move in a straight line; finally, he perfected the centrifugal governor, by whose agency the engine is maintained at a uniform speed, and a steam pressure gauge, which is to the engineer what the stethoscope is to the doctor. Thus Watt left the design of the steam engine much as it is today.

In two respects, however, Watt refused to develop his engine; by "compound expansion," which would have made it capable of driving a locomotive, and by the use of high-pressure steam. The former, he thought, would endanger the monopoly of his firm, the latter because he was afraid it would imperil public life by causing explosions. His prejudices thus left the way open for Richard Trevithick (1771-1833) and George Stephenson (1781-1848) to develop the steam-propelled locomotive, which brought about rapid transport by land. However, Watt was instrumental in developing steam-driven ships. Robert Fulton, the American designer of the first steamship, ordered his engines from Watt's firm.

Like most inventors, Watt was not fitted for the commercial exploitation of his inventions. He was fortunate in his association with Dr. Roebuck, the master of the Carron iron-works, and Matthew Boulton, the famous Birmingham manufacturer of silver-ware. These two men supplied him with the funds he so badly needed for his inventions. At a later date Boulton became Watt's partner, and had it not been for his business acumen it is probable that Watt would soon have given up his experiments. As it was this silversmith, who gave up the manufacture of artistic "Brummagem" ornaments, not only found the vast amount of capital required to finance the installation and upkeep of the engines, but also solved Watt's chief technical problem—he supplied workmen who could manufacture the parts of his engines.

The only available hands in Glasgow, where Watt had made his first engine, were blacksmiths and tinners little able to construct articles outside their ordinary run of business. The men Boulton employed in his works at Soho, just outside Birmingham, were skilled in all manner of metal work, and were thus able to turn out work as accurate as was possible without the aid of machinery. The beautiful self-acting tools made possible by Watt's invention had not yet come into existence, and even with the most expert handwork, carrying out specifications was often an intolerably slow and inaccurate process. Thus no tools were possible without cheap and efficient power, and no general development of power was possible without the exact work machine tools alone could perform. Watt broke the vicious circle.

There is something a little pathetic about the end of Watt. He retired from the vexations of business at the age of sixty-four. Invention now became his besetting passion. The man who had made a vital contribution to human welfare was unable to continue his great work and became a "tinkerer" with "gadgets." His last invention was a machine for copying sculpture! A pointer travelled over the surface of the work and controlled a revolving tool, which cut a corresponding surface on a suitable block of stone. Not long before his death, we find him presenting his copies of masterpieces of the sculptor's chisel to friends as the work "of a young artist just entering his eighty-third year."

He died in 1819 aged eighty-three; his memorial plaque is in Westminster Abbey.

If Savery and Newcomen were the pioneers, it was Watt who invented and perfected the modern steam engine, and he is outstanding among the pioneers of steam-power development. He paved the way for Trevithick, "the father of the locomotive engine," and so for Stephenson, whose railway fame has stolen the thunder from the earlier discoveries. To these men, and to those vaunted heroes such as Branca, Papin, Cugnot, and Murdock, was owed a new age of knowledge and power.

EDWARD JENNER

(1749–1823)

Acute observation, determination, long years of patient research and experiment, and courage: these, and the brain of Edward Jenner, fought and defeated the scourge of small-pox. Basing his work on the country belief that infection with cow-pox prevented the contraction of small-pox, Jenner worked for twenty years to establish at last his principle of vaccination. It rapidly came to be recognized as an effective preventive of small-pox, and its widespread use has practically stamped out this once rampant disease.

The sun drove off the twilight gray
And promised all a cloudless day;
His yellow beams danced o'er the dews
And changed to gems their pearly hues.
The song-birds met on every spray,
And sang as if they knew the day;
The blackbird piped his mellow note,
The goldfinch strained his downy throat,
To join the music of the plain;
The lark pour'd down no common strain;
The little wren, too, left her nest
And, striving, sang her very best;
The robin wisely kept away,
His song too plaintive for the day.
'Twas Berkeley Fair, and Nature's smile
Spread joy around for many a mile.
The rosy milkmaid quits her pail,
The thresher now puts by his flail;
His fleecy charge and hazel crook
By the rude shepherd are forsook;
The woodman, too, the day to keep,
Leaves Echo undisturbed in sleep;
Labour is o'er—his rugged chain
Lies resting on the grassy plain.

These lines were written by a young Englishman living in the county of Gloucester, in the last quarter of the eighteenth century. His name was Edward Jenner, and he had spent all his life in his father's vicarage at Berkeley, where he was born on May 17, 1749.

Surrounded by the lovely Cotswolds, in daily contact with

farmers and men to whom industrialism was as yet unknown, Jenner was steeped in a love of the countryside in general and his native Gloucestershire in particular. As a boy he could recognize the cry of every bird, and he could name every plant by the roadside. To him, therefore, observation came naturally, and it was not long before he began to turn his knowledge to good account. He so loved the beauties of nature that to him disease and sickness were as sacrileges against his beloved goddess, and he determined to become a doctor.

Poetry was abandoned, and he began his studies under Dr. Daniel Ludlow, a surgeon, of Sodbury, near Bristol. It was during this time that he noticed a local belief that if once a man had had the disease known as cow-pox, usually caught from sores on cows' udders when milking, he could not contract small-pox. Knowing that there is no country saying which has not some foundation in fact, Jenner determined to see what truth there was in this, and he made ceaseless enquiries among his medical colleagues to get to the bottom of the matter. But he did not receive much help. Most doctors seemed to think that this popular notion was just an old wives' tale and nothing else. Still Jenner was not satisfied and, after he had gone to London to study under the celebrated physician, John Hunter, he kept on with his enquiries and investigations, when he returned to begin practice at Berkeley in 1773.

Finally, in 1780, he discovered that there were in reality two different forms of cow-pox, only one of which acted as a defence against small-pox. At that particular period the cow-pox happened to be scarce in Gloucestershire, and some time passed before he could test his theory. But, in the meantime, Jenner collected every scrap of information he could, and published each step of his discoveries.

At last, after more than twenty years of research, his theory seemed to him to be irresistibly proved, and he resolved to carry out his first experiment of inoculation. On May 14, 1796, he inoculated an eight-year-old boy whose name, James Phipps, should be blazoned in the annals of medical history, with cow-pox vesicles from the hands of a dairymaid, named Sarah Nelmes.

On July 1 he inoculated the boy with "variolous matter," or small-pox germs. His medical colleagues awaited the result with ill-concealed excitement, not a few criticizing Jenner in the harshest and most unscrupulous manner for the risk he was taking. But Jenner was immeasurably above such criticism. He knew that the conclusions he had reached were, by all the standards of medical science as they were then known, unassailable; and finally, as he had predicted, James Phipps escaped the small-pox. As is the way with the small-minded, his colleagues turned from criticism to immoderate adulation, and it was not long before they advocated vaccination for almost every disease to which the human frame is liable.

Joseph Farington records in his famous diary: "Before he (Jenner) published his discovery, Sir Walter Farquhar said to him that if he chose to preserve it a secret, he might make £100,000 by it. It would be easy for him to prove its value to medical men of character who would recommend it and warrant its efficiency, which would enable him to get £10,000 a year by it; but Dr. Jenner determined to give it to the world."

And he was as good as his word. In 1798 Jenner published his *Inquiry into Cause and Effect of the Variolæ Vaccinæ,* which he followed a year later with *Further Inquiries* and, in 1800, *Complete Statement of Facts and Observations.*

By 1806 the great social reformer, Samuel Wilberforce, was able to say that "even in remote countries, and even in China, a country in which innovation is jealously opposed, it has been admitted. In India it is used."

Like all great men, Jenner was essentially modest by nature and yet impervious to unscrupulous opposition. He had two kinds of opposition to face. The first was the direct attack of the conservative medical men of the time, who regarded vaccination as a dangerous practice; the second was much more difficult to deal with.

No sooner had he published his results than every kind of doctor, both genuine and quack, took up the practice and advocated its adoption. The village fair-grounds were infested with quacks offering "the genuine vaccine operation of Dr. Jenner," and the people that were thus infected with diseases were innumerable.

One of the most notorious of the genuine medical men who advocated vaccination, while being completely ignorant of its real nature, was a certain Dr. George Pearson. This man published a pamphlet in November, 1798, in which he gave to a troubled world his theories on the subject without having even seen a case of cow-pox. He delivered frequent lectures on the subject, and inoculated hundreds with a virus which was found to produce not cow-pox, the slight disease produced by Jenner, but more or less severe eruptions very similar to small-pox.

Jenner at once proceeded to look into the sources whence Pearson had got his vaccine, and he found that, as he had suspected, this vaccine had come into contact with variolous matter. But this did not deter the amazing effrontery of Pearson. Hearing that Jenner was trying to found institutions where people could be vaccinated free, Pearson proposed founding such an establishment in London, and actually had the effrontery to offer Jenner the post of honorary consulting physician. Jenner immediately went to London to counter this move. The insult to himself did not disturb him, but what did cause him the most acute anxiety was the thought that an institution was to be formed where erroneous and dangerous practices would be carried on. There were, fortunately, at that time a few men of influence in London who recognized Jenner's worth, and George Pearson's scheme was sent to the obscurity it deserved.

Other and even more unscrupulous attacks were made against Jenner. A particularly vile calumny was the story that was spread that Jenner had given up vaccination, and was inoculating people with a mild form of small-pox. Colour was lent to this libel by the fact that Jenner had had his younger son, Robert, inoculated with the small-pox virus; and the tale went the round of England.

The real truth was that Jenner had vaccinated his son, and that the vaccine had not " taken "—that is to say that the expected mild infection of cow-pox had not taken place. But one day, a friend of the family called on the Jenners when they were at Cheltenham, and began to play with young Robert. In the course of conversation he remarked casually that he had just left a family where small-pox was raging. This plunged Jenner into a fever of anxiety and he exclaimed, " Sir, you know not what you are doing—that child is not protected. He was vaccinated but the 'infection failed.' "

As he was away from home, Jenner had no vaccine with him. So he did the next best thing, which was to have the child inoculated with small-pox, since he knew that the illness brought on by inoculation was only a very mild form of the disease. This action was perfectly natural, and in the circumstances the only proper thing for Jenner to do.

But still the story ran its round, until it came back to Jenner at a reception at St. James's, where he overheard a certain peer, who was personally unknown to him, repeating it as a tit-bit of gossip. Jenner's methods were always direct, and in none of his actions did he ever lose possession of his calm dignity. Going up to the nobleman, he said, " Sir, *I* am Dr. Jenner." That killed the spread of the calumny as far as London was concerned, and, little by little, the real facts became known.

In the meantime, Jenner's fame spread far beyond the shores of Britain. In France vaccination was widely practised, and Napoleon became an enthusiastic patron of the institution set up for its spread. On hearing of Napoleon's advocacy of his discovery, Jenner wrote to him on one occasion to petition for the release of some English prisoners. The letter was forwarded to the Empress Josephine, and she went to plead the cause of the imprisoned Englishmen. At first the Emperor was adamant, but when Josephine said that it was Jenner who was pleading, Napoleon said, "Ah! we can refuse nothing to that name."

So highly was the name of Jenner thought of that certificates signed by him acted as passports and secured the release of other prisoners in countries as far apart as Mexico and Austria. Those who ruled in England at the time were less large-minded, and Jenner's efforts for the release of certain French prisoners were unsuccessful.

Parliament did, however, vote him £10,000 towards spreading his discovery, but the money was not paid to him until two years after the vote, and then £1,000 was deducted in "government fees." The sum Jenner thus received was inadequate, and did little more than pay the expenses he had incurred in making his discovery. Some idea of the extent to which Jenner had to put his hand into his own pocket may be gained from the fact that he once wrote to a friend describing himself as "the vaccine clerk of the world," and Farington recorded in his diary in 1806 that Jenner's enormous correspondence alone cost him £100 a year.

But money never attracted Jenner, and he was as ready to vaccinate the poor as the rich. He offered free vaccination to those who were so poor that they could not afford a fee, and as many as three hundred of the poorest would wait at his door every day to be vaccinated.

Parliament was finally prevailed on, in 1806, to vote him a further £20,000, this time without any deductions, and with this money Jenner founded, in 1808, the National Vaccine Institution. He spent some months in London organizing the institution, and then one of his sons fell dangerously ill, and Jenner returned to Berkeley.

While he was away, Sir Lucas Pepys, President of the College of Physicians, formed a board composed entirely of that college and the College of Surgeons, in flat contradiction of Jenner's orders, and so Jenner immediately resigned his post as director of the institution.

A short while later, Oxford conferred on him the degree of M.D., and everyone believed that this naturally meant election to the College of Physicians. But that body refused to elect Jenner unless he passed an examination in classics. Jenner's refusal to brush up his Latin and Greek was characteristic. He said, "It would be irksome beyond measure. I would not do it for a diadem. That indeed would be a bauble; I would not do it for John Hunter's museum."

In 1810 his eldest son died, and this loss and the strain of his labours caused Jenner to have a breakdown. He retired to Berkeley, only going up to London on important business.

His last public appearance in London was in 1814, when he was presented to the allied sovereigns, who were in London following the Congress of Vienna and the banishment of Napoleon to Elba. Jenner then went back to Berkeley, where he had lived in retirement, enjoying, uninterruptedly for only too brief a period, the company of his wife, to whom he was devoted.

He had married, twenty-six years previously, Katherine Kingscote, the daughter of a Gloucestershire gentleman, and whenever he was able to snatch time from his many visits to London in connection with his discovery, he loved to take his wife and young family to Cheltenham for a holiday. He had a high opinion of the Cheltenham waters and recommended them to all his patients.

His biographer and friend, Dr. Baron, says that "his wife was gentle and mild, and exercised a great and peaceful influence on him . . . Jenner was always conscious of the presence of God, and Mrs. Jenner taught this lesson to the poor around her in schools she had set up for teaching the Scriptures." But Mrs. Jenner was always delicate, and this caused her husband constant anxiety. When she died, in 1815, Jenner's grief was overwhelming. He wrote to Baron shortly afterwards: "Every surrounding object reminds me of my irreparable loss. Every tree, shrub, flower seems to speak. But yet no place on earth would at present suit me but this . . . the bitter cup has a kind of relish in it which it could afford nowhere else."

Though Jenner had left London for good in 1814, he was not idle at Berkeley. He devoted himself to his boyhood pursuits of natural history and geology, and he kept well abreast of all the tendencies of his time. He built the first balloon that was ever seen in Gloucestershire, and he did much to further the geological knowledge of the county. In 1823 he presented his last paper to the Royal Society—of which he had been made a Fellow in 1780—"On the Migration of Birds."

But although to all appearances he seemed destined to live many years longer, his unflagging industry and care for others had taken its toll of his strength, and he was found on the morning of January 24, 1823, unconscious on the floor of his library. He had been stricken with apoplexy. His right side was completely paralysed, and it was clear that there was no hope. The next day this simple-hearted lover of Nature, poet and benefactor of mankind, passed to his reward.

ISAMBARD KINGDOM BRUNEL

(1806–1859)

The lives of the heroes of civil engineering rarely receive their due measure of praise. To those outside the profession they are more often unknown. Railways run, tunnels are thrust through the bowels of the earth, cuttings are carved out of mountains, bridges leap across rolling rivers, and from all these works of patience, ingenuity and skill, mankind benefits, while forgetting or ignoring the men who have accomplished them. One of these, Isambard Kingdom Brunel, stamped England with the products of his genius, and by his vision showed the world the way in railway construction and the building of mighty ships.

IN 1823, Sir Marc Isambard Brunel, a brilliant civil engineer and inventor, planned the Thames Tunnel. It was to be constructed by means of his own tunnelling shield, and a company was formed to put the wonderful project into operation. Although work was begun in 1825, it was not until 1843 that the tunnel was opened to the public, for every kind of difficulty and disaster dogged the engineers. Once, when the Thames burst into the tunnel, the workmen were rescued from the shield in the nick of time. Labourers and engineers fled to the shaft to escape the rising flood and the floating debris that had been torn from their uncompleted work. The young engineer-in-charge had seen the men safely to the shaft and was clambering up it himself, when a sudden cry for help came from the flooded tunnel. Without a second's hesitation he seized a rope and slid down one of the iron ties of the shaft to the water. There was every probability that the recoil of the flood would sweep him away to certain death, but he managed to slip the rope round the drowning engineman's waist and haul him up the shaft to safety. The young engineer who, after narrowly escaping death, returned to face it and rescue one of his workmen, was Isambard Kingdom Brunel, son of the famous Sir Marc and destined to become greater than his father.

Sir Marc was French by birth and had narrowly escaped the guillotine during the French Revolution by reason of his royalist sympathies. He had become a naturalized Englishman, and

Isambard Kingdom, his only son, was born at Portsmouth on April 9, 1806. Early in life the young Isambard showed a great talent for drawing; when he was at school in Hove at the age of fourteen, he drew a complete and accurate plan of the whole town.

After some years in England he was sent to the College of Henri Quatre in Paris, which had a great reputation for mathematical teaching. There he spent two years and returned to Britain for technical training before entering his father's office in 1823. When the work on the Thames Tunnel was started, Isambard was engaged on it, and later he was made resident engineer. His courage was matched by his devotion to work and his technical skill, while the job of tunnelling gave him valuable practical experience.

His first individual effort came in 1829, when he submitted plans for a proposed bridge over the Avon at Clifton. On the advice of the great Thomas Telford, builder of the Menai suspension bridge and founder of the Institute of Civil Engineers, the design was rejected, but two years later Brunel put forward another, which was declared to be the most mathematically exact of all the plans submitted, including Telford's own, and was accepted. Brunel was appointed engineer of the work, which began in 1836. But the money failed, and the famous Clifton suspension bridge was not actually completed until after his death.

Brunel, whose genius was now recognized, was appointed engineer to Bristol Docks, and there he made a series of improvements. In 1831 he designed Monkwearmouth Docks, and carried out dock and harbour works at various times at Plymouth, Briton Ferry, Brentford and Milford Haven.

At the age of twenty-seven he became engineer to the proposed Great Western Railway. It will be convenient in recording the increasing triumphs of his skill and vision to divide them into categories; the Clifton suspension bridge had given the first proof of his genius, and then comes his wonderful work as a railway constructor.

When Brunel became a candidate for the post of engineer to the proposed railway, an incident occurred which gives us a clear insight of the man's character and of the spirit in which he worked. He heard that the selection committee had decided to give the position to the engineer who would tender the lowest estimate for the line. Brunel immediately requested that his name should be withdrawn. But the committee evidently preferred value to cheapness, for on March 7, 1833, he received his appointment at a salary of £2,000 a year.

Brunel began work with characteristic energy. Within a month he had surveyed and planned a route from London to Bristol. Then he had to go to work on a detailed survey for the purposes of presenting the Railway Bill to Parliament. Railways were in their infancy, and men with knowledge of construction conditions and difficulties were few. Brunel had to supervise the work of his assistants as well as direct the whole business: "I am rarely much under twenty hours a day at it," he wrote at this time.

Brunel's conduct before the committee which sat on the Bill was admirable and his evidence was given clearly and straightforwardly. George Stephenson, called also to give evidence, heartily supported his choice of route, which lay north of the Marlborough Downs, between Reading and Bath, and agreed with Brunel that the proposed Box Tunnel was neither dangerous nor impracticable. The first Bill was rejected, and it was not until 1835 that Brunel could write in his diary:

"The railway now is in progress. I am thus engineer to the finest work in England. But what a fight we have had, and how near defeat, and what a ruinous defeat it would have been! It is like looking back on a fearful pass; but we have succeeded."

Brunel had planned a line for high speeds. He had chosen the easiest gradients and now he built his track to a seven-foot gauge. The standard gauge of today, and the one that was already in use in the north, is four feet eight and a half inches; but Brunel knew that, at that period, with his broad gauge he could use more powerful locomotives, have steadier carriages, and run faster trains. He also invented revolutionary methods of track-laying. Some of the innovations he adopted were modified after the opening of the first section of the line in 1838, but his longitudinal sleepers were retained. In this, as in many other details of construction, Brunel's genius put him in the forefront of railway pioneers.

The outstanding difficulties to be overcome in the construction of the line to Bristol were the Brent valley and Thames crossings, and the hills at Sonning and Box. To carry the line over the first, Brunel constructed a great viaduct at Hanwell, and for the second the remarkable bridge at Maidenhead. The latter crosses the river in two spans, and they are the longest and flattest spans constructed in brickwork. The flatness of the spans raised a storm of criticism, and the contractor wanted to throw up the job, until Brunel convinced him of the safety of his design. At Sonning he made a cutting over two miles long, while the Box Tunnel was a triumph of courage. It was nearly two miles long, easily the longest that had yet been driven. The public firmly believed that they would be suffocated if they travelled through it!

Brunel was not one who suffered fools gladly. There was but one chair in his office as a reminder to the visitor that he had no time to waste. If it was important business he offered the caller his chair; if not he occupied it himself. Inefficiency he could not and would not tolerate, hence this letter: "You are a cursed, lazy, inattentive vagabond, and if you continue to neglect my instructions and to show such infernal laziness I shall send you about your business."

It is not possible to enumerate the successes and the magnificent results of Brunel's work for the Great Western Railway. They are the more remarkable because he was tackling for the most part new and untried problems. For example, in constructing his bridge over the Usk, he used girders of his own design to meet the peculiar difficulties of the case, and nowhere is his ingenuity better displayed than in his famous Chepstow bridge.

His ideas did not always meet with success. He tried out the atmospheric system of Clegg and Samuda on the South Devon Railway in 1847. Although it started promisingly, it proved to be a failure, and Brunel lost both money and reputation in the venture.

His greatest achievement in railway engineering was his last. In 1854 he began work on the Royal Albert Bridge at Saltash. The River Tamar is there 1,100 feet wide, and the Admiralty required that any bridge across it should give at least one hundred feet headway for ships. Eventually Brunel designed a bridge of two main spans, each four hundred and fifty-five feet long, with long approach viaducts at each end. The rock on which the foundations of the central pier were to be placed was beneath a thick bed of mud and eighty feet of water. This, and every other obstacle, Brunel met successfully, and the wonderful bridge, "a combination of an arch and a suspension bridge, half the weight being placed on the one and half on the other," was opened by the Prince Consort in May, 1859. Brunel was not present, and later as a dying man he was driven slowly across his masterpiece on a truck.

His work for the Great Western led him to be consulted by other lines, notably those of Victoria and the Eastern Bengal Railway. It has been justly remarked that his great railway achievements "all exhibit boldness of conception, taste in design, and great skill in use of material."

While Brunel was cutting lines of communication on land, he was also revolutionizing the means of communication by sea. It was when he was building the first section of the Great Western Railway that he designed and supervised the construction of the steamship *Great Western*. She was the biggest vessel of her day, nearly thirty feet longer than her nearest rival, and she was of 2,300 tons displacement. Her first voyage, in 1838, was a triumph. She made the Atlantic crossing in fifteen days, a record, and was the first steamer to be put on a regular service between England and America.

During the next few years Brunel conducted a series of observations on screw propellers, and satisfied himself that the screw was practicable for driving large steamers. In 1841 he was commissioned by the Admiralty to make experiments with screw steamers, with the result that the navy adopted screw propellers in 1845.

The *Great Britain*, which he had designed as a paddle steamer, Brunel immediately had converted and built with screws. She was an even larger ship than the *Great Western*, and made her successful first trip to New York in 1845. The strength of her construction was proved when she was stranded off the coast of Ireland during the whole winter of 1846 and remained undamaged.

Brunel believed in building bigger and bigger ships, and advocated steamers with room for large supplies of fuel. When he was appointed consulting engineer to the Australian Steam Navigation Company in 1851, he recommended steamers of 5,000 tons, capable of reaching Australia with only one stop for coaling, but his ideas were not carried out.

The *Great Western* had been two hundred and thirty-six feet long and of 2,300 tons displacement: in 1853 work was begun on Brunel's *Great Eastern*, originally christened the *Leviathan*. She was six hundred and ninety-two feet long with a displacement of 32,700 tons, and embodied entirely new principles of construction, including the division of the hull by bulkheads and a double skin. Her launch in 1858 marked an epoch, and although the vessel was a commercial failure, she afforded magnificent testimony to Brunel's strength of construction and accuracy of design. The *Great Eastern* was the ancestor of all big ships.

Brunel's shipbuilding plans, like many of his railway schemes, met with strong criticism and opposition, but as his son wrote: "The conclusions he sought to establish are now so generally accepted that it is difficult to believe that they were ever questioned. No one now has any doubt that large vessels can with safety be built of iron, or that the screw propeller can be advantageously employed in ships of war and the mercantile navy; no one can now deny that it is practicable for steamships to make long voyages across the ocean with regularity and speed."

Even this wonderful pioneer work in railway and shipbuilding did not exhaust Brunel's engineering activities. During the Crimean War he turned his attention to gunnery, and invented a floating gun-carriage for an attack on the Kronstadt in 1854. The war also brought from him designs for military hospital buildings on a new principle: hospitals to these plans were erected on the Dardanelles in 1855 and were so successful that they were copied by the Americans in the Civil War, by the Germans in the Franco-Prussian War, and have been the basis of military hospital construction ever since.

He was a member of the building committee of the Great Exhibition of 1851, and was partly responsible for the acceptance of Paxton's design for the Crystal Palace. It was Brunel who designed the two great water towers that flanked the Crystal Palace at Sydenham.

Honorary degrees, the fellowship of the Royal Society, and the vice-presidency of the Institute of Civil Engineers were formal honours that were bestowed upon him, but his genius and his cheerful personality won him the regard of all. When once he accidentally swallowed a half-sovereign, which lodged in his windpipe for six weeks, and was then only got out by an apparatus he designed himself, the news of his relief was received by the whole nation with joy, and the cry went round: "It is out!"

His labours on land and sea, and particularly the worries incidental to building a ship of such unprecedented size as the *Great Eastern,* wore out Brunel's health. On September 5, 1859, he was watching the engine tests of the *Great Eastern,* when he was seized with paralysis. Ten days later he was dead.

He lies in Kensal Green cemetery. On the Royal Albert Bridge at Saltash his name is graven in huge letters, but he left his own memorial in stone and steel and iron, and in the great works that posterity has built upon the foundations of his vision.

MICHAEL FARADAY

(1791–1867)

Electricity has ceased to be an intangible phenomenon, it has become a domestic and industrial slave. Michael Faraday made this possible. His discovery of induced currents, which meant the production of electric current from magnetic force, was the dawn of a new epoch. By it he made the way clear for his followers to produce the dynamo, the generator of electric current: indirectly, we owe to him electric light and power, the telephone, telegraphy, and a thousand other devices made possible by tapping the vast sources of electricity which he discovered. On his work were based the researches which led to wireless telegraphy. His experiments in electrolysis were invaluable: he magnetized light: he was a great chemist as well as physicist. A humble, patient, brilliant scientist, his achievements are among the highest ever attained by humanity, for the fruits of them may never be exhausted: " The progress of future research will tend, not to dim nor to diminish, but to enhance and glorify the labours of this mighty investigator."

SIR HUMPHRY DAVY, the great chemist, was almost at the end of his days, when a friend, so the story goes, asked him to declare which of his discoveries he considered to be the greatest. Davy, who was somewhat jealous of his fame and professional reputation, considered for a while. Then he gave a short list, named an electrical discovery, the results of some of his chemical researches, his famous safety lamp, and concluded, " But the greatest of all my discoveries was the discovery of Michael Faraday." And Davy, who died in 1829, spoke more truly than he knew.

Michael Faraday was born at Newington Butts on September 22, 1791. His father, James Faraday, was a blacksmith who had come to London from Yorkshire. He was hard put to it to make ends meet, and the young Michael experienced the hardships of poverty throughout his childhood.

Some five years after Michael's birth, the family moved to Jacob's Well Mews, Charles Street, Manchester Square. From there he was sent to school. His education, he said years later, was of " the most ordinary description, consisting of little more than the rudiments of reading, writing and arithmetic at a common day school. My hours out of school were passed at home and in the streets." When he had become famous, Faraday would often frequent that part of London in which his early days had been spent, and point out the places where he had looked after his younger sister, or had played marbles in the street. But the young Michael was not allowed to run wild. His father had become a member of the Sandemanian Sect, and Faraday, as his later life showed, absorbed his deep religious convictions.

At the age of thirteen, Michael Faraday had to leave school and go out to earn his living. He became an errand boy for a neighbouring book-seller, named Riebau. His job consisted mainly of carrying and delivering newspapers; in the words of Professor Tyndall, Faraday's friend and successor, "he slid along the London pavements, a bright-eyed errand boy, with a load of brown curls upon his head and a packet of newspapers under his arm."

His trial year as an errand boy was so satisfactory that, in October, 1805, Faraday was apprenticed, without premium, to Riebau to learn the trade of bookbinder and stationer. For the next few years Faraday was busy, for, in addition to learning his trade, he had access to books, and Riebau, who was a considerate master, allowed him occasional leisure to attend shilling lectures on natural philosophy. Faraday made friends at the lectures and learned quickly from the books and papers: his interests turned particularly to science and chemistry. He was soon inspired with the ambition to leave trade and take up a scientific career.

And then occurred an incident which was the turning point of his life. The story has often been dramatized in the telling; hear it in the simplicity of Faraday's own words:—

> "During my apprenticeship I had the good fortune, through the kindness of Mr. Dance, who was a customer of my master's shop, and also a member of the Royal Institution, to hear four of the last lectures of Sir H. Davy in that locality. The dates of these lectures were February 29, March 14, April 8, and April 10, 1812. Of these I made notes, and then wrote out the lectures in a fuller form, interspersing them with such drawings as I could make. The desire to be engaged in scientific occupation, even though of the lowest kind, induced me, whilst an apprentice, to write, in my ignorance of the world and simplicity of my mind, to Sir Joseph Banks, then President of the Royal Society. Naturally enough, 'no answer' was the reply left with the porter."

Faraday sent the notes of Davy's lectures, which he had absorbed with interest and delight, to Sir Humphry himself, and asked to be allowed to quit trade, which he thought "vicious and selfish," and to devote himself to science. Davy replied courteously.

One evening, when Michael Faraday was undressing to go to bed, there was a loud knock on the door. Davy's carriage was outside, and Davy's servant handed Faraday a note, as a result of which he called next morning at the Royal Institution, where he was engaged as a laboratory assistant at twenty-five shillings a week. Faraday at once became a valuable help to Davy, and the two experimented together with chlorine. During his work at this period both he and Davy were several times injured by explosions of chloride of nitrogen, a dangerous gas.

In the autumn of 1813 Sir Humphry Davy and his wife went abroad, and Faraday accompanied them, partly as secretary and assistant, partly as valet. Davy, who was Faraday's life-long friend, treated his assistant with every consideration, but Lady Davy used him as a menial, and almost drove him to return home. At Geneva, Davy was the guest of his friend, De La Rive, father of the great electrician, who was shocked when he found out that Faraday, then living with the servants, was actually Davy's laboratory assistant. He at once suggested that Faraday should eat with the family, but Lady Davy objected; so the courteous host compromised by sending Faraday's meals to his own room.

Faraday was away two years with Davy. He kept an interesting journal of their tour through France, Switzerland, Italy and the Tyrol, and his affectionate letters to his mother at this period are typical of the man. One of the most interesting notes of the tour records how on June 17, 1814, he "saw M. Volta, who came to Sir H. Davy, a hale, elderly man, bearing the red ribbon, and very free in conversation."

The travellers returned to London in 1815 and Faraday was re-engaged at the Royal Institution. He now settled down to a life of research and discovery: "From May 7, 1815 (the date on which he rejoined the institution), onwards, his life was a time of steady intellectual growth, spent in chemical research, in the explaining of phenomena, and in what is by no means his least claim on our regard, the popularization of scientific knowledge."

In June, 1821, Faraday married a Miss Sarah Barnard, the daughter of an elder of the Sandemanian Church. The union was long and happy. "A month after his marriage," writes Bence Jones, in his *Life and Letters of Faraday,* "he made his confession of sin and profession of faith before the Sandemanian Church. When his wife asked him why he had not told her what he was about to do, he only replied, 'That is between me and my God.'"

Faraday's chemical researches were first made in directions opened up by Davy, and soon resulted in valuable advances and discoveries. He made a particular study of chlorine. On one occasion Dr. Paris entered the laboratory while Faraday was at work and, seeing an oily liquid in a tube, censured the scientist for his carelessness in using dirty vessels. The next day Dr. Paris received a note:—

"Dear Sir,

The *oil* you noticed yesterday turns out to be liquid chlorine.

Yours faithfully,

M. Faraday."

Faraday had succeeded in converting chlorine gas into a liquid by means of its own pressure. This was an important discovery, and led to many experiments with other gases, which produced like results. During this period of his life, Faraday, besides liquefying several gases, made the first rough experiments on the diffusion of gases, a phenomenon first pointed out by John Dalton. He discovered two new chlorines of carbon; investigated alloys of steel; produced several new kinds of optical glass; and in 1825 announced the discovery of benzol. In addition to these valuable discoveries, there must be credited to the careful, accurate and painstaking Faraday the general improvement in laboratory methods which dates from this time.

In 1823 Faraday was elected a Fellow of the Royal Society, and two years later was made director of the laboratory at the Royal Institution. In 1833 he was appointed Fullerian Professor of Chemistry in the Royal Institution for life, without the obligation to give lectures.

Meanwhile he had been conducting experiments and making the first of those electrical discoveries which have made his name a household word. Basing his experiments on the work of Oersted and Wallaston in the realm of electro-magnetism, Faraday explained the continual rotation of a magnet and the electrified wire round each other. That was in 1821. Ten years later he made his great discovery of electrical induction; "Faraday, in 1831," writes Tyndall, "had now reached the threshold of a career of discovery unparalleled in the history of pure experimental science."

In November, 1831, Faraday announced his epoch-making discovery to the Royal Society.

He showed that an electro-motive force is set up in a conducting wire when it is moved at right angles to a magnetic field. If the wire is part of a closed circuit, its motion results in an " induced " current.

Now, in 1824, Arago had discovered that a disk of non-magnetic metal had the power of bringing a vibrating magnetic needle suspended over it to rest, and that on causing the disk to rotate the magnetic needle rotated with it. When both were quiescent, there was no measurable attraction or repulsion exerted between the needle and the disk, yet when in motion the disk was competent to drag after it, not only a light needle, but a heavy magnet. To this, " the darkest physical phenomenon of that day," Faraday turned his attention. He placed a copper disk between the poles of a large horse-shoe magnet and, connecting the axis and the edge of the disk each by a wire with a galvanometer (an electric current-measuring machine), he obtained, when the disk was turned round, a constant flow of electricity.

Faraday then stated the law governing the production of currents in disks and wires. When iron filings are scattered over a magnet, the particles of iron arrange themselves in certain definite lines called magnetic curves. Faraday named these curves " lines of magnetic force "; and he showed that to produce induced currents neither approach to nor withdrawal from a magnetic source, or centre, or pole was essential, but that it was only necessary to cut appropriately the lines of magnetic force.

Or, to sum up the essence of electro-magnetic induction: electric current is induced in a conductor which cuts the lines of magnetic force, or whenever the number of these lines passing through the current of the conductor is in any way varied: any movement which causes an alteration to take place in the amount of magnetic conduction through the coil produces a transient current, the electromotive force of which is proportional to the rate of the alteration.

In fact, Faraday had tapped new and inexhaustible sources of electricity. Before these experiments, magnetism had been evoked by electricity; he had aimed, and succeeded, at exciting electricity by magnetism.

Faraday's spinning disk between the poles of the magnet—his " magneto-electric machine "—was, in fact, a primitive dynamo: he was the father of commercially practical generation of electricity.

Through this discovery of induced currents was made possible the invention of the telephone, the development of the telegraph, of electric lighting, and the production of electricity for the thousand and one uses of modern life.

Medicine was quick to benefit by the discovery, and faradic electricity is extensively used in medical practice. Faradic electricity is produced by a simple form of induction coil, consisting of a primary coil of thick wire bound round a tube in which slides a bundle of iron wire. A secondary coil of fine wire is fitted over this. The induced or faradic current is generated in the secondary coil only when the primary current makes or breaks contact (as Faraday discovered in his experiments), so an automatic "interrupter" is used to make and break the primary current and produce a flow of induced current. Faradic electricity was used in the diagnosis of nervous and muscular disorders, for the treatment of inflamed and painful joints in acute cases of articular rheumatism, and to combat neurasthenia and functional disorders.

Faraday himself was partially responsible for an early adoption of electric light. In 1858 Professor F. H. Holmes built an improved and powerful electro-magnetic machine on the pattern invented by Faraday, and Faraday, who in 1836 had been appointed scientific adviser to Trinity House, suggested the use of it for generating current for lighthouse lamps. Accordingly, a complete installation was made in the South Foreland Lighthouse, which was the first in the world to be lit by electricity.

But Faraday was not concerned in the commercial development of his discoveries—he even discarded the supplementary commercial work which added to his income. He went on with his experiments in the spirit of the true investigator. Four years later, investigating from observations made by a William Jenkin, Faraday discovered "extra current" or the current which is induced in the primary wire itself at the moment of making and breaking contact. In writing of this, Professor Tyndall made an illuminating comment on Faraday's thoroughness:—

"Seven and thirty years have passed since the discovery of magneto-electricity; but, if we except the extra current, until quite recently nothing of moment was added to the subject. Faraday entertained the opinion that the discoverer of a great law or principle had a right to the 'spoils'—this was his term—arising from its illustration; and guided by the principle he had discovered, his wonderful mind, aided by his ten fingers, overran in a single autumn this vast domain, and hardly left behind him the shred of a fact to be gathered by his successors."

In 1833 Faraday decided that the various kinds of electricity which had been discovered were all identical. Next he turned to electro-chemistry and electro-chemical decomposition, which he named electrolysis. At this time he invented a number of new terms: he abandoned the word "poles" for the ends of a decomposing cell and called them "electrodes"; substances which could be decomposed by an electric current he called "electrolytes," and constituents of the decomposed electrolyte became "ions." He was the first to make accurate quantitative experiments in electrolysis. The two great laws he formulated are: the mass of substance liberated from an electrolyte by the passage though it of electric current is proportional (1) to the total quantity of electricity which passes through the electrolyte and (2) to the chemical equivalent weight of the substance liberated. How valuable these discoveries have been may be imagined, when one considers the vast commercial uses of electro-chemistry in the refining of metals, metallic production from ore, and in the making of caustic soda, chlorates and gases.

It had been the intention of Sir Robert Peel to offer Faraday a pension, but a change in government left the task to Lord Melbourne, who performed it somewhat brusquely. Faraday proudly refused the offer until Melbourne sent him a written apology, and eventually he was granted £300 a year for the rest of his life.

In 1841 Faraday had a breakdown in health. His nerves were shattered and his mind was seriously shaken. For three years he did nothing, not even "reading on science." He visited Switzerland with his wife and brother-in-law. One of the entries in his journal gives us an insight on his warm affection for his family. At Interlaken, on August 2, 1841, he wrote: "Cloutnail-making goes on here rather considerably, and is a very neat and pretty operation to observe. I love a smith's shop and anything relating to smithery. My father was a smith."

There is a similar story told of how, when sitting for his bust to Noble, he was agitated when the sculptor made a clattering with his chisels. Noble apologized and said that no doubt the jingling of the tools had distressed him and that he was tired. "No, my dear Mr. Noble," answered Faraday gently, "but the noise reminded me of my father's anvil and took me back to my boyhood."

Faraday got back to work as soon as his health permitted, and in 1845 he announced his great discovery of the magnetic rotation of the plane of polarized light. He was the first to seek for and discover effects of magnetism on light; and he found that if polarized light is passed through a transparent substance placed in a strong magnetic field, the plane of polarization is rotated. This, in the science of magneto-optics, is known as the Faraday effect.

Faraday suggested that light might be a series of transverse vibrations travelling along his lines of electric and magnetic force, thus brilliantly foreshadowing the electro-magnetic theory of light later developed by Clerk Maxwell.

The discoveries of Faraday led to the work of Maxwell, and later of Hertz, in electro-magnetic radiation, which paved the way for the invention of wireless telegraphy.

All the experiments and discoveries of Michael Faraday, "the greatest experimental philosopher the world has ever seen," would take a volume to mention. Much of his later work was on diamagnetism: that is, he discovered that every substance reacts to a magnet; those that are attracted, like iron, he called paramagnetic; those that are faintly repelled, diamagnetic.

In all Faraday's work there appeared the same minute care in experimentation, the same wide grasp of possible theory and possible counter-theory, the same imagination, the intuitive grasp of developments, and finally the beautiful lucidity of his exposition. "He smells the truth," said Kohlrausch, but Faraday still tested the smell until it was inescapable. His fame as a scientist was equalled by his power and reputation as a lecturer. He exercised a magic upon his hearers, but he was at his best at the juvenile lectures which he delivered in the Christmas holidays.

For forty years Faraday lived in the Royal Institution, but in 1858 a house on the green at Hampton Court was placed at his disposal by the Queen at the instigation of Prince Albert. Here, at length, he retired, giving up his last active work in 1865. From then until his death on August 25, 1867, he spent his time, with failing memory, "just waiting."

Michael Faraday's achievements, his discoveries which mark a tremendous stride in the progress of the world, have overshadowed the man. Short, curly-headed, active, vivacious, with a hearty laugh, he was a man of strong emotions. He was generous, charitable and deeply religious. His affection for his parents and for his wife was strong and lasting. For some time he was an elder in the Sandemanian Church, in which he was an earnest preacher. But those who knew him stress, not his intellectual power, not his sincerity and his straightforwardness, but his natural refinement and delicacy of character.

"Faraday himself," said Sir Ambrose Fleming, "never gave attention to so-called 'useful' applications of his scientific work. His mind was entirely occupied with the endeavour to penetrate further into the secrets of Nature. . . . For nearly forty years he went every working day into his laboratory with some new question to put experimentally to Nature and he never paused until he had a sufficient answer, 'yea' or 'nay,' to his query."

There could be no finer summary of Faraday, the man, than the description of him given by one of his intimate friends: "Nature, not education, made Faraday strong and refined. A favourite experiment of his own was representative of himself. He loved to show that water, in crystallizing, excluded all foreign ingredients, however intimately they might be mixed with it. Out of acids, alkalis, or saline solutions, the crystal came sweet and pure. By some such natural process in the formation of this man, beauty and nobleness coalesced, to the exclusion of everything vulgar and low."

SIR JAMES YOUNG SIMPSON

(1811–1870)

The grim old days of surgery without anæsthetics seem removed from us by ages, yet it was little more than a century ago that the brilliant physician, James Simpson, introduced the use of chloroform, and saved succeeding generations incalculable suffering. Simpson's fame rests on this great innovation, but he was also pioneer of gynæcology and his work in this field and in that of obstetrics has conferred lasting and immeasurable benefits upon womankind.

To heal the sick and to save life—such were the two objectives of the medical profession in the early part of the nineteenth century. To add to those two admirable ideals only a third was needed—but it was seldom constructively countered—the elimination of pain.

For a man to be a surgeon in those days he had to have qualities not unlike those of a successful butcher. He had to be quick and nimble with his fingers, insensible to pain in others, and brusque in his manner. Otherwise no one had any confidence in him. It never occurred to anyone that there were any other qualifications needed in the medical profession.

But it was the seventh son of a baker in Linlithgow, James Simpson, " a wise wean " protected by the kelpies, as the superstitious peasants of the time believed, who was to cause the much-needed change and bring a great and permanent benefit to humanity. He brought it in a bottle of chloroform.

The operating tables of the time were only one degree less terrible than the torture chambers of the medieval barons. Except that they were there to be healed and not killed, the patients endured much the same agony and saw instruments every whit as terrible and often as dirty. The procedure, too, was much the same. To stop the patient from struggling and interfering with the surgeon he would be bound hand and foot. He could see the instruments spread here and there around him, and he could hear the bubbling and smell the smoke of the boiling tar which he knew would be used to seal the wound when the surgeon had done his task. Often he would faint, mercifully, before an operation was completed. These methods were so commonplace that the doctors and students of Edinburgh were astonished when Simpson expressed his disgust.

Born on June 7, 1811, at the village of Bathgate, Linlithgow, Simpson had spent his early years in the primitive and superstitious atmosphere of the Scottish countryside. The slaughter of animals was a commonplace event to him; and what was worse, he even witnessed such things as the burial alive of a cow because it was believed to have been the origin of a murrain that had afflicted the village cattle.

It may be that these early impressions helped him in his determination in later life to conquer pain. As a boy he was quick at his studies and practical in everything he did. When he came home from school he would mind the bakery when his mother went out. He was observant and athletic, and he soon became known as the brightest in the village school.

Poor though they were, the Simpson family decided that James should be given a chance of making a name for himself, and they pooled their money to send him to Edinburgh University. When he was fourteen years old he entered the faculty of arts, where he spent two years before deciding to specialize in medicine, and at twenty-one he took his degree as a doctor and became a licentiate of the College of Surgeons.

It was then that he had a stroke of luck which was to have a great influence on his career. To gain his doctorate he had written a thesis on "Death from Inflammation." The careful analysis, the balanced reasoning and the far-seeing discernment of this paper so impressed the Professor of Pathology, Dr. John Thomson, that he offered to make the young student his assistant. Simpson gladly accepted, and did so well that when in 1837 Dr. Thomson had to take a year's sick leave, Simpson took his place in the lecture room. The year's experience in pathology was of inestimable value to him, and he co-ordinated this work with other studies on obstetrics, on which he lectured the following year.

It was while he was lecturing at Edinburgh that he made the acquaintance of a distant relative, Jessie Grindlay, the daughter of a Liverpool merchant, and he became a welcome guest at Liverpool during his vacations.

In 1839 the Chair of Midwifery fell vacant at Edinburgh, and Simpson, in virtue of his special studies in obstetrics, applied for the post, which was the principal professorship of its kind in Great Britain. He was told that the occupant of that chair must be married —such was the prudishness of the time. Characteristically,

Simpson departed immediately for Liverpool, and a month later he returned with Jessie Grindlay as his bride. He applied for the professorship again, and this time he was not refused. Here he found his life's work.

Though a scholar and a professor, Simpson had none of the detached outlook of the academic mind. He was, above all, absorbed by the human side of his science, and to him pain and disease were hateful things rather than mere phenomena of interest to the scientist. Although the sight of the tortures undergone by patients on the operating table shocked him, Simpson was indescribably moved by the agonies of the women patients he had to deal with, and the memory of an operation in which the knife was used in a case of childbirth never left him.

Some years after he became professor of midwifery, news reached England in December, 1846, that an American dentist named Morton had used ether as an anæsthetic for the extraction of teeth. In doing this, Morton was carrying out a suggestion made in 1800 by Sir Humphry Davy, when he discovered laughing gas, that it should be used in surgical operations "in which no great effusion of blood takes place," but no one had dared to put Davy's suggestion into practice. Morton, curiously enough, did not use laughing gas, but decided on ether, as it produced a more profound sleep, and was more lasting in its effects.

Simpson saw the first operation to be carried out under a general anæsthetic performed by the famous surgeon, Robert Liston, and the drug used was ether. This so impressed Simpson that he resolved to use ether for midwifery cases, and the results were startling.

It was as if all the pent-up prejudices of the ages were unloosed at once, and a cloudburst of opposition broke out. Although he had to endure the attacks of the more conservative medical men, the chief assault came from the divines and theologians who have always abounded in Scotland. Taking as their text the passage in Genesis, "In sorrow thou shalt bring forth children," they accused Simpson of violating the divine ordinance. Others took an even more obscurantist line, and said that the deep stupor into which the patient was put rendered him or her subject to the machinations of the powers of darkness.

In this they were guilty not only of superstition but also of a confusion of thought. As far back as the seventeenth century there had been certain doctors who had hypnotized their patients before operating on them, though for this they had incurred the censure of the Church which had always taught the evil of surrendering the freedom of the will into the hands of another. But there had never been any prohibition, either biblical or ecclesiastical, of the use of narcotics or drugs for a legitimate purpose. In the thirteenth century, the age when the power of the Church was at its height, an Italian physician, Hugo de Lucca, had given mandragora as a sleeping draught to his patients to enable him to conduct surgical operations.

The logical mind of Simpson had no difficulty in refuting these objections, and his retort to the more serious attack out of Genesis was taken from the same authority. In a letter to *The Lancet,* he said: "Those who urge on a kind of religious ground that an artificial or anæsthetic state of unconsciousness should not be induced merely to save frail humanity from the miseries and tortures of bodily pain, forget that we have the greatest of all examples set before us. I allude to that most singular description of the preliminaries and details of the first surgical operation ever performed on man, which is contained in Genesis II, 21: 'And the Lord God caused a deep sleep to fall upon Adam, and he slept: and he took one of his ribs, and closed up the flesh instead thereof.'" This defence was unanswerable, and the attacks were smothered in general approbation.

Simpson, however, found that ether was not altogether a suitable substance for obstetric purposes, and he lost no time in searching for another anæsthetic. He worked ceaselessly in the daytime in the laboratory, and did not relax even after he came home in the evening, but would invite two or three doctor friends in to continue the research. These meetings had the form rather of friendly gatherings than scientific researches. The three doctors would sit round a table inhaling from their glasses various compounds of liquid that Simpson had prepared. But for long, success eluded them. Finally one night, that of November 4, 1847, Simpson remembered a small bottle of chloroform with which he had once experimented, but had rejected because he considered the liquid to be too ponderous. After much search, the bottle was found under a heap of waste paper in his work room. The chloroform was poured out into the glasses, and the three men began the nightly ritual of inhalation. After a while, they were all of them struck by the brilliance of each other's conversation. Joke capped joke with winged repartee, and the Simpson household took on an unwonted hilarity. The end came suddenly and dramatically. Like the drinking parties of the eighteenth-century squires, one after another of the doctors slid to the floor with a crash.

Simpson was the first to recover, and his first thought was for the success of his experiment. His next was one of intense amusement at the sight of his two staid colleagues straddled on the floor and snoring like drunkards. When the doctors of the party had recovered, one of the ladies, a Miss Petrie, courageously asked if she might repeat the experiment, and she was handed the glass. In a few minutes, crying, "I'm an angel! I'm an angel!" she, too, lapsed into unconsciousness.

This experiment convinced Simpson of the efficacy of the drug he had discovered, and he immediately used it in midwifery cases. He described his results as follows:

> "I have never had the pleasure of watching over a series of better or more rapid recoveries; nor once witnessed any disagreeable results follow to either mother or child; whilst I have now seen an immense amount of maternal pain and agony saved by its employment, and I most conscientiously believe that the proud mission of the physician is distinctly twofold—namely, to alleviate human suffering and to preserve human life."

How well he succeeded in getting his views accepted is testified by the fact that, in 1847, Queen Victoria made him her physician in Scotland, and that she herself submitted to anæsthetics when she bore her children.

In the same year he was honoured by being elected a Foreign Associate of the Academy of Medicine at Paris, even against the rules of the Academy. Other nations were quick to pay tribute to his work, and he was made a member of almost every medical society in Europe and America. In 1856 the French Academy of Sciences awarded him the Monthyon prize of two thousand francs for "most important benefits done to humanity."

Great though he became through this discovery, Simpson deserves imperishable renown for the light that he threw upon, and the improvements he made in, the science and art of gynæcology. It was through his efforts that the country is now covered with hospitals for the special treatment of women, and he may well be said to be the saviour of countless mothers. He brought, too, a new precision into the science of obstetrics, while his papers on both subjects are of permanent value. His foresight was remarkable. In one of his addresses he anticipates the discovery of X-rays:

> "Possibly even by the concentration of electrical and other lights, we may render many parts of the body, if not the whole body, sufficiently diaphanous for the inspection of the practised eye of the physician or surgeon."

In the actual practice of surgery, too, he added his contribution. He introduced a new method of binding arteries known as acupressure, and in this he supplemented the work of Joseph Lister, which unfortunately he could never rightly appreciate. His controversy with Lister, whom he always acknowledged to be a great surgeon, is the one blot on his career. He could never understand Lister's methods, and he failed utterly to see the value of antiseptics.

Accustomed to the violent methods of controversy of his time, Simpson employed them ruthlessly against Lister, but it is certain that had he lived to see the success of Lister's discoveries he would have been the first to make reparation for his attacks.

In 1866 he was created a baronet "in recognition of his professional merits, especially his introduction of chloroform," and he was the first Scottish professor and doctor in Scotland to receive this honour.

But he was not to enjoy his success and happiness for long. The congratulatory letters for the baronetcy had hardly ceased coming in when they were followed by letters of condolence, for his eldest son, Dr. David James Simpson, died suddenly a few days after, and only a month later he lost his daughter, Jessie, at the early age of seventeen.

Simpson was utterly shattered by these blows. His health broke down, though he continued to work until it was physically impossible to do so any longer, and on May 6, 1870, this man who had used sleep to conquer pain in others had to surrender; and he sank, not altogether regretfully, into that sleep from which no man could wake him.

CHARLES ROBERT DARWIN

(1809–1882)

Few books have been greeted with such a storm of controversy as the " Origin of Species," in which Charles Darwin set forth his theory of Natural Selection as the means of evolution. The new theory shocked the churchman and astonished the layman; but the scientist, after careful consideration, supported it; and today, although parts of the theory have been modified, the scientist still accepts it. The name of Darwin will always live, for his was the great mind that gave us a new conception of creation.

IN the second half of the eighteenth century there lived at Lichfield, one Erasmus Darwin, a physician. As a doctor he was famous, and King George III himself had asked Darwin to come to London. But Erasmus, until his second marriage, stuck to Lichfield and to the botanical garden he had made there, for he was famous as a naturalist and a poet, as a radical and a freethinker. As a poet Erasmus Darwin does not rank highly, but his ideas are interesting, for they contain hints and germs of great truths. Most scientists of his day still believed in the theory of special creation, that each species of life was created as it is and was and remains constant; but he believed in evolution.

Erasmus Darwin died in 1802, a year after the great French zoologist, Lamarck, had begun to produce the first results of his study of evolution. Lamarck, who had amplified his work in his *Philosophie Zoologique* in 1809, and his *Histoire naturelle des animaux sans vertèbres* in 1815, attempted to explain evolution by the influence of environment in animal life and by the inheritance of acquired characteristics in animal life. But lack of evidence to establish these theories as laws made them unconvincing.

By study of fossils, of geographical distribution, and of experiments in breeding, the *fact* that evolution had taken place was firmly established. Charles Darwin's principle of Natural Selection, which he outlined in the *Origin of Species*, provided a natural law for the working of evolution, and one capable of proof by observation and experiment.

Natural Selection has been summed up by Herbert Spencer's

phrase: "The survival of the fittest in the struggle for existence": it may be explained briefly as the combined effect of heredity, the struggle for existence, and variation. Darwin held that when varying organs were inherited, those that were advantageous were likely to survive: this in time led to an accumulation of favourable variations, which in turn led to an evolutionary change. "Favourable variations have a tendency to be preserved, unfavourable to be destroyed."

Erasmus Darwin's third son, Robert, became a doctor and settled at Shrewsbury, and there, in 1809, was born Charles Darwin, who gave to the world the only feasible solution of the method of evolution.

The Darwinian theory of the cause and progress of evolution was accepted by the leading scientists; subsequent research in embryology helped confirm it; it was used to advance men's knowledge in anthropology, ethnology, and psychology; and today, although it has been slightly modified in some respects, it is still accepted as valid.

Charles Darwin was born on February 12, 1809. He was the fifth child in a family of six, and he had only reached the age of eight when his mother died. He was looked after by his father and his elder sisters, and all his life he recalled the happiness of his childhood and of his home life.

In 1818 he became a boarder at Shrewsbury school, where the education, following the custom of the age, was on strictly classical lines. Charles said that the only real education he picked up during his school life was from private lessons in Euclid and from chemistry experiments in a home-made laboratory which his brother rigged up in a tool-shed at home. But chemistry was frowned upon at Shrewsbury, and Charles was actually rebuked at school for wasting his time upon it. Out of school he acquired a passion for collecting which was to stand him in good stead as a naturalist, and a love of shooting.

"By the time I went to this day school," he records, "my taste for natural history, and more especially for collecting, was well developed. I tried to make out the names of plants, and collected all sorts of things—shells, seals, franks, coins and minerals. The passion for collecting which leads a man to be a systematic naturalist, a virtuoso, or a miser, was very strong in me, and were clearly innate, as none of my sisters, or brother, ever had this taste."

It was intended that Charles should follow the profession of his father and grandfather and become a doctor, and so, in 1825, he left

When William Harvey presented his revolutionary theory on the circulation of the blood many thought him "crackbrained". Later, Harvey became physician to Charles I (*below*).

By his persistent investigation of natural laws, Galileo Galilei laid the foundations for modern experimental science. (*Above*) Galileo at Pisa where many of his important experiments were carried out.

In 1783 the Montgolfiers launched their captive fire balloon and man made his first aerial voyage. Pilâtre de Rozier and the Marquis d'Arlandes are shown (*above left*) ascending from the gardens of la Muette, Paris. The genius of Isambard Kingdom Brunel lay in showing the world the way in railway construction and ship building. His last great venture was the building of the *Great Eastern* and this photograph (*above right*) shows Brunel beside this famous ship in 1858. Charles Darwin startled the conventionally religious Victorian world with his theories of evolution. This portrait of him (*left*) was taken when he was still virtually unknown in 1854, five years before he published *Origin of Species.*

school for Edinburgh University. But medicine had no attraction for him, anatomy disgusted him, and the operating theatre, in those days before the discovery of anæsthetics, was a chamber of horrors to him.

He decided to abandon medicine and enter the Church; but before he left Edinburgh his friend, Dr. Grant, the zoologist, had turned his attention to nature study. Under his influence Darwin made an examination of some seaside fauna and also collected some of the rarer British beetles.

He entered his name at Christ College, Cambridge, in 1827, spent a year at home in getting up his forgotten classics, and went up in 1828. He joined in the life of the university with zest, did just enough work to get a degree, and divided his leisure between shooting, riding, cards, parties, and beetle-collecting.

"No pursuit at Cambridge," he tells us, "was followed with nearly so much eagerness or gave me so much pleasure as collecting beetles. It was the mere passion for collecting, for I did not dissect them, and rarely compared their external characters with published descriptions, but got them named anyhow. I will give a proof of my zeal. One day, on tearing off some old bark, I saw two rare beetles, and seized one in each hand; then I saw a third and new kind, which I could not bear to lose, so that I popped the one which I held in my right hand into my mouth. Alas! it ejected some intensely acrid fluid which burnt my tongue so that I was forced to spit the beetle out, which was lost, as was the third one."

While up at Cambridge he read Humboldt's *Personal Narrative*, and was fired with enthusiasm for natural history and travelling as a naturalist: he even started to get a party together to visit Teneriffe. At the same time he became very friendly with Henslow, the professor of botany. In fact, he became known in Cambridge as "the man who walks with Henslow."

It was Henslow who persuaded Darwin to attend lectures in geology, and it was Henslow who obtained for him the appointment of naturalist to the *Beagle* expedition. The *Beagle* was a brig which had been fitted out for the survey of the South American coasts, begun by Captain King in 1826, and for the carrying of "a chain of chronometrical measurements round the world."

Darwin had returned home from a geological tour of North Wales when he received a letter from Henslow with the offer of the *Beagle* appointment. "Don't put on any modest doubts or fears about your disqualifications," wrote Henslow, "for I assure you that I think you are the very man they are in search of; so conceive yourself to be tapped on the shoulder by your bum-bailiff and affectionate friend . . ."

Darwin's father objected to the proposal, so he wrote a refusal; but his uncle, Josiah Wedgwood, the son of the great potter, heartily supported the idea, and in the end Robert Darwin was won over. Charles started at daybreak the next day for Cambridge, where he saw Henslow, and then went on to London to see Fitz-Roy. This energetic captain was later to become one of the most violent opponents of Darwinism, and never ceased to lament the fact that it was he who had been responsible, indirectly, for producing it. Apparently he took an instant dislike to Charles, and, being somewhat of a student of physiognomy, complained to Henslow that he doubted whether anyone with Charles's nose, which was, incidentally, one of the most noteworthy features of his face, could possess sufficient energy and determination for the voyage. "But I think," Charles wrote later, "he was afterwards well satisfied that my nose had spoken falsely."

Charles Darwin joined the expedition as naturalist without pay, and on December 27, 1831, the *Beagle,* under the command of Captain Fitz-Roy, set sail for the south.

The voyage lasted five years, and in addition to the survey of the South American coasts the *Beagle* visited the Galapagos Islands, Tahiti, Australia, New Zealand, Tasmania, the Maldive Islands, Mauritius, St. Helena, Ascension, the Cape Verde Islands and the Azores. Darwin returned home with a magnificent collection and a thorough, practical knowledge of geology and zoology. And his study of South American fossils and of the unique bird life of the Galapagos Islands, together with the realization that all living things were interdependent, turned his thoughts to evolution.

"The voyage of the *Beagle* has been by far the most important event in my life," Charles tells us, "and has determined my whole career. I have always felt that I owe to the voyage the first real training or education of my mind; I was led to attend closely to several branches of natural history, and thus my powers of observation were improved, though they were always fairly developed."

The period immediately following his return found him busy with the publication of the results of his work on the *Beagle* voyage, and in 1838 he became secretary to the Geological Society, a post which he held for three years.

At the beginning of the year 1839, Darwin married Emma Wedgwood, the daughter of his uncle, Josiah, and they settled in London; but continued ill-health forced him to seek a retreat from the city, and in 1842 he retired to Downe, in Kent. "Its chief merit," he wrote, "is its extreme rurality. I think I was never in a more perfectly quiet country."

Ill-health, mainly dyspeptic trouble, dogged him all his life, although he was accustomed to conceal his suffering. It was his habit to work quietly in his peaceful retreat at Downe until at last his health broke down completely, and then he would recruit his strength with a short holiday and prepare for another spell of labour.

His first years at Downe he spent in producing his works on the Volcanic Islands and the Geology of South America, together with a valuable monograph on barnacles; but all the while he was drafting and planning his great theory on evolution.

That he held orthodox views in his early years is proved by an entry in his journal for 1834:

". . . It seems not a very improbable conjecture that the want of animals may be owing to none having been created since this country has been raised from the sea . . ."

But in 1842 he had sketched out his theory of Natural Selection in a draft of thirty-five pages. His reading of Malthus on *Population,* in 1838, had influenced the deductions he had made from his own observations. Two years later he improved and expanded the sketch to one of two hundred and thirty pages. From that time he began to collect evidence and make laborious experiments: he reconstructed the skeletons of birds, made breeding experiments with pigeons, inquired into the transport of seeds: all this while he kept up a valuable correspondence with his friends, Lyell, the great geologist, and Hooker and Asa Gray, the botanists. At last, in 1856, Lyell asked him to publish his results, and Darwin began to write them out.

Then one morning Darwin received a letter from the Malay States. It was from a famous British naturalist and explorer, Alfred Russel Wallace, and it contained an essay which elaborated the very theory on which Darwin had been working. "I never saw a more striking coincidence," wrote Darwin. "If Wallace had my manuscript sketch, written out in 1842, he could not have made a better short abstract!"

Darwin was perplexed by this new development. Wallace had said nothing about publication, but Darwin felt that it would be dishonest if he immediately published the results of his own work with the private knowledge that Wallace was in the field. He referred the matter to his friends Lyell and Hooker.

They decided that simultaneous publication of the theories of both men would be the fairest way out of the dilemma: Wallace's paper was read, and with it a letter of Darwin to Asa Gray, dated September, 1857, which gave an outline of his theory, and passages from the sketch of 1844.

Darwin now got to work on his book, but the work was hard and slow. He loved experimenting, but he hated the labour of writing, and his continued ill-health hampered him. But at last it was finished. On September 11, 1859, he wrote: "Oh, good heavens! The relief to my head and body to banish the whole subject from my mind."

As always, he issued the result of all his labour with a great deal of misgiving and diffidence. With one advance copy he wrote: "When I think of the many cases of men who have studied one subject for years, and have persuaded themselves of the truth of the foolishest doctrines, I feel sometimes a little frightened, whether I may not be one of these monomaniacs."

The *Origin of Species* was published on November 24, 1859, and the whole edition of 1,250 copies was sold out on the day of publication. The book created a storm of furious controversy. Religion, firmly believing in the Book of Genesis and special creation, rushed in to attack, and scientists leaped up in defence. The battle raged for years, but Darwin gained adherents among the men whose support he wanted.

He wrote to Hooker that he was "astonished and rejoiced" at the converts to his theory, and added a classified list of those who were convinced of its truth. They made an imposing body:

Geologists: Lyell, Ramsay, Jules, Rogers.

Zoologists and Palæontologists: Huxley, Lubbock, Jenyns (to a large extent), Searle Wood.

Physiologists: Carpenter, Sir H. Holland (to a large extent).

Botanists: Hooker, Watson, Asa Gray (to some extent), Dr. Boott (to some extent), Thwaites.

The most dramatic incident concerned with the publication of the book took place at the famous British Association meeting in Oxford at the end of June, 1860. At this meeting, at which Charles was not present, the enemies of his theory had planned a great attack, and the notorious Bishop Wilberforce, of Oxford, popularly known as "Soapy Sam," was known to be going to lead the onslaught. On the platform to defend Charles were Hooker and Huxley. The excitement was tremendous. "The lecture room in which it had been arranged that the discussion should be held proved far too small for the audience, and the meeting adjourned to the library of the museum, which was crammed to suffocation long before the champions entered the lists," runs an eye-witness account. "The bishop was up to time and spoke for full half an hour with inimitable spirit, emptiness and unfairness. It was evident from his handling of the subject that he had been 'crammed' up to the throat, and that he knew nothing first hand." At the very end of his speech he turned towards Huxley, seated beside him, and asked, with a sarcastic smile, whether it was through his grandfather or grandmother that he claimed descent from a monkey? After this schoolboy taunt he finished his speech by declaring Charles's views to be contrary to Biblical revelation. He then sat down, well satisfied with himself, amongst the applause of the many clergymen present and the waving handkerchiefs of many of the ladies in the audience.

Huxley, who at the bishop's talk had struck his hand upon his knee, saying: "The Lord hath delivered him into my hands," now waited silently, with the audience calling his name on all sides, for the president to call on him to speak. "I am here only in the interests of science," he said, in his usual incisive tone, "and I have not heard anything which can prejudice the case of my august client." Then, after showing how incompetent the bishop was to take part in the discussion, he referred to the question of creation. "You say that development drives out the Creator. But you assert that God made you: and yet you know that you yourself were originally a little piece of matter no bigger than the end of this gold pencil case." Finally, he made his famous retort on the question of descent from a monkey in a reference to "Soapy Sam's" ancestor, Samuel Wilberforce. "I would rather have an ape for an ancestor," he said. "I should feel it no shame to have risen from such an origin. But I should feel it a shame to have sprung from one who prostituted the gifts of culture and of eloquence to the service of prejudice and of falsehood." There was an immediate uproar. The bishop himself, as was his wont when attacked, smiled greasily, but throughout the audience men were on their feet, protesting and cheering. Lady Brewster achieved a passing fame by fainting and having to be carried out. From the holy ranks of the clergy present came forth the sounds of most unholy anger.

When order was at last restored, it turned out that the next speaker was none other than Admiral (as he had then become) Fitz-Roy, who was smarting under the thought that it was he who was indirectly responsible for the terrible heresies which his former protégé had produced. Waving a Bible in the air, he proclaimed its unshakable authority.

After the gallant admiral and one or two other speakers, came Hooker, who apparently thought that Huxley, in spite of having rendered one member of the audience unconscious, had not made sufficient impression, and it was up to him to save the day. And so, in his own opinion at least, he did—" smashing that Amalekite Sam " amid, as he told Charles afterwards, repeated applause. " I hit him in the wind at the first shot in ten words taken from his own ugly mouth; and then proceeded to demonstrate in as few more: (1) that he could never have read your book, and (2) that he was absolutely ignorant of the rudiments of botanical science. Sam was shut up—had not one word to say in reply, and the meeting was dissolved forthwith, leaving you master of the field after four hours' battle."

While the storm raged, Darwin worked quietly on developing his theory, although that was not the only study which occupied his mind. He spent much time in botanical research, and in 1862 published his work on the *Fertilization of Orchids*. Two years later he produced the *Movements and Habits of Climbing Plants*.

His first enlargement on his evolutionary theory came in 1868, with his *Variation of Animals and Plants under Domestication*. From that he went on to *The Descent of Man* (1871). In this he deposed man from his lordship of creation and made the human race to be descended from a hairy four-handed animal of the great anthropoid group, related to the progenitors of chimpanzees, orang-utans and gorillas. He also developed his theories of sexual selection. The theories he puts forward in the *Descent of Man* have not been universally accepted.

In 1872 Darwin made a further contribution to his work on evolution in *Expression of the Emotions in Man and Animals*. For the remainder of his life he devoted his writings mainly to botanical subjects.

He worked steadily to the end. He divided his days into short spells of labour and rest, and he worked to a regular programme. He accounted for his success by admitting that he seemed " superior to the common run of men in noticing things which easily escape attention, and in observing them carefully."

His chief relaxation was novel reading, and he would frequently " bless all novelists," provided they wrote books with happy endings.

His own ending came on April 19, 1882, at Downe, and science mourned the thinker who had changed man's whole conception of the world.

FERDINAND DE LESSEPS

(1805–1894)

The Suez Canal, that wonderful waterway which divides two continents, is the memorial of the greatness of Ferdinand de Lesseps. His vision, his courage, and his determination caused that canal to be cut, and by his achievement he brought the Far East nearer to the West and gave to Great Britain a new and important channel of empire communication. With the same spirit and enterprise de Lesseps tackled the task of cutting the Panama Canal, but the venture brought disgrace and ruin upon his head. In the story of these two canals, mighty feats of engineering, is the drama of his rise and fall.

THE life of Ferdinand de Lesseps is at once one of the great romances and one of the pitiful tragedies of the nineteenth century. Few men have achieved more in face of such overwhelming odds, and few men with such a record of success have died in such poverty and disgrace. De Lesseps battled his way slowly to the height of fame, a fame all the more glorious because of the rich gift it gave mankind, and then fell to the depths of ignominy.

He was the man responsible for one of the finest engineering feats of all time, the construction of the Suez Canal. He made a reality of what had long been a dream and, by cutting a passage between the Mediterranean and the Red Sea, shortened the journey to the East by thousands of miles. Unfortunately, his attempt to repeat his success and build a similar canal at Panama failed, and failure was made all the more bitter for being sullied by the breath of scandal and corruption.

Ferdinand Marie de Lesseps was born on November 19, 1805, at Versailles. For centuries his family had been servants of the State and Ferdinand followed the family tradition. In 1825 he entered the consular service, and was sent as assistant vice-consul to Lisbon.

It was when on his way to take up a similar post in Alexandria that he first conceived the idea of building the Suez Canal. His ship, the *Diogenes,* was quarantined off the port and to while away the time de Lesseps glanced idly through some books his chief had sent him. One of them dealt with the possibility of piercing the isthmus of Suez to link up the Mediterranean with the Red Sea, and thus cut out the Cape route to the East, which would mean an enormous saving of time and money. The memorandum had been drawn up on Napoleon's instructions by an engineer named Lapère in 1797, when the little Corsican had been on his ill-fated Egyptian expedition.

The idea fired de Lessep's imagination. From that moment he became a man with a mission. Henceforth his one ambition was to construct the Suez Canal. Though the time was not yet ripe, he was convinced that the opportune moment would come, and the work be accomplished. Without knowing it, he laid the foundations of his work almost immediately, for he became friendly with Mohammed Said, son of Mehemet Ali, the great ruler of Egypt. The work itself was not undertaken for more than twenty years.

Meanwhile de Lesseps had risen in the consular service. While consul at Cairo between 1833 and 1837, he distinguished himself by his bravery and energy during a terrible plague, and also in 1842, when at the Spanish port of Barcelona, he showed the most persistent bravery during an insurrection. Throughout a heavy bombardment he rescued, without distinction, members of both factions. Seven years later he was sent on a secret mission to Rome, which led to his resigning from the consular service. A new government repudiated the policy of the old, and de Lesseps was made the scapegoat. He felt the blow keenly, but ultimately it proved a blessing in disguise, for when the time came for him to begin his life's work, he was free to devote all his attention to it.

One morning in August, 1854, de Lesseps was supervising the work of masons who were altering his house at La Chenaie when he opened some newspapers that had been passed to him. Casually glancing through the pages, he noticed an announcement of the accession to pashalik of Egypt of his friend, Mohammed Said. Immediately the idea which had lain dormant for twenty-two years flashed across his mind. Hope was fanned by the receipt, soon afterwards, of an invitation from Said Pasha to visit him at Alexandria. He arrived there on November 7, 1854. The Pasha received him warmly, housed him in a palace, and placed servants and horses at his disposal.

De Lesseps was somewhat doubtful as to the Pasha's attitude, but after some hesitation he broached the matter. His personality was extremely attractive and his manner persuasive. The Pasha furthermore, realized the value to his country of such a scheme, and believed that it could be carried through. He listened, pondered the matter, and said simply, "I am satisfied. I accept your scheme." The first victory had been won.

The engineer now found himself confronted by a more formidable barrier. That barrier, ironically enough, was the hostility of the British Government.

From first to last, Palmerston, supported by his Cabinet, set his face against the project. He told de Lesseps bluntly that the Government would move heaven and earth to stop the canal being built. England, he said, regarded the canal as a French attempt to interfere in the East, and was convinced that its construction would have an adverse effect on Britain's maritime supremacy. Had Palmerston only known how things were to turn out and that within twenty years, through Disraeli's brilliant stroke, England would control the canal, he might have acted differently.

The country as a whole was more favourable to the scheme. Its imagination was fired by the project, and de Lesseps was well received when he held meetings in London and the major provincial towns. Despite public opinion, the Government tried to kill the project. Permission from the Sultan of Turkey, as overlord of Egypt, was necessary, and Lord Stratford de Redcliffe, who had great influence over the sultan, did all he could to persuade him not to grant it. De Lesseps never for a moment allowed his activities to flag. The rights were obtained and he floated a company in Paris, and on the plans of two French engineers in Egypt, Linant Bey and Mougel Bey, the work was put in hand. On April 25, 1859, the first blow of the axe was given by de Lesseps at Port Said.

His troubles multiplied. Apart from the difficulties involved in such work, England never ceased her attempts to undermine the scheme. When Said died in 1863, Ismail, who succeeded him, though willing for the excavations to continue, was less loyal than his predecessor, and caused de Lesseps much uneasiness.

The most severe blow came when, largely through the efforts of British agitation, the practice of using forced labour was stopped. At the outset it had been estimated that eight thousand men would be needed. Soon there were twenty thousand employed, and then forty thousand, and at one time there were as many as eighty thousand at work. The bulk of these wielders of pick and spade were Egyptian fellaheen. The conditions under which they worked were fairly good, and the pay was better than they would have received elsewhere, but they were drafted compulsorily.

The agitation in England was not entirely humanitarian. Lancashire had been badly hit by the cotton famine, due largely to the American Civil War, and England would have preferred to see these labourers at work in the cotton fields. To engage European labour was beyond the resources of the company, and for two years the work was held up. Yet de Lesseps, though badly hit, did not despair. It was decided to install machinery, at that time a novel measure. The change proved the salvation of the enterprise, and in 1869 the task was completed, not, however, without overcoming serious difficulties of construction.

The canal was opened amid gigantic celebrations, and de Lesseps tasted the sweets of success. The Emperor of Austria, the Crown Prince of Prussia and the Empress Eugénie, wife of Napoleon III and chief guest of honour, were present.

On November 16, 1869, the Khedive, Ismail Pasha, officially opened the canal. In the port, in addition to the royal yachts, were the battleships of nearly every nation, and for an hour onlookers were deafened by repeated salvoes.

Next day came the great test. Headed by the *Aigle,* on which was the empress, the ships of sixty nations sailed slowly through the canal without a hitch.

De Lesseps's success was complete. Disregarding all difficulties and surmounting obstacles as they came, he had forced his way to victory. No one now questions that it was one of the finest engineering feats ever accomplished. It shortened the voyage from London to Bombay by five thousand miles.

De Lesseps returned to France, full of honour and justly proud of his great achievement. Had he been content to rest on his laurels, he might have passed his last years in happiness instead of disgrace. Not that ambition caused him to stumble and fall. When the Geographical Society of Paris decided, in 1879, to construct the Panama Canal, de Lesseps was designated head of the enterprise. He had every right to feel confident that he could repeat his success. The venture attracted the attention of all classes in France, and thousands of small investors put their savings into the company.

Work was begun in 1881 and went on for eight years, throughout which extravagance and corruption sapped the vitality of the venture. While the engineers themselves were going ahead, the administrators were madly squandering the company's money. Everything was bought at an excessive figure; supplies were taken regardless of necessity, and included an item of ten thousand snow shovels.

Disease and death were taking toll of those employed. Sir Ronald Ross estimated that fifty thousand lives were lost, chiefly through malaria and yellow fever.

Panama became a pest-house. Froude, the historian, said of it, "In all the world there is not now concentrated in any single spot so much swindling and villainy, so much foul disease, such a hideous dung-heap of moral and physical abomination."

It is doubtful whether de Lesseps knew of the state of affairs. He spent most of the time in Paris, and was much too old to have a complete grasp of all that was happening. But in one respect he was at fault. He had determined to build the canal without locks, and his success in the case of the Suez had made him over-confident and unwilling to listen to the advice of his engineers. In vain they pointed out to him that he was wrong. The Culebra and the Chagres, the mountain and river that barred his path, could not be overcome in any other way. De Lesseps was obdurate, and against this obstacle his will, fortune and honour were broken.

In 1888 the company went bankrupt for £80,000,000. It was estimated that one-third was spent on the canal, one-third wasted, and one-third stolen. Thousands of investors were ruined, and a tremendous scandal ensued, stirred up by the opposition with all its power. The French Government was forced to institute an inquiry, and de Lesseps, his son and his assistants were made to stand trial. De Lesseps was sentenced to five years' imprisonment and fined, but the sentence was suspended. He died at his home at Chenaie on December 7, 1894, in his ninetieth year.

Much of the work done by the white-haired old genius, whom Gambetta had called "the great Frenchman," was of the highest value, as the Americans, who succeeded where he had failed, readily admitted. Their task was made much easier by the pioneer work of de Lesseps and his followers.

Of the character of de Lesseps, all who knew him spoke highly. He was charming, good-natured, and highly honourable. When he floated the Suez Canal Company he could easily have collaborated with one or two big Parisian bankers and netted a fortune. It is unlikely that he ever thought of such a thing. His one ambition was to construct the canal, and in that he succeeded.

LOUIS PASTEUR

(1822–1895)

The name of Pasteur has become a household word throughout the world. It is fitting, for he worked to bestow some of the greatest benefits that science has produced upon mankind. He discovered the existence of bacteria in fermentation and put medical science on the track of the cause of many diseases. His discovery of germs in the air enabled Lister to do his great work in the cause of antiseptics. He crushed the terrors of anthrax, hydrophobia, and rabies. Countless human lives have been saved and the sufferings of millions relieved, through the pioneer work of that mighty chemist and simple man, Pasteur.

THAT commonplace thing, the "average man," and yet a genius. Such was Louis Pasteur. It would be difficult to overrate the importance of his work for humanity and science, the brilliant discoveries that must stand for all time, the patient work that had led to them, the gigantic utility of his achievements. And it would be foolish to underrate the beauty and simplicity of the man's character, a nature that remained unspoiled amid his many triumphs of the mind and the honours that those triumphs brought him. Among his sayings there is this, which may be said to outline the guiding principles of his life:

"These three things, will, work and success, cover the whole of our lives. Will opens the door to brilliant and happy careers; work crosses the threshold, and, at the end of the journey, success comes to crown our efforts."

Pasteur was born two days after Christmas in 1822 at Dôle, Jura. He was the son of a tanner who had been a sergeant-major in Napoleon's army of the Peninsula, and was filled at an early age with that love of country and desire for achievement that characterized all who came into contact with the tradition of the Corsican.

As a boy he so loved the beauties of his native countryside that he began to make little drawings. He painted the portraits of his parents, and many of his village friends. Indeed, until his sixteenth year this love of art held him until he decided that there was greater and better work ahead.

The romantic chivalry that made the father snatch back his sword from the hands of the official of Louis XVIII, to whom he had been forced to deliver it after Napoleon's downfall, descended to the son. Throughout his long life, Louis Pasteur was utterly indifferent alike to danger or to the criticisms of the outside world. He remained steadfast to the ideals he had received from the old volunteer of the Republic, and yet to him patriotism meant something more than conquest by force of arms. The great aim of his life—and it is perhaps not his least achievement—was to rehabilitate the reputation of his vanquished and humiliated country.

His love of peace was such that at the outbreak of the Franco-Prussian War he did not hesitate to send a formal protest to the medical faculty of Bonn against the barbarity and hypocrisy of "those who, to satisfy a criminal pride, persist in the massacre of two great peoples. Men of science ought to be preoccupied by what would add to the glory of their country."

Thus did he fight France's battles, and in this spirit did he restore to her that leadership in the world of science that had been hers before the great revolution.

Shortly after Pasteur's birth, his family removed to Arbois, and there he first attended school. But in 1838 he was sent away to a school in the Latin quarter of Paris, where homesickness and loneliness caused a breakdown in his health. "If only I could smell the tannery once more, I should be well," he said.

So he returned to Arbois, but shortly afterwards he went to the Royal College of Besançon, where in 1840 he took his degree of Bachelor of Letters. He stayed at Besançon as an assistant mathematical master of the college, and after two years gained his Bachelor of Science degree, though his chemistry was classed as "mediocre"!

For some time now Pasteur studied chemistry under the great J. B. Dumas at the Sorbonne, and in 1848 he was appointed Professor of Physics at Dijon, but almost at once he removed to Strasbourg, where he taught chemistry. This recognition was largely due to his first original work, that on the optical qualities of racemic acid. This first triumph was one which was to win him the lifelong friendship of Professor J. B. Biot, of the Sorbonne, the most historical of Europe's universities, as well as gain him the Chair of Chemistry at Strasbourg University. Biot had been working on a problem which had baffled the scientists of the time—the theory of the polarization of light—and it was through Pasteur's acute observation that the key was found. This so delighted Biot that he took Pasteur's arm and said: "My dear boy, I have so loved science all my life that this makes my heart beat."

The problem consisted in the reason for the different reactions of two apparently identical acids to a ray of polarized light. One acid turned the plane of light in a right-handed direction; the other had no rotary effect at all. Pasteur showed that the inactive acid contained two compounds of the same composition, but with differing properties. One of these compounds was the ordinary right-handed acid, the other was an altogether new acid with an equally powerful left-handed action which neutralized the first.

One of Pasteur's first visits on his appointment to Strasbourg, in 1848, was naturally to the Rector of the Academy, M. Laurent, and this was to be the forerunner of many visits of a much more intimate character. Marie Laurent, the pretty young daughter of the rector, had captured the young scientist's heart and caused him to forget a resolution that he had made not to think of marriage for some time. A fortnight after his arrival, he wrote to M. Laurent the formal letter that was necessary in those days, announcing an imminent proposal. But Marie refused to give an immediate answer, and Pasteur wrote to her asking her not to judge him too quickly. "Time will show you that under this cold and shy exterior there is a heart full of affection for you," he said. She accepted him, and they were married on May 29, 1849.

Despite the fact that he was a young man very much in love, he was so absorbed in his work that it is said that they had to run to Pasteur's laboratory to get him ready for the wedding. However that may be, it is certain that his married life was idyllic, and that Mme. Pasteur proved a perfect wife to him.

When the prince-president, the future Napoleon III, visited Strasbourg, there were great entertainments in which, of course, the functionaries of the university took a leading part. On the day of the prince's arrival, Pasteur was so immersed in his laboratory that he forgot the passage of time, and so Mme. Pasteur missed all the fun; and when, returning in the evening, he remarked, "What would you have? I could not interrupt my experiments," Mme. Pasteur said not a word of reproach. She was as devoted to the work that made him glorious as he was himself.

His whole interest lay in his work. Had it not been for Mme. Pasteur's constant vigilance at the required times, he would never have attended the meetings of the academies and committees to which he belonged. To him, silence was indispensable when he was working. He once said to the great chemist, Wurtz, who was working surrounded by his pupils in a constant hubbub: "What! You can work in the middle of this turmoil?" "It stimulates ideas," replied Wurtz. "It would drive all mine away," said Pasteur.

Mme. Pasteur only opposed him, and then sweetly and gently, when she thought his work was affecting his health. "I am often scolded by Mme. Pasteur, whom I comfort by telling that I am making her a name which will be known to posterity," he once said. And, indeed, his wife understood him and appreciated more than anyone the value of his labours. "She was not only an incomparable companion to her husband, but also his best collaborator," said one of Pasteur's most devoted disciples.

In 1854, Pasteur was given a professorship and made dean of the new Faculty of Sciences at Lille, and here, in the centre of the brewing industry, he turned his attention to the mysteries of fermentation.

One day Pasteur was invited to go over a brewery and give an explanation of why the beer in certain vats was either of an inferior quality or was even definitely bad. Two vats were shown to him, one containing good beer, the other bad. The scientist examined the yeast in the vats, carefully noting its consistency, and trying the reaction of samples from each vat to various chemical tests. Suddenly, he noticed a curious phenomenon which had never seemed to strike anyone before. It was that the globules of yeast in the good vat were nearly spherical, whereas in the bad vat they were elongated. This difference in the shape of the globules suggested to Pasteur the idea that there might be some different substances that had been introduced into the vat during the process of fermentation which would, as it were, "sour" the beer. As a result of further researches he came to the conclusion that the change had not in any way been caused by any substance in the vat itself, but had come from contact with the outside air. In short, the organisms that caused fermentation had come from similar organisms existing in the atmosphere. From that he went on to prove the existence of germs in the air, and thus exploded the theory of spontaneous generation which had held the field until his day. That theory held that germs or living organisms were produced from inorganic (non-living) matter. But it was not until he had finished a series of exhaustive and intricate experiments, such as the filtration of pure air from the high Alps, that he finally announced his discovery.

That was in 1864. The results of his researches made Pasteur known as the greatest chemist of his day. His discovery was applied by Lord Lister to the treatment of wounds, who took steps to keep germs away, with the result that millions have been saved from the dread consequences of septicæmia.

In 1865, Pasteur was requested by the French government to investigate a disease which was attacking silkworms and threatening to ruin the whole industry. Within three years he had isolated the bacilli of two distinct diseases and had discovered a means of protecting silkworms from them as well as one of detecting diseased stock.

At this time he was stricken with semi-paralysis, but he was able to return to Paris and continue working—in 1867 he had been appointed professor of chemistry at the Sorbonne—and shortly afterwards he published his famous paper on fermentation.

He now turned his attention to bacteriology, and in 1877 began his researches upon anthrax. In two years he had demonstrated the whole natural history of the disease, when, in 1880, he was requested to investigate chicken cholera.

There was a logical sequence in his discoveries. From solving the problem of the fermentation of beer, he discovered the existence of germs in the air; from the investigation of the disease of chicken cholera, which had decimated the fowls of France, he found the microbe which was ultimately to lead him to the discovery of the cause of anthrax, the terrible disease that afflicted not only cattle but human beings; and, finally, to his great work—the diagnosis and defeat of rabies or hydrophobia.

It is said that he saved the poultry industry of France more than the whole amount of the war idemnity paid to Germany after 1870. The poultry farmers were suffering in the same way as the silkworm industry had been, when Pasteur began his examination of the dread disease. In an amazingly short space of time he managed to isolate the germ; then he cultivated an attenuated form of it and injected fowls with the culture. That rendered them immune from chicken cholera!

Returning to his work on anthrax, he made use of the same methods by which he had conquered the chicken cholera—and with the same success.

It was out of these researches into the causes of anthrax, and later, rabies, that came the process of inoculation, which will be for all time linked with the name of Pasteur, and the tremendous success he had in dealing with the latter disease led to his foundation, in 1888, of the Pasteur Institute.

These diseases are now so rare that it is hardly realized how terrible they were. Anthrax affects chiefly cattle and horses, but it is so highly infectious that contact, even with the hair of a diseased animal, may produce the symptoms in human beings. It is generally fatal.

The discovery and use by Pasteur of the serum as an antidote to this horrible disease has been of indescribable benefit to the human race, and especially to those who are engaged in manual labour. The mortality was chiefly great among wool sorters, and if the condition of the wool workers of Bradford is today healthier and cleaner, it is to Pasteur's discovery that the thanks must be given. But if anthrax was a disease which took its tribute of human life, the toll that it exacted from animals was far heavier. So old is the disease that some have supposed it to be one of the plagues that descended on Egypt at the time of the Exodus, and Virgil mentions it in the third book of his great rustic poem, the *Georgics,* as the only cattle disease worthy of mention. Not only, then, have the workers in the mills cause to bless the name of Pasteur, but also those who are dependent for their livelihood on the production of sturdy and healthy cattle.

Now hydrophobia, or rabies, as it is called when contracted by animals, is in its effects more terrible than anthrax, and it is more deadly. When a man has been bitten by a mad dog, the wound does not immediately get septic or declare itself as in anthrax. Indeed, cases have been known where a wound has apparently healed, and it was only weeks later that anything unusual appeared. The first symptoms are great mental depression, an unusual tendency to talkativeness, and an abrupt and rapid articulation. As the disease develops, the sufferer experiences intense thirst, and his every effort to slake this thirst causes such agonizing seizures that he acquires a dread of anything liquid. Even the sound of running water will cause a seizure when this stage is reached. Finally, after two or three days of intense suffering, the victim dies either from a paroxysm of choking, or from exhaustion.

All this the work of Pasteur banished to the limbo of forgotten plagues. His work was not without its real physical dangers. He kept whole kennels of mad dogs, which he would handle fearlessly. He was so eager to secure specimens of the germ of rabies that on one occasion he actually sucked through a tube the saliva of a mad dog. The sublime courage of this act will be realized when it is remembered that it is through the saliva that the mad dog transmits the disease. He ended by discovering a serum which, when injected into a recently bitten dog, cured it.

But could the same thing be done for human beings? That was

the problem. Hydrophobia was becoming a scourge in France, and the doctors were in despair of a cure. The difficulty was to discover the exact strength of serum which would be effective, and Pasteur spent agonizing months in thinking out how he was to effect the necessary experiments without endangering the life of a patient.

At last the opportunity came. A child, Joseph Meister, had been severely bitten by a peculiarly violent dog. He was brought to hospital, where they despaired of his life. As the case seemed hopeless, Pasteur, as he said, "decided, not without deep and cruel anxiety, to test on Joseph Meister the method that had been constantly successful on dogs."

For nine days the great scientist inoculated the child with varying strengths of serum, and after three weeks he was able confidently to predict that the boy would live. Three months and three weeks after the date of the accident, Joseph Meister walked out of hospital completely cured. But that cure had cost the boy's saviour a hell of mental anguish. Though he knew that his experiments on animals had all been successful, and that the disease was fundamentally the same, except for differing symptoms in humans, Pasteur as a scientist knew that there is always in science the possibility of some unknown law taking the matter out of human hands, and that something might have gone wrong. It has been said that the cure of this child was the "greatest recompense his brave heart desired for all his work."

But other recompense he did have. So great had his fame become that when the positivist, Joseph Littré, died, his chair at the Académie française was offered to Pasteur. When he began making the customary formal visits to the academicians, he was kindly received on all hands. Only Victor Hugo asked him, somewhat coldly: "What would you say if I presented myself at the Academy of Science?" Alexandre Dumas, however, would not allow him to pay his call, saying: "It is I who will go to thank him for kindly consenting to be one of us."

At his inauguration he affirmed before an assembly that had none other than the famous free-thinker, Renan, as its director, his faith in the supernatural. "Everywhere in the world I see the expression of the idea of Infinite. Owing to it, belief in the supernatural is found at the bottom of every heart. . . . Science and the passion for knowledge—what are they but the spur which the mystery of the Universe applies to our souls?"

And Renan, though compelled to disagree with the great scientist's declaration of faith, in an eloquent passage concluded by saying: "You will, above all, bring us your glory, your genius, and the fame of your discoveries. Sir, you are welcome."

He was welcome, too, at the University of Edinburgh, where his great contemporary, Lister, acknowledged his debt to him in regard to his own great discoveries in antiseptic surgery.

When the learned societies of the world gathered in Paris on December 27, 1892, to celebrate Pasteur's jubilee, Lister paid him this homage: "Your researches threw a powerful light which has illuminated the dark places in surgery, and have changed the treatment of wounds from an uncertain and too often disastrous business into a scientific and certainly beneficial art." Not only surgery, but medicine, too, said Lister, would recognize for all time the debt it owed to the name of Pasteur, and he added his own personal tribute of thanks for the knowledge he had gained from the work of this brilliant and humble-minded Frenchman. Then, in the midst of the terrific applause at the end of his panegyric, Lister stepped up to the dais, and embraced Pasteur, thus sealing with personal friendship the intellectual and scientific bond that had long existed between the two men.

In spite of all the honours that were heaped upon him, Pasteur, as has been said, remained simple of heart. Perhaps the imagery of his boyhood's days, when he limned the familiar scenes of his birthplace, and the longing to be a great artist, never wholly left him. In truth he did become a great artist, though after his sixteenth year he abandoned the brush for ever. Like every artist of worth, he put his whole soul and energy into his work, and it was this very energy that in the end wore him out. For to him, each sufferer was something more than just a case that was to be cured. He looked upon the fight against hydrophobia as a battle, and he was absorbed in his determination to win. The sight of injured children, particularly, moved him to an indescribable extent. He suffered with his patients, and yet he would not deny himself a share in that suffering. His greatest grief was when sheer physical exhaustion made him give up his active work. He retired to the estate at Villeneuve l'Etang, where he had his kennels for the study of rabies, and there he passed his last summer, as his great biographer, Vallery-Radot, has said, "practising the Gospel virtues."

"He reverenced the faith of his fathers," says the same writer, "and wished without ostentation or mystery to receive its aid during this last period."

The attitude of this man to the science he had done so much to perfect can be best summed up in a sentence that he is reputed once to have uttered, concerning the materialism of many of his contemporaries in similar branches of learning to his own: "The more I contemplate the mysteries of Nature, the more my faith becomes like that of a Breton peasant. Perhaps, if I learn still more, I shall have the faith of a Breton peasant's wife."

But even in retirement he loved to see his former pupils, and it was then that he would reiterate his life principles: "Work," he would say, "never cease to work." So well had he kept this precept that he began rapidly to sink from exhaustion.

Finally, on September 27, 1895, when someone leant over his bed to offer him a cup of milk, he said sadly: "I cannot," and with a look of perfect resignation and peace, seemed to fall asleep. He never again opened his eyes to the cares and sufferings of a world which he had done so much to relieve and to conquer. He was within three months of his seventy-third birthday.

Thus passed, as simply as a child, the man whom the French people were to vote at a plebiscite as the greatest man that France had ever produced. Napoleon, who has always been considered the idol of France, was placed fifth.

No greater tribute could have been paid to Louis Pasteur, the tanner's son, the scientist, the man of peace, the patient worker for humanity.

WILLIAM THOMSON, LORD KELVIN

(1824–1907)

One of the keenest and most versatile minds that ever answered the call of science was that of William Thomson, Lord Kelvin. He probed and studied in every branch of physical science, and by his inventions aided the development of industry and the welfare of his fellow-men. The submarine cable and the improved mariner's compass are two of his achievements that signalize the greatness and the value of a lifetime devoted to ingenious invention and patient research.

IT was examination day at Glasgow University. Crowds of young men were filing into the long hall where rows of desks stood, dressed like soldiers, at intervals of three paces. Among the candidates jostling their way into the examination room was a little ten-year-old boy, who took his place with youths seven and eight years his senior.

That boy's name was William Thomson, the son of James Thomson, professor of mathematics at the university. He was born on June 26, 1824, at Belfast, where his father had been a teacher of mathematics at the Royal Academical Institution. When William was eight years old, his father took up his appointment at Glasgow and, at the age of ten, William matriculated and thus began an association with the university that was to last until his death in his eighty-third year.

To matriculate at such an age was almost a phenomenal achievement, but it was looked upon as nothing out of the ordinary in the Thomson family. Mrs. Elizabeth King, William Thomson's sister, records in her book, *Lord Kelvin's Early Home,* that before he was ten years old, William would try to solve some of the problems his father had set his class at the university, and that one day a particularly difficult problem had been given. William, as usual, put his childish brain to the task, but when bed-time came no solution was forthcoming. Some hours later, when he was supposed to be fast asleep, a small voice was heard from upstairs, "Eureka! Eureka!"

The professor rushed up to see what was the matter, and there he found his small son, bare-footed in his nightgown on the landing, triumphantly holding a slate, on which he had scribbled, by the scanty light of the stair-gas, the solution of the problem.

But William Thomson's was a versatile mind, and he assimilated and loved the classics as well as solving the most abstruse mathematical problems. He once said, "I never found that the small amount of Greek I learned was a hindrance to my acquiring some knowledge of natural philosophy." At the age of twelve he won a prize for translating from the Latin Lucian's *Dialogues of the Gods,* and he won the university medal at sixteen for his essay, *On the Figure of the Earth,* on the title page of which he wrote a quotation which aptly describes his own life:—

> "Mount where science guides,
> Go measure earth, weigh air, and state the tides;
> Instruct the planets in what orbs to run,
> Correct old time and regulate the sun."

The mathematical handling of this essay has been described as marvellous, and it is interesting to note that during his life he frequently referred to it. There are three notes on the manuscript in his handwriting. One is dated October 16, 1844, another, "*Great Eastern* at Sea, September 13, 1866," and a third is signed "K, October 21, 1907." Thus, after fifty-seven years, and only two months before his death, this great man of science still found some use in speculating over the study of his boyhood.

When he was nearly seventeen, Thomson went up to Peterhouse College, Cambridge. While he was up, though he never neglected his work, he found time to row for his college. He once said, "I simply rowed for exercise every day, as I found it better exercise than walking." But that he was no mean oarsman is shown by the fact that he won the Colquhoun Silver Sculls. Though he regretted "the three weeks clean cut out of the time for working at Cambridge" through training for Peterhouse boat, he ended by being second wrangler, gaining the first Smith's Prize, and becoming a Fellow of his college. After going down from Cambridge, he went to Paris, where he studied under Professor Regnault, then engaged in his famous researches on the thermal properties of steam.

This apprenticeship was to set Thomson on his future career in life. He determined to specialize in research work in physics, and so great was his knowledge and so much promise did he show, that in 1846, when only twenty-two, he became professor of natural philosophy at Glasgow University. He was to hold this chair for fifty-three years, during which time he was to gain universal recognition as one of the greatest physicists of his time.

Many of the greatest researches of other physicists of the nineteenth century came from suggestions that Professor Thomson threw out at his lectures. One of his earliest papers was concerned with the age of the earth, and in these speculations he came up against what was known as the Uniformitarian school of thought. The Uniformitarians supposed that the earth existed in very much its present form some thousands of millions of years ago. Thomson showed conclusively by his calculations and experiments on heat and the dissipation of energy, that the sun had not illuminated the earth for more than about one hundred to five hundred million years.

These calculations were of inestimable value not only to geologists, but also to navigators, for in the course of arriving at his conclusions he had investigated the action of the tides, and had described in particular those in the Straits of Dover and the Mediterranean.

A meeting with Goule in 1847, whose theories on heat interested Thomson, led him to the enunciation, in 1851, of the now absolutely established dynamical theory of heat, and the law of the Conservation of Energy, which states that the earth retains the heat it derives from the sun, and that no energy is entirely lost, but must be developed or absorbed into some other kind of energy. Thomson showed this by giving instances of energy being transformed in all the major branches of physics, such as mechanics, heat, electro-statics and magnetism.

But although Thomson's work was pre-eminent in the world of physics, he is best known to the world at large for his discoveries and inventions. His greatest invention was the submarine cable. For years there had been attempts to exploit on a practical basis the long-distance telegraph. Hitherto all these efforts had been foiled by the fact that the greater the length of cable that was needed, the slower the transmission had to be. Thomson could not keep his mind from these cable problems, and arduous as was his work in the physics laboratory, he still laboured at the problem of telegraphy in his every spare moment. At last, in 1867, he produced his Mirror Galvanometer, which served not only as a "speaking" instrument for receiving signals, but also as an invaluable appliance for the most delicate operations of electrical testing.

Perhaps if Thomson had not decided to devote his energies to scientific inventions, he might have become a sailor. All his life he was devoted to the sea, and would never miss an opportunity of a voyage. He superintended the laying of the first transatlantic cable himself and, while engaged on this task, he noticed how imperfect were the ships' compasses of the time. The compass had to be corrected at regular periods on a voyage, to allow for the magnetism exercised by the ship itself. Thomson completely reconstructed the compass, and the accurate instruments of today, in which sailors the world over put their trust, is due to the genius of this man.

He also invented a machine which accurately recorded soundings taken at a speed of sixteen knots and to a depth of one hundred fathoms.

The simplification of the methods of taking bearings at sea are also due to Thomson, and his table for rapid reckoning simplified the famous Sumner formula for finding the position of a ship. He investigated the lengths and frequency of waves and tides, invented a tide-gauge and tide predicter, but perhaps his greatest work in connection with the safety of navigation is the improvement he effected in lighthouse lights.

Anything which would tend to lighten the labour of his fellow-men, or to further the progress of science, interested this genius. Faithful to the dedicatory lines of his first scientific essay, he measured not only the earth but the forces which control it. The first electric meter was the work of Thomson. He invented instruments that could measure tiny currents of one thousandth of an ampere to ten thousand amperes and electrical pressures from minute fractions of a volt to one hundred thousand volts. And even the ordinary bath-room tap was not beneath his notice.

In spite of all his great achievements and vast knowledge, though honours were heaped upon him by the governments and seats of learning of the civilized world, William Thomson remained the simplest, kindest and most easily approached of men. He always had a word of encouragement or praise for even the humblest student, and he would take as much care over the simplest thesis that was submitted to him as over any of the more abstruse problems that he had solved so successfully.

In his private life he was devoted to his family, and wrote regularly to his brothers and sisters.

In 1852 he married Margaret, the daughter of his father's great friend, Walter Crums, of Thornliebank. His married life was doubly happy in that his wife shared his affection for his family. A week after their engagement, she wrote to her sister, Elizabeth: "We have one interest in common that can never fail. I feel that in William's love for his sisters lies my best security for the continuation to me of those feelings on which the happiness of my life depends."

One cloud, however, disturbed this bliss, and that was that he had no children of his own. His wife was his constant companion on his many travels. Her health was always delicate and caused her husband so much anxiety that on several occasions he had to ask for leave of absence from Glasgow to take her abroad to recuperate. It was on one of these trips abroad that he met for the first time the great German physicist, Hermann von Helmholtz, who was afterwards to become one of his closest friends.

Helmholtz wrote to his wife his impression of his great confrère: "I expected," he said, "to find the man who is one of the first mathematical physicists of Europe somewhat older than myself, and was not a little astonished when a juvenile and exceedingly fair youth, who looked quite girlish, came forward. . . . He far exceeds all the great men of science with whom I have made personal acquaintance in intelligence, lucidity and nobility of thought, so that I felt quite wooden beside him sometimes."

But her travels did not restore Margaret Thomson to health, and she went into a rapid decline. Ailing though she always was, she was nevertheless a most accomplished woman, and wrote a number of poems, including translations from the German poets. A friend wrote of her that she was "sincere, bright and very keen-minded, and with a true insight into the real worth of things and thoughts."

When she died in 1870, Thomson was heartbroken. Shortly after her death, Sir William, as he had become since 1866, writing to console a friend in the death of a daughter, said: "I know well . . . that you cannot want the one great consolation. Yet I know too well how insufficient even the surest conviction that the loved one is happy, and the firmest hope of a transcendently happy meeting to come, are to mitigate the bitterness of the present gulf."

This grief cast a shadow over his life which nothing seemed to lighten. He travelled ceaselessly, chiefly to supervise the laying of the Atlantic cable, and it was on one of these voyages, four years later, in 1874, that he met, at Madeira, Frances Blandy, the daughter of a wealthy merchant of Funchal. She appeared to be the only person who could take him out of himself. They became engaged and were married in the British Consular chapel on June 24, 1874. This second marriage was to prove a real Indian summer to Thomson, and he seemed to take on a new lease of life.

Honours were showered upon him. In 1890 he became president of the Royal Society, and in 1892 he was raised to the peerage as Baron Kelvin of Largs. In 1896 the jubilee of his professorship at Glasgow was celebrated in a manner which was unique in the history of the university. The great library was filled with an exhibition of his inventions. More than two thousand guests were invited to the celebrations, and all the learned societies in the world were represented. A telegram was sent to him from the library, via Newfoundland, New York, Chicago, San Francisco, Los Angeles, New Orleans and Washington, and the message was in Kelvin's hand exactly seven and a half minutes after it was sent, having covered twenty thousand miles and twice crossed the Atlantic. This was a unique tribute on the part of the scientific world to the man who had shown it how to conquer time and distance.

After his retirement from Glasgow in 1899, Kelvin was seldom seen in public, though he was elected chancellor of the university in 1904, but he followed every new development of science with keen interest, and his pen was never idle. He wrote in the course of his long life more than three hundred works, dealing with almost every aspect of scientific development.

In his latter years the health of Lady Kelvin began to worry him, and in 1907 she had a stroke which partly paralysed her. He himself caught a chill which developed into a severe attack of sickness. He rapidly became worse, and septic fever set in. On December 17, 1907, this genius breathed his last, surrounded by his friends and those he loved.

Of a deeply religious nature, Kelvin was indifferent to questions of doctrine as taught by the Churches, and although he described himself as a Presbyterian, he was equally at home in the Church of England—thus it was possible to accede to the national desire that he should be buried in Westminster Abbey, next to the grave of Sir Isaac Newton.

Kelvin exemplified in himself the truism that between religion and science there can be no real conflict, and he would often insist that he was "a great believer in design." Huxley, his great antagonist in the realm of philosophy, once described him as a controversialist who, like Lancelot, was "the most perfect knight who ever broke a lance."

JOSEPH, BARON LISTER

(1827–1912)

Modern hospitals and modern surgery need no encomium. The greatness of their work for mankind is equalled only by their efficiency. Yet less than a century ago our hospitals were little more than mortuaries: the work of the surgeons was negatived by the dreadful toll of poisoning that killed patients after successful operations. It was not until Lister, basing his work upon the discoveries of Pasteur, applied the first antiseptic measures, measures which are now the commonplace basis of our aseptic surgery, that this dreadful mortality was checked.

"THE operation was successful, but the patient died from blood poisoning . . ." How often did those ironic words appear in the bulletins of the hospitals of England in the first half of the nineteenth century!

The discovery of anæsthetics had so revolutionized the practice of surgery that operations, which would have been unthinkable before, were successfully carried out. Hitherto the best surgeon had been the quickest, and thus many an operation was work only half done. With the discovery and application of anæsthetics, however, all this was changed, and deep-rooted complaints were tackled and successfully eradicated. But still the word "hospital" inspired an awful dread in the public mind. The mortality was so terrific that if only twenty-six per cent of the patients operated on in London died, the hospitals thought that they were to be congratulated. Public feeling was not appeased by this complacency, and the agitation reached such a pitch that there were many who even advocated the total abolition of the hospital system.

Frenzied efforts were made to meet the scourge of blood poisoning. The hospitals were swept clean of all dust. Windows were flung wide open, and stacks of clean towels and sheets were provided daily. But still the hand of Death lay heavy on the wards.

All this was to be swept away by the work of a young man whose name was as yet unknown to medical science. Joseph Lister, the son of Joseph Jackson Lister, who had been elected a Fellow of the Royal Society for his magnificent work in perfecting the microscope, was born at Upton Lane, West Ham, on April 5, 1827. As his family were Quakers, he could not go to any of the schools which might have assured him a career. He was educated privately and strictly, and grew up to be a young man of serious countenance and unobtrusive dress.

In spite of the extreme strictness of his upbringing, Lister was devoted to his parents, and his father was his closest confidant and friend. He wrote to his father regularly all his life, telling him of his experiments and researches. Even after he had left the Society of Friends he still used the "thee and thou" in his letters to his father. The old man, proud though he was of his son's success, still wrote to him in the same sober strain that he had used when Joseph was a boy.

There was nothing in this young man when he first went up to University College Hospital in 1848 to suggest future greatness and world-wide renown. Of average height but slender build, he had a large, intellectual head, dark, luxuriant hair, and side-whiskers. He wore the curious black coat favoured by the Quakers, and altogether presented a rather odd appearance. Nevertheless, he was of a gay nature, and this was thrown into greater relief by his sincerity and gravity on other occasions. He was fond of open-air exercise, and was a powerful swimmer, and he rapidly gained the esteem of his young colleagues.

After gaining his M.B. degree at University College, London, he went to Edinburgh, where he worked under the famous surgeon, James Syme.

Even then, though invested with the dignity of "Doctor," he was not beyond indulging in student "rags," and on one occasion he went on a raiding party to take down the wooden board of a quack doctor, and burn it ceremoniously in front of the infirmary.

Another time he climbed the "Cat's Nick," was thrown to the bottom of that perilous height by his more exuberant companions, and was brought back injured to the infirmary. "I aye kent something would happen wi' you Englishmen whustlin' on the Sabbath Day," was the only comfort that he got from Dr. Syme's famous nurse, Mrs. Porter.

Syme was not an easy man to work for, as he demanded more than was usually to be expected from his young doctors. He soon saw, however, that behind Lister's quiet manner there was great application and that no detail, however small, escaped him. It was not long before Syme appointed Lister his house surgeon, and it was then that Lister performed an operation that was to live in his memory and act as a spur to many of his future achievements.

A man had been dangerously stabbed in the neck in a brawl and the wound was so deep and so close to vital veins that it was doubtful if he would survive an operation. The danger lay chiefly in the patient's weakness through the amount of blood that he had lost, and also in the amount that he would inevitably lose in the course of the operation. This case had its importance for Lister not only because it was his first operation, but also because two lives depended on the result. If the man died, his assailant would certainly be hanged for murder. The interest in the case was enormous. The amphitheatre was thronged with students, while two police officers waited outside to learn the result. Syme and Lister got ready to perform the operation. The patient was wheeled in, and the ghastly pallor of his face made everybody despair of success.

The two doctors set to work as soon as the anæsthetic had taken effect. Syme worked as if he were conducting an autopsy, coolly but with the quick precision for which he was noted. Lister, on the other hand, was bathed in perspiration, as if he had been running a race, but his fingers were no less sure than those of his senior. All his life Lister could not help sweating when he operated, and it was the only outward sign of his intense interest in his work. At last the final stitches were made. A returning colour to the patient's face told the spectators that the operation was successful. Their relief was so great that they could not restrain themselves from giving loud and prolonged applause to the two doctors who had thus saved the lives of two wretched men.

Lister's association with Syme was thereafter to be much closer, and it was not long before he met and fell in love with Agnes, the great surgeon's eldest daughter. They became engaged and were married on April 23, 1856, in the Episcopalian Church. By this act of "marrying out" as the Quaker phrase has it, Lister joined the Church of England, of which he was to be a faithful member to the end of his days. There was the closest sympathy between Lister and his young wife and, indeed, their marriage can be described as a life-long honeymoon. Agnes Lister proved to be his best and closest assistant, and she would take notes for as much as seven to eight hours a day to his dictation. Most of the notes of Lister's lectures that are extant are in his wife's handwriting.

Skilful surgeon though he was, Lister was still unable to prevent the terrible loss of life from the after effects of operations, and he devoted his every spare moment to the study and elucidation of the diseases of the blood and the causes of inflammation. His first researches were in regard to inflammation and, as a result of a paper that he read to the Royal Society on "The Early Stages of Inflammation," he was elected at the age of thirty-two a Fellow of the Royal Society. From then on he became a marked man and his theories, if not always accepted, were at all events received with respect.

In 1864 Pasteur announced to the world his germ theory, which was that infection is due to germs, and that all fermentation and putrefaction come from these minute living organisms. Curiously enough, some time passed before Lister noticed Pasteur's discovery. He had been too preoccupied with his own researches into the composition of dead tissues to read much of what was being said and written outside Great Britain. When he did discover it, however, he knew that he was on the trail of the enemy that had so constantly eluded him.

The prevailing theory had always been that germs existed in the air only, and Pasteur's proof that they are to be found everywhere, even in the body, made Lister devote his attention to the state of the wounds themselves, rather than to the state of the surrounding atmosphere. Hitherto Lister had insisted on cleansing the parts round the wound and in eliminating as much as possible the entry of any foreign bodies. To achieve this end he used to spray the affected parts with carbolic acid the whole time that he was operating, and he was the first to insist on the use of clean towels and the constant washing of their hands by his assistant surgeons. But even so, patients died like flies from septicæmia. Pasteur's discovery showed Lister that a body could be infected before it had even come into contact with the outside air, and he therefore set to work to discover some means whereby the germs should be killed before more damage was done.

He spent months experimenting in order to get the best results, and he finally reached the conclusion that the only way to arrest the spread of sepsis was to keep the wound in constant touch with some disinfectant which would make it impossible for any germs to live. He thus applied dressings soaked in carbolic acid—or German creosote, as it was called in those days.

Lister finally chose carbolic acid as his antiseptic because its efficacy had been proved at Carlisle where it had been used as a disinfectant for sewage. It was in March, 1865, that he first used the acid in treating a case of compound fracture. Compound fractures were commonly aggravated by the poisoning of the flesh wounds in those days and formed one of the hardest class of case with which surgeons had to deal. Lister's treatment was successful, but it was not until two years later, after he had cured a difficult case of compound fracture with no resulting suppuration and no general illness, that he published his discovery in the *Lancet*.

His method was to introduce German creosote, which was in fact a crude form of carbolic acid, into the wound and then cover it with a layer of lint soaked in the acid. In order to alleviate the pain made by the application of the acid, he made many experiments in antiseptics introducing one after the other, carbolic oil, carbolized putty and carbolized shellac. He also experimented with types of dressings.

These measures brought a success he had scarcely dreamed of and, in a short time, a powerful body of opinion grew up in the medical world which attached itself fanatically and almost blindly to his methods. Any small deviation from the exact procedure adopted by Lister was condemned in heated controversies which were not always too scrupulously conducted.

But Lister was indifferent to all controversies. To him it was the result that mattered, and if experiment showed that he had previously been proceeding along wrong lines, he unhesitatingly abandoned his previous method. Thus, although he was the first to use the spray in the treatment of wounds, as soon as he discovered that the danger lay not so much in the elements of the air as in the tissues of the body itself, he abandoned the spray for a more direct and efficacious method. He soon insisted on the sterilization of all surgical instruments—a measure which today seems to be elementary—but which was greeted with derision by many in the medical profession.

Lister's method of sterilization was in the beginning almost entirely by the use of acids, and it was many years before he realized the aseptic properties of heat. When he did, he immediately applied the methods that are now commonplace in every hospital, and again the controversy broke out.

His most striking success was at Glasgow Infirmary. In the same building that stands today in Glasgow the mortality was appalling; nearly eighty per cent of the patients operated on died of septicæmia and gangrene and counsels of despair were beginning to prevail. Some even advocated the destruction of hospitals where gangrene had once got a hold and it was perhaps providential that when Lister went to Glasgow he entered an institution whose death-roll was the highest in the kingdom. The hospital was in the most insanitary quarter of the city, and the ward that Lister had to look after was the worst of all.

He began by taking a firm line with the managers of the hospital.

He steadfastly refused to allow any more beds in his ward than had been arranged for in the original scheme and it was as Lister said himself " fairly attributable to the firmness of my resistance in this matter, that though my patients suffered from the evils alluded to in a way that was sickening and often heart-rending, so as to make me sometimes feel it a questionable privilege to be connected with the institution, yet none of my wards ever assumed the frightful condition which showed itself in other parts of the building, making it necessary to shut them up for a time."

In spite of the appalling conditions in the other wards, during the first nine months that Lister practised his antiseptic system he did not have a single case in his ward of pyæmia, erysipelas or hospital gangrene. No greater proof was needed for the efficacy of his methods.

Besides being a great surgeon, Lister was above all a pre-eminent bacteriologist. Perhaps he inherited this interest from his father who had done so much to make the microscope the accurate instrument that it is today. His mind was as accurate as a machine, and the smallest detail never escaped his memory. Years after, when working on some new discovery, he would remember the result of an experiment he had carried out when a young man and put it to good use.

If he had a fault it was unpunctuality. He frequently kept whole assembly rooms waiting for more than half an hour before he arrived to deliver his lecture. This was not due in any way to laziness, but simply to the fact that he had probably thought of some new idea on his way to the lecture room which he would have to go back home to verify. The outstanding feature of Lister's work is that he never delivered a judgment which he could not substantiate with proofs. He even kept patients waiting for the same reason.

On one occasion when he had to go to a consultation on an urgent case of blood poisoning, an idea occurred to him when he was on his way, regarding a certain process to do with the coagulation of blood. Luckily he happened to be passing a slaughter house. He immediately went in and ordered a calf to be killed. Then and there, he proceeded to make his investigations. He was more than two hours late for the consultation, but he saved the patient's life.

His greatest discovery was, of course, antiseptics and their use, but he is also responsible for the perfection of the methods of stitching wounds. Hitherto very fine silk had been used for ligatures and this often caused poisoning to set in. It was Lister, who, after experimenting with animals, introduced catgut as a ligature which could be absorbed by the tissues of the body.

L'AÉRO-CLUB
DE FRANCE
PARIS
Certifie
que M. Orville
Wright
a été nommé
PILOTE-AVIATEUR
le 7 Janvier 1909
L. Cailletet

L'AÉRO-CLUB
DE FRANCE
PARIS
Certifie
que M. Wilbur
Wright
a été nommé
PILOTE-AVIATEUR
le 7 Janvier 1909
L. Cailletet

The most important flight ever made was that by Orville Wright (*above left*) at Kitty Hawk, North Carolina, in 1903, when the plane he and his brother, Wilbur (*above right*) had built remained airborne for all of twelve seconds. Louis Pasteur (*centre*) bestowed some of the greatest benefits that science has produced upon mankind. His discoveries made known the potency of bacteria in causing disease and revolutionized the treatment of wounds. The list of inventions by Thomas Alva Edison (*below left*) is endless and it can well be said that he contributed more to today's mechanical civilization than anyone else. Pierre and Marie Curie are shown (*below right*) in their laboratory at the time that they received the Nobel Prize for their work on radium and its compounds.

Alexander Graham Bell, the inventor of the telephone, inaugurating the New York-Chicago service in 1892 (*above*).

Marconi (*below*) with the receiving apparatus he used for the first transatlantic wireless signal in 1901.

Such innovations and epoch-making discoveries associated with his name, have obscured the fact that Lister was a magnificent surgeon. He devised many new operations, which would have made the reputation of lesser men. And his work for antisepsis has alone made possible the surgical treatment of diseased deep-seated organs in the body.

Nothing ever ruffled this remarkable man, and perhaps the only occasion when he ever felt nervous was on the occasion of Pasteur's jubilee in 1892, when he was greeted by the assembled scientists and students with the rhythmical applause that was the highest expression of esteem ever accorded by French University custom.

In 1883, a baronetcy was conferred upon him, but he valued this honour far less than the presidency of the Royal Society to which he was elected in 1894. In 1891 he founded the British Institute of Preventive Medicine on the lines of the Pasteur Institute, and the name has since been changed to the Lister Institute. This legacy of Lister's is perhaps among the most precious that we have. Here experiments and researches are constantly being carried on to discover the causes of disease, and it is the Lister Institute that examines and pronounces on specimens of germs that are sent in by doctors from all over the country.

By nature extremely reserved, Lister never hesitated to acknowledge the sources whence he derived his discoveries, and his recognition of the debt that he owed to Pasteur is the most touching tribute that has ever been paid by one man of science to another. In 1897 he was raised to the peerage and in 1902 became one of the twelve original recipients of the Order of Merit, but these were empty honours: for in 1893, his beloved wife and companion had died, and from that time on, life held no more joy for this great benefactor of humanity.

In 1903 he had a serious illness from which he never really recovered, and for the remaining nine years of his life he was practically a cripple. He never wrote a book because his life was so crowded with work, and when his days of leisure came, Lady Lister was not there to inspire him and help him as in the past. His faculties gradually began to fail him, and like a tired child, he fell asleep on February 10, 1912, at the great age of eighty-five. He had found the hospitals of England little better than mortuaries, and he made them the great healing centres that we know today.

His reputation was so great that public opinion clamoured for his burial in Westminster Abbey. But Lister had left in his will a record—if such a thing were needed—of his devotion to his wife, and stipulated that he should find his last resting place by the side of her who had been his constant comfort and helper in the difficulties he had had to face in life.

The funeral, however, took place in the Abbey, and the great building was thronged not only by those bearing the highest names in the land but also by the poor and the halt and the lame, whose sufferings he had soothed and whose lives he had saved.

ALEXANDER GRAHAM BELL

(1847–1922)

There is a monument to Alexander Graham Bell on almost every office desk—the telephone, which he invented. It was fitting that this expert on speech should discover the principle of telephony and make the instrument by which "nation may speak unto nation." The revolution which the telephone has made in the life of the whole civilized world is the measure of the gratitude we owe to Bell. By this one great achievement he stamped his name on the history of progress and crowned a life of patient work and painstaking invention.

"MR. WATSON, come here please; I want you."

With these commonplace words a stocky, bearded Scotsman ushered in a new era. That sentence marked the achievement of a man who changed the face of the world in his lifetime. For the speaker was Alexander Graham Bell, and the sentence was the first to be spoken *and received* over a telephone.

There is no need to expatiate on the importance of the telephone. It inaugurated the age of space-annihilation. No invention has surpassed it in usefulness. Today we have millions of telephone instruments, and the miracle of telephony has become a commonplace in the daily round. This is the story of the telephone's inventor.

Alexander Graham Bell was born on March 3, 1847, at Edinburgh. His genius provides a rare instance of inherited talent, for his father, Alexander Melville Bell, was a famous teacher of elocution, an expert on phonetics, and author of a system of "Visible Speech." Graham Bell was able to improve his natural powers by an extensive education. He was sent to Edinburgh High School, and from there went on to the university in that city. Later he was at University College, London, and at Würzburg in Germany, where he took the degree of Ph.D.

Even as a boy he had an inventive turn of mind. He used to tell how he had been taken with some schoolfellows over a mill at Edinburgh. The boys were given some ears of wheat and were invited to remove the husks. Young Graham Bell took home his wheat, and removed the husks quickly and neatly by using a nail-brush. He at once communicated the idea to the miller, who installed a machine for removing the husks working on the brush principle.

In 1870 Graham Bell's health began to decline; there were fears of consumption. So, with his father, he left his native country and went to Canada. Two years later he was at Boston, where he set up a school for training teachers of the deaf, and he also gave instruction in the mechanics of speech.

Bell's ability and knowledge were quickly recognized, and he was made professor of vocal physiology in the University of Boston. It was Bell's interest in teaching speech to the deaf and his inspiring work for deaf mutes that led him to his world-famous invention. He fell in love with a deaf girl, Mabel Hubbard, while he was experimenting on a machine which he believed would make the deaf hear, or, as he put it, "hear for the deaf." Mabel Hubbard, who later became his wife, persuaded him that lip reading was a more practicable way of giving the deaf hearing, so Bell continued his experiments to a different end.

He was trying to construct a "harmonic telegraph" with which he hoped to send several telegraphic messages simultaneously over one wire. While he was engaged upon this, he turned his attention to the transmission of speech by electricity. The twanging of a spring accidentally transmitted over a wire gave Bell the cue and the inspiration for his work. That was in June, 1875; his experiments on the harmonic telegraph had begun about a year previously.

Now Bell, unlike many previous experimenters in the same field, had grasped the correct principle of telephony. "If," he said, "I could make a current of electricity vary in intensity precisely as the air varies in density, during the production of sound, I should be able to transmit speech telegraphically." In his early work on the harmonic telegraph, Bell had attained a conception of undulating current. Now he studied the working of a dead man's ear, and the movement of air during the utterance of sound. He reasoned that as the small membrane which forms the ear-drum can move the comparatively heavy chain of bones in the ear, a larger membrane ought to be able to move an iron armature. If the armature could be moved as the air is moved, speech could be transmitted. So the twanging spring set Bell hard at work, and soon he had a rough apparatus which was the forerunner of the modern telephone.

On February 15, 1876, Graham Bell filed an application for a patent for his "improvement in telegraphy" at the United States Patent Office. Only two hours later Elisha Gray, of Chicago, filed a caveat at the Patent Office for almost the same invention! The great Edison, A. E. Dolbear, and Daniel Drawbaugh all were working in the same field: all claimed the invention or part of the invention of the telephone. The great telephone war was on.

Bell and his assistant, Watson, hid themselves in two rooms of a cheap Boston boarding house, rigged up apparatus, and worked day and night trying to transmit and receive sentences spoken by the human voice over the wire. On the afternoon of March 10, 1876, Watson was in the basement with the receiver glued to his ear. Suddenly he started. Words—real distinguishable words—had come through at last. Sharply and clearly the sentence came: "Mr. Watson, come here, please; I want you."

Watson flung down the receiver, rushed up the stairs like a schoolboy, clearing them two at a time, and burst into Bell's room, shouting: "I heard you: I could hear what you said!"

That year Bell exhibited his telephone at the Centennial Exposition at Philadelphia. Nobody thought much of the invention at first, until Don Pedro, the Emperor of Brazil, picked up the receiver. Bell, at the other end of the wire, recited the famous soliloquy from *Hamlet,* "To be or not to be . . ." "My God!" cried the emperor, "It speaks!" The telephone was from that moment given pride of place in the exhibition.

But still commercial development was slow. Bell found it hard to raise financial support, although at last a company was formed which included Watson and Bell's father-in-law, Gardner Hubbard. The fourth director was Thomas Sanders, who was the chief financier of the group. Sanders was the father of a deaf mute, in whom Bell had been so interested that he had gone to live with him; and it was in the Sanders homestead that Bell set up his first laboratory.

Meanwhile the telephone war raged. Bell fought lawsuit after lawsuit, defended action and action. He won every one. His patent stood. It was established that Alexander Graham Bell was the inventor of the telephone. But the story of the great battle between the Bell Company and the Western Union, of Edison's vital improvement of the telephone transmitter, do not really concern us here.

Bell soon withdrew from active work in the exploitation of the telephone. He had provided the first links of a new girdle for the earth: he left the final forging to others. But his invention had made Bell a rich man. He settled down in a fine country home at Baddeck, Nova Scotia, and devoted himself to invention.

It has been the fashion to scoff at Graham Bell. It has been said that he was no electrician, no physicist; that he was a man who had stumbled on the telephone by a lucky accident. Critics point out the many failures of his subsequent experiments and schemes, and cite them as a proof of his lack of inventive genius.

But the scoffers are wrong. True, many of Graham Bell's later inventions were useless or unsuccessful. But not all of them were: and his wide range of practical inquiry is proof of his mental resource. Whatever the adverse critics may say, Bell's greatness is manifest in his achievements. Bell *did* invent the telephone. Bell *did* invent the photophone. Bell *did* invent the graphophone.

His photophone is an apparatus for transmitting articulate speech along a beam of light. Bell saw and took advantage of the peculiar properties of selenium for this purpose. His graphophone, which he produced in 1887, was more or less on the same principle as Edison's phonograph, which was an earlier invention and overshadowed Bell's.

Almost the first thing to interest Bell, when he retired to Baddeck, was the problem of dynamic flight. He studied what he conceived to be the principles of aeronautics, and made a number of experiments in mechanically propelled aircraft. He constructed a huge kite, in which a man took his place as pilot. The kite, however, was never able to fly by itself, and although it was several times raised to a height of two or three hundred feet by being towed by a boat, nothing came of the experiments. In no way discouraged, he turned his fertile mind and scientific interest in every direction. He was willing to experiment in any field for the benefit of mankind.

In 1906 he was observing and practising new theories in sheep breeding. He was attempting to produce a strain of ewes which would always bear twins. The year 1910 found him back at his own speciality, speech. He tried a number of experiments in teaching speech to animals. Most of the attempts were absolute failures, but Bell did manage, by manipulative exercises, to make a dog imitate human vowel sounds. This achievement was of little value, but his next work was of real interest.

He put forward, in 1912, a plea for "World English," a universal language based on the phonetics of the English tongue. As a phonetic expert, he knew that the idea was practicable and exceptionally suitable for an international language. He knew, too, the chief objections that would be raised against it, and suggested that World English should only be used for speech, and that no interference should be made with written English. Bell's, of course, met the usual fate of universal languages. It received world-wide notice, and was promptly forgotten. But he went on inventing.

In 1919 he perfected a hydroplane, and in 1922, the year of his death, he produced an apparatus, which he claimed to be invaluable for explorers and travellers through deserts, for distilling the moisture from the breath.

Throughout his long life he poured forth papers and scientific monographs. He was widely recognized as an authority on speech, and his reputation as an inventor always procured him attention. But he did not receive a great number of scientific honours. He was the founder of the American Association to Promote the Teaching of Speech to the Deaf, and for some time he was president of the National Geographic Society. In 1898 he was appointed by Congress a regent of the Smithsonian Institute. So late as 1920 he crossed the Atlantic and revisited his native Edinburgh, which honoured him with the freedom of the city. These, with the addition of a few scientific medals, were the sum of his honours. But he lived to see the telephone which he invented installed throughout the world, and, linked by wireless, bring the continents within earshot of each other.

That, in brief, was the life of Alexander Graham Bell, who died at Baddeck on August 2, 1922. There is nothing outstanding, nothing picturesque in Graham Bell. He was just a kindly, pleasant, occasionally irritable Scotsman. He set his curious brain at one invention after another; but, strange enough, he lacked the typical business acumen of the Scot, and he fully acknowledged his own deficiency in commercial transactions. That was why, after the triumph of his patent and the formation of the Bell Company, he ceased to work in the telephone field.

But the most extraordinary thing recorded of Alexander Graham Bell, inventor of the telephone, is that he hated the telephone! When he retired to his country house at Baddeck to wrestle with the manifold problems of invention, he stuffed his telephone bell with paper, to prevent it from interrupting his work.

And there is a story told of a woman who met him at a social gathering. She was brought forward and introduced to Graham Bell, the great inventor. She expressed her pleasure in meeting the famous man, and then said, smilingly: "But I often wish you had never been born."

Bell looked surprised, indignant and somewhat hurt. The woman, startled by her own temerity and its apparent effect, was about to apologize, when a twinkle appeared in the inventor's eyes. "I know," he answered, with a smile. "I sympathize. I never use the beast."

THOMAS ALVA EDISON

(1847–1931)

Edison needs no introduction. His name, associated with a dozen different devices in everyday use, has long been a household word. By his own driving effort, by his persistent research and inexhaustible patience, and by his own peculiar genius, he made himself the greatest practical man of science of his age and the most successful inventor that the world has known. In the last century the western world led the way to mechanical civilization, and of that civilization Edison was the father.

WHENEVER you touch an electric light switch, or pick up the telephone, or turn on the gramophone, or watch a film, you are paying an indirect tribute to the inventive and mechanical genius of Edison. For by his long career of research, experiment and invention, of improving and making practical the inventions of others, Edison contributed more to our modern mechanical civilization than any other scientist. His effect upon the world has been incalculable: even Mr. George S. Bryan's neat summary is staggering in its implications:

"When Edison took up invention as a career, the Civil War was past. The energies of the country had been released for a burst of business enterprise, of speculation, of material progress generally. Edison had a faculty of making things work, of bringing things to pass, of overcoming obstacles thought to be insurmountable. His ingenuity and boldness of attack were exactly what capitalists and public were looking for—capitalists because he showed the way to profitable investment; public because he did 'stunts' with things near to its everyday life. He gave Bell's telephone a real transmitter and thus made it '. . . speak out loud and bold.' His name for years was placed on all Bell telephone sets. With his electro-motograph he furnished to Morse's telegraph a new sounder requiring neither a retractile spring to withdraw an armature from an electro-magnet nor any electro-magnet at all. He thereby delivered the telegraph from the menace of Jay Gould, who controlled the Page patent on a retractile spring. Using the principle of this same electro-motograph, he provided a loud-speaking receiver for the telephone. He thus established the fact that Bell's receiver was not indispensable in telephony any more than Page's retractile spring was in telegraphy. Such a man naturally convinced financiers that he was a handy person to have around when they wished to escape suits for infringement or to stake their investments on schemes that were likely to be 'practical' from the dividend-paying viewpoint. The public began to regard him as a marvel and to call him 'the Wizard'—a title bestowed on him by the newspapers.

"Then he invented the phonograph, by which he was the first, mechanically, to reproduce human speech and song. The phonograph aroused prodigious general interest. Edison was now looked upon as a 'wizard' indeed. To be applied to several practical uses, the phonograph had only to be developed. That development was postponed to make way for Edison's advance against a fresh impossibility—the subdivision of the electric current. From the invention-factory at Menlo Park issued the incandescent electric lamp, dynamos to supply it with current, and a long series of auxiliary devices through which the central-station system of incandescent electric lighting was organized and rendered commercially possible. On this spacious accomplishment was based a vast new industry. This industry in turn lent the first real impetus to the new profession of electrical engineering; and from it grew manufactures of great variety and wide extent."

Thomas Alva Edison was born on February 11, 1847, at Milan, Ohio. His mother was of Scots descent, his father of Dutch. When he was seven years old the family moved to Port Huron, Michigan, and there young Thomas went to school for three months. During that three months he was well at the bottom of the class, and the teacher described him as "addled."

Thomas then left school, and his future education was obtained from his mother and by his own experimental observations. As an experimenter he started young: he tried to imitate a hen by sitting on some eggs to hatch them, and he dosed the family odd-job man with Seidlitz powders to see if the gases generated by them would enable him to fly!

This last effort met with physical discouragement, and young Edison retired to the cellar where he began to assemble a laboratory. But chemicals cost money, so he applied for a concession to sell newspapers on trains running between Port Huron and Detroit. Edison soon saw the selling power of news: he installed a tiny printing plant on the train and produced his own paper. He also had a miniature laboratory in the luggage coach, while in his spare time he was experimenting with telegraphy.

His travelling laboratory brought disaster. One day the train lurched suddenly: a stick of phosphorus was thrown on to the floor and ignited: the coach caught fire. The angry conductor flung his laboratory and printing-press on to the next station and soundly boxed Edison's ears: from that buffeting came the deafness that afflicted Edison throughout his life.

On that same railway station Edison was standing one morning in 1862, when he saw a child playing on the line: running towards it at speed was a loaded truck. He flung down his newspapers, leaped from the platform, and snatched the little boy just clear of the wagon. The boy's father was the stationmaster, Mackenzie, who in gratitude taught Edison train telegraphy. Edison learned quickly and made the new hobby his job. He became a telegraph operator, and a good one.

He soon made his inventive faculty felt in his work. When he was night-operator at Stratford Junction, Ontario, he had to send an hourly signal to the train dispatcher. But as he spent his days in research, he needed sleep at night, so he contrived a clock device to send the signal automatically at the right time. When he was in Cincinnati the telegraph office was infested with rats, and Edison devised a "rat paralyser" which electrocuted the pests by making them complete a circuit. At Indianapolis he made an "automatic recorder" to take Morse messages, a device which was later to give him the inspiration for the phonograph.

It was in 1869, while he was working as an operator in Boston, that he applied for his first patent. The invention was an automatic vote-recorder, but nothing could be more objectionable to American politicians. Edison turned his attention to something more likely to meet with public approval. In 1867, E. A. Callahan had invented the tape-machine. Now Edison produced one of his own and started a small service, and devising also a private-line telegraph service, the life of invention and discovery beckoned to him. He flung up his job as a telegraph operator and left Boston for New York.

Edison arrived in New York penniless and hungry. For two nights he slept in the battery-room of the Gold Indicator Company, which ran a "ticker" service for brokers. On the third day he was sitting in the office when the transmitter broke down: the superintendent was frantic, the chief tore his hair, Edison repaired the machine. And after a couple of interviews with the chief, he was made manager of the entire plant.

In October, 1869, Edison went into partnership with a young telegraph engineer named Pope. They invented a "gold printer," and undertook to provide private telegraph lines. Their business was eventually absorbed by the Western Union, whose president asked Edison to improve the tape-machine: the result was the widely used Edison Universal Printer. Edison valued his inventions at five thousand dollars, but was nervously wondering whether he dared ask as much as three, when the company's president offered him forty thousand. The inventor reports that he came "as near fainting as ever I got."

Edison then opened a large shop in Newark, New Jersey, where he manufactured tape-machines and their parts. At that time he gathered round him a group of assistants, that formed the nucleus of the Edison pioneers. He picked good men—his workshops were always a kind of experimental school—and he worked them as hard and as unsparingly as he worked himself.

He next turned his attention to duplex and quadruplex telegraphy. Duplex telegraphy means the sending of two messages in opposite directions over the same wire at the same time. Edison, by obtaining a variation in the direction of the flow of current, invented the duplex system, by which two messages could be sent over the same wire at the same time and in the same direction. "It required," he said later, "a peculiar effort of the mind, such as the imagining of eight different things moving simultaneously on a mental plane."

His patents for duplex and quadruplex telegraphy were of first-rate importance, and saved millions of pounds in construction costs alone. But while he was working on them, he had other irons in the fire; a new system of call-boxes for district messenger service, for the introduction of which he organized a successful company; a mimeograph for producing stencils; and certain improvements in a typewriter invented by Sholes, which were later bought by Remingtons.

In 1876 he left Newark and set up his famous laboratory and workshops at Menlo Park. At Newark he had married Mary Stilwell, by whom he had three children. She died in 1884, and two years afterwards he married Mina Miller. But from now on until his death in 1931 we lose the man in the wonder of his work.

His first great work at Menlo Park was the improvement of the telephone invented by Bell. Orton, of the Western Union, asked Edison to overcome the defects of the Bell system and make the telephone thoroughly practicable. This he did by the invention of the carbon transmitter, which enabled speech to be clearly and distinctly heard in telephoning. His next production was the electro-motograph, and from that he developed his loud-speaking telephone, which Bernard Shaw, who worked as a young man for the Edison Telephone Company in England, described as "much too ingenious. It was nothing less than a telephone of such stentorian efficiency that it bellowed your most private communications all over the house, instead of whispering them with some sort of discretion. This was not what the British stockbroker wanted; so the company was soon merged in the National Telephone Company, after making a place for itself in the history of literature, quite unintentionally, by providing me with a job."

Towards the end of 1877 Edison gave one of his assistants a sketch of a model which he wanted to be made as piece-work for eighteen dollars. Edison explained the purpose of the queer machine, and the mechanic shook his head sadly. The "old man" was being ridiculous. The foreman of the machine shop wagered a box of cigars that it would not work. But it did. Edison put a sheet of tin foil round the drum of the machine, turned the handle of the shaft, and shouted into a speaking tube a verse of "Mary had a little lamb." Then, making a few adjustments to the apparatus, he again turned the handle, and from the machine came Edison's voice and Mary's verse. Edison had invented the phonograph!

The phonograph astonished the world. Edison was christened "The Wizard of Menlo Park." It was his pet invention, and it was his most amazing. Other work made him put it aside until 1887, when he began to improve the machine towards its modern efficiency and develop such kindred ideas as the ediphone.

And now he turned to the problem of electric lighting, and the results of his researches have illuminated the whole world. Electric arc lighting was already in existence, but although incandescent lamps had been made, none was satisfactory. Edison set out to subdivide the electric current; that is, to light a number of small separate lamps with the same current used to light a single arc lamp, a feat which many scientists declared to be impossible.

Edison and some fifty enthusiastic assistants started work. He had to find an incandescent substance with high resistance and small radiating surface. He made over 1,600 tests of various minerals and ores, and "I speak without exaggeration when I say that I have constructed three thousand different theories in connection with the electric light, each one of them reasonable and apparently likely to be true. Yet in two cases only did my experiments prove the truth of my theory. My chief difficulty was in constructing the carbon filament, the incandescence of which is the source of the light."

At last he tried carbonizing cotton sewing thread. A loop of thread was put in a nickel mould, which was placed in a furnace for five hours. Then the mould was allowed to cool and the thread had to be taken from it and sealed in a bulb. After working for two nights and a day and using a whole spool of thread, Edison and Batchelor got a piece of carbonized thread out of the mould without breaking it. Edison tells the thrilling story:

"It was necessary to take it to the glass-blower's house. With the utmost precaution, Batchelor took up the precious carbon, and I marched after him, as if guarding a mighty treasure. To our consternation, just as we reached the glass-blower's bench the wretched carbon broke. We turned back to the main laboratory and set to work again. It was late in the afternoon before we had produced another carbon, which was again broken by a jeweller's screwdriver falling against it. But we turned back again, and before night the carbon was completed and inserted in the lamp. The bulb was exhausted of air and sealed, the current turned on, and the sight we had so long desired to see met our eyes."

The lamp burned for forty hours while Edison and his assistants laid bets on how long it would last. That was on October 21, 1879. The electric lamp had come into existence. Edison now went on to complete the system of lighting.

First there were hundreds of experiments with filaments. Then he set out to devise a whole system of electric light supply. Generators were needed. Edison invented a new type of dynamo. Measuring instruments were wanted. Edison invented them. In brief, he worked and equipped the complete electric lighting system from generator to consumer bulb; and when the first central station was set up in New York Edison was superintendent, foreman, and even ganger on the job!

While he had been working on incandescent lamps he had discovered what is known as the "Edison effect" in connection with the emanation of electrons from incandescent bodies: that led Fleming to his discovery of the wireless thermionic valve.

In 1887 Edison moved from Menlo Park to West Orange. At the same time he began experiments on a machine that "should do for the eye what the phonograph does for the ear." Within two years he had produced the "kinetograph," which was the first motion picture camera. Then came the "kinetoscope"—the forerunner of the cinema. "When commercial expansion began in the motion-picture field in this country [America], the work of filming had to be done largely by processes and apparatus on which Edison had obtained patents." In 1912 he invented the kinetophone, which linked the invention of the film-camera with that of the phonograph and made a talking-picture possible.

The Edison effect helped to make radio history. But Edison himself had produced a satisfactory system of wireless telegraphy by means of induction: it was used to send messages to moving trains.

When X-rays were discovered by Röntgen, Edison invented a fluoroscope, which was an apparatus through which their effects could be seen. It was used successfully in surgical work.

During the Great War, Edison was made head of the Naval Consulting Board of the United States, and he provided his country with some forty inventions for use in naval warfare.

The list of his inventions and devices is endless. His first patent was taken out in 1869; by 1910 he had applied for over 1,300. There was hardly a field of electrical or mechanical development he had not entered. He gave his life unremittingly to work, and although he made money, he sought perfection in his productions: "even within the Edison sales organizations murmurs have been heard that the 'old man' was too much concerned with making things good."

Till his death on October 18, 1931, he was actively engaged in research, always finding some new problem for solution. Henry Ford has indicated his versatility and estimated his greatness:

"An inventor," he says, "frequently wastes his time and his money trying to extend his invention to uses for which it is not at all suitable. Edison has never done this. He rides no hobbies. He views each problem that comes up as a thing of itself, to be solved in exactly the right way. . . . His knowledge is so nearly universal that he cannot be classed as an electrician or a chemist—in fact, Mr. Edison cannot be classified. . . . The more I have seen of him the greater he has appeared to me—both as a servant of humanity and as a man."

If his achievements are his memorial, let that be his epitaph.

PIERRE AND MARIE CURIE

(1859–1906, 1867–1934)

Scientific research into radio-activity, culminating with the discovery of radium, opened men's eyes to a new world. And in radium they found themselves possessed of a new, and as yet incalculably potent weapon, for the war against disease. The scientist who conferred this priceless gift to her fellow men was Mme. Marie Curie, who, working in conjunction with her husband, Pierre, first obtained radium from pitchblende, and later went on to discover its properties. The colossal value of her work was soon apparent, but perhaps it will only be rightly assessed by future generations.

ONE bright, sunny morning in the eighteen-seventies, a laughing, curly-headed child ran down the Avenue Aleja in Warsaw to join a group of her playmates who were just ahead. An old, bent gipsy woman stopped her as she would have run past.

"Show me your hand, pretty one," she said.

Without a sign of fear the child thrust out her hand, and looked up with laughing eyes.

"Come on, Marja," cried the children, "don't listen to the silly old thing."

But the gipsy woman had tight hold of the little hand, and her old eyes were shining.

"What lines—such lines," she whispered, half to herself. "Oh, you will be famous."

The children had run up now, and danced round excitedly.

"Will Marja be a queen?" shouted one—and then: "Tell me my fortune, too."

But the old woman shook her head, and with one last look at the child went on her way.

And that was the first—and it must be acknowledged, most unscientific—tribute paid to Marja Sklodowska, known to the world today as Madame Curie. Working with her husband, Pierre Curie, she discovered radium, one of the most important factors in modern medical science.

In every true scientist there is, above all things, the desire to discover the truth—truth proven and without possibility of doubt. In Professor and Madame Curie that desire was stronger than anything else in their lives. They were a deeply devoted couple, more than ordinarily attached to their two daughters, but the sharing of their common interest in scientific research, and the dovetailing of their work, is the most remarkable feature of their lives together.

It is hard to separate their achievements. To Madame Curie goes the honour of actually discovering radium, but it is certain that her husband's work prepared the way. Until his sudden and tragic death in 1906, the two shared equal honours, and were more than content that it should be like that.

Pierre Curie was born in Paris in 1859. He was educated at the Sorbonne, the University of Paris, which later was to reward his work with the highest honours it had to give. His life was the story of a brilliantly clever man, working steadfastly towards scientific honours, and receiving due recognition as he worked. But behind the story of his wife lies a faint background of romance and of tragedy.

She was born in Warsaw on November 7, 1867. Her father, Professor Sklodowska, lectured on science in the Lycée there. It was natural enough then, that Marja and his other children should turn to science as a career, considering the atmosphere in which they were brought up. But there was the other and stronger factor which made Marja Sklodowska the woman she was—her nationality. Though later she became Madame Marie Curie, a Frenchwoman, she never forgot she had been born a Pole—and born at a time when Poland was suffering bitterly from the oppression of Russia.

As a child she had seen the Cossacks ride furiously through the streets of Warsaw, swinging their heavy whips, one blow from which was sufficient to split a skull. They were the hated foreign soldiers, there to enforce the authority of Russia. Two years before her birth there had been a terrible massacre of her people, and even then any faint murmur against the rule of Russia might mean banishment to Siberia. The national language was suppressed, and Russian was taught to all the children in the schools.

The Polish women are often beautiful, brilliantly clever, and of great and lasting charm. It is said that the only woman Napoleon ever really loved was Madame Walewska, a Pole. Marja Sklodowska had all the gifts of her people, but she had, too, the tragic look of those who are born of an oppressed race.

As a student in Warsaw, Marja became concerned with a

revolutionary body of young Poles. That reason alone would have made it advisable for her to leave Poland, but beside that, Warsaw offered no scope for further studies. She hoped at one time to study at the University of Cracow, at that time under Austrian rule. But when she demanded to attend the science lectures, the secretary laughed, and refused point blank. Science was not a thing in which women could meddle, he said, and offered to put her name down for cookery classes!

Finally she came to Paris. There were many reasons for her choice. The French were in sympathy with her people; she herself could speak the language; but most important—the Sorbonne was one of the few universities that encouraged women scientists. In England at that time, women were not allowed to take medical degrees, and many Englishwomen were studying medicine in Paris.

In 1888, when she had just attained her majority, began some of the happiest years of her life. True, money was not too plentiful. She lived on the fourth floor of one of the Paris apartment houses, waited on herself, carried up her coals those four flights, and had to live frugally. But there was the joy of her work. She both taught science and attended lectures at the Sorbonne, and worked in the laboratories there.

Here it was that she met Pierre Curie, then a respected and famous lecturer, and in 1895 they were married.

The marriage was ideally happy. Though they made scientific research their mutual life work, no other side of their life together was allowed to suffer. There were their two little girls, Irene and Eve, whose claims always came first with them. Though their household was not elaborate, it received careful attention from Madame Curie. Houses do not run themselves, as she acknowledged resignedly when a flustered cook or maid burst into the laboratory demanding instructions. Friends who visited them in those days would find Pierre sweeping the floor, and playing with his small daughters, while Madame cooked the meal.

And in the meantime, the unscientific world awoke to the fact that scientists were on the track of a great new discovery. For in 1895, the year of the Curie marriage, Röntgen discovered the famous rays that were named after him—the forerunners of the modern X-rays.

Henri Becquerel carried on the work a step further. By chance he discovered that certain compounds left in a dark room in the neighbourhood of photographic plates, affected the plates even when wrapped in black paper. The culmination of his work was the discovery of new rays, called after him, Becquerel rays.

The work of these two men had proved to scientists that there is all around us the great force known as radio-activity. It is in some metals, in the rays of the sun, in the mineralized waters we drink for our health—it is there, to be used. If they could track down and separate this power, it would be a tremendous thing; the benefits would be incalculable.

And it was Madame Curie, working with her husband, who achieved the miracle.

The substance used for the radium experiments was black and very hard; a compound called pitchblende. By fractionization—separating the substance up into its elemental parts by dissolving it—Madame Curie extracted a substance which she named after her native country, polonium, and a second element, radium.

Radium is the most powerful of the radio-active elements; that is, of the elements which give off rays capable of penetrating substances opaque to light. Becquerel had discovered that uranium possessed this property; but polonium, and lastly, radium, the discoveries of Madame Curie, possessed radio-activity in much higher degrees.

The benefits of radium in the realm of medicine are still incalculable, but it has been used with great effect against cancer both to cure and to relieve pain. The bacteria of such diseases as typhus, cholera, and anthrax, can also be killed by radium.

This story of the discovery is a bare statement of fact. Actually, the ordinary person can never realize how hard was the fight before victory was achieved. Sheer overwork caused Madame Curie's health to fail. Often she was forced to leave the laboratory to take a much needed rest. Her husband begged her to give up the fight, but she resolutely refused.

Then there was the question of expense. Pitchblende itself is an extremely expensive commodity. But the Emperor of Austria, who was an admirer of the Curies, sent to Madame a whole ton of the precious material. It was a costly gift, and perhaps the quaintest ever received by a lady from a crowned monarch.

Radium experiments are very dangerous. Some few years after, Pierre Curie, demonstrating radium experiments in England, was so badly burned that he could not hold his knife and fork at dinner. Such risks, and greater, had to be braved all the time. Enormous skill and judgment were necessary for extracting the radium in the final processes, and the amount obtained was infinitesimal. How infinitesimal can be judged from the fact that one ton of pitchblende treated with fifty tons of water, and from five to six tons of chemicals would yield, with any luck, about six grains of radium.

Madame Curie was not thirty-two when she discovered radium. The greater part of her research in that direction had been done since her marriage three years previously, and in those three years she had borne and reared her first child!

In 1903, when the truth of the achievement had been tested, the Curies shared with Henri Becquerel the Nobel Prize for physics. In the same year they received the Davy Medal of the Royal Society.

The Sorbonne honoured Pierre Curie by creating a special department of which he was appointed the head, and Madame Curie became his chief assistant.

Then, only three years later, Pierre Curie was knocked down by a dray and killed outright when crossing a Paris street. The shock was terrible, but Marie Curie found her greatest solace in carrying on her husband's work. She was appointed in his place at the Sorbonne, and four years later—in 1911—won alone the Nobel Prize for chemistry. The Sorbonne created for her a Radium Institute, and later she helped materially to establish a similar institute in her beloved native city of Warsaw.

During the World War she helped in the hospitals where the various forms of radium treatment were being carried out. She drove as near the firing lines as the authorities would allow in a car presented to her by the English people. In 1921 the people of the United States paid homage to her when President Harding presented to her a gramme of radium to help her in her work.

A similar gift in 1921, from the women of America, was accompanied by a small annuity. Madame Curie used the money to rent some radium for a hospital in her native Warsaw. She had not forgotten Poland. In 1929, after her second visit to the United States, the French Government voted a million and a half francs for a radium factory and research laboratory.

The two Curies had always been reserved, more than usually modest, and haters of publicity. After her husband's death, Madame Curie lived for nothing but her work and her children.

It was an additional happiness to Madame Curie that her daughter was deeply interested in her mother's work, and working with her husband carried it one step further; for in 1935, Madame Curie-Joliot and her husband received the Nobel Prize for chemistry, for the production of artificial radio-activity in the common elements.

Madame Curie lived to see the completion of the great work,

but by the time the great honour was conferred on her children, death had claimed her.

She died on July 4, 1934, in a sanatorium in the Haute Savoie. So quietly had she accepted her illness that the world who honoured her name knew nothing of her grave state until a day or two before her death. No woman was ever more sincerely mourned; but no woman died more happily in the conviction that her own work was done and that there remained those dear to her to carry it on yet further.

THE MARCHESE GUGLIELMO MARCONI

(1874–1937)

Of those seven wonders of everyday life, the telephone, the gramophone, the radio, the film, television, the motor car, and the aeroplane, the most far-reaching in achievement and existence must surely be the radio. Even in our own day, when broadcasting is a commonplace, there is still a thrill of wonder and awe in hearing a man speak to the whole world. And although so much has been done, it is clear from the rapid development and progress that is being made, that wireless and all the implications of wireless waves is still an infant study. So, while we acclaim Marconi as an inventor and a pioneer of incomparable genius, continuing research has revealed that his great work was only the beginning of a science with endless technical and social possibilities.

NOTHING is so commonplace as a wonder of the world. We live in an age of switchgear and miracles, but our only heed for the past is fleeting pity for the primitive nineteenth century, with never a thought for the miracle-makers. Today you may switch a button and hear a voice that has flown around the world: you may eavesdrop in all the capitals of Europe without moving from your fireside. By turning a dial you may rule the electric waves.

Those waves took some finding. As long ago, or rather as recently as, 1864, a mathematical genius named James Clerk Maxwell predicted the existence of the electric waves that we now know as wireless waves. Not only that, he estimated their properties, their wave-length measurements and their velocity.

For years Clerk Maxwell's theory was unaccepted and unproven. Orthodox scientists shrugged and turned away. And then a brilliant German physicist, Heinrich Rudolf Hertz, conducted at Karlsruhe a series of experiments which completely confirmed all Maxwell's predictions.

Hertz's discoveries, published in a series of papers between 1887 and 1889, set the scientists by the ears. Eager experimenters got to work on the newly discovered waves: Oliver Lodge in England, Alexander Popoff in Russia, Augusto Righi in Italy. Righi was professor of physics at the University of Bologna, and one of the pupils studying under him was a youth by the name of Guglielmo Marconi.

Guglielmo Marconi was born at Bologna on April 25, 1874, the son of an Italian father and an Irish mother. His father was a man of wealth, and the young Guglielmo was educated privately at Bologna, Florence and Leghorn.

As a boy he became keenly interested in physical science and electrical research, and it can be imagined how greatly he was affected by the news of Hertz's discovery of the electric waves, which was published when he was fifteen.

From that time Marconi's mind was turned in one direction, and it was not long before speculation on Hertz's work led him to the idea, or as he himself put it: "I might almost say the intuition, that these waves might, in a not distant future, furnish mankind with a new and powerful means of communication."

With Hertz's results published and eminent scientists at work, it might seem that others, too, would grasp this possibility, but although Lodge and Popoff came to the brink of the discovery, it was left for the young Marconi to apply the Hertzian waves to the invention of practical wireless telegraphy.

"I could scarcely conceive," said Marconi, "that it was possible that their application to useful purposes could have escaped the notice of eminent scientists." But it did. The young man, whom it had not escaped, began his experiments in the summer of 1895 at his father's country house at Pontecchio, near Bologna. Colonel Crawley describes his crude apparatus:

"His transmitter was a multiple spark gap as used by Righi, an induction coil, and a Morse signalling key. His receiver was a coherer as used by Branly, the filings being decohered by taps from the hammer of an electric bell, and the local circuit was closed by a relay, as used by Popoff. All the instruments, however, were improved in detail by Marconi, and, towards the end of these first experiments, he broke new ground by connecting one side of the spark gap to an aerial wire, and the other side to earth, thus producing for the first time a practical system of wireless signalling."

From his collection of primitive instruments Marconi got marvellous results: he managed to transmit a wireless message for a distance of over a mile. Early in 1896 he had increased the distance to two miles.

In the same year he brought his apparatus to England, where he applied for a provisional patent on June 2, and got immediately into communication with Sir William Preece, engineer-in-chief to the Post Office. Marconi's first demonstration in England was made from the roof of the General Post Office at St. Martin-le-Grand, London, in the presence of a number of post office and government officials. Army and navy representatives watched his experiments on Salisbury Plain, and finally, in an experiment between Penarth and Brean Down, wireless messages were flashed across the Bristol Channel—a distance of nearly ten miles!

Italy became aware of the wonderful discovery of her brilliant son, and the Italian government invited Marconi to conduct experiments at Spezia, where a land station was set up. From it messages were sent to warships twelve miles out to sea. Not only was the range of wireless telegraphy increasing: the world was beginning to realize its practical value.

In 1897 Marconi made tests of his apparatus in the presence of King Humbert and Queen Margherita of Italy, and also before the Italian Chamber of Deputies. In July of the same year wireless became a commercial reality with the formation, in London, of the Wireless Telegraph and Signal Company, which three years later became Marconi's Wireless Telegraph Company. This company developed and furthered the inventor's pioneer work, and stations were set up at Alum Bay, Isle of Wight, and Bournemouth.

While he continued to experiment in England, Marconi also saw his work being practically applied with success. In 1898 he installed the first wireless apparatus on a lightship, enabling the East Goodwin lightship to keep in communication with the South Foreland lighthouse, twelve miles away.

Almost immediately the value of the innovation was proved. In March, 1899, the East Goodwin lightship was run down by a steamer, and a message was flashed at once to the lighthouse. The lifeboats were sent out, and by their prompt arrival saved the crew.

In 1898 the English Channel was bridged by wireless for the first time, and in the summer messages were sent a distance of seventy-four miles between ships on naval manœuvres. By using higher aerials and longer waves Marconi was slowly increasing the distances of transmission. Now he had conquered the Channel he turned boldly to the conquest of the Atlantic.

The amazed public, still mistrusting the miracles that Marconi had already performed, were incredulous, and learned mathematicians proved to their own satisfaction that the feat was impossible. But Marconi was too busy at Poldhu, in Cornwall, to listen to them.

There, in October, 1900, he began building the first long-distance wireless station. He put up two-hundred-feet-high aerial masts, but they were smashed in a gale, and a set of masts thirty feet shorter was erected. When at last his transmitting station was complete, the inventor hurried across to St. John's, Newfoundland. After terrific difficulties he succeeded in raising an aerial to a height of four hundred feet by using kites, and then he established his receiving station.

On December 12, 1901, from Poldhu were transmitted a series of signals: they were received at Newfoundland. Marconi had bridged the Atlantic at his first attempt!

From that day wireless telegraphy ceased to be an experiment, and became an established and practicable service. But Marconi still went on pioneering, discovering, inventing. In 1902 he patented his magnetic detector, and three years later came his horizontal directional aerial. Colonel Crawley gives an impressive picture of its announcement:

"It was while on a visit to Poldhu that Marconi first demonstrated his discovery of the directional effects of low horizontal aerials. We all had dinner together at the hotel, which is a few hundred yards distant from the wireless station, and when the table had been cleared, Marconi placed a magnetic detector, with headphones for each of us, in the centre of the table. He connected one end of a piece of wire, a few feet long, to the aerial terminal of the instrument, and, holding the other end just clear of our heads, walked round the table. When the wire was in the direction of the station which was transmitting, we heard loud signals, and when it was at right angles to that direction we heard nothing. Personally, I was amazed, and I consider this to have been the most impressive demonstration I have ever witnessed. Next day, we had a full-dress demonstration with real aerials in the open country; but Marconi had shown us all that there was to be shown in those two minutes at the dinner table. I remember we looked wise and asked him for explanations. He told us that he had not had time to consider explanations, but that Dr. Fleming, in London, was tackling that part of the business!"

Meanwhile, John Ambrose Fleming had invented the thermionic valve, which, improved by Lee de Forest, revolutionized wireless receiving apparatus.

Marconi went on with his work. In 1910 he received a message from Buenos Aires at his station at Clifden in Ireland, a distance of six thousand miles. Two years later he invented his timed spark system for generating continuous waves: it was by means of this that he sent the first message to Australia in September, 1918.

With the outbreak of war in 1914, Marconi turned to the military uses of wireless, and in 1916 he was experimenting with ultra-short waves with the object of perfecting the beam system, by which wireless waves may be directed along a particular channel. In his early experiments in Italy and London Marconi had used short waves with reflectors, but the success of the long wave in long distance telephony, and his own discovery that by lengthening the wave it was possible to counteract the fading strength of signals in daylight (a fact which Marconi had first noticed in receiving messages from Poldhu in 1902), had allowed the short wave to be forgotten. But now, in 1916, short waves came to the fore.

The war brought other occupations besides experimentation to Marconi. He served both in the Italian army and navy and he was a member of the Italian War Mission to the United States. In 1919 he was appointed by the King of Italy, plenipotentiary delegate to the Peace Conference, and he signed several treaties on behalf of his country.

In 1919 his company at Chelmsford set up the first broadcasting station in the world.

Amateur experimenters had proved the usefulness of short waves for long-distance communication, and now from Poldhu a series of trial transmissions on short waves began. Marconi on his research yacht, *Elettra,* made an experimental voyage to the West Indies in 1923 and on the trip he continuously received the short wave messages from Poldhu.

As a result of these experiments Marconi announced his belief that a short wave service to South America was a commercial possibility. On the same trip he had at last proved that short waves could be concentrated into a beam and aimed in a particular direction.

" Although many different arrangements have been used," writes Mr. A. W. Haslett, " the result resembles the focusing of light by a mirror. We have only to think of how much illumination would be needed to give the whole sky the brightness of a searchlight beam to realize the saving of electrical power effected by the beam wireless system. It is today the basis of practically all commercial communication on short waves."

He followed up his short wave experiments and his establishment of the beam system with further research in the same direction. It was at first thought that ultra-short and micro waves (micro waves are those of less than a metre) travelled in straight lines, but in 1932 he proved that their path, like that of light, was not quite straight. On a wave-length of fifty centimetres he sent messages between Cap Figari in Sardinia and Roca di Papa near Rome, a distance of one hundred and sixty-eight miles. Had the micro wave travelled exactly in a straight line, the curvature of the earth's surface would have prevented the reception of the messages.

In 1933 Marconi returned to the practical side of wireless and made a great improvement in low-power short-wave transmission. It was clearly in ultra-short wave and micro wave transmission that the future of world communication lay.

The use of wireless to ensure safety at sea, which was one of the first advantages reaped from Marconi's inventions in the closing years of the last century, formed also the subject of some of his later experiments in invention. In July, 1934, he demonstrated his new blind harbour entrance device worked by ultra-short waves. Navigating from a curtained room, the captain of the *Elettra* steered the yacht between two buoys with uncanny accuracy. His course was directed from a beacon station giving directional signals and they were announced to him by loudspeaker and simultaneously by a needle on a dial.

Later that year, Marconi suffered a serious breakdown in health, but, despite the warnings of his doctors, was as active as ever again, working and travelling, by the following summer. Also, the war in Ethiopia claimed his attentions for its brief duration. (It is, perhaps, a rare item on the debit side of Marconi's account with humanity that he identified himself, right from the start, with the Fascist movement in Italy.)

The war over, he returned to peaceful research, and was in Rome when, on July 20, 1937, he had a fatal heart attack. The nations paid homage of silence to the genius who had taken them into a new dimension of sound.

Throughout the forty years Marconi conferred benefit after benefit upon the world, the great inventor was showered with honours. Chief of them was the Nobel Prize for physics, awarded to him in 1909. In 1915 he became a member of the Italian Senate: in 1929 he was created marchese.

It is a far cry to that silent age that existed before 1895. Radio, with its ever-increasing benefits in every sphere of human activity, knit a new world together and opened a new era in the history of mankind. In forty years we advanced an age: and the magician who tapped time with his wand was Guglielmo Marconi.

ORVILLE AND WILBUR WRIGHT

(1871–1948, 1867–1912)

The aeroplane has ceased to be a wonder of the world, although its breathless flights are ever taking us into a new age. Man's conquest of the air has been so rapid and far-reaching, that it comes with a shock to realize that the first flight made by a machine heavier than air took place in 1903. *Yet in* 1903 *the possibility of the aeroplane first ceased to be a fantastic dream. It became a reality through the vision, skill, courage and painstaking perseverance of two Americans, the brothers Orville and Wilbur Wright.*

DECEMBER 17, 1903.

To how many people is that day of any significance? How many who watch with awe the ever-more-wonderful feats being performed in the air think of that date as being the start of it all? Yet December 17, 1903, surely ought to be a red-letter day celebrated throughout the world. For on that day was accomplished one of the most outstanding, one of the most epoch-making feats of all time. It was then that Wilbur and Orville Wright, in a field at Kitty Hawk, North Carolina, flew for the first time in the history of mankind a heavier-than-air, power-driven flying-machine.

True, the longest flight of that day was but fifty-nine seconds, and the distance only eight hundred and twelve feet. But although the world was not aware of it, a revolution had taken place.

Man was about to realize the age-old dream and emulate the birds, taking to himself wings to enable him to travel through space. Before this men had flown in balloons and in airships. They had learnt to glide and some had even attempted heavier-than-air flight. But no one had succeeded, and not until this historic day was the feat that was to make possible transatlantic and other breathtaking flights accomplished.

Wilbur and Orville Wright were two American brothers. Wilbur was born in Millville, Indiana, in 1867 and Orville four years later at Dayton, Ohio.

Early in life the boys showed a mechanical turn of mind and, what was even more important, developed that scientific outlook necessary for pioneers in such a field. They were patient, careful and painstaking, and never took a step without first making sure that it was theoretically justified. This care was to be of the utmost value when they came to construct their machine.

Their aptitude for engineering they turned to good account in the construction of printing machines and bicycles, which were then becoming very popular. It was not until 1896 that the brothers seriously began to consider the possibilities of flying. Hitherto they had toyed with the idea, but in that year occurred the death of Otto Lilienthal, the German engineer who had startled the world by accomplishing long gliding feats. The death of Lilienthal drew the Wrights' attention to the problem and, still as a hobby, they decided to construct if possible a more successful gliding machine than Lilienthal's. They saw where the German's weakness had lain. Lilienthal had balanced his machine by movements of his body. The Wrights realized that a better method than this was essential. But there was absolutely no indication whatever as to what this method should be. The great feat of these two young men was to discover it.

Also, the Wright brothers realized that while gliding might be a good sport, flying could have no practical future unless it were harnessed to power. Using steam as a motive power, Sir Hiram Maxim had carried out experiments which, although they had not been successful, had resulted in the collection of a mass of invaluable data. It remained for the Wrights to invent a suitable engine.

Both these difficulties they were to overcome, though not without a vast amount of work and a great deal of disappointment that would have been more than enough to deter other men. Time and time again they were to find that the changes and improvements they had made were not sufficient. Yet they did not despair. Once started, they believed in the ultimate success of their labour, and nothing was allowed to stand in their way.

Their method of approach in building the glider was typical of them. Having made up their minds, they proceeded not to build but to study. First they collected all the available information on the subject of flying. They studied with the utmost care the writings of every pioneer in the field, the works of those who had tried and failed, and those who had flown in airships and balloons. Cayley, Maxim, Lilienthal, Pilcher, Ader, Langley and others were carefully combed for every scrap of information that could be of service. The Wrights wanted to learn all they could about air pressure and air currents, how to construct planes with the greatest lifting power, the secret of balance, the best way to gain initial acceleration, and the thousand and one other things necessary to achieve the conquest of the air.

Hours were spent collecting data, thrashing out in arguments every material possibility. Wilbur would take one point of view and Orville the other and the argument would wax bitter until one could prove his point conclusively to the other. This was the best possible method to adopt. It was unscientific to proceed to practical work until certain that the theoretical side had been properly clarified. What took up most of the time was the problem of balance and control. On the solution of that everything depended.

At last they decided to construct a glider. They set to work in their Dayton workshop and produced a biplane with several notable new features, the results of their long hours of study and deliberation. Whereas Lilienthal had sat upright in his machine, the Wrights decided that it would materially lessen wind resistance if the pilot were horizontal. Consequently in their machine the pilot lay full length on the lower plane. But more important still, the brothers had devised methods to control fore-and-aft and lateral balance, that is, means to prevent the machine from dipping at the front or back, or becoming depressed at either side.

Fore-and-aft balance was obtained by fitting in the front of the machine a small subsidiary plane called the elevator, which could be controlled by the pilot. To cause the machine to rise when in flight, it was necessary only to tilt the elevator to a higher angle, and vice versa.

The solution of the even more difficult problem of lateral balance was also solved. The wings of the machine were made warped, and the ends flexible, and these were connected by wires to the pilot. Thus, when one side of the machine became depressed, the pilot could lift the edge on that side, and the air pressure would right the machine.

This revolutionary discovery, now known as aileron control, proved to be the solution of the problem. From then on the conquest of the air was only a matter of time.

When the Wrights took their glider to Kitty Hawk in the summer of 1900, they saw, after trials and certain adjustments had been made, that the desired end was about to be achieved. They were on the right track, and further research would give them the control they sought.

The next step was to fit the glider with power. Fortunately the petrol engine, the only suitable motive-power, was to hand. It is the petrol engine which makes flying possible, because it gives one horse-power of energy for every three pounds of weight. Yet there was no engine built that could be used, for the automobile engine was much too heavy. The Wrights set to work to produce their own motor, and in due course constructed it.

It was a modest affair, with four cylinders developing fifteen horse-power and driving two propellers. Later, when Wilbur took his machine to France, European experts thought little of it until Wilbur actually convinced them with his flights. But the Wrights knew what they were doing, and surely enough the engine served its purpose.

In December, 1903, the machine was taken to Kitty Hawk and the engine fitted. All was now ready for the great experiment. The residents of Kitty Hawk were invited to witness the first aeroplane flight in history—though at this time the Wrights had not adopted that name, calling their machine the "Wright Flyer"—but so used had people in the neighbourhood become to what they must have considered mere antics, and so little importance did they attach to the occasion, that only five people turned up to watch history being made.

The morning of December 17 was icy cold, and a wind of about twenty-seven miles an hour was blowing when the Wrights drew their machine from its shed and fixed it on the apparatus they had devised for giving it initial acceleration.

The brothers tossed who should have the first try and Wilbur lost. Accordingly, Orville mounted the machine, and Wilbur, after starting the propeller and pulling the cord that released the plane, pushed it to the end of the wooden rail.

The machine left the ground, careered wildly in the currents and whirls of the air, and came down a hundred and twenty feet from its starting place, after being twelve seconds in the air. Twelve seconds! Scarcely a flight at all. Yet a flight it was, and more important than any made since.

Wilbur then took a turn, and succeeded in remaining in the air for fifty-nine seconds, covering a distance of eight hundred and twelve feet. And with that the day's work was ended by a gust of wind overturning the unguarded machine.

Man had flown. No matter how brief the flight; for the first time a power-driven, heavier-than-air machine had travelled through space. As Wilbur Wright said afterwards: "It was the first time in the history of the world that a machine carrying a man had raised itself into the air by its own power in free flight, had sailed forward on a level course without reduction of speed, and had finally landed without being wrecked."

The world remained in almost total ignorance of what was going on in that obscure region of North Carolina. Rumours crept out that two men were actually flying, but little credence was given them. By the lay mind the possibilities of such flight were regarded in much the same way as we now consider a trip to the moon.

The Wrights now set about constructing a stronger and more powerful machine. They gave up Kitty Hawk as being too far from Dayton, and transferred the scene of their operations to Huffman Prairie, eight miles east of Dayton.

It was now decided to give the world an insight into what was going on, and with this in view the Wrights invited fifty newspaper reporters to witness the trial flight of their new machine. Impelled more by curiosity than by belief, the pressmen came. But they saw nothing. The wind was unfavourable and the engine would not function properly. Some of them came the next day, but the results were no better. The reporters left with their doubts confirmed.

The loss of publicity was the last thing to worry the Wright brothers. Both were extremely modest and retiring and, though they were confident that they had overcome the major difficulties and might truthfully be said to have conquered the air, they had no desire to boast about it and were solely concerned with one thing—to perfect their machine. "If I talked a lot," said Wilbur, "I should be like the parrot, a bird that talks most and flies least."

Immediately after their failure before the pressmen, the Wrights began flying in earnest. The length of their flights increased steadily, and it became common to fly for several minutes and cover often more than a mile. In 1904, Patrick Y. Alexander created a sensation in the London Aeronautical Society by reading a letter from Wilbur Wright in which the latter described a flight of twenty-four miles. But still many people were sceptical.

In 1905 the brothers decided to give up flying for some time. Their exploits were now attracting wide attention and all their experiments were watched by a large crowd of amazed onlookers. Both brothers had for some time devoted the whole of their time and capital to the work. They had long ago ceased to treat it as a hobby, and had even given up their bicycle business to sink themselves wholly into their new work. Consequently they now depended on their invention to repay them for their efforts, and were fearful lest details of it might be copied for reproduction elsewhere. They therefore devoted their time to technical improvements and laboratory research.

In the years when the Wrights were absent from the flying field, much progress was made in heavier-than-air flying in Europe. Santos-Dumont, Henri Farman, Blériot and Voisin were among those eagerly seeking to perfect a good power-driven aeroplane. Yet so much in advance were the Wright brothers that when the time came for Wilbur to compete with the European experts he was easily the most successful.

Not until a syndicate had taken over the financial side of the business (to conduct the negotiations with the U.S. Government and a French syndicate that was interested), did the brothers emerge once more, to show the world how much they had accomplished.

Then, in 1908, while Orville remained in the States to satisfy the tests of his Government, Wilbur travelled to France. At Le Mans the simplicity of his mode of life surprised everyone. He slept in a cot near his beloved machine, and a chair and plain table were all the furniture he needed.

But that was nothing to their surprise when he began to fly. Beginning on August 8, every day he improved on his previous performance, soaring and circling freely in the air. On September 6 at Chalons he flew for an hour and four minutes with a passenger. No one before had ever flown for such a period with so great a load.

Meanwhile in America Orville was equally successful, though his triumph was marred by a fatal accident. While flying with Lieutenant Selfridge, an army officer, one of the propeller chains broke. The plane crashed to the ground. Orville escaped with severe injuries, but Selfridge was killed instantly.

When in France, on December 18, Wilbur flew for two hours, and climbed to a height of three hundred feet, both records at the time, the company formed to purchase the Wright patent in France was satisfied, and monetary reward at last came to ease the brothers' burdens.

From now on successes followed each other rapidly. Governments all over the world awoke to the value, civil and military, of the aeroplane, and offers of purchase came in a rush.

The Wrights' day had come. Everywhere they were fêted. In Europe, royalty came to witness the new marvel, and at home huge crowds would gather to see them give an exhibition. For a long time they remained at the very head of the aviation world, and their every deed was front page news. But while success after so much neglected toil must have been pleasant, it was nothing compared to the knowledge that they were responsible for one of the most revolutionary discoveries of all time.

The Wrights now gave up active flight to devote their attention to the construction of machines and to the training of new men.

But the partnership that had given the world so much was soon to come to an end. In 1912 the world learnt that Wilbur Wright had been taken ill with typhoid fever, and on May 30 he died at his home in Dayton. It may truthfully be said that his death inflicted on the world a loss it could ill afford.

Orville Wright lived to see their invention grow to proportions greater than he or his brother could ever have dreamed—lived to see it become the supreme tool of world transport, annihilating time and distance, bridging oceans and leaping land barriers; more unhappily, lived through two world wars to see it become a third fighting arm, swift in destruction and of limitless range; indeed, lived to see it transform existence.

Achievement followed achievement in the air with such bewildering rapidity that, by the year 1948 when Orville Wright died, the world could no longer marvel. But then, what flight that ever followed—no, not even man's rocketing into space—could match the wonderful achievement and sheer courage of those first breathless twelve seconds in the air that memorable day in December, 1903, or equal it in significance as the herald of a new age?

WRITERS AND POETS

HERODOTUS

(*c.* 484–408 B.C.)

"Herodotus," says Lemprière, "is among the historians what Homer is among the poets, and Demosthenes among the orators of ancient times. His style abounds with elegance, ease, and sweetness. . . ." That is a just summary: for as Homer was the first and greatest of the poets, so Herodotus was the first and fountain-head of prose writers. His great work set a standard and gave inspiration to the ages that have followed. No one has questioned the justness of the title of "the father of history" which Cicero bestowed upon Herodotus.

"HERODOTUS of Halicarnassus here displays his researches, with the intent that things which have happened may not perish from among men by the lapse of time, and that great and marvellous deeds, some displayed by Greeks, others by barbarians, may not lack renown; and, in particular, for what cause they fought with one another."

With those words begins the first of European histories and one of the most remarkable literary works that the world has seen. It was Cicero who dubbed Herodotus "the father of history," and posterity has endorsed the title. We might, indeed, go further and proclaim him the father of European prose.

It is ironical that the man who devoted his genius to recording the deeds, stories and legends of his world in order that "things which have happened may not perish," should himself be a misty figure almost unknown to history.

Herodotus was born at Halicarnassus, a city of Caria in the south-west of Asia Minor, some time about the year 484 B.C. Artemisia, the warrior queen who displayed such courage when she fought for Xerxes in the great sea battle of Salamis, was ruler of Halicarnassus at that time, and when Herodotus was a young man, her grandson, Lygdamis, was the tyrant of the city, with Artaxerxes, the great king of Persia, as his overlord.

Herodotus joined the revolutionary party, whose aim was to throw off the yoke of Lygdamis and the Persian king and establish once more a free Greek city. Panyasis, an epic poet and uncle to Herodotus, was the leader of the party, and when he was captured by Lygdamis and promptly executed, Herodotus fled to Samos, where, during the next seven or eight years, he learnt the Ionic dialect in which his histories are written.

Eventually the tyrant was overthrown and Herodotus returned to his native city. But the new party in power was as hostile to him as Lygdamis had been, and so he left Halicarnassus for good and set out on a life of wandering.

Athens, then at the height of its greatness and the cultural centre of the world, became his second home. Herodotus found a friend in Sophocles, the great dramatist, who wrote an ode for him, and it is not improbable that he was acquainted with Pericles and other great contemporaries in the brilliant city whose glory still illuminates the world. Tradition says that his readings from his own histories delighted the Athenians, who gave him a grant from the public funds as a reward.

A less reliable source states that his histories were publicly declaimed at the Olympic games and were received with riotous applause. Herodotus did not spend his life of exile in the pleasant society of the Athenians. He travelled, and he travelled extensively.

Many of the tales he tells and the descriptions he gives in his work are based on his own experiences, and when the difficulties and dangers of travel in those far-off days are considered, his extensive journeyings appear almost as remarkable as their fruits.

He went far south up the Nile into Upper Egypt; he travelled through Asia beyond Babylon to Susa and Ecbatana, which is now the modern site of Hamadân in Persia. He sailed into the Black Sea, saw the mouth of the Danube, visited the Crimea and went on eastwards to the land of Colchis, the modern Georgia and the mythical Land of the Golden Fleece. He sailed to Tyre and along the whole of the Syrian coast. The Thracian coast he also knew, while to the south-west he went as far as Cyrene and ventured into Libya. Greece he covered in every direction; he wandered through the Epirus, Thessaly, Attica and the Peloponnese, visiting all the places of the greatest interest.

Whatever the primary purpose of all this travelling—and it must seem that they were the journeys of the first historian in search of history—the results are apparent in Herodotus's work. And when he is reproached with inaccuracy and gullibility, it is well to remember that he tells us in the second book that he sailed specially to Tyre to verify one single fact.

In 444 B.C. the Athenians established a new colony in the south of Italy, founding the town of Thurii on the site of ruined Sybaris, proverbial for its luxury. The citizens of Thurii were drawn from all nations, and among them were Lysias, the Syracusan, who was to become at Athens a great orator, and Herodotus. How long he remained there is not known, but he was apparently in Athens after 432 B.C., and he died with his great work unfinished, or at least unrevised, some time betweeen 426 and 415 B.C.—although even these dates are conjecture.

Perhaps the clearest idea of Herodotus's work and of his attitude towards it will be gained from Professor Gilbert Murray's admirable summary:

"Herodotus, the father of history, was an exiled man and a professional story-teller; not, of course, an 'improvisatore,' but the prose correlative of a bard, a narrator of the deeds of real men, and a describer of foreign places. His profession was one which aimed, as Thucydides severely says, more at success in a passing entertainment than at any lasting discovery of truth; its first necessity was to interest an audience. Herodotus must have had this power whenever he opened his lips; but he seems to have risen above his profession, to have advanced from a series of public readings to a great history —perhaps even more than that. For his work is not only an account of a thrilling struggle, politically very important, and spiritually tremendous; it is also—more, perhaps, than any other known book—the expression of a whole man, the representation of all the world seen through the medium of one mind and in a particular perspective. The world was at that time very interesting; and the one mind, while strongly individual, was one of the most comprehensive known to human records. Herodotus's whole method is highly subjective. He is too sympathetic to be consistently critical, or to remain cold towards the earnest superstitions of people about him: he shares from the outset their tendency to read the activity of a moral God in all the moving events of history. He is sanguine, sensitive, a lover of human nature, interested in details if they are vital to his story, oblivious of them if they are only facts and figures; he catches quickly the atmosphere of the society he moves in, and falls readily under the spell of great human influences, the solid impersonal Egyptian hierarchy or the dazzling circle of great individuals at Athens; yet all the time shrewd, cool, gentle in judgment, deeply and unconsciously convinced of the weakness of human nature, the flaws of its heroism and the excusableness of its apparent villainy. His book bears for good and ill the stamp of this character and this profession."

The history of Herodotus is by no means a history in the modern sense of the word. Geographical descriptions, legends and moral tales, studies in different sciences, gossip and " news stories " are all jumbled together. On this account he has often been charged with inaccuracy and credulity, but his rambling garrulity has its purpose of interesting the reader or hearer, and it does not follow that Herodotus was merely an ignorant chronicler and an unscientific historian.

He gives us a glimpse of his method and of his own attitude towards the stories that are quoted against him, when he writes in the second book—the book that contains his wonderfully graphic account of Egypt and Egyptian life:

" Up to this point my observation, judgment, and research have been speaking. I am now going to utter Egyptian accounts based on hearsay; mingled with them will be something of my own observation."

Again, in the seventh book, he says explicitly: " It is my duty to repeat what is said, but to believe unreservedly is not; this remark applies to all my work." And the story, already cited, of his journey to Tyre indicates the spirit in which he approached his task.

It may be said that Herodotus had definitely the right attitude and method of a scientific historian, but he had also a weakness for a " good story," and would repeat the story whether it were true or not.

Herodotus has been attacked on another ground: that of ascribing favourable happenings to the direct intervention of divine power. It must be remembered that his profession depended on popular appeal, and the belief in the interest of the gods in one's own cause was, and still is, widely held. Moreover there are many passages in which he uses his own judgment cautiously to leave open the question as to whether such-and-such an act was caused by the gods. And, quoting Herodotus on the defeat of Xerxes: " The gods and heroes grudged that one man should be king both of Europe and Asia, and that a man impious and proud," Professor Murray pertinently remarks: " What Englishman did not feel the same at the news of the wreck of the Armada? What Russian, after the retreat from Moscow?"

In the same way it is unreasonable to accuse Herodotus of sententious moralizing when he produces such moral tales as that of Solon and Crœsus, or this little story, which was adduced to illustrate the madness of Cambyses in " deriding sacred and established customs ":

" Darius having summoned some Greeks under his sway, who

were present, asked them for what sum they would feed upon the dead bodies of their parents. They answered that they would not do it for any sum. Darius afterwards having summoned some of the Indians called Callatians, who are accustomed to eat their parents, asked them in the presence of the Greeks, who were informed of what was said by an interpreter, for what sum would they consent to burn their fathers when they die. But they, making loud exclamations, begged that he would speak words of good omen. Such, then, is the effect of custom: and Pindar appears to me to have said rightly that 'custom is the king of all men.'"

Such a story was added to embellish the tale and point the moral of his conclusions, but it cannot be regarded as evidence of the religious disposition or simple piety of the narrator.

Pindar is quoted at the end of the story. Herodotus sprinkles his whole work with interpolations from the poets, and it seems clear that he had perused and mastered all the Greek literature that existed in his day. Everything goes to prove that he was a well-read, intelligent man, who used his own observation and judgment, even if he did publish fairy tales.

The clear pictures that Herodotus gives, and the honest way in which he presents his matter may be best illustrated by two chapters from his second book:

"The following is the nature of the crocodile. During the four coldest months it eats nothing, and though it has four feet, it is amphibious. It lays its eggs on land, and there hatches them. It spends the greater part of the day on the dry ground, but the whole night in the river; for the water is then warmer than the air and the dew. Of all living things with which we are acquainted, this, from the least beginning, grows to be the largest. For it lays eggs little larger than those of a goose, and the young is at first in proportion to the egg; but when it grows up it reaches to the length of seventeen cubits, and even more. It has the eyes of a pig, large teeth, and projecting tusks, in proportion to the body: it is the only animal that has no tongue: it does not move the lower jaw, but it is the only animal that brings down its upper jaw to the under one. It has strong claws, and a skin covered with scales, that cannot be broken on the back. It is blind in the water, but very quick-sighted on land; and because it lives for the most part in the water, its mouth is filled with leeches. All other birds and beasts avoid him, but he is at peace with the trochilus, because he receives benefit from that bird. For when the crocodile gets out of the water on land, and then opens its jaws, which it does most commonly towards the west, the trochilus enters its mouth and swallows the leeches: the crocodile is so well pleased with this service that it never hurts the trochilus. . . .

"There is also another sacred bird called the phœnix, which I have never seen except in a picture; for it seldom makes its appearance amongst them, only once in five hundred years, as the Heliopolitans affirm: they say it comes on the death of its sire. If he is like the picture, he is of the following size and description: the plumage of his wings is partly golden coloured and partly red; in outline and size he is very like an eagle. They say that he has the following contrivance, which, in my opinion, is not credible. They say that he comes from Arabia, and brings the body of his father to the temple of the sun, having plastered him up in myrrh, and there buries him in the temple. He brings him in this manner: first he moulds an egg of myrrh as large as he can carry; then he tries to carry it, and having made the trial, he hollows out the egg and puts his father into it, and stops up with more myrrh the hole through which he put in his father; so when his father is inside, the weight is the same as before: then having covered up the hole, he carries him to the temple of the sun in Egypt. This, they say, is done by this bird."

These are two pieces of graphic reporting. But the first is concise, sure, and hard. There Herodotus was writing from his own observation and knowledge. The second is as lucidly written, but hedged about with reserves and doubts. It is a good story, but "in my opinion is not credible." So, generously sprinkled with "they say" and "as they affirm," it goes into history.

Herodotus presented the truth with a wide and sympathetic grasp and set down a story that has won renown through the succeeding centuries not only because it was the first of all histories and father of all our prose works, but also for its intrinsic interest and the beauty of its telling.

EURIPIDES

(*c.* 480–406 B.C.)

The thinker is the enemy of the mob. Euripides, the greatest of the Athenian playwrights, made men think by posing real—and awkward—problems before them. Like Mr. Shaw, he made men uncomfortable and he made them angry. They accused him of blasphemy and misogyny: they said he had a grudge against gods and men. But they had to listen to his ideas, ideas that were presented in superb poetry. They lampooned him and cursed him, until in weariness he left his native Athens. But after his death he became the most played and most honoured of all the tragedy-writers, and his fame has rested secure ever since.

IN the heat of the battle, when the warm air was heavy with the stench of blood and sweat, as armoured men writhed and struggled to get at grips with each other and sword clanged on shield or bit silently into flesh, while curses and groans made an accompaniment to death and destruction, one of the fighters staggered back for a brief respite and muttered: "Child-bearing must be like this, but not half so bad."

The speaker was Euripides, greatest of the Athenian dramatists, and the writer who won the reputation of being a crabbed, sour misogynist.

The battlefield remark provides the key, if any is needed after a study of his plays, to Euripides' attitude towards women. But there are ample explanations for the hatred and the scorn which were poured upon him by his contemporaries. For Euripides was a realist with the imagination of a poet. He made men think and he made them face problems that were unpleasant to contemplate. He told the old stories and wrote of the old gods, but his hearers were at last awakened from the complacency with which they had believed in them.

He was an intellectual rebel. He was a "modernist" in more senses than one, for much of his philosophy bridges the gap of two thousand years between his age and ours. Yet, while controversy raged around Euripides, his public were compelled to regard the products of his keen mind and to listen to the outpourings of his poetry. In his lifetime he was the most famous poet of all Greece; before he was dead he was assured of deathless fame.

* * * * *

Euripides was born about the year 480 B.C., the date of the great naval battle of Salamis, in which the Greeks met and defeated the mighty fleet of Xerxes, King of Persia. Tradition says of the three great Greek dramatists, that Æschylus fought at Salamis, Sophocles danced in the boys' chorus, and Euripides was born in the year of the battle. It says further that the father of Euripides was a rogue and a bankrupt, his mother a vegetable woman who sold bad greens. But this story is no more than the slander of contemporary critics and the invention of the comic poets who made Euripides their butt. We know that his father, Mnesarchides, was a member of an old and well-to-do family, and that he was the holder of an hereditary office connected with the shrine of Apollo at Phlya; while his mother, far from selling greengrocery, was a woman of noble birth.

Similarly there are tales of his wife: that his first wife was named "the sow" and lived up to her name, and that he divorced her to marry another who was no better and had also to be divorced. But these may be dismissed, together with the other stories that have sprung from myth and malice.

As a young man, Euripides studied painting and he intended to follow that art, but before he was twenty-five he had abandoned it for poetry and the writing of tragedies.

His first play, *The Daughters of Pelias,* was produced in 455 B.C., and from that moment the Athenian public realized that a new star was ascending the firmament. They were to learn that this new poet brought new ideas and a forcible and direct style without rhetorical frills or theatrical turgidity. A blast of realism had entered the Attic theatre of tradition and traditional story.

But there was a new excitement with this poet. He used novel tricks of technique to introduce thrills. Euripides displayed his highest powers in his handling of dramatic situations, and in his finest plays magnificent poetry and superb craftsmanship command our admiration as he creates each scene.

Some idea of his power can be gathered from the plot and handling of his *Telephus*, which made a great impression when it was produced in 438 B.C. The play is now lost, but fragments remain to us.

Telephus, King of Mysia, was wounded by Achilles while he was fighting for the Trojans against the Greeks. He is told by an oracle that only the spear of Achilles, which gave the wound, can cure him, so he sets out to obtain the only cure. Disguised as a beggar, and lame from his wound, he limps through the enemy land. At last the beggar comes to a gathering of the Greek generals. He speaks in the assembly and is struck for his insolence, yet he carries his point. Then Clytemnestra, the wife of Agamemnon, admits the beggar as a suppliant. He seizes her baby son, Orestes, tells who he really is, and threatens to dash the child's brains out if any one moves towards him. With the baby as hostage, he dictates his terms, and is healed by the spear.

The *Telephus* was remarkable, apart from the excitement of its story, for an innovation which struck at the Attic stage conventions. For the beggar appeared in real rags. It is difficult in our age to realize the impression made by this stroke of realism in a formal theatre, where the presentation of plays was part of religious festival.

Realism in staging and in treatment of story forms one of the bases of attack used by Aristophanes, the greatest of the Attic comic poets, who was the most savage of Euripides' critics. The beggar's rags and philosophic tags of Euripides were joy and ammunition to Aristophanes, who also levelled the accusation of woman-hater against Euripides. In his comedy, the *Thesmophoriazusae,* he makes the women of Greece conspire to have their revenge on Euripides for introducing unpleasant women characters in his plays.

But the women of Euripides, even when they were carried away by passion to deeds of bloodshed and revenge, were never unsympathetic. His women characters are carefully studied and built up. His heroines, such as Alcestis, who gave her life for her husband, and Iphigenia, the virgin sacrifice, are idealized, yet they are flesh and blood. Even Phædra, who lied away the life of Hippolytus, and the bloodthirsty Medea are drawn so that they win us to their side.

Euripides' sympathy with women is part of his understanding and feeling for the underdog. He felt more often for the slaves and the peasants, the humble folk, than for their chiefs, whose feuds and wars made the material for high tragedy.

In those myths, which were the common stock for the plots of tragedies, the treatment of Euripides also wrought new wonders and brought new misgivings into men's minds. Those fine old blood feuds, which Homer and Æschylus had sung in heroic lines, were they not merely sordid stories of craft and treachery? And those fabled gods, whose temples towered above the city, could they be truly honoured in their ungodlike bickerings and deceits? Such were the half-questions raised by Euripides in his tragedies.

There were, too, reflections of the troubled history of the times.

Euripides was a democrat, but he hated demagogues and bureaucrats and the heartless, impersonal leaders who brought war and disaster in their train. The gloom and horror of the dragging war with Sparta have left their mark in the *Suppliants* and the *Trojan Women*.

Of Euripides' life while he was composing the tragedies that have made his name imperishable there is little enough to tell. He lived on his own estate at Salamis, and wrote his poetry in a cave that faced the sea. He was a grave and austere man, who mixed as little as he possibly could with his fellow citizens.

It is a picture fitting the severe beauty of his work: that of the poet alone in his cave, far from the bustle and the noise of the city, with only the sound of the sea to accompany the music running in his head. But that chosen solitude helped to add to his reputation as a hater of mankind and of the gods, as a crabbed cynic who shunned all contact with his fellows.

As a citizen of Athens, Euripides could not entirely separate himself from public life. He served in the army and at one time performed his duty of providing service to the state at his own expense. He also held the office of consul for Magnesia.

His true life was in the plays that captivated and horrified the world. For all the while his "blasphemies" brought him execration from the Athenian public, the beauty and power of his poetry and the excitement of his action won him admirers throughout the civilized world.

Greeks who had been captured during the ill-fated Athenian expedition to Syracuse won freedom from slavery by reciting passages from the plays of Euripides. The people of Abdera were sent almost crazy by seeing his *Andromeda*. They walked about the streets declaiming verses "and especially sang the solos in the *Andromeda* and went through the great speech of Perseus, one after another, till the city was full of seven-day-old tragedians, pale and haggard, crying aloud, 'O love, high monarch over gods and men,' and so on."

But such pleasant tributes were overshadowed by the friction in Athens. The long war was sapping the life blood of the city, and with its deepening shadows Euripides seems to identify himself. He is alone in his cave, sceptical, bitter, hating the warmongers and the demagogues; still he writes the plays which prick his hearers and yet compel them to hear.

But the baiting of the comedians and of the mob was at last too much for him; it drove him from his native city to the court of a barbarian king.

In 408 B.C., after the production of the *Orestes,* the old man left Athens for ever. He was seventy-two, and he must have known when he set out that he would never again see the city for which he had fought and which he loved.

King Archelaus of Macedon received him kindly and made him welcome. Euripides seemed to take on a new lease of life. Says Professor Gilbert Murray, whose beautiful English versions of Euripides' plays should be read by every one, "He died about eighteen months after reaching Macedon; but the peace and comfort of his new surroundings had already left their mark upon his work. There is a singular freshness and beauty in the two plays, *Bacchae* and *Iphigenia in Aulis,* which he left unfinished at his death."

There were old friends of Euripides at the court, Agathon, the dramatist, and Timotheus, the musician, and life, for a little while, must have seemed pleasant once again. But the end was near.

Tradition says that Euripides was torn to pieces by the king's hounds, set on him by jealous courtiers; perhaps tradition confused him with Pentheus in his own play, the *Bacchae,* for it seems certain that the great poet's death was not so dramatic and unpleasant.

Euripides left three sons, one of whom followed his father's profession and produced the posthumous plays.

Of the vast output of some eighty or ninety tragedies which Euripides composed, only eighteen are extant: the *Alcestis, Medea, Phoenissae, Andromache, Electra, Orestes, Hippolytus, Hecuba, Iphigenia in Aulis, Iphigenia in Tauris, Supplices, Bacchae, Ion, Cyclops, Heraclidae, Helena, Troades, Hercules.*

In spite of the extent of his fame, his plays did not win great laurels on the stage at their first productions, for he only obtained four first prizes in the tragedy contests during his lifetime, and one posthumously.

Yet, from the moment he started writing, his fame was secure and it is as great today as at any time in the twenty-four centuries since his death.

The remark of Philemon will serve as a magnificent epitaph: "If I were certain that the dead had consciousness, I would hang myself to see Euripides."

PUBLIUS VERGILIUS MARO

(70–19 B.C.)

Virgil (as he is better known) was the greatest of the Roman poets who flourished in the Augustan hothouse of genius. With his friend and fellow poet, Horace, he enjoyed the patronage of Mæcenas, and he tuned his Muse to the pleasing of the minister of Augustus and of those who appreciated the good and the beautiful. His deep feeling for nature and the countryside, his gentle love of peace and mankind, his command of rhythm and his nobility of diction, are the outstanding merits of his poetical achievement.

A FRAIL, dark figure is seated in a sunny garden, lost in contemplation of the mysteries of nature. The dusty white road which leads to Nola stretches out before him until it disappears in the distance. The figure suddenly sits more erect, for his peace has been disturbed. The creak and rattle of carts on their way to the town come nearer and nearer. His eyes light up as he watches the wine-stained vehicles lumber along, and he smiles as he replies with upraised hand to the cheerful greetings of the carters. He stands up to follow their progress, and watches with visible pleasure the very ordinary group until it disappears. He sees in it a romantic beauty to which his matter-of-fact neighbours of Campania are blind, for he is Virgil—Publius Vergilius Maro—the first poet of his time, whom the entire Latin world already honours and reveres.

Although the printing-press was a thing of the future, there was then, as now, a demand for good books at a popular price. This eagerness on the part of the public was met by publishers who employed slaves for the purpose of copying manuscripts. Rome boasted of numerous bookshops, and announcements of new works were pasted on the columns of the colonnades. Free public libraries attempted to satisfy the requirements of those who could not afford to buy, and public recitations of their works were given by authors. No household of importance was without a slave whose duty it was to read aloud at meals and such times as might be required.

Virgil was neither a Roman nor a Latin. He was a Celt. He was born near Mantua on October 15, 70 B.C., and belonged to the race then inhabiting the Lombardy plain north of the Po, which was outside Italy proper, and formed part of Cisalpine Gaul. Roman culture and civilization had indeed penetrated to the farm of the yeoman who was Virgil's father, but the romantic and melancholy temperament, the sense of natural beauty, the appreciation of the spiritual meaning of nature on the part of the young man was Celtic, not Latin.

Virgil's father, busied with his farming, his forestry, and his bee-keeping, was not the type of cultivator who insists that his son should stick to the soil at all costs. The boy was sent at the age of twelve to be educated at Cremona, and then to Milan. After two years in each of these places he went to Rome to study rhetoric and philosophy. Practically nothing is known of his life there. It is more than probable that his studies were interrupted by the civil wars which troubled the country about that time, but neither he himself, nor any other of the ancients, has written anything of Virgil's life during that stormy period in the midst of which Julius Cæsar was assassinated.

We know only that in 42 B.C. his reputation as a rising poet had already reached the ears of Asinius Pollio, governor of the district north of the Po. After the overthrow of the republican forces at the battle of Philippi, Virgil's father's farm was one of the many in that part of the country which were confiscated to be distributed by way of gratuity among the ex-servicemen who had fought for the triumvirate of Octavian, Mark Antony and Lepidus. Appeals to the local authorities were in vain, so Virgil, on the advice of Asinius Pollio, went to Rome with special letters of recommendation to Octavian. Restitution was made, partly as a result of this personal mission and partly with the help of influential friends. A short time later we hear of the poet living in the capital as one of the protégés of that wealthy patron of letters, the prime minister, Mæcenas. It was about this period that he became friendly with his fellow-poet, Horace, whose *Epistles* rank with the *Georgics* of Virgil.

Before going to Rome, Virgil had started work on his *Eclogues* or *Pastoral Poems,* based on the Greek model of Theocritus, who had lived in the third century B.C. He finished these in 37 B.C., when they were published and immediately established his reputation. Their aim was to pay a tribute to the Latin countryside. The first eclogue refers directly to the events of the times and to his own personal circumstances, for it deals with the distress and confusion arising from the confiscations of land, of which his father had been one of the victims. The ninth eclogue is generally supposed to describe the actual site of the farm on which Virgil was born. The fourth, however, is the poem which has attracted the greatest attention on the part of posterity, because in it there is reference to the prospective birth of a child which was to be coincident with the dawn of a new era. Some of the phraseology of the poem caused the early Christians to read into it a Messianic prophecy of which Virgil had been the unconscious instrument. The avowed object was to give expression to the longing of the world for a return of peace and happiness after the troubles and disturbances of the devastating wars through which it had just passed.

The *Eclogues* as a whole express sentiments of appreciation for the beauty of the world and for the charms of human affections and relationships. They created an enthusiasm in Rome which was due as much to a recognition of their romantic beauty as to the realization that in Virgil a Latin poet had at last appeared who could compare with the great men of Greece. After this, all other Latin poetry was to be judged by the extent which it fell short of Virgil's.

Virgil was now in easy circumstances, and he purchased a villa in Naples and a country house near Nola. At the latter he appears to have lived from 37 to 30 B.C., busy with the composition of his next work, the *Georgics* or *Art of Husbandry*.

Mæcenas, even while he took a great personal pleasure in helping forward the cause of letters for its own sake, was not slow to use the talents of the writers and poets whom he had taken under his protection for the promotion of aims which were dear to him as a statesman, and it is believed that it was he who suggested to Virgil the subject of the *Georgics*. As a supporter of the policy of Octavian, then Cæsar Augustus, he had at heart the revival of the agricultural industry, which had fallen upon evil times as a result of war and unsettled political conditions. Virgil's name, as that of the son of a yeoman farmer and of a man whose early associations had been so closely bound up with the soil, suggested itself at once as being that of the one writer capable of arousing interest in the subject.

Virgil adopted as his aim in the composition of the *Georgics* the faithful description of the year's task of the yeoman farmer, and to give it a poetic glamour which had never been associated in the Latin mind with the cultivation of the land. He brought into relief the pleasure to be derived from the intimate contact with nature on the part of the cultivator, and he compared the security and beauty of life on the land with the vice and luxury and emptiness of the fashionable world. He showed that rural life was more in keeping with the glories of ancient Rome and the natural beauties of Italy than life in the towns.

The subject is divided into four books, the first treating of the cultivation of the fields, or agriculture proper, of the constellations by whose movements the farmer must regulate his year, and of weather portents, upon a knowledge of which farming must depend so much for its success. The second book deals with the growing of the vine and the olive, two of the principal sources of Italy's prosperity, and of arboriculture in general. The third treats of cattle and horse-breeding, and the fourth of bee-keeping.

The *Georgics* more than fulfilled the promise of the *Eclogues* and confirmed Virgil's position as the first poet of the age. After its publication from 29 B.C. until his death, he devoted his entire time and energies to what had been his earliest and greatest ambition, namely, the composition of a great national epic which would tell of the glory of Rome and celebrate the greatness of the Emperor Augustus. The story he chose was that of the wandering of Æneas, the legendary Trojan founder of the Roman nation, and the father of Julius, the ancestor of the great patrician family of the Julii. The poem was that which became known to the world as the *Æneid,* the most famous of his works.

The idea underlying it is that of the universal empire of Rome resulting from the dominant part already played and still to be played by its citizens in the making of the world's history. Virgil's conviction, suitably encouraged by his patriotic patron, was that that rôle had been confided to Rome by divine decree, and that the heroism and steadfast virtue of her children were the means given by the heavenly powers for the due and proper fulfilment of her destiny.

The character of Æneas himself is hardly that with which a modern writer, or even a contemporary of Virgil, would endow his hero, for he is held up not so much as a man of valour, but rather as the ideal of piety and steady and persistent purpose in the pursuance and attainment of his aims. He bears, indeed, more resemblance to the Christian ideal of a lover of peace than to the popular swashbuckling knight generally associated with heroism.

By 19 B.C., Virgil had practically completed the *Æneid,* but he still wished to revise it before giving it to the world. In the summer of that year he left Italy to travel in Greece and Asia, intending to make a voyage of three years' duration before the final revision of his epic. At Athens he met Augustus and was persuaded by him to return to Italy, but before he could embark he was taken ill. He sailed, however, but during the journey his illness took a turn for the worse, and by the time the ship made land at Brindisi, Virgil was a dying man. He died a few days after landing, on September 21, 19 B.C.

In his will Virgil had directed his executors not to publish any of his work which had been left unfinished or for the publication of which they had not received his explicit sanction, and during his final illness he was tormented by the thought that the *Æneid* would be given to the world with all the errors and imperfections which time had not enabled him to eliminate. His executors would have respected his wishes, but Augustus overruled them, and directed that the *Æneid* be published.

By his own wish Virgil was buried at Naples on the road to Pozzuoli. His tomb was regarded with nothing short of religious veneration, for during his life he had been the object of the deepest affection of his fellow men. His deep sincerity, his sweetness of temper and kindness of heart, combined with his love for humanity and his patriotism, had drawn towards him even his fellow poets, who never felt the natural jealously which they might well have evinced for a successful rival. His profound piety, which showed itself in the purity of his life in an age of luxury and laxity of morals, in the honesty of his dealings, and in the hope he entertained of happiness beyond the grave, have endeared him to all posterity.

From the day of his death to the present time, Virgil's writings have been used throughout the civilized world as school text-books. Christian writers as early as the third and fourth centuries regarded Virgil as someone apart from all the other pagan poets. It has been mentioned that the fourth eclogue was taken to be a prophecy of the coming of Christ, and Virgil and the sibyls were actually introduced into the liturgy of the Church, together with Old Testament prophecy, as witness of the coming of the Messiah. Divines as far apart in temperament and in time as St. Augustine and Cardinal Newman, bear testimony to his many excellencies as a man and a poet. Dante gives sufficient evidence of his opinion by choosing Virgil from among the ancients to be his guide in the *Divine Comedy*.

In the writings of the Middle Ages it became popular to transform all the eminent ancient philosophers and poets into necromancers. Virgil was no exception, and he became famous in those later days not only as a poet, but also as a supposed exponent of the black art. Tales of magic regarding him were invented, so that the life attributed to him by the biographers of the time became something very unlike the real life lived by the gentle poet who died nineteen years before Christ was born.

An English version of the "mervelus dedes" of this imaginary Virgil was published about A.D. 1520. It describes how, at an early age, Virgil got the better of the devil in much the same way as the fishermen in *The Thousand and One Nights* induced the djinn to get back into the bottle beneath King Solomon's seal.

Other stories, even more fantastic than this, were told, but they all bear a family resemblance to the other tales of enchantment which were so characteristic of the period during which they were written.

It was not only in the Middle Ages that a superstitious halo surrounded the head of Virgil. The beginnings can be traced back as far as the early years of the Roman Empire. Most people are familiar with the curious practice of seeking guidance at critical moments by opening a page of the Bible at random and reading the first verse which strikes the eye. Long before the Scriptures came into common use for this purpose, Virgil's *Æneid* was employed in the same manner for divination and fortune telling. The custom—called the *Sortes Virgilianæ*—began a few years after the poet's death, and prevailed in some circles until comparatively modern times.

It is said that Charles I of England visited the Bodleian Library at Oxford for the sole purpose of trying to foretell his lot by means of the *Sortes Virgilianæ*. We can imagine the effect produced on the superstitious and ill-fated king as his eyes fell on the lines which confronted him on his chance opening of the *Æneid,* for they were from Dido's curse when she prophesied for *Æneas* rebellion, defeat, and finally shameful death.

Until 1896 no authentic portrait of Virgil had been known to exist. In that year there was discovered at Sousse, in Tunisia, a mosaic which was executed not less than a hundred years after his death, and obviously a copy of a picture of earlier date. It is scarcely conceivable that a personage of his fame and popularity should not have been the subject of a painting or sculpture by one or other of his contemporaries. Perhaps one contributory cause to the loss of such works of art was that Virgil never married, and consequently left no descendants to cherish his memory. A half-brother, who possibly remained on the paternal farm, could hardly be expected to collect portraits or statues. Neither, however, has been necessary to keep his name and fame ever-green throughout the ages.

DANTE ALIGHIERI

(1265–1321)

In the middle of the thirteenth century, when the western world was struggling from the darkness of medievalism to the faint flush of light that was to herald the dawn of the new learning, there was born in the lovely and troubled city of Florence a man named Dante Alighieri. He spent the opening phase of his life in politics, fighting for his beliefs, first on the battlefield and later for his guild. His reward was disgrace and long years of exile. But in that period of exile he created one of the noblest poems that the world has seen, an epic which made a language and stirred a world with a vision of wisdom and new beauty.

"Do you see the man who visits Hell, and comes back when he pleases, bringing news up here of those who are below?" remarked a woman as Dante passed. "Yes, you must be right," answered her naïve companion, "don't you see how his beard is crisped from the heat and smoke down there?"

The poet who came to be called the "morning star of modern literature" was considered by his contemporaries "reserved and disdainful, and after the fashion of a philosopher careless of graces and not easy in his converse with laymen." Boccaccio describes him as a man of middle height, who in later life "walked somewhat bent over, with a grave and gentle gait. He was clad always in most seemly attire, such as befitted his ripe years. His face was long, his nose aquiline and his eyes rather big than small. His jaws were large and his lower lip protruded. His complexion was dark, his hair and beard thick, black and curly, and his expression ever melancholy and thoughtful."

Dante Alighieri was born in 1265, the son of a well-known lawyer who lived within sight of the mosaic-fronted baptistery of St. John in the little republic of Florence. The boy studied industriously under one Brunetto Latini, who, despite his notorious vices, contrived to make his pupil conversant with the known scientific principles. Despite his serious nature, he was not averse from the lighter pursuits of his companions. Florence was the cradle of the love-song and Dante was not behindhand in writing amatory verse. The

Renaissance, which was to spread over Europe and shed light in the dark places of medieval culture, was yet to come. Dante, indeed, has been termed " the glimmer of the dawn."

The romance which was to form the subject of so much of his writings followed a casual meeting, at the age of nine, with Beatrice Portinari, a girl of noble birth a few months his junior. In the *Vita Nuova* (New Life), dedicated to his passion for her, he described her dress as of " a most noble colour, a subdued and goodly crimson, girdled and adorned in such sort as best suited her tender age." He saw her only once or twice. " When so many days had passed that nine years exactly were fulfilled," Dante writes, " this wonderful creature appeared to me in white robes between two gentle ladies who were older than she; and, passing by the street, she turned her eyes towards that place where I stood very timidly, and in her ineffable courtesy saluted me so graciously that I seemed then to see the heights of all blessedness." It is doubtful whether Beatrice was ever conscious of his emotional agonies. But his worship was all the stronger for her remoteness. He fell ill from musing on the object of his affection. In the midst of delirious dreams, she appeared to die and be transfigured. He allowed the compassion of another to console him for his " loss " for a time, but he soon turned again to his true love, and studied feverishly in order to become worthy of her.

From being the earthly love of a highly-strung youth, Beatrice became the idol of his whole life. In *Divine Comedy,* which represents the best known contribution of Dante to the literature of the world, he ended his travels in hell and purgatory in the company of his mentor, Virgil, by climbing the purgatorial mountain. At the top he came upon the " Earthly Paradise," where he found Beatrice. He proposed to say of her " that which never was said of any woman." But the meeting was only the first stage of his journey towards the real goal of his life. In her charge he was led through the various spheres which, according to the theology of the time, composed heaven. Here, for one blessed moment, he was granted divine understanding of all mysteries, which was the aim of mystical fourteenth-century theology.

Dante, however, was living in an age of strife and change. The twin blows of Beatrice's marriage to Simone de' Bardi and of the early death of his " most gracious lady " in 1290, were not permitted to deflect him from the path of public service for which his estate assigned him. He did, indeed, indulge himself in lamentation in the shape of writing the *Convito* (Banquet), in which he told how, heartbroken after Beatrice's death, he married Gemma Donati, a relative of Corso Donati, later his implacable enemy, and of the two daughters and two sons he had by his wife. It may be that he was thinking of her when one of his characters in the *Inferno* refers to " my wife of savage temper."

His first experience of politics was on the battlefield. A feud had started between the Guelph and Ghibelline parties owing to the jilting of a member of a noble Florentine family by one of the Buondelmonte, who was subsequently murdered. The strife following this matrimonial squabble led to the intervention of Pope Boniface VIII in the Guelph cause and the Ghibellines then set up their standard to oust the traitors. Dante joined the Ghibelline army. But at Campaldino, at which he fought with conspicuous gallantry, the Ghibellines were defeated, never to recover their hold on Florence. Dante was also present at the later battle of Capranao. Then, his soldiering over, he returned to his career as a politician.

He was enrolled a member of one of the six guilds, that of Apothecaries. These corporations were the effective rulers, through their priors, of the city of Florence. It was arising out of the demand of Pope Boniface VIII that Dante came into prominence. His Holiness ordered one hundred knights to fight against his personal enemies of the Colonna family. Dante's well-organized opposition to this imposition led to his being appointed the prior of his guild. His rise to power was to be the beginning of all his misfortunes, for once again civil war raged.

The factions involved were the Cerchi and the Donati families, known respectively as the Bianchi (whites) and the Neri (blacks). To check a struggle whose consequences he fully foresaw, the guild of which he was the head banished the leaders of both parties, and the Pope was asked to act as mediator. The first Papal envoy was unsuccessful, and Charles de Valois was sent to establish peace. The French prince entered the gates of the city on All Saints' Day. The Blacks took his arrival as the signal for a rising, and for days the banks of the Arno were the scene of bloodshed, fire and rapine. When flame and fury had died down, a considerable part of the once fair city of Florence was no more than smouldering embers.

After the massacre, Dante found that, from being one of the rulers of his native city, he was now an exile, condemned to be buried alive if he returned. Further, he was fined heavily for the alleged crime of " barratry " or raising of discord.

From 1302 until his death in 1321, Dante led a wanderer's existence, ever plotting with his fellow-exiles for reinstatement in his native city. In 1316, he and his fellow, Bianchi, were granted an amnesty under humiliating conditions, but Dante's pride forbade him to re-enter Florence " except with honour, secure that the means of life will not fail him, and free to gaze at the sun and the stars, and meditate on the sweetest fruits of philosophy."

The poet, a dispossessed politician, was doomed to wander from one patron to another among the city states of Lombardy, Tuscany and the Romagna. Scant details of his travels are available, but it would appear that he went as far as Paris. One chronicler even pretends that he visited Oxford.

His first real refuge was with the Lord of Verona, to whose brilliant son, Can Grande della Scala, he dedicated the *Paradiso.* " Thou shalt make trial of how salt doth taste another's bread," he makes one of his characters say, though the allusion is to himself, " and how hard the path to descend and mount upon another's stair." Thence he migrated to the roof of Guido Novello da Polenta at Ravenna in whose service he undertook an embassy to the Doge of Venice. Unsuccessful, he made his way back to Ravenna, where he died in 1321, and was buried in the church of St. Francis. After death his remains, screened behind a sculptured tomb with a " little cupola more neat than solemn," of which Byron wrote, became one of the most treasured and embarrassing relics belonging to the Franciscan monks. But even in death he was not allowed to rest in peace, for shortly before his death he had aroused the ire of the clerics by his book *De Monarchia.*

De Monarchia, in which a modern Italian commentator finds the foreshadowing of the League of Nations, maintained that the ideal state was that of government by a universal emperor as lord temporal and a universal pope as lord spiritual. The book was unwelcome to the princes of the Church because it asserted that the emperor was the divinely appointed guide of the human race in temporal matters, and was to work in partnership with the pope to abolish all national conflicts. The pope contended that he ruled both spiritually and temporally, and therefore the treatise was put on the Index of forbidden books.

On the instructions of Cardinal de Polget copies of this book were burned publicly, and it was only through the representations of the worthy citizens of Ravenna that the French prelate was deterred from holding a public burning of Dante's disinterred bones. The monks of Ravenna at some period during the seventeenth century, fearing for the safety of the relics, removed them from the sarcophagus at the back of the tomb to another part of the church, where, with the exception of the jawbone, they were found in 1865, placed in an ornate urn and returned to their original resting place. Thus ended the travels of the mortal remains of Dante, an exile even in death.

Dante's fame rests upon the *Divine Comedy* wherein he sought "to put into verse things difficult to think." The word "divine" was added by a later hand, and "comedy" it is well to remember had not then quite the same significance as it has today. It meant "action moving on towards a happy ending." Chastened by his political misadventures, Dante wrote of what courses of life will meet with reward and what with punishment in the hereafter. His characters are men and women known to him either personally or by repute, but the hero is the narrator. Although his enemies figure in his wanderings in the depths of Hell, they are described without bitterness and with scrupulous fairness. Writing in an age of vendettas and of unscrupulous methods, the poet felt no resentment for those who had caused his downfall, and was pitiless to those "sorry souls who lived without infamy and without renown, displeasing to God and to His enemies."

In the great story of his journey with Virgil through Hell, Purgatory and Heaven he gives us an encyclopædic view of the highest culture of his age. History, philosophy, literature, physical science, morals and theology are dealt with in the most exquisite poetry, and the depth of his thought is matched by the beauty of his words.

"Before Dante," says a leading authority, "there was no Italian language; after there was one," and of the power of the pen which brought it into being no reader has ceased to marvel.

GEOFFREY CHAUCER

(*c.* 1340–1400)

Chaucer was the first poet to write in modern English. Had that been his only claim to fame, had his talents done nothing else but light the torch of English poetry, it had been greatness enough. But Chaucer was not only a pioneer and a craftsman of innovation; he was a genius who could paint pictures in words, tell stories in lilting verse, and bring to us swift drama in soft cadences. He gave not only forms to his followers; he bequeathed them a spirit and an example. " The Canterbury Tales " constitute one of the greatest poems in any language.

"When that Aprille with his shoures sote
The droghte of Marche hath perced to the rote,
And bathed every veyne in swich licour,
Of wich vertu engendred is the flour;
Whan Zephirus eek with his swete breeth
Inspired hath in every holt and heeth
The tendre croppes, and the yonge sonne
Hath in the Ram his halfe cours y-ronne,
And smale fowles maken melodye . . ."

Thus, with a breath of spring, begins the prologue to *The Canterbury Tales;* and aptly, for that poem is itself the April morning of English literature. Geoffrey Chaucer, to quote the expressive phrase of James Russell Lowell, " found his native tongue a dialect and left it a language."

We have only glimpses of Chaucer's life. They come from official records and the hints he gives in his own poems. Here is a brief record of the facts.

Geoffrey Chaucer was born about the year 1340. He was the son of a London wine merchant, who lived in Upper Thames Street, beside the little stream of Walbrook. There he spent his early life, and in " The Pardoner's Tale " betrays his knowledge of his father's trade:

"Now kepe yow fro the whyte wyn of Lepe,
That is to selle in Fish-strete or in Chepe.
This wyn of Spayne crepeth subtilly

In other wynes, growing faste by,
Of which ther ryseth swich fumositee,
That whan a man hath dronken draughtes three,
And weneth that he be at hoom in Chepe,
He is in Spayne, right at the toune of Lepe,
Nat at the Rochel, ne at Bordeux toun."

When he was about seventeen Chaucer became a page in the household of Elizabeth, the wife of Lionel, Duke of Clarence and third son of Edward III. His father may have had some influence at court, for John Chaucer had attended on the king and Queen Philippa in Flanders.

The reign of Edward was a period of battle and victory: the Hundred Years War was being waged relentlessly against France. Six years after Chaucer's birth, England had won the great battle of Crécy, and in 1356 the Black Prince had again crushed the French at Poitiers. Now, in 1359, Edward III again invaded France, and Chaucer took service in his army. He was taken prisoner at Retiers. In May, 1360, the peace of Bretigny was signed, but two months before that Chaucer had been freed, and the king himself had paid £16 (a sum equivalent to over £200 of present English currency) towards the ransom money.

We next hear of him in 1367, when he was granted a life pension of twenty marks as one of the valets of the king's chamber, a position which included the making of beds and the running of messages. Possibly he transferred his services to the fourth son of the king, John of Gaunt; certainly in 1369 he wrote one of his earliest poems, *The Book of the Duchess,* in memory of the duke's wife, Blanche.

From now on Chaucer was frequently sent abroad on embassies and missions. In 1372 he visited Genoa, Pisa and Florence, and was in Lombardy again in 1378. Secret service work in Flanders occupied part of 1377, and he was sent on frequent missions to France. His visits to Italy mark a new period in the history of his writing, for he was greatly influenced from that time by the work of Dante, Boccaccio and Petrarch. Dante was dead, but he may have met the other two.

Chaucer's rise to importance was accompanied by signs of great prosperity. In 1374 the king granted Chaucer a pitcher of wine daily to be received from the royal butler. In the same year he was given the important post of Comptroller of the Customs and subsidy of wools, skins and leather for the port of London, and John of Gaunt conferred on him a life pension of £10 for good service rendered by Chaucer and his wife Philippa to himself, his wife and the queen. Little is known of Philippa, although there has been much ingenious conjecture.

Money poured in upon the poet from feudal dues and fines as well as from his emoluments. In 1382 he received another appointment as Comptroller of the Petty Customs, and three years later was allowed the privilege of nominating a permanent deputy to do the work. It was about this time that he moved from London, where he had been granted a lease by the corporation of "the whole of the dwelling-house above the gate of Aldgate, with the rooms built over, and a certain cellar beneath the same gate." He spent most of his remaining years at Greenwich, until just before his death, when he took a house near the chapel of St. Mary in Westminster.

In 1386 Chaucer was elected as a knight of the shire for Kent in the Parliament which sat at Westminster, but in the same year disaster overtook him. In the absence of John of Gaunt, his brother, the Duke of Gloucester, deprived the youthful King Richard II of power and appointed a regency. Chaucer, as a protégé of John of Gaunt, was dismissed from his offices, and, faced with sudden poverty, was compelled to raise money on his pensions. In 1387 came a further blow: his wife died. And yet, at this period, with fortune at its lowest ebb, Chaucer was planning and composing his greatest poem, *The Canterbury Tales*.

Two years later the tide turned, though the poet never regained his old prosperity. But in 1389 Richard II dismissed the Council of Regency, and Chaucer was appointed clerk of the King's Works at Westminster. A little later he obtained a similar position at Windsor and was also made one of a commission to repair the banks of the Thames between Woolwich and Greenwich.

We know that in 1390 he was responsible for putting up scaffolds in Smithfield for the king and queen to view a tournament, and that he was twice robbed of the king's money: once at Westminster, where he had £10 taken off him, and again at Hatcham, in Surrey, near the "Foule Ok."

In spite of a pension of £20 a year for life received from the king in 1394 he was still in poverty, and four years later was sued for debt. On the accession of Henry IV in 1399, the poet addressed to him a "Compleynt to his Purs," which brought prompt response from the new monarch, who ordered the pension of twenty marks to be doubled, in addition to the grant of £20 made in 1394.

But he did not live long to enjoy his new good fortune. In 1400—October 25 is the traditional date—he died, and was buried in

Westminster Abbey, the first to sleep in Poets' Corner. Over seventy years were to come and go before any of his works were printed; until that time copies were made laboriously with the pen. In 1478 Caxton issued *The Canterbury Tales* from his press, prefacing the second edition (1483) with these words: "He [Chaucer] excelleth in my opinion all other writers in English; for he writeth no void words, but all his matter is full of high and quick sentence."

That is the scanty story of his life as it has come down to us, but the poet has given us a picture of Geoffrey Chaucer, the man, in his work. His character and personality are revealed in many passages. "We easily recognize in them," writes Professor Skeat, "a man of cheerful and genial nature, with great powers of originality, full of freshness and humour, a keen observer of men, and at the same time an enthusiastic and untiring student of books." With ready sympathy he understood many of the foibles and weaknesses of humanity, but failed to condemn. He summed up but gave no verdict.

In the prologue to Sir Thopas, Chaucer gives a little picture of himself:

> ". . . Our hoste japen tho bigan,
> And than at erst he loked up-on me,
> And seyd thus, 'what man artow?' quod he;
> 'Thous lokest as thou woldest finde an hare,
> For ever up-on the ground I see thee stare.
>
> Approche neer, and loke up merily.
> Now war yow, sirs, and lat this man have place;
> He in the waast is shape as wel as I;
> This were a popet in an arm t'enbrace
> For any womman, smal and fair of face.
> He semeth elvish by his contenaunce,
> For un-to no wight dooth he daliaunce."

We know from his poems and stories that he was a scholar and a lover of books, and in *The House of Fame* he tells us himself of the bookish seclusion to which he retired after his day's work:

> "And noght only fro fer contree
> That ther no tyding comth to thee,
> But of they verray neyghebores,
> That dwellen almost at thy dores,
> Thou herest neither that ne this;

And hast y-maad thy rekeninges,
In stede of reste and newe thinges,
Thou gost hoom to thy hous anoon;
And, also domb as any stoon,
Thou sittest at another boke,
Til fully dased is thy loke,
And livest thus as an hermyte,
Although thy abstinence is lyte."

But he was no mere bookman. The delightful pictures he draws in *The Canterbury Tales* are taken from the life, and there is a love of nature in his work that is fresh and genuine. It was the poetic convention of the time to deck the theme with references to flowers and spring, but there is sincerity in that delightful passage from the prologue to *The Legend of Good Women"*:

"And, as for me, though that my wit be lyte,
On bokes for to rede I me delyte,
And to hem yeve I feyth and ful credence,
And in my herte have hem in reverence
So hertely, that ther is game noon
That fro my bokes maketh me to goon,
But hit be seldom, on the holyday;
Save, certeynely, whan that the month of May
Is comen, and that I here the foules singe,
And that the floures ginnen for to springe,
Farewel my book and my devocioun!"

But his books stood him in good stead, for he was deeply read in the learning of his time and had a wide acquaintance with Latin, French and Italian literature. His true mastery, however, was over his own language. He was always a conscious artist, experimenting in verse forms and paying great heed to the technicalities of the literary craft. Yet although he was influenced first by the French, and later by the Italians, he was no mere adapter: in English poetry he was essentially a creator and a pioneer.

His works fall easily into three periods. The first lasted from 1359 to 1372, when he was under the influence of French poetry. It is to this period that *The Book of the Duchess* belongs, and we know also that he made a translation of the immensely popular—and incidentally immensely long—medieval love story, *Le Roman de la Rose*. At this time he used the couplet of eight syllables, the metre of *The House of Fame* in the quotation cited above.

After his visit to Italy, the literature of that country, foremost in love of art and letters, made a powerful influence upon his work. He was a fervent admirer of Dante, and Boccaccio provided him with inspiration and stories. This second period, roughly from 1372 to 1386, produced *The House of Fame,* usually regarded as the loftiest of his imaginative flights; *The Assembly of Foules,* an allegory of bird life; the unfinished *The Legend of Good Women,* said to have been written at the queen's request, and the beautiful *Troylus and Cryseyde,* based on Boccaccio's *Teseide.*

He slowly discarded the old form, as in the following stanza from *Troylus and Cryseyde*:

> " Criseyde was this lady name a-right;
> As to my dome, in al Troyes citee
> Nas noon so fair, for passing every wight
> So aungellyk was hir natyf beautee,
> That lyk a thing immortal seemed she,
> As doth an hevenish parfit creature,
> That doun were sent in scorning of nature."

Towards the end of the period he was turning to the heroic or rhyming couplet, which was to become, in large measure, the new standard metre of English verse.

The last fourteen years of Chaucer's life was the period of his maturity. He adopted the use of the heroic couplet and worked on the great scheme of *The Canterbury Tales,* although a number of these had been written earlier.

It is in this last poem, with its nine and twenty characters, grave and gay, refined and coarse, that his genius manifests itself. Chaucer could tell a story and tell it with dramatic clearness: the simplicity, the colour and the vigour of his word-painting have made the Tales immortal; the wide experience which they translate makes them not merely the poems of a master, but the embodiment of an epoch.

At the end of *The Canterbury Tales,* Geoffrey Chaucer wrote:

" Here taketh the makere of this boke his leve.

" Now preye I to hem alle that herkne this litel tretis or rede, that if ther be any thing in it that lyketh hem, that ther-of they thanken oure lord Jesu Crist, of whom procedeth al wit and al goodnesse.

"And if ther be any thing that displese hem, I preye hem also that they arette it to the defaute of myn unconninge, and nat to my wil, that wolde ful fayn have seyd bettre if I hadde conninge.

"For oure boke seith 'al that is writen is writen for oure doctrine'; and that is myn entente.

"Wherefore I biseke yow mekely for the mercy of God, that ye preye for me. . . ."

If lovers of poetry and of beauty have not answered this petition literally, we may be sure that they have expressed their gratitude by an inward satisfaction that may mean much the same.

FRANÇOIS VILLON

(1431–1465)

King of the beggars, brawler, thief, and roistering drunkard: that was François Villon. And he was also one of the most exquisite poets who ever turned a verse. His romantic life has been the subject of fable and story, but none has equalled in beauty or sincerity the poems that he gave the world. The noise and hubbub of the workaday world is silenced when one of her great poets speaks, and there is still silence when we hear that voice crying from the taproom: "But where are the snows of yesteryear?"

"I CANNOT afford to hang François Villon. There are a hundred thousand rogues in France as great as he, but not such another poet."

So said Louis XI when he gave the order for Villon's release from the prison of Meung-sur-Loire in 1461, and the wily French monarch proved himself a shrewd judge of men and books, for the wretched thief he freed is famous today as the first of the great French poets. He holds his place in history both because of the greatness of his work and its influence on other writers, and for the extraordinary contrasts of high-minded genius, religious feeling, and drunken knavery that made up his character.

His descriptions of Parisian life in the fifteenth century are biting in their realism. As a satiric yet humorous critic of humanity, he gave to French literature a smile of irony. His influence can be traced in the work of many great writers, including Rabelais and Gautier, Voltaire and Anatole France. In England he has been translated by such masters of English verse as Swinburne, Rossetti, John Payne and de Vere Stacpoole. Stevenson wrote of him in *Familiar Studies of Men and Books*, Justin McCarthy made him a hero of fiction in *If I Were King* and *Needles and Pins;* George Alexander presented him as a romantic stage figure in a dramatic version of the first of these novels, and the story of the burglar poet has been revived in post-war days as a musical play and a talking picture under the title *The Vagabond King*.

Let us consider the career of this extraordinary man who was a petty rogue and vagabond, despised, punished and broken in his own day, but whose fame as a poet has shone ever more brightly for over five hundred years.

François de Montcorbier, better known by his adopted name of Villon, was born in Paris in 1431, the year in which the ardent spirit of St. Joan was set free by the flames at Rouen. We know nothing of his parents except that his mother was a poor and pious woman who must have suffered many griefs and disappointments on account of her scapegrace son. This much he himself tells us.

A relative, Guillaume de Villon, Canon of St. Benoît, befriended the widow and her boy. He succeeded in obtaining admission for young François to the University of Paris in 1446, and at the age of twenty-one Villon became a Master of Arts and (ironically enough) a Licentiate in Theology.

How he lived for the next few years we can only guess. He may have earned money as a tutor or as a scribe. One thing is certain: he fell in with bad company. He roistered and rioted among the tavern blades and wasted his time and money with dubious light-o'-loves. Or so he tells us in his poems. And when his purse required replenishing he was easily led along the paths of crime.

Among his companions were such notorious evil livers as René de Montigny, who came to the gallows; Colin de Cayeulx, an expert picklock, afterwards broken on the wheel; and a foolish, garrulous fellow named Guy Tabarie. There were also Jehan, known as "The Wolf"; the Baron de Grigny, a coiner; and the "Abbess of Port Royal." This woman had been a real abbess, but the orgies held within her convent brought her to disgrace, and she became one of the notorious figures of the Paris underworld. She often masqueraded in man's attire with Villon and his unsavoury companions.

François, it seems, first fell into trouble through no fault of his own. While he sat with two friends under the clock tower of St. Benoît, a priest named Philip Chermoye, who had some grudge against him, rudely accosted the poet, and attacked him with a sword, wounding him in the face. A woman named Isabeau is mentioned in connexion with the affair, but whether she was the cause of the quarrel or merely a witness is not clear. Villon stabbed his assailant, struck him with a heavy stone, and took to his heels. Chermoye was carried away to die, but before his death he made a statement exonerating Villon. This did not save the poet from being banished for a time from Paris.

We can hardly blame Villon for acting in self-defence against Chermoye, but there is little excuse for some of the actions of his later career. Returning to Paris in 1456 (about a year after the fatal fracas) he joined Colin de Cayeulx and company in a campaign of organized robbery.

A priest named Coiffier was the first victim, his house being burgled to the tune of some six hundred crowns. Then came an attempt on the church of St. Mathurin (Villon, let us remember, was a Licentiate in Theology) but this was foiled by watchdogs. Next the gang broke into the College de Navarre and netted another rich haul of five or six hundred crowns. There were probably other crimes of which we have no record. There were certainly many petty rogueries. One little trick ascribed by tradition to the vagabond poet makes an amusing story.

Villon and a companion went with no money but with two eathernware jugs to the Fir Apple Tavern. Here the poet set one jug on the counter and called for white wine. The jug was filled and brought to him, at which moment the other rascal distracted the bar-tender's attention. Meanwhile, Villon substituted the second jug, which was filled with water, for the first. Then, sniffing at the water, he cried angrily: "What scurvy wash is this? Take back your mouldy wine, varlet." And having quickly emptied the water into the wine cask he departed, cursing and swearing, with his two jugs, one of them brimming with good liquor which had cost him nothing.

Many such pranks are attributed to François, whose "villoneries" became legendary in the underworld. But more serious matters soon invited his attention. Guy de Tabarie, babbling in his cups, gave away the secret of the gang's burglarious exploits, and Villon, on returning from a trip to the country (probably to plan a fresh robbery) was cast into prison. There he was put to the question by water (this torture consisted of forcing water down the victim's throat till he was likely to burst) and afterwards sentenced to death. The poet appealed from his dungeon to Parliament—we can well imagine with what fervour of genius he worded the appeal—and the sentence was reduced to banishment for life.

After this Villon wandered far and wide. We find him competing in a contest for poets at the court of Charles d'Orleans at Blois. We find him in prison again at Meung, whence he was saved by the clemency of the new king of France, Louis XI.

The next we know of him is that he returned to Paris and wrote his masterpiece, *The Great Testament,* in 1461. After that he was again exiled and completely vanished. He may have died of disease, for he was broken by dissipation and by his prison hardships. He may have ended on the gallows as did so many of his friends. We do not know, and it seems unlikely that we ever shall.

Villon's literary legacy to the world consists of *The Small Testament, The Great Testament,* and a few ballades and songs apart from these. He also wrote several ballades in the thieves' slang of the day.

The Great Testament, written as though it were his will, bequeathing jesting or bitter legacies to his friends and foes, gives numerous brilliant sidelights on the poet's life and times, and its eight-line stanzas are interspersed with several beautiful ballades and rondeaux.

One of these, written as *A Prayer for his Mother to Pray to Our Lady* is among the most beautiful and tender of religious poems. Another, the *Ballade of the Ladies of Old Times,* has been admirably translated by D. G. Rossetti:

Tell me where, in what hidden way is
Lady Flora, the lovely Roman?
Where's Hipparchia, where is Thaïs?
Neither of them the fairer woman?
Where is Echo, beheld of no man,
Only heard on river and mere?
She whose beauty was more than human?
But where are the snows of yesteryear?

Where's Heloise, the learned nun,
For whose sake Abelard I ween
Lost manhood and put priesthood on,
From love he won such dule and teen?
And where, I pray you, is the Queen,
Who willed that Buridan should steer,
Sewn in a sack's mouth, down the Seine?
But where are the snows of yesteryear?

White Queen Blanche, like a queen of lilies,
With a voice like any mermaiden?
Bertha Broadfoot, Beatrix, Alice
And Ermengarde the Lady of Maine?
And that good Joan, whom Englishmen
At Rouen doomed, and burned her there?
Mother of God, where are they then?
But where are the snows of yesteryear?

Nay, ask me not this week, Fair Lord,
Where they are gone, nor yet this year,
Except with this for an overword
But where are the snows of yesteryear?

This is one of the world's most beautiful lyrics. It is a strange and chastening thought that its author spent much of his brief and wayward life in sordid drinking dens and filthy dungeons.

The glaring contrast between the ugliness of his life and the beauty of his lyrics is no doubt one of the reasons why the vagabond singer has attracted so much attention from modern poets and romancers. There is also the mystery of his disappearance, which, of course, gives a fine opportunity for the imaginative novelist or playwright. Fifteenth-century traditions depict Villon as living to a good old age (two of these stories are related by Rabelais). From this hint has been built up an edifice of romance. Villon is portrayed as a gay, swashbuckling hero, winning the love of Katherine de Vaucelles and settling down to a respectable middle age.

It is true that this lady is mentioned in the poems, but the reference is not exactly romantic. Here is the verse from *The Double Ballade of Good Counsel* (Swinburne's translation) which tells how Villon was given a good thrashing at Katherine's instigation:

Next to myself I tell, poor me,
How thrashed like clothes at wash was I
Stark naked, I must needs agree.
Who made me eat so sour a pie
But Katherine of Vaucelles? Thereby
Noel took third part of that fun;
Such wedding gloves are ill to buy;
Good luck has he that deals with none.

The truth seems to be that the poet had pestered this Katherine with his attentions and that she led him into a trap where he was roughly handled by her lover, Noël Joly. There is no reason to suppose that Villon was ever reconciled with Katherine.

Yet he could sing with spirit and gaiety of the girls of his native city:

Albeit the Venice girls get praise
For their sweet speech and tender air,
And though the old women have wise ways,
Of chaffering for amorous ware,
Yet at my peril dare I swear,

Search Rome, where God's grace mainly tarries,
Florence and Savoy, everywhere,
There's no good girl's lip out of Paris.

And he concludes (again the translation is Swinburne's):

Prince, give praise to our French ladies
For the sweet sound their speaking carries;
'Twixt Rome and Cadiz many a maid is,
But no good girl's lip out of Paris.

There we have Villon in his lighter mood. If you would see the other side of the shield turn to the *Epitaph in Form of a Ballade,* which Villon made for himself and his comrades, expecting to be hanged along with them:

Men, brother men, that after us yet live,
Let not your hearts too hard against us be,
For if some pity of us poor men ye give,
The sooner God shall take of you pity.
Here are we five or six strung up, you see,
And here the flesh that all too well we fed
Bit by bit eaten and rotten, rent and shred,
And we the bones grow dust and ash withal;
Let no man laugh at us discomforted,
But pray to God that he forgive us all.

Thus opens this poem of a sinner's plea for pity. The last lines (Swinburne's rendering) read:

Prince Jesus, that of all art Lord and Head,
Keep us, that Hell be not our bitter bed,
We have nought to do in such a master's hall
Be not ye therefore of our fellowhead
But pray to God that he forgive us all.

We find here that religious note which often recurs in Villon's poems. It reaches its utmost tenderness in the ballade for his mother to which reference has been made. There the poet paints the picture of "a pitiful poor woman, shrunk and old," kneeling in prayer before the shrine of Our Lady. This poem is not only a beautiful and moving portrait in words; it is also a noble and simple expression of belief. "For in this faith I choose to live and die" is the refrain of the old woman's hymn of worship, and it is easy to believe that her son, scapegrace though he was, had a strong vein of true piety.

Another French vagabond poet, Paul Verlaine, wrote while in prison many beautiful religious poems. There is no doubt that Verlaine (who was known personally to many still living) was inspired by sincere religious feeling to write those hymns. There is no reason to doubt that Villon was similarly inspired.

Among his ballades is one, *Of the Lords of Old Time,* in which he recalls the fame of many soldier princes. When, banished for the last time, he passed through the gates of Paris and vanished into history, Villon was thirty-two. At that age Alexander had conquered Persia and established his fame as one of the world's great captains. Yet who will now deny that the verses of *The Great Testament* are a mightier memorial than the trophies of Persepolis?

FRANÇOIS RABELAIS

(*c.* 1495–1553)

"Cardinal Jean du Bellay . . . admired Rabelais so much that he refused a learned individual of the day a seat at his table because he had not read 'The Book,' for so Rabelais's singular narrative was called." Which only proves, if such proof were wanted, that the Cardinal was a man of sound judgment and right thinking. It may be doubted whether any work has given the world so much delight, and withal so much wisdom, as that "singular narrative" of François Rabelais's. His book has become more prized as the centuries have passed; it will make mirth for generations to come; for when Rabelais ceases to be read, on that day mankind will have lost the power to laugh.

SOME half-dozen years before the close of the fifteenth century at La Devinière, a farm near Chinon, that "famous city, noble city, ancient city, yea, the first city in the world," was born François Rabelais. Whether there were portents at his birth is not recorded, but if the earth did not shake then, mankind has shaken with laughter ever since. For Rabelais was the greatest story-teller and the mightiest maker of laughter that this weary world has ever known.

"Three of the four greatest creative literary geniuses that the whole Christian era has produced, were produced in this (the sixteenth) century; Cervantes in Spain, Shakespeare in England, Rabelais in France. Yet relatively little is known of Cervantes's personal life, almost nothing of Rabelais's, and nothing significant of Shakespeare's."

We have few accurate biographical details about Rabelais: we know nothing of his appearance, his habits, his goings out and his comings in. But we have those precious volumes addressed to us "most noble and illustrious drinkers," and if we have not there the essence and very soul of our man, then there is no truth in words and all good pantagruelists live in the Stygian gloom of error.

Rabelais was the son of Antoine Rabelais, a lawyer of moderate means. His education, says tradition, was received at the hands of the Benedictine monks at the Abbey of Seuilly, near Chinon, and from there, it is said, he went to the Franciscan convent of La Baumette near Angers. Be that as it may, we know that by 1521 Rabelais was a member of the Franciscan monastery of Puy-St.-Martin at Fontenay-le-Comte, in Poitou.

He had already acquired a first-class knowledge of Latin and some Greek: the tide of the Renaissance was sweeping across Europe, and Rabelais, who was to be one of the glories of humanism, turned eagerly to the new learning. Among the ignorant monks at Fontenay-le-Comte there was one other interested in classical scholarship, a young man named Pierre Amy. Amy had corresponded with Guillaume Budé, secretary to the king, Francis I, and the greatest Greek scholar in Europe, and he encouraged Rabelais to write also. Rabelais did so, and Budé acknowledged his letter, written in Latin and ending with a flourish of Greek, in a letter to Amy. A second letter was answered directly with praise for Rabelais's command of Latin and Greek, and for several years Rabelais continued to correspond with Budé, whose reputation for learning was second only to that of Erasmus.

In the town of Fontenay-le-Comte there was at that time a little group of lawyers who were interested in discussions and in culture, and they would meet for intelligent discussions and debates. Chief of them were Artus Cailler, his son-in-law, André Tiraqueau, Jean Brisson, and Aymery Bouchard. To this group Amy and Rabelais were welcomed, and they joined in the conversations that took place in Tiraqueau's pleasant garden.

The chief subject of their talks was feminism. The position of women was one of the most popular topics of the day, and it was of particular interest to Tiraqueau. At the age of twenty-four he had married Cailler's daughter when she was only eleven, and for her instruction had translated a Latin treatise on a wife's duties and published it in 1513. He also wrote an original work on the same subject, entitled *De Legibus Connubialibus*. Tiraqueau's book, which was rigidly based on the principle that "the wife is under the rule of her husband," was popular with the anti-feminists and caused much controversy.

He was already preparing a second edition, when, in 1522, Aymery Bouchard produced a counter-attack in *The Nature of Women,* to which Amy wrote a preface. Tiraqueau was furious. He and all his friends set to work to get out a new edition of his own, which they published in 1524. The work was loaded with learning and the citations of authorities, and Rabelais had a good hand in it. Tiraqueau acknowledged his debt to Rabelais and his brilliant scholarship, and Rabelais must have enjoyed the fun that the work had given him.

But in the meanwhile a disaster had occurred. In 1523 the opponents of intellectual progress at the Sorbonne, the University of Paris, made one of their drives against the new learning and decided that the study of Greek was irreligious. The Franciscans of Fontenay were shocked to find that they had Greek scholars in their midst, and the books of Rabelais and Amy were confiscated.

Amy could not stand this persecution. He fled to Orleans and thence to Switzerland, where it seems he died a Lutheran. In the tenth chapter of the third book, Rabelais tells how Amy acted on the advice of a Virgilian lottery:

"When Mr. Peter Amy did in like manner explore and make trial, if he should escape the ambush of the Hobgoblins, who lay in wait to bemaul him, he fell upon this verse in the third of the *Æneids*:

'Oh flee the bloody land, the wicked shore!'

Which counsel he obeying, got forthwith out of their hands, safe and sound, and avoided all their ambuscades."

Rabelais had other, and quieter, methods of dealing with the "Hobgoblins." He lay low, said nothing, and in a short time his books were returned to him. Nearby was the Benedictine Abbey of Maillezais, ruled by an enlightened and liberal lord of the Church, Geoffroy d'Estissac, and by the influence of powerful friends, Rabelais managed to get a special decree from the pope authorizing his transfer from the Franciscan to the Benedictine order. So, in 1524, Rabelais went to Maillezais, where the bishop welcomed the scholar and attached him to his household.

For the next three years Rabelais travelled with the bishop through the diocese and gained that intimate knowledge of Poitou which appears in the background of his work. Rabelais never missed and never forgot a detail. Most of the period he spent at Ligugé in a pleasant atmosphere of learning and scholarship; and then, in 1527, he left Ligugé and wandered off—to learn medicine, probably to visit Paris. But it is all conjecture, for there is no record of him from the time he left Ligugé until 1530.

In the September of that year he was registered with the faculty of medicine at the University of Montpellier, and in the December he proceeded to the degree of Bachelor of Medicine. During the next year he delivered his bachelor's lectures, making commentaries on the *Aphorisms* of Hippocrates and the *Ars Parva* of Galen. At

Montpellier, where his gown is still preserved, he took part in amateur dramatics, for Epistemon says in the third book:

"I do not remember to have seen you before now, since the last time that you acted at Montpellier with our ancient friends, Anthony Saporra, Guy Borgoyer, Balthasar Noyer, Tollet, John Quentin, Francis Robinet, John Perdrier, and Francis Rabelais, the moral comedy of him who had espoused and married a dumb wife."

From Montpellier, Rabelais went to Lyons, and there, in the summer of 1532, he published an edition of Hippocrates and Galen with his own notes. The work seems to have had a success, and certainly Rabelais's value as a doctor was recognized, for in November he was appointed house-doctor at the Grand Hôtel Dieu de Notre Dame de Pitié du Pont du Rhône. But before then there had appeared at the August fair at Lyons an anonymous volume of folk stories: *The Great and Inestimable Chronicles of the Huge Giant Gargantua*. The book was enormously popular. "The printers have sold more of them in two months' time than there will be bought of Bibles in nine years," wrote Rabelais in his preface to the second book, which was probably inspired by the success of the anonymous volume. At any rate there appeared in a short time *The Horrible and Dreadful Feats and Prowesses of the Most Renowned Pantagruel,* by Alcofribas Nasier.

Alcofribas Nasier was an anagram from François Rabelais, and his *Pantagruel* now forms the second book of his great work. It was two years before he turned his attention to the folk-lore figure of the great giant and produced his own *Gargantua,* which is now the first book.

The second book—it will be more convenient to refer to the books in their present order—was received with the popularity it deserved. It delighted Francis I and his court, and an attempt to ban it made by the Sorbonne only increased its popularity. And who could fail to be delighted by the horrible and dreadful feats of Pantagruel and by the tricks of his companion, Panurge? This Panurge "was of middle stature, not too high nor too low, and had somewhat an aquiline nose, made like the handle of a razor. He was at that time five and thirty years old or thereabouts, fine to gild like a leaden dagger—for he was a notable cheat and coneycatcher—he was a very gallant and proper man of his person, only that he was a little lecherous, and naturally subject to a kind of disease which at that time they called lack of money—it is an incomparable grief, yet, notwithstanding, he had three score and three tricks to come by it at his need, of which the most honourable and most ordinary was in the manner of thieving, secret purloining and filching, for he was a wicked, lewd rogue, a cozener, drinker, roisterer, rover, and very dissolute and debauched fellow, if there were any in Paris; otherwise, and in all matters else, the best and most virtuous man in the world."

The success of *Pantagruel* led Rabelais to turn out a comic almanac, a parody of the astrological almanacs of his times. And for several years he produced them, under such titles as: *The Most Certain, True and Infallible Pantagruelian Prognostication for the Year that's to Come and Ever and Aye. Calculated for the Benefit and Noddification of the Giddy-brain'd and Weatherwise Wouldbe's by Master Alcofribus Nasier, Architriclin to the Aforemention'd Pantagruel.* And here is a sample of the prognostications to be found therein:

"Of the Diseases this Year.

"This year the stone-blind shall see but little; the deaf shall hear but scurvily; the dumb shall not speak very plain; the rich shall be in somewhat better circumstances than the poor, and the healthy than the sick. Whole flocks, herds and droves of sheep, swine, and oxen, cocks and hens, ducks and drakes, geese and ganders shall perish; but the mortality shall not be altogether so great among apes, monkeys, baboons, and dromedaries. As for old age it will be incurable this year, on account of the years past."

In January, 1534, Rabelais drew twenty-seven livres* on account of his salary at the hospital and set off as personal physician to Jean du Bellay, Bishop of Paris, who was on a diplomatic mission to Rome concerning the proposed divorce of Henry VIII of England. While at Rome he worked on a book describing the topography and appearance of that city, only to find when nearly finished that an Italian, Marliani, had just published a volume on the same subject. Far from expressing disappointment or rancour, Rabelais congratulated the Italian and wrote a dedicatory letter to be published with Marliani's work at Lyons.

After the visit to Rome, Rabelais returned to his post at the hospital at Lyons. But in February, 1535, he drew six months' salary due to him and disappeared. He seems to have given his friends the tip, for the next morning three of them turned up at the hospital and applied for his post. The hospital authorities had heard nothing of any vacancy, and even when Rabelais did not come, they were reluctant to replace him for some time—testimony to their esteem of his professional worth.†

* About £2·25

† His successor received only 30 livres a year, 10 livres less than Rabelais.

There is no known reason for Rabelais's sudden flight. But there was at the time a reactionary persecution and an anti-Protestant drive, and learning, humanism, and intellectual superiority have always been fair game for heresy hunters. Rabelais, the mocker, had no relish for martyrdom.

It is probable that he spent the first part of the year at Maillezais: in the summer he once more accompanied du Bellay, now a Cardinal, to Rome. At Ferrara he met Clément Marot, the poet, who had fled there from persecution. At Rome he executed commissions for d'Estissac and sent him seeds for his garden, and at the same time he put some business of his own through the papal court to regularize his eccelesiastical position. He returned from Rome in 1536.

In the February of the next year he was guest at a banquet given in Paris by the brilliant young Etienne Dolet, scholar and publisher. Clément Marot, Budé, Salmon Macrin and other learned men were of the company. Six years later Rabelais quarrelled with Dolet for publishing an unauthorized version of his first two books—a dangerous proceeding with the heresy hunts that were prevailing, for Rabelais himself was revising his text. But Dolet was himself in trouble and in 1546 he was burned at the stake for heresy.

Rabelais took his Doctor of Medicine degree at Montpellier in 1537, and gave public demonstrations of anatomy—a daring innovation. Dolet has written of Rabelais as among those who were advancing the knowledge of medicine, while Macrin praised him as a practitioner. We know that Rabelais was as eminent in his profession as he was famous for his writing. About this time Rabelais had an illegitimate son, Théodule, who was born at Lyons and died in infancy.

In 1540 Rabelais was with a new patron, Guillaume du Bellay, Sieur de Langey, who was Governor of Turin. To him Rabelais was not only physician, but secretary, friend and confidant. Du Bellay's task in Piedmont ruined his health, and in 1543 he died, leaving to Rabelais in his will "fifty livres yearly, until such time as his heirs shall have provided for him, or seen to his provision, in the Church with the sum of three hundred livres a year." But the Sieur de Langey died heavily in debt, and it is doubtful whether Rabelais got the bequest or the living.

Two years later Rabelais obtained a copyright warrant from Francis I for his two books, "not less useful than delectable," and for the forthcoming third book, which he published in 1546. This book, which continues the adventures of Pantagruel, is mostly occupied with Panurge's indecision about marriage and such examination of women as that subject involves. It has been taken by critics, in conjunction with Rabelais's work for Tiraqueau, as an indication that Rabelais was a misogynist—as intelligent a case as was made out against that other "misogynist," Euripides.

A few months after the publication of the third book, Rabelais, "driven from France by the misfortune of the times," went to Metz, where he was promptly appointed city physician. In 1547 he left Metz presumably to accompany Cardinal du Bellay to Rome once again; at any rate he was in Rome in 1549. In 1551 du Bellay gave him the curacy of Meudon and also that of St. Cristophe-de-Jambet, both of which he resigned at the beginning of 1553. He published the fourth book in 1552: the fifth, edited, and perhaps partly written by an unknown hand, was published after Rabelais's death, which occurred in April, 1553.

And now what are we to say of the five books of Rabelais that have convulsed the world with honest laughter? In England, thanks to the inspired translation begun by Sir Thomas Urquhart and continued by Peter le Motteux, we are in a peculiar position of being able to appreciate fully the gusto and liveliness of the masterpiece. It is a magnificent piece of story-telling. First and last Rabelais is a story-teller, whose words tumble over each other with the vividness of spoken language. The story is suffused with satire—but it is not the satirical allegory that some critics would like to make it. It comments on the times, but it is not directed by a tendency; there are morals, but no motive. If it is vulgar and obscene in places, the vulgarity is honest and the obscenity is funny—there is no cleaner work in any language than the breezy, elevating story told by Master Rabelais. In short, it is a tale told by one who knew and loved and laughed at his fellow-men, the unsurpassed production of a many-sided genius mellow with the finest spirit of the new learning.

WILLIAM SHAKESPEARE

(1564—1616)

The man who is the outstanding figure in the history of English literature—and possibly of the world's—is one whose real self is a mystery. Scholars and critics who have analysed his plays will, by concentrating on certain aspects of his work, claim to show the man, but they seldom produce more than a shadow. Contemporary allusions and known facts would make us believe that Shakespeare was a shrewd business man and a pleasant and unassuming companion. But if his plays tell us little about himself they reveal a mind rich in the knowledge of his fellow creatures with their greatness and their faults; he understood men and women and the motives that lie behind their actions. His plays, so diverse in subject, have grandeur and tenderness, brilliance and depth, wit, passion and poetry. They are the products of a man typical of the Renaissance whose comprehension of man's life and interests never ceases to astonish those who read his works.

WHOLE libraries could be—and are—devoted to books about William Shakespeare. Yet the known facts of his life fill only a page or two. No great man—certainly none for whom claims for godhead have not been seriously made—has had more dissertations, speculations, appreciations, depreciations, castigations and elevations made and spent on him. He has moved lesser poets to foolish sonnets as well as fine ones. He has stirred and moved and fired and soothed humanity far more, immeasurably more, than any other breathing man who ever made writing his profession. His best plays have, ever since their first appearance, provided the theatre in which the highest, or most ambitious, acting talent most hopes to excel.

What do we know about the man himself? If mankind can be compared to a pond (and it has, in its time, been compared to things even smaller in bulk and scope—an antheap, for example, and even a molecule), what have we to say about the fiery particle which was thrown into its centre in the sixteenth century and has been surrounding itself with concentric wavelets of active comment and argument ever since?

The answer is, as near as maybe, the same as Cordelia's answer to Lear's request for a plateful of flattery. It is Nothing. Humanity, deprived of anything like a full biography, glares at the would-be biographer as Lear glared at Cordelia when refused his fulsome compliment, and Lear-like says: "Nothing will come of nothing: speak again." Well, one says it all once more, and notes, even when repeating it all, the "perhapses" and the "probablys" and the "almost certainlys" that must necessarily (if we love the whole truth) qualify the dubious stretches that lie between the few known facts.

He was born at Stratford-upon-Avon in Warwickshire in the year 1564, probably on April 23. His mother was Mary Arden and his father John Shakespeare. Both parents, in the words of the true-blue biographers of the bard, "appear to have been of that honest and substantial old English yeomanry from whose better-than-royal stock and lineage the great Poet of Nature might most fitly fetch his life and being." William had four sisters and three brothers, and several of these died in infancy. William himself somehow survived a severe visitation of plague which afflicted Stratford when he was less than a year old.

Of his infancy and boyhood we know nothing, and even inventive tradition has produced very little. John Shakespeare became an alderman at Stratford in 1565, and in 1568 was elected Bailiff, the highest office in the corporation. He held this position for a year. Throughout the year 1571 he was head-alderman, and he continued as an alderman until 1586, when "for persevering non-attendance at the meetings" he was deprived of his gown. Several times throughout his term of office John Shakespeare is found acting in his public capacity as a patron of the stage. The town records survive to prove this. Twice, for example, in the year 1568 when he was Town Bailiff, money was paid to different companies of visiting players. They are the earliest notices we possess of theatrical performances at Stratford. From that time forward until 1572, when an Act was passed for restraining itinerant players, it is probable that acted plays were often on view in the Warwickshire town. Furthermore, in spite of the Act, the Stratford chamberlain's accounts show that between 1569 and 1587 (William's infancy, adolescence and young manhood, in a word) no less than ten distinct companies performed at Stratford under the corporation's patronage. In the year 1587 no fewer than five of these touring companies performed there.

Now, one is very well aware of the dangers of "conjectural history." But surely it is taking caution too far to demand any direct evidence—it does not exist—that young Shakespeare first saw plays acted at his birthplace in his youth? One is tempted in this instance—and one succumbs to the temptation—to throw away "possiblys" and "probablys." Of course he saw the plays and players, and of course he was (as we would put it nowadays) "mad about them"! It seems certain that in his boyhood he dreamed and read and pondered and maundered by the Avon's gentle banks. It is quite certain that later, when philosophic solitude grew irksome, he took to courting as young men will, and made the chief object of his courtship Anne Hathaway, the daughter of a "substantial yeoman" who was a friend of his father's. But it is more certain still that William's mind was more engaged in these years with playwriting and play-acting than with anything else, and more than likely that he was often tempted to join and run away with one of the troupes of players which descended upon the town (just as, years later, he was to make one descend upon Elsinore) and left it dazed and stunned with the clangour of its grandiloquent rhodomontade. For those were the days—even more than the days of Shakespeare's maturity—when resounding words were far more the part and parcel of a play than intelligent philosophizing or even intelligent action. The *words* were the thing wherein the players at Stratford caught the conscience, literary and creative, of this broad-browed young son of the local alderman.

At the age of eighteen he obtained a special licence from the Bishop of Worcester to marry Anne Hathaway in the church at Temple Grafton, near Stratford. The first child, Susanna, followed only six months later. In 1585 twins, called Hamnet and Judith, were born and christened in the parish church at Stratford, as was Susanna before them. Nobody knows how William supported his wife (she was, as far as can possibly be ascertained, eight years older than he) and his growing family. Nobody knows why he suddenly (or more or less suddenly?) ran away alone to London. Nobody knows whether he continued to support them from London. John Aubrey is often quoted on these mysteries, or, at least, on the first of them. And John Aubrey is certainly quaint and charming on the subject:

"His father was a Butcher, and I have been told heretofore by some of the neighbours, that when he was a boy he exercised his father's Trade, but when he killed a Calfe, he would do it in a high style, and make a Speech. . . . This Wm being inclined naturally to Poetry and acting, came to London I guesse about 18 and was an Actor at one of the Play-houses and did act exceedingly well. . . . He began early to make essayes at Dramatique Poetry, which at that time was very lowe; and his Playes took well: He was a handsome well shap't man: very good company, and of a very readie and pleasant smooth Witt."

This is very pretty, and very much what we all want to believe of our "sweetest Shakespeare, Fancy's child." But Aubrey (1626—1697) was a whimsical gossip, not a responsible writer. His facts are too often unreliable, and his opinions had better be compared with more serious opinions before they are accepted.

It is certain, for example, from Stratford town records that John Shakespeare was a glover and dealer in soft-leather goods, and not at any time a butcher. Another persistent tradition, also perpetuated by the ingratiating Aubrey, is that William was, for some time at least, a Warwickshire schoolmaster. In estimating the value of such traditions one should always bear in mind the rule laid down by the great eighteenth-century Shakespearian scholar, Edmund Malone:

"Where a tradition has been handed down, by a very industrious and careful inquirer, who has derived it from persons most likely to be accurately informed concerning the fact related, and subjoins his authority, such a species of tradition must always carry great weight along with it."

A great Shakespearian scholar of the present century, Professor Peter Alexander, is of the opinion that Aubrey's schoolmaster story satisfies Malone's three requirements, *and that this is the only tradition about Shakespeare that does:*

"Aubrey did not sift and arrange his notes for publication; he set down what he heard; we have to judge for ourselves the various degrees of credibility that attach to them. The schoolmaster tradition is not merely strong in itself; it is supported by the type of play with which Shakespeare started as dramatist."

Incidentally, the traditional legends of Shakespeare poaching deer near Stratford, and of holding horses near theatre doors as a poor young adventurer in London, are completely discredited by modern scholarship. These, and other such, are part of the nineteenth-century schoolbook biography of Shakespeare, and should not nowadays be resuscitated.

Shakespeare's successful career as a London playwright is as disappointingly undocumented as that of any of his numerous rivals in the field. Is this a mystery? No, nothing like the mystery that has been made of it. In those days and times a playwright was a mere play-provider—a man of the theatre, a member of the company whose sole duty was to provide text, and then to hear it rehearsed and delivered if so the fancy took him. A biography of a mere playwright was a thing as yet unheard-of. Publishers might print his plays if some patron thought them good enough to be kept. But no publisher had yet had the notion of printing a mere playwright's life story—especially a mere playwright who was not even of courtly status.

Shakespeare did not live to publish a collected edition of his works. It was not until seven years after his death that two of his old friends and fellow actors, John Heminge and Henry Condell, saw to the production of the First Folio of his plays. Similarly it was not until nearly a hundred years after Shakespeare's death that his first biography appeared, written by Nicholas Rowe in the reign of Queen Anne. From these actual and factual circumstances, how can we expect not to find in his works abundant corruptions, obscurities, and examples of the author's own lack of revision and polish? And how can we hope not to find the known facts of his existence smothered in surmise and ornamented with legend? The wonder is not that we should have a questionable text and a dubious biography; it is rather that so much of the eternal Shakespeare should have survived in his works which are, after all, far more the essence of the man than any time-table of his worldly existence between 1564 and 1616. As one of the most succinct of his biographers, Dr. J. W. Mackail, has said: "However far additional knowledge might go in satisfying curiosity, its absence is not greatly to be deplored. The life of an artist survives not in his biography, but in the products of his art."

Shakespeare's career in London is soon summarized—so little is known of it. He appears to have been a handyman and a play-provider rather than an actor at the Globe and other theatres. Just after the turn of the century he appears to have a preoccupation with morbid subjects. But the psychological study of Shakespeare as man and artist at this period, or at any other, takes us very little distance: data are so few. It is no more safe to identify Shakespeare with Hamlet than with Othello. It is clear from old contracts that he worked with both Richard Burbage's, with Edward Alleyn's, and later with the Lord Chamberlain's Company. He published his two ornate narrative poems on his own account—*Venus and Adonis* in 1593 and *The Rape of Lucrece* in 1594. These were successful and gave him rank as an author, but he made no attempt to publish his plays as they were acted. This fact seems continuously to astonish people who fail to realize that plays in those times, even when printed, hardly counted as literature.

In letters patent of the year 1603 the Lord Chamberlain's Company was reconstituted under the title of the King's Servants. As such they might be called on for duty as ushers at Court. They received regular salaries and wore red liveries. The Globe Theatre on Bankside was their headquarters. Nine actors were named as shareholders, and Shakespeare's name is second on the list. With the death of his only son Hamnet, at the age of eleven, in 1596, Shakespeare seems to have resumed his connection with Stratford, though there is, indeed, no proof that he ever severed it. In that same year a grant of family arms was applied for at the Herald's Office. In 1597 Shakespeare purchased New Place, a large house at Stratford, and thus established himself as a burgess. Further freehold property in the town was acquired by him at his father's death in 1601. The local boy had obviously made good in the worldly as well as in the sense of Coriolanus's "world elsewhere." Nevertheless Shakespeare remained for another eight or nine years in London to present the greatest of his plays. He can be traced as living in Bishopsgate, in Southwark, in Bankside, and in Cripplegate. During the last half-dozen years of his life various Stratford records show him settled at New Place. A deposition in a lawsuit of the year 1612 describes him as "William Shakespeare, of Stratford on Avon, gentleman." His elder daughter Susanna married in 1608, his younger daughter Judith in 1616. The latter event occurred in February. In March Shakespeare made his will, and on April 23 (certainly St. George's Day and probably his birthday) he died. Little more is known about Shakespeare the man; infinitely more has been surmised and conjectural.

The fantastically and persistently elaborated theory that someone other than Shakespeare wrote Shakespeare's plays seems to one open-minded reader, at least, to be devastatingly disproved at the outset by the contemporary tribute at his death of his friend, Ben Jonson. The stiffness of this—as of all Jonson's verse—makes it less well known than it should be. Only an occasional single line—like "He was not of an age, but for all time!"—is ever quoted. But the whole address is a striking and not-to-be-overlooked illustration of how Shakespeare struck a distinguished and eminently honest contemporary:

"Sweet Swan of *Avon*! What a sight it were
To see thee in our waters yet appeare,
And make those flights upon the bankes of *Thames*,
That so did take *Eliza*, and our *James*!
But stay, I see thee in the *Hemisphere*
Advanc'd and make a Constellation there!
Shine forth, thou Starre of *Poets*, and with rage,
Or influence, chide or cheere the drooping Stage;
Which, since thy flight from hence, hath mourn'd like night,
And despaires day, but for thy Volumes light."

"Sweet Swan," be it noted. And elsewhere in the same poem he is "my gentle Shakespeare." Spenser in *Colin Clout* fairly obviously refers to our same superman when he writes:

A gentler Shepherd may nowhere be found;
Whose Muse, full of high thought's invention,
Doth, like himself, heroically sound.

Aubrey declared, "He was very good company, and of a very ready and pleasant smooth wit." And Jonson again, in a prose tribute later than the poem above cited, declared his regard for the man as a man: "He was indeed honest and of an open and free nature; had an excellent fantasy, brave notions, and gentle expression." His essential gentleness is insisted upon in a dozen other places, in commendatory and in memorial verses. In brief, he was likeable as a living man as well as deathless as a poet. To not one of the great geniuses of earth can higher praise be given.

JOHN BUNYAN

(1628–1688)

The Bible is still the best-selling book in the English language; second to it is " The Pilgrim's Progress." Ever since it was written this exquisite parable has made a constant appeal to young and old; every generation has enjoyed the excellence of the story and of its telling; its power to captivate has never languished. The life of John Bunyan, its author, is in itself an inspiration. It is a story of simple faith and courage; in very truth a pilgrim's progress.

IN 1678 a small book was published bearing the formidable title *The Pilgrim's Progress from this World to That Which is to Come. Delivered under the Similitude of a Dream.* It was an exquisite allegory of Christian life, written in simple, forceful, direct English seasoned with racy humour. The work was an instant success, probably to the amazement of Nathaniel Ponder, who issued it from the sign of the Peacock, in the Poultry, London, and was at once reprinted with additions. In the following year a third edition with still further improvements was called for. Copies, printed cheaply on coarse paper, sold rapidly to the poor and the lower middle classes; working folk read the book avidly. By 1684 it had run through nine editions, and the author wrote a second part. Still it went on selling, as it continues to do nearly three hundred years later. In the cottage and humble home it became the companion to the Bible.

The literary history of John Bunyan's most famous work is as remarkable as the book itself. For a century it was a best seller, but only among those whose tastes were not considered of consequence. In the middle of the eighteenth century the worth of the book began to dawn upon the educated classes, regarded as the arbiters of literary survival. Cowper praised it, but did not dare name the author. So, slowly, *The Pilgrim's Progress* won its rightful place in English letters.

" In general," writes Macaulay, " when the educated minority and the common people differ about the merits of a book, the opinion of the educated minority finally prevails. *The Pilgrim's Progress* is perhaps the only book about which the educated minority has come over to the opinion of the common people."

John Bunyan was born at Elstow, near Bedford, in November, 1628. He says himself: "My descent was of a low and inconsiderable generation, my father's house being of the rank that is meanest and most despised of all the families in the land."

Actually he came of a well-established family, which had been settled in the neighbourhood for hundreds of years. A William Buniun held land in Bedfordshire in the twelfth century, and there is abundant evidence that the Bunyans were decent, if humble, citizens. Thomas Bunyan, his father, was a "brasier" or white-smith, a mender of pots and pans; John, when he followed his father's trade, called himself a tinker.

Thomas Bunyan was not, as Scott and others have suggested, of wandering gipsy stock. He was established at Elstow and had a forge there. John had some schooling, but he confesses that he forgot what little he knew when he took up his trade. "I never went to school to Aristotle or Plato, but was brought up at my father's house in a very mean condition, among a company of poor countrymen."

In June, 1644, John was plunged into sudden grief at the death of his mother, and two months later into indignant rebellion on the remarriage of his father. He promptly left home and enlisted. The first period of the Civil War was drawing to a close when the sixteen-year-old Bunyan became a soldier. He was in the Parliamentary army for two years, but nothing is known of his service, except for a reminiscence which he always recounted with gratitude to Providence for having saved his life:

"When I was a soldier, I with others was drawn out to go to a place and besiege it. But when I was just ready to go, one of the company desired to go in my room; to which, when I consented, he took my place, and coming to the siege, as he stood sentinel he was shot in the head with a musket bullet and died."

Shortly after he left the army, when he was about the age of nineteen, he married. He and his wife were "as poor as poor could be" and had not "so much household stuff as a dish or spoon between them."

His young wife was a pious woman, whose parents, it would appear, were dead, and she brought to her new home two religious books—*The Plain Man's Pathway to Heaven* and *The Practice of Piety*. Bunyan had always been one of the gay youths of the village, always ready for a game on the green, taking delight in bell-ringing and dancing. But there was no real vice in him, and his only bad habit was one of swearing richly and profanely.

His wife's books impressed him in a way. He accused himself of having been vicious and depraved and adopted a new air of piety: he still swore as generously as before, but he was filled with a Pharisaic self-satisfaction. "I thought no man in England could please God better than I."

He was still in this mind when one day, while plying his trade of tinker, he heard some poor women in Bedford "sitting at a door in the sun and talking about the things of God." Their conversation, the richness of their spiritual experience which had passed him by, made a profound impression on him. For four years he was in a state of spiritual conflict, and the story of his doubts, his questionings, his yearnings, and his sincere strivings, is told in his *Grace Abounding to the Chief of Sinners*.

But at last his doubts were settled and a holy peace took possession of him. In 1653 he joined the Nonconformist body to which the old women had belonged. The pastor was the "holy Mr. Giffard," who had once been an officer in the Cavalier army, and the body occupied the church of St. John at Bedford.

Two years later Bunyan moved to Bedford. The new home was early the scene of misfortune, for his wife died, and Bunyan himself was taken seriously ill and threatened with consumption: but the tinker's sturdy constitution pulled him through, and once again he devoted himself to his trade and to his newly-found faith.

He became a deacon of his church in 1655, and two years later was a preacher. He discovered in himself a gift for speech, and his preaching soon won him a reputation. People heard, too, that the swearing tinker had turned preacher, and they flocked to hear, or mock at, this wonder. Bunyan toured the county, preaching to the populace in barns and on village greens, and in some cases even the pulpits of the churches were thrown open to him.

The orthodox clergy were for the most part "wide against him," however, and most of them were eager to put obstacles in his way. They "were angry with the tinker because he strove to mend souls as well as kettles and pans."

He was actually indicted for preaching at Eaton Socon, at the assizes of 1658, and was charged with being a "witch, a Jesuit, a highwayman," and with bigamy and other monstrous and meaningless crimes. Nothing is known of the result of the case.

His first writings belong to this period. In 1656 he produced *Some Gospel Truths Opened,* which was directed against the mystic elements in the teachings of the Quakers. One of the Friends, Edward Burrough, answered the pamphlet with no mean invective, whereupon Bunyan launched *A Vindication of Gospel Truths* in 1657. A year later he wrote *Sighs from Hell, or the Groans of a Damned Soul.* These early works all show that nervous, forcible style, the vivid imagination and the deep knowledge of the Bible which were to make his name and work famous throughout the world.

In 1659 Bunyan married his second wife, Elizabeth, who became a stepmother to four children. He was soon parted from her. The Commonwealth had come to an end, and the Restoration of Charles II saw the restoration also of the old Acts against Nonconformists.

It became dangerous to preach, but Bunyan carried on his work. On November 12, 1660, he was arrested in a hamlet near Bedford, where he was holding a service in a private house. Bunyan had known that the warrant was out, but he disdained flight and refused to alter his plans. He was brought before Mr. Justice Wingate, who would probably have let him go but that Bunyan obstinately refused to give an undertaking to stop preaching. The judge had no option but to commit him to the county jail.

In January, 1661, Bunyan stood his trial at the quarter sessions. The indictment, brought under an Act of Elizabeth, ran: "That John Bunyan, of the town of Bedford, labourer, being a person of such and such conditions, hath devilishly and perniciously abstained from coming to church to hear divine service, and is a common upholder of several unlawful meetings and conventicles, to the great disturbance and distraction of the good subjects of this kingdom, contrary to the laws of our sovereign lord the king. . . ."

Bunyan confessed to the indictment and said that he would repeat his offence at the first opportunity. After he had had a short argument with the justices, who sat without witnesses or jury, he was sentenced.

"You must be had back again to prison, and there lie for three months following; and at the three months' end, if you do not submit to go to church to hear divine service, and leave your preaching, you must be banished the realm; and if you be found to come over again without special licence from the king, you must be stretched by the neck for it, I tell you plainly," avowed the judge.

Towards the end of the three months the clerk of the peace visited Bunyan in prison, but the preacher was adamant. Shortly afterwards, on April 23, 1661, the coronation of Charles took place, and all kinds of prisoners awaiting trial were released, while those who were convicted were allowed to sue for pardon, and handsome concessions were made. It was held that Bunyan's committal was a conviction, so that to be freed he had to sue for pardon. He did not do so.

His wife was made of the same stern stuff as her husband, and now she began to make determined efforts to have him set at liberty. She journeyed up to London and presented a petition to the House of Lords. Some of the peers expressed sympathy with her case, but they declared it was a matter for the judges.

At the August assizes she three times presented petitions to the judges, and urged them to give her husband a proper and legal trial with witnesses. One of the judges, Sir Matthew Hale, received her kindly, but he was powerless to act. "I tell thee, woman," he said, "seeing it is so, that they have taken what thy husband spake for a conviction, thou must apply thyself to the king, or sue out his pardon, or get a writ of error."

So Bunyan stayed in his "close and uncomfortable" quarters, and there he remained, except for a brief interval in 1666, for twelve years.

It was long thought that he was confined in the tiny town lock-up on Bedford bridge, but he was actually imprisoned in the county jail, which was larger and healthier. The conditions of his life in prison varied with his jailers; in his early years he was actually allowed out to attend the services of his own church, but when these excursions were discovered, his jailer was dismissed, and he was strictly confined, nor even allowed "to look out of the door."

He found opportunities for exercising his gifts as a preacher, for the prison was often filled with Nonconformists, and Bunyan held services for them: his constant companions were the Bible and Foxe's *Book of Martyrs*.

As he could not pursue his trade to support his family, he spent much of his time in prison making long-tagged laces, which he sold in hundreds to pedlars. But there was time also to write. A constant stream of works flowed from his pen: the greatest of them was *Grace Abounding*, which he wrote in 1666. It is unlikely that he wrote *The Pilgrim's Progress*, which we know was written in prison, during this long sentence, and the probability is that his masterpiece was produced while he was serving a short term later, probably in 1675.

"The parting with my wife and poor children," he writes, "hath often been to me in this place as the pulling of the flesh from the bones, and that not only because I am somewhat too fond of these great mercies but because I should have often brought to my mind the many hardships, miseries and wants that my poor family was like to meet with—especially my poor blind child, who lay nearer to my heart than all besides. Oh! the thought of the hardship my poor blind one might go under would break my heart to pieces. Poor child, thought I . . . thou must be beaten, must beg, suffer hunger, cold, nakedness and a thousand calamities, though I cannot now endure the wind should blow upon thee. But yet, recalling myself, thought I, I must venture you all with God, though it goeth to the quick to leave you."

Charles II was at heart a Catholic, and in 1672, in order to relax without suspicion the laws against Popish recusants, he repealed those against Nonconformists as well.

So Bunyan was released, and at once applied for and received a licence to preach. At the Restoration the Church of St. John, in Bedford, had been given back to its rightful establishment, and Bunyan's brethren now met in a barn. But Bunyan was soon travelling the roads again; he had a regular circuit, and was known as "Bishop" Bunyan.

Religious questions still vexed the country. The Test Act, passed in 1673, and equally operative against Catholic and Nonconformist, made preaching, other than in accordance with the beliefs of the Church of England, a dangerous occupation. Bunyan went resolutely on, and tradition tells how he drove to one meeting disguised as a wagoner and preached with the whip in his hand. Whatever the conditions of the country, his purpose was steadfastly adhered to; he was concerned only with spreading the gospel, and at no time did he heed political tendencies or meddle in affairs outside his ministry.

He was now writing his greatest works. *The Pilgrim's Progress,* published in 1678, was followed in 1680 by *The Life and Death of Mr. Badman,* a delightful piece of work that has been somewhat neglected. Two years later came *The Holy War,* which, in the opinion of Macaulay, would have procured Bunyan his present fame had he never written *The Pilgrim's Progress.* The second part of the latter followed in 1684, and up to the very end of his life Bunyan was writing and publishing, for he was a voluminous author. In our own time £6,800 has been paid for a copy of the first edition of the world's second "best seller."

He often travelled to London at this time and preached to huge congregations in the Zoar Street Chapel, Southwark; as many as twelve hundred people assembled to hear him on a cold winter's morning. In 1688 he was an unofficial chaplain to the Lord Mayor of London.

It was in that year he died. He had ridden from London to Reading in pouring rain to effect a reconciliation between a father and son. He caught a cold, fever set in, and on August 31 he died at the house, on Snow Hill, of his friend, John Strudwick. He was buried in the Strudwick vault in Bunhill Fields, Finsbury.

Such is the plain tale of Bunyan's life. Here are two contemporary accounts of the man:

"He was tall of stature, strong-boned though not corpulent, somewhat of a ruddy face with sparkling eyes, wearing his hair on the upper lip after the old British fashion, his hair reddish, but in his latter days had sprinkled with grey; his nose well-set, but not declining or bending, and his mouth moderately large, his forehead something high, and his habit always plain and modest."

"He appeared in countenance to be of a stern and rough temper, but in his conversation mild and affable, not given to loquacity or much discourse in company, unless some urgent occasion required it, observing never to boast of himself in his parts, but rather seem low in his own eyes and submit himself to the judgment of others."

The judgment of posterity has raised the author of *The Pilgrim's Progress* to the heights of the immortals.

JEAN JACQUES ROUSSEAU

(1712–1778)

Jean Jacques Rousseau died eleven years before the French Revolution began, yet he, if any one man can be held responsible, started that Revolution. His writings, in which he had insisted on the rights of the poor and on the free and equal citizenship of every member of the state, had enormous influence on the minds of his fellow men and on the subsequent history of the world. He displayed originality and force not only in his works on social evils, but also in his educational theories, which were as startlingly "modern" as they have been influential. Yet Rousseau's life, with its strange passions, adventures, and final mania, makes a weird and chequered background to his great work.

THAT genius is akin to madness is none the less true for being a platitude, and surely there is no more striking example of this than the fantastic dreams of a mind, latterly clouded by the mists of insanity, leading the way to freedom for an enslaved nation and blazing new trails for ethical exploration that have not even yet been followed to their ultimate destination.

The dreamer was Jean Jacques Rousseau, and we shall glance at the conditions that gave rise to his dreams—squeezed the good out of the man, as it were, while his grosser parts struggled impotently against the destiny that dragged him always over the rough places of life.

Rousseau was born in Geneva on June 28, 1712, the second son of a watchmaker who added a few sous to his scant income by giving dancing lessons in his spare time. His mother died a fortnight after Jean's arrival, and the first ten years of his life were spent happily enough in the company of his father, his nurse Jaqueline, and of an aunt, who together endeavoured to fill the gap in his affections left by his mother's death.

In 1722 his father, who had taught Jean to read and enjoy the classics as well as the languishing novels of the period, became entangled in a dispute that forced him to choose between banishment or prison. He chose the former and fled to Lyons, leaving the boy in the care of his brother. Uncle Bernard had a son about the same age as Jean Jacques, and they were sent to Boissy to be tutored by the pastor of that town, M. Lambercier. The worthy pastor kept house with his sister, then aged thirty. The young Rousseau promptly fell in love with her, and he confesses that this childish passion for an unconscious subject had a powerful effect on his character which persisted throughout his life. Allowing for the exaggerations of a vain man, we may assume that this early emotional disturbance made his childhood a period of storm and stress until it found an outlet six years later in the enthusiasm of a change of faith.

In the meantime he had returned to Uncle Bernard, been apprenticed to a notary and later to an engraver, with whom he remained three years. But the mild-mannered, moody boy did not fit in with the boisterously practical atmosphere of the engraving studio. He learned to improve his drawing but he also learnt to steal and lie and play stupid jokes with his fellow apprentices. His master was honest, if hard-handed, but Jean Jacques felt his pride as well as his hide was being too roughly used. He ran away.

He expected the world to welcome him as a rebel against the conventions of ordinary life. The world ignored him, and it was by no nobler methods than common begging that he reached Confignon, some little distance from Geneva. There he met a Catholic priest who drew such vivid pictures of the consolations of the Church that all the confused, shapeless ideas that had seethed in the youth became clarified. Life would be simple if one were a Catholic. The universe had a plan, after all. He, Jean Jacques Rousseau, would find his place—be accorded his due recognition.

He was instructed to go to Annecy, where dwelt a recent convert, a Madame de Warens, who would shelter him and complete his religious education. He went, and was installed in her household, acting at times as a private secretary and others as a footman. Jean Jacques was then sixteen, a well set up young man with sparkling eyes, dark hair, white skin, a well-turned foot and ankle, and a tremendous opinion of himself. His mistress was a widow of twenty-eight, an ash-blonde with plenty of money and a generous disposition. She belonged to a type that is never happy without some scheme in hand for helping someone or something, and her interest was naturally increased when that someone was a personable young man who obviously adored her.

But he was young, and his adoration was tainted with the irritating obtuseness of youth. He was too meek—or too jealous;

he presumed too much, or failed from an excess of timidity. He was abominably self-conscious.

It was suggested that, in company with a M. and Mme Sabran, he should go to Turin, where "in a hospital instituted for the instruction of catechumens he should find food both spiritual and temporal" and be reconciled to the Church. The three of them set out to walk from Annecy to Turin. It is impossible to judge from Rousseau's own *Confessions,* which are not altogether reliable, whether Mme. de Sabran had—to put it vulgarly—designs on him. But a silver sword ribbon that Mme de Warens had given Rousseau disappeared. He says she stole it from him. More important, as throwing light upon Rousseau's character at that period, was the disappearance of another ribbon from the house of M. de Vercellis, with whom he had found employment. This had actually been stolen by Rousseau, but he accused a servant girl of the theft when it was discovered. They both protested their innocence, so much that they were both dismissed as the best way out of the difficulty.

Rousseau's next situation was with the Comte de Gouvon, who treated him kindly and well. After a short while a sudden longing to see Mme de Warens made him behave with deliberate impropriety so as to get himself dismissed and be free to return to Annecy. His patroness welcomed him back, but soon packed him off to St. Lazare seminary to complete his education. Theirs was a curious relationship. He was a servant in so far as he received a small salary. Yet she paid for his education, taught him music and received attentions that accorded ill with his pet name for her of "Maman." He was continually leaving her and then, after varying periods of wandering, turning up again. He started off from St. Lazare with a fellow student, whom he left, somewhat inconsiderately, in a fit by the roadside, and returned to Annecy to find madame had gone. After wandering about the Savoie giving music lessons at Neuchâtel and Lausanne, where he even gave a concert, he became secretary to the Greek Archimandrite. With a letter of introduction from the French ambassador at Soleure he went to Paris, where he mixed in good society, learnt manners, and polished off most of the rough corners that had given offence to his friends at home. Finally, at the age of twenty, hearing that Mme de Warens was at Chambéry, he walked half across France to see her.

Their meeting was affectionate. He became her lover again, and they embarked on one of those typical associations of the period when country estates were used as "retreats" for the study of chemistry, music and the arts.

Mr. WILLIAM
SHAKESPEARES
COMEDIES,
HISTORIES, &
TRAGEDIES.
Published according to the True Originall Copies.

LONDON
Printed by Isaac Iaggard, and Ed. Blount. 1623.

Geoffrey Chaucer, the first poet to write in modern English, is depicted here (*above left*) as a traveller in the Ellesmere manuscript of *The Canterbury Tales.* The title-page of the first folio of William Shakespeare's *Plays,* London, 1623 (*above right*).

The fame of François Rabelais (*below right*) rests on two works, *Pantagruel* and *Gargantua,* noted for their broad and racy humour and grotesque invention. John Bunyan (*below left*) spent a great many years in prison because of his Nonconformist teachings and writings and it was whilst in prison that he wrote *The Pilgrim's Progress.*

The writings of Jean Jacques Rousseau (*above*) can be said to have directly contributed to the mood and ideals of the French Revolution of 1789. "The Great Cham of Literature", as Dr. Samuel Johnson was known, in his travelling dress, as described in Boswell's *The Journal of a Tour of the Hebrides* (*left*). A contemporary was the French writer, Voltaire, who is shown here being crowned by France (*below*).

In 1738 she took "Les Charmettes," a country place near Chambéry, in order that Rousseau might recuperate after a severe illness. Rousseau, however, had other plans. He decided to go to Montpelier for his health. Madame de Warens discovered that his cure apparently necessitated the company of a certain Mme. de Larnage, and that was the end of their intimacy. When Rousseau wandered back to "Les Charmettes" he found his position had been successfully filled during his absence. Unperturbed, he took a post as a tutor and, in 1741, returned to the capital.

This year marks the end of what has been referred to as Rousseau's "useless" period. From now onward his genius began to manifest itself.

In Paris his acquaintance with Diderot, co-editor of the *Encyclopédie,* and his friends the Dupins, was to prove useful. Through the latter he obtained the post of secretary to the French ambassador at Venice, whence he returned to Paris in 1745. He had worked out a scheme of musical notation that had been unfavourably received by the academy. Now his opera *Les Muses Galantes* was performed, and Diderot gave him articles to write.

In 1742 he met a seamstress, Thérèse le Vasseur, whom he afterwards married, according to the *Confessions* "ugly, ignorant, stupid, and a detestable mother." It is difficult to discover where the attraction lay; but they had five children, each of which was deposited on the steps of the foundling hospital "to save expense." Yet this extraordinary man was able later to write the most sensible and "modern" treatise on infant welfare and education of his time!

During these years he had been writing persistently, but it was not until 1750 that he gained success with a prize essay for the Dijon Academy on *Has the Progress of the Arts and Sciences Helped to Corrupt or to Purify Morals?* His next success was even greater when, with the production of *Le Devin du Village,* an operetta, he was offered a pension and a position at court. But for the first time he lived up to the principles he advocated. His chequered career had taught him a lot that was bad, but it had at least demonstrated the vice and extravagance flaunted by the French court before the hungry eyes of the people. He would not accept the pension and court position even though it meant the end of all financial worries.

Shortly afterwards he published *The Origins of Inequality,* and in 1754 revisited Geneva, where he renounced Catholicism. On his return to Paris he accepted a little cottage, "The Hermitage," near Montmorency, from Madame d'Epinay, who was the "friend" of

Madame Dupin's son-in-law. Here he wrote *Julie, ou La Nouvelle Héloïse,* which appeared in 1760 and was an instant success although condemned in certain quarters as immoral because of its "free thinking" propensities, for it treated on the rights of the poor and the duties of the rich.

Long before *La Nouvelle Héloïse* was published he had quarrelled with Madame d'Epinay and her friends and left her for Montlouis nearby, where he came under the patronage of the Duke and Duchess of Luxembourg. There had been more than hints of scandal and a suggestion, that must have been particularly insulting to Rousseau, of his playing the part of decoy duck in Madame d'Epinay's affairs. Perhaps it was all for the best that he left her, since most of his best work was written at Montlouis.

In 1762 appeared *Le Contrat Social,* published for safety in Amsterdam, which "endeavoured to base all government on the consent, direct or implied, of the governed." It started from the assumption that the basis of society is an original compact by which each member surrenders his will to the will of all on condition that he receives protection. In it Rousseau demanded a republic with universal suffrage and put forward the citizen's claims to liberty, equality and fraternity that later was the battle-cry of the Revolution.

In the same year appeared *Emile, ou de L'Education,* which contained revolutionary pleas for the home training of children, for "natural religion" instead of Church doctrine, and dealt with matters of diet and hygiene in a novel and unheard-of way. The book was a powerful argument for less pedantic methods of training and developing the mental, physical and moral faculties of the young, and it undoubtedly influenced, in later years, such prominent educationists as Froebel and Pestalozzi.

Threatened with arrest for the publication of *Emile,* Rousseau fled to Luerdon and then to Motiers, whose owner was that celebrated patron of arts, Frederick the Great. He attacked his attackers in *Lettres de la Montagne* (1763), with the natural consequence that even Switzerland became too dangerous to live in; so he fled (as Voltaire had done) to the safety of England and the sympathy of David Hume. Through all these adventures poor Thérèse, had followed him, and it is interesting to note that she was escorted to London by James Boswell. We can imagine what Johnson thought of the affair! But London lionized Rousseau, even while it was inclined to whisper in drawing-rooms and coffee houses at the new celebrity's curious behaviour. By royal command a performance was given at Drury Lane in his honour.

Whatever may be the causes that transform an injured pride into a shrinking sense of persecution, and an open sweetness of mind into bitter delusions of mistrust and treachery, these symptoms now asserted themselves in Rousseau's intercourse with his friends. Hume took him down to Wootton, in Derbyshire, where he astonished the neighbourhood by donning an American costume and wrote most of the *Confessions,* that curious document of warped personality; but the English visit was not a success. After a peculiarly violent quarrel with Hume he returned to France in 1762, and wandered from patron to patron, perpetually wretched, quarrelling with them all, and pursued by ghostly tormentors that whispered despairingly in his brain.

By 1770 he was able to return to Paris, where he lived quietly enough for a time, finishing the *Confessions* and his *Dialogues,* and beginning the *Promenades d'un Solitaire,* which is perhaps the best of his books considered purely as a work of art. In 1778 a rich financier offered him a house at Ermenonille, and there he might have lived peacefully for years had not Thérèse, after so many years of fidelity, wounded him and inflamed his mania by her open affair with a stable boy. That Thérèse should fail him was conclusive evidence that the whole world had turned against him.

On July 2, 1778, his body was found with the face suffused and swollen. The medical officers were unable to state whether death was the result of apoplexy or suicide.

So died unhappily one of the strangest of the world's reformers. Supremely selfish, Rousseau realized that the monarchy of his time meant the greatest misery of the greatest number, and he was man enough to say so. Without much sense of moral responsibility, he was yet able to write a sane and valuable text-book for the guidance of youth. His *Social Contract* has been described as an impassioned version of Locke's *Treatise on Government.* Yet, as Lord Morley says, "it was due to his work more than that of any other one man that France arose from the deadly decay which had laid hold of her whole social and political system and found that . . . energy which warded off dissolution within and partition without."

In other words it was Rousseau who started what is known as the French Revolution, even though more than a quarter of a century elapsed before any concrete results could be observed.

FRANÇOIS MARIE AROUET DE VOLTAIRE

(1694–1778)

While in England, the great Dr. Johnson drank gallons of tea and thundered for piety with his mighty wit; in France a shrivelled manikin swilled litres of coffee and attacked orthodoxy with powerful and pungent irony. He was Voltaire. He was the greatest journalist who ever lived. He was a writer supreme in craftsmanship and versatility, a magnificent expounder of criticism and of the truth, an inimitable wielder of the sharp weapons of irony and sarcasm. And, by virtue of "Zadig," it may be fairly claimed that he was the inventor of the detective story.

When Notary Arouet's youngest boy was born at Paris in 1694, no one expected it to live. A sickly, miserable infant, it wailed in the nurse's arms, wriggling convulsively, and twisting its pinched little face into wry grimaces. Hurriedly it was baptized—François Marie Arouet—but, in spite of the somewhat haphazard methods of nursing at that period, the child survived. Though never physically strong, he became something of a prodigy, since we learn that he was able at the age of three to recite the whole of La Fontaine's fables.

His godfather taught him these, the Abbé de Châteauneuf, a gentleman with a shady reputation in the eyes of all good churchgoers, and the sly old rascal, finding an apt pupil, continued to instruct the boy in the rudiments of learning, and at the same time to inculcate some of his own unconventional views.

"He already knows *The Mosaïdè*," said the abbé gleefully to his old friend, the celebrated Ninon de l'Enclos.

Now *The Mosaïdè* was a notoriously agnostic poem, and later, when young Arouet was composing similar poems of his own, Ninon, who had bewitched three generations with her beauty before she began to depend upon the attractions of intelligence alone, sent for him. We may imagine with what interest she gazed upon the boy who was fated to dazzle a world even she could never live to see; for that boy was to become famous as Voltaire, the satirist, the wit, the philosopher, the bitter enemy of orthodox religion. It was not until his majority that Arouet decided to call himself by the more aristocratic name of Voltaire, but by that name he lives, and by that name we call him.

At ten he was sent to a Jesuit school, where he astonished the fathers with his quickness, his charm and his inexhaustible curiosity. His school career was as brilliant as any parent could wish, and it must have been a severe blow to his father, after he had bought a legal situation for his son, to be told, "I desire no profession save that of a man of letters."

Godfather Châteauneuf was useful at this point. He had watched the boy grow up and away from his parents and his devout, strait-laced elder brother; now he stepped in and introduced his protégé to all his elegant and vicious friends at court. Success went to the young man's head. He was fêted by princes and petted by pretty ladies. So frail he seemed, and yet with so vigorous a mind! From epigrams and naughtier lampoons he aspired to drama, and wrote his first tragedy, *Œdipe*. "A charming thing," said his friends, few of whom had seen the manuscript. The court producers did not scramble for the work as rapidly as the spoilt young author would have liked. But there was plenty of time. Meanwhile, to rid him of the graceless and scandalous company which he kept, his father packed him off to the Marquis de Châteauneuf, his godfather's brother, who was then ambassador to Holland.

At the Hague, Voltaire had his first recorded love affair. He met Olympe Dunoyer. But the mother of Pimpette (as he called her) complained loudly and at length, to Châteauneuf; and, as it does not do for an ambassador to be mixed up in a scandal, he did the best he could, and sent Master Voltaire off home to Paris.

In 1715 Louis XIV died and, with the accession of the fifteenth Louis under the Regent Duc d'Orléans, all the restraint that the "Grande Monarche" had imposed on his people melted away. At last men could talk and write what they pleased—and most of them did, Voltaire among them. Unfortunately, his misguided pen attacked the Regent a little too keenly, and he was immediately sent to the Bastille for eighteen months to remember his manners.

He spent the time in beginning a long epic on Henri IV. On his release he was invited by the Duc de Béthune to recover his health at Sully, where he fell under the spell of Mlle de Livry, and there began to write plays in which she was to perform.

Back in Paris he managed at last to have *Œdipe* produced. It was a tremendous success, not because it was a good play, but because rumour whispered that the Regent was guilty of its hero's crime. The world believed that *Œdipe* had been specially written to attack the vices of the court, and the public crowded to the theatre. The performance led directly to an enormously enlarged reputation, but his next plays were failures. So Voltaire turned his attention to the publication of his poem on Henri IV, eventually entitled the *Henriade*.

(He had now assumed the name of Voltaire, which is generally taken to be a rather sketchy anagram of Arouet l.j., the last two letters standing for *le jeune*.)

Permission for the publication of the *Henriade* was refused, because the poem championed the causes of Protestantism and religious toleration. Nevertheless, in 1723, Voltaire had it printed at Rouen, and personally supervised its publication. While doing so he fell ill with smallpox and for a time was at death's door.

A more violent misfortune befell him in 1725. He was insulted by the Chevalier de Rohan, and he replied with witty and scathing epigrams. The sequel was swift. One day, while dining with Sully, Voltaire was summoned without and was set upon and beaten by hirelings of de Rohan, the latter watching the proceedings in person. No one, not even the Duc, would take Voltaire's part, and at last he challenged de Rohan to a duel. But on the morning the engagement was to have taken place, Voltaire was seized and once more cast into the Bastille. There he was kept for a fortnight, and was then, at his own request, packed off to England.

Voltaire left France in a white-hot fury of rage against the indignities and injustices that had been piled upon him. England, he felt, would sympathize.

There he was able, through an introduction to Lord Bolingbroke, to meet the best minds of the period. He met Swift, whom he called "The English Rabelais," Pope, Young, Gay, Congreve and scores of celebrities such as the Duchess of Marlborough, Chesterfield and Peterborough.

Voltaire was much impressed by English society and by the English toleration for personal freedom of thought, while Bolingbroke and the English deists furnished him with ideas. He made some thousands of pounds out of an edition of the *Henriade*, which was dedicated to Queen Caroline, and when he returned to France in 1729, it was with his completed manuscript of *The History of Charles XII* and the material for his *Letters on the English*.

His stay in Paris was short. Infuriated by the unconsecrated burial of Adrienne Lecouvreur, the famous actress, he protested in a slashing poem that was regarded by the Church as a horrible impiety. Voltaire fled to Rouen, and there published *Lettres Philosophiques,* the fruits of his stay in England, that attacked most forms of religion and some of the most cherished institutions in France, and contained as well what must be some of the earliest *Popular Philosophies* ever written for the general public.

The book was burned by the public hangman in 1734; the bookseller was sent to the Bastille, and Voltaire's position was more insecure than it had ever been before—especially as there was now a new and terrible rumour of an unspeakably coarse satire on *St. Joan* that the authorities itched to lay hands on. A certain Madame du Châtelet offered him shelter in her husband's castle at Cirey in the independent Duchy of Lorraine, and there began the great passion of Voltaire's life that was only to end fifteen years later with her death.

He was thirty-nine, she was eleven years younger, married and without children. Her husband did not seem to mind this three-cornered arrangement whereby his wife spent weeks on end studying astronomy, chemistry and philosophy with the fascinating yet dangerous writer. She was ugly—one of her friends said she had a skin like a nutmeg-grater—but she was intelligent and sympathetic. And so they lived happily together, quarrelling and abusing each other (in English so as to be more insulting), making it up, working hard at their studies, writing innumerable plays for their visitors to perform in the private theatre; making love and quarrelling all over again.

One day in August, 1736, Voltaire received a flattering letter from the Crown Prince of Prussia, to which he replied eagerly and politely. Four years later the prince became the Emperor Frederick, and he invited Voltaire to grace his court. But Madame du Châtelet would not go to Prussia, and so Voltaire remained in France.

Fate was beginning at last to smile on him in his own country. In 1745 the influence of Mme de Pompadour at court procured for him the post of histographer royal, in spite of Louis XV's dislike. In 1746 he was elected to the Academy. King Stanislas of Lorraine invited both of them to his court, and this time Madame du Châtelet did not refuse a royal invitation. They entertained the king " with concerts, fêtes and spectacles."

Madame du Châtelet entered on a wonderfully gay and crowded life, acting and singing and meeting all kinds of charming and amusing people. Among these there was the gallant young M. de Saint-Lambert, whose attentions were perhaps more marked than his intentions. Voltaire was elderly, she was eleven years younger than he was. Saint-Lambert—well, Saint-Lambert had a way with him!

Voltaire soon discovered everything. It may be that Madame confessed to him certain misgivings that arose out of her new love. There was a quarrel between the three of them, a hasty journey back to the Marquis du Châtelet, and a period of anxious waiting. Poor Madame was forty-four and she felt frightened of this unforeseen thing that had happened to her. The unsuspecting Marquis told all his friends of the happy event he was expecting. Voltaire ground his teeth. Six days after the birth of a little girl, Madame du Châtelet died (1749). Voltaire, after one agonized outburst to Saint-Lambert, "It was *you* who killed her for me!" returned to Paris to work off his intolerable grief in plays and novels, and to forget, in the splendour of his ultimate arrival at the Emperor Frederick's court, that *she* was no longer there to forbid him.

It was not long, however, before the emperor quarrelled with his prickly and outspoken guest. By 1753 Voltaire had outstayed his welcome, but he could no longer return to France, and England no longer seemed to offer refuge for an embittered republican. He turned his tired footsteps towards Switzerland, and finally settled, at the age of sixty, in the village of Ferney near Geneva, with his niece, Mme. Denis.

At Ferney, Voltaire became a craftsman, an industrialist, a farmer and a host of other things besides. He planted and dug, experimented in horse-breeding, built houses for his workers, started a silk stocking factory, a lace-making establishment, a trade in watches. And always he wrote and wrote. But now his vitriolic pen was devoted to concrete causes. He no longer railed against law, the Church in general; he was able to vindicate Jean Calas after his frightful torture and execution for the alleged murder of his son; he fought to prevent the Chevalier de la Barre from being burned alive, and strove with all his power to mitigate the savage criminal laws of his time. Last, but not least, it was at Ferney that his genius crystallized in the perfection of *Candide,* the one work whose mature humanity and ageless irony has secured for him a niche in the gallery of immortals.

The years passed on, and with their passing came peace and honour to Voltaire, after a life of storm and travail. Ferney became a place of pilgrimage. Frederick once more made friends with him. France beckoned smilingly. Voltaire, at eighty-three, had finished *Irène,* a tragedy that was to be performed in Paris. He must—he *must* return to Paris for the performance.

The journey was a triumphal procession, culminating in a coronation with laurel wreaths upon the stage of the theatre. *Irène* was a stupendous success. But the end was near. Agonizing pains seized him in the midst of his triumph.

On May 30, 1778, still surrounded by a clamorous throng of visitors, he died. His last words were, "Do leave me to die in peace!"

Thus passed one of the most remarkable figures that ever graced, and sometimes disgraced, the literary world. His wit, his magnificent irony, his sarcasm and his acute judgment stamped all his enormous output. The theatre was his passion, and he wrote over fifty pieces for the stage; the best are the tragedies of *Zaire* (1732), *Merope,* and *Mahomet* (1741). His satirical poem, *La Pucelle,* which was published at last in 1755, is uneven but amusing. In the vast number of his historical and philosophical works and in his enormous correspondence he gives constant proof of his versatility, his penetrating mind, and his perfect craftsmanship.

DOCTOR SAMUEL JOHNSON

(1709–1784)

The eighteenth century in England was a golden age of genius. Burke, Reynolds, Gibbon, Garrick, Goldsmith, Fox, Burney, Adam Smith, these were the leaders of the arts, the aristocracy of intelligence. But one man bestrode them like a Colossus; one man was their acknowledged leader—Dr. Samuel Johnson. His learning was greater than his writing, his wit greater than them both. He was England's greatest conversationalist; an arbiter of elegant common-sense. Yet these do not make the sum of his worth: he was a genius, but in the courage and conduct of his life he becomes supreme. Johnson has not won fame from Boswell. Boswell's "Life" is the finest biography in the language because its minute faithfulness shows us the true Johnson.

A MIGHTY roar breaks the stillness of a summer's night and fills all Fleet Street with its shattering explosion. Good citizens stir uneasily in their sleep and stir again as a second roar bursts on the echoes of the first. The noise grows louder; shouts reverberate from Temple Bar, and are borne on the still air across the Fleet Ditch to St. Paul's. Is this a murder? A riot? A cautious nightcap peers from an upper window. Ah! Beneath the lamp over Temple Gate can be seen the cause of the commotion. A gross man is clasping a post on the pavement; his hat is on the ground, his wig is awry; his body rolls and reels in violent convulsions: it is he who is uttering these horrible sounds, while another man stands by silent and helpless.

"Only some poor devil having a fit, or a madman," murmurs he of the nightcap, and jumps back into bed to escape the still rising torrent of ululation. He is wrong. The writhing figure is Mr. Samuel Johnson, the most learned and one of the most respected men in all England. The noise is his laughter.

That is a picture of Sam Johnson which Boswell, then the silent companion, has given us. It is a picture that might well be symbolical: that great Englishman, "the awful, melancholy and venerable Johnson," standing in his beloved Fleet Street at midnight, laughing like an earthquake. For Johnson's mirth—"he laughs like a rhinoceros," said one of his friends—was like the man, generous and great. Great is his adjective: he was great of body, great of mind, great of soul: he enriched the world with his works and with his wit, but more than either with his life. His shadow bestrides Fleet Street like a Colossus; that laugh from the belly is echoing still.

Sam Johnson had one companion of longer standing and of more constancy than Boswell—poverty. He was born in September, 1709, at Lichfield, at a time when his father, who was a bookseller, was "forced by the narrowness of his circumstances to be very diligent in business." Sam spent most of his life forcing his great body through the same narrows. In his childhood he was afflicted with scrofula, the king's evil, and he was actually brought to London to be touched by Queen Anne. The queen's touch in this case was ineffective. She wrought no cure. The scrofula disfigured Johnson's face and affected one of his eyes so that it was useless all his life.

Young Sam was lazy, but he had a remarkable gift for learning. He devoured books in all languages, read them haphazardly, but absorbed their contents like a sponge. At nineteen the lumbering lad went up to Oxford. He had no money, but a friend had promised to support him. The support never materialized, and eventually Johnson had to come down without a degree.

He was an unusual undergraduate. He would startle his tutor with a quotation from some little known Latin author. He would startle him again by excusing an unauthorized absence with a cool: "I was sliding in Christ Church meadow." When Boswell heard of this answer to the tutor, he was struck by the young man's nonchalance, and remarked to Johnson: "That, sir, was great fortitude of mind." "No, sir," answered Johnson, "stark insensibility."

Johnson's poverty at Oxford was so extreme that he gave up attending certain lectures, because his feet showed through his worn-out shoes. Someone left a new pair at his door, but Johnson was so independent that he flung them angrily away.

After Oxford, Johnson tried schoolmastering, and in 1736 set up on his own at Edial, near Lichfield; but he could only obtain three pupils, one of whom was David Garrick, the actor.

The year previously he had married Mrs. Porter, a widow many years older than himself. It was an extraordinary match: it started with a wedding-day tiff, which Johnson relates himself:

> "Sir, she had read the old romances, and had got into her head the fantastical notion that a woman of spirit should use her lover like a dog. So, sir, at first she told me that I rode too fast, and she could not keep up with me; and, when I rode a little

slower, she passed me, and complained that I lagged behind. I was not to be made the slave of caprice; and I resolved to begin as I meant to end. I therefore pushed on briskly, till I was fairly out of her sight. The road lay between two hedges, so I was sure she could not miss it; and I contrived that she should soon come up with me. When she did, I observed her to be in tears."

But it was a love match. Johnson was a good husband and he loved his wife to her death and beyond.

Schoolmastering at Edial was not fattening. Johnson, with his friend and pupil, Garrick, came to London. He struggled with poverty as a journalist and a bookseller's hack. In 1738 he published *London, a Poem, in imitation of the third Satire of Juvenal.* It was the foundation of Johnson's reputation, but reputation does not fill a man's belly.

Sam battled on against poverty, against illness—he suffered bad health throughout his life; he had a convulsive infirmity, and in middle life and late years had asthma. He wrote parliamentary reports, essays, pamphlets and prefaces. His *Life of Richard Savage,* published in 1744, increased his reputation, and in 1747 he announced his Plan for the Dictionary of the English Language, that immense undertaking which alone would have secured him immortality. He worked on the dictionary with intermittent bursts of energy for eight years, and in addition to this, from 1750 to 1752, published a bi-weekly paper called *The Rambler,* which enjoyed much success.

In 1752 Johnson's wife died. He was overcome with grief, but he struggled on with work, calling upon his deep, almost superstitious, piety. The great dictionary, the first of the English language, was published in 1755. It was a stupendous achievement for one man, who had to contend with lack of encouragement and support. His letter to the Earl of Chesterfield, written just before its publication, is the most dignified retort ever penned in reply to an offer of help that came when no longer needed:

My Lord—I have been lately informed by the proprietor of *The World,* that two papers, in which my *Dictionary* is recommended to the public, were written by your lordship. To be so distinguished is an honour, which, being very little accustomed to favours from the great, I know not well how to receive, or in what terms to acknowledge.

When, upon some slight encouragement, I first visited your lordship, I was overpowered, like the rest of mankind, by the enchantment of your address, and could not forbear to wish that

I might boast myself *Le vainqueur du vainqueur de la terre*—that I might obtain that regard for which I saw the world contending; but I found my attendance so little encouraged, that neither pride nor modesty would suffer me to continue it. When I had once addressed your lordship in public, I had exhausted all the art of pleasing which a retired and courtly scholar can possess. I had done all that I could; and no man is well pleased to have his all neglected, be it ever so little.

Seven years, my lord, have now passed, since I waited in your outward rooms, or was repulsed from your door; during which time I have been pushing on my work through difficulties, of which it is useless to complain, and have brought it, at last, to the verge of publication, without one act of assistance, one word of encouragement, or one smile of favour. Such treatment I did not expect, for I never had a patron before.

The shepherd in Virgil grew at last acquainted with Love, and found him a native of the rocks.

Is not a patron, my lord, one who looks with unconcern on a man struggling for life in the water, and when he has reached ground, encumbers him with help. The notice which you have been pleased to take of my labours, had it been early, had been kind; but it has been delayed until I am indifferent, and cannot enjoy it; till I am solitary and cannot impart it; till I am known, and do not want it.

I hope it is no very cynical asperity not to confess obligations where no benefit has been received, or to be unwilling that the public should consider me as owing that to a patron, which Providence has enabled me to do for myself.

Having carried on my work thus far with so little obligation to any favourer of learning, I shall not be disappointed though I should conclude it, if less be possible, with less; for I have been long wakened from that dream of hope, in which I once boasted myself with so much exultation, my lord: your lordship's most humble, most obedient servant,

SAM JOHNSON.

The rest of his writings may be chronicled briefly. His dictionary brought him world-wide fame. In 1759 he published *Rasselas,* a philosophical romance, and during the same year published a weekly paper called *The Idler*. In 1773 he toured the Hebrides with Boswell, and two years later published the *Journal* of the tour. His *Lives of the English Poets,* in which he displayed his critical faculties, appeared in the years 1779-81. He was made a Doctor of Laws by Oxford University in 1775, but he never called himself Doctor Johnson. His last work, *Prayers and Meditations,* was published in 1785, the year after his death. But Johnson lives, not in his published works as much as in the dominance of the literary world of his day.

In 1763 James Boswell met Samuel Johnson, for which the world may be truly thankful. Bozzy played moon to Johnson's sun; in his *Life,* one of the best biographies ever written, he has given us the man and his talk; both unique.

Here is Johnson at home in 1763:

> "His brown suit of clothes looked very rusty; he had on a little, shrivelled, unpowdered wig, which was too small for his head; his shirtneck and knees of his breeches were loose; his black worsted stockings ill drawn up; and he had a pair of unbuckled shoes by way of slippers. But all these slovenly particularities were forgotten the moment he began to talk."

The moment he began to talk; then this shambling, shaggy man became a magician, an alchemist in words. At the Literary Club, with its galaxy of talented members, he was the king. The great men of his day, Sir Joshua Reynolds, Goldsmith, Garrick, Gibbon, Burke, Fox, Burney, gathered round him, came to hear him and to love him. "No, sir," he would thunder, and "Why, sir," he would expound; but he was as kind-hearted as his manner was rough. He was poor, but always generous. His Christianity was composed of piety, fear, and superstition. But his charity was practical.

Once in Fleet Street he stumbled on a woman of the streets lying helpless in the gutter. He picked her up, slung her on his broad back, and took her to his lodgings. There he had her attended to during a long illness, and when she had recovered found work for her. He had a strange household of indigent friends and dependants; he could not do too much for anyone who had a claim upon his affection.

"What signifies giving halfpennies to common beggars?" objected someone to Johnson. "They only lay it out in gin and tobacco."

"And why should they be denied such sweeteners of their existence?" retorted Johnson.

For in spite of his poverty, and his melancholia and his afflictions, Johnson had a gust for life. He could roar with laughter; he drank little, but he loved eating; he liked good talk, speed, and pretty women. "If," he said once, as he was travelling along the road at speed, "if I had no duties, and no reference to futurity, I would spend my life in driving briskly in a post-chaise with a pretty woman; but she would have to be one that could understand me, and would add something to the conversation." And women liked him in spite of his peculiarities. He had strange habits of rolling and contorting his body, of muttering and whistling under his breath, of shaking his head and blowing out his cheeks. But none of his physical infirmities affected his brain. To his last hours his reason and his wit were invincible.

The quality of his talk may be judged by the number of his aphorisms that have become commonplaces in our language.

His gibes are sabre-strokes. Boswell has heard a woman's sermon. "Sir," says Johnson, "a woman preaching is like a dog's walking on his hind legs. It is not done well; but you are surprised to find it done at all."

A Scot, forgetting Johnson's prejudice against his race and country, praises Scottish scenery. "Sir, let me tell you," comes Sam's crushing answer, "the noblest prospect which a Scotsman ever sees, is the high road that leads him to England." And he saves a phrase for Ireland: "The Irish are a fair people; they never speak well of one another."

Johnson strove mightily for victory in conversation; yet his most characteristic retort was that to the Plymouth woman who asked him why he had made a wrong definition in his dictionary. "Ignorance, madam, pure ignorance."

Even in the dictionary he could fool and thunder. His definition of "Oats" is famous: "a grain which in England is generally given to horses, but in Scotland supports the people." "Pension" he describes as: "An allowance made to any one without an equivalent. In England it is generally understood to mean pay given to a State hireling for treason to his country." While in more playful mood he defines "Lexicographer" as: "a writer of dictionaries, a harmless drudge."

Sometimes he will browbeat in conversation: "Sir, we know our will is free, and there's an end on't." Or he will snub Bozzy when he goes too far. Boswell: "But I wonder, sir, you have not more pleasure in writing than in not writing." Johnson: "Sir, you *may* wonder."

But his gruffness was only of manner. Goldsmith, who had often suffered at Johnson's hands, said of him: "He has nothing of the bear but his skin." And Edmund Burke said finely at the end of Johnson's life: "It is well, if, when a man comes to die, he has nothing heavier upon his conscience than having been a little rough in conversation."

And that, perhaps, is the perfect epitaph for this extraordinary man; this huge, afflicted provincial, of booming voice and golden heart, who towered over London in the eighteenth century; this bookseller's son who became the most learned man of his age; this uncouthly dressed fellow who could thrash a band of street ruffians, pink an earl with his wit, and talk easily with his king; this poor pensioner who paid the debts of others; this bear who could charm the wisest and the wittiest; this devout Christian who would sup with sinners; this stern moralist who hated cant; this paragon who had no priggishness; this man, Samuel Johnson.

PERCY BYSSHE SHELLEY

(1792–1822)

A youth in revolt, a fervent apostle of liberty, a man who wronged yet knew no wrong, who bound himself by the conventions he defied, who set before himself the ideals of consistency and perfection, who shocked his contemporaries by his life's work and dazzled posterity by his genius. That was Shelley. The man and his actions will ever be the cause of argument, criticism, censure and explanation, but we may forget them all in the immortal music that he has left as his memorial.

It is the year 1792. In London, William Blake is hard at work following up the lovely lyrics of the *Songs of Innocence* with the dark fire of his first prophetic poems. In Edinburgh, a young Scotsman named Walter Scott, who is reading for the bar, spends his leisure in collecting the ballads of his country. A gloomy genius, Samuel Coleridge, is idling at Cambridge, and in Paris an enthusiastic young republican, William Wordsworth, glories in the progress of the Revolution. In the far north, at Aberdeen, a limping boy, named Byron, attends his first day school, and a livery-stableman called Keats grooms his horses at Moorfields where, three years later, his grandson genius will be born. And on August 4, Percy Bysshe Shelley is born at Warnham, in Sussex.

Percy Bysshe Shelley was the eldest son of Timothy Shelley, of Field Place, Warnham. His grandfather, Bysshe Shelley, a rich old eccentric who became a baronet in 1806, disliked his son, and from an early age Shelley disliked his father. "Shelley," writes Mr. Clutton-Brock, "from an early age was fastidious about manners and appearance; and his father was absurd in both. Shelley could love no one whom he did not think perfect; and his father's imperfections were obvious. Shelley, like a clever girl, expected every one to be consistent; and his father had no consistency. . . . To Shelley he seemed morally, intellectually, and æsthetically contemptible, a symbol of all that irrational authority against which it was his duty to rebel. Shelley's moral sense was precociously and morbidly developed. He was too much in love with abstract perfection to make any allowances for the concrete imperfection of his father; and since he turned every one he knew into a character of romance, he turned his father, who was unfitted for the part, into a villain of melodrama."

The boy Shelley lived his early years in a romantic, make-believe world of his own; and certainly, when at the age of ten he became a boarder at Sion House Academy, at Isleworth, he was a strange, delicate creature in the rough schoolboy world. A contemporary at the school pictures him—" like a girl in boy's clothing, fighting with open hands, and rolling on the floor when flogged, not from the pain, but from a sense of indignity."

At Sion House, Shelley received some hard knocks and conceived a love of science, which led him to make dangerous experiments throughout his school and university days.

In his early teens he was sent to Eton, where he was bullied unmercifully, and it is said that the cause of his leaving Eton early was that he had been provoked into stabbing the hand of one of his tormentors and pinning it with a penknife to the desk.

While he was at Eton he made the acquaintance of Dr. Lind, who became a benevolent friend and for whom Shelley had a warm affection. Shelley used to tell how: "Once, when I was very ill during the holidays, as I was recovering from a fever which had attacked my brain, a servant overheard my father consult about sending me to a private madhouse. I was a favourite among all our servants, so this fellow came and told me, as I lay sick in bed. My horror was beyond words, and I might soon have been mad indeed if they had proceeded in their iniquitous plan. I had one hope. I was master of three pounds in money, and, with the servant's help, I contrived to send an express to Dr. Lind. He came, and I shall never forget his manner on that occasion. His profession gave him authority; his love for me ardour. He dared my father to execute his purpose, and his menaces had the desired effect."

Of this story, Shelley's friend, Hogg, wrote: "I have heard Shelley speak of his fever, and this scene at Field Place, more than once. . . . It appears to myself, and to others also, that his recollections were those of a person not quite recovered from a fever, and still disturbed by the horrors of the disease." And Mr. Clutton-Brock comments: " It took less than a fever to produce romantic delusions in Shelley's mind."

In 1810, Shelley entered University College, Oxford. He had already blossomed forth as an author with a highly-coloured romance in the fashionable "gothic" style, called *Zastrozzi.* He had also begun his first love affair with a passion for his cousin, Harriet Grove, but Harriet married "a clod of earth."

At Oxford he formed a close friendship with Thomas Jefferson Hogg, who has given us a vivid picture of young Shelley with his passions for chemistry, poetry, and philosophy: "His figure was slight and fragile, and yet his bones and joints were large and strong. He was tall, but he stooped so much that he seemed of a low stature. His clothes were expensive, and made according to the most approved mode of the day; but they were tumbled, rumpled, unbrushed. His gestures were abrupt and sometimes violent, occasionally even awkward, yet more frequently gentle and graceful. His complexion was delicate and almost feminine, of the purest white and red; yet he was tanned and freckled by exposure to the sun. . . . His features, his whole face, and particularly his head, were, in fact, unusually small; yet the last *appeared* of a remarkable bulk, for his hair was long and bushy . . . he often rubbed it up fiercely with his hands, or passed his fingers through his locks unconsciously, so that it was singularly wild and rough. . . . His features . . . breathed an animation, a fire, an enthusiasm, a vivid and preternatural intelligence, that I never met with in any other countenance. Nor was the moral expression less beautiful than the intellectual. . . ." Hogg goes on to mention that his only physical blemish was his strident voice.

Shelley's philosophy and his abandonment of religion soon led him into trouble. In 1811 he published a tract, *The Necessity of Atheism,* for which he was expelled by the master of the college. Hogg protested against this summary treatment and received similar sentence. The two friends left Oxford together and took lodgings in Poland Street, London, but in April, Hogg left for York and a legal career. Shelley had refused to be reconciled to his father, and was consequently without means, but his sisters, at school at Wandsworth, sent him gifts of money by one of the girls who was allowed to go home. In this way he made the acquaintance of Harriet Westbrook, the fifteen-year-old daughter of a retired coffee-house proprietor, and of her elder sister, Eliza, who seems from the first to have been a determined match-maker.

By the end of the year Shelley was married to Harriet. He tells the story of the affair in a letter to his friend, Miss Hitchener. He was in Wales when Harriet wrote to him complaining of her father's tyranny. "Suicide was her favourite theme. . . ." (It remained so throughout her life.) "Her letters became more and more gloomy. At length one assumed a tone of such despair as induced me to quit Wales precipitately. I arrived in London. I was shocked at observing the alteration of her looks. Little did I divine the cause. She had become violently attached to me, and feared that I should not return her attachment. Prejudice made the confession painful. It was impossible to avoid being much affected. I promised to unite my fate with hers. I stayed in London several days, during which she recovered her spirits. I had promised at her bidding to come again to London. They endeavoured to make her return to a school where malice and pride embittered every hour. She wrote to me. I came to London. I proposed marriage for reasons which I have given you, and she complied. Blame me if thou wilt, dearest friend, for still thou art dearest to me; yet pity even the error if thou blamest me."

The couple eloped to Edinburgh, where they were married on August 28. It was a foolish marriage, prompted by chivalrous pity on his side and by infatuation on hers; yet for two years they lived happily together and the pretty, charming girl was a loyal wife to him. His uncle, Pilfold, who had been one of Nelson's captains, supplied Shelley with money, and they lived a wandering life. York, Keswick (where he met Southey), Dublin, the Isle of Man, Wales, Lynmouth found homes for them. But at York they had been joined by Eliza Westbrook, who was still determined to manage her sister. From then until his death Shelley was haunted by the disasters of a *ménage à trois*.

At Lynmouth, in 1812, he wrote *Queen Mab,* the first of his works which contains the promise of his genius. "The past, the present, and the future are the grand and comprehensive topics of this poem," said Shelley at the time.

In the summer of 1813, Harriet had a daughter, who was named Ianthe after the heroine of *Queen Mab,* and in the March of the following year, owing to the questionable validity of the Edinburgh marriage, Harriet and Shelley were re-married in London.

From that fact it would seem that Shelley had no thought of separation from his wife; yet it seems clear that he had lost what love he had had for Harriet and that his home had been made hateful to him by Eliza; and soon he was madly in love with Mary Wollstonecraft, the daughter of William Godwin. Shelley had read and been inspired by Godwin's *Political Justice* at Eton, and had been in correspondence with him from his Keswick days. In London he tried to raise money for the always hard-up philosopher, and his frequent calls at Godwin's house inevitably led to his acquaintance with Mary, who, though less beautiful, was certainly more intelligent than Harriet.

Shelley asked Harriet to agree to a separation, but she would not. The shock made her ill—she was expecting a child, and Shelley danced attendance on her. But in July, 1814, he fled to France with Mary, taking with them Jane Clairmont, the daughter of the second Mrs. Godwin by her first marriage. From Troyes he wrote to Harriet inviting her to join them in Switzerland!

But after wandering for six weeks on the Continent the three returned to England. Shelley found that Harriet had drawn all his money, and went to see her, and he had several meetings with her in the next few months. In November her son was born.

"Those who are inclined to think of Shelley's desertion of his first wife as a romantic event, or a symptom of his genius, or an heroic protest against the tyranny of convention, or anything else it was not," writes Mr. Clutton-Brock, "should give attention to the squalid incidents of his life at this time, when he was getting money from the wife he deserted, and trying to persuade her and himself that he had not deserted her, dodging bailiffs, and haggling with money-lenders."

The bailiffs and the money-lenders were appeased when, early in 1815, Sir Bysshe Shelley died. Timothy bought out his son's interest in the entailed estate and gave him an income of £1,000 a year, of which Shelley allowed £200 to Harriet.

In 1815, Shelley wrote *Alastor,* a masterpiece in blank verse. It was published in March, 1816, and two months later Shelley, with Mary and Jane Clairmont, who now called herself Claire, set out for Geneva. Claire was already a burden to the household, but she had her own reasons for accompanying the party, for she was with child by Byron, and Byron, too, was bound for Geneva.

Byron and Shelley met for the first time in Switzerland. Shelley already admired Byron's poetry, and he was interested in the man; while Byron, the cynical trifler, recognized Shelley as a great and disinterested man. During their sojourn at Geneva, Byron wrote his *Prisoner of Chillon,* but Shelley's only productions were the poem on *Mont Blanc* and the *Hymn to Intellectual Beauty*. Mary, urged on by Shelley and Byron, wrote a story that has won her lasting fame —*Frankenstein*.

In August the Shelleys and Claire set out for England. On his return Shelley made the acquaintance of Leigh Hunt, who had favourably reviewed his poetry. He stayed with Hunt in December, and immediately afterwards he heard that Harriet had drowned herself in the Serpentine. By the end of the month he had married Mary, but he was grieved and angry when a chancery decree deprived him of the guardianship of his children by Harriet, and he vented his rage in a bitter poem addressed to the lord chancellor, who had given judgment.

In 1817, Shelley took a house at Marlow on the Thames, and there he began *Rosalind and Helen,* completed *The Revolt of Islam,* and produced the fragment, *Prince Athanase.* The hard work, and the climate, had its effect on his health, and he was ordered by his doctor to rest and have a change of scene. Shelley wanted to see Italy, and so, in March, 1818, he left England with Mary and their children and with Claire and her child.

They wandered from Milan to Leghorn and from Leghorn to Lucca. Claire's child had been sent to Byron at Venice. Byron had conceived a violent hatred of Claire, but he was determined to keep the child. Shelley was sent to intercede, and he paid two visits to Byron. He was shocked at Byron's way of living. In his poem, *Julian and Maddalo,* he records his impressions of Venice and conversations between himself and Byron.

It was during this period, while wandering through Italy without a fixed home, that Shelley reached the full height of his genius. In 1818 he began writing his magnificent *Prometheus Unbound,* and in the next year finished it and wrote *The Cenci,* one of the finest poetical dramas in the English language. Now, too, he began to produce those lyrics which have made him known as the finest English lyric poet. The *Ode to the West Wind* belongs to 1819, and in the next year came *The Cloud, The Skylark, The Hymn of Pan, Arethusa,* and the *Song of Proserpine.*

Late in 1820 Shelley met, in the convent in which she was imprisoned, the beautiful Emilia Viviani, who inspired his *Epipsychidion.* "This poem," said Shelley, "is a mystery; as to real flesh and blood you know that I do not deal in those articles; you might as well go to a gin shop for a leg of mutton as expect anything human or earthly from me."

When Keats died in Rome in February, 1821, Shelley was enraged by the news, that was then rumoured, that he had been killed by adverse criticism of *Endymion.* In June, Shelley produced one of his finest poems, *Adonais,* an elegy on the death of Keats. Yet he knew Keats only slightly, and of his poems admired only *Hyperion.* Later in the year Shelley was inspired by the Greek War of Independence to write his lyrical drama, *Hellas.*

In the meantime he had been persuading Byron to help Leigh Hunt, who was always in trouble over money, and Byron offered to start a magazine to publish their joint works. Shelley sent money to Hunt and invited him to come to Italy at once. At this time he was living as Byron's neighbour at Pisa. He had made new friends in Edward Williams and his wife, Jane, and in Edward John Trelawney, who afterwards became one of his biographers.

In the spring of 1822 the Shelleys and the Williamses took a house together on the Bay of Spezzia. Shelley and Williams, who had once been in the navy, ordered a new boat, but when she was delivered, Trelawney did not like the look of her. As a member of the crew, Shelley, who could not swim, "was worse than useless. He was set to steer, and did so with a book in his hand, saying that 'he could read and steer at the same time, as one was mental and the other mechanical.' When Williams cried 'Luff,' he would put the helm the wrong way. Then he was put in charge of the main sheet. He was told to let it go, whereupon it jammed and the boat became unmanageable. His hat was knocked overboard, and he would have followed it if Trelawney had not held him. Then Williams blew him up, whereupon he put his beloved Plato in his pocket and gave his mind up to the fun and frolic."

During the early summer Shelley was alternately in high spirits or gloomy with forebodings about death, and many stories are told of his strange moods.

In June they heard that Leigh Hunt had arrived at Genoa, and Shelley and Williams sailed to Leghorn to meet him. On July 8, after a visit to Pisa with the Hunts, they set out to sail back in spite of warnings by the local sailors. They stood out of Leghorn early in the afternoon, and Trelawney watched them through a glass. In the evening a thunder squall broke. . . .

Ten days later a slight, tall body was washed up on the shore near Via Reggio; in one of the pockets of the jacket was a volume of Sophocles, in the other Keats's poems, opened and doubled back. Thus, in his youth, the poet of youth had died, drowned in the waters he had loved.

Trelawney, Leigh Hunt, and Byron made a funeral pyre and burned the body. Byron could not stand the sight and leaped into the sea to swim out to his yacht. Trelawney snatched the unburned heart from the flames.

And on the tomb at Rome in which Shelley's ashes were placed was carved:

"Nothing of him that doth fade,
But doth suffer a sea-change
Into something rich and strange."

GEORGE GORDON, LORD BYRON

(1788–1824)

That strange, wild, handsome lord, who made Childe Harold's pilgrimage, became the lion of London and its Don Juan, was thrown from his pedestal by a scandal of mystery and hounded from his country by public outcry, lived and loved with wild extravagance in Italy, scalded his enemies with satire and inflamed the youth of England with his poetry, flung himself into the cause of liberty, died a hero in the eyes of all Europe, and was compared at his death with Napoleon. Byron and Napoleon, said men, were the two greatest men of the century; the comparison was not inapt, for as Napoleon remoulded Europe, so Byron gave it a new pattern for its literature.

In the year 1785, while William, fifth Lord Byron, known to his servants and tenants as the "wicked lord," was amusing himself with toy ships and cockroach racing at Newstead Abbey, his nephew, "Mad Jack" Byron, married Catherine Gordon of Gight at Bath. It was not "Mad Jack's" first venture in matrimony. Ten years before he had seduced the wife of Lord Carmarthen, and she, when she had inherited a title and £4,000 a year from her father, had run away with him. Carmarthen divorced his wife; John Byron married her and took her to France, where a daughter, Augusta, was born. But in 1784, soon after Augusta's birth, her mother died, and John Byron was left without wife and income.

So he returned to the fashionable spa of Bath and there he met Catherine Gordon, the daughter of an ancient Scottish family, and, more important, an heiress. They were married on what is traditionally the unluckiest day of the unluckiest month, May 13, and on January 22, 1788, their son, George Gordon Byron, was born. Two years later, "Mad Jack," who had successfully ruined his wife, now reduced to living on £150 a year, borrowed some money from her and fled to France. Within twelve months he was dead—at the age of thirty-six.

Mrs. Byron, pathetic, generous and affectionate, but with a violent and uncontrollable temper, was left in Aberdeen with her little son. The boy, who appeared to inherit the violence and virtues of both sides of the family, had a malformation of one foot, which made him limp, and this lameness was the cause of much physical suffering in childhood and of mental anguish throughout his life.

Byron's first education was at a day school in Aberdeen. "I was sent, at five years old or earlier, to a school kept by a Mr. Bowers, who was called *Bodsy* Bowers, by reason of his dapperness. It was a school for both sexes. I learned little there except to repeat by rote the first lessons of monosyllables (God made man. Let us love Him), by hearing it often repeated without acquiring a letter. Whenever proof was made of my progress at home, I repeated these words with the most rapid fluency; but on turning over a new leaf I continued to repeat them, so that the narrow boundaries of my first year's accomplishments were detected, my ears boxed (which they did not deserve, seeing it was by ear only that I had acquired my letters), and my intellects consigned to a new preceptor. He was a very devout, clever little clergyman, named Ross. . . . Under him I made astonishing progress; and I recollect to this day his mild manners and good-natured painstaking. The moment I could read, my grand passion was history, and why I know not, but I was particularly taken with the battle near Lake Regillus in the Roman History put into my hands first. . . . Afterwards I had a very serious, saturnine, but kind young man named Paterson for a tutor. He was the son of my shoemaker, but a good scholar, as is common with the Scotch. He was a rigid Presbyterian also. With him I began Latin in Ruddiman's Grammar, and continued until I went to the grammar school."

In 1796, after an attack of scarlet fever, Byron was taken by his mother for a holiday in the Highlands, and there he acquired his great love of mountain scenery. At this time, too, he formed his first romantic attachment—to his cousin, Mary Duff. He was only eight at the time, yet he declared that eight years after, when he heard of her marriage, it "was like a thunderstroke; it nearly choked me, to the horror of my mother and the astonishment and almost incredulity of everybody."

When Byron was ten, his grand-uncle, the "wicked lord," died, and the boy succeeded to the barony. Newstead had been left in a state of ruin and decay, but Mrs. Byron was given a Civil List pension of £300 a year, while Byron was placed under the guardianship of his distant relative, Lord Carlisle.

Byron's foolish mother subjected him to the tortures of a Nottingham quack in an attempt to cure his lameness, and when that failed he was brought to London and sent to school at Dulwich.

But his mother alternately spoilt and abused the boy. "Byron," said one of his schoolmates, "your mother is a fool." "I know it," was the gloomy answer.

At last in 1801 he was sent to Harrow, where he was brilliantly lazy. He boxed, swam exceedingly well and, in spite of his foot, played in the cricket match against Eton in 1805. There is one well-known story of his schooldays which illustrates the chivalry of the small Byron. Robert Peel was being beaten by a school bully, when Byron, not strong enough to fight the torturer, came up to him with tears of indignation in his eyes and asked in a quivering voice how many stripes he was going to inflict. "Why, you little rascal, what's that to you?" was the reply. "Because, if you please," said Byron, "I would take half."

When he was on holiday, at the age of sixteen, Byron fell madly in love with Mary Ann Chaworth. But she, two years his senior, was already engaged, and Byron's forlorn suit made bitter changes in him.

From Harrow he went, in 1805, to Trinity College, Cambridge. He divided his time between the University, London, and his mother's home at Southwell, and lived a conventional life of extravagant dissipation. But he cultivated the friendship of Gentleman Jackson, the prizefighter, and under his training lost the fatness that had marred his beauty. He returned to Cambridge slim and handsome, healthy, with the appearance "of a beautiful alabaster vase lit from within."

Already he was amusing himself by writing verses, and in 1807 he published his first collection of poems under the title of *Hours of Idleness*. The talent displayed in them was mediocre, but promising, yet they provoked a violent attack in the columns of the *Edinburgh Review*. Byron, stung by the unfair criticism, sat down immediately to compose a retort, but after he had begun his poem he decided to wait and produce a really biting reply from the coolness of reflection; so it was a year later that his satire, *English Bards and Scotch Reviewers,* was published. It was an immediate success, and a second edition was called for a month after publication.

Meanwhile Byron had come of age, had taken his seat in the House of Lords, and was feasting his friends on a feudal scale at Newstead. His mother's violent temper had made their separation inevitable, but Byron had no intention of settling down at Newstead. He was well in debt, but he managed to borrow more money, and in June, 1809, he left London with his old Cambridge friend, John Hobhouse, for a journey to the East.

They sailed from Falmouth to Lisbon, where Byron swam the Tagus, thence by horseback to Cadiz and by sea again to Gibraltar. After a stay of three weeks in Malta, they crossed to the continent again and landed at Preveza for a tour of the wild and little-known country of Albania. The wild scenery and semi-barbarian people delighted Byron, and so did his reception by Ali Pasha, the bandit-despot, whose "first question was, why at so early an age I left my country, and without a 'lala' or nurse? He then said the English minister had told him I was of a great family, and desired his respects to my mother. . . . He said he was certain I was a man of birth, because I had small ears, curling hair and little white hands. He told me to consider him as a father while I was in Turkey, and said he looked on me as his son. Indeed he treated me like a child, sending me almonds, fruits and sweetmeats twenty times a day."

The amiable bandit, who was a neat hand at poisoning and torture, provided the travellers with an armed escort, and while he travelled on towards Greece, Byron began writing the poem that tells the story of the tour, *Childe Harold*.

At last he reached, for the first time, Missolonghi, and then on to Patras, Delphi, Thebes, and finally Athens. In the memories and the association of Attica, Byron found inspiration, yet he seemed little moved by the remnants of Grecian grandeur. "Very like the Mansion House," he said of the Parthenon.

After three months at Athens, the travellers sailed to Smyrna, where Byron finished the second canto of *Childe Harold*. His companion, Hobhouse, thought very little of it. On his way from Smyrna to Constantinople Byron swam the Hellespont from Sestos to Abydos in company with Lieutenant Ekenhead. He was tremendously proud of the feat and of his emulation of Leander—"I plume myself over this achievement more than I could possibly do on any kind of glory, political, poetical or rhetorical."

From Constantinople Hobhouse returned to England and Byron went back to Greece, where he composed the *Hints from Horace* and the *Curse of Minerva*. At last creditors and lawyers demanded his return to England, and he arrived in London in July, 1811. On August 1, before he had seen her, his mother died at Newstead.

Byron placed the manuscript of his *Hints from Horace* in the hands of his friend, Dallas, who was frankly disappointed in it. "Have you no other result of your travels?" he asked, and Byron replied, "A few short pieces, and a lot of Spenserian stanzas, not worth troubling you with, but you are welcome to them." And with that he gave him the first two cantos of *Childe Harold*. Dallas immediately saw their worth and took them to John Murray, the publisher.

On February 27, 1812, Byron made his maiden speech in the House of Lords against the proposal to inflict the death penalty on the frame-breakers of Nottingham. The speech attracted some attention. Two days later the first and second cantos of *Childe Harold* appeared. The poem took the town by storm. Seven editions were sold in a month. "I awoke one morning and found myself famous," wrote Byron.

London society opened its doors to the romantic author, whose pale beauty was as much admired as his poetry. The lonely young man became the lion of society, and at once plunged into a series of love affairs—with Lady Caroline Lamb, with Lady Oxford, and, it seems indubitable, with his own half-sister, Augusta.

Meanwhile he was pouring out poems and verse romances, which were seized upon by the public as fast as they appeared. *The Waltz* was published in April, 1813, *The Giaour* in May, and *The Bride of Abydos* in December. In the following year came *The Corsair, Lara* and the *Hebrew Melodies*.

In January, 1815, Byron married Annabella Milbanke, an heiress cousin of Lady Caroline Lamb. He had first proposed to her in 1813 and had been refused, but in September, 1814, they were betrothed. The marriage is one of the mysteries of Byron's story—he was not in love with his wife and the money he stood to gain was not considerable. The match was foredoomed to disaster. In December a daughter, Augusta Ada, was born; five weeks later Lady Byron left her husband never to return.

The mystery of the separation has been argued and disputed since the time it occurred, and a volume could be written about it without producing a clear conclusion. But one clear result the separation did produce—a violent public outcry. Indignant in its ignorance, the Press, the pamphleteers and the people attacked Byron in the fiercest terms. Bankrupt—and yet he still refused to accept money from his publisher, for he felt it beneath him to publish for profit—and an object of hatred to all except a few constant friends like Hobhouse, he was hounded from the country. In April, 1816, Byron set out once more on his travels: *Childe Harold* resumed his pilgrimage.

He landed at Ostend and travelled to Geneva, where he met his last mistress in England, Claire Clairmont, who had travelled with her half-sister, Mary Godwin, and Mary's lover, Shelley. With all their differences of character and ideals, the two poets were attached to each other and recognised each other's greatness.

With Shelley he toured Lake Geneva, during which time he wrote the *Prisoner of Chillon*. In July he finished the third canto of *Childe Harold,* poured out half a dozen shorter poems, and began *Manfred*. When the Shelleys and Claire returned to England in August, Byron made a short tour of the Alps with Hobhouse and wandered through northern Italy, finally settling at Venice. Here he lived in magnificence and loved with prodigality, but still he worked: *Beppo, Mazeppa* and the first two cantos of *Don Juan* were the products of his Venice days.

Claire Clairmont had borne a daughter, Allegra, in 1817, and when she accompanied the Shelleys to Italy in the following year, Allegra was sent to Byron. He despised and disliked the mother, but he received the child and placed her in a convent. Her mother's desire for the child, and her request that she should be placed with a family in a more healthy climate than that of the Romagna, a request which was supported by Shelley, met with cold refusals; but when, in 1822, the girl died, Byron was genuinely grieved.

It was in the spring of 1819 that Byron met the Countess Guiccioli. She was the very young wife of a sixty-year-old nobleman. She became Byron's mistress in Venice and when she left with her husband for Ravenna she summoned her lover to follow. And from Ravenna he followed her to Bologna, escorted her thence to La Mira, near Venice, where he scandalized the neighbourhood by living with her until the indignant count appeared. The countess smoothed matters over, departed with her husband for Ravenna, and in a few months summoned Byron once more! In July, 1820, matters came to a head. A Papal decree of separation was made, and the countess retired to live with her father, Count Gamba, at Ravenna.

In the next year, while he was writing *Sardanapalus* and *Cain,* Byron was plotting with members of the Gamba family against the Austrian power, but the prospective revolt came to nothing. Byron could not be touched, but the Gamba family were banished. Meanwhile *Cain* had raised a storm in England and was violently attacked by the defenders of religious orthodoxy.

We have two clear pictures of Byron at this time. His old friend, Tom Moore, the poet, visited him at Venice in 1819 and wrote that he "had grown fatter, both in person and in face, and the latter had suffered most by the change, having lost, by the enlargement of the features, some of that refined and spiritualized look that had in other times distinguished it, but although less romantic, he appeared more humorous." And Shelley, who came to Byron at Ravenna in the summer of 1821, remarked that "Lord B. is greatly improved in every respect—in genius, in temper, in moral views, in health and in happiness. His connexion with La Guiccioli has been an inestimable benefit to him. He lives in considerable splendour, but within his income. . . ."

Towards the end of the year Byron followed his mistress to Pisa, where he had the Shelleys for neighbours. Shelley admired Byron the poet, Byron liked Shelley the man. Trelawney joined the group and then came Leigh Hunt and his family, who had been invited out to Italy by Shelley. The idea was that Byron and Hunt were to start a magazine together, and Shelley had already prevailed on Byron to send money to the impoverished Hunts.

After Shelley's tragic death, Byron, with the Hunts (there were six children), removed to Genoa. Their magazine, the *Liberal,* published in London, was a failure, and the two men, who had nothing in common and hardly knew each other, quarrelled; yet Byron kept the Hunts until they left Genoa in 1823.

Meanwhile he had resumed work on *Don Juan,* which had been laid aside at the request of La Guiccioli, and was pouring out the successive cantos of his masterpiece.

In Greece the War of Independence against the Turks was being fiercely waged, and Byron, inspired by the vision of liberty for the country that gave liberty to the world, flung himself into the cause. He corresponded with the Greek Committee in London, placed his money generously at the disposal of the fighters, and in July, 1823, he embarked for Greece.

His courage, his generosity, his clear thinking and his name were an inspiration to the Greek rebels—but the end was near. A few months after joining Prince Mavrocordato at Missolonghi, his health gave way, he contracted a fever, and on April 19 the cry went forth in Missolonghi and echoed through the mourning land of Greece, "Byron is dead."

So died this strange, generous, romantic figure, who had blazed like a meteor through Europe. His poetry had hit the mood of the moment—no poet has made a greater material success in his own lifetime—his genius inspired the literature of Europe: Hugo, Lamartine, Heine, Pushkin revered him as their master; and today we turn to him for his colour and above all for his masterly satire. His greatness, like that of Scott, lies as much in his influence as in his matter, and no figure looms larger in the history of European literature of the nineteenth century than that of George Gordon, Lord Byron.

WILLIAM BLAKE

(1757–1827)

An artist whose designs and drawings are breathtaking in their magnificent conception; a poet whose lyrical sweetness and purity is unsurpassed in our language: that is William Blake as we know him. Add to that the lost Blake—the complete artist who sang his poems to his own settings, printed and engraved his own works, bound and published them; and the inspired mystic, fighting for his own vision of beauty and art, a brave man struggling against poverty and neglect—and you have a picture of one of the finest and rarest figures that has graced the art and literature of England.

It is probable that everyone has attempted, in youth, to become a poet, and the verses of childhood and adolescence soon feed the flames of every kitchen fire. But there could be no doubt of the genius of the boy who sang at the age of thirteen:

> " How sweet I roam'd from field to field
> And tasted all the summer's pride,
> Till I the prince of love beheld,
> Who in the sunny beams did glide!
>
> He shew'd me lilies for my hair,
> And blushing roses for my brow;
> He led me through his gardens fair
> Where all his golden pleasures grow.
>
> With sweet May dew my wings were wet,
> And Phœbus fir'd my vocal rage;
> He caught me in his silken net,
> And shut me in his golden cage.
>
> He loves to sit and hear me sing,
> Then, laughing, sports and plays with me;
> Then stretches out my golden wing,
> And mocks my loss of liberty."

The boy who wrote this poem was William Blake, who "became an artist at the age of ten, and a poet at the age of twelve." Already his imagination, the imagination that crowded his life with visions as vivid as reality, was leaping ahead to illuminate the way for his talent.

"The first time you ever saw God," his wife later recalled for him, "was when you were four years old, and He put His head to the window and set you screaming." From that time his visions became regular occurrences. On the return from one of his childhood walks he told his mother that he had seen the prophet Ezekiel under a tree: she was shocked and beat the boy. But when on another occasion he came home from Peckham and told how he had seen a tree filled with angels, she stopped his father from thrashing Blake for telling lies.

That Blake understood the true significance and value of his visions is clear from his own attitude towards them. When, late in life, he was drawing the *Spiritual Portraits,* he said: "You can see what I do if you choose. Work up imagination to the state of vision, and the thing is done." Once Blake's supersensitive imagination is related to the early influences of his home life and apprenticeship, it is not difficult to understand his development as an artist-mystic.

William Blake was born on November 28, 1757, the third child of James Blake, a hosier, of Broad Street, Golden Square, London. James Blake was a dissenter and a believer in Swedenborg, and his religious theories naturally coloured the boy's early learning, especially as William was never sent to school. James and Catherine Blake seemed to have been intelligent and helpful in bringing up William. As soon as they realized from his accounts of his visions that he was an unusual child, they determined not to send him to school where he would be at the mercy of uncomprehending and impatient ushers. So William Blake learned his reading and writing at home, and his undisciplined reading soon fired his own imagination to imitative composition.

His father naturally intended William for the shop, but the boy quickly manifested a talent for drawing, and he was more interested in making sketches on the backs of bills than in selling socks. Mrs. Blake encouraged his love of art, and again the father showed himself anxious to be helpful. He sent the ten-year-old William to Par's drawing school, in the Strand.

Par's school was recognized as the best of the day, and there Blake remained for four years, drawing from the antique. In his spare time he wrote poems and, helped by his father, collected prints. He would take the pocket money James had given him to the

This painting by Fournier (*above*) depicts Byron, Leigh Hunt and Trelawney, all friends of Percy Bysshe Shelley, watching the funeral pyre of the dead poet.

The Greek philosopher, Socrates, is shown (*below*) about to take hemlock in this drawing for a painting by the celebrated French artist David.

Sir Thomas More, Lord Chancellor of England, lawyer and author of *Utopia,* with his family and household drawn by Holbein (*above*).
Possibly the proudest moment of American statesman, scientist and philosopher, Benjamin Franklin, was the signing of the Declaration of Independence. He stands to the right of the group at the table (*below*).

auction sales of old prints at Christies' and Longford's. Longford "called him his little connoisseur, and often knocked down to him a cheap lot with friendly precipitation." The poems he wrote between the ages of twelve and twenty were printed in 1783 under the title *Poetical Sketches*. The lyric quoted is a fine example of their quality.

When he was fourteen years old Blake was apprenticed to James Basire, the engraver. Tatham in his *Life of Blake* gives the reason for this move: "His love of art increasing, and the time of life having arrived when it was deemed necessary to place him under some tutor, a painter of eminence was proposed, and necessary applications made; but from the huge premium required, he requested, with his characteristic generosity, that his father would not on any account spend so much money on him, as he thought it would be an injustice to his brothers and sisters. He therefore himself proposed engraving as being less expensive, and sufficiently eligible for his future avocation. Of Basire, therefore, for a premium of fifty guineas, he learnt the art of engraving."

Basire was engraver to the Society of Antiquaries, and he taught Blake a respect for strict form and severe outline in drawing, imposing a discipline on his art which was lacking in his writing. Basire sent Blake out to copy monuments in Westminster Abbey and old city churches, with the result that Blake came completely under the influence of Gothic art. Says Mr. Osbert Burdett: "Lost in the corners of these old churches, Blake's romantic imagination was completely Gothicized, and for the future he completely closed his mind to every other influence or interpreted it by the light of these impressions, for which he had been unconsciously prepared by the religious atmosphere of his home." And again: "His active mind was besieged in his boyhood by the symbolism of the Abbey, and it is to his lonely hours within its peopled walls that we can trace the origin and leanings of his later mysticism."

Blake's apprenticeship lasted until 1778, and then he became a student in the antique school at the recently founded Royal Academy. At the same time he began making engravings for London booksellers. The year 1780 was a busy one for Blake: he met Stothard, the artist, who introduced him to Flaxman, and made another friend in the painter, Fuseli; he exhibited for the first time at the Royal Academy with a water-colour, "Death of Earl Godwin"; and he was accidentally involved in the Gordon Riots.

And now he fell in love. Her name was Polly Wood, and she was "a lively little girl." Too lively, in fact; for she liked the society of men, and when Blake remonstrated with her, she laughed at him. The sensitive Blake was upset at his treatment and retired for a holiday to Battersea, where he stayed with a market-gardener named William Boucher. Boucher's daughter, Catherine, was of a very different stamp from Polly Wood. She was modest and demure, yet when she saw Blake for the first time she at once recognized him as her future husband and had to leave the room to recover from the faintness that overwhelmed her.

Blake poured out his story to her and she heard it with obvious emotion. He noticed the effect that his tale had had, and blurted out: "Do you pity me?" "Indeed, I do." "Then I love you," he said.

With that he returned to London to earn the money for a home, and a year later, on August 18, 1782, they were married in the village of Battersea, and settled down at Green Street, Leicester Fields. Mrs. Blake had chosen the most difficult and thankless of all lives—that of wife to a genius: she managed it with such devotion, sympathy and tact, and adapted herself so admirably to the ways of her extraordinary husband that it may be said that in its own way her genius was no less than his.

Flaxman, the designer and sculptor, was a neighbour of the Blakes, and he introduced them to the Reverend Henry Mathew and his wife. Mathew was a patron of the arts and Mrs. Mathew a bluestocking: Blake was welcomed at their parties, where he recited or sang his own poems. He was the complete artist, for he set his songs to music of his own composition, and sang them.

Mrs. Mathew persuaded her husband to share with Flaxman the cost of printing Blake's poems. This was done, and in 1783 the printed sheets of *Poetical Sketches,* unbound, were presented to Blake for distribution as he wished.

A year later Blake moved to Broad Street, next door to the hosier's shop now kept by his brother, James, and set up as a print-seller in partnership with James Parker, having his own brother, Robert, as a voluntary apprentice. The firm lasted until the death of Robert in 1787, and then broke up. Blake removed to Poland Street, and from there, in 1789, he published his *Songs of Innocence.*

This work was not only remarkable for the beauty and purity of its lyrics; it was also Blake's first piece of illuminated printing. By this new method—Blake's own invention—"the text and the surrounding design were written in reverse in a medium impervious to acid upon small copper plates about five inches by three, which were then etched in a bath of aqua-fortis until the work stood in relief as in a stereotype. From these plates, which to economize copper were, in many cases, engraved upon both sides, impressions were printed, in the ordinary manner, in tints made to harmonize with the colour scheme afterwards applied by the artist."

In this way William Blake and his wife printed, bound, coloured, and published the works which he wrote and illustrated. The true beauty of the work lay in the interdependence of design and matter.

"The text and the illustration," writes Mr. Burdett, "are interwoven into a harmonious whole, and as the colour can be varied no two copies need be exactly alike. Little but the use of a press distinguishes the books so made from illuminated manuscripts, and the etching in reverse makes the new method even more laborious than the old. . . . Only those who have compared his originals with the printed pages in which his poems are ordinarily read are fully aware of the loss now suffered by his writings, which require to be read as much by the eye as by the mind on pages suffused with life and colour."

Songs of Innocence and its companion book, *Songs of Experience,* which appeared in 1794, contain Blake's finest lyrics. They have a rare simplicity and a purity that is not matched by any other poet.

But besides the two volumes of lyrics, Blake was writing and engraving tracts and the first of those works known as the Prophetical Books. *There is No Natural Religion* and *All Religions are One,* two tracts consisting of short propositions in prose, came out in 1788. In the same year he wrote *Tiriel,* followed in 1789 by *The Book of Thel.* Working furiously, he produced in rapid succession *The Marriage of Heaven and Hell, The Vision of the Daughters of Albion, The Book of Urizen, The Book of Los,* and *The Book of Ahania.* Much ink has been spilled on the significance and value of these prophetical works, in which Blake, using a mythology of his own, pours out poetry cloudy with grandeur.

While he was writing and decorating his own works, Blake was engraving for Johnson, the bookseller, to whom he had been introduced by Fuseli. Johnson was Godwin's publisher and a friend of Thomas Paine; at his house Blake met a circle of sympathizers with the French Revolution, and Blake himself wore the red cap in the street.

In 1793 Blake had moved to Lambeth, where he took pupils "of high rank." As a result, he was offered the position of drawing master to the royal family, which he promptly refused, at the same time dismissing, with a grand gesture of courtesy, his own pupils.

This loss of income, and the decline in demand for his engraving, brought the Blakes to extreme poverty, from which he was saved in 1799 by Thomas Butts. Butts was a remarkable man; he was a patron who believed in the genius of Blake and who was willing to buy whatever that genius produced. From 1799 he bought Blake's work steadily, and by doing so saved the artist from starvation.

Another patron came into Blake's life at this period. He was William Hayley, a fashionable poet of no talent and a country squire. Blake was introduced to him by Flaxman, and it was arranged that Blake should do the engravings for a *Life of Cowley* which Hayley was writing. He was invited to live at Felpham, and so he took a cottage near his new patron's home, and there he lived for three years, from 1800 to 1803.

While he was there Blake worked hard at miniature painting, at the heads of the poets for Hayley's library (they are now in the Manchester Art Gallery), and at illustrating Hayley's ballads and his Cowper. But it was not to be expected that the passionate poet could live long under the patronage of an urbane platitudinarian such as Hayley: the break came in 1803, but not before Hayley had helped to save Blake from an absurd charge of sedition brought by a soldier whom he had turned out of his cottage garden.

Once more in London, Blake again set to work on prophetic books and in 1804 engraved *Jerusalem* and *Milton*. The preface to the latter contains that magnificent lyric, beginning:

> "And did those feet in ancient time
> Walk upon England's mountains green:
> And was the holy Lamb of God
> On England's pleasant pastures seen!"

A year later Blake was made the victim of a shabby trick by Cromek, an engraver, who, writes Blake, "came to me desiring to have some of my designs; he named his price and wished me to produce him illustrations of *The Grave,* a poem by Robert Blair; in consequence of this I produced about twenty designs, which pleased so well that he, with the same liberality with which he set me about the drawing, has now set me to engrave them."

But, at the last moment, Cromek handed Blake's designs to the more fashionable engraver, Schiavonetti, and all Blake received was twenty guineas for the designs. Meanwhile, Cromek saw a drawing by Blake of Chaucer's *Canterbury Pilgrims,* and asked him for a finished design, but Blake refused to sell it unless the commission included the engraving. Then Cromek went to Stothard, suggested the subject to him, and commissioned him to paint it for sixty guineas. The picture was exhibited in 1807, and created great interest. In 1809 Blake held an exhibition of his own works, and published his *Descriptive Catalogue,* perhaps his most important prose work, in which he gives his views on art.

The worthy Butts bought Blake's *Canterbury Pilgrimage,* and he also ordered the *Inventions to Job,* Blake's greatest engravings. John Linnell, a rising young painter, ordered a duplicate set of these and also a series of designs for *Dante.* At this time Blake became acquainted with John Varley, for whom he drew the spiritual portraits. Varley would say : "Draw me Julius Cæsar." And Blake would look up and answer: "There he is," and begin drawing as from a living model. Sometimes he would stop, and say: "I can't go on; it has gone," or "It has moved, the mouth has gone." So they would go on, with Blake drawing far into the night.

In the last years of his life a little group of artists gathered round Blake like disciples. Linnell, who made use of his own success to help Blake in his poverty; Tatham, Calvert, Richmond and Palmer were the friends who were inspired by his genius. Palmer has left a vivid picture of Blake as an old man:

"His eye was the finest I ever saw: brilliant, not roving, clear and intent; yet susceptible; it flashed with genius, or melted in tenderness. It could also be terrible. Cunning and falsehood quailed under it, but it was never busy with them. It pierced them and turned away. Nor was the mouth less expressive; the lips flexible and quivering with feeling. I yet recall it when, on one occasion, dwelling upon the exquisite parable of the Prodigal, he began to repeat a part of it; but at the words: 'When he was yet a great way off, his father saw him' could go no further; his voice faltered and he was in tears. . . . He saw everything through art, and in matters beyond its range exalted it from a witness into a judge."

Blake went on working in his rooms at Fountain Court in the Strand until the very end. When failing health compelled him to take to his bed, he still continued with the designs for *Dante.* In December, 1826, he heard of the death of his old friend, Flaxman, and remarked: "I thought I should have gone first," and, after a pause, "I cannot think of death as more than the going out of one room into another."

As he lay in bed in August, 1827, he cried suddenly to his wife: "Stay as you are! You have been ever an angel to me; I will draw you." He seized his pencil and began: It was almost exactly forty-five years since their wedding day. But Blake was sinking. He lay back in the bed composing and singing songs to God. And thus singing, he died "like a saint," on the evening of August 12, 1827. His wife, whose love and loyalty is as inspiring as her husband's inspirations, was provided for by the kindly Linnell, and lived until October 18, 1831.

Thus died William Blake, designer, poet, mystic. And since his death the little circle that knew of his works has widened until today we know and proclaim him as one of the supreme artists that the world has produced.

RABINDRANATH TAGORE

(1861–1941)

To the peoples of the world outside India there have appeared to be two great leaders of India's millions during the twentieth century. One is the politician Mohandas Gandhi, the other, the poet Rabindranath Tagore. But Rabindranath was more than a writer of verses; he, too, was a politician and a patriot. His efforts to further the well-being of his countrymen sprang from his overwhelming desire to help them to perfect world citizenship, and his support of the nationalist movement lay more in its promise of social reform than its political freedom. An extensive and tireless traveller, his personal dignity and burning sincerity did much to enlist the sympathy of the world for the cause of India's self-government.

IN India the Sanskrit word *Kabi* is generally accepted as denoting a poet, but the word, correctly interpreted, does not mean a person who, having been endowed with high powers of imagination and expression, is purely and simply a writer in verse; it means a seer, an enlightened and wise person. And Rabindranath Tagore was much more than a mere versifier having high powers of imagination and expression; he was a *Kabi* in the strictest sense of the term. It is undoubtedly true that, in the course of his long life of eighty-one years he wrote magnificent verse, songs, dramas and other works in prose, yet the real impression that his life and works give of him is not that of a poet but of a prophet, a searching but serene spirit in a tumultuous world, which he was ever striving to calm by pouring in ceaselessly the messages of truth. He travelled extensively, visited many lands and peoples, studied deeply their different principles of philosophy and life, enriched his various experiences with life-long contemplation, and gave out to the world the wealth of his wisdom that " the wakeful ageless God calls today on our soul—the soul that is measureless, the soul that is undefeated, the soul that is destined to immortality and yet the soul which today lies in the dust."

Rabindranath Tagore was able to trace his ancestors as far back as the eleventh century, when the family line was founded by a native Brahmin of Kanauj, named Bhattanarayna, who, as the leader of a group of five Brahmins, was sent by the King of Kanauj to Bengal at the request of King Adisura, of Bengal, to assist him in a sacrificial ceremony in or about the year A.D. 1072.

The poet was born on May 6, 1861, in Bengal, a province which was, at that time, the most progressive in India. At the beginning of the nineteenth century Raja Rammohan Roy, himself a native of Bengal, and a man of great vision and versatility, had inaugurated a movement that was destined to enliven every aspect of Indian life and to rouse his fellow countrymen to action. Rammohan Roy directed his energies chiefly towards the reformation of religion; as a Hindu Brahmin himself he was keenly aware of the decadence which had developed and which he wished to modify. Like other religious reformers before and after he was forced into the position of initiating a schism within the Hindu fold. The new faith which he propounded was called Brahmoism, and was based on liberal ideas which he gleaned from Christianity, Islam and the ancient Hindu religio-philosophic literature.

His zeal in the field of politics, literature and social reform was also remarkable in that he helped to revive the interest of Indians in themselves and their country. Rammohan might fairly be said to have laid the foundations of modern Indian thought and ideals, and he was certainly among the first of those Indians responsible for directing the consciousness of intellectual and artistic men towards the development of a new Indian culture, of which Rabindranath Tagore was both a disciple and an apostle.

Rabindranath's family was closely associated with Rammohan, and after the latter's death his task was taken up by one of his most competent and sound lieutenants, Prince Dwarkanath Tagore, the poet's grandfather. However, it was Devendranath Tagore, the poet's father, who was responsible for bringing Rammohan's religious reformation to maturity. Devendranath was given the title of *Maharshi* (the great sage) for his profound religious nature and activities.

This, then, was the family and cultural background of Rabindranath, youngest son of Devendranath. The boy, in his childhood, was brought up strictly; attempts to send him to school failed, for it was found that the conventional type of discipline and education cramped his already independent spirit. He was driven more and more into mental reflection, and having no access to the world beyond the walls of the grounds of his home, he used to spend much of his time in a quiet garden adjoining the house. The natural beauty of the garden was a source of joy to the little boy and infused in him a spirit of serenity and, even at that early age, an idea of the grace and harmony that reign in the universe. Private lessons were regularly imparted to him at home, and as the Tagore family was one of the most progressive and cultured families in Bengal, and as Devendranath, the head of the family, was the pillar of the new faith, it attracted enlightened people from all parts of the country. Rabindranath was brought up in this cultured atmosphere, and came into contact with many people. Once his father, who was constantly away from home in his journeys to the Himalayas, proposed to take him there. The close company of the father served to intensify the latent sympathetic and mystical temperament of the boy, and he soon came to learn and understand the ancient wisdom of India.

The early impression of the *Upanishad* (the religio-philosophical literature of India) which he received under the tutelage of his father stirred him so much that later on he became a poet of the *Upanishad*, his ideas and works being thoroughly permeated with the spirit of the sacred literature. The elder brothers of Rabindranath were men of great talent, and so were the women of the household. They gave the boy every encouragement in self-development, and never clipped his poetic wings. Rabindranath read extensively the works of the medieval mystics and the *Vaishnav* poets of India. These, along with some of the contemporary lyricists of Bengal, considerably influenced him in his boyhood.

On September 20, 1877, he sailed for England for the first time, with his second brother, with the intention of studying law there, but the profession did not appeal to him and he returned to India after a stay of only one year. Bengal at this time was an awakened province, and was animated with new ideas and a new spirit in religion, literature and politics. Rabindranath entered the scene with the incentive to create a new art and new standards. One break with the past had already occurred, but Rabindranath broke away completely from the still conservative traditions, and inaugurated a fresh era of literary activity. His works at this period, though not quite mature, were full of life and showed promise of further development. The clarity of his writing and the simplicity of thought of his earlier poems fascinated the younger generation and he came to be quite a prominent figure in Bengali literary circles. He was criticized with intense hostility by powerful and conservative writers, but this only served to rouse in him the urge for further creative activity. At this point it is necessary to mention a collection of poems which he wrote at the age of about twenty-two, and which were published under the name of "Song of the Morning" (*Prabhat Sangeet*). The poems in this book were a witness to the joy of life which suddenly one morning flashed into his heart, and they mark a distinct stage in the development of his poetic faculties. For in them was revealed the intense delight which a poet both discovers and enjoys at the revelation of the identification of his soul with the natural and beautiful. The same mystic perception of the sense of communion with the vast and grand natural world became more and more distinct, deep and calm as he grew older, and enriched his works with the wealth of perfect sincerity, penetration and harmony. The closing years of the nineteenth century saw the poet in the full vigour and ebullience of youth, completely immersed in the joy of his ever-developing power and in giving realization to his perceptions in the form of poetry, drama and novels.

Bengal, at this time, was bubbling with new life. In addition to the new religious and literary movements the province was showing signs of organized nationalist upheaval as the result of the growing political consciousness. This, in turn, was due to the deplorable social and economic condition of Bengal, and the increased knowledge of the West through the medium of the English language. Being imbued with nationalist aspirations, Rabindranath flung himself into the political arena, and used his pen with increased vigour to write political poems, songs and essays. A few lines from a speech which he delivered on the occasion of a Hindu festival show the strength of his political feelings and his idealistic attachment to his country: "In this meeting there is no sweetness alone, there is the heat of the blazing flame. It is not the satisfaction alone, it gives strength. Whether the people of England listen to our piteous cries or do not listen, our country is our country eternally, the land of our fathers and our sons and descendants, the giver of life to us, the giver of strength, the giver of good."

The political movement reached a critical stage following the proposal and execution of the plan to partition Bengal in 1905, and Rabindranath rushed headlong into the fray. As a result of that his writing at this period was saturated with politics.

The year 1901 was very important in his life. It saw the foundation of his school, Santiniketan (The Peace Retreat) at Bolpur. He became the editor of the old and famous Bengali literary journal *Bangadarshan*, at one time edited by Bankim Chatterji, a famous literary personality of the nineteenth century in Bengal. The intention behind his establishment of the school at Bolpur was to form the nucleus of a cultural organization based on the model of the ancient Indian forest schools which, through the imparting of education, would gradually become a centre of international culture. Here, in such a school, was evolved his conception of the perfect world citizen. The world, he had found, was full of sound scholars but not of sound men, and it was with the purpose of bringing out sound men that his school was started. According to his teaching the sound man should come before the sound scholar. This spiritual attitude was made abundantly clear in all his works and was the mainspring of his life.

In 1902 his wife died, and Rabindranath retired from his many organized activities to the serene solitude of the Himalayas with his children. The years 1907 to 1912 were rich in his literary activities. In 1909 appeared the famous *Gitanjali* ("Song Offering"). In the year following he made an attempt to revive the Brahmoism which, by that time, probably owing to the impact of political forces, had lost its former importance. Moreover, a schism had already divided the followers of Brahmoism into three camps opposing each other on some doctrinal and social questions. Rabindranath strove, however, to unify the three but failed just when he was within sight of success. He then returned to his school at Bolpur, where he remained in quiet meditation for a year, only to emerge as an international figure.

He came to England with his *Gitanjali* which had already been translated into English, and there he made the acquaintance of W. B. Yeats. In 1912 the India Society published the translation of *Gitanjali* with an introduction by Yeats. What Yeats, himself a poet of great sensibility, perception and imagination, wrote in the introduction is a witness to the value and quality of *Gitanjali*:

"I have carried the manuscript of this translation about with me for days, reading it in railway trains, or on the top of omnibuses, and in restaurants, and I have often had to close it lest some stranger would see how much it moved me. These lyrics . . . displayed in their thought the world I had dreamed of all my life long. The work of a supreme culture, they yet appear as much the growth of the common soil as the grass and the rushes."

Rabindranath was awarded the Nobel prize for literature in 1913, and a shower of honours followed that. An honorary Doctorate was conferred upon him by the University of Calcutta in the same year. In 1914 he was knighted.

In 1919, in protest against the Amritzar massacre in the Punjab, Rabindranath renounced his title, but although the renunciation was declined he himself never used his title again.

In 1921 he opened Viswabharati at Bolpur, turning his original Santiniketan into a world university. An invitation came from Oxford in 1928 to deliver the Hibbert lectures. This he accepted but could not deliver the lectures on that occasion owing to illness. He visited Russia in 1931 and wrote a book on the impressions he gathered about the life and thought of the people.

In 1940 he received from Oxford University the degree of D.Litt. in a special convocation held in Santiniketan. The honour seemed a little belated.

His death occurred on August 7, 1941. Thinking men throughout the world paid tributes to his work as poet and educationist, humanist and artist, social reformer and philosopher. The position of Rabindranath Tagore might be summed up in the words of Shelley: "A poet participates in the eternal, the infinite and the one. . . . It is impossible to read the compositions of the most celebrated writers of the present day without being startled with the electric life which burns in their works. Poets are the hierophants of an unapprehended inspiration . . . the unacknowledged legislators of the world."

LEADERS AND REFORMERS

GAUTAMA BUDDHA

(*c.* 560–480 B.C.)

Of the great religions of the world, some 1,000,000,000 *people are adherents of Christianity and* 300,000,000 *of Buddhism. In spite of the often-made comparisons between the two faiths, they are basically dissimilar, and so, too, were their founders, Jesus and Gautama. Yet in the Christian religion of love and in the Buddhist Rule of Life, based on unbounded Love for Mankind and personal salvation from suffering, sacrifice of their founders, and broad and all-embracing humanity, there are many points of contact and fellowship. So, too, in the fleeting yet surer glimpses that the Buddhist scriptures give us of Gautama, there seem to be easily recognizable outlines of the Personality of Jesus—the first thus being the commencement and the latter being the flowering of human perfection.*

THE son of a princeling of the Sakya, or warrior caste, which ranks second in the four great divisions of Hindu society, Gautama Buddha was probably born about the year 560 B.C., and, reared in an aristocratic home, lived a life of luxurious ease throughout his youth and early manhood.

At what period his mind first became troubled, when first he found the futility of the pleasures of the senses and was confronted with the problem of suffering, we cannot say, but certain it is that it was on the birth of his son that Gautama, then twenty-nine years of age, took the decision that was to alter the whole course of his life, and along with him eventually to revolutionize religious thought in the Orient.

On that day it was revealed to him that he must leave home and wife and child and, divesting himself of all worldly possessions, concentrate his thoughts upon the ultimate realities of life. He did not reach this decision without much struggle of spirit, nor was the parting easy.

Waking in the dead of night, his mind fully made up, he yet could not resist the impulse to take one last look at his wife and child. As he gazed upon them sleeping sweetly amid heaped-up flowers, the gifts of those who had gathered for the natal feast, a burning desire came upon him once more to clasp his infant son in his arms. Yet he would not, lest he wake his wife; so, conquering desire, he crept silently away, mounted his horse and rode into the darkness.

Far from his native land he wandered, travelling across the fertile Ganges plains till he came to the tree-covered spurs of the Vindhya hills that separate Hindustan from the barren uplands of the Deccan, the "land of the south." Here he lived for six years, seeking wisdom by the direst penances of the ascetic practised as a rule throughout the length and breadth of India.

He shaved his hair and his beard, put on the yellow garments of the wandering friars, and subjected his body to exhausting fasts and every known form of physical mortification. With five disciples he lived alone in the jungle, striving through self-discipline and torture of the body to achieve through certainty of mind unqualified peace.

He became known far and wide as a pure man, yet the truth he sought seemed distant as ever until one day, on waking from a fainting fit brought on by his extreme asceticism, light came like a flash to his mind. All this fasting and refraining from leading a normal life, this suppression of the breath and the like was leading him nowhere, was producing nothing but increased enfeeblement of mind as well as of body. To be able to ensure unclouded reason, flawless thinking, surveying the processes of thought, and acquire clarity of vision and unadulterated experience, a man must normally have proper food and lead a healthy life.

Thrilled by his discovery, Gautama hastened to share it with his five disciples. But they, when they heard their revered master renounce the ascetic life and demand food, were so shocked and horrified by a suggestion revolting to all their preconceived ideas, that to a man they deserted him. The day that followed was pregnant with consequence to the Eastern world. Left to himself, Gautama wandered through the forests of Gaya, now called Bihar, till he came to the banks of the River Neranjara, where he sat down in the shade of a spreading bo-tree or wild fig. There a lady presented him with a dish of milk and he partook of it and was sufficiently invigorated to carry on his search.

And there, after enduring hour upon hour of fiercest mental and spiritual anguish, after ranging through every emotion known to man, from blackest despair to sublimest hope, Gautama found at last the peace and certainty he sought. Truth was revealed to him; he became the Buddha, the Enlightened One.

The joy of his discovery was at first so overwhelming that he was tempted to keep it to himself, to spend the remainder of his life in happy solitude and to share with no one the bliss achieved at so great a cost. But so selfish a desire could not long possess the heart of one who had reached ultimate truth only by sublimation of all human craving, and soon the Buddha was on the road to Benares, inspired to impart to all men the realization which possessed him.

In the precincts of the city he sought out his late disciples. Quickly they became again his devoted followers, for he spoke to them with a dignity and calm confidence, a tranquil and serene assurance, that banished every doubt and hesitation. The band built themselves dwelling-places in the Deer Park, the Sages' Town at Benares, and there the Buddha taught all who would learn of the enlightenment he had discovered.

"There are," he said, "four noble truths which must be understood. The first is that of Suffering. It is universal and persists throughout life. Birth is suffering; old age is suffering; sickness is suffering; death is suffering; to be united with the unloved is suffering; to be divided from the loved is suffering; not to obtain what one desires is suffering; in short, the five-fold basis of the elements of personality is suffering."

That truth being established, the next to be discovered is the cause of suffering. This, Buddha taught, is engraved in man's craving which he likened to a hankering (tanha), "the lust for being which leads from birth to birth, accompanied by lust and desire, which finds gratification now here, now there; it is the thirst for continued existence; it is the thirst for power."

The third noble truth is that "of the annihilation of suffering; the extinction of this craving, forsaking it, expelling it, breaking loose from it, giving it no room."

The fourth noble truth, which is designated as the Noble Eightfold Path, expounds the way of deliverance by way of "right vision, right thoughts, right speech, right action, right livelihood, right efforts, right mindfulness and right concentration," and thus covers the three main avenues of human activity—body, mind and speech.

He who has learned and understood these four noble truths, declared the Buddha, has reached the state of the Arhat, the perfected disciple. He has now mastered the way of deliverance which is called the Middle Path between the two extremes of sensualism and asceticism, and has thus reached that state which leads, beyond death, to Nirvana, the state of perfect blessedness, of utter freedom from selfish desire, of utter reconciliation and harmony in which the individual soul is absorbed in the peace of the infinite.

Buddha's doctrine, while exceedingly beautiful, has to be placed against the contemporary background of Hindu life and thought before we can appreciate its significance. The dominant religion of North India in his day was Hinduism as primarily taught by the Brahmins, or priestly caste. Life according to them was essentially ritualistic; only faithful observance of vows, rules and regulations could ensure one's moral and material well-being. Life was reduced to a mere mechanical process, without change, without progression, without elevation or dignity, and the rigorous following of this pattern of life was styled as the Dharma, or the duty of profession. Society was divided into four castes, or divisions, and caste was determined by a man's birth. His position was thus determined and unalterably fixed from the day he was born until the day he died. This rigidity of caste divided society into watertight compartments and thus an aristocracy of birth was created and tried to dominate the poor and ignorant. For the latter there was no scope for self-expression. Their duty lay in serving and showing utter subservience to the privileged castes, thus fulfilling the doctrine of predestination. This doctrine was a great handicap; it gave no hope for the masses whose well-being and happiness were entirely neglected, and prevented any development of independent thought or ideas. The idea of religion forging a link between man and man, irrespective of any consideration of caste, of enhancing human relationships was incomprehensible. The cardinal creed was a blind belief in the ways of God and subservience to his will.

A sombre picture of the helpless conditions of the majority of the people, with their narrow life, is thus presented at the time when Gautama preached his doctrines to the people. He approached them without any sensational appeal, but he spoke to them in their own language and taught on the basis of love and non-violence in speech, thought or act. His extraordinary personality attracted equally the young and old, the rich and poor, the privileged and the downtrodden.

Buddha accepted the doctrine of the transmigration with its endless succession of rebirths, but he provided a way of escape. By attaining, through knowledge of the four noble truths, the blessed state of Nirvana, a man could rid himself of all individuality and be free of the possibility of rebirth.

More important to the masses of his followers than this philosophical conclusion, which could only be attained by the keenest and ablest minds, and then through great self-discipline and self-restraint, were the practical results of Buddha's teaching. The Eight-fold Path imposed a lofty standard of morality, and the promise of Nirvana gave morality a motive. Hitherto the good life had been no more than an unthinking observance of ritual; now it became a concentrated striving after virtue and created a tie of love to bind the whole of humanity.

Buddha rejected the idea of caste. To him all men were equal, and all were to be treated as brothers and friends. No living being was to be killed, for all life was sacred; and to this day the ground around Buddhist temples and pagodas is cleared of vegetation, lest unwittingly one tread upon and kill any small animal or insect. He forbade his followers to lie, to steal, to commit adultery and to indulge in intoxicating liquors or to make any claim to superhuman powers.

To spread his doctrines for the betterment of the masses the Buddha established an order of monks, the Sangha. The rules of this order were very strict; all who joined were required to renounce the world and all family ties and to live a life of absolute chastity and abnegation of self. They put on the yellow robe, furnished themselves with the begging bowl, which is the mark of all mendicant orders in India, and went out into the highways and byways to spread the teachings of the Buddha.

Lay believers were admitted, their duties being to receive and maintain the brethren of the order and, in return, to receive lessons from the monks. Many princes and nobles were numbered among them. Later, through the influence, it is said, of Gotami, the foster-mother of Buddha and Ananda, one of his favourite disciples, an order of nuns was established, but it remained inferior and subordinate to that of the monks, for in accord with Hindu thought throughout all the ages, the Buddhists believed man to be a superior creature to woman. In the Buddhist church, however, equal opportunities were given to women with those of men, and there are examples to show that the Buddha did not share in the general opinion that the women's abilities were very limited. The Buddha, in fact, made woman more conscious of her latent powers.

The Buddha set his disciples the example by becoming, and remaining, for the remainder of his long life, an itinerant beggar-monk. Little is known in detail of his wanderings, which were probably confined to northern India and concentrated in the districts of Oudh and Bihar, but for some forty-five years he continued to teach and preach.

During the rainy season he would retire to some town or village, where for the period of the monsoon he would journey from place to place, begging food and shelter like the meanest of his monks.

Kings received him kindly; wealthy people entertained him and set apart gardens for him and his followers—gardens because in these could be accommodated the crowds of inquirers and followers who daily sought him out, and because in them he and his disciples could retire for meditation and quiet thought.

Yet princes' gardens and the palaces of the wealthy were by no means always the lot of Buddha and his followers, as the following anecdote, which reveals clearly also the sublime serenity of the great teacher, will show.

One day a dweller in Alavi in the Simsapa forest came upon the Buddha seated wrapt in thought by the side of the cattle path. Approaching him with great respect, he asked, "Master, does the Exalted One live happily?"

"It is so, young man; I live happily. Of those who live happily in the world, I also am one."

"Cold, master, is the winter night; the time of the frost is coming; rough is the ground trodden by the hoofs of the cattle; thin is the couch of leaves; light the monk's yellow robe; sharp the cutting winter wind."

With sublime equanimity the Buddha replies, "It is so, young man. I live happily. Of those that live happily in the world, I also am one."

Through all his many years of wandering, amid all his varied experiences, Buddha retained his lofty serenity of mind and assurance of purpose. With the Brahmins and other sects like the Jains he would hold disputations, in which he lured them to contradiction and confusion by a form of catechism similar to that of Socrates, the great Greek philosopher.

He has no fear of being worsted in argument. "That in disputation with anyone whatsoever," he declared, "I could be thrown into confusion or embarrassment, there is no possibility; and because I know of no such possibility, on that account it is that I remain quiet and confident."

Gautama adapted his methods of instruction to his audience and to common people he spoke in parables and fables. We cannot resist the temptation of narrating the talk with the farmer Bhardwaja, who told Gautama not to be an idler, but work as a farmer like himself and earn his bread. Thereupon, Gautama told him that he also was a farmer and maintained himself by ploughing and tilling. The Brahmin was astonished since Gautama never possessed any agricultural implements. So said Gautama: "Faith is my seed, torment is my rain, knowledge is my yoke and plough, shame is the pole of my plough, mind constitutes my yoke straps and mindfulness is my goad. Protected in body, in speech and mind, and restrained in my meals and belly, with the truth I cut and gentleness is my deliverance. Energy constitutes my yoked oxen, and it leads me to the incomparable safety of Nirvana. It takes me from whence there is no turning back to the place where there is no suffering. This is my farming and it gives me the fruit of immortality." Similarly, to a mother who had gone mad following the death of her dear child, Gautama taught the most difficult teaching of the inevitability of death with a parable of the mustard seeds.

He was close upon eighty when illness warned him that his end was impending. Yet by an effort of will he deferred it, for, he reflected, "it would not be right to depart from existence without first having spoken to my disciples."

So, though racked by illness, he lived on through the rainy season, and then called his disciples together. His life, he said, would end in three months, and they were not to expect another leader. He urged them to be firm and a refuge to themselves, and to remain ever eager to learn. Then, calling Ananda to him, he spoke these words, "I, too, Ananda, am now grown old and full of years; my journey is growing to its close; I have reached the sum of years, I am turning eighty years of age; and just as a worn-out cart, Ananda, can only with much additional care be made to move along, so, methinks, the body of the Enlightened One can only be kept going with much additional care."

Yet with indefatigable persistence he set forth again on his travels, only to be seized again with illness accompanied by great pain. Arrived at Kusinara, he spent his last hours addressing his monks: "Behold now, brethren, I exhort you, saying, decay is inherent in all component things. Work out your salvation with diligence." So saying, the Enlightened One passed to his rest.

His teachings have enriched the thought and lives of countless generations of Oriental peoples. Though the purity of his doctrines soon became obscured to all save the few, though the masses early raised him to divine rank and ignorantly worshipped the founder of Buddhism in place of trying to understand his precepts and endeavour to put them into practice, Buddhism has conferred two priceless benefits upon its adherents: it has freed them from the bondage of caste—a relief which only those who have travelled in the East and understood the Eastern mind can fully appreciate, and it has taught them that life is not without hope.

Buddha's philosophy of change and development meant that man was made entirely responsible for his own deeds, and this doctrine infused a new spirit into the dormant masses. His teachings had the great effect of producing tolerance, so that throughout the long history of two thousand years of Buddhism its adherents have never appealed to the sword but to intellectual and moral suasion; moreover, there has been no religious persecution. Buddha's teachings, in fact, paved the way for a religion of active piety based on a belief of the perfectibility of the human spirit.

CONFUCIUS (K'UNG FU-TZU)

(*c.* 550–479 B.C.)

Loyalty, benevolent authority and dutiful submission thereto, courtesy, moderation, chastity and the abhorrence of violence, with the golden social rule "What you do not want done to yourself, do not to others." Those are the fundamental principles of Confucianism, the ethical code which for centuries swayed the soul of China. Confucius, the sage, teacher and reformer, whose wisdom and virtue gave birth to the movement that has taken his name, died in the fifth century before Christ, but in his work he is living yet.

IN February, 1917, there took place in the Chinese parliament a lengthy and interesting debate. Five years previously, when the Emperor of China, the "Son of Heaven," had abdicated, and China had become a republic, Confucianism, which for more than two thousand years had been the state religion, had been abolished. Now it was proposed to re-establish it, and in addition to make Confucius the god of China.

The proposal was not carried, in spite of the fervour with which the more scholarly among the statesmen supported it, but the incident shows how strong had remained the hold upon the Chinese mind of their "most sagely ancient teacher." The force of the incident is redoubled when it is remembered that, although for many generations Confucius had been worshipped by the Chinese, and had had sacrifice offered up to him, he had never before been regarded as a god.

The idea of his divinity would probably have been faintly amusing to him, for of all the great teachers of antiquity he was the least religious. According to one authority* he "was not a religious man, practised few religious rites, and taught nothing about religion." Were he living today he would be called an agnostic, for while he admitted the existence of spiritual powers he did not concern himself overmuch with them. "Respect the spirits," he said, "but keep them at a distance."

He was interested neither in where man came from before birth nor whither his soul departed after death, but only in the practical

* Du Bose

conduct of life while it lasted. "I have striven," he said of himself, "to become a man of perfect virtue, and to teach others without weariness." His ideal was "the superior man, carrying out in his conduct what he professes." For the pursuit of this ideal he was supremely fitted, for he was that very rare combination, the idealist who is also a practical business man.

There is a saying that "the age produces the man"; in the case of Confucius it is indubitably true, for the state of China in the sixth century B.C. was such as both to sharpen a naturally penetrating intellect, and also to give him a rare opportunity to exercise his talents as a man of affairs. The Shang dynasty, which had ruled China as priest-emperors for more than one thousand years, and from which Confucius traced his descent, had come to an end in 1125 B.C., and for more than five hundred years China had been gradually breaking up into a larger and larger number of petty states, until by the sixth century B.C.—the "Age of Confusion," as Chinese chroniclers called it—there were said to be between five and six thousand of them.

It was in the winter of either 551 or 550 B.C. that Confucius was born, in the state of Lu, which occupied part of the modern province of Shantung. His father, Shuh-liang Heih, was commandant of the district of Tsow. A man of some importance, he had many daughters, but no lawful male heir, so at the age of seventy he married again, and in due course was presented with the son he desired.

As with so many other great men of old time, legend has played busily around the birth of Confucius. It has related how his young mother, Ching-tsai, prayed for a son, performing many propitiatory rites, and how a god appeared to her in a dream and said: "You shall have a son, a sage, and you must bring him forth in a hollow mulberry tree." On hearing this, Shuh-liang Heih read the oracle aright and arranged for her confinement to take place in a cave in a hill that was called "Hollow Mulberry Tree."

When the child was born, dragons and nymphs appeared, mounting guard at the entrance of the cave and pouring out aromatic potions; and his mother heard sweet strains of music, and a voice saying: "Heaven is moved at the birth of thy holy son, and sends down harmonious sounds." On the baby's body were found forty-nine marks, and the words: "He will originate principles and settle the affairs of men." In the floor of the cave a spring welled up miraculously, and a unicorn brought a tablet inscribed: "The son of the essence of water shall succeed to the withering Tsow and be a throneless king."

More certain than these lovely fables it is that Confucius at a very early age gave clear signs of extraordinary ability. His father's death, which occurred before Confucius was three years old, left the family poor, so the boy was compelled to work for his living, but his mind was set upon learning, and it is said that by the age of fifteen he had determined to become a sage.

At nineteen he married, but though his wife bore him a son and two daughters, marriage and home life seem to have imposed but light bonds on one who was becoming increasingly conscious of a dual combination—to become not only a learned man but also a wise ruler. Shortly after his marriage, Confucius obtained an official post as a storekeeper, and he was later promoted to be superintendent of parks and herds.

At twenty-two he began his career as teacher and sage by founding an academy or school in which he expounded the principles of right conduct and government. His students were young men. From them, if they were rich, he accepted considerable fees; but none was turned away on the score of poverty. Ability and enthusiasm were the criteria by which he judged his pupils. "When I have presented one corner of a subject," he said, "and the pupil himself cannot learn the other three, I do not repeat the lesson."

His reputation grew, both as a teacher and as an administrator. As an official he became known as a zealous reformer who did not hesitate to attack and sweep away old-established abuses; as a scholar he mastered history and philosophy, till at the age of thirty, he tells us, he "stood firm" in conviction, having studied exhaustively the records of the past and formulated his principles of government and moral behaviour.

In 517 B.C. two youths of high rank in the state of Lu became his disciples, and with them Confucius paid a visit to the capital of the empire, where he continued his historical research in the imperial library, and studied music, of which he was passionately fond, in the imperial court. Music was to have great influence upon him; not only did he love melody so much that "it made him forget the taste of food," but he came to regard it as a key to the balance of things, and incorporated it in his scheme of government.

It was during this visit, so we are told, that he met his most distinguished contemporary, the philosopher Lao-tsze, his opposite in character but his rival in greatness, founder of one of the three religions of China, whose adherents, the Taoists, came to be numbered in their scores of millions.

It was hardly to be expected that these two men should find much in common, for in mind and outlook they were utterly unlike. Lao-tsze, dreamer, idealist and mystic, believed devoutly in a Supreme Being, and held that to find truth one should empty the heart of earthly longing and to allow a consciousness of *Tao,* the way, the mystery of mysteries, permeate the soul. Confucius, practical, business-like, and earthly-minded, never acknowledged a personal God, but referred always to heaven, and devoted himself to the sedulous cultivation of virtue in all outward observances, which he held to be a fitting vehicle for the expression of spiritual perfection. Nevertheless, it is recorded that while Confucius made little impression upon Lao-tsze, he was himself greatly impressed by the father of Taoism.

In the year of this visit, just as everything seemed to point to a prosperous career for Confucius, a sudden revolution in the state of Lu caused the lord of it to flee into the neighbouring land of Ts'i, whither Confucius followed him, for he felt it was not consonant with his honour to countenance rebels. A famous story is told of his journey into exile.

Passing with many of his disciples by the mountain T'ai, Confucius was moved by the sight of a woman prostrate with grief by the side of a grave. He sent one of his disciples to inquire the cause. "My husband's father," sobbed the woman, "was killed here by a tiger, and my husband also, and now my son has suffered the same fate." Asked why she did not leave the place, she replied that it was because the government was not oppressive. Confucius was not slow to point the moral. "Remember this, my children," he warned his followers, "oppressive government is fiercer and more feared than a tiger."

For many years Confucius remained without public office. He did not stay long in Ts'i, for the prince of that realm was baffled to know how to treat with due honour a man of high reputation yet of low rank. He offered Confucius a pension, but the sage would accept no income unless his services were made use of and his counsels followed. Some of the time he spent travelling, teaching men everywhere the precepts of virtue and the practice of good government, but much he devoted to study and to the instruction of his disciples, who flocked in ever-increasing numbers to hear *K'ung fu-tzu,* "the philosopher K'ung" (Confucius is a Latinized version of his name, first used by Jesuit monks in China).

During these years he moved "amid a company of admiring followers" who treasured every word he uttered, and studied reverently his every act. Thanks to their devotion, we possess a detailed picture of Confucius the man, as well as a voluminous record of the sayings of the sage.

He was tall, frequently walked with his arms extended like the wings of a bird, and had "a back like a tortoise." Though he ate and drank moderately, he was particular about his food, liking fine rice and meat minced small, and insisting upon having the correct sauce for each dish. With due regard for good food, "when eating he did not converse," and there is a deliciously human touch in the record that : "He must always have ginger on the table." We can imagine him as exquisitely precise and courteous in manner and punctilious to a degree in all ceremonial observances.

Not a character for which one could feel deep love; he was too cold, too formal, too remote for that. Rather one that compelled distant admiration and reverent loyalty; a man whose every word one treasured as a pearl of wisdom, but with whom one could never dare to be familiar, or aspire to call one's friend. That he had human frailties his disciples well knew, for it is recorded that on hearing thunder he would change countenance or at night would dress quickly, but the constant impression he must have given was that of a character so elevated by wisdom and the practice of virtue as to stand aloof from the common run of mankind.

When put to the test the virtues and learning acquired by Confucius were to be triumphantly proved in the field of practical politics. At the age of fifty-two he was recalled to office in his native state, and made governor of the city of Chung-tu, with results that caused all to marvel. Before long he was promoted, until he reached the highest offices of state. Then, thanks to his genius and the aid of two of his disciples—"A transforming government went abroad. Dishonesty and dissoluteness hid their heads. Loyalty and good faith became the characteristics of the men, and chastity and docility those of the women. He was the idol of the people, and flew in songs through their mouths."

The reforms of Confucius were strangely modern in conception. Some of them, indeed, are in advance of social ideas of today. He not only fed the poor, but assigned different food to young and old. In organizing labour he allotted different tasks to strong and weak. He fixed the prices of goods and used state revenue for the development of trade. Communications were improved, roads and bridges being repaired, and the brigands that infested the mountains being rooted out. The power of the nobles was curbed, the common people were freed from oppression, and all men made equal in the eyes of justice.

Such a policy, though immensely popular among the masses, could not fail to excite the hatred both of individuals and of powerful vested interests, particularly as Confucius did not hesitate to strike at the greatest in the land if they obstructed his reforms. Actually, the stroke that caused the downfall of Confucius came from the state of Ts'i, where he had spent the first part of his exile.

The ruler of that state, with whom Confucius had been in negotiation concerning the restoration of full sovereignty to his own prince, realized the danger of having a model state next to his own. Would not his own people cry out for reform? And might not the kingdom of Lu, grown strong and confident, cast covetous eyes upon the lands and possessions of its neighbours?

He devised a plan typically Chinese in its subtlety and appeal. Selecting a company of eighty beautiful women, accomplished in music and dancing, and a number of magnificent horses, he sent them as a present to the Duke of Lu. The Oriental finds it hard at all times to resist the attractions of sensuous pleasure, and the duke and his courtiers proved no exception to the rule. Duty was neglected for the charms of the dancing girls, and the counsels of Confucius could command no attention while such attractive toys absorbed the interest of the court.

Slowly and reluctantly the sage determined upon his departure from Lu; slowly and reluctantly he journeyed forth a second time into exile, his eyes ever turning backward to glimpse the messenger posting to recall him to favour and to power. But no messenger came.

Confucius had held office but for three years, but thirteen were to drag out their weary length before he saw again his native land. Thirteen years of growing disappointment, during which he passed from state to state, ever hoping to find some prince who would entrust his realm to his care and give him power to transform it into Utopia, and ever being compelled to turn away with his desire unfulfilled.

In many a place he received kindly welcome and princely entertainment, but he would have none of these. He would become the pensioner of no one. To a ruler who offered him the revenues of a town for his maintenance he sent the sublime retort: "A superior man will only receive reward for services rendered. I have advised the duke; he has not obeyed, and now he would endow me. Very far is he from understanding. With coarse rice to eat, water to drink, and my bended arm for a pillow, I still have joy in these things. Riches and honour acquired by unrighteousness are to me as a floating cloud."

He was constant in suffering as in times of prosperity. "Must the superior man endure like this?" asked his disciple one day, sad and angry at seeing his master without food. "The superior man may have to endure want," came the tranquil reply, "but he is still the superior man. The small man in similar circumstances loses his self-command."

At length the longed-for message of recall reached the sage. The ruler whose neglect had terminated his active career was dead, and his son, interested to learn from one of his successful generals that the latter owed his military skill to the instruction of Confucius, was persuaded to send for the master and ask him to take charge once more of the destinies of Lu.

But Confucius was now close on seventy, and the sad years of exile had added to the weight of years. Though he returned to Lu, it was to a quiet retreat in a pleasant valley, and not to the busy life of political office, that he came.

Five years of life remained to him, and these he spent in writing and instructing the disciples who sat at his feet. It was during this time that he composed the only book that is entirely his own original work, the *Ch'un Chi'u King,* or book of *Spring and Autumn,* a collection of annals covering a period of two hundred and forty-two years.

Confucius said of this book that "by the *Spring and Autumn* men would know him and men would condemn him." If we did not know so much of the sage from other sources, we should certainly condemn him on its evidence, for, though it has ever since been regarded as a perfect model of Chinese scholars, it is, as an historical summary of events, about as bad as it could be.

But few great men, particularly those of ancient days, would live up to their reputation if they had to be judged only by what they can be proved to have written; and the greatness of Confucius has to be judged, not on the *Spring and Autumn,* but on the influence he has exerted on China throughout the ages right down to the present day.

Two hundred years or more after his death a reforming emperor strove with might and main to sweep out of China all traces of the work of Confucius. He burnt all the books which the sage had written and from which he taught, and he put to death every scholar who upheld his doctrines. He failed; and succeeding emperors based their power on restoring the reputation of "the most sagely ancient teacher."

Confucius was above all things conservative. "The cautious never err," was a favourite saying of his. He looked to the past for wisdom, and had the profoundest respect for authority. "It is better to be mean than insubordinate," he taught. He based his principles of government on his idea of the family; just as a son owed and paid obedience to his father, so a subject owed and paid obedience to his ruler. This respect for paternal authority is the foundation of ancestor-worship, for centuries the fundamental religion of the Chinese.

Confucius made no claim to be the founder of a religion or a philosophy or a system of government. He expressly denied such claim, saying that he was a "transmitter, not a maker." He was the champion of the old-established, the proved, of the order which has been from the beginning, is now, and ever shall be; whereas his contemporary, Lao-tsze, represented the spirit that is ever searching for a new and better order.

Confucius was, as we have seen, a Northerner, and the descendants of his family, the K'ung clan, are to be found in their thousands in his native city of K'iuh-fow. Outside the city, on a tree-covered hill, is the K'ung cemetery, and there, isolated in solitary splendour and approached by an imposing avenue of cypress trees, a marble statue commemorates the last resting-place of China's "most sagely ancient teacher; all-accomplished, all-informed king."

He died in 479 B.C. a disappointed and disillusioned old man of seventy-one. "There is none who knows me," was his despairing cry. "No intelligent ruler arises to take me for his master."

But the love his disciples bore him was to prove a stronger force than the patronage of any prince. For three years they mourned beside his tomb, so that in death the fame of the sage went abroad throughout the land and spread in ever-widening circles that have persisted throughout the ages.

SOCRATES

(*c.* 469–399 B.C.)

There are those who pretend that the fame of Johnson depends entirely upon Boswell. Others, with equal folly, maintain that the greatness of Socrates owes all to the pen of Plato. But Socrates was not the first nor the last of great teachers who wrote no word, who founded no school, but spent their lives seeking and asking for the living truth. It was the aim of Socrates to turn men's minds in the same direction, so that they might have knowledge of goodness; with that knowledge he was sure that men would have no other aim. For his virtue the Athenians killed him, and crowned his life with immortality.

SOCRATES was an ugly, snub-nosed, paunchy, bolt-eyed little man, who talked a lot and did little. He wrote nothing that was published. Yet we know him as one of the finest philosophers of the ancient world, perhaps the greatest of the great men produced by Athens. His name commands admiration, honour and reverence.

For his genius he became conspicuous; for his virtue he was condemned to death—the world cannot stand the completely honest man. His life-story is a golden thread in the dark fabric of the world's history.

All we know of him is gathered from the writings of his friends and pupils, Plato and Xenophon the historian. Plato in his dialogues has revealed the living Socrates; his talk, his arguments and questionings in search of truth, his opinions, his attitudes to life and death, his greatness. Although he talked in a little intimate circle, the echoes of his speeches still reverberate.

Socrates was born *c.* 469 B.C., and lived through the golden age of Athens, when she was the most powerful of the Greek states, and learning, the arts and commerce flourished as never before. His father was a sculptor, and for a time the young Socrates followed the same profession. His mother was a midwife. Later Socrates claimed that he followed her profession in his dialectic. He called himself a midwife of thought, which shows that he had a sense of humour.

Like all Athenian citizens, he saw military service. He fought in the Potidæa campaign, and he fought bravely and well. During one battle he saved the life of the great Alcibiades, who became his friend and disciple. Later he fought at Delium and at Amphipolis, and bore himself with the same fearlessness that he showed in the less conspicuous but greater crises of civil life.

Socrates spent the remainder of his years in talk. Never was there such a talker, but the quality of what he said gained for him, even in his lifetime, the reputation of being the world's wisest man. He wandered out into the open early in the morning. His wretchedly dressed figure was probably the best-known in Athens. Winter and summer he wore no coat; his feet and legs were always bare. But there was no ostentation in his poverty. He inured himself to physical hardships, for he was concerned only with things of the mind and of the soul. "If a slave were made to live so, he would run away," wrote Antiphon.

But Socrates did not run away. In fact he rarely went outside the gates of Athens. He had no interest in the country; men and women were his objective, to them he had a mission. He wandered through the streets and down to the market-place, or often he would go to the public gymnasium. Then he started business—the business of talking. He would talk to all and sundry. High and low, great personages and folk of no importance would listen to him and answer or pretend to answer the teasing questions by which he made his points.

It was his pretence to be the most ignorant man in any discussion. He would use simple illustrations, and ask simpler questions—the famous Socratic "irony"—to draw his hearers to the examination of good. Goodness was his objective. Without goodness a man was nothing. Socrates believed that all men would seek goodness if they had true knowledge of it; that all virtue was the knowledge of goodness, all sin, ignorance of goodness.

Unlike most Athenians, he took little part in the public life of the time. When he did, he adopted the honest, resolute course, which might be expected of a man of his courage and indifference to public opinion.

He was once a member of the council. Some Athenian generals were put on trial for their lives, and through the force of public opinion were illegally condemned to death. The whole of the council supported the verdict, with the single exception of Socrates. In spite of the popular outcry, he was firm in the interests of justice and of the established law. Again, in the "Terror" of 404 B.C., when the Athenian Empire came to an end, Socrates was ordered by the

Thirty, who were ruling Athens, to make some illegal arrests. He refused, though he knew the refusal might cost him his life. In fact he was only saved by a public uprising and the overthrow of the Thirty. Such was the man's courage. It was even greater at his own trial and death.

But Socrates cared little for death. He believed in the survival of the soul, and he believed in virtue. His religion was not that orthodox acceptance of mythological gods which was the official worship of Athens. His code of ethics and of conduct more nearly approached that of Christianity than any other.

The man was something of a mystic and yet he was essentially practical. It is told of him that he stood for twenty-four hours wrapped in thought. And he himself referred to his "daemon," or still, small voice, a restraining influence which warned him not to do certain things. Socrates, of course, could not continually discourse in public and please everybody. In fact the outspokenness of his remarks annoyed a number of people. Aristophanes, the great writer of comedies, ridiculed him in his play, *The Clouds,* which was produced in 423 B.C. He represents the philosopher as a half-crazy old man who keeps a "thinkshop," and teaches young men high-falutin' and disrespectful ideas. The playwright's views of the philosopher were probably shared by a large class of Athenian citizens, but this did not prevent a little band of disciples, rich and poor, from gathering round Socrates. Some came for their own ends, to learn his skill in dialectic and his powers of argument and refutation, others to learn from him how to make their lives better. They were a diverse company. Critias, one of the thirty tyrants, Alcibiades, the brilliant and vicious, Crito, Plato, Xenophon, the younger Pericles, Cebes, the Theban philosopher, and Euripides, the great tragic playwright, were some of those who sat at his feet. The attendance of his "disciples" was casual and voluntary. Socrates founded no regular school of philosophy. He merely questioned and reasoned, and tried to lead men towards the light.

It is strange to think of him as a married man. Yet he was twice wed—first to Myrtone, by whom he had two sons, and afterwards to Xanthippe, who bore him another boy. Xanthippe has acquired the reputation of being a shrew. It is probably unjust, although we have accounts of her violent temper. Yet it must be admitted that the life of a woman married to a poverty-stricken philosopher who spent most of his time talking and reasoning with strangers, must have been a severe trial.

In 399 B.C., when Socrates was seventy years of age, his enemies at last had their way. He was put on trial. Two principal charges were preferred against him: that he neglected and disbelieved in the gods of the republic and that he was corrupting the youth of the city.

Lysias, one of the greatest Athenian orators of the day, wrote a speech in defence of Socrates and offered it to the philosopher. He read it, courteously thanked Lysias for it, and declined to use it. A professional defence, he explained, did not express manliness. It was like a pair of Sicyonian shoes which, though fitting, were proofs of effeminacy. A philosopher ought to be conspicuous for his magnaminity and firmness of soul.

He started his own defence by saying, "I do not know, men of Athens, how far you have been influenced by my accusers; for my part, in listening to them I almost forgot myself, so plausible were their arguments; however, so to speak, they have said nothing true."

He did not trouble to refute the evidence of the prosecution. He made a noble and simple exposition of his own aims. Whatever he possessed he gave to the service of Athens. It was his wish to make his fellow citizens happy. That was a duty which he performed by special command of the gods, "whose authority," he told the judges, "I regard more than yours."

There is no doubt that his speech annoyed the court, but worse was to come. "If you propose to acquit me," he said, "on condition that I abandon my search for truth, I will say: I thank you, O Athenians, but I will obey God, who, as I believe, set me this task, rather than you, and so long as I have breath and strength I will never cease from my occupation with philosophy. I will continue the practice of accosting whomever I meet and saying to him, 'Are you not ashamed of setting your heart on wealth and honours while you have no care for wisdom and truth and making your soul better?' I know not what death is—it may be a good thing, and I am not afraid of it. But I do know that it is a bad thing to desert one's post and I prefer what may be good to what I know to be bad." He was condemned by a small minority. The penalty proposed by his judges was death. By Athenian law it was for Socrates to suggest an alternative penalty, such as exile. He did. He proposed that he should be treated as what he was—a public benefactor. That he should be feasted and maintained at the public expense, like a winner at the Olympic Games. Eventually he offered to pay a fine of a mina (about £6) instead of suffering death. His friends entreated him to make it thirty minae. He refused.

The court was now really angry. Socrates had shown an utter disdain of so-called wisdom. Without further ado he was condemned to death by drinking hemlock, the Athenian method of capital punishment. The philosopher accepted the verdict calmly, and continued his dignified address to the court. "But now it is time to depart, for me to die, for you to live," he concluded, "but which of us is going to a better state is unknown to everyone but God."

Owing to the celebration of religious festivals, the carrying out of the sentence was delayed for three weeks. He was kept in prison and loaded with chains, but he continued to receive his friends and talk with them cheerfully. Crito, one of his most faithful disciples, who had been present at his trial and had offered to assist in paying the suggested fine of thirty minae, came to Socrates in his cell and told him he had arranged for his escape. Socrates refused the offer. He had been condemned to death by a legitimate court and would obey the laws of his country.

Plato in the *Phaedo* has movingly described the final scene. A group of his friends came to see Socrates on his last day. They found him in his cell, just freed from his bonds, with Xanthippe and his youngest son. Xanthippe was weeping. "Socrates," she cried, "your friends will now talk with you for the last time, and you with them." But Socrates looked towards Crito and said, "Crito, let someone take her home." After she had been gently led away, the condemned man sat up in bed, rubbed his leg where the chains had been, and began to discourse calmly on the relationship between pleasure and pain. So they sat round and talked of life, of death and of man's immortal soul. Late in the afternoon Socrates left them and went to bathe. When he returned it was almost sunset, the hour of execution.

A state officer came in and apologized for the office he was about to perform. He asked Socrates not to be angry with him, and then turned away and burst into tears. Crito tried to persuade Socrates not to hurry, for the sun had not quite set, but Socrates smiled at him and ordered him to fetch the man to administer the poison. Socrates took the cup, poured out a libation to the gods, and drank off the rest of the poison. His friends standing round could not restrain their anguish. But Socrates reproved them.

"What are you doing?" he asked. "It was chiefly for this reason that I sent away the women, that they might not commit any folly of this kind. For I have heard that it is right to die with good omens. Be quiet, then, and bear up."

The poison gradually crept through his limbs, chilling them;

then, just before he lapsed into unconsciousness, he gave instructions about a minor sacrifice which he had forgotten.

Plato thus concludes the account: "This was the end of our friend, a man, as we may say, the best of all of his time that we have known, and moreover the most wise and just." It was an epitaph as true as it was noble.

No sooner was Socrates buried than the Athenians repented. His accusers were universally boycotted, until some in desperation hanged themselves. Now that the ragged philosopher was no more, the Athenians commissioned Lysippus to duplicate his features in bronze.

The life of Socrates was a living example of his ideals; his philosophy, which is set forth by Plato, marks an epoch in human thought. "He brought philosophy down from heaven to earth," wrote Cicero. For Socrates was the founder of moral philosophy. He was not concerned with abstract metaphysics, but with mankind and its conduct. He was scoffed at for taking his examples from common life, but he did so to lead plain men to goodness, truth and beauty. He ruled his life by reason.

Once an individual, looking at the rolling eyes, the thick lips and the flat nose of the short, thick-set little man, said that he could tell by his face that Socrates was of a licentious disposition, that he was one of the most depraved, immodest and corrupt men in the world. The philosopher's admirers nearly murdered the physiognomist, but Socrates stopped them, and remarked that all that the man had said was true but that he—Socrates—had curbed and corrected his vicious propensities by means of reason.

But if we are to judge by his life, the ignoble tendencies of that ugly body were ruled and checked not so much by reason and the exercise of mind as by that which Socrates sought throughout—greatness of soul.

ARISTOTLE

(384–322 B.C.)

"Aristotle," writes Lemprière, " had a deformed countenance, but his genius was a sufficient compensation for all his personal defects," and has the grace to add with all his passion for grandiloquent understatement, " He has been called by Plato the philosopher of truth; and Cicero compliments him with the title of a man of eloquence, universal knowledge, readiness, and acuteness of invention, and fecundity of thought." All these " compliments " reflect a facet of the truth: one penetrates the genius of Aristotle. He was the professor of Universal Knowledge: for centuries Europe acknowledged him as the master, and no philosopher has ever had such a profound and lasting influence on the thought and life of the western world.

"PHILIP to Aristotle, greeting. Be it known that to me a son is born. I am thankful, therefore, to the gods, but not so much at the birth of the child as that he was born in thy time. For I hope that, trained and educated by thee, he will prove himself worthy of us and of succession to the throne."

Thus ran the message sent by King Philip of Macedon to Aristotle on the birth of the child who was to become Alexander the Great and to weep because " there were no more worlds to conquer." The letter was a fitting tribute to the philosopher who, perhaps, has most influenced human thought.

The great Greek thinker took for his province almost every important department of intellectual activity; his *Politics* laid the foundation of modern political philosophy; his *Poetics* contained the first conception of the dramatic " unities " in tragedy; his essay, *On the Soul,* laid the foundation of psychology as we know it today. He was the pioneer biologist, the first to formulate the law of the association of ideas, and the father of many theories now accepted without question. When King Philip's letter was written he was not yet thirty.

Aristotle was born in 384 B.C., at Stagira on the Ægean Sea, whence his familiar title of " the Stagirite." He was the son of a learned doctor, Nicomachus, who for some time had been court physician to Amyntas II, father of Philip of Macedon. This connexion of his father with the Macedonian court was to have a great influence on the life and career of Aristotle. He began by studying at the Academy under Plato, who called him the intellect of the school. When Plato died his place was taken by his nephew, Speusippus, whereupon Aristotle, after composing a noble epitaph on his old teacher, retired to Atarneus, where he took up his abode with Hermias, another former pupil. The niece—some accounts say the sister—of Hermias became Aristotle's wife. By her he had a son, whom he called by his father's name. Undoubtedly there was a marked affection between the two men, and when Hermias was captured and crucified by the Persians, Aristotle wrote a beautiful ode to his memory.

While studying marine zoology and other subjects at Mitylene he received a summons to undertake the education of the young Alexander, as had been promised at the boy's birth. A writer has said of this conjunction of philosopher and world-conqueror; "The one had the power and the will to rule and master the world. The other had discovered and had subjugated a new world for the human mind."

We must not think of Aristotle as a kind of private tutor to the heir to the Macedonian Empire. The Greeks had ideas of a different kind. Aristotle was allowed to set up a school of his own at Mieza, near Pellas, in the province of Emathia. Here, in the Grove of the Nymphs, Alexander and the sons of various nobles pondered the teachings of Aristotle. The boys would gather round the great stone chair of the master, or walk with him in the shady paths about the temple of learning.

One and all had an admiration for their teacher that amounted to worship, but Alexander never allowed his veneration of the wisdom and knowledge of Aristotle to become slavish. One morning Aristotle asked a pupil whose rank was more than patrician, "What wilt thou do when, in the ordinary course of events, thou ascendest the throne of thine ancestor, and becomest king?" The youth modestly replied that in every crisis he would seek the advice of his old master and abide by it. Another prince, also questioned, replied in like manner. The same question was put to the young Alexander, who responded, "I cannot tell, nor can any man, what the morrow will bring forth. When the time comes, ask me that question again, and I will answer thee according to the circumstances."

Philip rendered every honour possible to the teacher of his son. The tyrant had at some previous time seen fit to lay waste Stagira.

To mark his admiration for the philosopher, he caused the city to be rebuilt, and recalled from banishment its former citizens, some of whom were living in slavery, and all in great misery. It was a magnificent gesture and worthy of a great king, though we must remember that in ancient Greece a city was often no larger than a small town of today.

Aristotle implanted in the young Alexander a love of Homer which lasted him all his life. In other ways, too, his teachings were such that Philip exclaimed to Alexander in a transport of generous admiration, "Verily, not in vain have we honoured Aristotle and rebuilt his native town, for a man is deserving of the highest reward who has given thee such doctrine of the duties and the functions of kings!"

Alexander's admiration and affection for his master lasted long after he had ceased to be a pupil. "To my father," he avowed, "I owe my life, to Aristotle the knowledge how to live worthily." When the latter was engaged in his biological researches, Alexander placed the services of a thousand men at his disposal. They were to help in observing and reporting on the habits and characteristics of birds, beasts and fishes. Alexander was also extremely generous in money gifts. Many valuable manuscripts were thus placed within the reach of a man who otherwise would not have been able to afford them.

When Alexander set out for Asia, Aristotle returned to Athens, then the cultural centre not only of Greece but of the world. Here, at the age of fifty, he opened a school. This was called the Lyceum, from its nearness to the temple of Apollo Lyceius. Pupils flocked to it in order to benefit by the teachings of one who was now, by common consent, the foremost philosopher of the age. The word "Lyceum" still survives though few of those who use it connect it with the site of a heathen temple. Those who frequented the Lyceum soon became known as the peripatetic philosophers, possibly from their habit of walking up and down as they conversed.

The teachings of Aristotle covered a wide range. His was a philosophy founded on facts, for he possessed the exact and scientific mind that characterizes the best type of physician. Indeed, he first intended to follow his father's profession and had already gained some experience in dissection and other branches of medical study when he abandoned the idea. To the end the study of biology was his favourite pursuit.

The death of Alexander at Babylon left Aristotle exposed to suspicion. He was accused of being a Macedonian favourite, and a plan was set on foot to convict him of impiety. Aristotle knew too well the fickleness of the Greeks. He remembered the fate of Socrates and had no desire for a draught of hemlock. Accordingly, he left Athens and took refuge at Chalcis, in the island of Eubœa. In 322 B.C., not long after this act of self-exile, he died.

Contemporary accounts of Aristotle speak of his firm lips and intent eyes, though they add that he talked with a lisp and was excessively careful in his dress—an unusual trait in a philosopher.

Centuries afterwards, the English poet, John Dryden, wrote in a passion of admiration: "He made his torch a universal light!"

Aristotle was indeed a light-bringer; and as such he has been recognized by the finest minds of succeeding ages. Ethics, metaphysics, poetics, politics and rhetoric were not only taught by him but illuminated anew. His philosophy profoundly influenced such diverse minds as those of Thomas Aquinas, Dante, Spenser and Goethe, besides many lesser men.

We shall better appreciate the immense effect that Aristotle has had upon the ages during which our civilization has been built up if we consider, however briefly, the work that has made his name immortal. To begin with, his philosophical method formed the basis of the great scholastic system which was the glory of the Middle Ages, and which today, amid a thousand warring philosophies, still holds its place. The intellectual giants of the Christian Church assimilated almost bodily into their theological systems the method of thought of this great "pagan."

Aristotle's works, which seem to have been his notebooks, form almost an encyclopædia of philosophy. In his *Organon* he laid down the laws of logic, and his examination of reasoning and of the laws of thought pointed a way which the world has followed, with modifications, ever since. His *Rhetoric* is a masterpiece on the art of persuasion, and the versatility of his mind, the variety of his knowledge and the acuteness of his thought are displayed in *Physics, Metaphysics* and *Topics*. In his treatise, *On the Soul,* he enters the realms of biology and psychology, while his slender *Poetics* has had more influence than any other work of literary or dramatic criticism. But the two works which have had, and have, the most far-reaching influence on the western world are *Ethics* and *Politics*. Both in medieval and in modern times the systems he propounded have commanded the attention of both statesmen and philosophers. There has hardly been a department of human thought in which the teachings of Aristotle have not had an illuminating and a vivifying effect.

His life was a romance of mind in a day when little enough was known of matter. He remains a supreme example of the truth that genius knows no age or time, but in its essence belongs to eternity.

"So it comes to pass," writes D'Arcy Thompson, "that for two thousand years and throughout all lands men have come to Aristotle, and found in him information and instruction—that which they desired . . . Where he has been, there, seen or unseen, his influence remains; even the Moor and the Arab find in him, to this day, a teacher after their own hearts: a teacher of eternal verities, telling of sleep and dreams, of youth and age, of life and death, of generation and corruption, of growth and of decay; a guide to the book of Nature, a revealer of the Spirit, a prophet of the works of God."

MOHAMMED

(*c.* 570—632)

About four hundred and fifty millions of the world's inhabitants are followers of the religion of Mohammed. The importance of Mohammed, therefore, needs no further emphasis. His life is indeed remarkable. Within its range of some sixty years the whole gamut of human experience seems to have been played through, from poverty to riches, from failure to success, from friendlessness to unquestioned power, from persecution to kingly authority. By inspiration he awoke religious life in the East amongst a humanity sunk in the depths of ignorance and profligacy. During the years 609-632 the light of faith flashed out from the sincerity of his heart, and heralded one of the mightiest movements that have ever influenced the history of the world.

"ALLAHU! AKBAR! La Ilaha Ill' Allah! Mohammed ur-rasul Ullah!" "God excelleth in greatness! There is no God but the one true God! Mohammed is the Messenger of God!" The cry from the minarets echoes down the centuries. In these words for thirteen hundred years the glory and greatness of God has been extolled throughout the East. In these words the heavenly reminder has been proclaimed, and a continual respite sounded amidst the daily hubbub of human affairs.

Now we may well ask: what sort of a man was it who awoke and cleansed the East, who in roughly a score of years in Arabia produced the greatest religious revolution known to history?

Mohammed was born in or about the year A.D. 570. He came from the nobility of Arabia. His family belonged to the tribe of the Quraish, and his descent has been traced back to Ishmael and Abraham. Muslims believe that Ka'ba was built by Abraham. So from birth Mohammed was associated with an important centre of religious worship, though at that time Mecca was steeped in the grossest idolatry.

His father, Abdullah, the son of Abdu'l Muttalib, died before Mohammed was born, while his mother, Amina, died a few years later. Mohammed, at the age of six, was thus left alone in the world, an orphan bereft of both father and mother.

Mohammed was now taken care of by his grandfather, Abdu'l Muttalib, who, however, died before two years had elapsed. Mohammed then passed into the guardianship of his uncle, Abu Talib, who soon developed a deep affection for the lad and would have him sleep by his bed, eat by his side and go with him whenever he walked abroad. The depth of mutual affection between the lad, Mohammed, and his uncle, Abu Talib, was soon after this put to an open test. Abu Talib was about to make a distant journey to Syria. The prospect of such a lengthy separation from his kindly protector so distressed Mohammed, then a lad of twelve years of age, that Abu Talib decided to take the lad with him to Syria. The journey, which lasted several months, gave Mohammed his first impressions of the outside world, and must have brought him into contact with men of different races and varying religious beliefs.

Another incident of external interest occurred during the youth of Mohammed. The valley of Mecca and the surrounding country became involved in a sacrilegious war, arising out of a dispute between two Arab tribes, the Quraish and the Beni Hawazin, at the annual fair of Okaz. Mohammed attended his uncles of the Quraish, but his part in the actual conflict seems to have been confined to gathering up the arrows of the enemy as they fell and handing them to his uncles.

Some part of Mohammed's youth, like that of David of old, was spent as a shepherd tending the sheep and goats of Mecca upon the neighbouring hills and valleys; but whatever his pursuit and whatever the duties or transactions that fell to his lot, he discharged them all with such an honourable sincerity as to win for himself, by common consent, the title of *Al-Amin,* the Trustworthy.

It is also everywhere historically agreed that the youth of Mohammed was one of singular purity and modesty. When one considers the profligacy rampant at that time in Mecca and throughout Arabia generally, the merit of Mohammed must in this respect shine the more brightly by sheer contrast. Endowed with a refined mind and delicate taste, reserved and meditative, he lived much within himself and, not covetous of wealth, it seems that the quiet and retired life he was living in the family of Abu Talib was well suited to his disposition.

Abu Talib, however, was by no means wealthy. He therefore suggested to Mohammed the advisability of his earning his own livelihood by taking charge of the caravan to Syria of Khadija, a wealthy and distinguished lady of the Quraish. Mohammed readily complied, and under his guidance the Syrian caravan was conducted so successfully that Khadija was delighted. Mohammed's serious bearing and personal charm, moreover, made so deep an impression upon the lady Khadija, then a comely widow of forty years of age, that shortly afterwards, in 595, their marriage was celebrated, Mohammed being at that time twenty-five years of age.

Although Khadija was fifteen years older than Mohammed, the marriage proved fortunate and happy, the more perhaps by mutual esteem and affection than by the solace of children; for although two sons and four daughters were born of the union, Mohammed lost all these children in his lifetime with the exception of one daughter, Fatima, who was married to Ali.

During the lifetime of Khadija (she died at the age of sixty-five, when Mohammed was fifty years old), Mohammed, although in the prime of life and living in a country where polygamy was customary, remained strictly faithful and devoted to his one affectionate companion and wife, the staunch-hearted lady Khadija.

At Mecca, after the death of Khadija, Mohammed married Sauda, a widow, and later, at Medina, Ayesha, the daughter of his faithful companion, Abu Bekr.

In 605, some years after the marriage of Mohammed with Khadija, the necessity arose for rebuilding the Ka'ba, the sacred house of Mecca. The requisite material being provided, the Quraish jointly undertook the work. In the course of construction a serious dispute arose as to who should have the proud privilege of laying the sacred black stone in position in the wall of the Ka'ba. The much-prized honour was hotly contested by the various families of the Quraish. At the height of the dispute, Mohammed, then about thirty-five years of age, entered the court and was chosen as arbiter. Spreading his mantle upon the ground, he placed the sacred stone thereon and bade one from each of the four contesting divisions of the Quraish to come forward and take each a corner of the mantle and lift the stone thus. This was done; the stone was raised, and Mohammed with his own hand guided it to its place in the wall of the Ka'ba. Honour was thus shared and peace established.

Deeply religious by nature, Mohammed would often retire to a cave at the foot of Mount Hira, some three miles north of Mecca, and spend days at a time in prayer and meditation. Upon one occasion, when the world was thus set aside, the call came to Mohammed, the call that was to overthrow the gross idolatry of Arabia and to restore to the East the brightness of the religion of

Abraham, the belief in the One True and Only God, the Merciful, the Mighty, the First and the Last.

Mohammed at first listened with fear and trembling, but at length, putting his whole trust in God, he accepted the call to declare the unity of God, to overthrow idolatry and to revive the ancient lustre of true religion, consisting in the worship of God and the service of humanity; faith and good deeds; submission to God and the practice of brotherhood towards humanity.

But the task before Mohammed was well-nigh superhuman. His own tribe, the Quraish, were the chief upholders of the gross idolatry of Mecca. It is said that the idols worshipped at that time in Mecca numbered as many as three hundred and sixty-five. In the face of the bitterest opposition, persecuted, stoned, insulted and his very life in danger, Mohammed, undaunted, continued to denounce idolatry and to proclaim the mercy and magnificence, the power and punishment, the wisdom and forgiveness of the Eternal, the One Creator, the One Upholder of all humanity, of all existence.

Converts came slowly. First was his own devoted wife, Khadija. Of others, Abu Bekr, a Meccan notable, wealthy and influential, whose soundness of judgment commanded great respect amongst his compatriots; Ali, the Prophet's youthful cousin; and Zaid, a liberated slave, were three of the earliest converts; while at the end of the first three or four years of Mohammed's prophetic mission the converts to the faith probably numbered nearly forty.

Then the period of persecution set in more sharply, and in 615 it was found necessary for a band of the Muslims (as the followers of Mohammed were called) to flee for safety into Abyssinia, where the emigrants were well treated. But the persecution of the Quraish became hotter than ever, and, in the following year, a second detachment of Muslims fled from Mecca and sought refuge with the Negus of Abyssinia. Mohammed himself remained at Mecca, the object of continual invective and abuse. The Quraish endeavoured to make the influential Abu Talib abandon his nephew, Mohammed; but Abu Talib remained staunch, and continued to give Mohammed his protection.

The Quraish then announced a ban of outlawry against Mohammed and his family, the Hashimites. The ban remained in force for some two or three years, and brought in its train much suffering and hardship by the state of blockade and social ostracism under which Mohammed and his relatives were compelled to live. In 619 the ban was removed, but in the same year Mohammed sustained a severe loss in the death of his faithful wife, Khadija, while the following year saw the death of Mohammed's great protector, Abu Talib.

The Prophet's position in Mecca thereupon became critical. His followers, though devotedly attached, were but a handful against a host, and the greater part even of them were now in Abyssinia. Mohammed, hard pressed, resolved to make trial of Tayif, a city of importance sixty or seventy miles east of Mecca; but there met only with insults, stones and imprecations. With blood flowing from both his legs, he was obliged to flee the obdurate, idolatrous city. But though clouds were so dark, the persistence of the Prophet in preaching Islam (submission to the will of the One True God, even the religion of Abraham) had not been without effect. Some pilgrims from Medina had heard and been converted. In 621 they plighted themselves to Mohammed by the first pledge of Aqaba, thus: "We will not worship any but the One God; we will not steal, neither will we commit adultery, nor kill our children, nor bring false accusation against others; nor will we disobey the Prophet in anything that is right."

This was followed the year after by a still greater success from Medina, some seventy-three men and two women swearing allegiance to Mohammed by the second pledge of Aqaba. The Muslims at Mecca now began in small parties to emigrate from that city of persecution to the more hospitable atmosphere of Medina, and soon the Prophet was left at Mecca with but two companions, Abu Bekr and Ali.

The Quraish now thought to make an end of Mohammed. They laid siege to his house in an armed band, ready to fall upon him in a body as he came forth. But Mohammed received news of the plot beforehand, and secretly escaped with Abu Bekr under cover of night to the cave of Thaur, three miles distant from Mecca. The next day, the Quraish, finding themselves balked in their intent, made an extensive but fruitless search for Mohammed, who, upon the third night, quitted the cave of refuge and set out for Medina on June 20, A.D. 622. This was the Hegira (flight), and from this date begins the Muslim calendar.

Medina now became the city of Islam. Mohammed was welcomed there. The Muslims soon established themselves in the city, and amid scenes of general enthusiasm built in Medina the first mosque in the history of Islam.

But the Quraish were not satisfied even with the departure of the Muslims from Mecca. They seemed determined to use their utmost endeavours to exterminate the Muslims. The course of the next ten years is consequently marked by bitter hostility and continual warfare between the idolaters in Mecca and the Muslims in Medina.

In the second year after the flight, the Quraish, with a force of some thousand strong, advanced upon Medina. Apprised of the attack, the Muslims, a mere three hundred and thirteen, left their city to engage the enemy. A decisive battle was fought at Badr, thirty miles from Medina but two hundred and twenty miles from Mecca. Viewing the disparity of the opposing forces and seeing the Muslims outnumbered by three to one, Mohammed was filled with deep anxiety. Before the battle, therefore, he retired for a moment to his hut with Abu Bekr, and engaged in earnest prayer. Then the battle began. The Meccans were defeated with heavy loss, and many notable chiefs of the Quraish were slain on the field.

The victory of Badr greatly inspirited the Muslims, but the Quraish fled only to renew a more desperate attack the following year, when, about three thousand strong, they advanced to Uhud, some three miles north of Medina. Mohammed led the Muslims forth from Medina to repel the attacks, and once again his forces were outnumbered by the enemy by three to one. To make matters worse, with the enemy already in sight, Abdullah ibn Ubay, with his three hundred followers, deserted. Thus the forces remaining with Mohammed were reduced to seven hundred. The fighting was fierce; the fortune of battle fluctuated for some time; the Muslims sustained heavy losses and were compelled to retreat, but the stout resistance they had offered gave the Meccans no heart to pursue their advantage, and they withdrew their armies from the field.

It should be noted that in both these battles Mohammed was upon the defensive, fighting against an aggressor, who had come from a distance to fall upon and exterminate the Muslims.

Two years later the Quraish, with allied tribes, made a yet more ambitious attack upon Mohammed and the Muslims. With an army of some twenty-four thousand they advanced and laid siege to Medina itself. But after a month's efforts, not succeeding in breaking through the defence, the Meccans became exhausted. Their provisions ran short, and discomfited by tempest and hurricane which demolished their tents, Abu Sufyan, the Meccan commander, gave the order to retire.

The truce of Hudaibiya was now proclaimed. Mohammed made pilgrimage to Mecca and, in an atmosphere of general peace, Islam gathered strength and numbers.

After some years tribal feuds broke out again, and Mohammed and the Meccans found themselves once more arrayed in opposing camps. But now the Muslims were strong. Mohammed advanced upon Mecca and obtained a bloodless victory, the Meccans surrendering without resistance.

This was the final triumph of Islam. The sacred house of the Ka'ba was purified of idols, polytheism was overthrown and before long arose an Arabia united in the worship of the One True God.

In the tenth year after the flight, in an atmosphere of peace from which every vestige of idolatry had been swept away, Mohammed donned the pilgrim's garb and went up to Mecca for his last, his farewell pilgrimage. He invoked the blessing of God upon the Holy Temple at Mecca. Then, having performed the ceremonies of pilgrimage, he went in procession to Mina and Arafat, where he concluded his prayer and recitation with the Quranic verse: "This day I have perfected your religion for you and fulfilled My favour upon you and chosen Islam to be your religion."

In the year 632, having seen the complete success of his prophetic mission, having magnanimously pardoned his bitterest enemies and won respect and affection upon every side, Mohammed died in the arms of his youthful wife, Ayesha, and was interred at Medina. His last thoughts, his last words were still of heavenly things, as he whispered prayerfully: "Lord! . . . Eternity in Paradise! . . . The blessed companionship on high!"

So passed away from the affection and devotion of his followers the figure of the great Arabian Prophet.

His greatest reform was the overthrow of idolatry, while amongst other salutary measures he limited polygamy, forbade adultery, usury, gambling and the use of intoxicants. He abolished infanticide, discouraged slavery and proclaimed the essential brotherhood and equality of mankind in the sight of God, irrespective of race or class.

The Quran (the sacred book of Islam) has remained undimmed in its pristine beauty and sublimity for over thirteen hundred years and has been translated into many different languages.

SIR THOMAS MORE

(1478–1535)

In the second half of the fifteenth century the world took on new life. The new learning of the Renaissance swept across Europe, stirring men to great adventure and to higher realms of thought. Every country produced pioneers, artists, philosophers, according to its genius, and these men laid the foundations of our modern world. In England, the greatest of the adventurers upon the new seas of learning was Thomas More, the gentle wit who was loved by all who knew him; who rose by his own genius to the highest office in the land; who died for his faith and was canonized four hundred years later.

IT is Christmas, 1491. In the great hall of Cardinal Morton, Archbishop of Canterbury, a company of players are performing, and the prelate, with his household and friends, are enjoying the pleasures of the festivity and the play. Suddenly, among the actors appears a thirteen-year-old page. He steps on to the stage and begins to take part, making up his words as he goes along and keeping the company in constant laughter with his wit and extempore sallies.

The archbishop smiles approval. As he has said before: "That boy will become a marvellous man."

The boy was Thomas More, and within a year Thomas Morton had suggested that he should leave his service and go to Oxford.

Thomas More was born in Cheapside, in London, in 1478. His father was Sir John More, butler at Lincoln's Inn, and later barrister and judge. He was sent to St. Anthony's school in Threadneedle Street, where only a few years earlier William Latimer and John Colet had also been scholars. From there he entered the service of the archbishop, on whose advice he went up in 1492 to Canterbury Hall, Oxford, which has since given place to Christ Church.

His allowance was small. Even had he wished there were but few pence for frivolity. His natural intelligence enabled him to grasp subjects without a great deal of effort.

The "New Learning" had reached England, and men were turning to the study of Greek and the exercise of their own wits: the stilted doctrines of medievalism were giving way before the freedom and keenness of Renaissance scholarship.

More took his first lessons in Greek from the great Thomas Linacre, and he also studied under another eminent Oxford scholar William Grocyn. The classics did not occupy his whole time, for he read French, history, mathematics, and learned to play the flute and the viol.

After two years, his father, fearing that Greek and the new learning might affect his son's orthodoxy, removed Thomas from Oxford before he had taken his degree and brought him to London, where he became a law student. Again he devoted himself to his books, was called to the Bar in a shorter space of time than was usual, and was appointed lecturer on law at Furnival's Inn.

Now he turned his attention to literature and spent much of his time writing little comedies and verses. He continued his acquaintance with Linacre and Grocyn, and through them met other scholars, among whom were William Lilly, an old Oxford man, and John Colet, who was to be his lifelong friend. Colet, who became Dean of St. Paul's in 1505, and founded St. Paul's School in 1510, was one of the greatest humanists of the Renaissance.

Soon afterwards More made a close friendship with Erasmus, the glory and figurehead of European culture. Erasmus came to England in 1499, and when he saw More he was at once attracted by the man's wit, charm and intelligence. From that time the two were bound to each other in that close correspondence of learning and intelligence which was the splendour of the age. Both were early and enthusiastic champions of education for women.

More took Erasmus to the royal nursery, and there they met the young Prince Henry, who was to be King Henry the Eighth. The little excursion was typical of More's whimsical personality, for the great Dutch humanist had no idea where he was being led until he saw More present the prince with some verses. Erasmus had brought none, and had to promise to write some at once, and when they left the royal presence he soundly scolded the irrepressible More.

More was now twenty-one, and spiritual questionings began to loom largely in his life. For four years he retired from the world and spent his time in spiritual contemplation, and he seems to have considered becoming a priest. From then onwards he wore continually next to his skin, that "sharp shirt of hair" that is the constant proof of the man's asceticism.

It was during this period that he lectured on St. Augustine's *De Civitate Dei* at the church of St. Lawrence Jewry by the invitation of Grocyn, who was rector. His audience included some of the most learned men in London.

Some time in 1503 More decided definitely against entering the Church, but we have no hint of his reasons. He returned to public life, and in the following year became a Member of Parliament.

He at once distinguished himself in a characteristic and dangerous manner. King Henry VII had asked the House for an "aid" of three-fifteenths, which amounted to a sum of about £113,000. It was at least a third more than he was entitled to, but the king's creatures had paved the way, and the servile members were about to grant the money when young More rose to speak.

He "made such arguments and reasons there against" the king's proposals "that they were thereby overthrown; so that one of the King's Privy Chamber, named Maister Tyler, being present thereat, brought word to the king out of the Parliament House, that a beardless boy had disappointed all his purpose." The result was that Parliament granted only £30,000, and in revenge the king cast Sir John More into the Tower and would not release him until he had paid a fine of £100. Thomas again retired from the public scene. He shared chambers with William Lilly, and the two bent over their desks making translations of Greek verses and epigrams into Latin.

But a new attraction claimed some of More's time. He found it at "the house of Maister John Colte, a gentleman of Essex, the honest conversation and virtuous education" of whose daughters impelled him "there specially to set his affection. And albeit his mind most served him to the second daughter, for that he thought her the fairest and best favoured, yet when he considered that it would be both grief and some shame also to the eldest to see her younger sister preferred before her in marriage, he then, of a certain pity, framed his fancy towards the eldest."

So in 1505 he married Jane Colte and set up house in Bucklersbury. The gentle More made a model husband, and he settled to a quiet life of literature. Soon he invited Erasmus to stay with him, and together they translated some of the dialogues of Lucian from Greek to Latin. In 1508, after More had paid a visit to the universities of Paris and Louvain, Erasmus again came to Bucklersbury, and there he wrote the *Moriæ Encomium* (Praise of Folly), with its punning title on his host's name.

When Jane, who had borne him four children, died in 1511, More took as his second wife, Alice Middleton, a widow seven years older than he, neither beautiful nor well-educated, but a thoroughly capable housewife. Their life together was one of continuous happiness. More, and his bride, moved to Bishopsgate Street

Without; it was not until 1523 that he built his famous mansion at Chelsea.

He now devoted himself to his Bar practice. His skill and honesty won him success and high reputation, and he was soon making £400 a year; equal to roughly £5,000 a year of our present money. He had become a Bencher of Lincoln's Inn in 1509, and had been made an under-sheriff of London in the following year. As already noted, Henry VIII had known More in his boyhood, and Wolsey recognized his power as a lawyer and planned to make use of him. In 1515, More was sent on a commercial embassy to Flanders, and on his travels he found time to sketch his most famous work, *Utopia,* which he finished and published in the following year.

Utopia—the title means Nowhere—was a satire on the abuses of the times. It described an ideal state, in which communism was in force, where everyone worked for a limited number of hours and spent the rest of the day in amusement and learning; where there was education for all, both men and women, complete religious toleration, humane legislation, and a proper provision for hospitals, sanitation and social necessities of every kind.

Utopia made a great impression in More's own time and in the succeeding centuries, but, admirable as the reforms of his ideal state are, they must not be regarded as those advocated by More in real life. The views expressed in the satire are not compatible with the actions of the author.

Wolsey was pleased with More's first work for him. In 1516, More wrote to Erasmus: "When I returned from my embassage of Flanders, the king's majesty would have granted me a yearly pension, which surely, if I should respect honour and profit, was not to be contemned by me; yet have I as yet refused it."

But Wolsey and the king were not to be put off: they wanted the service of the brilliant young lawyer, and in a few months he accepted a pension of £100 a year for life.

It was after his return from another embassy that his brilliant and successful arguments against the crown in a Star Chamber case so impressed Henry VIII that the king at once declared that More must be in his employ. So More became Master of Requests in 1518. His task was to examine the petitions presented to Henry, and he was in constant contact with the king.

Henry delighted, as all men did, in the conversation of the brilliant lawyer. He would summon him to his own chamber to talk of "matters of astronomy, geometry, divinity, and such other faculties," or invite him to supper with the queen, "to be merry with them." But More knew the value of Henry's friendship. At the height of his favour, after the king had walked for an hour with him in the garden at Chelsea, during which the royal arm had been placed about More's neck, More told his biographer that he had "no cause to be proud thereof, for if my head would win him a castle in France, it should not fail to go."

One result of More's rise was that he won the king's approval of the new learning, and persuaded Henry to make the university diehards give more scope to the teaching of Greek and the writings of the moderns.

In 1520 he accompanied Henry to the Field of the Cloth of Gold, and at Calais met Erasmus, who introduced him to the French king's secretary, Budæus, the greatest Greek scholar in Europe. In 1521 More was knighted and made the king's sub-treasurer. He accompanied Wolsey on embassies to Calais and Bruges, and when Charles V visited England it was More who made the Latin speech of welcome, as he had also done to the Papal Legate, Cardinal Campeggio.

On Wolsey's recommendation, More was elected Speaker in 1523, and such was his zeal in procuring a subsidy for the king, that the cardinal suggested that he should be given a gratuity of £100 over and above his fee. "I am rather moved to put your highness in remembrance thereof," wrote Wolsey, "because he is not the most ready to speak and solicit his own cause."

The gift was made, and More thanked Wolsey effusively. Yet later the two were at loggerheads over the creation of a new office.

"You show yourself a foolish councillor," said Wolsey.

"Thank God the king has only one fool in his council," replied More.

Wealth had come to More with his rise to power. Henry made him large gifts of land in Oxfordshire and Kent in 1522 and 1525. In 1526 he was granted a licence to export a thousand woollen cloths. But in his increased comfort More continued to live simply.

On October 19, 1529, Wolsey was deprived of the chancellorship. Warham, Archbishop of Canterbury, was offered the appointment, but he declined on the score that he was too old. On the twenty-fifth, More became Chancellor of England, the first layman to hold that office.

"I do indeed congratulate England," wrote Erasmus, "for a better and holier judge could not have been appointed."

As chancellor, More made himself notable for the rapidity of the despatch of his cases. He dealt with his business efficiently and well, and he even encouraged litigants to lay their claims before him at his own home. As ever, he seasoned his law with jokes: on one occasion he handed back an unimportant paper to a lawyer with "a tale of a" written in before the lawyer's signature—which was Tubbe! The speed of his work evoked a popular rhyme:

When More some time had chancellor been,
No more suits did remain;
The like will never more be seen,
Till More be there again.

His leniency and clemency stopped short at heretics. In spite of the religious toleration advocated in *Utopia*, More was zealous for his Church. Heresy must be hunted, and when found it had to be whipped, racked, or burned out. Mild man as he was, he was harsh and uncompromising on this point. He could even declare, when some unfortunate was burned for heresy: "There was never a wretch, I wene, better worthy."

The bitter question of Henry's divorce from Catherine of Aragon soon came to disturb More's peace of mind. At first he was silent on the point, but when Henry taxed him he could not agree to the king's views. In March, 1531, the decisions of the universities were read out to the House of Lords by More, who, when asked his own opinion, cautiously said that he had already told it to the king. But the chancellor saw the trend of events, and in 1532 he resigned. He went home and informed his wife with light-hearted indifference, and at once made plans for a new life in straitened circumstances.

A year later he was named as one of the disciples of the Holy Maid of Kent, and was charged as guilty of treason. He was called before four privy councillors, and in spite of his danger, treated them with cool disdain. Only his great popularity saved him then, and Henry grudgingly struck his name out of the Bill of Attainder.

But in April, 1534, Sir Thomas More refused to take the oath of adherence to the new Act of Succession, by which Anne Boleyn's issue became heirs to the throne. He was willing to take an oath of loyalty to the king, but he could not swear one which abrogated the authority of the Pope. So he was committed to the Tower.

He was a sick man. Congested lungs, gravel, stone and cramp made his body a torment, but his spirits were as cheerful as ever. His wife asked him to take the oath and regain his liberty, but More answered: "Is not this house as nigh heaven as mine own?"

In 1535, Henry was declared supreme head of the Church in England, and in April, Thomas Cromwell went to the Tower to ask More whether this were lawful in his eyes. More replied that he was a faithful subject of the king. In May and June, Cromwell repeated the visits, and then sent the solicitor-general to interview More.

Meanwhile, More was still cheerful, believing that: "A man may live for the next world and yet be merry." He wrote to his wife and daughters, but when it was discovered that he had exchanged notes with his friend and fellow-prisoner, John Fisher, Bishop of Rochester, his writing materials were taken from him. From that time More closed the shutters of his cell.

On June 25, Fisher was executed. More knew what to expect. He was charged with high treason at Westminster Hall on July 1. The evidence was based on the solicitor-general's reports of his conversations and on the notes to Fisher. More, seated as a sick man, denied the charges with great dignity. He was found guilty and sentenced to be hanged at Tyburn, but five days later Henry commuted the method to decapitation.

His behaviour at the final scene on Tower Hill on the morning of July 7, 1535, was as magnificent as it was moving. As he reached the steps of the scaffold, he said to the lieutenant there: "I pray thee see me safely up, and for my coming down let me shift for myself." With a joke he told the executioner to do his job fearlessly, and then he moved the beard, which he had grown during his imprisonment, away from the block, saying: "It has never committed treason." Finally, he prayed God to send the king good counsel.

Then came the end.

All Europe was shocked at the news of his death. It paid then, as it has done since, homage to More, the great and good. In 1886 he was beatified: in 1935 he was made a saint of the Roman Church.

More needs no epitaph but the story of his life. Let his friend Erasmus complete for us the picture of the man and his household:

"There is not any man living so affectionate to his children as he, and he loveth his old wife as if she were a girl of fifteen.

"Plato's academy was revived again: only whereas in the academy the discussion turned upon geometry and the power of number, the house of Chelsea is a veritable school of Christian religion. In it is none, man or woman, but readeth or studieth the liberal arts. Yet is their chief care piety. There is never any seen idle. The head of the house governs it, not by lofty carriage and frequent rebukes, but by gentleness and amiable manners. Every man is busy in his place, performing his duty with alacrity, nor is sober mirth wanting."

DESIDERIUS ERASMUS

(*c.* 1466–1536)

In the first quarter of the sixteenth century, when our civilization was changing the cloak of medievalism for the lighter garb of modernity, when the Renaissance was in flower and the first discords of the Reformation were rumbling across Europe, the whole of the educated world looked to one man—Erasmus. He was the arbiter of learning, the fountain-head of culture, and he swayed Europe with his pen. The pope, the emperor, kings, princes, scholars and divines sought his company and his help. This scholar with the biting wit and the frail, fastidious body, "with a Catholic head and a Lutheran stomach," was the greatest humanist of his age, the founder of a tradition of scholarship and tolerance that the world today need strive to maintain.

IN 1466 a Dutchman named Gerhard became the father of a love-child. When the son grew to manhood he was smallish and slight, with fair hair and blue eyes of steady gaze. But there was a twinkle in those eyes, a satiric gleam in their calm watchfulness. They were set over a long, pointed nose and a large mouth. The whole head was poised timidly, like a bird's.

Of this little, illegitimate Dutchman at the age of fifty, it has been written: "Three young kings, the greatest in Europe . . . contend which shall have him as a voluntary subject. Popes write to him to announce their accession and offer him public hospitality at Rome. Little states as well as great ones, provinces and cities as well as states, invite him to enjoy in their midst a glorious repose. Everyone flatters him, even Luther. All the presses of Germany, England and Italy reproduce his writings. All the reading world reads nothing but Erasmus. . . . All who write imitate his way of writing; even his enemies cannot attack him without casting their rejoinders into his own style. The world is pregnant with wars to come . . . but it keeps silence for a moment around Erasmus."

Gerhard's son had become one of the most influential men in Europe, the intellectual spearhead of the Renaissance, the transmitter, in a way the founder, of the tradition of liberal knowledge.

Gerhard was a man of learning; a Latin and Greek scholar

and with a knowledge of law. He was very much in love with a girl named Margaret Brandt. Unfortunately, Gerhard's parents would not allow him to marry her; they wished him to enter the Church, and celibacy was essential. Margaret bore him a son, and as Gerhard's family were still as adamant regarding the priesthood, he shut the door of his home behind him and set out for Rome, where he earned what must have been a precarious living by copying manuscripts. Still insistent on satisfying their ambition, his parents sent him a false story about Margaret's death, and in despair he took holy orders. Then he returned to Holland to find how grossly he had been deceived. Margaret was not dead, and another son had been born while he was away. So the story goes, and perhaps the truth with it. The younger son received the paternal name of Gerhard, which means "beloved." To the world he is known as Erasmus.

"Desiderius," we are reminded by Sir Richard Jebb, is barbarous Latin for "beloved," "and Erasmus is barbarous Greek for it. . . . The combination, Desiderius Erasmus, is probably due to the fact that he had been known as Gerhard Gerhardson. It was a singular fortune for a master of literary style to be designated by two words, which both mean the same thing, and are both incorrect."

Gerhard kept his priestly vows, but Margaret devoted herself to her children. Erasmus was sent to school at Gouda, about twelve miles from Rotterdam, when he was four years old. Later he became a chorister of Utrecht cathedral, and at nine was taken to Deventer, where he went to school with Adrian of Utrecht, afterwards Pope Adrian VI. At Deventer, Erasmus learned a store of Latin with a little Greek, logic and physics.

Bereaved of both parents by the year 1484, the frail, sensitive youth with a keen wit, a nimble intellect, and love of learning, came under the care of guardians, who wished Erasmus to enter the monastic life. He hated the idea. They sent him for three years to the Fratres Collationarii, who prepared candidates for religious orders. His life there was a torment. According to his own account of the method of the brethren: "If they saw any youth of unusually high spirit and quick disposition, it was their chief care to subdue him by means of blows, threats, scoldings and other devices which they called 'breaking in,' and thus to fit him for the monastic life."

This training, even allowing for possible exaggeration, was hardly calculated to make Erasmus more docile, but his guardians still insisted on him entering a monastery. Erasmus fell ill, they pressed their case, until, mentally and physically exhausted, he gave in. Still protesting, Erasmus became a novice in the house of the Canons Regular of St. Augustine at Stein. He was then eighteen. Two years later he made his solemn profession and received the religious habit.

He spent five miserable years at Stein, loathing the whole round of monkish life. Insomnia tortured him, and the frequent rising for night offices accentuated the trouble. He hated fish; it made him ill; even the smell of it turned his stomach.

Yet Erasmus pursued his studies in spite of difficulties. Rummaging in the neglected library, he came across some dust-stained manuscripts that gave him many a happy hour. His knowledge of Latin stood him in good stead, for after he had been ordained priest the Bishop of Cambrai offered him a post as his Latin secretary. Erasmus accepted with alacrity, got leave of absence from his monastery, and left it for ever. He was with the bishop for about a year and then received permission to proceed to the University of Paris, but he left it in disgust. The place was insanitary; the food, both mental and physical, was meagre and unwholesome; the cold on occasion was intense.

"The theologians or theologasters of Paris," wrote Erasmus, "have the most rotten brains, the most barbarous tongues, the most stupid intellects, the most barren learning, the coarsest manners, the most spiteful tongues and the blackest hearts." Perhaps he succeeded in taking the degree of Bachelor of Divinity in spite of the professors; or it may be that they were not quite so foolish after all.

For the next few years he struggled with illness, lived by tutoring, and studied Greek. One of his pupils was William Blount, afterwards Lord Mountjoy, who invited Erasmus to England. Erasmus accepted, and went there in 1499.

He found happiness and scholarship. At Oxford he met John Colet, later Dean of St. Paul's and founder of St. Paul's School, a man of liberal tendencies and a disciple of the new learning. He also made the acquaintance of Thomas More, "the saint of the Renaissance," and of Warham, future Archbishop of Canterbury. They all became devoted friends of Erasmus until their deaths. He met, too, the boy of nine years who was to become Henry VIII. The child took to him and afterwards corresponded with him. "Your England is most pleasant to me," Erasmus tells Colet, "for many reasons, and chiefly because it possesses so many men well skilled in sound learning." The quiet scholar came out of his shell. He wrote to Andrelini, poet laureate of the French king, telling how he was becoming quite a man of the world, a fair horseman, a courtier.

"I know how to bow gracefully and smile pleasantly, even when I feel least inclined." He ends the letter with a generous measure of praise for English womanhood. "English ladies," he says, "are divinely pretty, and too good-natured. They have an excellent custom among them that wherever you go, the girls kiss you. They kiss you when they come, they kiss you when you go, and they kiss you at intervening opportunities." It is an amusing tribute and a reminder of the writer's humanity; he was never the dry-as-dust school-man. He was a lover of life, of delicate living, and of old Burgundy.

Erasmus returned to the Continent early in 1500 and published his first considerable work, the *Adagia*. It was dedicated to Lord Mountjoy, who had settled a pension upon him, and also carried some verses in praise of Prince Henry. The *Adagia* was a collection of proverbs from ancient and modern literature to which Erasmus had added interesting and witty comments. The book gained him a European-wide reputation. It sold in thousands of copies. It has been described as "a prodigious monument of patience and knowledge," but its wit and satire gained its popularity. Erasmus himself regarded it as one of the best among his numerous works. Warham was so delighted with it that he carried it everywhere and offered Erasmus a benefice if he would return to England.

In 1502 he published *The Christian Soldier's Manual*. It was a plea for rational Christianity as opposed to monkish theology and monasticism. For example: "You honour the bones of St. Paul hidden in a shrine," he writes, "but you do not honour the mind of St. Paul hidden in his writings." This book, too, was very popular.

Erasmus was now toiling away at Greek, in an age when Greek scholars were few. His object, as always, was to disseminate the knowledge and diffuse the good influence of ancient learning. He revisited England in 1505, when he lectured on Greek at Cambridge, and in the next year departed for Italy, where at Turin the university conferred on him a doctor's degree in sacred theology. While he was at Bologna the plague broke out. The civic authorities ordered that all doctors who attended the sufferers should make use of main thoroughfares as little as possible and don a white scarf so that people might recognize and avoid them. The Augustinian scapular, which Erasmus wore as part of his habit, caused him to be mistaken for a medical man, with the result that he was almost lynched by a crowd among whom he was innocently wandering. The unhappy victim of ignorance promptly applied for and received a papal exemption from wearing the scapular. From that time he dressed in a costume half cleric, half lay, " in which," writes Lilly shrewdly, " we may see the outward and visible sign of the inner man of the heart."

While in Italy Erasmus supervised a second and considerably enlarged edition of the *Adagia* at the famous Aldine Press at Venice, and in the city which is the glory of the Adriatic he met some of the finest scholars of the age. Efforts were made to keep him in Rome, which he visited and stigmatized as " ruins and rubbish," though he afterwards thought better of it. Clerical appointments with chances of high preferment were offered, but he refused them all. " I prefer to serve no one, and be of service, if I can, to everyone." Such was his policy.

When Henry VIII succeeded to the throne in 1509, Lord Mountjoy wrote to Erasmus, heralding a golden age of literature under the new reign and asking the scholar to visit England again. Erasmus went. He stayed with Thomas More, and at his house in Bucklersbury wrote *Moriæ Enconium* (Praise of Folly). This stinging satire is usually regarded as his finest work. In his own lifetime it went through no fewer than twenty-seven large editions, an astonishing success when it is remembered that most people were illiterate and that reading was regarded as an accomplishment. With graceful but biting wit, he scourges theologians, lawyers, grammarians, writers, scientists—all professional folk. He flays the pedants, the enemies of good learning, and hurls shafts at the ecclesiastical corruption of the age. Pope Julius II made no objection to the book and his successor, Leo X, received it with delight.

Erasmus followed the *Moriæ Enconium* with a still more important work. In 1511, Fisher sent him to teach at Cambridge, and while there Erasmus started on a version of the Greek New Testament with a Latin translation and critical notes. Meanwhile, Warham presented him to a benefice at Aldington, Kent, which was commuted for a pension of £20. "Although I am not a native, but an adopted child of Great Britain," Erasmus wrote, " yet when I reflect how many years I have lived in England, how many protectors I have found in her, how many honourable and sincere friends she has bestowed upon me, how much of my fortune—such as it is—is owing to her, I feel as great a love for her as if I had drawn my first breath in her territory." In 1514, Erasmus proceeded to Basel to superintend the publication of his Testament.

It awoke fresh interest. Scholars looked again at the Vulgate, which had been the only version in use, and saw a new method in

Biblical scholarship. His *Paraphrases on the New Testament,* completed in 1524, were deemed of such value in England that a translation of them was placed in every parish church. A part of this work contained a dedication to the Emperor, Charles V, and a passage from it may be cited as likely to be of topical interest until the globe ceases to pursue its daily course: "May Your Majesty always remember that no war, however just the causes for which it is undertaken, can be carried on with such moderation that it shall not bring in its train a whole host of villainies and of misfortunes; and that the evils of war fall, for the most part, upon the innocent." Erasmus was uncompromising in his rejection of violent conflict, which offended his sweetness of reason even as it shocked his deep humanity and outraged his sense of justice. Thus he writes to a friend in much the same vein, and with far less restraint: "I often wonder what it is that urges, I will not say Christians, but men, to such a pitch of madness that they will make every effort, incur any expense and meet the greatest dangers, for their mutual destruction. For what else are we doing all our lives but waging war? We are worse than the dumb animals, for among them it is only the wild beasts that wage war, and even they do not fight among themselves, but with beasts of a different species, and that with the weapons with which nature has furnished them; not as we do with machines invented by the art of the devil, nor for all manner of causes, but either in the defence of their young or for food."

Erasmus became the most talked-of man in Europe. Everybody who was anybody was writing to him and reading him. Some criticized him. Already he had become involved in controversy. A converted Jew of Cologne, named Pfefferkorn, proposed that all Hebrew books, except the old Testament, should be examined and, if deemed undesirable, destroyed. Ruechlin, a distinguished Hebrew scholar, protested violently, but the Inquisitors approved the idea. Erasmus knew no Hebrew, and was little interested in it, but in the cause of liberalism and learning he earnestly supported Reuchlin against the obscurantists. The Dominicans were angry: there was a long struggle.

Then, suddenly, Luther appeared with his condemnation of indulgences and their traffic, and in many points gained the sympathy of Erasmus. But Erasmus was a gentle scholar, and by comparison Luther was a boisterous revolutionist and reformer. Erasmus could not help sympathizing with some of Luther's aims, but he disliked the violence of his methods. As for Luther's opinion of Erasmus, the former remarked: "With him the purely human is of more account than what is divine. Though I am loath to judge him, I must admonish you not to read all his works, or rather not to accept them without exercising judgment." It must also be noted that he flattered the humanist not a little by writing to him: "For who is there whose entire, inmost thoughts are not dominated by Erasmus?" He considered that Pope Leo's Bull of 1520, which Luther burnt at Wittenberg, drove him to rebellion: "most evangelically minded men were not incensed by Luther's opinion but by the Pope's Bull." The split in the Church put Erasmus in a quandary. He was not heart and soul with the Lutherans, nor could he be with the reactionaries and enemies of true learning who were among Luther's opponents.

Erasmus was ill at ease. Unwilling to be drawn into theological controversy, he was accused by the Church of being a sympathizer with Luther, and the Protestants condemned him for favouring the Church. In 1524 he at last broke silence and wrote a work on free will against Luther's doctrine of predestination, though he had really not much heart for the battle. His opponent replied in an abusive pamphlet, but later acknowledged "the freedom of the will in all men who have the use of reason." Erasmus answered with an equally vitriolic pen, and Luther confessed that whenever he prayed he prayed for a curse upon Erasmus.

In 1521 Erasmus had settled down permanently at Basel, where he had become general editor and adviser to the press of Johann Froben, whom he had first met in 1514. Under the direction of Erasmus, Froben's press began to turn out excellent editions of the classics and of the works of the early Fathers. The publishing house acquired fame and Erasmus became monarch of the realm of letters.

Men looked to him as the arbiter of education, so much so that it might be said that he conducted a correspondence school long before that aid to culture was officially invented. "I receive daily letters from remote parts," he tells us, "from kings, princes, prelates and men of learning, and even from persons of whose existence I was ignorant." Sometimes his answers extended to many pages.

In 1526 Erasmus published the final edition of his *Colloquies,* in which he held up to ridicule many of the follies of the age. It was enthusiastically received, later became a school text-book, and is enjoyed to this day.

When Froben died, Erasmus removed to Freiburg, but he returned to Basel in 1535, not a little weary of life, anxious only for God to take him "from this furious world." Money came to him from crowned and uncrowned heads, but friends passed away, and their deaths, as those of his old friends, Fisher and More, were not always due to the natural running down of the clock of life.

His last years were troubled by the ecclesiastical dissension, and he strove hard for peace within the Church. "Contention grows hot, and charity grows cold," he avowed. Honours pursued him, but he was old and ill, and in 1534 he refused the offer of a cardinalship. He preferred the substance of independence to even the shadow of servitude.

He died at Basel on July 12, 1536. So passed the man who educated Europe; who revived the glories of the classics and re-established their tradition of culture. He taught learning not for its own sake but for the disciplining and freeing of the mind.

Too reasonable to be a thorough-going partisan, an instinctive foe of fanaticism and violence and the tyranny of ignorance, the sworn friend of common-sense and sweet reasonableness, Erasmus said what many other men thought and wrote what they could not, or dared not, express. He founded no cast-iron system, and if on occasions he changed his opinions, let us be frank and admit that consistency is often the genius of mediocrity.

MARTIN LUTHER

(1483–1546)

When Martin Luther nailed his theses attacking the sale of indulgences upon the door of the castle church at Wittenberg, his hammer broke Christendom in twain. From that time he became the leader of the Reformation, the dominating force in the creation of Protestantism. His was the dynamic figure that headed this break with Rome, and the influence of his life and work has never ceased to be felt in the subsequent history of the western world.

NEVER since the establishment of Christianity in Europe has there been such a period of religious decadence as the early years of the sixteenth century. The glories of the Italian Renaissance and the great movements that followed had decayed; in northern Europe the re-birth was only dawning. Sloth and vice had lowered the prestige of the Church. Corruption was not universal, but it prevailed in high places for all men to see. The Mendicant Orders had largely fallen from their great ideals, and had become grasping and indolent; pluralism was rife and bishoprics were held by nobles whose only thought was worldly gain; while popes such as Alexander VI and Julius II put the temporal power of the papal states before their spiritual office. Times were ripe for a change. So great was the spiritual unrest arising in men's minds that when, on November 1, 1517, Dr. Martin Luther, professor of theology at the University of Wittenberg, nailed on the door of the castle church ninety-five theses attacking the hawking of indulgences, a storm broke over Europe such as their author had certainly never expected. Here let it be noted that the posting of the theses for debate was in accordance with custom and no new form of propaganda.

Luther was a strange figure for a religious leader—a vast, dynamic man, gross of speech on occasion, though he could write with rare beauty; a man of the people, always apt to be perplexed and ill at ease in the company of his social superiors. Yet he had the fire of spiritual fervour within him. For years after leaving his native Eisleben, where he was born in 1483, he had tortured himself with doubts and perplexities in the matter of saving his soul. In an excess of enthusiasm he abandoned law and joined the Augustinian monastery of Erfurt, and once there, with the vision of God as an implacable judge firmly fixed in his mind, he practised the strictest asceticism, fasting and scourging himself far beyond prescribed custom. All to no purpose. His doubts remained unassuaged, his difficulties increased rather than decreased. "If ever a monk got to heaven by monastic observance," he afterwards said in his downright fashion, "I should surely have done so."

In 1507 Luther had become a priest, and in 1508 was lecturing on philosophy at the newly created University of Wittenberg. A year later his subject was the exposition of the Scriptures in which he did not always see fit to follow tradition. In 1510 he went to Rome, and there saw abuses in high places that later drew him into conflict with his Church. Seven years later, at the age of thirty-four, he was professor of theology at Wittenberg, was indeed made a doctor of the subject on the instructions of the elector. He had established a considerable reputation by his preaching, which showed distinct originality of thought, "getting at the kernel in the nut, the grain in the wheat, the marrow in the bone," as he said, but he had, as yet, given no hint of rebellion against ecclesiastical authority, although he had criticized abuses. Then came the attack on the sale of indulgences.

This custom was one which had been much abused during the decline of faith. Stated simply, the theory of indulgences was that the temporal punishment due for sin could be remitted in whole, or in part, in the case of those who, after confessing and showing contrition for their sins, received holy communion and performed some act of penance. In course of time the most popular act of penance became that of making a contribution to the temporal needs of the Church, and in the hands of unscrupulous or over-zealous ecclesiastics, the matter had developed into a ready-money transaction.

It was this development, and not the doctrine of indulgences itself, that Luther attacked in 1517. There was much that was controversial in his theses, but nothing positively heretical. Certainly the last thing Luther desired at this time was to break away from the Church. His followers were more ardent, and the professor of Wittenberg found himself dragged into the welter of European politics. The Dominican prior, John Tetzel, one of the chief offenders at whom Luther aimed his shaft, replied roundly to the theses and accused Luther of heresy. Wordy warfare began, and its echoes reached the Vatican.

Leo X, the learned, charming, worldly Medici, was not at first particularly interested. He considered the matter a trivial university dispute that would drown itself in a sea of rhetoric. It did nothing of the kind, and at length the pope was compelled to alter his opinion. The controversy was spreading to all parts of the Continent, and Dr. John Eck, an Ingodstade professor, also denounced Luther. Luther defended his theories, and began to extend them. It is now that we find him first advancing the fundamental doctrine of the Reformation—justification by faith without works: "Good works will never make a good man, but a good man does good works; bad works will never make a bad man, but a bad man does bad works." Man can never be anything but a sinner, said Luther. Let him acknowledge this fact and throw himself on God's mercy. If he only believes that he will find salvation, salvation will come to him. It was this idea which led him in after years to write to his friend and disciple, Melanchthon, whom he first met as a fellow professor at Wittenberg: "Be a sinner and sin for all you're worth. But even more heartily rest your faith and your joyful hope in Christ, who triumphs over sin and death." It was a hyperbole, of course, to enforce a belief that only a student could appreciate.

Luther could no longer be ignored at Rome, and, in 1520, Leo took the decisive step of issuing a bull, or papal edict, denouncing some, but not all, of Luther's opinions. If their author did not retract within sixty days he would be excommunicated. Luther replied by publicly burning a copy of the bull. The great step had been taken. Papal supremacy had been defied, and the Reformation was launched.

From now we see Luther borne on the flood he had unwittingly released; always in the front, yet with no fixed plan beyond tomorrow; a violent, irrational, rather bewildered leader, holding the public imagination with his personality, improvising as he went along; the central figure of the Reformation, yet apparently never having a very clear idea as to what ultimate goal he was leading it.

He was next summoned by the new emperor, Charles V, a Spanish youth barely twenty years of age but the supreme head of the temporal power, to appear at the Diet of Worms. An edict was issued against Luther, and he was ordered to recant his heretical opinions. His appearance at the Diet was not particularly impressive; he was never at his best in such an august assembly. But he maintained his views. "I can and will retract nothing," he stoutly asserted, "as it is dangerous and dishonourable to act against one's conscience." Consequently it was proposed to outlaw him and declare him liable to be put to death as a heretic. But the safe-conduct he had been granted was still in force, and while he was returning with the imperial herald he suddenly vanished. The wildest rumours gained credence. It was popularly believed that he had been murdered by his accusers, and the anti-Catholic movement became strong and more bellicose.

Actually, what had happened was that his good friend and practical patron, Frederick the Wise, Elector of Saxony, had had him kidnapped and carried off to his own castle on the Wartburg to get him out of danger. And in this Thuringian stronghold, with his native town of Eisenach in view, the reformer was kept for nearly a year.

He occupied himself mainly with writing, reading and meditation, not unmixed with melancholy. He was a prodigious worker, for in addition to completing his excellent translation of the Greek Testament in the German vernacular, he wrote tracts on the abuse of the mass, on monastic vows and the confessional, and filled in odd hours with a commentary on the Psalms of which he was very fond. Here, isolated from the turmoil of the world for a time, he was enabled for once to think out his opinions. He definitely decided to abandon many of the fundamental doctrines of the ancient faith. He denied the spiritual power of the clergy, and proclaimed the priesthood of every true believer. He asserted the right of the clergy to marry, and denounced monastic vows. Above all, he rejected the private mass, and held that Christ was bodily present in the Eucharist.

It was on this point that he later had his great disputation with Ulrich Zwingli, the Swiss reformer. They debated for days upon the words: "This is My body." Luther held firmly to his doctrine, while Zwingli maintained that there was only a spiritual presence.

In spite of the bitterness of this dispute, Luther maintained friendly relations with the Zwinglians and later with Bullinger, Zwingli's successor. He was also impressed by the work and attitude of Calvin, but he countenanced the persecution of the Anabaptists with as much venom as the Catholics.

Meanwhile, the Reformation movement was splitting Europe asunder. Powerful German princes, Philip of Hesse foremost among them, adopted the Lutheran views. The inevitable fanatical extremists appeared in the new party, and a section arose that advocated rebellion and anarchy. When Luther left the Wartburg, he had no longer to fear the imperial edict. His followers were strong enough to defy the greatest power in Europe. In 1522 Luther wrote a vigorous reply to an attack on him by Henry VIII, whom he calls among other things ninny, crass liar, twister and rogue, and three years later published his work on predestination against that of Erasmus on free will.

In 1525 came the Peasants' War. It was partly economic in its causes, but there can be no doubt that the results of the religious revolt inspired the peasantry to rise against their masters. At all events the insurgents looked to Luther for support. They were disappointed. Luther condemned both sides. When the revolt actually broke out, he denounced the rising in the most uncompromising terms. "O Lord God," he wrote, "if such a spirit reigns among the peasants, it is high time to cut their throats like mad dogs." And again: "A man who is convicted of the crime of rebellion is under the ban of God and the emperor, and every Christian can and should slaughter him and will thus be doing a good deed." Strange words from the man who had himself incurred the wrath of both pope and emperor.

The Reformation was now pursuing a political course. In 1526 the Diet of Speyer proclaimed a measure of toleration for the new opinions, but three years later this was revoked, and Luther's influential supporters made a formal protest. Thus was the word "Protestant" born.

Charles next re-affirmed at Augsburg the Edict of Worms, and demanded that all church property taken possession of by the Protestant princes should be restored. Luther was once more outlawed, and the breaking out of a war of religion in Germany was only a matter of time. The Protestant princes consolidated their position, and formed the League of Schmalkald to resist the Roman and imperial enemy.

From this time on Luther's importance declined. His influence in doctrinal matters was as great as ever; he never ceased to be the acknowledged spiritual leader, and to the end he continued to preach and develop his opinions. But the centre of gravity in the Reformation had shifted, and it was the princes and their armies that bore the brunt of the battle.

Luther settled down at Wittenberg. In June, 1525, he had married Catherine von Bora, a nun of noble birth who had forsaken her convent. He had always said that, in spite of his declaration in favour of marriage for the clergy, he himself would never break the vow of chastity which he had voluntarily sworn when he entered the monastery at Erfurt. Luther defended his conduct by the strangest of arguments. "I am married and to a nun," he wrote to a friend. "I did it to defy the devil and his host, the objectors, the princes and bishops, since they were all foolish enough to forbid the clergy to marry. And I would with willing heart create an even greater scandal if I knew of anything else better calculated to please God and put them in a rage." In the same spirit he wrote: "Oh! if I could only conceive some enormous sin to confound the devil and make him understand that I do not confess to any sin, that my conscience reproaches me with none!" To such lengths had the doctrine of justification by faith alone brought him.

He spent his last years working as hard as ever, despite a constant decline in health. He revised his translation of the Old Testament, which he had made in 1523-32, and also that of the New. Luther's contribution to the literature of the Reformation would alone have made him a great figure and a benefactor of his country. Besides his excellent translations of the Bible, he published commentaries, and also wrote those rugged hymns which are impressive in their sincerity.

In his public life he continued to oppose compromise with Rome, for he knew that any accommodation with the Church would mean the sacrifice of many of the principles for which he had fought.

It was his views on marriage, views which he expressed more and more frequently and more strongly, that exposed him to the greatest censure both from his contemporaries and from those who came after him. He cannot have meant all he said. He was a man of extremes, who habitually overstated his case. He never knew how to moderate his speech. Few of his admirers have attempted to justify his approval of the bigamy of Philip of Hesse. Here his obsequiousness before princes —the peasant trait which he could never overcome—is apparent. When Philip wanted to take a second wife, Luther signed a paper condoning the transaction and setting forth the principle, that, although bigamy was forbidden by God, the pastorate, in single exceptional cases, could override that law, and that such a union was a true marriage in the sight of God. It was not an edifying document.

Luther died in 1546, at the age of sixty-three. He had undertaken a journey to Eisleben, where he had spent most of his childhood, to settle some small dispute. The weather was cold, and his health broke down. He managed to get to the church to preach his last sermon, but stopped abruptly before the end, and retired. His death took place four days later, on February 18, 1546. At the end he was asked whether he still clung steadfastly to the faith he had taught, and with his dying breath answered: "Yes."

His body was taken back to Wittenberg, escorted by nobles and troops, while thousands of peasants lined the long route. He was buried in the castle church where, twenty-nine years before, he had nailed his ninety-five theses to the door.

Luther was by far the greatest figure in the Reformation. In spite of the fact that he at first had no desire to die outside the Church of Rome, he was the inspiration of the whole movement. He was not by nature a theologian. The doctrines he formulated were often a contradiction, and before his death his followers had split into three separate groups, a state of confusion in which they have remained ever since. But as a personal force he eclipses all those who followed—Zwingli, Melanchthon, Calvin. His vigour and his energy were the guiding forces of the movement that transformed the medieval world into the modern.

BENJAMIN FRANKLIN

(1706–1790)

When, in the eighteenth century, the American colonies were beginning their final dispute with England, a dispute which led to the Declaration of Independence and the establishment of the United States, the eyes of the world were focused on the greatest and most famous American of the time—Benjamin Franklin. Franklin, who had begun life as a poor printer, rose to be the wisest statesman of his day. He achieved success in many other spheres beside that of public life. His writings were world famous, he was acknowledged by two continents as a philosopher and scientist, by posterity as a philanthropist and a genius. But all his activities, all his inventions, all his works on philosophy, economics, politics and science were directed to one end—the benefit of mankind.

IN 1751 Dr. Thomas Bond conceived the happy idea of establishing a hospital by subscription in Philadelphia, but he found the task impossible until he had enlisted the help of Benjamin Franklin, for every one he approached for a subscription asked, "Have you consulted Franklin upon this business? And what does he think of it?"

For Benjamin Franklin, then forty-five, was recognized as a kind of universal uncle; for which the United States of America had, and has, every reason to be grateful. To sum up his life in one sentence: Benjamin Franklin was a poor boy who set out to improve himself, and ended by improving everything he had a mind to.

He was born in Boston, New England, in January, 1706. His father, who was a Nonconformist, had left England late in Charles II's reign owing to religious difficulties. Benjamin was his fifteenth child. As he was intended for the Church, the young Benjamin was sent to the grammar school when he was eight; but that proved too expensive, and after a couple of years' education he was taken home to help his father in the tallow-chandling and soap-boiling business.

Soap had no attractions for little Benjamin. "I disliked the trade," he writes, "and had a strong inclination for the sea, but my father declared against it; however, living near the water, I was much in and about it, learnt early to swim well, and to manage boats; and when in a boat or canoe with other boys, I was commonly allowed to govern, especially in any case of difficulty; and upon other occasions I was generally a leader among the boys, and sometimes led them into scrapes. . . ."

Sea and soap chafed each other, and at last his father looked round for another trade for Benjamin. The boy had always been fond of books, had read everything he could lay hands on, so the father hit upon printing as suitable. At twelve years of age, then, Benjamin was apprenticed to his brother, James, at Boston. The composing room gave Benjamin further opportunities for reading, and a chance of writing when James started the *New England Courant*, the second newspaper to be published in America.

Franklin himself gives us a little picture of his apprenticeship days, important because it shows the lad's interest in experiment, his desire for improvement and his determination:—

"When about sixteen years of age, I happened to meet with a book, written by one Tryon, recommending a vegetable diet. I determined to go into it. My brother, being yet unmarried, did not keep house, but boarded himself and his apprentices in another family. My refusing to eat flesh occasioned an inconveniency, and I was frequently chided for my singularity. I made myself acquainted with Tryon's manner of preparing some of his dishes, such as boiling potatoes or rice, making hasty pudding, and a few others, and then proposed to my brother that if he would give me, weekly, half the money he paid for my board, I would board myself. He instantly agreed to it, and I presently found that I could save half what he paid me. This was an additional fund for buying books.

"But I had another advantage in it. My brother and the rest going from the printing-house to their meals, I remained there alone, and, despatching presently my light repast, which was often no more than a bisket or a slice of bread, a handful of raisins or a tart from the pastry-cook's, and a glass of water, had the rest of the time till their return for study, in which I made the greater progress, from that greater clearness of head and quicker apprehension which usually attend temperance in eating and drinking."

There is the young Franklin. But to complete the portrait, to show his humour and remove any trace of priggishness, let us hear how, about a year later, he forsook vegetarianism:—

". . . in my first voyage from Boston, being becalmed off Block Island, our people set about catching cod, and hauled up a great many. Hitherto, I had stuck to my resolution of not eating animal food, and on this occasion I considered, with my master Tryon, the taking of every fish as a kind of unprovoked murder, since none of them had, or could do us, any injury that might justify the slaughter.

"All this seemed very reasonable. But I had formerly been a great lover of fish, and, when this came hot out of the frying-pan, it smelt admirably well. I balanced some time between principle and inclination, till I recollected that, when the fish were opened, I saw smaller fish taken out of their stomachs; then, thought I 'If you eat one another, I don't see why we mayn't eat you.' So I dined upon cod very heartily, and continued to eat with other people, returning, only now and then, occasionally to a vegetable diet. So convenient a thing it is to be a *reasonable creature,* since it enables one to find or make a reason for everything one has in mind to do."

Benjamin could not get on with his brother James. At seventeen he quarrelled finally with him and made his way to Philadelphia, via New York. He arrived, after much travelling, poor, tired, dirty and very hungry, and walking into a baker's shop asked for three-pennyworth of bread.

"He gave me, accordingly, three great puffy rolls. I was surprised at the quantity, but took it, and having no room in my pockets, walked off with a roll under each arm, and eating the other. Thus I went up Market Street as far as Fourth Street, passing by the door of Mr. Read, my future wife's father; when she, standing at the door, saw me, and thought I made, as I certainly did, a most awkward, ridiculous appearance."

Has there ever been a more delightful picture of a man's first encounter with his wife? Have you noticed how Franklin tells his story; neatly, tightly and in a few words?

The awkward, ridiculous figure was soon working at his trade in Philadelphia. Then in 1724 he came to England, where he worked as a printer in London for two years. He had been considered too young to marry Miss Read, and in London, as he wrote years afterwards, "I forgot . . . by degrees my engagement with Miss Read, to whom I never wrote more than one letter, and that was to let her know I was not likely soon to return. This was another of the great errata of my life, which I should wish to correct if I were to live it over again." The girl married in his absence, but she was deserted and widowed. Franklin married her in 1730 and lived happily with her until her death in 1773.

Franklin the swimmer was closely allied to Franklin the scientist.

On this first visit to London he excited great interest when he "stripped and leaped into the river, and swam from near Chelsea to Blackfryar's, performing on the way many feats of activity, both upon and under water, that surprised and pleased those to whom they were novelties."

These glimpses have shown us Franklin the man. Now let us see what he did.

He returned to Philadelphia in 1726, and shortly afterwards set up with a partner as a printer. He worked hard, soon acquired the whole business, and made a success of it. In 1729 he took over the publication of the *Pennsylvania Gazette,* and four years later published *Poor Richard's Almanac* for the first time.

Almanacs were the most popular and in many cases the only reading enjoyed by the American colonists, and "Poor Richard's" multitude of sententious saws and homely quips became a best-seller. Franklin had launched a type of proverbial humour which is still popular in the United States. More than that, he had laid the foundations of his fortune, for if it were Franklin the scientist, Franklin the philosopher and Franklin the statesman who became a world-famous figure, it was "Poor Richard" which gave that Franklin riches and success.

And now Franklin had already commenced his public-spirited career of improving.

As soon as he returned to Philadelphia, he formed a club for mutual improvement called the Junto, and many of the papers which he read before this society and afterwards published formed the bases for reforms. Franklin had his eye on everything—he was interested in anything.

First we find him advocating the issue of more paper money, and writing pamphlets on the subject. Then in 1730 he organized the first circulating library in America. He followed up this fine idea by founding the first fire assurance company in the United States, and in arranging for adequate fire-fighting measures. That was in 1737. In 1744 he established a philosophical society. Then anxiety about the defence of the town arose—Britain was at war with Spain and France. Franklin raised volunteer regiments and had a battery built. He was always a masterly organizer.

Franklin's next work was to found an academy, which in his own lifetime became the University of Philadelphia, and is now the University of Pennsylvania. The academy was opened in 1749. Two years later Franklin assisted his friend, Dr. Bond, to establish the first hospital in America. In these enterprises he always prepared the way by pamphlets, contributions to the newspapers and other modern means of publicity and propaganda. Next we find him interested in cleaner and better streets. He organized street scavengers and promoted a bill for paving the roads of the city.

Now the ever ingenious Franklin turns once more to science. He had already, in 1742, invented a new kind of open stove, for which he declined a patent, on the grounds "that, as we enjoy great advantages from the inventions of others, we should be glad of an opportunity to serve others by any invention of ours; and this we should do freely and generously."

He became interested in electricity. The recent discovery of the Leyden jar aroused Franklin's ever eager scientific curiosity and he began experiments with newly acquired apparatus. Soon he had framed a new theory of electricity, involving two kinds—positive and negative, a distinction which is still made to this day.

Franklin discovered the identity of lightning with electricity in 1752, and although he was not the first to think of the connexion, he was the first to prove it. He followed up this discovery with the invention of the lightning conductor, an event which gained for him enormous public prestige.

His invention, his experiments and his papers raised great interest in England and France. He was made a member of the Royal Society, and granted the Copley gold medal for 1753. Later, when he visited England, he received honorary degrees from the universities of St. Andrew's (1759) and Oxford (1762).

Franklin was particularly admired by the logic-bound eighteenth century scientists for his practical and realistic talents. His ideas and theories on natural phenomena, although not always correct, were invariably precise and neatly expressed, and his medical theories were held in equal esteem.

In 1730 Franklin was a struggling printer; by 1749 he was a public figure, and could afford to retire from business. He gives a neat sidelight on his rise:—

"We kept no idle servants," he writes of the period about 1730, "our table was plain and simple, our furniture of the cheapest. For instance, my breakfast was a long time bread and milk (no tea), and I ate it out of a twopenny earthen porringer with a pewter spoon.

"But mark how luxury will enter families, and make a progress, in spite of principle. Being called one morning to breakfast, I found it in a china bowl, with a spoon of silver!

"They had been bought for me, without my knowledge, by my wife, and cost her the enormous sum of three and twenty shillings, for which she had no other excuse or apology to make, but that she thought *her* husband deserved a silver spoon and a china bowl as well as any of his neighbours. This was the first appearance of plate and china in our house, which afterwards, in a course of years, as our wealth increased augmented gradually to several hundred pounds in value."

When Franklin retired from business he had already made his mark as a printer and publisher. The witty and wise sayings from his *Poor Richard's Almanac* had been many times translated and republished in England, France, Germany and Italy.

He was, as we have seen, always interested in public affairs. In 1736 he had become clerk to the Pennsylvania Assembly. In the next year he was made postmaster of Philadelphia, and in 1753, joint controller of the Colonial Postal Service. Meanwhile, in 1750, he was elected to the assembly and was a member until 1764. He visited the motherland of his ancestors in 1757 and again in 1764. He was known in England as the most famous citizen of America, and for some years he acted as agent for the American colonies.

Franklin's work as a statesman between his retirement and his death was full of notable achievements and worthy of greater results than were actually obtained. It was his ideal to see America flourish and expand as a member of the British Empire. Had the British Ministry possessed some of Franklin's great qualities, that ideal would have become a fact.

Nevertheless, Franklin did good work for the empire of which, at that time, he was still a citizen. In 1760, while he was in England, he published *The Interest of Great Britain considered with regard to Her Colonies,* which had considerable influence on the English decision to retain Canada rather than Guadeloupe, when considering the peace terms with France.

In 1761, Franklin toured Holland and returned home to Philadelphia in the following year. In 1764 an old quarrel between the State of Pennsylvania and the Penn family regarding the payment of taxes broke out again, and Franklin, as a leader of the popular party in opposition to the Penns, sailed for England to ask the king to take over the state as a royal province.

He was handicapped in this mission by the fact that the unpopular Stamp Act was passed at the time of his arrival. It was largely owing to Franklin, who was examined by the House of Commons, that the Stamp Act was repealed in 1766. Franklin was a loyalist, but he felt bound to oppose the British taxation of colonies without representation.

The Commons examination made Franklin the most famous American in the New World and the Old. He achieved an extraordinary popularity. Georgia made him its agent in England in 1768, and two years later Massachusetts followed suit. Franklin visited Germany in 1766, France in 1767 and 1769, Ireland and Scotland in 1771; everywhere he received an enthusiastic welcome.

In 1744, one of his craftiest pieces of statesmanship went awry. Franklin conceived the notion of mitigating the harsh British attitude towards the American colonies by claiming that the Ministry had been inspired by extremist American Tories, and as a result a petition for removing one of them, Governor Hutchinson of Massachusetts, was set on foot.

The English could have made excellent use of Franklin's wily stratagem; instead, they hauled him before the Privy Council, where he was insulted and called a "thief" by Wedderburn, the Attorney-General. There was even talk of arresting him, before he sailed for home, a famous, but a beaten man.

When the War of Independence broke out, Franklin's organizing genius was placed at the disposal of his country. He became a member of Congress and was made Postmaster-General.

In 1776, he was sent as a delegate to France, and after two years he managed to conclude an alliance with the French and to obtain money and military help in the war against England. He was preceded by his reputation as a scientist and as a liberal philosopher, and he was warmly welcomed by the French. His clear mind and his genius had great influence on the French philosophers and on the radicals. He continued to help his country's cause in France and on the Continent generally, and before his return to America in 1785 he had concluded commercial treaties with Prussia and Sweden.

In his last years Franklin was still working, still interested in everything, still doing everything he could for mankind. On his return to America he became president of the Supreme Executive Council of Pennsylvania, and 1787 he assisted in drawing up the Federal constitution. All the while he was publishing scientific pamphlets. In his extreme old age he was leading the movement in Congress for the abolition of slavery, and was hard at work when he died, after a short illness, in 1790.

It is difficult to sum up Benjamin Franklin. He did so much, he did so much good, and he did so much well. If he was ambitious, his ambition benefited others; if he stooped to cheap journalism and subtle propaganda, it was in a good cause; if he had a finger in any pie, it was an honest finger.

He wrote, and he wrote well, on science, philosophy, politics and economics. He was willing to undertake anything for the public good. He was against the split with England, but when war came he chose his cause and prosecuted it with all his heart.

And Franklin, you will have gathered from his writings, was a pleasant man. Witty, humorous, forceful when need be; a good story-teller, popular with men and women.

As for his honesty, it was quixotic. He once organized transport and furnished provisions for General Braddock's army. He was partly paid and later asked for the balance from Lord Loudoun, Braddock's successor. Loudoun put him off, and Franklin protested; to which "'O, sir,' says he, 'you must not think of persuading us that you are no gainer; we understand better those affairs, and know that everyone concerned in supplying the army finds means, in the doing of it, to fill his own pockets.' I assured him that was not my case, and that I had not pocketed a farthing; but he appeared clearly not to believe me; and, indeed, I have since learnt that immense fortunes are often made in such employments. As to my ballance, I am not paid it to this day. . . ."

But that "ballance" has been paid since by the gratitude of the United States to a wise and benevolent father, and by the homage of the whole world to a very human genius.

WILLIAM WILBERFORCE

(1759–1833)

In 1833 the Slavery Abolition Bill was passed in the Houses of Parliament, and Britain's national conscience was awakened to give the world the lead in abolishing slavery. The leader of the agitation which pricked the country into action, the man who stamped his personality and his sincerity upon the anti-slave campaign, the undauntable spirit who gave nearly fifty years of his life to the task, was William Wilberforce, a philanthropist whom his bitterest opponents could not but hold in affection and respect.

"Look here upon this picture, and on this . . ."
—*Hamlet.*

IT is the year 1780. A sailing ship is making heavy weather across the Atlantic, pitching through the great rollers under her spread of canvas. She is loaded well down to the limit of safety, her holds are full, and the cargo is as precious as it is heavy. It is a black cargo, well packed and corded, free on board, to be sold at port of delivery: it is a cargo of slaves. They are chained together and crowded into the smallest possible space; a sweating, stinking, suffering mass of humanity. A little while before they had been free, living with their tribes in their native Africa: then had come the slave raiders from the West Coast, who had seized the likely men and the strongest women, shot down those who resisted, and carried them back to the coast. They were sold as slaves to the traders, and now were on their way across the sea to where the West Indian planters and those of the southern states of America would buy their bodies and set them to work.

It is the year 1780. An elegant young man is sitting in a London club, amusing the fashionables with his wit and charm, as they crowd round the gaming tables. It is an exclusive club, and there are famous faces round the tables—Fox, Sheridan . . . a score of others whose names are household words. But the most charming of them all is the young man of twenty-one, just down from Cambridge, already a Member of Parliament, who wins or loses with equal indifference. He has a fortune behind him and all life before him.

There could hardly be two pictures more dissimilar or with less in common. Yet it was that young man in the gambling club who became the chief instrument in abolishing the slave trade and in sweeping slavery from the British Empire.

His name was William Wilberforce. He was born in August, 1759, the only son of Robert Wilberforce, a merchant in the Baltic trade.

The Wilberforces were an old-established Yorkshire family, and Robert's business was in a flourishing condition. At the age of seven William went to the grammar school at Hull, but when his father died, in 1768, he was sent to his uncle's house at Wimbledon, and attended a school in Putney. But his mother, scared of the aunt's Methodist influence, brought the boy back to Hull, and finally settled him at Pocklington Grammar School.

There young Wilberforce did little work: but he was a charming schoolfellow and blossomed out as a good singer. In 1776 he went up to St. John's College, Cambridge, where he gained a reputation for hospitality and good fellowship. Even his tutors told him that there was no need for a rich young man to work, but Wilberforce had enough natural ability to do well in his classical examinations.

As soon as he came down from Cambridge, Wilberforce decided to give up the business and enter public life; and at the general election in 1780 he put up for Hull. He spared no money in his campaign: there were three hundred freemen of Hull working on the Thames, and Wilberforce came down to address them and entertain them afterwards to lavish suppers in the inns of Wapping. He spent over £9,000 on the election, but he reaped the reward of success, and in September, 1780, was returned as Member for Hull.

London received the rich young man with open arms. He was elected to a number of clubs, the famous Goosetrees among them, and he quickly cultivated a friendship with Pitt, whom he had first met at Cambridge. His charm of manner and his wit made him popular in all circles. The Prince of Wales liked his singing, and he became renowned as a mimic until he was quietly warned not to "take off" his political opponents in public. He was often at the gaming tables, but he gave up gambling suddenly, after he had won £600 in an evening from men who could not afford to lose.

His friendship with Pitt developed warmly both in public and in private. Wilberforce voted for and with Pitt in Parliament, and Pitt had rooms in the Wimbledon house that Wilberforce had inherited from his uncle. In 1783, he and Pitt, together with Edward Eliot, afterwards Pitt's brother-in-law, went to France. They stayed at Rheims, and were later presented to the king and queen at Fontainebleau. In the December of that year Pitt became prime minister, and throughout the session Wilberforce supported him. On dissolution, Wilberforce went into the country as an adherent of the Pitt faction, and was returned for Yorkshire.

And then, in October, 1784, Wilberforce went on a journey which changed the whole of his life. He took his mother and sister to Nice, and then, after a brief visit to London in February, 1785, rejoined the party at Genoa, toured Switzerland, visited Spa, and came home in the November. Throughout the tour Wilberforce had been accompanied by the Reverend Isaac Milner, and together they read Doddridge's *Rise and Progress of Religion,* and afterwards studied the Greek Testament, with the result that Wilberforce was converted to evangelical Christianity. He came home determined to lead a strictly religious life.

Religious conversion is usually accompanied by a marked change of character and demeanour, but Wilberforce, although inwardly changed, did not lose his old charm of manner, his easy address, and his wit.

When he returned to London he told Pitt of his new resolves and explained that as a result he would probably be less of a party man, but the cordiality between the great statesman and Wilberforce was not lessened, and Wilberforce still supported Pitt in the House.

The first public sign of the new Wilberforce came in 1786, when he introduced a bill to amend criminal law. The Lords threw it out, not without complimenting its sponsor on his benevolent intentions. A year later he procured a royal proclamation against vice and founded a society to enforce it: known as the Proclamation Society, the new body took a prominent part in prosecuting blasphemous and indecent publications: in 1802 it was superseded by Wilberforce's Society for the Suppression of Vice.

And now Wilberforce turned his attention to slavery. Thinking men had already been attacking the slavery question. In 1772, Granville Sharp won a law-suit, which resulted in the formulation of the principle that as soon as a slave set his foot on English territory he became free. In 1785, Thomas Clarkson attracted attention with a prize essay on slavery. Bennet Langton offered to bring the cause to the notice of Parliament. In 1787, a committee, consisting mainly of Quakers, with Sharp as president and Clarkson as a member, was set up to work for the abolition of the slave trade.

Wilberforce had already been urged to take up the question of slavery, and now his friend Pitt also advised him to champion the cause of slave-trade abolition in the House, warning him that "he must not lose time, or the question would be taken up by another." At the foot of a tree in Holwood Park, near Bromley, in Kent, Pitt's country residence, Wilberforce made up his mind. From that moment he became the champion of the slaves.

He had not been the originator of the agitation for the abolition of slave trading, but he was admirably fitted to become its leader. His "high principle, independent position, and singular charm of character" combined to make him an inspiring, and respected, champion. The committee continued its work of collecting evidence and presenting facts: Wilberforce conducted the campaign in Parliament.

At that time there was no consideration of freeing slaves. The sole aim of the agitators was to stop the slave trade, and prevent the extension of slavery.

Pitt allowed evidence on the African slave trade to be read before a committee of the Privy Council, and in 1787 Wilberforce tried to get anti-slave trade clauses put into the treaty that was being drawn up in Paris. Then, in January, 1788, Wilberforce had a serious illness involving "a total decay of all the vital functions." In April he was sent to Bath and given a fortnight to live. But by the means of "a moderate use of opium" he recovered, and although he had to use opium for the next twenty years, he did so without increasing the dose.

Meanwhile, Pitt took up his cause and put a resolution through the House to deal with the slave trade in the next session. On May 12, 1789, Wilberforce spoke for three and a half hours, moving twelve resolutions against the slave trade. Pitt, Burke and Fox spoke in support, and they were carried without a division. But the planters obtained leave to produce evidence at the bar of the House, and the matter was deferred until the next session.

Throughout the summer of 1790 Wilberforce worked nine hours a day getting up evidence, and in 1791 he received a dying message from John Wesley, asking him to persevere. On April 18 of that year Wilberforce asked leave to bring in a bill for the abolition of the slave trade; the debate lasted until half-past three in the morning, and ended in defeat for the abolitionists by one hundred and sixty-three votes to eighty-eight.

They were discouraged by this reverse, and Wilberforce urged the necessity for open-air meetings throughout the country.

Meanwhile, troubles in St. Domingo and the changed attitude of the king, who considered that the slave trade abolition agitation savoured of Jacobinism, lost Wilberforce the support of the government. Nevertheless, Pitt spoke with unusual brilliance on behalf of a resolution to abolish the slave trade by gradual steps, a resolution which was carried on April 2, 1792. The date of beginning the abolition was fixed, after a further debate, for January 1, 1796. Encouraged by this success, the enthusiasm of the abolitionists abated somewhat, and the opponents of abolition dug themselves in and availed themselves of delaying tactics.

Wilberforce did not stop hammering at Parliament. In February, 1793, he introduced a motion to hasten abolition measures through the House of Lords. It was rejected by sixty-one votes to fifty-three. In June, he sponsored a bill to prohibit the supply of slaves to foreign powers. It was thrown out on third reading by thirty-one votes to twenty-nine, was carried through the Commons in the next year, only to be thrown out by the Lords, on the plea of waiting for the general inquiry. In 1795 Wilberforce asked leave to introduce a bill for the abolition of the slave trade; in vain. In 1796 he was defeated on the third reading by seventy-four to seventy—and enough of his supporters to carry the motion were at the first night of a comic opera! He tried again during each of the three succeeding years, meeting defeat every time; and a new proposal to limit the slave trade area was also overruled in 1799.

The war with France distressed him, and he was constrained to vote for peace against his friend Pitt, who—he thought at first—had not been pacific enough in his negotiations. It is said that the mutiny at the Nore and Wilberforce's defection were the only two calamities that caused Pitt to lose sleep. But the breach was only temporary.

In that year Wilberforce published *A Practical View of the Prevailing Religious Systems of Professed Christians in the Higher and Middle Classes of this Country Contrasted with Real Christianity*. The book became an immediate best-seller in England and America, and was translated into half-a-dozen languages: it was a classic of evangelical Christianity.

He married Barbara Spooner in 1797, and they settled at Clapham Common, where Wilberforce became a member of the Clapham Sect. Meanwhile, his philanthropy took many and practical forms. He was continually helping people with his money, as well as contributing to charitable causes. He gave Hannah More, in 1798, £400 a year to further her good work in founding Sunday schools, and in the same year founded the Church Missionary Society. In 1796 he had started the Society for Bettering the Condition of the Poor, and in 1803 co-operated in the foundation of the

Bible Society. The extent of his practical charity in the years of distress may be judged by the fact that in 1801 he spent £3,000 more than his income.

In 1804, Wilberforce made another effort to end the slave trade, and the planters fought him tooth and nail. He piloted the bill through the Commons, but again the Lords threw it out. Next year saw a similar defeat. But at last public opinion was swinging; there was no longer the fear of Jacobin ideas; the long campaign, too, was having its effect. In 1807 Wilberforce's bill was carried through two readings in the Lords. It was referred to the Commons on February 10 and counsel was heard against it. The debate took place on February 23, and Wilberforce was too overcome with emotion to heed the cheers which greeted him and his triumph; for the motion was carried by two hundred and eighty-three votes to sixteen. The bill received the royal assent on March 25, 1807, and the African Institution was founded to carry out its provisions.

Wilberforce was now a national hero, deeply respected by men of all shades of opinion. A public subscription was raised to pay his election expenses in 1807, and his house at Kensington was constantly thronged with friends and visitors, whom he received with his still youthful charm and lavish hospitality. Madame de Stael met him in 1814, and said that she had known that he was the most religious and now discovered him to be the "wittiest man in England."

The renewal of the East India Company's charter in 1813 gave Wilberforce an opportunity to make proposals for propagating religion in India, and thus he was responsible for the foundation of the Bishopric of Calcutta, first held by Thomas Fanshawe Middleton.

By now he was convinced that the emancipation of all slaves was necessary, although his previous work had only been concerned with trading in slaves, and he worked hard for the total abolition of slavery. One of his eloquent appeals led, in 1823, to the foundation of the Anti-Slavery Society.

Illness had now caused his retirement, but the old Wilberforce was still the charming, kindly, witty man who had charmed London in his youth. His fortune failed with his health, and he divided the last two years between the homes of his two sons.

In July, 1833, he heard the second reading of the Slave Emancipation Bill, and on the twenty-ninth of the month he died. The bill, which was to become law in August, was a nobler epitaph than that which was carved above his grave in Westminster Abbey.

KARL MARX

(1818–1883)

When in 1917 the second revolution took place in Russia and the Bolsheviks came into power, the hand that led the people was the hand of Lenin, but the voice was the voice of Marx. For Karl Marx was the founder of scientific communism, and on Marxism the principles of modern communism are grounded. The tremendous influence of Marx's teachings has already made itself felt, for better or worse, in recent history: and in the social, economic and political struggles that are still to come that influence will play an even greater part.

In the summer of 1851, the year of the Great Exhibition, a man sat poring over tomes and notebooks in the reading-room of the British Museum for hour after hour, day after day. He was a striking figure: his broad face and high brow were framed in a black bushy beard and a shock of unkempt hair, and there was a set, grim expression on him as he worked. At the end of the day he would gather up his notebooks and tramp off to Soho, to Dean Street, where he climbed the stairs of No. 28 to the little rooms that formed his home. And there the grim, bearded man became a new man. His wife and six children greeted him lovingly; they bantered each other with pet nicknames; and the man forgot his work and became the happy father. Unless, as was often the case, there was no money and no food in the two-roomed home, and he had once more to slip out to the pawnbrokers with some forlorn trinket or a remnant of his wife's family plate: and if there were nothing to pawn there would be a desperate effort to raise a small loan. But on happier evenings he would talk to the children, puff cigars as he arranged the notes he had made during the day, or play chess with the family nurse. And so to bed, and a long day's work in the Museum on the morrow.

The man was Karl Marx, and the work that he hatched in those hours of labour at the British Museum has been the greatest consistent influence on the politics of the modern world.

Karl Marx was born, the son of a Jewish lawyer, at Trier (Trèves) in the Rhineland, on May 5, 1818. When Karl was six the whole of the Marx family became Christians, but neither the influence of religion nor of race seemed to make itself felt in the development of the lawyer's son. Early in life he showed signs of the independence, the truculence, the rebellious ruthlessness, and the complete subordination of emotion to reason, which, harnessed to his belief in his own infallibility, were to make him an outstanding figure and a tremendous force in a changing world.

At the age of seventeen, Karl became a law student at Bonn University, and in the following year he went on to the University of Berlin. In the summer vacation between the change he fell in love with Jenny, the daughter of Baron von Westphalen. With considerable boldness, the eighteen-year-old son of the middle-class Jewish lawyer wrote to the baron and, after Jenny had fought loyally with "her pious aristocratic relations, who regarded the Lord in heaven and the lord in Berlin with equal veneration," he was accepted as her future husband.

The love affair had one remarkable result: it made Marx a poet. He sent volumes of verse to Jenny, and in 1841 he had two lyrics published in the Berlin *Athenæum*. Thus Karl Marx, the political thunderer, first appeared in print as a poet.

In 1841 Marx took his degree of doctor of philosophy at the University of Jena, and returned to Bonn, where he came under the influence of Bruno Bauer and others of the "young Hegelian" school of philosophy who were the originators of the "higher criticism" of the Bible. At that time Marx definitely embraced the anti-religious attitude which is an essential part of his doctrine.

Soon after he arrived in Bonn a group of "young Hegelians" founded a radical daily newspaper, the *Rheinische Zeitung,* and Marx became a contributor. His slashing articles made a great hit, and in a few months he became editor. Now he lashed out at the Prussian Government and at the philosophers, such as Bauer, who had once been his friends but whom he now denounced as academic and dilettante revolutionaries. As always, Marx was on the top of his form when flaying his old friends. But his reign as editor was as brief as it was glorious, for the censor stopped publication of the newspaper.

It was proposed to start another radical sheet outside the limits of the Prussian censorship, in Paris, and while preparations were being made by Arnold Ruge, Marx took advantage of the lull to marry his Jenny. The fact that he was working hard throughout the honeymoon did not detract from the supreme happiness of the lovers.

"I can assure you without any sentimentality," wrote Marx to

Ruge, "that I am in love from head to foot and in all seriousness. . . . My bride and I have, for years on end, had to fight more exhausting and unnecessary battles than many other people who are three times as old and who are always talking of their 'experience of life.'"

The original Paris venture fell flat, and Marx transferred his vitriolic pen to *Vorwarts,* a radical German paper published in the French capital. Once again his invective was too strong to be stomached: at the request of the Prussian Government Marx was expelled from France, and in January, 1845, he left Paris for Brussels.

But before he left France an important event had taken place which was to have a lasting effect on Marx's life. He had struck up a firm friendship with Friedrich Engels. Engels, two years younger than Marx, was the son of a German cotton manufacturer, and had early embraced radical views. He had spent some time in Manchester in the English branch of his father's firm, and there had made the acquaintance of Robert Owen and the Chartist leaders. He had first met Marx when the latter was editing the *Rheinische Zeitung,* but it was not until 1844, when they again met in Paris, that any cordiality sprang up between them. In that year they collaborated in writing a pamphlet against Bruno Bauer: it was the beginning of a partnership that was to last a lifetime. For Engels became the friend, disciple, collaborator, popularizer, hack and, most important, the constant source of income of Karl Marx.

In the spring of 1845, Engels joined Marx at Brussels, and in the summer of the same year took him on his first visit to England. He introduced Marx to the founders of the German Workers' Educational Union that had recently been started in London, and on his return to Brussels Marx founded a similar organization, the German Working Men's Association, whose object was to study and preach the principles of communism. From this beginning, Marx established a Communist Correspondence Committee to draw together the communists in different countries, and Engels was sent to Paris to start a similar centre of activity. In 1847 a congress was held, in London, of representatives from the Brussels, Paris and London organizations, and it resulted in the formation of an international Communist League, on whose behalf Marx and Engels issued their famous *Communist Manifesto.*

The *Communist Manifesto,* the first chapter in the dogma of Marxism, begins: "The history of all past society is the history of the struggle between classes." It is a development of the materialist conception of history. Hegel held that each idea produced its negative, and from the conflict between them a new and better idea was born. Marx, under the Hegelian influence, translated this into the world of economics. Classes are the social results of the methods of economic production, and the class war in its most active forms is the social reflection of necessary changes in methods of production. The growth of the capitalist class—the buyers of labour—necessarily created its negative, the proletariat—who have only themselves to sell. As the capitalist class increases in economic strength but grows relatively fewer in numbers, it represses the proletariat more and more, but in doing so it gives the proletariat a common social life and discipline, and hence enables them to form a common aim, until at last the proletariat, unwilling to support the conditions decreed by capitalism's needs, will overturn capitalism, smash the social structure of the capitalist state, and build a new state to meet the needs of the changed forces of production. The communists are the class-conscious section of the proletariat—that part of the populace conscious of the separate interests of the working class in face of capitalism; and their work is international.

After this preliminary statement the *Manifesto* demanded these immediate reforms:

The taking over of landed property, and the use of rent to cover state expenditure; progressively graded income-tax; the abolition of the right of inheritance; the confiscation of the property of all emigrants and rebels; the centralization of credit and transport in the hands of the state, and the establishment of a state bank with exclusive monopoly; increased state ownership of factories and redistribution of agricultural land; universal obligation to work, with labour armies recruited specially for agriculture; unification of agricultural and industrial labour; public education of all children, and abolition of factory labour for children in its present form.

The *Manifesto* concludes:

"The communists consider it superfluous to conceal their opinions and their intentions. They openly declare that their aims can only be achieved by the violent overthrow of the whole contemporary social order.

"Let the governing classes tremble before the communist revolution. The proletarians have nothing to lose in it but their chains. They have the whole world to gain.

"Proletarians of all countries, unite!"

A year of revolutions was 1848, and at the first outbreaks Marx was ordered out of Belgium. But the revolutions that were shaking

Europe opened to Marx the gates of Paris, and then of his native land. In April he was established at Cologne as editor of the *Neue Rheinische Zeitung*. But the revolution died, and a year later Marx once more fled Germany, was ordered out of Paris, and finally settled in London.

For many years the life of the Marx family in London was a dreary struggle against poverty. Karl had a loving wife, affectionate children, a faithful nurse, but no money and no source of income. They were turned out of their lodgings at Camberwell, and took the two rooms in Dean Street, Soho. Ill health followed poverty, and two of the children died in infancy. Marx himself suffered from carbuncles and other painful ailments, and at last his wife, soured and crushed by the burden of poverty and shame throughout her life, became embittered and seemed to turn against him.

Only the generosity of Engels enabled Marx to live. Engels was again working in Manchester, and he was continually sending Marx gifts of money and allowing him to draw bills upon him. Marx never appealed to him in vain, but he received Engels's help with cold, businesslike gratitude; it is difficult not to judge harshly this ruthless worker, who buried all warmth and feeling beneath his pride.

In 1851, Marx was asked to contribute articles to the *New York Tribune,* and again he called on Engels, who wrote them for him, and afterwards for some time translated Marx's articles from the German, until Marx could take over the work himself. Engels, the devoted disciple, was always willing to write for or collaborate with the master.

Research for his great work on political economy, journalism, and quarrels with his fellow emigrés occupied Marx's time. He discarded everyone who did not thoroughly absorb and submit to his own principles. To save the Communist League from the influence of a rival, Willich, he had its headquarters transferred to Cologne, which effectively killed the league. Marx would brook no competitor.

There is a vivid picture of him in his Brussels days:

"With a thick black mop of hair on his head, with hairy hands and crookedly-buttoned frock coat, he gave the impression of one who has the right and the power to command respect, whatever his appearance and whatever he did. His movements were clumsy, but firm and self-assured. His manners defied the accepted forms of social intercourse, but were haughty and almost contemptuous. His sharp, metallic voice suited remarkably well the radical verdicts which he was in the habit of pronouncing on men and things. Even at this time Marx invariably spoke in the form of judgments without appeal, in which was heard the uniform, disagreeably sharp note which dominated everything he said—a note which seemed to express the firm conviction that his destiny was to sway men's minds, to be their law-giver and to lead them in his train."

Current politics and journalism kept him busy, but all the time Marx was planning and drafting a work on "capital in general." The first section, dealing with the nature of value, was published at last in 1859 under the title *A Critique of Political Economy*. It was not until 1867 that the first volume of *Capital* was published, while the second and third volumes were edited by Engels after Marx's death, and appeared in 1885 and 1894.

This enormous work is devoted to analysing and describing capitalism with a view to discovering the economic laws that produced it, controlled its growth, and ultimately brought about contradictions, which, if Marx is right, are insoluble within capitalism.

In the *Critique* Marx had pointed out that the value of a commodity was measured by the amount of labour which had gone into its production. In *Capital* he now produced the theory of surplus value; that is, the difference in time or time-value between the amount of work necessary to keep a labourer and the amount of work he does. Thus, if a man is paid five shillings a day, and the man can do five shillings-worth of work in four hours, but works eight hours a day, the extra four hours, producing four hours' labour-value, is surplus value.

The labourer, concludes Marx, has not the right to his own produce, but the whole body of labourers have the social right to the whole of their co-operative production. The proletariat must learn the necessity to smash the social superstructure of capitalism. For when a system has passed its maximum and is beset by internal contradictions, evolutionary changes only prolong its life in the interests of the dominant class at the expense of those whose needs involve a new system and new promises. Hence: "Force is the midwife of every old society pregnant with a new one." Then will come the dictatorship of the proletariat, but that again is only transitional, for in a socialist world, "when history begins," there is no economic basis for an exploiting class; class antagonisms and classes themselves tend to disappear, and what starts as a proletarian dictatorship becomes in practice a classless government. But in such a world even government in the old sense will begin to fade. As one class is no longer engaged in keeping another in its place, government becomes less a matter of administrating *men* and more a matter of controlling *things*. In such a world, states in the old sense, with their armies and prisons, begin to "wither away." That, in brief, is Marxism, the creed founded on the writings of Marx, the creed which inspired Lenin and the makers of the Russian Revolution. Whatever we may think of his analyses and theories, his work gives a background and a scientific handbook to a movement that draws its main strength from moral grounds. Yet for Marx the forms of morality, of religion, of the family, of politics, and of patriotism, are conditioned in time and place by the form of man's struggle with nature and specifically modified by the struggles between economic classes—to be further modified, perhaps out of recognition, when class domination ceases. For Marx the revolution was inevitable: he taught the proletariat to wait and prepare.

While he was writing *Capital,* Marx was again active. In 1864 the International Working Men's Association—the First International—was formed, and he rapidly became its dominating influence. The organization looked like becoming of real importance, when the Franco-Prussian War split Europe; then members of the International broke with each other; Marx was involved in feud with Bakunin, and he repeated the tactics he had adopted with the Communist League. In 1872 he moved the transference of the general council to New York, and with the change the First International died.

He was still struggling along with the second volume of *Capital.* He was more comfortably off now, and had long been living in North London. In 1869 Engels had retired from business and allowed Marx £350 a year; but poverty and ill-health had taken their toll, and Marx was finding it harder to work.

In 1881 his wife died, after suffering for years with cancer, while he was lying seriously ill with pleurisy. Marx recovered, but his span was nearly over, and on March 14, 1883, he died in London.

In a speech over his grave in Highgate Cemetery, Engels declared that "his name and works will live on through the centuries."

"He combined in his own person and nature," writes Hyndman, "with his commanding forehead and great overhanging brow, his fierce glittering eyes, broad sensitive nose and mobile mouth, all surrounded by a setting of untrimmed hair and beard, the righteous fury of the great seers of his race, with the cold analytical power of Spinoza and the Jewish doctors. It was an extraordinary combination of qualities, the like of which I have known in no other man."

And Mr. Edward Hallet Carr, in his admirable study of Karl Marx, has summed up:

"A name which, fifty years after the death of its possessor, has still the power to excite passionate loyalties and passionate hatred, will not soon be effaced from the annals of mankind. Marx was not, in the strict sense of the world, a great philosopher. He was not in any sense of the word at all, a great economist. He was not a statesman or an orator or a leader of men. He was not inspired by any deep love for humanity; and he was not, in his dealings with his fellow men, a particularly estimable or lovable character. But he imposed himself on his contemporaries, and he has imposed himself upon history, with all the sheer force of a unique and dominant idea."

To his opponents, Marx was a prophet claiming for his teaching a universal validity which future generations will not concede to it. To his friends, he is a scientist whose work must be gauged by the extent to which his predictions are verified by history. But no such reserve can minimize its importance for the generation to which Marx belonged or for its immediate successors. Marx was one of the few—perhaps the first since Luther—whose life constituted a turning point in human thought. Marx was the enlightened prophet of the newly-created, inarticulate, many-headed proletariat which, emerging from the throes of the industrial revolution, dominates the present age. Marx perceived that this emergence heralded the end of the three-hundred-year period of history to which he gave the convenient, though not entirely appropriate, label of "bourgeois civilization." Only a powerfully original mind can emancipate itself as completely as Marx's did from the tyranny of universally accepted, but already obsolescent ideas. He could see—as hardly any one else of his time could see—that not only Metternich and Bismarck, but Bright and Gladstone, belonged to an outworn epoch. While such men still seemed to occupy the centre of the stage, the advance of the proletariat was thrusting them gently and imperceptibly to one side. Marx proclaimed the coming of the new age. He knew that its leaders and heroes would be men of another mould, of other traditions and other methods.

MOHANDAS KARAMCHAND GANDHI

(1869–1948)

Many figures have moved across the modern world stage with a more spectacular flourish and a greater aplomb than Mahatma Ghandi; few, though, have wielded an influence so momentous on the history of our time. With a frail and puny body, and with few of the traditional qualities of leadership, but endowed with a clear vision and a tenacious faith, this remarkable man awakened in oppressed peoples a sense of their dignity and a resolution to strive for their independence. His long struggle on behalf of the Indians of South Africa and his emergence later as a prophet in the hearts of millions of his fellow-countrymen; his political shrewdness and legal acumen enabled him to translate his faith into effective action. Above all, he won world renown by his doctrine of non-violent resistance. Abjuring property, he spent his life in service. His achievement, rare if not unique, was to bring to politics the moral force of a great religious teacher.

THE Gandhis are a family of Bania caste who for several generations had held high positions in the political life of the states of Kathiawar. The Mahatma's father, Kaba Gandhi, was Diwan in Rajkot and Vankaner. Mohandas was the youngest son of Kaba by his fourth wife.

Gandhi was brought up in an orthodox religious atmosphere, his mother especially being very strict in the performance of religious duties. She was also a very intelligent and well-informed woman. His father had little academic education, but had gathered much practical knowledge and wisdom from a busy life.

Gandhi was born on October 2, 1869, at Porbandar. He lived there until he was seven. He attended school, but he tells us that "it was with difficulty that I got through the multiplication tables." The family then left Porbandar for Rajkot, where Kaba Gandhi was to take up duties at the court.

At thirteen, Gandhi was married. His next eldest brother and his cousin were married at the same ceremony. After a year's break, he continued his studies at high school. With difficulty he learned a little Sanskrit, but afterwards he was always glad of the effort made, as it enabled him to read some of the Hindu scriptures. He came to consider that all Indian children should be taught Hindi, Sanskrit, Persian, Arabic and English.

During this period Gandhi's father was ill and bedridden. Gandhi was his devoted attendant and nurse. His father's death was a sore blow to the boy.

Gandhi passed his matriculation and went for a term to Samaldas College in Bhavnagar. But he could not accustom himself to the life there and returned home. Then an old Brahmin friend of the family advised sending him to England to study law. After much hesitation and heart-burning, it was decided that he should go. This step caused a scandal in the Bania caste, and the Sheth declared him to have forfeited caste. He sailed from Bombay in September, 1887, leaving behind a son a few months old.

In London he met leading theosophists, including Mrs. Besant, newly converted, and Madame Blavatsky. Through them he developed an interest in Hindu sacred literature. He also turned his attention to Christianity, which he had hitherto regarded with some hostility. He was much moved by the Sermon on the Mount, with its insistance on returning good for evil, and he compared it in his mind with similar passages in Hindu scriptures.

With Narayan Hemchandra, he obtained an interview with Cardinal Manning, to whom the two Indians expressed their admiration for his championship of the dock labourers in their famous strike of 1889.

After nearly four years, he completed his studies in London, was called to the Bar, and returned to India. He set up practice in Rajkot, but met with indifferent success. Then came an invitation from a Porbandar firm of merchants, which had a branch in South Africa, to go out to that country to help in an important lawsuit, covering many thousands of pounds, in which the firm was engaged.

In April, 1893, Gandhi went out to South Africa for one year. He stayed there for over twenty. Almost immediately on his arrival in Natal, political consciousness was awakened in him by a series of humiliating shocks. So far he had only encountered race prejudice in the rudeness of an official in Kathiawar. In Natal it appeared everywhere in the most degraded insults, social and political, heaped on the Indian community individually and collectively.

On the day after his arrival, Gandhi attended the magistrate's court at Durban. The magistrate stared at him for some time, then ordered him to remove his turban. Rather than do so he left the court room. A few days later he took train to Pretoria. This humiliating and hazardous journey fully showed him the abject social position of his fellow Indians in South Africa. Although he had a first-class ticket, he was ejected by force from the first-class compartment, and on that part of the journey which in those days was completed by coach, he was forced to sit outside with the driver and later, he was even assaulted and beaten by the conductor. He was addressed by railway officials by the name of " Sammy "—the contemptuous nickname given by the Europeans to all Indians, just as they referred to all Indians as " coolies." Gandhi was thus called a " coolie " barrister.

The case he had come to work on dragged out at Pretoria for months. Gandhi's clients were Moslems, and it was at this time that he first took a serious interest in the Mohammedan faith. He read the Koran in translation. At the same time the followers of several Christian sects in Pretoria were trying to convert him to Christianity. At length, largely through Gandhi's personal efforts, the protracted lawsuit was settled out of court by arbitration.

Gandhi returned to Durban intending to sail for home. While in Pretoria he had made a study of the wrongs of the Indian community in South Africa and had addressed meetings on the subject. At a farewell party given for him in Durban, someone pushed into his hand a Natal newspaper, where he read a report that the Natal Government was about to take away the Indian franchise. At the urgent instance of his friends, Gandhi agreed to stay on temporarily in South Africa to fight the measure.

That same night he drew up a petition which was soon presented to the Natal Legislative Assembly. This was the first parliamentary petition ever presented by Indians in South Africa. It aroused great enthusiasm and support among the Indian community. A memorial with 10,000 signatures was sent to Lord Ripon, the Colonial Secretary.

Gandhi now wished to leave for home, but his compatriots begged him to stay and lead them. He consented, but refused the salary they offered him. It was arranged that he should be given the legal work of the big Indian firms and thus support himself.

Straightway he started the work of organization. In May, 1894, he founded the Natal Indian Congress. He also initiated a drive to raise the standards of cleanliness, sanitation, housing and education among the Indians of Natal.

In 1896 Gandhi went for a six months' holiday to India. While in the home country he delivered a number of speeches at public meetings on Indian conditions in Natal, and also wrote a pamphlet which had a wide circulation.

News of these activities aroused the anger of the Natal Europeans. Feeling rose to such a pitch that the white inhabitants of Durban determined to prevent Gandhi and his family, and the 800 other Indian passengers on Gandhi's boat and another steamer, from setting foot on Natal soil. The Government held the steamers in quarantine for twenty-three days, and all sorts of efforts were made to induce the (Indian) steamship company to send the boats back to India.

At last the passengers had to be allowed to disembark. Gandhi, however, was mobbed, beaten, and but for the intervention of the police superintendent's wife, might well have been murdered. Later in the same day the crowd stormed the house where Gandhi was staying, but he was rescued by a ruse of the police.

The next important event in the Mahatma's life was the Boer War. Many of the Indians in Natal were too hostile to the British to wish to aid them, but Gandhi won them over to his view that, since they had never ceased to consider themselves British subjects, it was their duty as citizens to help the British side in the war. Gandhi himself was at this time quite unshaken in his loyalty to the empire. So he organized an ambulance unit, which did heroic work at the front, very often under fire, and with Gandhi always in the fore.

After the war Gandhi left South Africa and set up as a barrister in Bombay. But it was only to be for a few months. The South African Indians implored him to return to take up their battles once more. Under the British administration of the Transvaal after the defeat of the Boers, the position of Indians in that province had worsened. All existing colour-bar regulations were tightened; a strict control on immigration and a system of permits and registration was enforced. Gandhi started a paper in Natal to voice Indian grievances, and called it *Indian Opinion*. The paper was issued from a communal land settlement, which Gandhi, inspired by reading Ruskin's *Unto This Last,* had set up at Phoenix, near Durban. Gandhi himself went to live in Johannesburg, the focal point of the Transvaal Indians.

At the outbreak of the Zulu rebellion in Natal, however, he sent his family to Phoenix and himself led an ambulance unit for the British. His work lay entirely among the Zulu wounded prisoners,

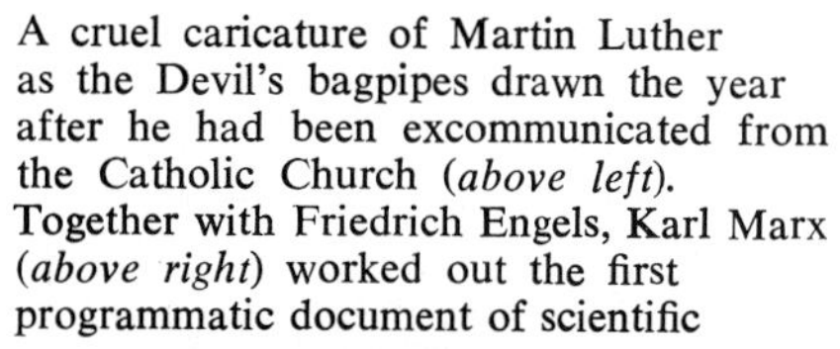

A cruel caricature of Martin Luther as the Devil's bagpipes drawn the year after he had been excommunicated from the Catholic Church (*above left*). Together with Friedrich Engels, Karl Marx (*above right*) worked out the first programmatic document of scientific communism, the *Manifesto of the Communist Party,* which was issued in 1847. Mahatma Gandhi, the prophet of a new India and a tireless worker for the cause of his country's independence, lying in state at Birla House, New Delhi (*below*), after his assassination on January 30, 1948.

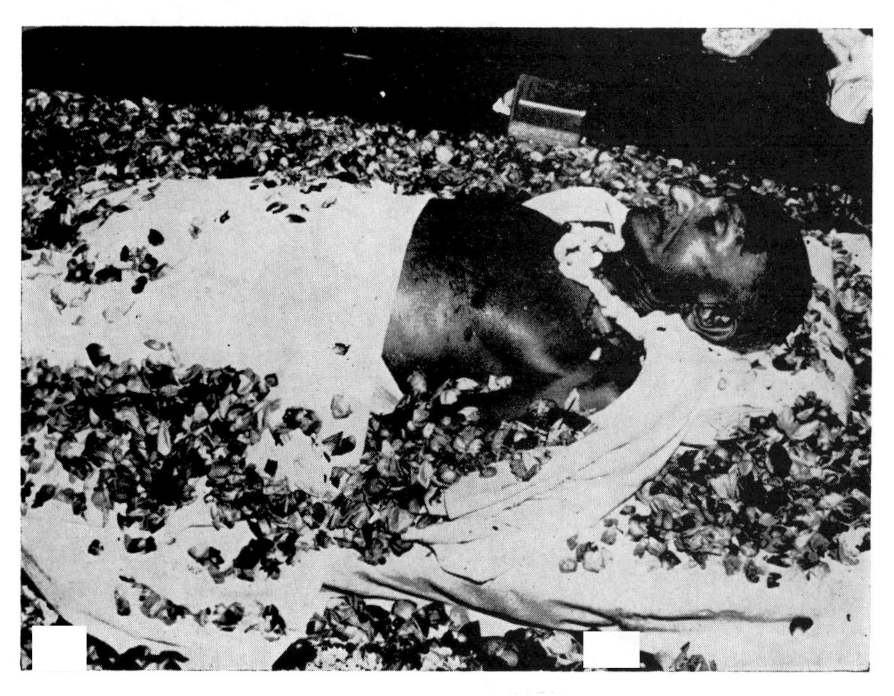

(*Above left*) A self-portrait of the greatest genius of the Renaissance, Leonardo da Vinci, who is also a famous sculptor and engineer. (*Above right*) *Peasants Dancing,* an engraving by the great German artist Albrecht Dürer. It took three years for Michelangelo to paint the ceiling of the Sistine Chapel in Rome. A detail from *The Creation of Man* (*below*).

whom no one else would tend. The unit was disbanded after a month with the highest praise for its work.

At the same time, the Transvaal Government was proposing to pass a stringent registration law to control the movements of Indians in the Transvaal. Among other things, the law proposed compulsory registration of the fingerprints of every Indian adult.

In September, 1906, a momentous mass meeting of Indians was held in Johannesburg. The three thousand Indians present took an oath to resist the "Black Act," as it was dubbed, to the last, *but by non-violent means*. Thus the Indian passive resistance weapon was forged.

Gandhi had no name for this new movement, and offered a prize in *Indian Opinion* for a suitable name. Maganlal Gandhi won the prize for the word *Sadagraha,* which Gandhi altered to *Satyagraha*. So the great movement was born.

The struggle against the "Black Act" went on. Gandhi led a deputation to England to interview the Secretary of State for India and the Secretary of State for the Colonies. On the way back the deputation received a telegram at Madeira telling them that the "Black Act" was to be disallowed. But when they reached Capetown they found that on the granting of responsible government to the Transvaal, which was to take place almost immediately, the Transvaal would be at liberty to pass what measures it pleased.

The Act was passed. Very few came forward to register. A number of arrests were made, including Gandhi himself. Eventually Gandhi reached a compromise with Smuts, by which, if the majority of Indians registered voluntarily, the Act would be repealed. This compromise bitterly disappointed many of Gandhi's followers. They felt he had betrayed them, and so strong was the resentment of a small section that Gandhi was even assaulted and wounded in the street.

General Smuts did not carry out his side of the agreement. The struggle was resumed. A new Act was passed prohibiting "Asiatics" from entering the Transvaal, and at the same time another even more insulting blow fell on the Indian community. A judgment in the South African Supreme Court ruled that only Christian marriages registered by the registrar were legally valid in South Africa. A fresh wave of indignation swept the Indian community. Under Gandhi's leadership, Indians in the Transvaal deliberately got themselves jailed in their scores as a protest.

Then the indentured labourers in the coalmines of Natal came out on strike against the £3 tax which they were forced to pay at the end of their term of indenture. Gandhi went to Natal to be with them. He led a vast mass of thousands of illiterate, poverty-stricken strikers in a great march into the Transvaal. Gandhi and his helpers were arrested.

Gandhi was separated from the others and taken to prison in Bloemfontein, where there were no Indians except a few hotel waiters.

The strikers were arrested in a mass (under Gandhi's influence they submitted peacefully), herded back to Natal, and then forced, by flogging and shooting, to resume work in the mines. This treatment so outraged feeling in India that the Viceroy, Lord Hardinge, made a stinging speech condemning the action of the South African Government.

General Smuts was obliged to climb down. A commission was appointed to enquire into the whole matter, and Gandhi and the other leaders were unconditionally released.

At length the famous Gandhi-Smuts agreement was reached, and took form in the Indian Relief Act, which abolished the principal grievances. This was the victorious culmination of Gandhi's first period of public work, in which he had shown the world the immense possibilities of the new weapon of the oppressed—*Satyagraha*.

Gandhi sailed for England. The Great War broke out while he was on the high seas. No sooner had he arrived than he asked and gained permission to recruit an Indian ambulance unit from the Indians in Great Britain. A severe attack of pleurisy forced him to give up the work and on doctor's orders he returned to India.

Here, in 1916-17, he led an agitation for the abolition of emigration of indentured Indian labour to other parts of the empire. The Government agreed in principle but did nothing. Gandhi toured the country stirring up an All-India agitation. Already he was being honoured by being watched by the police. The agitation was successful; the indenture system was abolished.

Then Gandhi went to Champaran to help the peasants oppressed under the system of indigo growing. He had to face bitter hostility from the landlords and the Government, but he conducted the struggle to a victorious conclusion by means of peaceful *Satyagraha* agitation. "Hence it was," in his own words, "that this age-long abuse came to an end in a few months."

This struggle brought him face to face with India's greatest problem—the poverty and backwardness of the villages, and from this time onwards his mind became increasingly occupied with the regeneration of the peasant.

From Champaran he passed to Khaira to aid the peasants there in their revolt against the Government assessment of their crops after a bad harvest. The struggle ended in an unsatisfactory compromise. But Gandhi was now a force in India. The Viceroy invited him to attend the War Conference at Delhi in order to gain his support for the recruitment of Indian volunteers for service overseas. To the surprise of many, Gandhi offered his support, and went himself to conduct the recruiting campaign in Khaira. He met with very indifferent success, and then fell seriously ill with dysentery.

While in South Africa, Gandhi had taken a vow not to drink milk, owing to the cruelties practised on cows in dairies. During this illness his wife and the doctor persuaded him to take goat's milk, which he continued to take after his recovery. Nevertheless, he considered even the drinking of goat's milk to be a fall from grace.

Then came the first great civil disobedience campaign against the Rowlatt Act. It started with an All-India hartal of unprecedented success. The temper of the people grew dangerous, and, in flat contradiction to *Satyagraha* principles, outbreaks of violence occurred. But in the Punjab the agitation led to reprisals by the Government. Martial law was declared. The notorious Amritsar massacre took place. Gandhi had been refused entry into the Punjab by the police. To the disappointment of many of his followers, Gandhi called off the campaign.

The Amritsar massacre proved to be the turning point in Gandhi's attitude to the empire and Great Britain. Until then he had preserved a waning loyalty, but now he felt that Britain brought evil to India, and that India must obtain *swaraj* within or without the empire.

At the same time he realized that India could never reach this goal if she were rent by Hindu-Moslem hostility. He threw himself into the struggle to heal the breach between the two communities. He supported the Moslems in the Khilafat campaign, and agitated for the release from prison of the Ali brothers. It was about this time, too, that the Khadi movement was inaugurated on a large scale.

At first Gandhi supported the Montagu-Chelmsford reforms in Congress, but in the following year, April, 1920, he launched the non-co-operation campaign. With the agitation for *swaraj* he also coupled his drive for reforms, such as the abolition of the liquor trade, the removal of untouchability and the boycott of foreign goods. He himself adopted an untouchable girl into his home.

The boycott of foreign cloth was an important feature of the campaign which led, then and later, to many terrible clashes with the police. The great bonfire of foreign cloth which Gandhi had organized as a counter-demonstration at the arrival of the Prince of

Wales in Bombay proved the occasion of an outbreak of violence. The Bombay riots were followed by murder and arson at Chauri Chaura.

This violation of the *Satyagraha* spirit was a mortifying blow to Gandhi. Feeling that he was to blame in having entrusted the weapon of non-violence to the people before they had been properly trained to use it, he called the movement off. He himself retired to his *Ashram* at Sabarmati to do penance by fasting. There he was arrested, for the first time in India.

At his trial at Ahmedabad, he made a great speech defending the *Satyagraha* movement and his own principles. The judge acknowledged the purity of his motives, but under the law sentenced him to six years' imprisonment. He served the sentence in Yeravda jail, Poona, until January, 1924, when he fell very ill. He was removed to Poona Hospital and operated upon for appendicitis. He always expressed the deepest gratitude for the care and kindness he received at the hospital. He had barely recovered when he undertook his first great fast at Delhi, as a protest against the increasing conflict between the Moslem and Hindu communities.

In 1927 the Simon Commission was appointed. It was boycotted throughout India. On its report, the British Government decided to call a Round Table Conference. Gandhi, as leader of Congress, notified the Government that Congress would not participate in the conference, and threatened a civil disobedience campaign if India's demands were not granted.

The new campaign was launched in March, 1930. Previously Gandhi had written to the Viceroy to inform him that he proposed to lead a movement to defy the Salt Laws by non-violent means. On March 12 he set out from Sabarmati at the head of a band of followers from his *Ashram* on his famous march to the sea. As the marchers passed through the villages, Gandhi appealed to the inhabitants to join the non-co-operation campaign. Especially he addressed himself to the *patels,* urging them to resign their offices as representatives of the Government and to throw in their lot with the people.

The march commanded a growing interest not only in India but throughout Europe and America. It took the band of *Satyagrahis* a month to reach the sea coast at Dandi. There, on April 6, Gandhi ceremoniously picked up a piece of salt from the beach and thus, by a symbolic breach of the law, inaugurated the new civil disobedience movement.

At the end of the month he announced that he would lead a

non-violent raid on a Government salt depot at Dharasana. The raid was never carried out, for on May 5 Gandhi was arrested under the Bombay State Prisoners Regulation for 1827, whereby persons may be imprisoned for indefinite periods without trial.

His arrest was followed by a hartal in all the chief towns of India. A truce was at last brought about by the Irwin-Gandhi agreement. Gandhi agreed that Congress should suspend direct action, while the Viceroy promised to withdraw repressive measures.

Six months later, Gandhi attended the second Round Table Conference as representative of Congress. He achieved little at the conference, and meanwhile strife had again broken out in India. Gandhi's truce was broken, and the Rule of Ordinances in full swing.

On his return to Bombay, Gandhi sought an interview with the Viceroy, now Lord Willingdon. His avowed purpose was to settle the issue by negotiation. A series of telegrams passed between Gandhi and the Viceroy's private secretary. The Viceroy was intransigent. Little more than a day after the last telegram had been sent, Gandhi was arrested at dawn. It was commonly rumoured in Bombay that the order to arrest him had gone out while the exchange of telegrams was still in progress.

Gandhi was taken once more to Yeravda jail, and kept in custody without trial. The arrest precipitated a widespread movement of resistance.

Gandhi in jail was as great a force as Gandhi at liberty. Later in the same year he made the greatest gesture of his life on behalf of the untouchables. This was the fast "unto death" to undo Mr. Ramsay MacDonald's Communal Award. The fast was successful. Indians of all classes worked frantically to bring about the agreement which should save the Mahatma's life, and the Poona Pact came into being.

Gandhi was released, and again imprisoned without trial. He undertook another fast as a protest against the lack of facilities to carry on from inside the jail his activities for the uplift of the Depressed Classes whom he termed Harijans (God's men). He was later released and then, at a conference in Poona which he attended, it was decided to give up civil disobedience on a mass scale but Gandhi himself was to have the liberty to offer individual *satyagraha*.

He was arrested again and released in August, 1933, following another hunger-strike against "nobody in particular but in the cause of truth." Thereafter Gandhi confined himself to Harijan work and it was only in 1934 that he resumed advising Congress leaders. A few months later, he felt his association with the Congress was a source of embarrassment to those who could not follow the ethics underlying his political activities, and he resigned his membership of the Congress. He was still a virtual preceptor of the Congress and his views on subjects like prohibition, village uplift and improvement of the condition of Harijans were acted upon by ministries in the provinces.

In 1938, on the eve of the Haripura session of the Congress, he staved off a first-class political crisis following the sudden resignation of the Bihar and U.P. ministries over the issue of the wholesale release of political prisoners. Gandhi's appeal to the Viceroy resulted in the ministers being enabled to examine individual cases of prisoners on merits.

The differences between Hindus and Muslims were widening and Gandhi attempted to bridge the gulf by entering into negotiations with Jinnah, President of the Muslim League. Their prolonged discussions, however, broke down.

Gandhi became the focal point on the Indian political stage again in 1939 when, shortly before the Tripuri session of the Congress, he undertook a fast in Rajkot State over a breach of the agreement between the ruler and leaders of a movement for responsible government in the State. Gandhi's condition became critical and he was persuaded to end the fast after the dispute had been referred by the Viceroy to Sir Maurice Gwyer, the then Chief Justice of the Federal Court of India.

Gandhi issued an appeal to every Briton to accept the method of non-violence. He also formulated a demand that Congressmen should be free to preach against aid being given in any form towards the prosecution of the Second World War. This was followed by a campaign of civil disobedience which, beginning with individuals, assumed the proportions of a mass movement. A large number of Congressmen went to jail during the year that the campaign lasted.

On August 9, 1942, Gandhi was arrested in Bombay along with several members of the Congress after the passing of the "Quit India" resolution· He was kept in the Aga Khan Palace in Poona while members of the Congress Working Committee were sent to the Ahmednagar Fort prison.

A fast "according to capacity" was begun by Gandhi on February 10, 1943, on the moral issue of a *satyagraha* "crucifying his flesh." His condition caused grave anxiety during the second week of the fast. At this crisis, three members of the Viceroy's Council resigned. The fast ended on March 3. Gandhi's wife died on February 22, 1944.

India was convulsed by a mass movement against the Government following Gandhi's arrest, which lasted several months and seriously hampered the war effort. The casualties were heavy and thousands were sent to prison. Gandhi corresponded with the Viceroy from his prison camp, protesting against the Government's repressive policy and received the reply that the Government could not possibly tolerate lawlessness.

Gandhi was released after a severe attack of pernicious malaria. He met Jinnah again in an effort to arrive at a settlement over the League's demand for a separate Muslim state. The talks again broke down.

Then followed the Simla Conference convened by the then Viceroy, Lord Wavell, to which representatives of the Muslim League, the Congress and others were invited. The conference failed on the issue of communal ratio. Gandhi refused to be an active participant but remained as "adviser to all parties and the Viceroy."

The Government in Britain had in the meantime changed and the Labour Party had assumed power. The new Prime Minister, Mr. Attlee, announced in Parliament that India's independence was no longer a disputed issue and that Britain would be willing to help India to frame her own constitution. The British Cabinet Mission of three arrived and, after prolonged discussions and on the failure of the parties to agree, announced their compromise proposals. Gandhi hailed the Mission's efforts as a sincere and honest endeavour to help India.

The Muslim League first accepted the Mission's plan. The Congress accepted the long-term plan but rejected the interim plan on the basis of the Viceroy's proposals. The League then rejected both the long-term and interim proposals, and decided to launch a direct action campaign.

The Viceroy in the meantime had called on Pandit Jawaharlal Nehru, as leader of the majority party, to form a government. The inauguration of this Cabinet was the signal for widespread communal riots in the country. League representatives were later included in the Cabinet but the riots continued.

On February 20, 1947, the British Government announced their decision to leave India, and offered to hand over power to the provinces or other authorities. This was followed by a bid to capture power in the Muslim majority provinces where the League was not in charge of the administration.

Unprecedented violence broke out in East Bengal, followed by reprisals in Bihar and later in the Punjab and the North-West Frontier Province.

Gandhi, who was in Delhi advising the Congress Party in Government, left for East Bengal where he started on a village-to-village tour to restore confidence among the panic-stricken people and to inculcate ideas of mutual trust and goodwill. He later went to Bihar on a similar mission.

During the period of the transfer of power and the establishment of India and Pakistan as two separate self-governing dominions Gandhi continued to give his strength for his fellows, touring riot-affected areas and preaching the need for peace and goodwill.

He lived to see his great ambition for a free India realized, but strife between Muslims and Hindus was intensified by the division of the continent in 1947.

Early in 1948, Gandhi, now a frail old man of seventy-eight, in a further effort to bring peace to his country, embarked on another fast. This stimulated substantial peace offerings to Pakistan and the Muslim minority, and Gandhi ended the fast after five days. All India rejoiced.

All, that is, save certain Hindu sectarian fanatics who could only see any softening to the Muslims as treason. Two attempts were made on Gandhi's life at prayer meetings. The first, a bomb, hurt no one, and Gandhi desired that the thrower should not be punished. A few days later, on January 30, 1948, the Mahatma was shot dead at point-blank range.

India's joy was turned to grief. Hindu and Muslim mourned alike and paid homage in the miles-long funeral procession to the burning ground near the sacred river Jumna, where his ashes were scattered on the waters. Gandhi, the man, was gone for ever; his significance to India had been absolute. But the teaching of Gandhi remains, and his wider significance to a world torn with violence may yet await its fulfilment.

ARTISTS AND MUSICIANS

LEONARDO DA VINCI

(1452–1519)

One of the ideals of perfection in mankind is that of perfect balance. A man whose brain is many-sided and can grasp the details and see the inner laws of arts and sciences, and yet have creative faculties as well as analytic; whose body is healthy and beautiful and vigorous, a worthy temple for that brain; whose personality is pleasant and kind, and whose whole being is animated by a spirit of lofty enterprise; such a man has the gifts of life in just balance, he approaches completeness. Such a man was Leonardo da Vinci, the greatest light of the Italian Renaissance, whose many-sided genius is unique in the history of the world.

It is evening in Florence. The citizens of the republic are taking their ease. The great painters, the sculptors, scientists, philosophers gather together to talk. But they are not talking now. They are listening.

They are listening to a young man of striking beauty, whose face lights up as he warms to his subject. His features are remarkable and they are framed by the luxuriant curls of his golden hair, which fall about his shoulders and down over his rose-coloured cloak. Beneath the cloak ripple the muscles of an athletic body; the young man is poised in a striking attitude; and the beauty of his appearance is matched by the beauty of his voice; and the beauty of his voice is but worthy of the wisdom and the fire of his talk. The wise men of Florence listen.

The young man is Leonardo da Vinci, known in Florence as a youth of charm and address, a man of wit, a singer and a poet, a rising painter, sculptor and architect. But they do not know him, as we do today, as one of the finest painters the world has seen, a draughtsman, sculptor, architect, mechanician, military and civil engineer, natural philosopher, a pioneer in many realms of science, an anticipator of Galileo, Newton, Bacon, Harvey, Watt, Fulton: a genius whose versatility has never been paralleled in the history of the world.

This man, one of the greatest lights and most dynamic forces of the Italian Renaissance, was born in 1452. He was the illegitimate son of a lawyer, Ser Piero Antonio da Vinci, and he was born in the fortified hill village of Vinci, whence his family took its name. His mother, Catarina, afterwards married another man, and Leonardo was brought up entirely in his father's house.

Vasari, the famous biographer of painters, tells us of Leonardo's early education: "In arithmetic he made such rapid progress that he often confounded the master who was teaching him by the perpetual doubts he started, and by the difficulty of the questions he proposed. He also commenced the study of music and resolved to acquire the art of playing the lute, when, being by nature of an exalted imagination and full of the most graceful vivacity, he sang to that instrument most divinely, improvising, at the same time, both the verses and the music."

But drawing and modelling were the favourite tasks of his childhood, and this led his father to place him under Verrocchio, the Florentine artist. Leonardo came under the tutorship of Verrocchio in 1470. He rapidly became a proficient painter, and we know he was employed to finish and assist in works undertaken by his master. In June, 1472, we find the name of "Lyonardo di Ser Piero da Vinci" entered in the account books of the Florentine Guild of Painters as an independent artist.

With the exception of an unfinished canvas of the "Adoration of the Kings," in the Uffizi at Florence, nearly all of Leonardo's early work has been lost. It is said that he painted one of the angels in Verrocchio's "Baptism of Our Lord," and we know that in this period of his life he did a water-colour cartoon of "The Fall" and a painting of the Medusa. He had already begun to make his mark, too, as an architect and sculptor, and we are told that, while still a youth, he executed a number of fine heads in terra-cotta.

From about 1477 to 1482, Leonardo worked as an independent artist under the patronage of Lorenzo the Magnificent. During all this time he was not only concerned with his own chosen arts of painting and sculpture. He was the first painter to go to Nature for his example. He owed nothing to the old classical rules and patterns. Leonardo, again, was the first painter to realize the effects and to appreciate the beauties of light and shade; he attempted to reproduce their interplay in his pictures—a mighty advance from the simple concentration on colour and form of the old school.

But Leonardo did not stop there. He had an insatiable thirst for knowledge. He not only saw, and attempted to reproduce, the beauties of light and shade; he wanted to know the laws that governed them. He studied optics, and the physiology of the eye.

He gained a knowledge of the laws which govern the movements of waves, and applied them to light and sound. And this was in the fifteenth century! His painting and sculpture opened up other fields of enquiry. He studied human and animal anatomy, enquired into the laws of muscular movement, and was the first to examine physiology and botany. In these sciences he was a pioneer. We find the evidence of his genius and of his great, enquiring mind in the notebooks in which he jotted down his observations and his knowledge for forty years of his life.

In 1482, Leonardo went to Milan, "with," says Vasari, "a lute which he had himself constructed almost wholly of silver, and in the shape of a horse's head, a new and fanciful form calculated to give more force and sweetness to the sound. When playing this instrument, Leonardo surpassed all the musicians who had assembled to perform before the duke; he was, besides, one of the best improvisatori in verse existing at the time; and soon the duke became enchanted with the admirable conversation of the young Florentine artist."

Ludovico Sforza was then ruling Milan. In a remarkable letter, Leonardo offered his services to him. He set forth nine new and original ideas in military science and in the conduct of warfare, and concluded:—

"10. In time of peace, I believe I can equal anyone in architecture, and in constructing buildings, public or private, and in conducting water from one place to another.

"Then I can execute sculpture, whether in marble, bronze or terra-cotta, also in painting I can do as much as any other, be he who he may.

"Further, I could engage to execute the bronze horse in lasting memory of your father, and of the illustrious house of Sforza . . ."

Leonardo was not boasting, and Ludovico was quick to accept his offer. Thus, for the next seventeen years Leonardo lived and worked in Milan.

He employed his genius in many ways. Ludovico prized him as much for his personality and charm as for his art. He was the court pageant master. He arranged and presided over all festivities. He wrote satires, fables, allegories and songs. And all the time he was working at his chief tasks.

The plague in Milan, in 1485, gave him the idea of a new city. He drew up plans for rebuilding Milan on new and sanitary lines, and in the following year, he was submitting plans for beautifying and strengthening the Castello, the stronghold of the Sforzas. A year later he put forward drawings for Milan Cathedral. Meanwhile, he was studying geometry, astronomy, statics, dynamics, the art of lyre construction, and mathematics, and in his spare time he was engaged on the model of the colossal equestrian statue of Francesco Sforza. He made many drawings and studies for this work, some of which are still preserved. After years of labour, the model, twenty-six feet high, was completed and exhibited in Milan in 1493. But the giant statue was never cast in bronze, and when, six years later, Milan was sacked by the French, " this wonderful work became a target for the Gascon archers," and was later destroyed.

The year 1494 found Leonardo still hard at work. He produced plans for a complete system of irrigation and waterways throughout the Lombard plain. He made a number of observations on storm and lightning. With Bramante, he was the architect to the Castello. He painted a Madonna. And it was in this year that he began the greatest and indeed the most famous of all his paintings, "The Last Supper."

The work was painted on a wall in the convent of Santa Maria delle Grazie. It was executed in tempera, and unfortunately the tempera did not take well to the plaster, nor the plaster to the wall. (The old legend of Leonardo mixing tempera with oil as an experiment has been discounted.) The painting soon began to flake and decay. Many attempts were made at restoration, but most of them made matters worse, until Cavaliere Cavenaghi succeeded in preserving what was left of the original, and in restoring the parts that had vanished.

In spite of its decayed state, "The Last Supper" is recognized as one of the very greatest paintings in the world. It has been called " the first masterpiece of the perfected Renaissance" and " the most perfect composition in the history of painting of all ages." The perfect technique of the work is only surpassed by the painter's spiritual insight.

The picture at once made a tremendous impression. When Louis XII entered Milan, in his victorious campaign against Ludovico Sforza, less than two years after " The Last Supper" was completed, he saw the picture and " was greatly struck thereat, and closely contemplating it, he asked those about him if it were not possible to hew out the wall whereon it was painted, being minded to take the picture with him to France."

Other works Leonardo executed while he was at Milan include the " Virgin of the Rocks," now in the Louvre, the National Gallery "Virgin of the Rocks," which he painted with his pupil, Ambrogio de Predis, the interior decorations of the Sala della Torre in the Castello, and innumerable sketches and drawings.

In 1499, Ludovico was driven from his duchy, and at the end of that year Leonardo left Milan for Venice. He was kindly received by the duchess, Isabella Gonzaga, of whom he did a chalk drawing; he promised a portrait later. But science claimed him once more, and he seems to have spent most of his short stay in Venice in the study of mathematics and cosmography.

In April, 1500, the news came of the complete overthrow of Ludovico, and Leonardo set out for his own city of Florence. His thirst for knowledge had now turned to geography. We find him writing and enquiring about the tides in the Black and Caspian Seas. At the same time, he produces plans for the canalization of the Arno and for other civil engineering projects. Isabella Gonzaga, who writes to him for a painting, is informed that the master is engrossed in geometry, and is " very impatient of the brush." It is interesting to note that at this period Soderini offered him, in vain, the block of marble from which Michelangelo later carved his colossal " David."

Michelangelo disliked Leonardo, and there is a story of a street encounter between the two in which Michelangelo shouts the taunt: ". . . horse modeller, who couldn't cast a statue in bronze and had to give up the attempt in shame."

In 1502, Leonardo took service with Cesare Borgia, for whom he travelled through central Italy as chief engineer. Six excellent and accurate maps, which he made on these journeys, are in the royal library at Windsor. They are a marvel of scientific cartography and of draughtsmanship.

Leonardo was soon back in Florence, and work was at once found for him. According to Vasari, " the Servite monks had at that time commissioned Filippino Lippi to paint the altar-piece for the principal chapel in their church, Santa Maria dell'Annunziata, when Leonardo declared that he would himself very willingly have undertaken such a work. This being repeated to Filippino, like the amiable man that he was, he withdrew himself at once, when the monks gave the picture to Leonardo."

Filippino had already begun upon his picture of " The Descent from the Cross," but Leonardo had no wish to continue this. He delayed a long time, then prepared a cartoon of the " Madonna with the Infant Christ and Saint Anne," " so admirably depicted that it not only caused astonishment to every artist who saw it, but, when finished, the chamber wherein it stood was crowded for two days by men and women . . . all hastening to behold the wonders produced by Leonardo, which awakened amazement in the whole people." But the picture never got beyond the cartoon stage, and eventually the monks cancelled the contract, and gave it back to Filippino Lippi.

During the years 1504 and 1505, Leonardo was engaged on a cartoon of a battle piece for the council hall in the palace in the signory of Florence. He was to do one more, and Michelangelo another. Leonardo's cartoon of—to use his own phrase—" the bestial frenzy " of battle, was exhibited beside Michelangelo's and was the wonder and admiration of all the artists who saw it. Its influence on the younger men, such as Raphael, was tremendous and lasting. During this time, too, Leonardo was working on what is perhaps his most celebrated painting, the " Mona Lisa " (now in the Louvre, Paris), which he finished in 1506. The face of the woman there portrayed is famous for its strange and subtle smile.

In that year he went once more to Milan, and there he stayed until he transferred his services from the city of Florence to Louis XII of France. In 1512 he went to Rome, but did not find the atmosphere congenial, and two years later he accepted an offer of Francis I of France and retired to the castle of Cloux, near Amboise, where he remained until his death in May, 1519.

That, in brief, is a chronicle of Leonardo's life. It would take a volume to chronicle his achievements.

Had his notebooks been published at the time of his death, science and scientists would have been saved centuries of labour; but they were neglected until the nineteenth century, when it was found that Leonardo had anticipated discoveries in every sphere.

We have given his achievements as an artist. As a writer he helped to mould Italian prose. As a theoretician in art, he discovered and laid down immortal principles. A century before Bacon, he showed a finer grasp of the principles of experimental science than Bacon did.

He designed an aeroplane which, if he had had some agent such as the petrol engine, would have flown. He anticipated the use of steam, sketched a steam cannon, and designed paddles for ships. He even made drawings for breech-loading cannons. Some of the machines that he constructed and designed, such as the saw in the marble quarries of Carrara, have survived for over four centuries.

He was the originator of the science of hydraulics, and discovered the camera obscura. He was convinced of the molecular structure of water, had knowledge of sound and light waves, and was the first to study the structure and arrangement of flowers and foliage. And he was a great philosopher.

His virtues are not ended. As a man he was handsome, strong enough to bend horse-shoes, charming, tactful, athletic; he was popular and deserved to be; he was a generous and loyal friend, and devoted to his followers and pupils.

There can only be one summary of Leonardo da Vinci, that almost perfect example of the civilized mind wedded to a healthy body: He was the complete man.

ALBRECHT DÜRER

(1471–1528)

Albrecht Dürer was one of the greatest artistic geniuses that the world has produced. If there be need to add to that—he was a painter who produced the finest paintings in the whole history of German art, he was a supreme draughtsman, he was both a pioneer and master of etching. The mastery of drawing which he displays in his etchings and engravings has never been excelled. His work has, since its first appearance, delighted and inspired the world. He was . . . he was Dürer.

THREE small boys crouch together in a top floor room of an old house in Nuremberg. Two of them are on the alert, straining their ears to catch every sound in the house, while they eagerly watch what the third is about. Their companion, a good-looking boy, with large, soft eyes, long curling hair, cut short over the brow in the fashion of the times, is working calmly with pencil and paper, to please himself and delight his friends. He is making a sketch of a woman, with a falcon on her hand, an odd Burgundian cap on her head.

His drawing lies now in the British Museum, and the inscription says: "Albrecht Dürer did it for me before he went to Wohlgemuth's as a painter. . . ."

Dürer was at that time less than fifteen, and had not yet made known to his father his great desire to work as a painter, rather than to follow his father's trade of goldsmith. Though fully conscious of his special talent, the boy said nothing about it until secret and diligent practice had assured him that his inclination was fixed. In his free hours he would delight his playfellows by drawing little figures in the nooks and crannies of his father's house, or of those of his friends.

The old house in Nuremberg was actually a sort of appendage to the great mansion of the Pirkheimers, leaders of the city interests and of the city's culture. There, Albrecht Dürer the elder had settled with his young wife, when he became a master goldsmith, and there, in 1471, his second son, Albrecht, was born. In him the father's hopes ultimately settled.

The young Albrecht showed a keen desire to learn, and his father gave him the best education he could. The boy was taken from school to his father's workshop at an early age; but he quickly discovered in what branch of art his talents were centred. He told his father at last. The old man was not pleased, thinking the years at the goldsmith's workshop entirely wasted. But he gave in, and Albrecht was apprenticed to Michael Wohlgemuth, the painter to whom Nuremberg was indebted for the introduction of the art of engraving on copper. Dürer's training in this studio set him on the path to supremacy.

Dürer was apprenticed in 1486. He passes over his apprenticeship with the remark that God gave him industry, and that he learned well, but that he had much to suffer from his fellow-apprentices. After four years of this he set out on his wanderings, for it was the old trade custom for apprentices to go from town to town, working in the different studios, to obtain a wider and more varied experience. From the very beginning Dürer showed signs of marked individuality in his work, and now during these travels, he tried to shake off the traditions of the Wohlgemuth school, retaining principally a feeling for the charms of landscape.

It is difficult to trace his route during the four years he was away from Nuremberg. He visited Colmar, and was kindly received by the brothers of the celebrated artist, Martin Schongauer. At Basle he visited another Schongauer, then worked in Strasbourg for a time, and finally returned to his home town in 1494.

Dürer's special study at this time was landscape. He made a series of studies of castles and cities in the Tyrol. He copied the details of nature in a way which entitles him to be considered the founder of independent modern landscape painting.

Within a month of his return, Dürer was married to Agnes Frey, the daughter of a wealthy Nuremberg merchant.

"Häns Frey," says Dürer, "was in treaty with my father, and gave me his daughter Agnes and two hundred gulden with her, and celebrated the wedding." The bride was charming as well as wealthy, and the young people made a handsome couple. Albrecht took his bride to his father's house, where they lived until the old man died, in 1502.

There the young man set up a studio and eagerly devoted himself to his work, at the same time sharing the burdens of his father's domestic cares. To this period belongs the Dresden Altar-piece, a water-colour on fine linen; but much of the work done in this first studio was carried out by the apprentices. The Baumgartner

Altar-piece marks the transition between the school pictures and the larger ones of Dürer's own.

In 1498, Dürer published his great *Apocalypse*. He had been developing the idea for this work even on his youthful travels, and had been engaged on the actual work of making the woodcuts since 1495. The first two editions appeared in the same year, one in German, one in Latin, printed by Dürer himself and adorned with fifteen woodcuts. The fourth cut, "The Four Horsemen," is one of Dürer's most powerful drawings, and has for centuries commanded universal admiration.

As regards execution, Dürer introduced a new epoch in the art of wood engraving. He needed no colouring; his skilful use of light and shade was far more effective than colour. His meaning was so precisely set forth that his designs were very easily worked out by the wood engravers who actually carried out the task of cutting the blocks.

Dürer was, at this time, engrossed in the study of the nude. He could never be satisfied with anything but the best; and the best for him was the exact representation of nature. The "Nemesis," of 1503, shows an unflinching realism in depicting a common type of mature, muscular, unshapely German woman. By 1504, under the influence of Jacopo de Barbari, he had arrived at a new conception of the human figure. His first large panel painting, the "Adoration of the Magi," was completed in that year, and his largest copper engraving the "St. Eustace."

In 1505, Dürer went to Venice, with the chief object of carrying out a commission for the German colony there. He was to paint a panel for an altar-piece, and it appears that he was well pleased with his work. "It is so good and beautiful in colour," he writes. "I have got much praise but little profit from it. I have silenced all the painters who said that I was good at engraving but could not manage colour." The painting was the "Adoration of the Virgin," or the "Feast of Rose Garlands," and when it came into the possession of Rudolf II, he had it carried from Venice to Vienna on men's shoulders, as a thing beyond price.

His fame in Italy was already great, and when he visited Bologna he was extravagantly fêted. In Venice he passed two prosperous and successful years. "How cold I shall be after this sun," he writes to his friend, the scholar, Pirkheimer, and adds: "Here I am a gentleman."

On his return, Dürer spent much time in painting after the fashion of the Italian masters. His "Adam and Eve," of 1507, shows the advance he had made, during his stay in Venice, in the study of the nude. They are the most perfect nude figures which then had come from the hand of any northern artist. His work was hindered for some time by attacks of fever, but he persevered at, and soon finished, a panel commissioned by Frederick of Saxony.

In 1508 he made his first sketch for the wonderful "Trinity," which was eventually completed in 1511. The following year he produced the small but perfect "Madonna with the Pear."

All this time he was hard at work on his great series of woodcuts and engravings. Before he went to Venice, sixteen of the twenty cuts for the "Life of the Virgin" were completed, and in 1511 that work was published. By the following year sixteen plates of his "Passion," engraved on copper and never published, were completed and the series was ended within a year.

In 1510, Dürer made many experiments which were to be of great importance in the future of the art of engraving. He took the first steps in dry-point etching, and invented the process of etching with aquafortis. He used this process on copper plates at first, but gave up copper in favour of iron, which succeeded perfectly. About 1514, he adopted a method which combined the old style of working with a dry needle and graving tool, and his later discovery of the use of acid.

The engravings which were completed by this method showed softer tones than his earlier work. Among them were the celebrated "Melancolia" and "The Knight, Death and the Devil." About the same time appeared a whole series of engravings of Biblical subjects, including the beautiful "St. Jerome in the Cell."

In 1511, he had completed the great series of woodcuts on which he had been at work for so long, and issued them as books. These were the twelve cuts of the "Great Passion," and the thirty-seven cuts of the "Little Passion," perhaps his most renowned work. He had a printing-press set up in his house, and had probably the assistance of his godfather, Koburger, the well-known printer. His books obtained a big sale in every direction.

To the portraits of himself of 1484, 1493, and 1497, must be added the one dated 1500, which is the most popular likeness of the great painter. He appears in this a magnificent man, with rich brown hair falling in full curls to his shoulders. His full-pursed lips are shadowed by a delicately curling moustache and beard; his eyes are large, clear and thoughtful. His friend, Camerarius, speaks of the noble form "well adapted for the abode of so glorious spirit," of the charm of his language in conversation, of the greatness of his mental and moral qualities, and extols him as "the truest preserver of modesty and chastity."

So far Dürer had been working in the pursuit of fame, or of wealth. Having established himself in both these spheres, he turned to the service of his emperor.

The Emperor Maximilian stayed in Nuremberg during 1512, a visit of great importance to Dürer. He was commissioned to work on a book, "The Triumph of Maximilian," consisting of ninety-two separate blocks which, put together, formed one colossal woodcut, ten feet six inches high by nine feet wide. In four years the work was finished. For the Prayer-book of Maximilian, Dürer supplied marginal drawings in pen and ink, which show to perfection his richness of invention and the airy freedom and playfulness of his hand. At the same time Dürer was busy with portraits, religious paintings, and designs for wall paintings for the civic buildings of Nuremberg.

In 1520 came the journey to the Netherlands. The plague was raging in Nuremberg, and Dürer, with his wife and a maid, set out for Antwerp. Throughout the journey he was handsomely received in all the towns he visited, not only at Antwerp, where he met Erasmus, but in Brussels, Bruges and Ghent. He attended the coronation of the emperor, Charles V, at Aachen, and was appointed court painter to that monarch.

Visiting Zeeland, to see a whale that had been washed up there, he narrowly escaped shipwreck, and in the Lowlands he contracted the fever which ultimately caused his death.

Throughout the twelve months that he was away from Nuremberg, he was incessantly working on portraits and on small paintings as gifts for the many friends he made.

In July, 1521, he returned to Nuremberg with his mind full of schemes for great religious paintings. These he never carried out. The only evidence of them remaining is in the many sketches he left. He devoted himself instead to the preparation of his books on the theory of engraving, on geometry, perspective, proportion and fortification.

He was now continually wearied by sickness. He had never been a very strong man, and was always liable to attacks of illness. The Netherlands journey had permanently undermined his health, both by the costly feasts with which he had been entertained, and by the hardships of the actual travelling. There is a coloured sketch of himself, half naked, the right hand pointing to a round yellow spot on his left side. Above he has written: "Where the yellow spot is on which I put my finger, there it pains me." Another self-portrait shows him vastly changed from the handsome man he had once been. The shoulders are bent, the features gaunt, the hair and beard thin and wretched.

He died suddenly and unexpectedly in April, 1528, before even his devoted friend, Pirkheimer, could see him again.

Of his published works the most important are: the first book of four he had planned on *Human Proportion;* the *Instruction in Mensuration; Instructions in Fortification,* and a work on fencing. He had also planned an encyclopædic work on the art of painting, and had made careful studies in the proportions of the horse.

It is chiefly in Dürer's engravings that we are able to get an insight into the depths of his character. By nature and upbringing a devoutly religious man, he was restless in his pursuit of knowledge, humble and faithful in his search after good, and he was rewarded by revelations which he strove to communicate.

His temper and his life were free from all jarring elements. He enjoyed the most honoured and fortunate career as an artist, and as a man had the friendship of the greatest men of his age, painters, statesmen, humanists and reformers. He commanded the sincere admiration of men such as Raphael and Bellini, Erasmus and Luther.

Dürer's genius lies in his individuality, which can easily be seen by comparing his works not only with those of former engravers, but with those of foreign contemporary masters. As an engraver he enormously advanced the progress of the art. No one before him etched with such skill and vigour; no one ever showed so delicate and yet so powerful a talent.

His genius has been summed up by Roger Fry, who says:

"Dürer was, perhaps, the greatest infant prodigy among painters, and the drawing of himself at the age of twelve shows how early he had mastered that simple and abrupt sincerity of Gothic draughtsmanship. One is inclined to say that in none of his subsequent works did he ever surpass this in all that really matters, in all that concerns the essential vision and its adequate presentment. He increased his skill until it became the wonder of the world and entangled him in its seductions; his intellectual apprehension was indefinitely heightened, and his knowledge of natural appearances became encyclopædic."

MICHELANGELO BUONARROTI

(1475–1564)

Michelangelo Buonarroti, or Michelangelo, made his own monuments to the loftiness of his genius. He carved them in marble, limned them in paint, built them in stone, and wrote them in ink. He was a giant in an age of giants; one of those amazing men of the Italian Renaissance who not only mastered an art, but enslaved the arts. Throughout a long and painful life, he worked and toiled to give fresh beauty to the world, and, as long as civilization lasts, the beauty that he created will move mankind and keep alive the name of Michelangelo, " the man with four souls."

An old man stands in the darkness of a musty room, listening. He stands broad-shouldered and erect in his old clothes, and his small eyes strain towards the door. Although he is aged and weary, those eyes are keen, and the flesh above his short, forked beard is of good colour. His large, square-topped head is surmounted by a cardboard hat, in which is stuck a lighted candle: there is a chisel in his hand. The knock on the door is repeated, and the old man shuffles across to open it. Outside stands a servant with an armful of candles—a present. They are special candles of goat-fat, which do not gutter so much as tallow, to be worn in the cardboard hat. The old man is annoyed and makes an irritable gesture of refusal.

" Sir," cries the servant, " they have almost broken my arms carrying them, and I am not going to take them home again. I'll stand them all up in the mud outside your door and light them."

" Put them down then," snaps the old man. " You're not going to play pranks at my door."

And he shuffles back into the darkness of the room and continues his work.

Who is the old eccentric to whom his friends send candles? A pensioner? A broken-down acquaintance? No. It is old Michelangelo, at work on a statue. Michelangelo the artist. Michelangelo, " the man with four souls," who has crowned a lifetime of work with achievements of the highest rank in architecture, sculpture, painting and poetry.

* * * * *

Michelangelo Buonarroti was born at Caprese, where his father was *podestà* (mayor), on March 6, 1475. The Buonarroti were a Florentine family of ancient burgher nobility, but by the year of Michelangelo's birth poverty had robbed them of everything save pride. When his six months of office as *podestà* of Caprese expired, Ludovico Buonarroti returned to Florence, and Michelangelo was put out to nurse with a stonecutter's wife. "I drew the chisel and the mallet with which I carve statues in together with my nurse's milk," he said in after years.

As a boy, Michelangelo was taught to read and write his native Italian, but he was soon attracted to art. His father and uncles tried to thrash art out of him, but the boy and his passion were too strong for them. So in 1488 he was apprenticed "to Domenico and David Currado, commonly called Ghirlandaio." Domenico Ghirlandaio was reckoned among the finest artists of the day, and it is interesting proof of Michelangelo's rapid development that the master was jealous of the pupil.

Condivi, Michelangelo's friend and pupil, tells how from the first the artist studied reality and based his work on naturalism. At the age of thirteen "Michelangelo coloured no particular without going first to Nature and comparing her truth with his fancies. Thus he used to frequent the fish-market, and study the shape and hues of fishes' fins, the colour of their eyes, and so forth in the case of every part belonging to them; all of which details he reproduced with the utmost diligence in his painting."

Michelangelo soon left Ghirlandaio, and turned to sculpture in the school formed under the patronage of the great Lorenzo de Medici—Lorenzo the Magnificent. Soon afterwards he attracted the attention of Lorenzo himself. He had carved a grinning mask out of a piece of waste marble, and was polishing it when the great Lorenzo walked by. Lorenzo admired the mask, but said: "You have made this faun quite old, and yet have left him all his teeth! Don't you know that men of that great age are always wanting in one or two?"

Michelangelo picked up his chisel and without hesitation knocked a tooth off the upper jaw. Lorenzo was struck with the clever way he had performed the task. He sent for the boy's father and arranged to take the young sculptor into his household. And there Michelangelo remained until Lorenzo's death in 1492.

These were the years of Michelangelo's moulding. He met Politian, the poet and the finest scholar of his age, and we know from his work of this period that he was inspired by the paganism and the Greek influences cultivated by Lorenzo.

After Lorenzo's death, Michelangelo fell under the spell of that fierce prophet, Savonarola. He turned also to those diligent studies of the Scriptures which so deeply affected his life and work. In poetry and philosophy, Dante provided the inspiration, for it was at this time that Michelangelo first studied and admired the master. In his own realm of art, he soaked himself in the rich examples of Ghirlandaio, Masaccio, Ghiberti, Giotto, and most of all, Donatello. Life was pleasant in the Medician gardens. Rare were incidents such as the famous one described by Torrigiano:

"This Buonarroti and I used, when we were boys, to go into the Church of the Carmine, to learn drawing from the chapel of Masaccio. It was Buonarroti's habit to banter all who were drawing there, and one day, when he was annoying me, I got more angry than usual, and, clenching my fist, I gave him such a blow on the nose that I felt bone and cartilage go down like biscuit beneath my knuckles, and this mark of mine he will carry with him to the grave."

Torrigiano's boast was unfortunately true. Michelangelo bore the mark of the blow all his life.

It was at this time that he experienced one of the great passions of his life, but even here, artist as he was, his emotions became fuel for his art. He met and fell in love with the beautiful Luigia de Medici, and his love, entirely unrequited, found expression in a series of exquisite sonnets.

Not until his sixtieth year was that fountain again to be unsealed. Then we find him addressing a further series of sonnets to the young Tommaso Cavalieri—a series that reminds us vividly of Shakespeare's poems to the unknown "W. H." But even more important were his poems to Vittoria Colonna, the widow of the Marquis Pescara, who is the real Egeria of Michelangelo's poetic life. To her he poured out his soul in noble numbers. To her he addressed live poetry, mystical poems and works dealing with the Christian religion, the joys of Platonic affection and the mysteries of art.

Walter Pater points out that in Michelangelo's poems frost and fire are almost the only images—the refining fire of the goldsmith, once or twice the phœnix ice melting at the fire, fire struck from the rock it afterwards consumes. His biography, in the *Encyclopædia Britannica,* says:

"Michelangelo's poetical style is strenuous and concentrated like the man. He wrote with labour and much self-correction; we seem to feel him flinging himself on the material of language with the same overwhelming energy and vehemence with which contemporaries describe him as flinging himself on the material of marble —the same impetuosity of temperament combined with the same fierce desire of perfection, but with far less either of innate instinct for the material or of trained mastery over its difficulties."

But the formative years at San Marco were not to last. Lorenzo the Magnificent died in 1492, and Michelangelo returned to Settignano, where he devoted himself to dissection and anatomy. The fruits of his studies may be seen in his works.

In the next three years Michelangelo visited Venice and Bologna, and then returned to Florence. He was now a young man, and had commenced the period of his maturity which gave so many masterpieces to the world.

In 1495, he executed his beautiful "Sleeping Cupid," which was sold to the Cardinal di St. Giorgio as an antique. A year later the artist went to Rome, where he carved his marble "Bacchus." From now on he was prolific. The year 1499 marks his first real work of Christian sculpture, the beautiful "Pieta" now in the Vatican Basilica.

Michelangelo returned to Florence in 1501, and here he produced the "Bruges Madonna" and, three years later, the colossal "David." This last work he wrought from a spoilt block of Carrara marble, nine cubits in height. The marble was ill shaped, and made the task difficult, but in eighteen months Michelangelo had carved from it a statue of amazing beauty.

There is an amusing story of his way with art critics. One of his admirers told him that he thought the nose of the David was too large. Michelangelo immediately ran up the ladder, taking with him his hammer, chisel, and a concealed handful of marble dust. He pretended to work off a portion of the nose, letting the marble dust fall as he did so. Then he shouted: "Look at it now!" And the friend answered: "I am far more pleased with it; you have given life to the statue."

At this period, too, Michelangelo carved the "St. Matthew," and drew his great cartoon of the battle of Pisa. In 1505, he was summoned to Rome by Pope Julius II, who set him to work on the construction of his own tomb. This task dragged on for years, caused trouble and bitterness between the sculptor and the pope's executors; it was never completed, but the famous "Moses and the group of slaves" were part of the scheme.

Three years later Michelangelo unwillingly accepted the commission to decorate the ceiling of the Sistine chapel. The fame and beauty of this work are known to all. The trials and agonies of the three years' painting of that ceiling are best told in some humorous verses addressed by Michelangelo to a friend:

> "I've grown a goitre by dwelling in this den—
> As cats from stagnant streams in Lombardy,
> Or in what other land they hap to be—
> Which drives the belly close beneath the chin:
> My beard turns up to heaven; my nape falls in,
> Fixed on my spine: my breast-bone visibly
> Grows like a harp: a rich embroidery
> Bedews by face from brush-drops thick and thin.
> My loins into my paunch like levers grind;
> My buttock like a crupper bears my weight:
> My feet unguided wander to and fro;
> In front my skin grows loose and long; behind,
> By bending it becomes more taut and strait;
> Crosswise I strain me like a Syrian bow:
> Whence false and quaint, I know,
> Must be the fruit of squinting brain and eye;
> For ill can aim the gun that bends awry.
> Come then, Giovanni, try
> To succour my dead pictures and my fame,
> Since foul I fare and painting is my shame."

The next decade saw Michelangelo busy on the work for Julius's tomb and on the colossal figures for the Medici chapel. In the period from 1527–1534 he was involved in Florentine politics. We find him nominated as Commissary General of the Fortifications, and the fortifications which he built were later much appreciated by the great Vauban. In 1534 he left Florence for ever, and went once more to Rome.

Now he was in his sixtieth year. Pope Paul III issued a brief appointing Michelangelo chief architect, sculptor and painter to the Vatican. In the same year the artist began his fresco in the Sistine chapel, "The Last Judgment." It took him seven years; and even then his life work was not done. He went on with the frescoes in the Pauline chapel, with paintings, drawings, and statuary. In 1547 he was made architect of St. Peter's, whose cupola is his great memorial in that art.

It was about the year 1538 that Michelangelo met the widowed poetess, Vittoria Colonna. She is the only woman in his ascetic life, and his friendship for her was mental and spiritual. She inspired him to return to one of his early loves—poetry, and it is to this period of his life that we owe the bulk of his sonnets. His poems are statues in words, rough-hewn and beautiful in their rugged vitality.

Their charming friendship was broken by her death in 1547. Condivi gives a pathetic picture of their parting: "He, for his part, loved her so, that I remember to have heard him say that he regretted nothing except that when he went to visit her upon the moment of her passage from this life, he did not kiss her forehead or her face, as he did kiss her hand. Her death was the cause that oftentimes he dwelt astonished, thinking of it, even as a man bereft of sense."

He wrote two touching sonnets to her memory. But he had still many years before him, and he worked right to the end. In 1554 he wrote his sublime sonnet:

"Now hath my life across a stormy sea,
Like a frail bark, reached that wide port where all
Are bidden, ere the final reckoning fall
Of good and evil for eternity.
Now know I well how that fond phantasy
Which made my soul the worshipper and thrall
Of earthly art is vain; how criminal
Is that which all men seek unwillingly.
Those amorous thoughts which were so lightly dressed,
What are they when the double death is nigh?
The one I know for sure, the other dread.
Painting nor sculpture now can lull to rest
My soul, that turns to His great love on high,
Whose arms to clasp us on the cross were spread."

But he still had ten years of work and pain before that afternoon of February, 1564, when the frail bark of his life reached port. In his last moments, writes his friend Vasari, "he made his will in three sentences, committing his soul into the hands of God, his body to the earth, and his substance to his nearest relatives: enjoining upon these last, when their hour came, to think upon the sufferings of Jesus Christ."

Thus died "the prophet or seer of the Renaissance." He had lived a hard life. He had spent the long years alone, "wedded," as he used to say, "to his art, a wife who was too much for him."

He bestowed his love upon children, upon his faithful servant, and upon his family, who sponged upon him mercilessly.

Michelangelo was generous to them and mean to himself. He lived parsimoniously, grudgingly. He seemed to thrive on work; he ate little and lived in poor lodgings.

Condivi describes his daily life: " He has always been extremely temperate in living, using food more because it was necessary than for any pleasure he took in it; especially when he was engaged upon some great work; for then he usually confined himself to a piece of bread, which he ate in the middle of his labour. . . . Often have I heard him say: 'Ascanio, rich as I may have been, I have always lived like a poor man.' And this abstemiousness in food is practised in sleep also; for sleep, according to his own account, rarely suits his constitution, since he continually suffers from pains in the head during slumber, and any excessive amount of sleep deranges his stomach. While he was in full vigour, he generally went to bed with his clothes on, even to the tall boots, which he has always worn, because of a chronic tendency to cramp. . . . At certain seasons he has kept these boots on for such a length of time that when he drew them off the skin came away together with the leather, like that of a sloughing snake. He was never stingy of cash, nor did he accumulate money, being content with just enough to keep him decently. . . ."

His contemporaries declared that he was irritable, quick-tempered and arrogant. True, he had the ascetic's fire; but his anger was quick to melt; he was generous with his money, with his works, with his ideas, and with his acceptance and praise of work by fellow artists.

A priest friend once said to Michelangelo that it was a pity he had not married and had children to inherit the profit and honour of his labours. He answered: " I have only too much of a wife in this art of mine. She has always kept me struggling on. My children will be the works I leave behind me. Even though they are worth nought, yet shall I live awhile in them. . . ."

By the same token he is living yet.

SIR CHRISTOPHER WREN

(1632–1723)

"Sir Christopher Wren," runs a famous quatrain, "went out to dine with some men. He said, 'If anyone calls, tell them I am designing St. Paul's.'" The light quotation is not inapt: our subject is Wren, and surely Wren's preoccupation was St. Paul's? But, in fact, it was not. The greatness of his masterpiece has almost buried the greatness that came before it. By St. Paul's he proclaimed himself a genius, but he was already a genius: his feats in astronomy, mathematics, medicine, were overshadowed by his skill as a builder and his magnificent conception as an architect, and it is well to remember that almost in the shadow of St. Paul's he raised sixty other churches that are monuments to his genius.

WHILE Cromwell ruled in England there was a staunch old royalist dean living at East Knoyle, in Wiltshire, whose name was Wren. We know of him that he was not only a follower, but actually a friend, of Charles I, and that he was an able man in many ways; not only a fine scholar but something of an architect, too. He designed a good roof for his parish church, and his son's success in every subject he touched at Westminster School was evidence, as well as reward, of the old dean's wise tuition and admirable guidance.

At the vicarage at East Knoyle, as pleasant a home as any that has ever been, he lived for God and King Charles—and for learning. A dull boy with such a father would have progressed well; a boy with talents must, with such fostering as young Wren received, have become great. But to talk of young Christopher Wren as having talents is to call Everest a steep hill, to class leviathan as a big fish.

From Westminster young Wren went to Oxford, where he made a brilliant reputation for himself as a mathematician and astronomer. In 1653, at the age of twenty-one, he became a fellow of All Souls, at twenty-four he was professor of astronomy at Gresham College, and five years later was appointed Savillian Professor of Astronomy at Oxford. The value of his geographical work was acknowledged by Newton in his *Principia*, while his research work in connexion with the barometer and in the fields of anatomy and medicine was equally remarkable. Then at the age of thirty, this genius turned his attention to architecture and became the greatest practical builder Britain has ever known, and one of the greatest of all that country's artists.

The success of Wren's early career—or rather the success of his several early careers—is made all the more marked by the fact recorded of him that he was unusually modest, with nothing of the opportunist in his nature. When, at Oxford, we find him being offered the chair of astronomy at Gresham, we also find him declining—because he felt himself too young—and only accepting after long persuasion. Again he turns down opportunity, and this time more firmly, when first he finds himself in Charles II's favour. Part of the dowry of Catherine of Braganza, the king's betrothed, was Bombay and Tangier, and Charles decided that Tangier should be rebuilt. He offered the work to Wren, but Wren did not relish so long a journey—and said so. This, to say the least, was risky, but Wren remained in the king's favour—and in England, where he wished to be.

It seems, however, that the more he spurned opportunity, the more opportunity pursued him. To this man in a million came the chance in a million: in 1661 he was made Surveyor-General of His Majesty's Works, and five years later His Majesty's capital was burnt down.

The chance that the Great Fire of London gave to Wren was no less magnificent because it was tragic. We do not know exactly how many lives were lost; thirteen thousand two hundred houses were burnt, four hundred and sixty streets, eighty-nine churches—and old St. Paul's. It remains that the new surveyor was asked to plan a new capital of England—a new London.

Wren's plans for the city can still be seen, but they were never carried out. We can see the glory that might have been, the London that would have been the eighth wonder of the world. We can grasp the genius of this artist-astronomer who offered England a city in which air and sunlight and proper drainage would defy sickness and disease, for Wren planned with the memory of one hundred thousand dead of plague fresh and vivid in his mind. And beside this dream London, we see the city that is; the tangled web of narrow, basemented streets, the traffic helplessly congested that might have flowed freely—Wren, who can hardly have foreseen modern motor traffic, admirably provided for it in his plan.

But there were "vested interests." Those whose houses had been

After the Great Fire of London in 1666 it was Sir Christopher Wren who proposed plans for rebuilding the City of London. He built fifty-two churches in London, but his masterpiece was the rebuilding of St. Paul's Cathedral, which today remains a high point in baroque architecture and one of the most famous London landmarks (*above*). (*Right*) Richard Wagner, the German tone poet, composer and writer on music, who is especially celebrated for his dramatic operas such as *Der Ring des Nibelungen, Die Meistersinger von Nürnberg* and *Tristan und Isolde*.

Cleopatra (*left*), Queen of Egypt, is established as one of the great romantic heroines of all time. Though apparently not beautiful, she was both magnetic and fiercely ambitious. She became the mistress of Julius Caesar and later the wife of Mark Antony, but she was hated by the Romans, and after being defeated by Octavian, both Cleopatra and Mark Antony committed suicide. Joan of Arc (*below*) is France's national heroine. Born the daughter of a farmer, at the age of sixteen, she began to hear "voices" exhorting her to help the dauphin regain his throne from the English. Her eventual leadership of the dauphin's forces provided spirit and morale more than military prowess, but her campaign proved successful and the dauphin was crowned. Later she was captured by the Burgundians and sold to the English, and eventually burned at the stake on charges of heresy and sorcery Although hardly recognized for her services by her king, she was canonized by the Pope in 1920.

burnt down wanted them rebuilt just where they had stood before; those whose land lay in the way of widened streets made difficulties, and those in power grudged the money that Wren asked. A few hundred thousand pounds were saved after 1666 by rejecting Wren's plan for rebuilding London: how many hundreds of millions London has consequently lost in the centuries since can only be guessed at.

* * * * *

For many years before the Great Fire of 1666, St. Paul's had been so badly neglected that it had become unsafe. The soaring spire had fallen, leaving only the massive, two hundred feet tower on which it had stood. In the May before the fire, Wren himself had submitted plans for remodelling the greater part, "after a good Roman manner," he said, and not "to follow the Gothick Rudeness of the old Design." After the fire, only the massive walls and the old tower remained. These stood for some years. London was too busy rebuilding its homes and shops and markets to attend to its cathedral.

Charles's first suggestion was to patch up poor "Paul's" charred remains, but it was soon made clear that nothing less than an entirely new foundation was needed. When this was agreed, Wren prepared plans for the new cathedral. One of his first designs, not altogether unlike his final building, was strikingly magnificent, but his plan was almost entirely pulled to pieces by ignorant busybodies, and he was driven to re-design the whole thing. His next design, which he himself must have laughed at, was a strange mixture of Classical and Gothic architecture, with a lofty spire—very like the spire he afterwards put on St. Bride's Church, Fleet Street—perched on top of an elongated dome.

On May 14, 1675, nine years after Wren had submitted his first plan, the king issued a warrant for the re-building to begin—and to be executed according to this last surprising plan. Wren undertook the work, but upon one subtle condition—that he was permitted "in the prosecution of his work to make some variations, rather ornamental than essential, as from time to time he should see proper." The result of these merely "ornamental" changes was the cathedral as it now stands—resembling far more Wren's original plan than the plan that was approved by the restoration committee.

The king next opened the necessary subscription list with a "promise" of "£1,000 by the year to be paid quarterly." This example encouraged others, not only to promise, but to pay, and the work began. With it came difficulties that almost any other man but

Christopher Wren would have found insuperable. Even the demolition of the old building would have been almost impossible without his genius. For seven years the ordinary slow methods of house-breaking had been battling helplessly against the massive old walls and tower, and Wren at last decided to blow them up with gunpowder. His first mine was exploded successfully and safely, and brought down the tower. His second, prepared by a subordinate during Wren's absence, unfortunately shot a stone into a neighbouring house where some women were working. No one was injured, but from then onwards gunpowder was forbidden by the authorities. What other method remained? Wren's imagination found one. Out of the dusty pages of ancient history he designed a battering ram. He took "a strong mast of about forty feet long, arming the bigger end of this with a great spike of iron fortified with bars along the mast and ferrules. This mast in two places was hung up to one ring with strong tackle and so suspended level to a triangle prop, such as they weigh great guns with; thirty men, fifteen on a side, vibrated this machine to and again, and beat in one place against the wall the whole day; they believed it was to little purpose, not discerning any immediate effect; he bid them not despair but proceed another day; on the second day the wall was perceived to tremble at the top and in a few hours it fell."

Wren next examined the ground for the new foundations. It is well known that the site of St. Paul's Cathedral is ill-suited to carry its vast weight. The ground is sand and gravel, and the sub-soil consists as much of water as of earth; the rains that fall on Hampstead and Highgate filter through to the Thames under the city; and while the presence of water is no great obstacle to the builder, Wren fully realized the danger—which our generation has proved—of the water draining away from the sand and causing a sinkage. He did his best to overcome this difficulty on the insufficient funds allowed him by cheese-paring authorities, but in the following century the foundations began to give way, and considerable repairs had to be hastily carried out by Edward Strong, the son of Wren's master mason.

Throughout the whole of the building of St. Paul's there were continual set-backs. The authorities would not allow this, and insisted on that; Sir Christopher Wren was spending too much, he was not doing what was wanted; he must be stopped from doing this, made to do the other. And, throughout, Wren carried on steadily, ingeniously getting over colossal difficulties, conscientiously watching every detail himself—during the building he would be drawn up in a basket several times a week to see how things were going—working as if discouragement did not exist.

Whoever looks at St. Paul's sees proof of Wren's supreme genius. The inscription on his tomb in the crypt reads: *Si monumentum requiris, circumspice*—"If you seek his monument, look around." But to appreciate the man himself, his character and his courage, one must look not at the building complete, but at those long and patient years—five reigns—when the building was slowly going on.

Writers who lived when Wren lived, tell us little about his character. He was honest, modest, upright and God-fearing—which is just what we hear of so many people in history. But they tell us the conditions under which he built St. Paul's, the sort of men he worked for, the salary he was paid—less than four pounds a week—and that this trifling price was held by many to be too high for Wren's genius, and was partly withheld during the latter years of the rebuilding to urge him to work faster.

Slowly, Wren fought his way through the obstacles that lay at every step along his path. Slowly St. Paul's arose out of her own ashes. There is a story that when Wren was marking out the ground at the outset of the work, he told someone to fetch a stone and mark a spot. The workman picked up a fragment of tombstone from the old cathedral which bore the one word *resurgam*—"I shall rise again." Wren never forgot that word. In the finished cathedral a sculptured phœnix on its fiery nest was set over the south portico with that same word, *resurgam*.

Twenty-two years after the laying of the first stone, the great choir was opened. The first service was the thanksgiving service for the Peace of Ryswick, which acknowledged William of Orange King of England. Since that day services have been held regularly in Wren's cathedral. But the work was still far from finished. Another five years passed before Wren's son laid the highest stone of the lantern on top of the dome. Wren was seventy-eight, and probably watched his son from the ground. One story says, however, that they climbed to the dizzy height together, and that the old man looked down as the stone was laid, and saw his masterpiece complete below his eyes. The cathedral cost £747,661 10s., and even allowing for the higher purchasing power of money in those days this sum is extraordinarily small for such a vast work.

There is hardly a city in England that does not possess some example of Wren's industry and artistry, or at least a building deriving directly from his inspiration; to the City of London alone he gave sixty churches and countless other buildings. Always his work is sincere, tending to marked simplicity; always practical, efficient, eminently fit for its purpose. A renaissance in English architecture had begun with Wren's predecessor, Inigo Jones, who had first rebelled against Tudor Gothic, and returned to the Græco-Roman classical style in building. With Wren's genius in design and Wren's influence and industry on the side of the Classical, the Gothic era was finally ended.

Another instance of Wren's influence is in the use made of bricks in his time and since. To the Gothic mind, bricks were the cinderellas of building—not permitted to be seen. Facings should be of stone. To Wren, bricks were the standard material and nothing to be ashamed of. Dignity and fine proportion were controlled by the designer, not by his materials, and superb examples of his brickwork have survived on all hands.

His earliest great work was the chapel of Pembroke College, Cambridge, which was begun in 1663. In the same period he built the Sheldonian at Oxford, and the chapel of Emmanuel College. Chelsea Hospital, Trinity College Library at Cambridge, the Ashmolean and the Tom Tower at Oxford, and his additions to Greenwich Hospital and Hampton Court, are among Wren's most noted works, with St. Mary-le-Bow, Cheapside; St. Clement Danes, Strand; St. Bride's, Fleet Street; St. Michael's, Cornhill; and St. Stephen's, Wallbrook, his finest churches.

When we remember the difficulties that obstructed him all the time he was surveyor, the constant hindrance and interference from every incapable busybody in Charles II's court and government, it becomes clear that great as his works were, they might have been greater still. He performed miracles for architecture; allowed his own way, he would have done much the same for the lives of men and women. His cathedral shows us how he could handle stone: it was through no fault or failing of his that nothing stands to show how he would have handled the more flesh-and-blood problems of town planning, how he would have rebuilt London for the benefit of the community and sacrificed the interests and sentimentality of individuals to give a new standard of living to the majority of the people.

But we do know that centuries ahead of other men, Christopher Wren knew how a modern city should be built, and that he might have enjoyed in his great life the supreme gratification of seeing, as he sat at the window of his little house across the river, not only a new St. Paul's rising from the ashes of the Great Fire, but a new London around it, where men would live healthier and better lives

—an altogether new type of city that the whole world would thenceforth take as its model. This was the chance that destiny offered, and the government denied, to Wren. The tragic yet glorious opportunity fell at his feet. To rebuild London! Then came the years of thought and work and expectation. Then the final perfect plan. And then the slow, bitter realization that petty officialdom, personal greed, stupidity, obstinacy, prejudice and sentimentality were massing their dead and deadening weight against him until finally his dream city was utterly lost.

Few men, let alone an artist and a genius, could have taken that blow as Wren took it. If he could not build a new capital for England, if Londoners preferred their bedroom windows to overlook mean alleys instead of sweeping avenues and broad piazzas, if London liked dirt and darkness, and must crowd into every acre so many buildings that no architect's work could properly be seen there —very well! What he would do instead would be to give London one of the finest cathedrals in all the world, to stand half unseen amid her crowded shops and houses.

When Wren was eighty-six, jealousy and intrigue dealt their final card. On a trumped-up pretext, he was dismissed from the office of surveyor. But intrigue and treachery for once were powerless. The pettiness of politicians, the insolence of office, the greed of private interests, might steal England's chance of setting a great example to the world: Christopher Wren did not depend on chance. It could rob England of a properly built and ordered capital and rob London of health, wealth and happiness. It took nothing from Wren's immortal reputation.

He died on February 25, 1723, and lies buried beneath his own greatest monument to his genius—St. Paul's.

SIR JOSHUA REYNOLDS

(1723–1792)

Sir Joshua Reynolds occupies a unique niche in the hall of fame. He was the greatest of English portrait painters, and one of the finest masters of colour that the world has seen. He helped to found, and was first president of, the Royal Academy, whose early destinies he moulded ably. His care for the Academy schools, and the "Discourses" on art, which he published, helped to mould the traditions of the English school. He was a member of the intimate Johnsonian circle, which comprised the wits and the intellectual leaders of his age, and he was the actual founder of the famous Literary Club. In his lifetime he achieved material success; posterity has granted him undying fame.

A SPECTACLED gentleman with a long nose and dark, luminous eyes, and wearing a short powdered wig of the seventeen-eighties, was pacing up and down a large studio off Leicester Square, then a fashionable quarter of London. He was expecting a visitor, whom his servant shortly announced. She entered, heavily beautiful, with a statuesque presence that swam commandingly forward, sustained, it seemed, by her voluminous trailing skirts. The gentleman greeted her with marked pleasure, then led her to the platform at one end of the room.

"Ascend your undisputed throne," he said. "Bestow upon me some idea of the Tragic Muse."

With these words Sir Joshua Reynolds began the portrait of Mrs. Siddons that was to be his greatest achievement, and to set a seal upon his genius as one of the supreme masters of painting.

There had been endless discussions and cogitations over the picture. It had kept the artist in a fever for months. The previous year his exhibits at the Royal Academy, of which he was the first president, had not met with the unqualified approval of the public. "Reynolds is falling off," they said. Now he resolved to create a work of art that would conclusively prove that he was still far from being at the end of his power and strength.

At first Mrs. Siddons had been horrified at the brilliant tints he had laid on his canvas, but he explained that it was merely a matter of technique so that the sombre draperies of the "Muse of Tragedy" should pulsate with an inner glow, as of the living flesh beneath. When the picture was completed, Reynolds insisted on inscribing his name on her robe. "I cannot lose the opportunity thus afforded me," he said, "of going down to posterity on the hem of your garment."

He could not foresee that Mrs. Siddons would come down to posterity to a greater extent as Reynolds's "Tragic Muse." We who have never seen a gesture or heard a syllable of hers can at least see what the great actress looked like from the portraits of her, and best of all from this particular portrait. For Reynolds knew how to reveal the innermost character of his sitters, whether the sweet innocence of childhood or the vices and debaucheries of a Cardinal Beaufort. Sir Joshua Reynolds is the greatest of British portrait painters.

The seedling from which this mighty growth of genius sprang was nourished in Devonshire soil. He was born on June 16, 1723, at Plympton, the sixth child of the Rev. Samuel Reynolds, the kind and genial master of Plympton Grammar School. His father gave him his only education, and was eager that young Joshua should become a doctor. The boy, however, showed so much precocious talent that at seventeen he was apprenticed to Hudson, the portrait painter, himself a Devonshire man, who was then enjoying a tremendous vogue. In October, 1740, the young Reynolds took up his abode in his master's house in Great Queen Street, London, and began his four years' apprenticeship.

Only two of these were accomplished. Hudson was by no means a great painter, and it is probable that he was jealous of his brilliant pupil. They quarrelled, and Joshua returned to Devonshire, where he set up business for himself at Plymouth Dock, now known as Devonport. His father, unlike most of the parents of genius, seems to have sympathized with his son, for he resolved to persevere in his resolution "not to meddle in the controversy between Joshua and his master. . . . In the meantime I bless God and Mr. Hudson . . . for the extreme success that has attended Joshua hitherto."

Business at Devonport did not, however, prosper; and the next year Joshua returned to London and made up the quarrel with Hudson. The latter, now that their friendship was secure, invited Joshua to join the Artists' Club, and gave him every possible encouragement. It was at this period that Reynolds painted the portraits of Captain Hamilton, his first important patron, Mrs. Field and "The Reading Boy." The period did not last long. In 1746

Reynolds hastened home to be with his father during his last illness, and on Christmas Day of that year, old Samuel Reynolds died. The home was broken up, and Joshua, not without a sigh for the lost opportunities of life in London, took a house for himself and his two sisters at Devonport, and tried to reassemble his former circle of clients.

Here he came under the influence of another Devonshire painter, William Gandy. He had died some years before, but his ideas and technique were strong enough to revolutionize the work of his disciple and transform Reynolds's then somewhat harsh and dry style of painting into the rich warmth that was to bring him fame. Gandy's father had been a pupil of Van Dyck, and it is interesting to try and trace in Reynolds's work the influence thus indirectly transferred. From Gandy, too, he learned to love landscape; and though there is hardly a single canvas without figures by Reynolds now in existence, yet many of his portraits are embellished by delicious vistas of trees and fields that betoken an acute observation and keen feeling for nature.

Quite unexpectedly, Reynolds was to receive a new gift from fortune. He had been friendly since childhood with the Edgcombe family, and at Lord Edgcombe's house he met young Captain, afterwards Viscount, Keppel, then serving with the Mediterranean squadron, and *en route* for the African coast and Italy. He offered to take Reynolds with him in order that he might have an opportunity of studying the great Italian masters. This was the chance of a lifetime, and Reynolds sailed on the *Centurion* in May, 1749.

The main object of Keppel's expedition was to deal firmly with the Dey of Algiers, whose association with certain acts of piracy had made him more than unpopular with the admiralties of Europe. After calling at Lisbon and the Balearic Isles, Reynolds was landed at Minorca, where he stayed with the governor and painted to his heart's content, though not always to his satisfaction.

In December he travelled to Rome with the express purpose of seeing the works of Raphael. He was bitterly disappointed. Reynolds could appreciate intellectually the value of Raphael's work; but he had expected to be swept away by the grandeur of the compositions. His imagination had led him to expect something different from the reality, and his enthusiasm sank proportionately.

He spent two years in Rome studying, and occasionally copying pictures on commission. It was here, in the Vatican, that he caught a severe cold that resulted in a deafness that persisted for the rest of his life. It is one of the minor tragedies of his career that this most "clubbable" of men was ever afterwards unable to converse save with the aid of an ear-trumpet.

In the spring of 1752, Reynolds left for a five-months' tour of Parma, Florence, Venice and other Italian cities. Of the painters he studied, Titian and the Venetians were those who most delighted and impressed him. Then, after a rest in Devon on his return to England, he settled down once more in London.

The first ripples of a rising tide of success that was never to ebb were soon discernible. Lord Edgcombe proved to be a valuable patron; Hudson renewed his intimacy with his former pupil; the Artists' Club welcomed back its absent member. Most important of all was his meeting with Dr. Johnson, and the formation of a friendship that lasted till the death of the great Cham of Literature.

In 1755 his notebooks record one hundred and fifty clients. In 1757 the number is six hundred and seventy-seven. Portraits of folk famous, fair and frail, left the studio in St. Martin's Lane in rapid succession: the beautiful Duchess of Hamilton; a masterly rendering of his old friend Keppel; the Home Secretary, Lord Holderness, whose congested face presented no easy problem; and later the young Prince of Wales, Garrick the actor, and Kitty Fisher, the reigning toast of the time.

The growing procession of celebrities showed St. Martin's Lane to be inconvenient. Reynolds moved to Great Newport Street, but that was as bad, and finally, in 1760, he took the house in Leicester Square, where he was to end his days. The same year the Society of Artists held their first public exhibition, which included four portraits by Reynolds. It was at this time that the famous "Lady Waldgrave" was painted, causing a sensation that was only eclipsed by his portrait of Sterne, the great novelist, the next year.

Reynolds was now the focus of two worlds. His income had reached the then enormous figure of £6,000 a year, most of which he spent in buying pictures. Fashionable society thronged his studio and dining-room, while the leading lights of literature and the arts were equally friendly. His name shines in a Pleiades of great ones: Johnson, Sterne, Burke, Goldsmith, Sheridan, Percy, Garrick—the whole galaxy that led to the formation, in 1764, of the Literary Club, which Reynolds founded to "give Dr. Johnson unlimited opportunities for talking."

In the meantime the Society of Artists had been holding annual exhibitions and growing in strength and popularity. In 1765 it received a royal charter, becoming the Incorporated Society of Artists. Its rise, however, was accompanied by great rivalry and dissension among its temperamental members. Matters reached a climax when a body of members seceded from the Society of Artists, elected George III as their patron and Joshua Reynolds as their president, and formed, on December 18, 1768, the Royal Academy. This important event was followed in the succeeding year by the bestowal of a knighthood on Reynolds—significant evidence of royal approval.

Sir Joshua made a particularly fine president. His urbane, diplomatic manner, the charm and wit of his conversation, his generosity and friendliness, gave distinction to the society that helped it over the first difficult period of its existence. Moreover he put all his energy into the task of organizing the new academy and in instituting its famous schools.

At his suggestion an annual banquet was held, at which he delivered his presidential addresses. These were printed as *Discourses,* and remain among the clearest and sanest expressions of art theories than any student can have. They go far towards indicating the lines on which every artist, of no matter what " school " or " genre," should proceed. Reynolds's prose style has the perfection of simplicity. Indeed, his *Discourses* are so good that when they first appeared Johnson was believed to be their author. One unlucky conversationalist was bold enough to ask the doctor directly if rumour in this matter spoke truly. The reply was characteristic. " Sir Joshua, sir, would as soon get me to paint for him as to write for him."

For the first exhibition of the Royal Academy, Reynolds sent four pictures, including the exquisite " Miss Morris as Hope Nursing Love." Even the arduous duties of president could not interfere with or diminish his energy. Year by year portrait after portrait was painted, as well as innumerable studies of children, sacred subjects, and incidents from great literature.

It was not to be expected that Sir Joshua would be without rivals. Gainsborough had come to London and was attracting a good deal of attention. Relations between them were not harmonious. The position is best revealed by Gainsborough's outcry at Reynolds: " Damn him, how *various* he is!"

More irritating was the malice of one Nathaniel Hore, who accused Reynolds of copying other artists' tricks of technique. His spite was the more effective since it was founded upon a tiny half-truth. Reynolds undoubtedly did borrow. But he borrowed in the same way that Shakespeare borrowed the plots of his plays or Milton the argument of his greatest poem.

By 1782, Gainsborough was half-way towards friendship with his rival. He went so far as to begin a picture of Reynolds, but after the first sitting the latter had a paralytic stroke that necessitated a holiday at Bath. The portrait was never finished, but it is pleasant to record that, six years later, as Gainsborough lay on his death-bed, he sent for Sir Joshua, and we may assume that peace was finally concluded between them.

By this time Reynolds was in the fulness of his career. The great masterpieces of his life had been painted: "The Age of Innocence," "Heads of Angels," "The Strawberry Girl," "The Duchess of Devonshire," "Lady Powis," and the incomparable "Tragic Muse." In 1789 his sight began to fail, but he was busy as ever, not only at his painting but at a multitude of philanthropical works, including strenuous exertions to raise a memorial to Dr. Johnson in St. Paul's. In 1790 he delivered his fifteenth and final *Discourse,* after the only disagreement he ever had with the members of the Academy. The matter was a small one—a question of the election of a friend of the president, his casting vote, and the subsequent rumpus among the Academicians. Reynolds resigned; the members apologized and begged him to withdraw his resignation, which he readily did; but the end was nearer than anyone expected. In October of the following year, increasing blindness compelled him once more to tender his resignation, but the members refused to accept it.

On February 23, 1792, he died, the first president of the Royal Academy, "in full affluence of foreign and domestic fame, admired by the expert in art and by the learned in science, courted by the great, caressed by sovereign powers and celebrated by distinguished poets." Thus Burke, who continues what is perhaps the best summing up of Reynolds's life and character: "his native humility, modesty and candour never forsook him, even on surprise or provocation; nor was the least degree of arrogance or assumption visible to the most scrutinizing eye in any part of his conduct or discourse. His talents of every kind, powerful from nature and not meanly cultivated by letters, his social virtues in all the relations and all the habitudes of life, rendered him the centre of a very great and unparalleled variety of agreeable societies, which will be dissipated by his death. He had too much merit not to excite some jealousy, too much innocence to provoke any enmity. The loss of no man of his time can be felt with more sincere, general and unmixed sorrow."

LUDWIG VAN BEETHOVEN

(1770–1827)

It is said of Beethoven that he composed in three styles. When he was young he used the methods of his predecessors, and many of his early works are indistinguishable in style from those of Mozart. Then, as his own genius developed, his music became stronger, richer and more beautiful than music had ever been. And in his last years, when deafness had blotted out the world, a rare and unearthly feeling pervaded his themes. That is the record of Beethoven's triumphant career in its simplest terms. It was a triumph of the spirit over adversity, and courage as well as genius, made him the greatest of all tone poets.

THE hands of the pianist on the dais at the far end of the room swept up the keyboard in a last passionate crescendo. Then the music died away, peacefully, almost breathlessly.

There was a moment's tense silence, followed by a crashing wave of applause. Polite and languid men, exquisite and powdered women, rose from their gilt chairs and shouted, hammered on the floor, broke unnoticed their costly fans. The room rang and echoed with enthusiastic approval.

The man at the piano made no movement. He sat there, crouched and unconscious of it all. The shouting and applause grew louder, became almost frantic. Then an elderly man approached the immovable figure and turned him round that he might see his audience; placed him so that he might *see* the applause. For the pianist who had just finished translating the sublime tone poetry of his own emotions was almost stone-deaf. He looked at the shouting people with pathos and nobility; his lips moved dumbly. That was all.

There can have been few lives more ironically tragic than that of Ludwig van Beethoven, a man whose whole being breathed beauty in sound, whose inmost thoughts created sublime harmony. Before he reached thirty, the one faculty he deemed essential to his happiness was slowly being destroyed, until at last he lived in a soundless world. Shut up in his terrible little prison-house with few windows from which to communicate with his fellows, this great genius produced some of his mightiest works and "heard" them only as they ran through his brain.

Beethoven was born in the little Rhineland town of Bonn, Germany, on December 16, 1770. His father, a tenor singer at the court of the Elector of Cologne, was a tyrant and a dissolute scamp, but he taught his son to play the violin and the clavier, and because he saw in the child's precocious musical gifts—before he was four years old he had already composed three sonatas!—the opportunity of blazoning forth to an amazed and admiring world a second Mozart, he kept him constantly at his musical studies. The scene is not hard to picture.

In a rather small room near the top of the house the child sits, playing with intensity of purpose a singularly monotonous scale passage. His fingers stray off soon into a quaint little trilling fugue which pleases him, and he weaves fanciful arabesques, half-dreaming. He plays on softly. It is getting dark, and long past his bed-time. Then the door opens, and he hears his father's petulant voice, a little thickened and a little slurred: "Get on with your work!" he says. "Get on to something useful. There is time for pretty tunes afterwards. Now you go on with your practising." An unsteady shadow is thrown on the wall, the heavy figure closes the door, and the child sighs, then bends obediently over the harpsichord to resume the laborious, uninteresting and never-ending scales. Downstairs his gentle, long-suffering mother is listening anxiously.

Slowly the child's genius developed. With triumph the father realized the brilliance of his playing. For the pretty pieces he composed he did not care over-much, but they served to keep little Ludwig at his instrument.

The boy went to a common school, and stayed there until he was thirteen. His father only sent him because it was necessary, and fumed at the interference with the boy's real work.

Ludwig sits cramped at a scored desk, jammed knee-to-knee with his schoolmates, some of them not over-clean. The master dozes at his high desk, and the pupils enter their crabbed arithmetic in dog-eared copy-books, and play furtive tricks on one another when he nods. The boy Ludwig does not concentrate much; the rudiments of reading, writing and arithmetic are taken in vaguely, with no thought of retention.

Yet this schooling did not interfere altogether with the boy's musical life. When he reached the age of nine, his father—a tyrant, but still a man who knew already that his son was to be famous, called him and said (a little tenderly now, for he has completed his task): "Ludwig, little son, I have taught you all I know. I have found you someone more able. Be diligent and always remember . . . it is your life's work."

So the boy went to the court organist, Van den Eeden, and then was trained under his successor, Christian Gottlob Neefe.

In 1782, when Ludwig was not yet twelve, he was already deputy organist, and in a few months was conducting the opera band in the elector's theatre. There were jealousies—bitter jealousies—scoffing and malicious words were muttered behind his back, but the boy was blissfully unaware of all. He was becoming the musician who "felt, thought and dreamed in tones."

All this time he was composing steadily, but his output was not large. He had already developed that care, that exactitude which was to last throughout his life.

He sits at a table, pen in hand, staved paper in front of him. He crosses out a bar, goes thoughtfully to the piano, and plays—rather uncertainly at first, then with a great light on his face. For an hour he fingers and thumbs the phrase, over and over again. Then he returns to the table, and writes in a new bar. Tomorrow, and the day after, and the day after that, for weeks and months, perhaps a year or two, he will be seated in front of that same manuscript, crossing out, re-writing and interpolating. Nothing that Beethoven ever penned was altered once he had completed the score, and the score was never completed until it was as perfect as he could make it. That is, perhaps, the secret of his relative paucity of composition.

It was his reputation as a pianist which brought him to the notice of men. In 1784, Max Franz became elector. He recognized something of the genius latent in the young composer, and so Ludwig was given his first paid post. He became second organist at a salary of one hundred and fifty florins. Then, in 1787, occurred one of the outstanding events of his life. He was sent by the elector to Vienna, and received a few lessons from the great Mozart. The master, after hearing Ludwig play only two or three of his own compositions, leant thoughtfully back in his chair, made play with his hands, and impressively remarked to some of his friends: "Pay attention to him; he will make a noise in the world some day or other."

Ludwig was now seventeen. Sorrow cast a dark and lingering shadow across his mind. His gentle mother died, and his father became increasingly dissolute. Tyrant no more, he now hiccuped to his son, who was becoming famous, pathetic but alcoholic reminders that if Ludwig had not had a father who realized his boy's genius. . . . And so Ludwig had more and more responsibility on his hands. Small wonder that when the old man was gathered to his fathers, the elector reported to his marshal: "The tax on drink has just suffered a great loss by the death of Johann Beethoven."

Still Ludwig's life, so far untainted by illness, was very pleasant at Bonn. He had many friends. They invited him to their homes and then sat enraptured while he played to them. It was here that he got to know the von Breuning family to whom he gave piano lessons, receiving in return the rudiments of Italian and French. There were merry parties too, and gradually he began to pick up some of the niceties of culture which he had never known in childhood. At one of these congenial gatherings he met the young and rich musical dilettant, Count Waldstein, an intimate of the elector. He was to be immortalized later (1803), by the dedication to him of Beethoven's Opus 53, the Waldstein Sonata.

The second important event in Beethoven's life occurred when he was twenty-two. The great and kindly composer, Haydn, visited Bonn, and heard the youth playing some of his compositions. He was so impressed that he told Ludwig to continue, and for two hours Haydn sat in amazement. He went to the elector afterwards, said kind things about the young musician, and it was decided that Beethoven should finish his studies in Vienna.

So Beethoven left Bonn for ever, and began his career in earnest. All the tragedy and success, the bitterness and adulation, the despair and triumph that were in store for him came together. He received lessons from Haydn for nearly a year, but the boy had sadly changed. The pupil had become eccentric, a creature of strange fads and fancies. If the windows were open when he was about to play he asked for them to be shut; if they were closed he demanded air. He found fault with the piano stool, became increasingly impatient, would not listen to the kindly voice of his teacher, explaining and describing. He wanted to get on faster. The good nature of Haydn was imposed upon. A breach formed between them—a breach never properly healed. He continued his studies under Albrechtsberger and Salievi. The latter was a fashionable Italian composer who first attracted attention with his opera *Armida,* produced in 1771. He was a bitter rival of Mozart and at one time legends were current that Salievi had actually poisoned him.

Everything was changed with Ludwig now. He was slovenly.

He visited the house of a friend unwashed, half-dressed, unkempt, and returned the most gentle of remonstrances with overbearing pride and abuse.

One evening Beethoven presented himself at a magnificent mansion in the aristocratic quarter of Vienna. He sat at dinner with his friend and his guests, who were among the richest and most courteous in the city. Throughout the meal his manners were execrable. He spat on the floor, spattered his clothes with liquids, and used his napkin as a handkerchief. "But I—I am Beethoven." He did not say so much on this occasion, but on another he did.

He was full of suspicious pride. He sometimes walked out of a house if the name of another musician was mentioned. His temper was terrible. Ungoverned gusts of anger shook him, until the veins of his head stood out like ropes. He would bring his clenched fist crashing on the keys when he found a note slightly out of tune. He would throw a dish of stew at a waiter's head. Yet he was popular, and his popularity steadily increased. He made and kept friends because they understood his amazing personality better than he did himself.

After all these unseemly outbursts and eccentricities and rudenesses, Beethoven would invariably sit down quietly and pour out his soul in the lovely melodies he had created. He was either in heaven or hell.

Most of his friends were among the nobility. He had long successions of trifling love affairs with silly women who were far above him in station but flattered by his acquaintance. Most of them told him that they were "twin souls" or "soul mates," and that none could hear his music and not love its creator. To this Beethoven listened, perhaps, with a little amusement. He hated talk about the "artistic temperament" and such affectation, but was mildly interested in love. The breath of scandal never touched his name.

Beethoven was now nearly thirty. His habits were still almost unbearable, his anger, suspicion and rudeness a constant source of pain to his friends. Tragedy, relentless and remorseless, was slowly creeping on.

Little by little he became aware that his hearing appeared to be getting dull. He could not differentiate between subtleties of pitch and tone. He went to doctor after doctor. They examined him and shook their heads. Beethoven became almost frantic. The malady grew worse. He took a final opinion. There was little hope in the suggestion that the trouble originated in a disease dating from his early youth, and possibly inherited.

The broken man returned to his study and sat down at his piano. His heart was almost breaking. He saw nothing but a succession of blank, empty years, with no music in them. He struck some chords, pressing down the loud pedal, then the soft pedal—torturing himself. Perhaps the doctors were wrong; they sometimes made mistakes. But no, they seldom erred. So the pendulum of his thoughts swung from hope to despair and from despair to hope and back again. At last he moved from the beloved piano, now become an instrument of torture. He sat at the table with his head buried in his hands.

For weeks he did not leave the house. He would not see his friends, but those who did manage to pass the threshold were received with something that approached to meekness. His character had changed under the stress and horror of tragedy. Nobility and heroism were emerging.

In 1802 he wrote the letter known as his will. In it he told his brothers, with a heart-rending nobility and pathos, in clear, unhysterical language, exactly what his terrible affliction meant to him.

So Ludwig van Beethoven was condemned to a life of loneliness —of loneliness with friends about him. He was locked in a silent tomb through which no sound could penetrate.

To add to all this came the worry and sorrow caused by a wild nephew who proved himself utterly unworthy of his uncle's great devotion—a devotion coupled with a loyalty which never permitted Beethoven to relinquish his self-imposed trust. It is, however, only fair to record that the nephew reformed, and in later life married and settled down.

It has been said that the tragedy of Beethoven's life was not his deafness so much as the lack of outlet for his affections. He might have—and tried hard to—pour out his love on this nephew who was essentially incapable of appreciating or returning it. Gradually Beethoven began to realize this and, without any great heroics or hysteria, but with a noble resignation, he went on with his work. It seemed that his afflictions were rather a spur than a scourge. For this deaf man, who must have suffered every day, poured out some of the most glorious music ever penned. He wrote colossal masterpieces, the Third, Fourth, Fifth, Seventh and Eighth Symphonies, which he heard only in his brain. He composed overtures, the opera *Fidelio,* piano and violin concertos, the perfect Rasoumoffsky

Quartet, and finally the unearthly *Missa Solemnis*, passionately triumphant, a pæan of praise to the man's own spirit.

Towards the end of the autumn of 1826, Beethoven went to visit his brother, Johann, and contracted a violent chill. On his return to Vienna it developed into dropsy. Doctors were summoned, but nothing could be done. "You seem to me like Moses striking the rock with his staff," he remarked to the surgeon who tapped him. He put up a great fight for several months, trying to soothe his pain by planning new works. His face, lined by mental struggle, but indicative of strength and rugged simplicity, grew paler with increasing exhaustion.

On March 26, 1827, he was sinking fast. Suddenly the distant rumblings of thunder were heard. The storm approached rapidly, and in a few minutes was raging over the city. Vivid flashes of lightning lit up the room; the bombardment shook the house. The dying man heard nothing. During a mighty crash he stretched out his arm, and fell back dead. Twenty thousand people bowed their heads as his coffin left the house.

* * * * *

There is no space here to examine Beethoven's works. It must be sufficient to say that they are generally divided into three styles not strictly separable. The first period is known, loosely, as the Mozartian, for obvious reasons, although even as a child his harmonic and melodic derivations from the earlier master reveal a markedly different personality.

To this period belong the early piano sonatas, the 'cello sonata (Opus 5, No. 1), the piano and wind septet and quintet, and the horn sonata Opus 17.

The second period shows a deepening and broadening of his creative genius. Mozartian, clear melodic lines are emphasized by daring harmonies, and the composer is already breaking away from conventions, and a new spaciousness is now apparent. The most outstanding example of this period is the Waldstein Sonata (Opus 53).

The third period is really an extension of the second, and has little to do (as some critics have suggested) with his developing deafness. Here his genius found its fullest polyphonic expression. To this period belong his colossal fugues, the Mass in D, the Ninth Symphony, and the terrific piano sonata Opus 106.

"We have then," writes J. W. N. Sullivan, "in the person of Beethoven, a musical genius with all the conditions for writing great music. He has a realization of the ultimate character of life; he has a force adequate to any trial, however arduous; his growth will be free from the distorting effects of mere convention, and his response is pure and sincere to a wide range of expression. No other musician who ever lived has united so many advantages."

And to this, as a final word, we may add the following tribute from that great musical critic, Ernest Newman:

"It is the peculiarity of Beethoven's imagination that again and again he lifts us to a height from which we revaluate not only all music, but all life, all emotion and all thought!"

WILHELM RICHARD WAGNER

(1813–1883)

Richard Wagner lived, worked and wrote on the grand scale. He was a giant. In a dynamic life of passion, poverty and magnificent creation he stamped his personality and his art upon the world. His music was new, as new as it was stupendous. His aim was to reorganize the whole structure of opera, to make dramatic unity the one aim in that art. In short, opera was not to depend merely upon the music, but upon the story, the poetry, the acting, the staging and *the music. And in his music, too, he was an inventor and an innovator. Today, in spite of the storms and the controversies that have surrounded the man and his work, Wagner stands assured of fame among the supreme artists of the world.*

IN the silence of a dusty schoolroom in Dresden, a little boy sat reading. Nothing disturbed the silence except the monotonous ticking of the clock on the wall and an occasional rustle as a page was turned over. The boy's mind was far away, re-living the lives of the old giants of mythology. An hour passed, then the boy closed his book and remained gazing into the distance, visualizing the monstrous figures of the heroes. Thus the seed was planted which was to bring forth the most astounding conceptions the musical world had ever known.

Richard Wagner was born at Leipzig in 1813, just after the outbreak of the War of Liberation against Napoleon and a few months before the Battle of the Nations was fought there.

He was brought up in the world of the theatre. His father, Frederich Wagner, who died too soon to know the child, was a police actuary, but devoted to the theatre and literature. His stepfather, Ludwig Geyer, was an actor, a dramatist, a painter.

He was an amazing man. He would rush off to rehearsal in the theatre with little Richard holding his hand. Often enough Ludwig, after a period of muttered grumblings at the wooden work of some novice player, would leap on to the empty stage and act, in delicious pantomime, some tale of marvels with which he had sent Richard to sleep the night before. In the darkness of the auditorium, perched on the edge of a plush seat, the child watched with glistening eyes. When the lights were put out the two trotted off home together, hand-in-hand.

When Richard went to school, according to his own story, the boy translated, unaided, the first twelve books of the *Odyssey*. No easy task for a lad of thirteen to translate 6,000 lines of Homeric Greek. He had begun piano lessons a year before, but had shown no particular promise.

The awakening came when he heard a Beethoven symphony at one of the Gewandhaus concerts. Wretchedly performed though it was by a scratch orchestra, Richard listened with tense excitement and a quickened pulse. He was so overcome that he could not join in the applause but remained seated until long after the orchestra had packed up their instruments and left the hall.

In his early teens he wrote a tragedy. And what a tragedy it was! He introduced at the very beginning scores of characters, but the carnage which ensued was so wholesale that he had to resurrect many of the principals as ghosts in order to bring the play to a successful conclusion. With the memory of Beethoven fresh in his mind, the boy determined to set this leviathan to music. Here is the mature Wagner already, at least in one respect—he believed himself fully capable of doing it. So he borrowed from a library a copy of a text-book on thorough-bass, and in the secrecy and solitude of his own room composed a quartet, an aria and a sonata. Finally he told his family that he was going to be a musician. When the first incredulity had worn off, the family agreed.

Soon after, he was taking lessons. He wrote an Overture in B flat, 6/8 time, which was performed at the theatre as an entr'acte and excited the derision of the audience. It is easy to picture the scene. The burghers and their wives, one or two Hans with their Gretchens, and, perhaps, a sprinkling of the clerical side of the town. The curtain has just gone down, and Wagner's overture begins. But the persistent reiteration at every fourth bar of a fortissimo thud on the big drum brings forth titters until, finally, the audience are crashing into the time with great stamps of their feet.

In 1830, the young Richard matriculated at Leipzig University and set out for Vienna, eager for a glimpse of that famed city of music. But the theatres and concert halls were a deathly waste of *Zampa* and other heroics, and Wagner left in disgust. His mind was already occupied with thoughts of immense music-dramas based on the legends and sagas for which his thirst was not yet quenched. He studied the Greek tragedies and later put forward his theories in a book entitled *The Art Work of the Future.* Always he sought a large canvas. When handling words he was often dull. In his private life he was selfish and unscrupulous. But in his music, he was vast and sublime.

In 1834, Wagner had completed his first opera. It was called *Die Feen* ("The Fairies") and abounded with magicians, caves, fairies, oaths and secrets, and there was plenty of fire—for Wagner was already a pyromaniac. His score passed from hand to hand, and finally was shelved. It was not produced until five years after his death.

He was now conducting the opera at Magdeburg, and in the company of artistes was a young girl, an actress of small parts, named Wilhelmina Planer, known later as "Minna." She was to become his first wife.

By 1836 Wagner had finished another opera, *Das Liebesverbot* ("Love Forbidden"). The company attempted to give it after ten days' preparation and the whole thing was a fiasco. None of the singers knew their parts, and as there was a good deal of "tra-la-la" in it, the artistes, it would appear, substituted the monosyllables for phrases they forgot. The next night it was put on again, and this time the members of the cast chose to quarrel. The money was given back at the door, while Wagner, beside himself with rage, stood in the wings.

Soon afterwards Wagner married Minna, who already had a daughter old enough to be passed off as her younger sister. He was then just over twenty-two; she was twenty-seven.

The following year Wagner secured the post of musical conductor of the theatre at Riga, then just across the Russian border and the capital of the Baltic state, Latvia. Here he started on the composition of *Rienzi*, an enormously long and glittering opera. It was unfinished when his contract at Riga expired and the Wagner *ménage* thought it well to leave on account of accumulating debts. It was not easy to get away for Wagner was refused a passport. His wife had to flee in disguise, while he was forced to hide himself in an empty sentry-box until the vigilant eyes of the guards were turned in an opposite direction. *Rienzi* was given its first performance at Dresden in 1842. The theatre was crowded but many of the audience were asleep by the time it was over, for the opera started at six o'clock and went on until midnight. Still, the work was a great success, and Wagner took courage.

The next opera was *The Flying Dutchman*, an idea tentatively suggested at Riga, where Wagner had read Heinrich Heine's version of the famous legend and amplified by a perilous voyage from Pillau to London *en route* for Paris. It was less enthusiastically successful than *Rienzi*. The production suffered from inadequate rehearsals and was withdrawn.

Soon afterwards Wagner was made Royal Saxon Hofkapellmeister for life, and the post brought with it a fixed salary. Creditors gathered round like crows in a newly ploughed field (for twenty years or more of his life it is impossible to unravel the tangle of his finances). Minna struggled to help him as much as she could. *Tannhäuser* was introduced to the public in 1845 and *Löhengrin* in 1848. Neither did conspicuously well.

Now came an involved part of the composer's life, covering years of unrest and homeless wandering. Germany was in chaos. Ludwig of Bavaria was amusing himself with the dancer, Lola Montez, the Berliners had driven out Prince William of Prussia, afterwards the first German emperor.

Wagner became involved in politics. For his part in the rising of the Saxon people against the government, a warrant was issued for his arrest. He fled, and found sanctuary at Zürich, in Switzerland. From here he went to Paris, and from Paris to Bordeaux.

For five years he composed nothing, but the gigantic conception of *The Ring,* based on a German folk-saga, the *Nibelungenlied* was gradually taking shape in his mind. He was never dismayed by the immensity of the task he was undertaking—for he was writing the whole of the lengthy text himself. Liszt, the famous Hungarian composer and pianist, with whom he was now friendly, was enthusiastic over the grandeur of the theme. The music of *The Ring* took twenty years to write and is sublime, but the text is difficult. The whole work ably illustrates Wagner's theory of opera—first the essential part of the work, "the book," then the music.

In 1855 Wagner visited London to conduct the London Philharmonic Society in a series of concerts and then returned to Zürich, which he left in 1858, when his itinerary becomes bewildering. He went to Venice, then to Lucerne, then to Paris, to Brussels, to Paris again, and to Vienna, where he worked at *Tristan and Isolde*. "The passages depicting suffering always take me a long time," he avowed, "the fresh, lively, fairy parts proceed much more quickly. Thus do I, even in the technical execution, live in my work, sad or joyous according to the situation." His private life was bewildering, too. He was urged on to write his latest opera by love of Mathilde Wesendonck, the wife of a German merchant who was one of Wagner's most generous patrons. "*With* thee I can do all things," he writes to her, "*without* thee nothing." He quarrelled daily with Minna, who stolidly went on with her duty as a housewife until they separated in 1861. And now began the influence of Cosima von Bülow, the younger daughter of Liszt by the Comtessa d'Agoult. "You," she had told Wagner, "are a poet great as Shakespeare—your poetry is even more wonderful than your music." Doubtless he believed the first part of the phrase, if not the second.

In 1859, the Paris Opera, at the suggestion of the Emperor of Austria, accepted *Tannhäuser* for production. More than £8,000 was spent and new Venusberg music had been composed. But the production was deliberately wrecked by an anti-Austrian claque, together with the members of the Jockey Club, who objected to the ballet being placed at the beginning of the opera instead of, more conventionally, in the second act.

Three performances only, punctuated by howls, catcalls and whistles, were possible. Then the opera was withdrawn and Wagner, heartbroken, returned to Vienna befriended by the Princess Metternich. Through her intervention Wagner's exile was curtailed and by 1862 he was once more able to return to Germany.

In 1864, an event of great importance occurred. At Stuttgart, whence Wagner had fled to escape his ubiquitous creditors, the secretary of Ludwig II of Bavaria called upon him and gave him a ring with a red stone as a token of goodwill, and a letter from the young king inviting him to Munich. Wagner went, and found that Ludwig had conceived a great admiration for him.

At Munich, in 1865, the first performance of *Tristan* was given and was met by the audience with something approaching bewilderment. The conductor was Hans von Bülow, the husband of Cosima, who had now been living with Wagner for some time. Just two months before this performance, Cosima had given birth to a daughter, the paternity of whom was claimed by both von Bülow and Wagner.

In 1866, his sad, misunderstanding, and perhaps misunderstood, wife died. Even while separated from him she published a letter in which she declared that through everything—poverty, wealth, ill-health—Richard had always supported her. And she declared this to the last.

Two years later, *Die Meistersinger* was performed. Wagner hoped that this would meet with such generous approval that it might win sufficient help to enable him to build the "Ring" Opera House, on which his mind had been set for years. The work was conducted by von Bülow, who remained always a fast friend of Wagner. It gained an immediate success.

In 1869, von Bülow and his wife were divorced, and in the following year Cosima married Wagner. The same year their son, Helferich Siegfried Richard, was born. In 1876, his ambition of an opera house at Bayreuth was realized. Wagner societies all over the world raised funds for the purpose; it received the support of kings and princes.

Wagner's dream castle had become reality. It was all his idea, a German opera house, set in Bavarian uplands, peopled with the gods, dwarfs and magicians of German legend. Moreover, it was a huge success.

Tier upon tier of people sat through *Das Rheingold, Die Walkure, Siegfried,* and *Götterdämmerung,* and thundered applause. People walked about murmuring the song of the Rhinemaidens of Wotan's song. Wagner became almost a national hero. He sat dreamily at his home in Bayreuth and smiled. Over its portico he had inscribed the motto, "I call my house 'Wahnfried,' because here my aspirations found peace." He no longer thought of suicide and regarded what he referred to as the "sharp knife" of composition with impunity.

Wagner had dramatized the German soul in tones of rich colour. He had swept aside the propriety of the Italian form of opera, and had invented "drama-music"—music welded to words, not words clothes-pegged to music. He did not take the world by storm. Recognition other than in the Fatherland came slowly. In 1877, Wagner conducted his own works at a series of concerts in the Royal Albert Hall. The place was not over-crowded, and the Press anything but enthusiastic, but one discerning critic referred to Wagner's compositions as "the music of the future."

It only remained for him to write *Parsifal,* a work in which the Holy Eucharist is represented in melting—but perhaps cloying—sweetness. It is bewitching music, but it is pagan. It was performed at Bayreuth in 1882, a year before Wagner's death, and it was his *Nunc Dimittis.*

It was in the Palazzo Vendramini, in Venice, that Wagner died from a heart attack. The household was wintering there after *Parsifal.* On February 10, 1883, Wagner's physician, Dr. Keppler, arrived to find the composer in a state of great excitement in consequence of a conversation with Levi, the conductor of *Parsifal* at Bayreuth. Wagner suggested to the doctor that it would be better for his agitated state of mind if he could get away from Venice for a while and take his son, Siegfried, with him. The doctor agreed, and it was decided that a short trip to Verona should be taken.

Three days later a friend arrived at the house to see Wagner at lunch-time. He found Cosima at the piano playing Schubert's *Lob de Tranen*. Siegfried, afterwards to become a famous conductor, was with her, and she was weeping bitterly. At that moment a maid came in and said that Wagner was not feeling well and would not be down to lunch. Cosima jumped up, white-faced, and rushed upstairs. Soon she came down and cried that her husband had had a severe paroxysm. The doctor was sent for hurriedly. Half an hour after his arrival, the great composer was dead from angina pectoris. He died with his hand held fast in his wife's.

No one knows all the details of his life, but all pay homage to one of the greatest composers the world has seen—a man who was described by Liszt as a sort of "Vesuvius shooting out flames and fire, mingled with roses and lilacs," who triumphed over scorn and derision and gave to music and mankind new beauty.

The music of Wagner is distinguished by two outstanding characteristics. In his operas, the music, unlike that of his predecessors, is an integral part of the drama, supporting, interpreting, and in some cases superseding the words. This revolutionary move was not received without antagonism nor did the general public at first approve of his use of the *leitmotif,* a tune or musical phrase symbolizing a character or incident and used wholly or in part whenever that character or incident is referred to. Sometimes, with dramatic irony, the *leitmotif* is heard as a revelation to the audience of part of the plot while the characters then on the stage are not supposed to know anything about it.

As may be imagined, a new kind of listening was demanded by this kind of music and, together with his shimmering, tremendous orchestral sweeps with their unexpected resolutions, aroused much the same kind of antagonism that Stravinsky aroused in 1913 with his *Sacre du Printemps,* or the German atonal composers do today.

GREAT WOMEN

CLEOPATRA

(69–30 B.C.)

Whether Helen of Troy, whose beauty launched a thousand ships " and burned the topless towers of Ilium " really existed, is still a matter of some conjecture, but her rival in beauty, fame and influence, was a very real figure in the world's history. Cleopatra fascinated the great Julius Cæsar, and, after his death, Mark Antony, who in turn held the world in their hands. But she conquered the conquerors, and it was she who led Antony to ruin, a ruin that left Octavian in a position to become the first Emperor of Rome. Yet the oft-quoted remark about the length of Cleopatra's nose does her an injustice, for although she attracted men by her beauty and presence, she held them by her charm, her wit, and her learning.

IN the Palace of the Pharaohs, at Alexandria, sat Julius Cæsar, surrounded by his generals. The problem facing him was how best to serve the interests of Rome in the crisis that had then arisen: a bitter quarrel had broken out between the twenty-one-year-old Cleopatra and her brother Ptolemy XIV, a child of thirteen, who shared between them the throne of Egypt.

Cleopatra, who had been exiled, had gathered an army in Syria, and was marching on the Egyptian frontier to reconquer her kingdom. At this time, Cæsar, returning from his victorious war on Pompey the Great, arrived in Alexandria, and Ptolemy's faction asked him for the Roman army's support in the imminent civil war.

The council of Roman generals was about to break up. The decision in favour of Ptolemy's cause was all but taken, when into Cæsar's presence was ushered a Greek merchant with a present of rugs. A silence of astonishment filled the great hall as the bundle was unrolled, for there emerged from it a small, laughing, dishevelled young woman, Cleopatra, Queen of Egypt, Daughter of the Sun, Sister of the Moon. She was the woman whose charms and beauty, over two thousand years after her death, are still fresh in the minds of men, whose luxury and extravagance have never been surpassed, who, accused of fratricide and all heinous crimes, never lost the love of those around her. It has been said of her that " kings swooned on entering her presence," and two great Romans made their life work the gratification of her desires.

Cæsar, the war-worn general and libertine, fell at once under the spell of this beautiful child, who had cared in such fashion to enter her hostile capital and plead her cause in person; and that night, the most beautiful voice that had ever charmed men's ears set so well before Cæsar the cause of Cleopatra that at dawn Ptolemy had lost his prospective ally.

From that night dates the great partnership and romantic attachment between the queen of one of the wealthiest and most cultured countries of those times, and the leading citizen of invincible Rome. The partnership was to endure until Cæsar's death.

In Cleopatra, Cæsar, the ambitious warrior, had found an ally worthy to share his dream of a world empire. She was steadfast, courageous, intelligent; a woman who, when he had secured her throne for her, would have all the resources and riches of the east at her command. Cæsar had found in one woman all he had sought separately in others—beauty, charm, wit, intelligence, and above all a spirit of youth that owed nothing to her lack of years. The Roman in him admired in her the product of a civilization greater and older than his own, for Cleopatra, like all the Ptolemy dynasty, was of pure Macedonian blood. When Alexander the Great died, his empire had been dismembered, and Egypt had fallen to the lot of one of his generals, Ptolemy Lagos, who founded the Ptolemy dynasty, and thus Greeks ruled over Egypt for nearly three hundred years, making of their capital, Alexandria, first the rival and then the superior of Athens in beauty, culture and wealth. Cleopatra, the last of the Ptolemies, surpassed them all in artistic and literary patronage, in luxury and learning. We are told she spoke ten languages, including Latin, Hebrew and Syriac.

To Cleopatra, Cæsar was not only the means by which she would ultimately substantiate their shared ambitions; she instinctively gave him a heart-whole affection and the admiring respect of a pupil for her teacher. This woman, whom legend has taught us to think of as an immoral voluptuary, seemed, according to the known facts, to have regarded Cæsar as her husband, and she appears to have acted in all ways as an exemplary wife.

For many months Cæsar fought King Ptolemy's faction, and secured Egypt's throne for Cleopatra by victories at Alexandria and Pharos. Young Ptolemy, flying from defeat, was drowned, and Cleopatra became the absolute sovereign of Egypt. During these months of civil war, Cleopatra and Cæsar found time for feasting and love-making. Through days and nights, the beautiful laughter of Cleopatra echoed through the palace. Cæsar was happy, and in joy and happiness the son of Cleopatra and Cæsar was born. They named him Cæsarion Ptolemy, as became the heir of two great houses. A few hours after his child had been placed in his arms, Cæsar sailed away from Alexandria. The conqueror's holiday was at an end, new kingdoms must be won for the heir of Egypt and Rome.

For a year Cleopatra waited, while Cæsar made victorious warfare in Asia and North Africa. Then, in answer to his summons, she set sail for Rome. With her went her son, Cæsarion, and her ill-fated younger brother, Ptolemy Dionysius (Ptolemy XV), who nominally shared her throne. They went as guests of honour to participate with Cæsar in the applause of the people, but, according to the Roman custom, Cleopatra's rebel sister, Arsinoë, came in chains to be exhibited to the Roman mob. The Romans looked on in amazement at the retinue of this glamorous queen, whose beauty and riches had never been equalled. They feared her influence on Cæsar, whose boundless ambition these stern republicans already mistrusted.

Cleopatra took up her residence in Cæsar's villa on the bank of the Tiber, living openly as Cæsar's mistress but taking no part in political life. She remained in Rome for several years, during the period in which more and more honours were showered upon Cæsar. But Cæsar, if he had many friends, had also many enemies, and one day, in 44 B.C., to the villa by the Tiber came the tragic news of his assassination.

Cleopatra knew that she was unpopular in Rome, and lost no time in returning to her native land. Her brother, the young Ptolemy XV, was dead, poisoned at her behest, and she proclaimed her son, Cæsarion, as joint ruler, with herself, of Egypt.

* * * * *

For three years Cleopatra watched from afar the civil wars in Rome. Then, one day, there came a summons for her to meet Mark Antony, the leading Triumvir of Rome, at Tarsus, and explain why, as an ally, she had on certain occasions withheld her help. Cleopatra had been waiting, before giving her support, to find the likeliest Roman to embrace her cause. The long awaited moment had come, and with a smile on her lips and hope reborn in her heart, Cleopatra, Queen of Egypt, incarnation of the goddess Isis-Aphrodite, prepared to answer the summons of the most powerful Roman.

She had heard much of Antony's character, and she brought her limitless personal and material resources to the task of charming this giant with the heart of a child, this soldier for whom men died without asking questions, this hero on whom Cæsar's mantle had fallen.

* * * * *

Antony sat on the dais in the deserted market-place awaiting Cleopatra. The multitude which half an hour ago had surrounded him had herded towards the shore where her ship was anchored, and from the quay great cries of adulation reached his ears. Time passed, and still Antony waited. At last, irritated, he sent a message inviting the queen to dine with him. The queen's answer was an invitation to dine with her, and Antony, ever courteous to women, accepted. As he approached the river the most beautiful sight charmed his eyes. On a ship with a golden prow, with sails of purple and oars of silver, lay Cleopatra, apparelled as Venus. Beautiful slaves surrounded her, music filled the air, rich perfumes sent up a heavy smoke from wrought censers. Then the voice that had once charmed Cæsar greeted Antony, and he, " the colossal child, capable of conquering the world, incapable of resisting a pleasure," forgot his remonstrances in a wave of exhilaration and happiness. Cleopatra had found her champion.

The feast prepared for Antony was the most magnificent he had ever known. Costly gifts were presented to all the guests; such taste and riches had never been witnessed before even by him whose feasts and orgies were world famous. The populace on the shore gazed upon the beautiful, lamp-lit ship, and declared that " Venus had come down to earth to feast with Bacchus for the common good of Asia."

Nights of feasting followed; for Cleopatra's entertainment was succeeded by a banquet given by Antony, and that in turn gave place to a further feast by way of reply from Cleopatra. And Cleopatra's magnificence always outshone Antony's. So that at last he was forced into a happy admission of inferiority.

It is told that one night, to win a wager, Cleopatra dropped a pearl worth £150,000 into vinegar; the pearl dissolved and she drained the goblet. This incident is often quoted to prove her wanton extravagance, but it is more likely that, needing Antony's alliance, she hoped by such action to impress upon his mind the immensity of the wealth he would have at his disposal should he throw in his lot with hers.

Day by day, during these few brilliant weeks in Tarsus, Antony fell more and more under the spell of Cleopatra. Her powers of conversation, wit and charm, together with that childish gaiety which was so much a part of her, enthralled him, while she, though never losing sight of her ambitions, was attracted irresistibly to Antony.

It was at this period that Cleopatra enlisted Antony's help in the deed that has so blackened their story. Her sister, Arsinoë, who had fought against her in the days of Cæsar, and had followed his triumph in chains, was again in Egypt, plotting against Cleopatra. So also was a man, one who claimed to be the drowned Ptolemy XIV. With Antony's help, Cleopatra planned the assassination of these menaces to her throne, and the fratricidal policy was duly carried out.

Antony had followed Cleopatra to Alexandria after the meeting at Tarsus, and they spent the winter there together. For many months the queen entertained him with her characteristic extravagance—an extravagance rarely known to the world before or since. They formed the celebrated society of "The Inimitable Livers," the object of whose members was to outdo one another in luxury, patronage of the arts, culture, and all the pleasures of the mind and body. Antony gave himself wholeheartedly up to enjoyment, until at last the affairs of Rome would wait no longer. The rulers of the world were straining apart, but the break was not yet to be. Antony met his fellow triumvir, Octavian, at Brundisium, and once again they made a compact and divided the world between them: Octavian remained at Rome and ruled the west; Antony's task was to subdue the east. To seal the bargain, Antony married Octavian's sister, Octavia.

Then, in 37 B.C., he returned to Syria and to the arms of Cleopatra. Love and luxury were again the order of the day—and night. And then Antony set out on his campaign against the Parthians. On the victorious termination of this enterprise, he and Cleopatra hoped to found their empire. But disappointment was again in store for the queen. A fourth child had been born to her but a few weeks, when news came that disaster had overtaken the expedition. Cleopatra, the steadfast ally, set off at once with help for Antony.

When her ships sailed into the harbour of the White Village, where the remnants of Antony's forces rested, it was to find an army in rags, and a haggard, unkempt Antony, drowning in wine his hatred of facing her in defeat.

But this was soon forgotten in new alliances and a victorious campaign against the Armenians.

Meanwhile, Antony, by his attitude to his wife, Octavia, had long insulted Octavian, her brother, and relations between the triumvirs were strained. But on his return from Armenia, Antony insulted Rome. He held his triumph at Alexandria, thus robbing Rome of the glory of the conquest, and tacitly suggesting the supremacy of Alexandria. More than this, in a magnificent ceremony, where thrones of gold were placed on a dais of silver, he allotted kingdoms, lawfully belonging to Rome, to Cleopatra and his own children. War between the Antonian and Octavian factions was inevitable; the great struggle for the empire, which was to end at the battle of Actium, was at hand. The senate deprived Antony of his honours, and war was declared in 32 B.C.

In Cleopatra arose a growing doubt. Antony was no longer the young lieutenant, dauntless and born to success. His identification with Bacchus, the god of wine and joy, had been too complete. His preparations for war were half-hearted, the pleasures of life as an Eastern potentate claimed him, and in Cleopatra's heart resentment and contempt had begun to poison love. Then came the day when Cleopatra, at the head of her fleet, and Antony at the head of his legions, set out for the gulf of Ambrosia, in Greece, there to meet Octavian's forces. Hatred had nearly supplanted love. They disagreed on all points in the campaign. Cleopatra, who had been once deceived, distrusted Antony, unable to see that in him alone lay her hope, and Antony, his intelligence addled by wine, distrusted Cleopatra.

Thus things stood when Octavian's fleet and those of Antony and Cleopatra met, and the great battle of Actium was fought in 31 B.C.

This battle has remained a mystery to historians. The fighting had raged six hours, neither side having gained the advantage, when Antony saw the ship carrying Cleopatra, hoist sail and leave the fight, followed by her sixty ships. He followed in quick pursuit, flying from the yet undecided battle, leaving Octavian a vanquisher without a victory. It has been suggested that Cleopatra thought the battle lost and dreaded falling alive into Octavian's hands, or that a sudden attack of cowardice in this bravest of women compelled her to retreat. But in Antony's flight we can still less believe in cowardice, nor can one credit, as Plutarch suggests, that his wild infatuation for Cleopatra made him abandon an empire, fearing to be separated from her.

However it was, owing to this never explained conduct, the Egypto-Roman empire was lost, and Octavian became Augustus Cæsar, first Emperor of Rome.

Cleopatra had fled to Alexandria, where she made preparations for a defence—preparations on an heroic scale. Antony returned to Libya in a vain effort to find loyal troops. Both knew that they were doomed, and bitterness and reproaches died in their hearts, leaving only the desire to be together at the end. So to Alexandria Antony returned, and as once they had formed the society of "Inimitable Livers," so now they formed yet another magnificent society—the society of "Those Who Die Together." In glorious yet desperate feasts they awaited their end.

Near the temple of Isis, Cleopatra built her mausoleum, a splendid palace for the dead, in the true fashion of the Pharaohs. To this building all her treasures and jewels were carried.

Then from the prisons those condemned to die were brought to the palace and poison was administered to them or snake bites inflicted. Cleopatra was searching for the easiest way out of a world too strong even for her indomitable spirit.

Octavian was at the gate of Alexandria, and Antony, for a brief moment recovering his manhood, attacked him with success. Octavian's horsemen fled. Encouraged by this return of fortune, Antony determined to find death or victory in one last battle, but his allies deserted him at the last moment, and he found himself alone, save for a handful of faithful men. He returned to the palace. Here the news came to him that Cleopatra had killed herself. With Cleopatra dead, the world and all that it meant was lost to him and "in the high Roman fashion" Antony fell upon his sword, "a Roman vanquished by a Roman."

The wound did not kill him, and though he implored those around him to finish his work, none dared. A second messenger arrived contradicting the news of the first; Cleopatra was alive, and waited for him in the mausoleum.

Antony, dying of his wound, bade his weeping soldiers carry him to the great tomb where Cleopatra and her two faithful women, Charmian and Iras, had barred themselves in. Fearing to be taken alive by Octavian, their frantic hands had shot the bolts so far into their sockets that they were unable to open the grille. So, with the strength that only despair and love gave them, they hoisted the dying giant up the walls of the tower by cords and chains. Thus Antony died, clasped in Cleopatra's arms, all their hatred forgotten, and only the love of their early days in their hearts.

Antony dead, their kingdom lost, herself doomed, if she lived, to follow the triumphant chariot wheels in chains, Cleopatra made one last effort to charm yet another Roman, the cold Octavian, and he, fearing that she might take her life, and so rob his triumph of the spectacle of the humiliation of Rome's great enemy, made overtures and lying promises to her, offering her her kingdom and safety for herself and her children.

But news of Octavian's real intentions reached Cleopatra. So, to the splendid mausoleum, she and her two faithful women escaped to pour the last libations on Antony's tomb.

With the slow tears that come when only grief remains and hope is dead, Cleopatra placed crowns of flowers on her lover's coffin. whispering tender words. Then, having bathed in costly perfumes, she was adorned in her regal splendour, and feasted for the last time—alone.

At the end, a slave carrying a basket of figs approached her, and, smiling, she took it from him, saying: "So it has come." Her devoted slaves had not forsaken her; for she knew that, at her request, they had hidden an asp beneath the fig leaves. There would be no jeering Roman crowds, no ignominious death; Cleopatra would die as the goddess she was, in her own way, at her own hour. And that hour had come.

She pressed the lithe, small reptile to her breast almost lovingly. And the last Ptolemy slowly fell asleep.

* * * * *

After death, this great woman's ambition was ironically fulfilled, for Rome adopted Alexandrian civilization and culture, and formed in truth an Egypto-Roman empire. But Octavian, and not Cæsarion, sat on the throne.

Cæsarion had died by the assassin's knife; there was no room in the empire for two Cæsars.

JEANNE D'ARC

(1412–1431)

The peasant girl who heard the voice of God; who roused a spineless prince and a cowed people, and freed her country from the conqueror's yoke: that was Joan of Arc. All the world knows her story, for Joan is one of the world's heroines; but the tale of Joan is one that is always worth the re-telling, and here in this gallery of great lives, her example of faith and courage glows afresh in a brilliant setting.

THE town and castle of Chinon, on the banks of the Vienne, housed, in the first quarter of the fifteenth century, the shadow of a royal court. Officers of state in threadbare garments kept up what dignity they could in decrepit dwellings, most of the furniture of which had been pawned by a queen in a faded, shabby dress, desperately trying to keep the wolf, in the shape of a host of creditors, from the door. Grasping courtiers who found nothing to grasp intrigued and grumbled and, one by one, took their chance to desert for more lucrative employment. And at the head of all this tragic establishment lurked an ungainly, cowering figure, a timid young man of poor physique, the as yet uncrowned Charles VII of France, scorned and bullied by everyone, tortured by doubts of his own legitimacy, expecting every moment to be driven even from his humble home at Chinon by the dreaded soldiers from across the Channel.

Never had a monarch of France sunk so low. The victories of Henry V had made the English masters of all France north of the Loire, apart from the domains they already held in the south. The infant son of the dead conqueror had been proclaimed king in Paris, though he had not been anointed with the sacred oil of St. Remy, which alone could make him king in the eyes of France. The great Duke of Burgundy, richer and more powerful than many monarchs, had allied himself to the invaders. Crowning blow to Charles, his own mother, the German Isabeau, widow of the lunatic Charles VI, had also given her support to the English, and had declared that her son had not a drop of the blood royal in his veins—an assertion which those who knew Isabeau found no difficulty in believing.

At this moment, when all seemed lost, the miracle occurred. At a time when it seemed that at last, after all the miseries of the Hundred Years War, the English claim to rule France must become a complete reality, the Capetian dynasty was saved by the inspiration of an illiterate peasant girl.

Her name was Jeanne d'Arc, and she was born in the year 1412, the daughter of a peasant proprietor—the most influential personage of the village of Domrémy, on the Meuse. She was a pious child, unable to read or write, but proud of her skill in needlework, and able to help her father with his flocks and herds. Her home was in country partly French and partly Burgundian in sympathy, and she was from her earliest years familiar with the troubles that beset her native land.

When Joan was twelve, she declared that she had heard a voice from God, and from then on she vowed that she would remain a virgin and lead a holy life. During the next few years she continued to hear voices, and to see visions, and she became convinced that it was her mission in life to save her country and crown the true king in Rheims Cathedral.

It seemed a wild and fantastic notion to her companions and her parents. Her father, a prosaic country man of sound common sense, said he would drown her rather than let her yield to such ideas. But Joan had made up her mind, and nothing would stop her. In 1428, when she was sixteen, she bearded in his castle Robert de Baudricourt, who held Vaucouleurs for the dauphin, and demanded an escort to Chinon. Robert was flabbergasted. He was a rough, simple soldier, not the man to be impressed by the story that the apparitions of St. Michael, St. Catherine and St. Margaret had entrusted to a peasant maid the task of freeing France from foreign invaders. In short, he told her not to be a little fool, and sent her home.

But Joan was convinced of the genuineness of her inspiration and no initial failure would daunt her. She tried again, and this time won over certain of Baudricourt's followers, with the result that he was prevailed upon to give her the escort she demanded. In January, 1429, dressed as a man, and with six followers, the maid set out for Chinon.

For the moment her difficulties were over. Charles, in utter despair, and ready to jump at the vaguest hope, received her with open arms, and after a private conversation with her, in which she reassured him as to his legitimacy, and convinced him of her own divine mission by a revelation which she ever afterwards kept secret, he publicly declared his confidence in her, and, in spite of the blusterings of the gross and incompetent La Trémouille, announced that, provided she would submit herself to examination by theologians at Poitiers, he would give her command of a force to relieve Orleans, which was then being besieged by the English in their efforts to penetrate south of the Loire.

She went to Poitiers, satisfied the theologians, and Charles fulfilled his promise. On April 28, Joan, in white armour, wearing a sword with five crosses, which she had previously declared would be found in the church of St. Catherine de Fierbois and which was so found, with an army of 4,000 men, accompanied by the Duke of Alençon and escorted by a procession of priests, arrived before Orleans, and joined the commander of the garrison, the Bastard of Orleans, afterwards Count of Dunois.

What followed is one of the most astounding stories of the history of war. The French had been cowed by the continued success of the English. Their spirit was broken, and two hundred of the invaders could strike terror into the hearts of a thousand Frenchmen. The coming of the maid transformed them. With her inspiring figure to lead them, confident of her divine destiny, they suddenly became new men. They sallied forth from the town, attacked the English, stormed the "bastille" of the Augustines; and then, after a week of increasing triumph, came the final victory, with the capture of the Tourelles, the towers commanding the bridge across the river, held by the English. This was Joan's greatest exploit. The Tourelles seemed impregnable, but she planted the first scaling ladder, and led assault after assault, rallying her men to deeds of heroic valour that would have seemed incredible ten days before. Only when she fell with an arrow through her shoulder did she leave the front of the attack. But not for long. She had her wound dressed, and came back to her place, and when Dunois was in favour of retiring, saying the Tourelles could not be won that day, she spurred him on to one last, glorious effort. It was successful. The French entered the Tourelles, with the maid's banner borne aloft in triumph. The English commander, Glasdale, with his attendants, was drowned as the fired bridge sank beneath them, and Joan went apart to pray for their souls. Orleans was saved.

The effect was tremendous. The tables were turned at last, and it was the turn of the English to be demoralized by the feats of an all-conquering foe. Jargeau and Beaugency fell before Joan's troops; Sir John Fastolfe was defeated at Patay and, with joy and thanksgiving, the dauphin welcomed the victorious maid at Lyons.

Now, she felt, her hour had come. She would lead Charles to Rheims, and there crown him according to the traditions of nine hundred years. Then, an anointed king, he would, with her help, take possession of his capital, and drive the English from the soil of France.

The march through Burgundian country to Rheims was accomplished in triumph. Auxerre surrendered at once, Troyes submitted after a show of force, and on July 14, the royal cavalcade reached its destination. Two days later the Abbot of St. Remy brought the sacred oil, with which every French king since the legendary Pharamond had been anointed, and Joan knelt by the side of Charles as the Archbishop Regnault de Chartres, Primate of France, placed the crown upon his head.

"Gentle king," she cried, "now is the pleasure of God fulfilled, Whose will it was that I should raise the siege of Orleans and lead you to this city of Rheims to receive your consecration. Now has He shown that you are true king, and that the kingdom of France truly belongs to you alone."

Her destiny was fulfilled. She had touched the highest point of her glory. Thenceforward, though her spirit remained undimmed to the end, she was to meet, through no fault of her own, with nothing but failure. Charles, who had been inspired and awakened from his lethargy by the maid's enthusiasm, now fell back into his customary state of indecision and vacillation. Joan never ceased to urge an immediate assault on Paris, but the king chose rather to indulge in fruitless negotiations with Philippe of Burgundy, endeavouring to detach the duke from the English cause. Meanwhile, Compiègne, Senlis and Beauvais submitted to the royal army, and from the last place the bishop, Pierre Cauchon, was expelled. Not long afterwards he was to be the moving spirit in the trial of Joan of Arc.

At last Joan got her way, and was allowed to attack Paris. But the assault was a miserable failure. Charles was scheming behind her back. He was afraid of offending Burgundy, and he allowed her insufficient troops. Her courage and leadership was as great as ever, but she was alone. Everyone else was half-hearted. She was wounded in the encounter, and the assault on the Porte Saint Honoré was beaten off.

Charles now ennobled Joan and her family, and granted her village relief from taxation, but he would not grant her what she wanted—troops to complete the recovery of France. She chafed at the inactivity, and when at last she heard that the English and Burgundians were marching against "her good friends of Compiègne," she insisted on riding forth to help them. In a sally outside the town she was captured by John of Luxembourg and, at the instigation of the infamous Cauchon, thirsty for revenge, she was sold to the English, who regarded her as a witch and intended her to be tried by the Court of the Church known as the Inquisition which in this case was largely composed of French bishops. If she were condemned by an ecclesiastical court she would be discredited, thought the English, in the eyes of those who now thought her a saint. She would then cease to be an inspiration.

Accordingly she was brought to Rouen, and there put on trial for heresy and witchcraft before a tribunal composed of forty carefully selected theologians, presided over by her arch-enemy, Cauchon, and the vice-inquisitor, Jean Lemaistre. Between the time of her capture and her death a year elapsed, but during that period Charles lifted not a finger to save her.

There is no need to enter into the details of the trial. It was one of the most appalling travesties of justice ever seen, in spite of modern attempts in certain quarters to prove the contrary. For weeks on end, first in public, then in the prison, where she was guarded by blackguardly soldiers, she was subjected to remorseless interrogations and innumerable charges, many of them childish and trivial. Twelve points were alleged against her, the most important being that her visions were of the devil, that her prophecies were false, that she shamed her sex by wearing male attire, and that she claimed to appeal to God over the heads of the Church.

Cauchon's only purpose was to procure a confession of guilt, and a judge who declared the proceedings illegal was expelled from the court. Above all, Joan's demand to be allowed to appeal to the pope was ignored.

Through all the tragic farce Joan's composure remained undisturbed, and her country wit frequently disconcerted the learned examiners. "Light does not shine only on you," she said to Beaupère, when he asked if light accompanied her voice. And when another interrogator, whose accent was not of the purest, asked what language St. Margaret had used in her converse with her, she replied, "Better French than yours." To the ever-repeated charge of immodesty and defiance in continuing to wear a man's dress, she pointed out with simple common sense that, being as she was in prison, at the mercy of lewd English soldiers, it was a mere act of prudence.

But Cauchon won the day. There was a limit even to Joan's endurance, and at last, with the stake before her, her spirit broke, and she signed a recantation of her "errors." She was condemned to imprisonment for life, and the Earl of Warwick, the English leader, was furious with Cauchon for allowing her to live. But the bishop's wiles were not exhausted, and he reassured his accomplice. "We shall catch her yet," was the comment of this impartial judge.

And catch her he did. She had promised never again to wear man's dress, but by the simple expedient of allowing her no other, her captors succeeded in making her break her vow. On this extraordinary evidence she was proclaimed a relapsed heretic, and condemned to the stake.

The last scene took place in the market square of Rouen on May 30, 1431. After receiving communion, she was handed over to the secular arm and led to her death. She asked for a cross, and a soldier gave her two pieces of stick tied together. And then the cross was fetched from a neighbouring church and was held before her eyes as she died. As the flames gathered around her she kissed the cross in her hands and cried out the one word, "Jesus!" Then she spoke no more.

Her heart was found unburned in the pyre. Her ashes were thrown in the Seine from the bridge of Rouen.

Twenty-five years later her memory was publicly rehabilitated at a trial held at the instance of Charles VII, and the judgment of Cauchon was annulled. And nearly five hundred years afterwards, in 1919, Pope Benedict XV raised the peasant maid of Domrémy to the altars of the Catholic Church among the saints of God.

Posterity's two points of view are summed up by these two following quotations. Lamartine, the great French poet, says of her: "Joan of Arc, the prophetess, the heroine, and the saint of French patriotism, the glory, the deliverance, and equally the shame of her country. . . . Angel, maiden, warrior—she has become a fit blazon for the soldier's banner."

Bernard Shaw's tribute is none the less sincere for being less romantic. "We may accept," he says, "and admire Joan as a sane and shrewd country girl of extraordinary strength of mind and hardihood of body. Everything she did was thoroughly calculated; and though the process was so rapid that she was hardly conscious of it, and ascribed it all to her voices, she was a woman of policy and not of blind impulse."

ELIZABETH I

(1533–1603)

Of all the epics of English history, no period is so rich in romance, adventure, gallantry and poetry as the reign of Elizabeth I. She came to the throne of a country in despair, and when at last death forced her to relinguish her grasp, she left a prosperous country, rich in a renaissance of art, literature and architecture. She left a country that had triumphantly defied all the great powers of Europe. Hers was an age of great men: Shakespeare, Marlowe and Spenser in literature; in her time Drake and Raleigh sailed the seven seas, while Cecil and Walsingham managed her affairs of state. Here was a woman, ruthless, cold, clever and unscrupulous; yet made of such stuff that men counted it an honour to die for her whom they called "Gloriana." It was said of her that she loved nothing and nobody but England, and it can be said with truth that her England achieved a brilliance that has never again been reached.

ELIZABETH I, Queen of England, faced her first parliament with memorable words—perhaps the first and last utterly sincere words she spoke.

"Nothing," she said, "no worldly thing under the sun is so dear to me as the love and goodwill of my subjects."

She won their love though she stepped to the throne through the blood of the people spilt by Tudor hands. She kept their love, though she tricked and defied both her noblemen and her common people—kept their love even in the last dark pathetic days of her reign when, as a painted, raddled harridan, she tried to hold the love of young men—and then sent them to their doom. To the love of her people Elizabeth clung; it was the only true love she ever knew —she, the world's most courted woman.

She came to the throne in her twenty-fifth year, beautiful, young, brilliant and hard-headed. People might question the legitimacy of her birth—quibble whether the annulment that set aside Catherine of Aragon's marriage and made Anne Boleyn the lawful queen were worth the paper it was written on—but none would deny that Elizabeth, the child of that second union, was Henry VIII's daughter. Even more than the red-gold tint of her hair, the blue eyes, and fresh, fair skin, which were the physical characteristics he handed on to this despised daughter of his, she inherited his shrewd, quick brain, his imperiousness, his grasp of statesmanship, his love of learning, his cold egotism, and, it must be admitted, his complete lack of scruples. She added to these characteristics all the feminine wiles and artifices natural to a daughter of Anne Boleyn. The envoy of Spain expressed the general opinion of Elizabeth when he wrote bitterly to Philip—" this woman is possessed of a hundred thousand devils."

Elizabeth was born in 1533, and her father, Henry VIII, accorded her a cold reception. He wanted a male heir to carry on the Tudor line, and the least Anne Boleyn could do after all the trouble he'd been put to to make her queen, was to produce a son. Had Elizabeth been a boy, it is possible that Anne Boleyn would not have ended her ambitious career on the scaffold when her daughter was three.

As a child, Elizabeth knew more of sorrow, loneliness, bitterness, and fear, than any child should. From her earliest days, the fear of sudden death was always with her, and the stigma of her birth always before her. She spent much of her early years in virtual imprisonment. Yet, with good tutors, plenty of books, and in the company of her young step-brother, Edward, she found contentment, and the quiet months spent at Hatfield House under the tutelage of Roger Ascham and Baldassare Castiglione were among her happiest memories.

In 1547, Henry VIII died, and Edward VI, then aged ten, ascended the throne with his mother's brother, the Duke of Somerset, as Protector. Immediately, plots and intrigues darkened the horizon again. Somerset was ambitious for power, and not particularly clever—and it was pathetically plain that the frail boy king would never reach man's estate. By Henry VIII's will, Mary Tudor, daughter of Catherine of Aragon, stood next in the line of succession, then Elizabeth. In France, a menace to them both, was Mary Stuart, granddaughter of Henry VIII's eldest sister, Margaret, wife of the Dauphin of France, and heiress to the throne of Scotland. In actual fact, Mary Stuart had a better claim to the throne of England than either of the Tudor princesses, but like Mary Tudor, her Catholic adherence alienated the sympathies of the English people, added to which she was wedded to France.

Nevertheless, the situation gave full scope for plots, counter-plots, spies and intrigues. Edward VI's death, in 1553, was the signal for a rising in favour of Lady Jane Grey. It was put down, but since Elizabeth, with some justice, was accused of complicity in it, Mary sent her half-sister to the Tower. She escaped a traitor's death only by the intervention of Philip of Spain and his father, and in the later, long-drawn-out duel between Philip and Elizabeth, he did not neglect to point out that she owed her life to him.

Elizabeth passed the five tragic years of " Bloody Mary's " reign in the household of Lord Seymour, the second husband of Catherine Parr, Henry VIII's last queen.

Elizabeth grew to be fond of her stepmother's new husband. He was a handsome man, younger than his wife, and no doubt flattered by the pleasure he seemed to arouse in the fifteen-year-old princess. When Catherine died, in 1548, he may have made definite proposals to her. What the actual circumstances of Elizabeth's relations with Seymour were we shall never know, but he led them both into a public scandal that very nearly caused a double execution. Seymour was accused of treason on the grounds that he desired to marry Elizabeth and ascend the throne; and only the public proclamation of her innocence, after a terrific cross-examination by a battery of lawyers, saved their heads and their reputations.

But however Elizabeth amused herself in amorous dalliance, it is certain that she watched with clear, hard, unforgiving eyes, the mistakes made by her half-sister Mary. England was crying aloud for vengeance for the blood of Protestant martyrs. At length Mary died, in 1558, childless, unloved, a tragic failure. Elizabeth's accession was greeted with shouts of joy—joy that Mary was dead.

Thus it was that on November 17 of that year Elizabeth became the queen of a country ravaged by pestilence and sickened to the verge of revolution by an expensive war in France that culminated in the uncertain peace conference at Cateau-Cambrésis. In Mary's five-year reign the country had been ruined. England's credit was gone, her currency debased, and her people torn by religious dissension. The cheers at Elizabeth's coronation, some have said, were shouts of joy at her sister's death rather than rejoicings for the new queen, of whom they knew little.

She was a royal figure, all the same, with her red-gold, curly hair, her pale face, shrewd blue eyes, and her long white hands of which she was so vain. The fact that she was unmarried was, of course, the main interest in diplomatic circles, and almost immediately the English court was filled with whispering ambassadors and emissaries eager to pander for half the kings and princes of Europe.

With the approbation of her privy council she showed her genius for surrounding herself with the best possible advisers: not for a little while did the other aspect of her genius become evident—that of taking advice and transmuting it through her character into individual and personal decisions. William Cecil, Lord Burleigh, was her chief minister, and remained true to her till his death, forty years later—" the perfect servant," as a modern historian has written, " of a woman who preferred not to let her right hand know what her left was doing."

With Cecil and her new government, Elizabeth set to work to redeem her country. With stringent economies and heavy taxation for the first few years she reclaimed the nation's credit. She dealt tactfully with Philip of Spain, who threatened and cajoled her to part with Calais when peace with France should ultimately be signed. As a last resource he proposed marriage, with one anxious eye on the dwindling power of Catholicism in England. Elizabeth hummed and hawed, and then, after months of deliberately dawdling negotiations, sold Calais for five hundred thousand crowns and refused the hand of Philip once and for all. In the same month the Church of England came into being.

Elizabeth has been accused of being a flirt. This is, paradoxically, true and untrue. She flirted madly with the young manhood about her, possibly she may have been in love with Essex; but her coyness with Philip of Spain, with his cousins Don John and the Archduke Charles of Austria, with Henry of Anjou and his brother Francis, were all matters of cold politics. Her coldness was part of her success. In a country blazing with the fires of youth and adventure, with the excitements and lusts of wealth and freedom, she was a figurehead of ice more splendidly inspiring than burning gold.

She loved and encouraged shows and richness, and loved to display royal pageantry before the eyes of the common people, whom she dazzled. She became the inspiration which men hymned and praised—for which many courageous, brilliant, and often unscrupulous men strode the earth, sailed the seas, fought and died.

She could not afford to allow religious toleration. She knew only too well that the reforming Jesuits sent over from Spain to re-convert England were sowing the seeds of revolt and treason. However single-minded they were in their zealous faith, an England in sympathy with Catholicism menaced her throne. So Elizabeth persecuted the Catholics but, to quote Green, " she was the first English ruler who felt the charge of religious persecution to be a stigma on her rule; the first who distinctly disclaimed religious differences as a ground for putting men to death."

She had some sympathy with the Catholic faith. Nevertheless, the Church of England was of her making, and because it was her country's religion she would uphold it before all the world. That was the reason why Mary, Queen of Scots, rode over the border from the defeat at Langside, in 1568, and knocked for shelter at a door that opened only to imprison her. Elizabeth did not hate her cousin, but she was not going to alienate the Protestants by recognizing any claims made by a Catholic. So Mary went to prison for eighteen years, first in one castle and then in another.

Meanwhile, Elizabeth had cleverly taken advantage of other people's belief in Mary's claim to the throne by making peace with Spain for twenty-five years. She pointed out that if Philip should be ungentlemanly enough to conquer her, Elizabeth, then Mary's right to the throne would precipitate an Anglo-French alliance—which was the last thing Philip wanted.

During the eighteen years of Mary's imprisonment, plot after plot was hatched to usurp the throne. For eighteen years Elizabeth knew again the fears of assassination that had shadowed her youth, but still she was unwilling to put Mary to death. Even at the end, in February, 1587, frightened and perhaps irritated by the whole shabby business of yet another plot, she wanted Paulet, Mary's custodian, to take responsibility; and she tried to make a scapegoat of Davison, her secretary, over her signature to the warrant.

The very next year Philip, exasperated at the treatment of his galleons by English adventurers, sent his Armada to crush the dangerous power that was endangering his interests in the Netherlands and in the Americas.

Nothing seemed to be ready. There was not nearly enough ammunition. Elizabeth was compelled to retire from London in case the worst should happen. Pessimists talked about a Catholic rising in sympathy with the invaders. But, when the moment came, England—the England that she had built out of the devotion of men to an ideal—did not fail her.

"I do not desire," she cried to her troops at Tilbury, "to live to distrust my faithful and loving people. . . . I know I have but the body of a weak and feeble woman, but I have the heart of a king . . . and scorn to think that Parma or Spain or any prince of Europe should dare to invade the borders of my realm. . . ."

Suddenly—before the cheers had died away—a messenger ran to her side with the news from Drake that her faith was not in vain. God and the English had dispersed the Armada. And even while Elizabeth piously ordered the medal to be struck: "God blew with his wind and they were scattered," she was also angrily considering the cost of sending out the fleet, and insisting that she must find a profit on the food supplied to the ships.

That famous date, November 17, 1588, marks the climax of a famous reign. Thereafter, England was to float upon the calm waters of its own greatness while its queen grew more and more out of touch with her people. The figurehead had served its purpose. She had made a nation and saved it from destruction. Now, battered and lonely, she was to offer love and be spurned. Essex, the young, the beautiful, the wayward knight, snapped his fingers at royal favour. He had known a proud queen and lived to see her grow old and ugly. He thought she had grown humble, too, till he found the Tudor flame still fierce enough to consume him. On February 25, 1601, he perished on the block, and with him died the heart of Elizabeth.

Pride had killed her love. Pride would keep her alive, but the heart was dead. Sometimes there gleamed quick flashes of her old fire—of that resonant laughter and forthright speech that had shocked ambassadors into telling the truth and charmed rough seamen into poets—but they were only the last flickerings of an expiring flame.

Almost exactly two years after Essex's death—on March 24, 1603—Elizabeth I, Queen of England, died. Her monument, mightier than a Pharaoh's pyramid, was the country she had raised to the captaincy of the world.

By the simple expedient of knowing how to use good advice and never doing today what could possibly be put off till tomorrow—in case anything more suitable might turn up!—she had weakened for ever the maritime supremacy of Spain and Portugal. She had played off Lutherism against Catholicism to produce an established Church; and she was the inspiration of a glittering crowd of poets, soldiers, explorers, scientists and philosophers such as the world had never hitherto seen and will possibly never see again.

She had never married. Gossip of the time points to a physical defect. But it is pleasanter and more probable to believe historians who state that England itself was her only lover.

JEANNE ANTOINETTE POISSON LE NORMANT D'ÉTIOLES, MARQUISE DE POMPADOUR

(1721–1764)

Madame de Pompadour. The very name is scented with the atmosphere of the court, with the glamour of royal France in the eighteenth century. She was the favourite of the king, Louis XV, and through him she ruled France. Ministers rose and fell at her command, traditional policies were thrown overboard, new alliances made, and war begun to satisfy her whim. Writers, artists, courtiers were given protection and encouraged by her patronage. Her life and her work (and throughout her life she worked hard) were devoted to one end—the possession of the King of France and of his power.

On April 15, 1764, the Château of Versailles was agitated by a strange excitement. Madame de Pompadour was very ill. Inflammation of the lungs, it was, and Madame was likely to die. It was weeks since the court had glimpsed that ravaged, imperious mask, now hidden in the private apartments, waiting for death. That morning she had had her will read out to her; she had given audience to Janette, Intendant of the Post Office, and examined carefully the documents he had presented to her. When he had gone, she lay back upon the silken pillows of her bed, her face streaked with rouge and powdered pearls. M. le curé was due to visit her. After that—the end.

"My life has been a battle," she thought, and her tired mind swept back the curtains of memory till she saw again, like a tiny, brilliantly-lit stage, the interior of her mother's house—Madame Poisson, the butcher's wife—surrounded by a furtive crowd of "friends and acquaintances."

* * * * *

As a girl she had been shocked by her mother's immorality—but she could not fail to admire her indomitable character that pushed past every obstacle to train her daughter into the position of royal mistress. That had been the idea from the first. The fine education in the arts and sciences, the loveless marriage at twenty to the young Le Normant d'Etioles, resulting in the birth of a daughter, poor little Alexandrine, and the four long years of waiting while she encouraged the young wife to hope and scheme for an opportunity—just one!—to meet and captivate the king.

It came soon. She remembered that afternoon vividly. The sudden thunderstorm and a soaked sovereign with his attendants bearing the carcass of a deer he had just killed. Would M. d'Etioles be so kind as to offer shelter, and to accept this small present of game?

He had joked with her, and invited her to accompany him when next he hunted. Nothing happened. And when she tried to bring herself before the notice of the king at court, that odious Madame de Chateauroux had tried to interfere. A vindictive piece! Oh, the agony of a high, sharp heel ground into one's instep! She had not forgotten to repay that particular favour with interest!

By Easter of that year—1745, was it not?—she was acknowledged *maîtresse en titre* and Madame de Chateauroux was nowhere.

Binet, the king's *valet-de-chambre*, had helped. It was he who had persuaded the king, almost against his will, to receive her. She had been lovely then. Boucher, when he painted her—not so very long after—had expatiated upon her delicate, regular features. It was a pity her lips had always been a little pale, but a sharp bite with those pretty teeth she was so proud of soon brought colour to them. How clever he had been to get the exact green-brown of her eyes, and to bring out the chestnut gleam of her hair under the powder.

How many men had sung her praises! She had made the Abbé Bernis a minister of state for his serenade to her dimples. Yes, she had been lovely—though how she managed to keep her looks with all the worry and disturbances of those early years, remained a mystery. The fuss that her husband caused! One would have thought that the fool was really in love with her! How she had laughed when he had stormed and wept and even threatened suicide. It was positively a relief when the king became irritated at such low manners and had sent him into exile. And then her mother's death, and the careful negotiations that led to her being transformed from common Jeanne Louise Poisson into La Marquise de Pompadour. Her brother, too, had risen. What a stir among the people when he became Marquis de Vandière! And the jealousy of poor papa! For even the king had thought it was too much to include the butcher among the new arrivals at court.

In those days she had had to be careful. A king is not easily held, especially when the affection is one-sided. Louis was known as the Well-Beloved—but not by her. "You frigid bird of the sea," he had once said. At once she had seen to it that he was placated and diverted by the variety of her accomplishments. It was then she thanked *Maman* for her careful education.

She sang and danced all day and most of the night. She comforted him in his black moods. She humoured his every whim, yielded to him when necessary, and withstood his anger in just such a way as to win his admiration. Later—but she did not care to remember too clearly the period of the orgies in the Parc-aux-Cerfs, when the latent viciousness of a decadent mind burst the slender bonds of human decency, when the all-powerful king and his minions performed those acts that had made the little temple in the pleasure grounds a place of horror haunted by the ghosts of bestial, criminal pleasures.

She had perforce been involved in all that. It was part of the duties of her insecure position. And for that the queen hated her, and the populace crossed themselves at the mention of her name.

Louis the Well-Beloved! So called because his people had been grateful for his occasional charities, had shown some concern at his illness twenty years ago—afraid, perhaps, of losing one tyrant to whose iniquities they were accustomed, and gaining another, younger king with greater strength to persecute them.

She had worked hard, and to repay herself she had seized as much as she was able without appearing to ask for it. Louis, after all, was stupid when it came to dealing with a clear-headed, intelligent woman.

A wistful desire for a country cottage—and the Château of Belle Vue had been built; a fluttering of household bills increased her allowance; and because Louis was fundamentally lazy and hated the endless draughty corridors of Versailles, she obtained the best suite of apartments immediately below his with a specially constructed private staircase between.

The queen, Marie Lesczinska, had been annoyed, of course; and the dauphin—well, they always hated each other, ever since the first time she met him as a little boy, sulking and sticking out his tongue. He was sent away with boxed ears for that!

But much more dangerous enemies were the Jesuits. Always she had tried to overcome their power, but always, even in her moments of supreme achievement, the shadows of black robes darkened the brilliance of her triumphs.

The priests were near her now. Nevertheless, she could look back and remember with pride the great events she had influenced in spite of them. Could they have engineered a Seven Years War as easily as she had done? After all this time she still reddened with anger at the insult Frederick had offered her. Probably Voltaire had mismanaged things, but he was friendly with the Prussian king then, and had been entrusted with the message that Madame de Pompadour desired to present her respects. The unspeakable little man had dared to say: "I do not know her." Not know La Pompadour! A smile curled her lip as she remembered her fury. "I hate him!" she had cried. "Let us crush this Attila."

It had seemed like fate that Queen Maria Theresa sent her just then that friendly letter suggesting the advantages of an Austrian alliance. "*Ma chère cousine*" it had begun—just as if she was genuine royalty!

Louis had wondered why she had made such a fuss about dear Maria Theresa, but he had agreed to the alliance in the face of popular opinion. She had accomplished this thing alone. It seemed unfortunate now that the war had not turned out quite so successfully as she had expected. The defeat at Rossbach worried her still. All the same, she had shown her strength; had demonstrated a woman's power before the assembled nations, and had proved to her own satisfaction that politics—that fascinating game—need not be played by men alone.

If the affairs of nations were not easily managed, she had more spectacular effects with the lives of men. As her finger beckoned they rose and fell. Bernis—he of the serenade—failed her, and he went. Maurepas went, too, and revenged himself with filthy poems about her which he circulated in the streets of Paris.

It seemed there was another food shortage. She had heard that the common people were dying in the streets for want of bread. A pity, but economies were necessary all round just then. Had not the court subscribed a hundred thousand livres to keep the opera going? In one way, therefore, Maurepas was useful, since his dirty doggerel kept the crowds amused, though he must be taught the imprudence of offending a favourite. She liked to think of the twenty long years of exile he had to serve.

Maurepas' poetry brought home to her the advantage of being friendly with high officials—such as the Director of the Post Office. It was most convenient to be able to read exactly what the court said in its letters. . . . She had been able to put a spoke in the wheel of several dangerous intrigues. Even with cabinet meetings held in one's bedroom, information seemed to leak out, and it well repaid the care and trouble of dissolving wax and forging seals to gain some idea of where the leakage was.

She was feared for her power, and it was pleasanter now to recall the occasions when she had used it for the public good.

Choiseul's election as Minister of Foreign Affairs had been a good thing. His rise had begun out of personal gratitude. He had noticed his beautiful cousin's designs on the king before even her sharp eyes perceived it, and brought her an incriminating letter from the minx. She did not need to expend much energy to stop *that* little affair. But Choiseul was made ambassador to Rome for his trouble. Again, he helped her to negotiate the alliance in Vienna, and afterwards in the war gained Corsica and San Domingo for the French. A further bond between them was his hatred of the Jesuits. She was glad and proud of his present success. She had made him. France would remember them both.

Boucher, too, owed much of his success to her—as did those clever Messieurs Voltaire, Montesquieu, Diderot, and the rest. Yes, she had controlled the destinies of men, but destiny had in the end been stronger. She had never quite recovered from the shock of Alexandrine's death. The child had been so young—she was only thirteen—so sweet—so different from the rest; and even though M. le Maréchal de Richelieu had refused to allow his son to marry her, there might have been greater things in store. Strange, to look back on that period when she fled for comfort to the Church she had despised, when she had written to her husband and been rebuffed!

Her luck had turned, it seemed, from that date. Three years later came the attempted murder of the king. He was only slightly wounded, and the assassin was caught, but the remembrance of it haunted her still. Cracks appeared on the face of a society that appeared civilized, and yet could punish the wretched Damiens for his unsuccessful crime by drawing him apart with horses, and dropping boiling lead into his wounds.

That was seven years ago, and now she was forty-two. Somehow, those last seven years had seemed the hardest of all. Her power over the country had waned. What of the king?

It was better in this hour of approaching death to face the fact: Louis no longer loved her. Was it because his Immaculate Wonder had presented such an inelegant display of vulgar grief over Alexandrine's death? Was it because she weakened at the horror of Damiens's execution. Was it because her strength, that enabled her to cling so tenaciously to her position, tired with its own effort? She no longer cared. She had conquered life: it was restful by comparison to be conquered by death.

* * * * *

The door of her chamber opened. The curé entered. Seeing her awake, he bowed and made as if to retire.

"One moment only, Monsieur le curé," she said, "and we will take our departure together."

She smiled and closed her eyes. The priest gazed at her for a moment, and then began to whisper softly the prayers for the dead.

* * * * *

She could not have foreseen that evening of wind and dismal rain when Louis stood bareheaded at his study window to watch the coffin pass.

"Madame has bad weather for her last journey," he said lightly, and turned back towards the warmth and luxury of the room within.

CATHERINE THE GREAT, EMPRESS OF RUSSIA

(1729–1796)

A German woman, who as Empress of Russia became more Russian than the Russians: a woman of tolerance, learning and culture, ruling in a land which had known only despotism and the knout: an empress who attempted to do something for the under dog, and whose proposed reforms were banned in France as being "revolutionary"; a cunning diplomat and a skilful director of war, by which she increased her dominion and strengthened her country; a lover, whose amours have become a byword: that is Catherine II of Russia, who earned for herself the cognomen of "Great."

A COACH thundered along the frozen roads of Germany. It was bitter winter, the winter of early 1744, and snow and wind made the occupants shiver in their furs. There were two passengers in the stately equipage—a fourteen-year-old girl and her mother. They had set out from Zerbst, in the little German state of Anhalt, and were travelling post-haste eastwards. They had driven to Berlin, where the great Frederick himself had welcomed them, and given them God-speed. And now they were pressing on through the snow. At Riga the galloping horses swayed into a new country—Russia. The fourteen-year-old girl had arrived. She never left Russia again.

There was a warm welcome for the travellers at Riga. Then they sped on over the Russian wastes to St. Petersburg—the Leningrad of today—and from St. Petersburg to Moscow. And there the young girl was welcomed by the Empress Elizabeth with all the ceremony due to her as Sophia Augusta Frederica, Princess of Anhalt-Zerbst-Bernburg, and as a matrimonial prospect sent on approval.

Elizabeth was looking for a wife for her nephew, the Grand Duke Peter. She had invited the young German girl to pay a visit—and be looked over. Sophia Augusta Frederica, who since her birth in 1729 had lived with Christian Augustus, Prince of Anhalt-Zerbst-Bernburg, her warm-hearted, backboneless father, and her clever shrew of a mother, was bundled off to Moscow.

The fourteen-year-old girl was introduced to her prospective husband. He was just sixteen: an ugly, uncouth lad, sickly, weak and slow-witted. Mentally and physically backward, he was degenerate in every way, and already a drunkard and a rake. He told the young German girl at once that he was resigned to marrying her, but that he was in love with one of his aunt's maids of honour. The princess must have been charmed at the prospect of her match.

Meanwhile her mother was busy quarrelling with the empress; and then Sophia herself fell ill. Physicians applied the universal remedy and bled her sixteen times in a month. In spite of them, she recovered, and found herself, she writes, "frightfully ugly."

Even at this early stage she showed signs of enthusiasm for things Russian, for at the height of her illness she demanded an Orthodox priest instead of a Lutheran parson, in whose faith she had been brought up.

After due consideration, Elizabeth decided that the girl would be a good match for Peter, so the young Sophia set to work to learn Russian and study the Greek faith. She was converted to the Greek Church and, in spite of her father's opposition, received the name of Catherine Alexeyevna. Then she was betrothed, and in August, 1745, at the age of sixteen, was married to Peter. Mother, still quarrelling, galloped off home to Germany; Catherine had seen the last of her parents.

Life as the grand duchess was grim. Her husband was just as bad as his appearance at their first meeting gave promise of being. He made no pretence of loving or of tolerating his wife, and the Empress Elizabeth was a tyrant. The young girl, who had been well educated at home, who had been nourished on the finest traditions of French culture, who had taste and a keen mind, was wedded to a boor in the bondage of an autocrat.

But the girl was charming and, though not beautiful, pleasing to look upon. There was one distraction for her. She had been married some six years when she took her first lover. No one cared, least of all Peter, so Catherine continued to show young men the royal way to love. In 1754, Catherine bore a son, Paul, and four years later a daughter. Neither was believed to be Peter's child. The Empress Elizabeth took the children away to bring them up, and Catherine was left nothing but her lovers.

The dreary years dragged on, while clever Catherine drugged the passing time with affairs, while Peter debauched and Elizabeth tyrannized. Then in January, 1762, the empress died and Catherine's husband became the czar—Peter III.

It was a crisis in Catherine's life, but that astute brain was not unprepared. She knew her danger. Peter was still devoted to his maid of honour, Elizabeth Vorontzov, and wanted to marry her. He hated Catherine; but he was hated himself by his people. For Peter had become thoroughly Germanized. He grovelled before Frederick the Great. He had a craze for all things German; he talked German and even modelled his army uniforms on German patterns. But his German wife had become thoroughly Russianized, and the Russian patriotic party, who hated Peter's Germanism—Germanomania would be an apter term—rallied to Catherine.

It was a strange paradox. The Russians were supporting a German girl against their pro-German czar. Catherine was seen to be in danger. Peter insulted her, and threatened her with arrest and divorce. Then he drove away from St. Petersburg with Elizabeth Vorontzov to his palace at Oranienbaum. That was on May 22, 1762. When Peter drove to Oranienbaum, he rode out of his empire. When Catherine let it be known that she was prepared to benefit by the removal of her husband, Gregory Orlov, Catherine's lover, and his brothers appealed to the army, and regiment after regiment declared for Catherine.

"Long live the Empress Catherine!" cried the Orlovs, and the soldiers echoed the shout. Catherine herself, dressed in the uniform of a colonel of the Guards, rode at the head of the troops to the Peterhof. Peter was arrested at Oranienbaum. The wretched man was nearly paralysed with fear. He was removed to Ropscha and there imprisoned, and that was the end of the active career of Peter III. His death a short while afterwards was naïvely assigned to colic by a manifesto of Catherine, and there is still some doubt as to the details of his murder.

Catherine II was now the sole ruler of Russia. And this German-born woman performed her task so well that she earned her cognomen, "the Great." Catherine really ruled. She still took her lovers, made them her ministers, and inspired them to work for Russia. But Catherine ruled, and the success and prosperity of Russia in her reign was due entirely to her. She was politically shrewd and astute and she allowed no love affair or lover to sway her judgment.

Catherine left her stamp on Russian history in four ways: as a lover, as a domestic reformer and legislator, as a conqueror and author of foreign policy, as a woman of culture. Let us consider these influences in order.

It has been said, foolishly, that Catherine introduced loose morals and loose living to the Russian court. But lovers and wine-bibbers were familiars of the Russian court long before Catherine was born, and if she surpassed previous empresses in the number of her amours, she at least did not follow them in gluttony and drunkenness. Catherine loaded her lovers with money, presents, estates and offices. She called them her pupils, and maintained that she was training them to serve Russia.

Gregory Orlov was her lover when Catherine succeeded to the throne. He was nothing of a man, and his services seemed to be limited to his part in the overthrow of Peter, in 1762. Orlov suggested marriage to Catherine, and she actually toyed with the idea, but her ministers' hints made her drop it. "The empress can do as she pleases," they said, "but Madame Orlov can never be Empress of Russia." Gregory Potemkin succeeded Orlov as favourite in 1776. He was a large, gross brute of a man, with some force of character and a genius for taking the credit due to other people. Potemkin had some ability as a statesman, but his part in the aggrandizement of Russia has been overrated, and a large amount of it was due to the generalship of Suvorov, who had military genius of a high order. Catherine had other lovers during her reign, but they were of no account, except for the last of them. He was Plato Zubov, a callow youth of twenty-two (Catherine was sixty), who managed to take advantage of his position, as no other lover had done, by interfering in politics. Such was Catherine as a lover. She has been censured for her licence, but her licence was never allowed to interfere with Russia.

In home affairs, Catherine began her rule as a reformer. She had absorbed French culture and French ideas. She was determined to do something for the under dogs. In 1766, Catherine published her *Instructions*. They were based on Montesquieu and Beccaria and were to form the basis of a new scheme for internal reform to be considered by a grand commission in Moscow. The *Instructions* were considered so revolutionary that they were banned in France. The nobles and landowners in Russia opposed them, because by the adoption of the constitution outlined in the *Instructions* their own power over the serfs would be limited. Eventually Catherine gave in to them, and actually made concessions which rendered the conditions of the serfs more desperate than ever, and in 1773 a revolt of the Volga peasants under a Cossack named Pugachev, who proclaimed himself Peter III, brought matters to a head. The revolt looked serious at first and the peasants met with some success, but the movement collapsed and Pugachev was executed.

Then in 1775, Catherine achieved real success as a lawgiver. After a long study of Blackstone, the great English lawyer, and with the advice of a German jurist, she at last issued the "Statute of Provinces." This statute provided for local administration and provincial self-government, and it set up a regular local judiciary. It was a definite measure of improvement, and remained in force until superseded by the further reforms of Alexander II in the latter half of the nineteenth century. Catherine's domestic policy would probably have continued to be liberal, but the French Revolution drove her, as it did other absolute monarchs, to reaction.

Her foreign policy was to enlarge Russia. She knew just how far to go and how far to rely on her allies. In 1768, she undertook the first Turkish war in alliance with Frederick the Great of Prussia against the Turks and Austrians. The conflict lasted six years. Russia was victorious and gained territory in the south. Then in the second Turkish war of 1787, Catherine allied with Austria against Prussia and Turkey, to gain further lands. These campaigns, thanks to the fine victories of Suvorov, enlarged Russia to the shores of the Black Sea, the Crimea and the Caucasus. Meanwhile, Catherine had been acquiring Poland. She and Frederick the Great took part in the first partition of Poland in 1772, and Catherine annexed further portions until its final absorption in 1795. In the realm of foreign politics Catherine's reign was a triumph.

And all the while she remained the cultured woman with the keen intellect. She corresponded with Voltaire, with Diderot and other French encyclopædists and read constantly. Blackstone's *Commentaries* and Buffon's *Natural History* she regarded as light literature. She collected art treasures and imposed a new culture and new manners upon her court. She herself wrote history, tales, fables and proverbs.

And the woman herself? We get little glimpes of her. "She forgave easily, and hated no one" she had said of herself. But if she did not hate her husband, she did not forgive him, and she treated her son Paul as tyrannically as the Empress Elizabeth had treated her. Yet she always maintained that he was not Peter's son. But Paul behaved strangely like Peter, and "the old woman," as he called her, kept him in subjection.

On the other hand, she loved Paul's sons, Alexander and Constantine. She positively doted on the grandchildren. There is an intimate little note in one of the letters describing how she dressed little Alexander at the age of six months: "All is sewn together and is put on at a go, and is fastened at the back by three or four little hooks. There is a fringe round the garment and that dresses him quite well. The King of Sweden and the Prince of Prussia have asked for, and have got, the pattern of M. Alexander's garment. There is no tie in it at all, and the child hardly knows that he is being dressed. His arms and legs are put into the garment at once and that ends it. This garment is a stroke of genius of mine which I did not wish you not to know of." Catherine is all woman there.

We know, too, that she was charming. She captured men by her address, gathered genius around her by her intellect, and drew others by graceful and clever correspondence. And she worked so hard that she would rise at five in the morning and light her own fire in order to get a flying start at the duties of the day.

In 1787, by the suggestion and under the escort of Potemkin, Catherine made a voyage down the Dnieper and a grand tour of South Russia. Potemkin anticipated the propagandists of the modern Soviets. He turned deserts into flourishing provinces, by the simple process of building wooden cities and hiring crowds to populate them while the royal procession passed. Catherine travelled in state, and courtiers flung gold coins from her carriage to the grovelling people. Palaces were run up overnight for her accommodation, and many cities were founded—and left. Catherine laid the foundation stone to a mighty new city to be called after her, Ekaterinaslov. The Emperor Joseph laid a second stone and murmured after the ceremony, "The empress and I have this day achieved a great work; she has laid the first stone of a great city, and I have laid the last." He was right.

A marriage brought Catherine to Russia; a marriage removed her. She had arranged a match between her granddaughter Alexandrina and King Gustavus Adolphus of Sweden, and everything was to be settled with great pomp at the Winter Palace. The empress and Alexandrina were dressed in state and waited while the young king was given the marriage contract to sign in his apartments. But Catherine had inserted articles therein which had not been agreed on, and Gustavus refused to sign.

Trembling, Zubov took the news to the empress. The blood rushed to her face. She staggered, but controlled herself. Then she dismissed the court. That rush of blood was the symptom of her end. A few weeks later, on November 10, 1796, she was dead of apoplexy.

She had been a great ruler, and Russia, with the exception of her son, mourned her. Russia had flourished under her reign, and she left it powerful. She had made her mark upon the country, and there is a pleasing story that again reminds us that the imperial autocrat was a woman.

When Bismarck was Prussian ambassador at the court of Alexander II in the early sixties of last century, he looked out of a window at the Peterhof Palace and saw a sentry on duty in the middle of a lawn. He asked the czar why the man was there. The czar asked his aide-de-camp. The aide-de-camp did not know. He sent for the officer in command. The officer in command did not know. The general commanding troops at Peterhof was summoned.

"General, why is that soldier stationed in that isolated place?"

"I beg leave to inform your majesty that it is in accordance with ancient custom."

"What was the origin of the custom?" put in Bismarck.

"I do not recollect at present," answered the general.

"Investigate and report the result," ordered Alexander.

The investigation took three days. They found that the sentry was posted there by an order put on the books eighty years before! For one morning in spring, Catherine the Great had looked on that lawn and seen the first flower thrusting above the frozen soil. She ordered a sentry to be posted to prevent anyone picking the flower. And in 1860 there was still a sentry on the lawn—a memorial to a flower, and to Catherine the Great.

ELIZABETH FRY

(1780–1845)

They called her the Genius of Mercy. She was a humble Quakeress, who dared to enter the terrors of our early nineteenth century dungeons and minister to the prisoners she found there. She walked where even the prison governors feared to tread, and her faith won great victories. The wretched prisoners responded to her call, her efforts made Parliament move in prison reform. The whole of Europe listened to her teaching, and prison reform took on a world-wide aspect. Not only prisoners, but beggars, the destitute, and all those less fortunate than herself, received help from this courageous and meek woman who conquered the world by mercy.

ELIZABETH GURNEY sat apart in the grounds of Earlham Hall, heedless of eleven brothers and sisters who kept trying to persuade her to join in some game or other. So far she hardly understood the change that had come over her—she was only seventeen—but a small voice within seemed to tell her that she had finished with games. That was the river where she had watched for tadpoles, these were the trees she had climbed; everything reminded her of some youthful sport. But it was no good—she felt herself different and unable to capture again the spirit of past amusements.

And why? Because the day before she had listened to William Savery, the American preacher, and he had made her feel for the first time that there was a God. The candid sisters had naturally not refrained from telling Elizabeth that her new air of solemnity was distasteful to them—even faintly ridiculous—but the change was so genuine, so deep-seated, that these remarks drew from her no resentment. Elizabeth had felt the call, and hers was no fickle nature. Henceforth she must dedicate her life to the service of humanity, for she did not believe in half-measures. It mattered not that her father was a wealthy banker, that he had brought up his children to dance and hunt and entertain—she would have to give it up and become a "plain Friend," living only to aid the afflicted.

However, it seemed rather ludicrous to talk about giving up "the world" when she had no idea of what it was like, so she prevailed upon her father to let her visit London, that she might perceive to the full the extent to which pleasure might be indulged. There she painted her face and visited the play. But she was convinced that public amusement tended to promote evil, and returned all the more determined to become an out-and-out Quaker. She adopted a plain style of dress, gave up music, dancing, and ornaments, and looked about for charitable work. The most obvious thing seemed to be to start a school for village children, which she did, gathering seventy urchins together for instruction twice a week, and holding a little service for them on Sundays. Even at this age Elizabeth showed the firmness of character for which she was to become celebrated. Her eldest sister writes: "When she said she could not dance it was more than I could bear, and I persecuted her. But in vain. I never remember her to have been shaken in one single point which she felt to be her duty. The Bible became her study, visiting the poor, especially the sick, her great object."

Mr. Gurney, though a devout enough member of a Quaker family, highly disapproved of Elizabeth's rigid code of life. It caused friction in the family, and he felt that an attractive young girl ought not to waste her youth in this manner. Accordingly, he welcomed Joseph Fry, the plain Friend who had fallen in love with Elizabeth's flaxen-haired, unassuming beauty and devout nature, and invited him to Earlham with a view to encouraging the match. Elizabeth was not at all certain whether it would be right to marry, but after much persuasion, and Joseph's promise never to hinder her in her mission to humanity, she accepted him by the prearranged signal of picking up a watch that he had laid on a garden seat.

In 1800, when Elizabeth was twenty, they were married, and went to live in St. Mildred's Court, London. Joseph was wealthy, but Elizabeth would have no useless ornaments about her, and disapproved of lavish meals. They kept open house, however, in the manner of Quakers, and entertaining and the advent of children in rapid succession kept her busy. Soon she began to visit the London poor, but though she was appointed visitor of the Islington workhouse, she was far from being satisfied. After a few years of marriage she wrote: "Instead of being a useful instrument in the Church militant, I am a care-worn wife and mother merely devoted to the things of this life."

In 1811 she was recorded a minister in the custom of Friends, an honour which she greatly appreciated. She arranged schools for the poor, depots for the distribution of garments, medicines, and food, and learnt how to vaccinate, believing strongly in the efficacy of this operation. She began to address meetings, and was at first very nervous, not realizing that her real gift lay in oratory, and that chiefly through the power of the voice she was to achieve one of the greatest reforms of the time.

Elizabeth Fry was not the first person to become interested in prison life; John Howard had given his life to prisoners' relief in the eighteenth century, but he described himself as "the plodder who goes about collecting materials for the man of genius to make use of." As it happened, the "man of genius" who brought his work to the practical issue of a reform was Elizabeth Fry.

Prisoners in those days were treated as animals would scarcely be treated now. Hundreds died of starvation, of filthy diseases caused by foul air and herding together, and once when a fire broke out in an Irish jail, fifty-four were left to perish. Men and women, murderers, lunatics, debtors, pickpockets and children were thrown together in fœtid underground cellars without light or bedding. Drink was sold to anyone who could pay, and no limit was set to the amount consumed. "At every session, criminals in scores were sentenced to death. Even as late as 1833, sentence of death was passed on a child of nine who poked a stick through a pane of glass and stole some tubes of paint worth twopence."

When Elizabeth Fry first visited Newgate Prison in 1813, she found three hundred women with their numerous progeny lying about on the floor in a state of indescribable filth, unclassified, unemployed, and abandoning themselves entirely to bad language, fighting, and lawlessness. Those with money bribed the jailers for drink. Elizabeth's heart was especially filled with pity for the children—what chance would they have in life after being subjected to such experiences? She read the women the parable of the vineyard, and appealed to them to co-operate with her in some scheme for educating the children.

Though the response was great and touching, Elizabeth was unable to return for some time. Another child was born to her, and two people died in the family—one of her children and her brother John. With illness, trouble, and a family so far numbering nine to care for, she had to leave the prisoners alone for a time.

Her mind was restless: how could she arrange to devote herself to the work which she felt was her mission? Her sister, Rachel, came to the rescue, and took four girls to live in the country, while the boys were placed at school. Elizabeth went straight back to the prison, and at once started a school for the children under a

Elizabeth I (*above left*) was exceedingly successful as Queen of England. She commanded the love and allegiance of the English people, who recognized her immense courage and responsibility as a ruler.

A portrait by Bencken of the Marquise de Pompadour, mistress of Louis XV (*above right*). (*Below*) Elizabeth Fry reading to prisoners in Newgate Gaol. From 1813 she worked untiringly to improve the conditions in prisons.

This photograph of Florence Nightingale (*above left*) was taken in 1858, shortly after her work in bringing discipline and sanitary conditions to the hospitals of the Crimea had made her legendary. (*Above right*) A facsimile of a wood engraving of the *Epistola Christoferi Colom* printed about 1492 shows the discovery of San Domingo by Christopher Columbus after a sketch which is attributed to him, and in which he himself is made to appear. Sir Walter Raleigh (*left*), one of the most celebrated of the great Elizabethans, was distinguished as a statesman, courtier and poet. He was a favourite of Elizabeth I, founded the colony of Virginia and explored Guiana before being unjustly imprisoned and eventually put to death by James I.

governess chosen from among the prisoners. The governor of Newgate approved of Elizabeth's ideals, but was sceptical as to the results of her efforts. The women were so depraved that even he only entered the cells reluctantly. Elizabeth, however, had her own ideas as to the cause of their depravity, and was not to be deterred. F. A. Beaumont has vividly described her first visit to the female prison:

> For a moment, the crowd of infuriated women fell back in dumb amazement. They stared open-mouthed at this lady who had so calmly ventured among them. Then, almost in one movement, they surged forward with the avid curiosity of animals around a prey.
>
> Her Quaker dress, expensive but sober and simple, offered no fine laces and flounces, no scarves or frills for a malicious hand to seize and begin the savage sport of disrobing her. But already they had their eyes on that gold chain. She was in dire peril, surrounded by so dense a crowd, pressing ever closer, that the turnkey could no longer see her.
>
> If she betrayed the least sign of fear, if she did or said anything to provoke them in the slightest, they would leap and rend her. Swiftly her eyes roved to and fro; what could she do to convince them she was their friend, that she was there only to help them?
>
> In one corner she saw a grey-haired hag swaying to and fro, clutching a bottle of brandy, and screeching a bawdy song. In another, two women fighting like tigresses, rolling over and over, their clothes torn, their faces slashed to bleeding by vicious nails. In another, a woman tossing and moaning in fever on a pallet of dirty straw.
>
> Then, a few yards away, she observed two women stripping a dead child for rags to put on a boy, four or five years old, who was playing by their side. Quickly, Elizabeth Fry strode towards them and picked up the grimy little toddler, who instantly began fingering her bright chain. Then she held up her hand imploringly:
>
> "Friends," she said, "many of you are mothers. I, too, am a mother. I am distressed for your children. Is there not something we can do for these innocent little ones? Do you want them to grow up to become real prisoners themselves? Are they to learn to be thieves, and worse?"
>
> She had struck the only chord in their hearts that still rang true. Their hard, fierce hatred, vice and cunning, fell from them as at the touch of a magician. Marvel of marvels, here was

someone who might save their children. They themselves might be abandoned in the nethermost pit, but if their little ones could only be given a chance . . .

Sobbing, they fell on their knees all around her, kissed her hands and her dress. They brought their children to her, gave her a chair, began to pour into her patient ear tales of woe, betrayal, injustice, crime, and remorse, harrowing enough to have inspired a new Dante. But Elizabeth Fry had ever a simple heart; she saw her new friends not as wrongdoers, victims, or wretches, but merely as women who could be made respectable and useful.

When, later in the day, she took her leave, she had lit in the black hell of women's prisons in Europe a spark that was to grow into the floodlight of reform.

With a committee of twelve women she devoted herself entirely to the reformation of the women prisoners, having separated the children from their contaminating presence. The visitors almost lived at the prison. The city sheriffs had said "it was vain to hope that such turbulent spirits would submit to the regulations of a woman, armed with no legal authority, and unable to inflict any *punishment!*" But Elizabeth tried the experiment, and "they saw no more shameless creatures, half naked and half drunk. The prison no longer resounded with obscenity and licentious songs, but it exhibited the appearance of an industrious factory or a well-regulated family."

Elizabeth Fry founded the association for the Improvement of Female Prisoners in Newgate in 1817, with the object of establishing separation of sexes, classification of criminals, female supervision for women, religious and secular instruction, and useful employment. The improvements that resulted soon became obvious, and other institutions became interested and desirous of adopting similar methods. But it is certain that the first great step, the winning of the sympathies of the most desperate set of creatures in London, was necessary before authority could be won over, and only such a woman as Elizabeth Fry could have done this. She seems to have had some special magnetism in her person and voice, which endeared her where the mere quoting of texts and Bible-readings would only have alienated. One woman, sentenced to death, was so desperate that she could not be managed, but when Elizabeth entered she became perfectly docile.

When preaching to the prisoners, Elizabeth always classed herself with them, saying "we" instead of "you," implying that all are sinners in the sight of God. The effect of her teaching was marked. Says one divine: "The looks of tender reverence the women cast on her, as she moved among them, and the way in which some whispered a blessing after her, testified to the influence she had obtained over them."

Hangings were frequent in those days—the Old Bailey alone furnished about a hundred victims a year—and Elizabeth, who did not believe that capital punishment tended towards the security of the people, strove to procure the release of a young girl sentenced to death for uttering forged notes under the influence of the man she loved. This brought her into conflict with Lord Sidmouth, who believed firmly in killing off even mild criminals, and she did not succeed in obtaining the reprieve of the girl, who was hanged.

Though she failed to mitigate the severity of sentences, however, her work in connexion with prison conditions was eminently successful. In 1818 she visited the Scottish prisons with her brother, Joseph John Gurney, where she found the usual horrible conditions prevailing. One man had been fastened for several days to an iron bar with his legs passed through rings some feet apart. He was unable to rest or undress, and the position amounted to slow torture. Elizabeth's pleadings for the alleviation of his distress were unavailing. She also saw five men confined day and night in a closet nine feet square, and never let out for any purpose: they were debtors. There were no lunatic asylums, and the insane were thrown into prison along with the criminals. Elizabeth and her brother, impressed by the fearful cruelty prevailing, published a book on the subject after their tour. The publicity thus given, together with the recognition of Elizabeth's reforms by the House of Commons, led gradually to the improvement of prison life all through Scotland, Ireland, and the English provinces.

Meanwhile, the terrible conditions of the convicts transported to New South Wales had attracted her attention. She induced the government to make proper regulations for the voyages of the convict ships and to arrange that the arrivals in Australia should be provided with homes and employment.

Nor did her philanthropy stop at prison reform. The severe winter of 1819-20 drew her attention to the pitiable condition of beggars and the destitute. She opened a shelter for the homeless in London, and provided a soup kitchen, and later started a similar scheme in Brighton. Finding that the men of the preventive service were surfeited with idleness and boredom, she arranged to supply them with books, and started a library service to supply coastguard stations.

Her reforms attracted the attention not only of England, but of the whole of Europe. In 1820, Elizabeth became a correspondent of the Dowager Empress of Russia, who instituted reforms based on Elizabeth's teaching. From other countries, too, came letters seeking the advice and aid of the Genius of Mercy.

Now Elizabeth did not feel that her work had gone far enough. In 1838 she began her Continental journeys, visiting France, Switzerland, Prussia, Holland and Belgium. She obtained permission to view all prisons and was received with courtesy. Foreign travel was something of an undertaking at that time, for most of the ground had to be covered by coach. But in spite of the slowness of the journeys and her own failing health, Elizabeth managed to interview many people in high places, especially winning the sympathy of the King of Prussia. She inspected prisons, schools, and asylums, expressing her views everywhere and giving advice for reformation. In Prussia, the religious persecution upset her greatly. She found Baptist ministers of excellent character imprisoned, and petitioned the king for religious toleration. He was so struck with her sincerity that he visited her in her own home when visiting England in 1842.

During her visit to Germany she went to the Institute at Kaiserwerth, where Florence Nightingale received her early training in nursing, and the founder, Fliedner, told Elizabeth how greatly his work had been influenced by hers.

She was gratified in her last years to receive many letters from abroad, saying that the reports of her investigations were leading authorities to put her suggestions into practice. But her physical strength, worn by a life of unceasing labour, was waning and she developed a lingering illness from which she was never to recover. A series of deaths among her numerous children and grandchildren afflicted her sorely and though she kept her faith through all the mental and physical anguish that was heaped on her, vitality did not return, and she died on October 12, 1845, tended by her daughters.

Some of Elizabeth's convictions are worthy of note, even now, when criminal treatment has improved beyond recognition. She protested against solitary confinement, the silent system, and the darkness of cells. Solitary confinement, she said, was too cruel even for the greatest crimes, and sufficient to unhinge the mind. The silent system was unnecessary, as, "without word or action, a spirit may pervade any collection of persons, either of resistance, opposition and defiance, or of comparative kindness." Also, she believed that man should not be treated as a machine, having his conduct bent through strong coercion and dread of punishment. "The more hateful the restraints of virtue become to a person, and the stronger his dislike of the authorities, the more ready is he for the commission of fresh crime." Dark cells and dark windows were condemned, because the culprit should at least be able to see the sky. "I am certain," she says, "that separate confinement produces an unhealthy state of mind and body, and that therefore everything should be done to counteract this influence which is baneful in its moral tendency. I am satisfied that a sinful course of life increases the tendency to mental derangement as well as bodily disease, and that an unhealthy state of mind and body has a demoralizing influence; and I consider light, air, and the power of seeing something beyond the mere monotonous walls of a cell, highly important."

Such views strike a modern note, and it can easily be imagined that they created a sensation at the time they were first uttered by this quiet Quakeress. But, docile wife and mother and religious devotee that she was, she did not fear to stand against public opinion and fight to the death for her convictions, and from the day she heard William Savery preach to the day of her death she was a faithful and bold worker in the cause of humanity.

FLORENCE NIGHTINGALE

(1820–1910)

"The Lady of the Lamp" has become a great and picturesque figure in Britain's national history, but there are few who realize the debt which the whole civilized world owes to Florence Nightingale. Nursing was in the hands of such terrible creatures as Dickens's "Sairy Gamp," when this gentle daughter of a country squire sacrificed her social life to become a pioneer in clean and devoted attention to the sick. The Crimean War gave her the chance to put her principles into practice, and by her heroism there Florence Nightingale lit a lamp which will blaze for all time. Modern nursing and hospital routine are the blessings which we owe to her actions and ideals.

THE year 1850 saw a revolt. It was a disturbance not recorded in the histories of the time, for it was the drawing-room outcry of a young woman—a revolt against the futility and fatuity of the social life which surrounded and imprisoned her. "In my thirty-first year," she wrote in her diary, "I see nothing desirable but death. Everything has been tried—foreign travel, kind friends—everything. My God! What is to become of me?"

She was endowed with all the good things of life; well nurtured, educated beyond the stage of most young women of the period, and yet obsessed with an innate impulse to devote her apparently useless existence to the service of mankind, by which she understood the one and complete way of serving God. Within five years of her vehement expression of revolt, the woman's name had become world famous, beloved, and cherished by rich and poor alike; and, to this day and for all time it is revered and honoured by all civilized peoples.

The woman was Florence Nightingale, than whom no one person in history has done more to alleviate the sufferings of the sick and to establish a system which, by its adaptation, created and has maintained at so high a standing the honourable profession of nursing.

Before Florence Nightingale took up her self-imposed and arduous task, the condition of hospitals and the nursing profession —if profession it could be called—was in a disreputable state. Nurses were drawn from the most undesirable sections of the community. Scarcely any facilities for the training of nurses existed, and the pay was less than that for a common labourer in field or household. There were no such aids to hospital work as are ready to hand in these days—it was before the time of Lister, and antiseptics were unknown. Nurses were mere vulgar drudges, uneducated, unclean, and notorious for their drunkenness and immorality. Yet it was upon this profession that Florence Nightingale had set her heart. It was there that she saw the field in which woman could be of greatest service to mankind; and there, indeed, was need for a reformer, a pioneer who would be prepared to cleanse this Augean stable, even at the cost to herself of physical suffering, mental pain and social ignominy. For among the prejudices that at first precluded this ardent young woman from following the call that pealed through her soul, the strongest and hardest to combat was that of "class prejudice."

Florence Nightingale was born at Florence, in Italy, on May 12, 1820. It was her parents' fancy to call their children after the name of their birthplace, so that, although Florence was until then always understood to be a man's name, it was given to this future reformer in whose honour so many women have since borne it.

Her parents were wealthy, well connected, and associated with leaders in society and politics. It may be imagined with what repugnance they regarded this strange desire on the part of their younger daughter to take up a career that would bring her into contact with the fearful conditions then prevalent in hospital life. Every method was used to distract her from these interests. She was sent travelling with friends of the family, Mr. and Mrs. Bracebridge, who took her first to Rome, hoping that she would forget. But what were the glories of Rome to one who there discovered the beneficent work being done by the Roman Catholic sisterhoods? She left the holiday party to dwell for ten days in the Convent of the Sacred Heart, where she studied the organization. She knew a little of the work that was being done in Germany at Kaiserswerth, where Fliedner, a Protestant minister, had a school for the training of hospital nurses. These things only stirred in her mind a firmer determination to do something of the kind in England; but it was to be on secular and not religious lines.

It was at this time that Florence Nightingale met a man who was to be of tremendous influence in her career—Sidney Herbert, the gifted son of the Earl of Pembroke. Herbert and his wife were neighbours of the Nightingales in Wiltshire. Florence was at once attracted by this former cabinet minister, who was now a man of thirty-eight. She was then in her twenty-eighth year, "tall, slender, elegant and very straight, her hair of a rich brown, her complexion delicate, her grey eyes pensive, yet ready to light into mirth, and her smile the sweetest and most winning." Her personal charm, her culture, her attractive appearance, and the deep sincerity of all her actions, naturally brought many friendships—close and lasting friendships—but with all the opportunities Florence Nightingale had of marrying, and finding in the administration of a home an employment that would take her mind off her main obsession, she regarded with contempt any idea that there could be no attachment between man and woman without the thought of sex intruding. The friendship that was formed with Sidney Herbert, afterwards Lord Herbert of Lea, was cemented "by the humanitarian impulses common to both," and it was that friendship that did so much to effect the purpose to which this remarkable woman devoted her life.

Again Florence Nightingale went travelling. In 1849, while in Paris, she met two sisters of the Society of St. Vincent de Paul, who gave her introductions to their order in Alexandria. Florence travelled through Europe to Egypt, and in Alexandria visited the society's schools and hospitals. It was here that she first learned the importance of discipline in hospital management.

On her return journey she visited Fliedner's Institute of Protestant Deaconesses, to which she returned shortly afterwards for four months' training.

Wherever she went in her journey through Europe, she always sought first the places where some kind of good work was being done for the afflicted and needy. More than ever, she was convinced that it was useless trying to be a pioneer in a movement that did not exist in her own country. She must not merely point the way. She must make the way and lead. From her Continental travels, Florence Nightingale returned home firmly resolved upon the course which she knew her life must take. The prejudices and the drastic oppositions must be removed by her own hand. About her and around, in the atmosphere of a London season, she suddenly realized the sterile vacuity of her life that, because of social prejudices, was denied access to that service for God and mankind on which her heart was set. In such a mood and in such surroundings, Florence Nightingale cried out: "Oh, God! What is to become of me? How can I get away from all this? Let me *do* something!"

Through the persuasive intervention of Sidney Herbert, her family gradually resigned themselves to the position. Accompanied by her sister, she visited again those various institutions of which she had learned while on holiday. She enrolled herself at Fliedner's pioneer institute—it was the first modern establishment for hospital training—at Kaiserswerth on the Rhine. Here she lived the true Spartan life, underwent the strict training of a deaconess, rising at dawn, doing all the menial services, sharing the frugal meals of the sisterhood, and attending lectures on nursing. To one of so tender and delicate a nature, it was a life of peculiar hardship and self-denial. But, "it was an experience glorified by the consciousness that at last she was gathering in knowledge the strength necessary for the noble task to which she had dedicated her life."

On her return to England, Florence Nightingale spent much time in learning the conditions and the necessities of her craft at the hospitals of London and Edinburgh. In 1853, she was again in Paris, studying the details of nursing organizations there.

Then, in August, 1853, came the time when Florence Nightingale was given the chance of managing and directing such an institution as she had conceived to be needed in England. It was a philanthropic institution entitled the Establishment for Gentlewomen During Illness—a nursing home for ladies of restricted means, which had been established in Chandos Street, London. So successfully did she conduct the work that larger premises had soon to be acquired. They were found at No. 1 Harley Street, where the future "ministering angel" had her first opportunity of proving her theories. In the treatment of the sick, her first principle was cleanliness, and for that, fresh air was necessary. Contrary to all the tenets that then held sway, the reformer began by insisting upon open windows. From this and many other reforms which she effected in this institution, there began to be built up the modern systems of hospital treatment, and Florence Nightingale's fame began to spread through the "thoroughness, initiative and hygienic value of her dispositions." She was about to assume the superintendence of the nurses at King's College Hospital, where she saw her longed-for opportunity, when a national calamity occurred which caused the taking of the first step towards reaching the "Ideal." The Crimean War broke out in September of 1854.

Within a few weeks of the Battle of the Alma, *The Times* special correspondent denounced the shameful lack of proper provision for the care of the wounded after the heroic victory. Summed up, the denunciation declared "there were not sufficient surgeons; no dressers and nurses; no linen for bandages—and yet, no one was to blame." An outcry of indignation arose throughout the country.

Sidney Herbert, who was again Secretary for War, wrote to Florence. He told her there was no one to superintend "the whole thing" in the matter of organizing the care of the wounded. Would she go? Within a few days she had settled the details, and received a letter from the War Office officially appointing her as Superintendent of the Female Nursing Establishment in the English General Hospitals in Turkey. Two days later, on October 21, 1854, she set out for Scutari, accompanied by a group of voluntary nurses she had assembled, and whose abilities she had proved.

With the announcement of her government appointment, there came to Florence Nightingale immediate celebrity. Here was a gentlewoman, rich, popular, young and attractive, who was prepared to abandon a life of ease and luxury to face dangers, horror and fearsome toil. Funds were to be provided by the Commander of the Forces, the Purveyor-General, and the Chief Medical Officer at the front. Donations and gifts were showered upon her. Out of the forty assistants she and Herbert had decided would be the first necessary complement of the nursing force, she was only able to recruit thirty-eight. They were composed of ten Roman Catholic sisters, eight Anglicans, six nurses from the St. John's House, and fourteen from various hospitals.

Then arose a new kind of prejudice. She was denounced for the very composition of her relief party because of its sectarianism! It was only when Queen Victoria gave her personal benediction to the leader that the absurd accusations against her subsided. But even then, high officials carped at the idea of a woman taking charge of what was essentially a man's job. Encouraged by the queen's message, Florence Nightingale took no notice of her critics' shouts.

She reached Scutari on November 4, just in time to receive the wounded from the Battle of Balaclava. She and her staff were coping with the herculean task of tending them, when, a few days later, a further six hundred casualties from Inkerman arrived.

Meanwhile, a commission was appointed to inquire into the accusations in *The Times,* which had led Herbert to send his friend to the seat of war, but while the commission was "inquiring" the ministering angel went on working. The commission advised the appointment of an individual with plenary powers to correct the wrongs on the spot. Florence had herself taken on those powers, and men were being saved from the very ills with which the inquiry was concerned. They were being saved by one woman and her staff of nurses. Money came to her from *The Times* fund, and from private benevolence, and to it she added from her own purse.

Scrubbers and sacking for washing floors were her first need. To obtain them through the office of the purveyor-general would have meant weeks of delay. She approached *The Times* fund. The officer of the fund was told by the ambassador that no money was needed except enough to build a new church at Pera! When the contractors for the laundry work—of which there was very little under the existing system—failed in the fulfilment of their contract, Florence Nightingale took a house in Scutari, and equipped it as a laundry. A consignment of twenty-seven thousand shirts, urgently needed for the bedraggled sufferers, had been landed and awaited opening pending the report of the Board of Survey. With a high-handed action, Florence commanded that the bales should be opened at once, and the materials delivered to the hospital—" red tape or no red tape." They were.

Such conduct naturally incensed the staff. One of them wrote: " Is this the way to manage the finances of a great nation? Miss Nightingale coolly draws a cheque. A divine afflatus! Priestess Miss Nightingale! Magnetic impetus drawing cash out of my pocket!"

The Lady-in-Chief, by which she had come to be known among the wounded soldiers and the medical staffs, continued her work of cleaning up the shambles she had found. Those of her helpers who would not submit to discipline or the necessary privations were promptly sent home. They were soon replaced by others, by this time trained in the courses which she had set on foot in England. Hospital mortality, which before her " taking over " had been as high as forty-two per cent, rapidly fell to two per cent. This was directly attributed to the work of the sanitary commission of engineers and medical men appointed to carry out her own schemes of health. Officialdom impeded her actions at every step; but she overcame it with her persistent power of being able to find out the cause of an evil and at once suppressing it.

She wrote some astounding letters to her friends at home describing the conditions in the hospitals before and after her arrival. " In a time of such calamity . . . I have little compassion left even for the wretched purveyor-general, swamped amid demands he never expected. But I have no compassion for men who would rather see hundreds of lives lost than waive one scruple of the official conscience."

She made out plans in detail for the running of the entire staffs of hospitals, buying departments, housekeeping, furniture, clothing and supervising a daily routine. Those plans are working today, though certainly much improved. But when she found that officialdom would not help her to carry out these plans, this gallant woman during a twenty hours working day, often performed the duties of cook, housekeeper, scavenger, washerwoman, general dealer and storekeeper combined.

"It was her custom, late at night, or in the early hours of the morning, when her administrative and clerical labours were done, and before retiring to such rest as she allowed herself, to make a last tour of the wards; a tall, slender figure in black merino, her rich brown hair covered by a white cap, she would pass, camp-lamp in hand, down those long aisles, between the rows of beds, bestowing comfort in isolated cases." It was thus that she came to be called "The Lady of the Lamp"—a name by which she has become immortal.

She was laughed at when she began catering for the "other side" of the British soldier. Games, amusements, books and cafés were provided for the convalescent and eventually for the resting soldier. What such innovations meant then may well be understood from the present-day soldier's opinion of those blessings. And all the while the hospitals under her care were taking on an entirely new aspect.

She visited the front line, and realized that the need of hot food and other amenities was as essential to the soldier's efficiency as strict training and ammunition. In all, she made three visits to the scene of war during activities, each time to accomplish some new reform. Then she, too, succumbed to the fever through which she and her staff had nursed so many who might have perished but for her work. It was a severe attack, and for a time her life was despaired of. She came out of it with the loss of her beautiful hair, her health so impaired that she was never again the same woman.

After her recovery from the illness, the whole nation gave itself over to public thanksgiving, and the queen wrote: "It will be a great satisfaction to me, when you return at last to these shores, to make the acquaintance of one who has set so bright an example to our sex. And with every prayer for the preservation of your valuable health believe, always, yours sincerely, Victoria R."

In spite of her sickness and its weakening effects, Florence Nightingale refused to leave her post of duty until the British evacuated Turkey in July 1856. Then she returned to England and to the acclamation of the whole nation. She avoided the enthusiastic receptions that were arranged for her, but in September she was received by the queen at Balmoral.

Her work in the Crimea was a beginning only: she proceeded

to carry her principles into action in the hospitals of England. She was in fact, as well as name, the founder of the modern nursing system in England.

The nation raised fifty thousand pounds for her services during the war, and with this sum she founded the Nightingale Home for Training Nurses at St. Thomas's Hospital. She was still particularly interested in the work of the Army Medical Corps and in the hospital arrangements for soldiers. In 1858 she published an eight-hundred-page report entitled *Notes on Matters affecting the Health, Efficiency, and Hospital Administration of the British Army,* which formed the basis of the work of the royal commission appointed to inquire into health in the army.

Florence Nightingale would have liked to go out to India during the Mutiny, but she was not asked. She took a deep interest in the sanitary and health measures adopted in India, and was in constant communication with the Secretary of State for India and with high officials in India on these matters.

Her active days were now over, but she had lived to see hospital reform and the establishment of nursing as an honourable profession effected, through her pioneering work, not only in England, but the world over. She had been received by and was a friend of the queen, who had personally rewarded her for her devotion to duty.

In 1907, she was given the Order of Merit, being the first woman to receive so high an honour, and, in the next year, the Freedom of the City of London was bestowed upon her. She was then approaching ninety years of age; her memory and eyesight were failing, and it is not known whether the old lady fully understood or appreciated the meaning of the honours and their significance. But before her death, which took place on August 13, 1910, Florence Nightingale had the highest satisfaction of knowing that her work had been accomplished; that which she set out to do she had done.

The answer to her agonized question: "What is to become of me?" may be found in the words of Lord Stanley who, in a memorable eulogy of the Lady of the Lamp, said: "I know no person besides Miss Nightingale who, within the past hundred years within this island, or perhaps in Europe, has voluntarily encountered dangers so imminent, and undertaken offices so repulsive, working for a large and worthy object, in a pure spirit of duty towards God and compassion for man."

DISCOVERERS AND EXPLORERS

MARCO POLO

(1254–1324)

"In Xanadu did Kubla Khan
A stately pleasure dome decree . . ."
sang Coleridge, and the splendour of the Great Khan's court which he celebrates seems to us like that of a fairy tale. And so, too, it must have seemed a fantastic dream to Europeans of the Middle Ages, when they heard of the magnificence and the might of the Mongolian emperor in his far city of Peking. But it was no dream to Marco Polo and his father and uncle, who faced stern realities enough in their journey from Venice to China and back. In the thirteenth century they crossed the entire continent of Asia and travelled through country that no white man had ever seen, or saw again for more than five centuries after their passage.

IN the year 1295 three weary and travel-stained men arrived in Venice. They made their way to the Parish of St. John Chrysostom and halted before the door of a great mansion. "We have come home at last," they said when the door was opened.

The inhabitants of the house stared at the travellers, whose clothes were of outlandish appearance, besides being ragged and worn. Then they asked, "Who are you?" "Our name is Polo. We have just come out of the East." The Polos in the family mansion stared again. They had heard how the two brothers, Nicolo and Maffeo Polo, and Nicolo's son, Marco, had sailed away to the almost mythical land of Cathay; but that had been twenty-four years ago, and they had been presumed long dead.

But the travellers earnestly repeated their assurances and at last convinced their relatives that they were the long lost Polos. As soon as Nicolo, Maffeo and Marco had settled down in their old home, they issued an invitation to all members of their family and to friends to a banquet. The board was sumptuously set, and the three hosts were dressed in magnificent robes of crimson satin. When the guests were seated, they stripped off their satin robes and assumed others of crimson damask, giving orders that the discarded satin ones should be cut up and divided amongst the servants. Halfway through the meal the Polos again left their guests and changed into crimson velvet, and again they presented the cast-off robes to the servants. After the meal they changed the velvet robes for ordinary clothes, and then came the explanation of their display of wealth which had dazzled the banqueters: the three had come home dressed like beggars, and now they were entertaining like millionaires. . . .

Marco brought in the filthy old clothes in which they had arrived after their long and perilous journey. Then he and Nicolo and Maffeo slit open the seams and from the linings there poured a glittering stream of jewels—a hoard of wealth that staggered even the men of wealthy Venice: that was the legacy of their long journey.

Or rather one legacy. For the tale of their travels is one of the most stirring of all chronicles, and it gave Europe new knowledge and new outlook beyond the boundaries of its own narrow world.

The Polos did not talk a great deal of the wonders they had seen. Nevertheless, their fame spread, the story of their wealth became known, and men asked them questions about the Far East. Most of the stay-at-homes looked askance at the travellers' tales. They could not swallow the stories that Marco told about the vastness and wealth of China, and he was lost for words in describing them. He nearly always had recourse to the word "millions" in talking of the miles they had travelled, the multitudes they had seen, the wealth, power and wonder of the mighty Mongolian Empire, with the result that he was nicknamed Messer Marco Millioni, or Master Marco Millions.

But Marco Polo was not the kind of man to sit at home and talk. Three years after his return, the rivalry between Venice and Genoa came to a head. Marco Polo joined the Venetian fleet as gentleman-commander of his own war galley, and he fought at the decisive battle off Curzola Island. The Genoese were victorious and Marco Polo was taken prisoner. Another prisoner was "a respectable literary hack" named Rusticiano, of Pisa, and Marco wiled away his captivity by dictating the story of his travels to him. Thus the world came at last to hear of the wanderings of the Polos into the unknown East, to hear the story of the courage and perseverance of three white men who had walked right off the map.

And what a story it was! As far back as 1260, when Marco was a boy of six, Nicolo and Maffeo, who were merchants in partnership together at Constantinople, had made trading journeys to the Crimea and thence far eastwards to Bokhara. And there they fell in with envoys of the great Kublai Khan, chief of the mighty Mongolian empire that reached from China to the boundaries of Europe. The envoys were returning from their mission, and the adventurous Polos joined them and accompanied them to the imperial court.

The Great Khan had never set eyes upon a European, and he received Nicolo and Maffeo with delight. When they set out to return home, he gave them letters to the pope, asking that a hundred educated men should be sent out to teach his people Christianity and the liberal arts.

The Polos made the long journey back in safety and arrived at Acre in 1269. But they found that no new pope had been appointed after the death of Clement IV, and so they went home to Venice.

For two years they waited, and then, when there was no sign of the papal interregnum coming to an end, they once more set out for the East, taking with them this time Nicolo's seventeen-year-old son, Marco. They had no sooner started than they heard that a new pope had been elected, and so they turned back to carry out their promise to Kublai. Gregory X received the Great Khan's message with enthusiasm, but his enthusiasm was not translated into action. Instead of the hundred missionaries that had been requested, he dispatched only two Dominicans, who soon became disheartened by the length of the journey and the warlike state of the countries through which they had to pass, and turned back. It was a golden opportunity lost, for only when the pope had failed him did Kublai Khan turn to Buddhism as a civilizing influence for his subjects.

But the Polos had executed their commission and delivered the khan's letter. (It was a characteristic of these three remarkable Venetians that they did what they undertook to do in the face of dangers known and unknown.) They now set out for the second time, and left Acre in 1271.

They made their way from Italy to Hormuz, at the mouth of the Persian Gulf, whence they intended to sail to China. But they abandoned the idea of proceeding by sea and turned northwards through Persia to Kerman, through Khurasan to Balkh, "in Tartary," now Afghanistan. After a rest at Balkh, they turned eastwards to Badakshan and then ascended the upper Oxus through Wakhan to the plateau of Pamir.

Pamir is a name that occurs for the first time in Europe in Marco Polo's book, but to emphasize the daring and the pioneering spirit of the Polos it is necessary to mention that the journey they had made to the Pamir plateau was through country hardly known to another European until Lieutenant John Wood's expedition in 1838!

They descended from Pamir towards the south-east, passing through Kashgar and Yarkand to Khotan. No European passed that way again until after 1860!

From Khotan they made north-eastwards to Lob Nor. The Polos

were pioneers of exploration indeed. The next visitor from the West was Prjevalsky, the Russian traveller, who reached Lob Nor in 1871.

Now they entered the vast Desert of Gobi. They were well aware of the dangers ahead, but they provided for them with foresight and their own courage, for they made the crossing safely. Says Marco in his book:—

"Merchants who desire to pass over the desert cause all necessaries to be provided for them. And when victuals begin to fail in the desert they kill the asses and camels and eat them. They most willingly use camels because they are sustained with little meat, and bear great burdens. They must provide victuals for a month to cross it overthwart; for to go through the length would ask a year's time. . . . In it are neither beasts nor birds. They say that there dwell many spirits, which cause great and marvellous illusions to travellers to make them perish. . . . They go, therefore, near together, hang bells on their beasts' necks, and set marks if any stay."

So, at long last, the Polos came to the north-western boundaries of China, and in 1275, after a journey lasting three and a half years, they reached Shang-tu, the summer city of the Great Khan.

Kublai greeted them with pleasure and honour, well pleased with the messages from the pope (although they brought no friars) and with the oil from the Sepulchre.

"Who is this?" he asked when his eyes fell on Marco, who by now was a fine young man of about one-and-twenty.

"Sire," answered Nicolo Polo, "'tis my son and your liegeman."

"Welcome is he, too," then quoth the Great Khan.

A splendid feast was celebrated in their honour, and there they stayed at Kublai's court.

Marco quickly adapted himself to his new surroundings. He learned the language of the khan's people and entered the public service. Soon he was appointed a second-class commissioner or agent to the imperial council and began to be employed on public missions.

Unlike the average envoy of the Great Khan, young Marco Polo was a man of acute observation and he was interested in all he saw. He made notes on his travels, and when he returned to the court, instead of giving a formal report of official business done, he would entertain the khan with his accounts of the tribes he had met and other happenings on which he had chanced. The khan was delighted, and he advanced Marco rapidly in the public service.

In his work for Kublai, Marco Polo travelled all through the provinces of Shansi, Shensi and Szechuen. He went westwards to the boundaries of Tibet and southwards to the remote province of Yunnan and to North Burma.

The commissions that he was given became of increasing importance, and at last he was made Governor of Yangehow, a position he held for three years. Then once more he was sent far and wide in the imperial service: east to Kangchow, north through the Gobi Desert to Karakorum, south to Cochin China, and even across the seas to Southern India.

We hear little of his father and uncle all this time, but they assisted Kublai in the capture of Siang-yang on the Han River, inventing powerful new engines of war for the purpose.

By now the Polos were rich, but they were homesick. Moreover, the Great Khan was growing old, and they were fearful of their position should their friend and protector die . . . and Venice was a long way away. But Kublai would not hear of their departure, and every time they suggested it he positively refused to let them go.

At last, after they had spent seventeen years in China, there came an unexpected opportunity for their departure. In 1286, the favourite wife of Arghun, Khan of Persia, and grand-nephew of Kublai, had died: her dying request was that a girl of her own Mongolian tribe should take her place. So three ambassadors made the journey from Persia to Peking, the imperial city of the Great Khan. (It had, Marco tells us, four walls, each six miles long, and twelve gates: "At each gate a thousand men keep guard, not from dread of enemies, but in reverence of the monarch who dwells within it, and to prevent injury by robbers.") The ambassadors made known their business, a seventeen-year-old maiden named Kukachin was chosen, and the party prepared to return to Persia.

But the overland route, difficult and long by nature, was now made more dangerous by war, and so the ambassadors decided to return by sea. They had met the Polos at the imperial court and, knowing them to be experienced travellers, begged for their company.

Kublai Khan fitted out a magnificent expedition, loaded the Polos with jewels as parting gifts, and gave them letters bearing friendly messages to the pope and the kings of France, Spain and England. In 1292, they sailed from the harbour of Amoy in Fu-kien with a fleet of fourteen four-masted junks, each manned by two hundred and fifty seamen.

It took them three months to reach Java, and then they were delayed by storms for five months off the coast of Sumatra. They met with further delays off Ceylon, and it was only after a voyage of over two years that they arrived at length in Tabriz.

On the way two out of the three ambassadors had died, and so had most of their suite; but the hardy Polos and their young charge, Kukachin, who had come to regard them with filial affection, turned up safe and sound. Once again the Polos had executed their commission.

They found that Arghun Khan had died before they had left China, and his brother was reigning in his stead. The new khan's son, Ghazan, put a satisfactory conclusion to the embassy by marrying the girl, and the Polos turned their steps homeward. From Tabriz they made for Trebizond, thence to Constantinople, and so to Venice.

That was the substance of the wonderful tale that Marco Polo dictated to Rusticiano, of Pisa. It soon passed the time of his captivity, for in 1299 Marco was liberated and he returned to Venice. We know little more of him. He married a wife called Donata, and by her had three daughters, Fantina, Bellela, and Moreta. On January 9, 1324, he sent for a priest and for a lawyer to make his will, and on that day he died.

The greatly improved maps and charts of the fourteenth century and the direct trading contacts made between Europe and the Far East, were the immediate result of Marco Polo's work. He had brought to men a wide store of new knowledge about the world in which they lived, he had broadened their conceptions of the earth, he had inspired others with the desire to travel and explore. . . Among the books of Columbus, who went into the unknown to discover the New World, was a well-thumbed and annotated copy of Marco Polo's story of the men who went into the unknown to discover the Old.

COLUMBUS

(1451–1506)

Every schoolboy knows that Christopher Columbus "discovered America." And that is often the full meed of acquaintance made with the story of this strange, fearless adventurer, who, with his head stuffed full of travellers' tales, legends and madcap fancies, sailed with three tiny ships and a crew of ruffians across the unknown wastes of the Atlantic. It is a chequered story of courage and brutality, of mismanagement and misfortune, of faith, determination and magnificent achievement.

SHORTLY after midnight on October 12, 1492, a sailor in the crew of the caravel, *Pinta,* sailing westwards across the Atlantic, saw ahead of him, by the light of the moon, a long tongue of sand. He fired a cannon shot and cried out that land was in sight at last. Some days earlier this cry had been a familiar one, for, tempted by the reward offered by the admiral to the man who should first see land, the sailors had yielded to the illusion of sea and weather, and every low-lying cloud near the horizon was heralded with shouts of enthusiasm. This state of affairs had at length so infuriated Columbus that he prescribed heavy penalties for any future false alarms, and a measure of caution had been introduced.

Consequently, when the look-out raised his joyous shout, the crews of the three ships shook off the lethargy that had begun to possess them, and swarmed on deck breathless with expectation. Their hopes were realized: it was really land. And on Friday morning, October 12, Christopher Columbus, bearing the Royal Standard of Castile and Aragon, with his captains, Martin Alonso Pinzon and Vicente Yañez Pinzon, each with a banner of the Green Cross, set foot on an island which Columbus named San Salvador and is now called Watling Island. The first step in the discovery of the New World had been accomplished.

Attempts have been made recently to deprive Columbus of all the credit for his great discovery. It is said that the real leader of the expedition was Martin Alonso Pinzon, that Columbus was an ignorant adventurer with no knowledge of navigation, that he was in search of purely legendary islands, and obstinately refused to realize the real nature of the land reached.

That he was not the first explorer from Europe to arrive in America is true, for the continent was known to Norwegian navigators nearly five centuries before, and Columbus did not reach the mainland till 1498, a year after John Cabot, a Genoese in English pay. It is likewise true that he had stuffed his mind with all kinds of legends concerning the East and the Atlantic, and with a natural inclination towards the fantastic, had swallowed stories which were unhesitatingly classed as fables by the more sober-minded of his contemporaries. He died believing that he had found the western route to Asia. None of these facts affects the essential points, that Columbus was the first in modern times to brave and achieve the crossing of the unknown Atlantic, and that from this stupendous feat all further discoveries in that direction developed.

The events that led up to the landing on San Salvador on that bright October morning in 1492 comprise the efforts of several weary years to gain a hearing for Columbus's plan, with many disappointments and renewed hopes, and trampings from country to country and from monarch to monarch as his prospects seemed to change, or as new ideas came into his head.

His origin is uncertain. He is believed to have been a Genoese, the son of Domenico Colombo, a weaver, and to have been born about 1451. When he rose to fame and power, he claimed illustrious descent, but there is no reason to suppose that this was anything but a figment of his imagination; " window dressing " we should term it. As a youth, he probably assisted his father in his trade, but it was not long before he took to the sea.

The stories of the voyages of his early years we have only on his own authority, and Columbus was not always strictly truthful when recounting his own achievements. Thus, his claim to have visited Iceland about 1477 is generally rejected. Nevertheless, we may believe him when he tells us that he travelled extensively during this period, and that England was among the more remote places that he visited.

About 1478, he was in Lisbon, and it was here that he married a woman of rank named Felipa Moñiz de Perestrello. Here Columbus's history really begins, for at this time undoubtedly he began to fill his mind with visions of such a voyage of exploration as never man had accomplished before, a voyage that would bring him fortune and fame through all the world, that would be a source of wealth and glory undreamed of to whatever sovereign was far-sighted enough to offer him his patronage.

Felipa was the daughter of Bartholomew Perestrello, who had been a captain in the service of Henry the Navigator, the prince who had been the moving spirit and the inspiration behind the development of the great Portuguese empire overseas.

It was a period when men's imaginations ran hot in speculation as to the mysterious and unexplored portions of the earth's surface. The invention of the compass had made it possible to fit out expeditions of exploration with some hope of a safe return, and the Portuguese had become the pioneers of travel into strange and perilous seas. The stories brought back by the early navigators, soon magnified into fantastic legends, inflamed the minds of sailors, and roused the spirit of adventure to such a pitch as had never been known before. Far out in the Atlantic had been found the body of a man not belonging to any known race; strange pieces of carved wood and reeds of immense size, and gigantic trunks of pine trees of a kind that did not grow in any European land had been picked up. The Islands of the Seven Cities, where it was said that seven bishops from Spain had in the dim past established their sees, but which had never been visited since, were sighted; the floating island of St. Brendan, with its lofty mountains and deep valleys, bewildered voyagers by appearing now here and now there and ever eluding the most skilled and the most venturesome. Above all, there was the vast and mysterious island of Antilia, in the existence of which even hardened sceptics found it difficult to disbelieve.

The stories of the far distant East were even more magnificent. Marco Polo had told of the fabulous wealth of the Great Khan of Cathay (China) and of the huge and remote island of Cipangu (Japan), where the houses were roofed with gold. And somewhere in the far domains of Asia or Africa was the realm of Prester John, the mysterious potentate whose fame filled three centuries, and who was believed to rule a mighty Christian empire richer than any known to history.

Columbus devoured all these tales with the ardour of his nature. He was at once a visionary and a man of action, and there is not the slightest doubt that he fervently believed most of the wild tales of the day. And so he came to conceive his great project. He would sail west into the Atlantic until he came to India, exploring the ocean islands, and particularly Antilia, on the way; he would convert new nations to the glory of God and the Catholic faith; he would join forces with Prester John, and unite East and West; finally, with the wealth and strength he had accumulated, and with the alliance of the great Eastern prince, he would fulfil the dream of every true

Christian, and rescue the Holy Sepulchre from the power of the infidel.

Such were the dreams of Columbus. How could he make them realities? Here his difficulties began. To fit out such a voyage he must have a royal patron, and it was not easy to find one who would, in the midst of the political uncertainty of the end of the fifteenth century, willingly finance an unknown adventurer in a seemingly fantastic expedition. Moreover, his demands were almost incredible. Perhaps because he had such great faith in himself. He asked to be granted the rank of admiral, to be viceroy of all he should discover, and to be entitled to a tenth share of all precious metals discovered within his sphere of operations. The daring of the grasping company promoter of a later age is cowardice when compared to the exacting terms of Columbus.

First he tried John II of Portugal. The king was interested, but the mission was unsuccessful. After various attempts, with the help of Juan Perez, the Franciscan prior of La Rabïda, and of the Count of Medina Celi, Columbus then obtained an interview with the joint sovereigns of Spain, Ferdinand of Aragon and Isabella of Castile.

But Ferdinand and Isabella were involved in their Moorish wars in Granada, and had no money to venture on speculative voyages in the Atlantic. Moreover, advisers to whom his scheme was submitted pronounced it impracticable. Once again he had failed, and he next sent his brother Bartholomew to England to try to interest Henry VII, while he himself set out for France. But at the last moment he was recalled, and Isabella announced that she would grant him an interview. In January, 1492, Granada surrendered, and on the 17th of the following April the agreement between Columbus and their Catholic Majesties was sealed.

He had been for ten years attempting to secure a patron. Execrations have been poured forth on the shortsightedness and the parsimony of those who would not support him, but when we consider the extravagance of his demands, and the apparent impossibility of the feat he proposed to accomplish, the wonder is that he succeeded at all. The solution lies in the character of Isabella the Catholic. Mother of Catherine of Aragon, and grandmother of Mary Tudor, she was the noblest of a race the peculiar glory of which was the number of great-hearted women it produced. The gift of statesmanship and a devout religious fervour were alike hers, and she alone saw the possibilities of Columbus's plan. Above all, she was determined not to miss such a glorious chance of converting vast numbers of heathen souls to the true faith.

Columbus's troubles were not yet over. The town of Palos was ordered to provide him two ships, but even when an indemnity was offered to criminals who would accompany him, he found it almost impossible to get a crew together. At length, however, with the assistance of the influential brothers Pinzon, he succeeded in his efforts, and on August 3 with a mixed band of cut-throats, adventurers and genuine sailors, numbering eighty-seven in all, he set sail from Palos with three small vessels, the *Santa Maria* (100 tons) and the caravels *Pinta* (50 tons) and *Niña* (40 tons), the last two only partly decked and commanded by the brothers Pinzon.

None of the portraits of Columbus was painted from life, but Las Casas has left us a delightful literary miniature of his shipmate's appearance. "The admiral," he writes, "was a man of sturdy stature, rather above the average height, of a very ruddy complexion, with freckles and red hair when he was young. The latter soon turned white, which was also the colour of his beard."

It was not long before trouble began to arise among the crews of the three ships. The fear of the unknown took possession of them, and when days and weeks went by with no sign of land, there was danger of mutiny. But Columbus retained control of the situation and at last, on October 12, giving thanks to God, kneeling on the shore of San Salvador, and kissing the ground for joy, he took possession of the island in the name of their Catholic Majesties.

The main interest of Columbus's first and greatest voyage lies in his dealings with the natives. He was lyrical in his enthusiasm for their way of life. He found them, he tells us, gentle and peaceful, without a trace of malice, and hospitable and kind to those with whom they came in contact. He was later to find that he had somewhat idealized them, but in these early days there is no doubt that on both sides relations were astonishingly cordial. Columbus gave strict orders that the natives were to be treated with all kindness, and his men were effectively restrained from the excesses which afterwards ruined the fame of their leader. No marauding was allowed, and for all gifts accepted from the natives, trinkets, toys, or other presents were given in exchange.

Consequently, Columbus was enabled to continue his voyage in peace, unhampered by the bloodshed usually inseparable from the expeditions of the early explorers. He cruised the Bahamas and, among others, discovered Cuba, which he thought to be the mainland. Here, at last, he believed, he had found the Asiatic continent, or at least the great island of Cipangu. Here at last he would find wealth immeasurable.

From now on Columbus was continually searching for the country of his dreams, the country where the precious metal was so plentiful that all he would have to do would be to load his ships and carry it home. But gold in any quantity was always just beyond his reach. He could not understand the native language, but his fertile imagination persuaded him that always they were telling him of some vast and wealthy district further on, where the Great Khan reigned, and where the streets were paved with the glittering stuff. To the end of his life he believed that if he could but penetrate a little further, he would accomplish his great design.

The final stage of the first voyage was the discovery of Hispaniola (Haiti, or San Domingo). Here the *Santa Maria* went aground and had to be abandoned, and Columbus decided to return home in the *Niña*. He left a colony of forty-two Europeans on the island and, taking with him half a dozen natives for baptism and as evidence, set out for Spain.

His royal patrons received him with the utmost magnificence. He was the idol of the moment, and the natives in his train, the parrots, the unknown animals and strange fruit he brought with him excited wonder wherever he went. "Some days have now gone by," runs a contemporary letter, "since there came from the Antipodes a certain Christopher Columbus, a Genoese, who had obtained at great pains, from my sovereigns, three ships, in order to risk this expedition. It was deemed, in truth, that his projects were chimerical. He is, however, returned, bringing with him precious merchandise, and, above all, gold which is gathered naturally in those parts. These things are the proof that he has made this voyage."

The pope granted bulls confirming to the Spanish crown all the lands newly discovered, and a second and far greater expedition was planned by Ferdinand and Isabella. It sailed on September 25, 1493. But the history of Columbus's glory ends with his return from the first voyage. From now on he had his great moments. But his main work was done and the rest was comparative failure. It was not, primarily at any rate, his fault. When he reached Hispaniola, he found that his colony had been massacred, and from then on the peaceful tradition of the first voyage was no more than a memory. The colonists were grasping, licentious and cruel; the rabble collected from the Spanish ports let loose in an unhealthy climate among an uncivilized people indulged in all manner of excesses. The new colony which Columbus established at Isabella Island was to be the bane of his life.

It was in February, 1494, that Columbus, having failed repeatedly in his search for the gold country, though he had always succeeded in obtaining certain quantities of the metal, decided to establish the slave trade. This was the beginning of his fall. Slavery, of course, flourished in Europe already, and was not universally condemned in itself, while Columbus's calculation that any cruelty inflicted would be counter-balanced by the conversion of the slaves to Christianity was merely an example of the current notion that a man's soul is of more value than his liberty. But Columbus was not a merciful man, and his dealings in this matter aroused the disgust of people not accustomed to be squeamish. He sent home shiploads of women and children to a climate to which they were unused, and they died by hundreds, while he represented to his sovereigns that only prisoners of war, and those the dreaded Carib cannibals, were being enslaved. Moreover, though many approved of slavery, such a one was not Isabella, and from this moment Columbus's favour at court began to wane.

Columbus resumed his exploration of the Cuban coast on this expedition and he discovered Dominica and Porto Rico as well as sighting many other islands. But at last his health gave way, and he was carried back to his base at Isabella unconscious. His boundless energy had led to his undoing, and he was not expected to recover. When he did so, it was to find that a commissioner from Isabella, Juan Aguado, had been sent to inquire into his administration. Finding himself in the position of a suspected criminal, he sailed for home. He reached Cadiz in June, 1496, and no doubt to his astonishment was cordially received by Ferdinand and Isabella. The title of duke was even suggested. His reputation was restored, and he was given permission to equip a third expedition.

But Columbus's star was setting. The colonists were becoming unmanageable, the natives were treated barbarously, and revolt and conspiracy were rife. Moreover, as time went on, Columbus himself became more haughty and more cruel, and Hispaniola became a place of bloodshed and brutality. Isabella heard stories of the misgovernment, and in 1500 Columbus, who had meanwhile discovered Trinidad and the mainland of South America, arrived home from his third voyage in chains, while a new governor was left at Hispaniola.

Once again he was restored to favour, though not to his former office. He was allowed to undertake a fourth voyage only on condition that he did not visit Hispaniola. His spirit was undaunted and, ill though he was, he set his heart on penetrating still further west.

There is little of interest to record of this last voyage. He cruised among the West Indies, and spent some time in Jamaica. His crew was decimated by disease, there was much discontent and much trouble with the natives. At length, after two dismal years, he returned to Spain, broken in health, discredited and almost forgotten.

He died in 1506, in a plain little house in a quiet street in Valladolid. His last two years were spent in an atmosphere of anxiety and disappointment, but he never sank into poverty, and he was never completely disgraced. He had risen from an obscure origin to wealth and fame, and he had brought glory to Spain, but he suffered less than many adventurers who put their trust in princes.

His discoveries have placed Christopher Columbus in the front rank of explorers. He found the New World and brought knowledge of it to the Old. Even a brief list of his chief discoveries is a token of his worth. On his first voyage he found Santa Maria de la Conception (Rum Key), San Salvador (Watling I.), Isabella (Crooked I.), Long Island, Cuba and Haiti; on his second, Dominica, Porto Rico, Guadaloupe, Antigua, Santa Cruz and the Virgin Islands; while on the third he sailed to Trinidad and actually came upon the continental coast of South America near the mouth of the Orinoco. His fame is secure—and the West Indies are his lasting memorial.

SIR WALTER RALEIGH

(*c.* 1552–1618)

Sir Walter Raleigh. The name conjures up the hero of the heroic age of England, the romantic, piratic, adventurous, fighting sailor, who was courtier, scholar, poet, historian, soldier, navigator, explorer. A self-seeking careerist and favourite of the queen, yet a man who poured out his own fortunes for a dream of empire: an adventurer, but a man that all England admired and whom the sailors of Devon worshipped. A man of lion-heart, of wit, of nerves, who courted life with courage and faced death with a smile: the hero of the heroic age of England. Sir Walter Raleigh.

"WHERE shall we find another such head to cut off?"

This cry was wrung from one of the spectators of the execution of Sir Walter Raleigh in Old Palace Yard on October 29, 1618. It sums up the opinion of many contemporaries and admirers of this brilliant and many-sided man. Few men played so many parts on the vast Elizabethan stage. He was at once soldier and navigator, poet and historian. At one moment he was dandy and courtier at one of the most brilliant courts in Europe; at the next he was pushing his way at the head of a small, ragged band through trackless wildernesses infested with savages. Honoured and caressed by one of the greatest monarchs who ever sat on the English throne, he was first imprisoned and then put to a shameful death by her morally-degenerate successor. In his life a good deal of an adventurer and a pirate, he died like a hero.

Like other seamen of the Elizabethan period, Raleigh was born in Devonshire, at Hayes Barton, the son of a country squire. The elder Raleigh, also called Walter, was not wealthy, but he contrived to give his son a good education, and sent him to Oxford. Here, his contemporaries at Oriel relate that he was a brilliant scholar, but often in great straits for money. After this the history of his early years becomes rather obscure. It is known that he was in France during the Huguenot wars, being present at the battles of Jarnac and Moncontour, and it is also probable that he fought in the Netherlands with the Dutch against Spain. In London again, he took up his residence in the Temple, and began to study law in a desultory way; but it was under his kinsman by marriage, Sir Humphrey Gilbert, that he began his real career.

Elizabeth, after much petitioning and urging, granted to Gilbert a patent to discover "remote, heathen, and barbarous lands, not actually possessed of any Christian prince or people," with this right, not only to discover but to colonize. Raleigh sailed with his half-brother, some say in command of one of the smaller vessels of the fleet. The expedition was a failure. Gales and scurvy did nearly as much harm as the everlasting quarrels between the various captains; and some Spanish ships of war made an end of the miserable story by falling on the English flotilla off Cape Verde and dispersing it.

His hopes crushed in this direction, Gilbert turned to Ireland, still in active revolt against the English power, and Raleigh went with him. Of his exploits in Ireland we may say that he was, to the full, as ruthless and bloodthirsty as any of the other English commanders. Stern measures were necessary in dealing with the Irish kerns, savage, treacherous, and skilled in elusive guerrilla warfare; but Raleigh's action in dealing with the surrendered garrison of Fort-de-Ore is not in accordance with any code of civilized conflict. The surrender having been made, Lord Grey, the commander of the English forces, sent into the fort Captains Raleigh and Mackworth with instructions to put the garrison to the sword. The garrison included a Spanish force; but the only difference which Raleigh and Mackworth made between the two sections of the enemy was to slaughter the Spaniards on the spot and hang the Irish afterwards. The few persons who escaped this revolting massacre were certain high officers whom Lord Grey held for ransom. A more creditable exploit of Raleigh's in Ireland was his taking Lord Roche out of his own strongly garrisoned castle, and conveying him prisoner to Cork, the twenty-mile march back being made at dead of night in pouring rain through a hostile country.

Raleigh was not happy in his Irish service, and several times asked to be relieved. So it was with a joyful heart that he returned to London, in 1581, the bearer of dispatches touching the rebellion, to be laid before the queen in council. The tall, handsome young soldier, with his dandified air and his caressing manner, at once attracted Elizabeth's attention, and this was the beginning of Raleigh's rise.

There is a well-known story of Raleigh flinging his handsome cloak down in a muddy puddle that the queen might pass dryshod, thus bringing on himself her favourable notice. There is no historical

A painting (*above*) depicting the tragic murder of the great explorer and navigator, Captain James Cook, by natives of the Hawaiian Islands in 1799.

The most famous meeting in the history of exploration took place between Dr. Livingstone and H. M. Stanley at Ujiji, Lake Tanganyika, in 1871 (*below*).

Captain Scott's journey to the South Pole constitutes one of the great epic events of British exploration. (*Above*) Scott writing in his diary during the fatal expedition.

Alexander the Great, King of Macedon, undoubtedly one of the greatest leaders of all time, is shown (*below*) in the battle of Issus against Darius of Persia in 333 B.C.

evidence for this, but the son of Devon was in no need of such theatrical tricks to advance his fortunes. His own subtle brain and invincible determination to succeed and win for himself riches, honours, and fame, were his best helpers. In a later age, Raleigh would have been called a "careerist." He meant to be a "somebody," and he wrought so well in his efforts to raise himself that very soon he was first favourite with the queen.

She showered benefits on him. He was made Captain of the Guard, created a knight, granted Durham House in the Strand, formerly a bishop's palace, and came into possession of forty thousand acres in Ireland, besides an estate in Dorset. He was also granted the privilege of exporting certain cloths and of selling wines throughout the realm. These concessions brought him in much money, and added to his importance, with the inevitable result of causing much envy and jealousy among his compeers.

And now came one of Raleigh's most far-sighted ventures, and one of his most glorious failures. In 1584, after the death of Sir Humphrey Gilbert, Raleigh applied to the queen for a patent similar to that his kinsman had held, and one was granted "to discover new lands, take possession of them in the name of the queen, and to hold them for six years." An expedition, planned and financed by Raleigh, and headed by two of his trusted friends, Philip Amadas and Arthur Barlowe, was sent to America. They sent back enthusiastic reports both of the country and of the natives.

They reported to Raleigh that "a more kind and loving people than the Virginians is not to be found in the whole world," and that the land itself was "the paradise of the world." They brought back several novelties in the way of plants and foodstuffs. Cotton they called "grass silk," and described it as a kind of grass on whose blades grew a thin, glittering skin that could be stripped off and used like silk. Potatoes they called *Pater nostri,* because they grew in ropes, like chaplet-beads. There was also, they said, a herb which the natives called *uppowoc,* but which was known to the Spaniards in the West Indies under the name of *tabacco.* The Indians dried the leaves, pulverized them, and inhaled the smoke of the powder through long clay pipes. This *tabacco* the natives used as incense is used in Catholic churches; some was sprinkled on the holy fire on the occasion of a sacrifice, and a handful was thrown to the winds when a new fishtrap was to be dedicated. The sailors brought samples of the powder back to England. They found it efficacious as an aperient; doctors recommended it; and Raleigh was able to astonish Elizabeth's court with the sight of a smoking pipe.

The natural wealth of the country was immense, the soil yielding three harvests a year by merely scratching the ground. The captains, however, had to confess to one great disappointment. Both pearl and copper were known to the savages, although the copper mines and oyster beds had yet to be discovered. But of gold there was not a sign.

After staying only a few weeks, the ships left Virginia, arriving in England towards the middle of September. They brought with them two natives, Wanchese and Manteo.

These reports made Raleigh feel justified in sending another expedition to colonize the new territory of Virginia, named after the queen.

In the following year he sent his cousin, Sir Richard Grenville, with the first colonists. But the experiment was doomed to failure. The colonists became frightened and discouraged in the vast, wild and lonely land. Some made their way back to England, others were slain by Indians, while yet others wandered off into the trackless forests and disappeared. Raleigh made several attempts to establish the colony, pouring out thousands of pounds of his own money on successive ventures. But a few years convinced him that his great and courageous attempt to found an empire was premature. One good result came of the Virginia failure; it introduced tobacco and potatoes into England. Other men were to carry the Virginian idea to success, but it sprang originally from the brain of Raleigh.

Raleigh then became active in organizing and financing the English raids on Spanish commerce. Such able and formidable sea-rovers as Frobisher, Grenville and Cumberland were in actual command of the expeditions, and Raleigh burned to join them. Elizabeth, in spite of all his entreaties, would not allow him to leave England for some time; but eventually—the handsome young Earl of Essex had attracted the queen's notice in the meantime—he was placed in command of a large fleet, formed and financed partly by himself, partly by Elizabeth, partly by some London merchants, and partly by Cumberland.

The enterprise was more successful than its promoters had ever hoped, and enormously rich were the prizes that fell into the hands of the buccaneers. Raleigh, however, was not present at these remunerative captures, for he had been recalled by the queen. While his officers and men were rejoicing over the capture of the huge *Madre de Dios* with its cargo of treasure, Sir Walter was being committed to the Tower. Elizabeth had discovered him in a love affair with Bessie Throgmorton, one of her maids-of-honour, and this was an affront which the imperious daughter of Henry VIII could not overlook. Both the maid and her seducer were imprisoned, and Raleigh's submissive appeals to the queen fell on deaf ears.

However, Elizabeth was forced to release him at last, for only he could control the sturdy men of Devon, who were disputing violently over the *Madre de Dios* prize money. Raleigh rapidly settled the situation, and the queen, mollified, perhaps, by her own large share of the spoils, gave him his freedom. But he could not regain her favour, so he married Bessie Throgmorton and retired to semi-exile in his house at Sherborne.

Yet London soon saw him again, not as Raleigh the courtier, but as Raleigh the scholar and scientist. He was interested in literature and gave much advice to Richard Hakluyt, who was then preparing his famous *Voyages*. During his sojourn in Ireland, after the rise of Essex in 1588 had eclipsed his position at court, he had cultivated the friendship of Spenser. Now, in London, he became the centre of an intellectual and scientific circle. The group was suspected of atheism, and one of them, Christopher Marlowe, the dramatist, was openly accused of this crime just before his death.

Now he conceived his great plan for the penetration of Guiana, then a remote and mysterious region reported to be teeming with treasure of all kinds. His ambitious spirit felt keenly his fall from his position at court, and he desired to retrieve his reputation with the queen. Also his patriotism glowed at the thought of carrying the English flag into South America, for, self-seeking and personally ambitious as he was, he had his country's interests at heart.

The commission eventually granted by Elizabeth contained the usual warning against violating the territory of any Christian monarch, and in the early part of 1595 the fleet set sail. After much misery and suffering, with brighter intervals when they were hospitably entertained by native chiefs, the expedition reached a region which certain indications promised to be rich in gold. Satisfied with that, and bearing in mind that he had but inadequate resources, Raleigh resolved to return to England, relate what he had seen and discovered, and obtain permission to lead a larger and better equipped expedition later on. On his return he wrote his *Discovery of the Large, Rich and Beautiful Empire of Guiana,* which remains one of the best travel books ever composed.

To the end of his life Raleigh retained his belief in the riches of Guiana, now called Venezuela, and in the great gold mines of Manoa, the Eldorado of the Spaniards. And there is no doubt that the mines were there: the quartz that his expedition brought home was rich in gold. He brought, too, from this venture, the first mahogany to England.

But his next work was to be the moving spirit in an action directed against Spain. In 1596 a great fleet was manned and fitted out, with the object of striking a blow at Cadiz, the principal port of Spain, sinking or capturing as many Spanish ships as possible, and, as fate might have it, obtaining treasure.

Admiral Lord Howard, the Earl of Essex, and Raleigh were named the principal naval commanders, with Sir Francis Were in command of the troops. The fleet consisted of one hundred and fifty vessels, manned by six thousand four hundred sailors and carrying about the same number of soldiers. The action was a brilliant success, the Spanish fleet being for the most part burnt or sunk, the town of Cadiz stormed, plundered, and afterwards laid in ashes as regards the larger part of it, and a ransom of 120,000 ducats exacted. Then the jubilant conquerors sailed home again, with Raleigh groaning in pain in his berth. During the naval action he had received a severe gunshot wound in the leg.

He was still compelled to walk with the aid of a staff when he was again engaged in fighting the Spaniards, but the long war was drawing to its inconclusive close. Philip was dead, and both countries were weary of the continual strife. Strictly speaking, victory rested with neither nation, but the power and prestige of England had been immensely strengthened.

Then followed years of tranquillity and useful activity in parliament and elsewhere for Raleigh, but his enemies were preparing his downfall. Cecil and Lord Henry Howard were among the most active, and in anticipation of the old queen's death were already in communication with her heir, James of Scotland. It was slowly and cunningly instilled into James's mind that Raleigh was a dangerous man, leader of a hostile faction favouring Arabella Stuart as Elizabeth's successor.

In 1603, within a short time of James's accession, Raleigh was cast into the Tower of London to await his trial on a charge of high treason. The trial was the merest parody of judicial proceedings. The accusation was false, most of the evidence perjured, and at least two of the judges were bitter enemies of Raleigh. Raleigh was sentenced to die the death of a traitor.

That sentence was not carried out, but held in abeyance. The unjustly condemned man was carried back to the Tower, where he remained for thirteen years, perpetually chafing against his loss of liberty, and addressing appeals and complaints to the king, Cecil, and various others. He occupied his time in making chemical experiments and in writing. Historical essays, discourses on war by land and sea, and political treaties flowed from his pen, and he also began his gigantic *History of the World*. He dedicated the work to Henry, Prince of Wales, who had an immense admiration for him. "Only my father could keep such a bird in a cage," exclaimed the generous prince on one occasion.

The book contains that celebrated passage which is constantly quoted to this day:

"O eloquent, just and mighty Death! Whom none could advise, thou has persuaded; what none hath dared, thou hast done, and whom all the world has flattered, thou only hast cast out of the world and despised. Thou hast drawn together all the far-stretched greatness, all the pride, cruelty, and ambition of man, and covered it all over with those two narrow words: *Hic Jacet!*"

It was with the magic word "Guiana" that Raleigh at last opened the doors of his prison. James was induced to release the illustrious captive (though not to pardon him outright) on condition that he sailed for El Dorado, there to do such things as might enrich his country both in gold and fame.

In May, 1617, seven ships of war and three pinnaces sailed out of Plymouth Harbour to the sound of drums. But Walter Raleigh did not know that his doom was already sealed. James, with incredible duplicity, had taken pains to inform the Spanish Ambassador in London of the object of Raleigh's expedition. The Spaniards in Guiana were more than likely to resist any attempt at trespass by gold-seeking adventurers from England.

As a matter of fact, that is what they did. There was a fight, Raleigh's son was killed, the weary and disheartened men mutinied, the second-in-command shot himself, and Raleigh returned home. He was at once arrested, and was told by Chief-Justice Montagu, in the King's Bench, that the fourteen-year-old sentence of death—which had never been commuted, but only suspended—would be carried out.

Raleigh went to his death with a stoic courage which is amazing. He gaily warned an acquaintance to come early so as to get a good place for the final scene. "As for myself," he said, "I am sure of one." Seeing an old man in the crowd with a bald head exposed to the bitter cold, he took off his own cap and threw it to him, saying: "Thou hast more need of this than I." Arrived on the scaffold, he took up the axe, and running his finger along the edge, mused: "This is a sharp medicine to cure all my diseases."

The headsman was overcome by the sight of so much gallantry and achievement doomed to a shameful death, and hesitated. "What dost thou fear? Strike, man, strike!" cried the condemned; and his head fell. Self-seeking adventurer he may have been, but he died in a manner that inspired a bystander in Palace Yard to write:

> "I saw in all the Standers by
> Pale Death—Life only in thine eye.
> Farewell: Truth shall this story say—
> We died, thou only livedst that day."

CAPTAIN JAMES COOK

(1728–1779)

Captain Cook made the world infinitely smaller, and the British Empire magnificently greater. It was he who sailed to the unknown South Seas in the eighteenth century and claimed Australia and New Zealand for the crown. It was he who charted the expanse of the Pacific, discovering, re-discovering, and exactly locating its scattered islands and archipelagos. As a navigator and map-maker he was supreme, as a commander he was admirable. On long voyages in tiny ships he kept his crew efficient and healthy: he was the conqueror of scurvy, that scourge of the seas. His courage and determination may be gauged by his work: he spent his days in unknown seas, finding unknown lands and confronting the strange races that inhabited them; in a ship of less than five hundred tons he sailed the length and breadth of the Pacific Ocean from South Australia to Tierra del Fuego, from the Antarctic Circle to the Bering Straits.

"I HAD ambitions not only to go farther than any man had been before; but as far as it was possible for man to go." wrote James Cook, the explorer who added Australia and New Zealand to the British Empire. The area of the one is twenty-five times that of the British Isles, and the other the size of England and Scotland combined.

This Yorkshireman who gave the British peoples such vast areas in which to expand and who was the father of Antarctic exploration, was the son of a simple farm labourer from Marton village, Cleveland. He was born there on October 28, 1728.

At the age of twelve, Cook was apprenticed to a haberdasher of Staithes, near Whitby, who was a little too fond of the stick for his apprentices and of the grog for himself. It was not a pleasant life for a spirited lad. Young James was expected to put up and take down the shutters, run errands for his master, sweep out the shop and kill the cockroaches, which he thought was poor sport. His one distraction was to steal away from the shop and escape to the haunts of the seafaring men of the the tiny port. Here, open-mouthed, he would listen to their fantastic tales of piracy, of strange cities and stranger peoples. One day the lad made up his mind; he, too, was going to sea in order to visit glamorous lands.

No sooner said than done. Packing up his few belongings in a pocket handkerchief, he stole a shilling from the till and ran away to Whitby to be apprenticed to a coal shipper named Walker. During the next fifteen years he sailed before the mast on ships serving the Norwegian and Baltic ports, enduring all the drudgery and dirt of small coasting ships.

At the age of twenty-seven, Cook had risen to the proud position of first mate. Then, in order to escape the brutalities of the press-gang, which was active at the beginning of the war with France, he joined the Royal Navy as a volunteer. The first service Cook saw was in Canada, where he was employed in the dangerous task of surveying the St. Lawrence. Constantly liable to attack by Indians and French look-out boats, he made a chart of the river from Quebec to the sea, which served to guide the British fleet before Wolfe's famous attack on the Heights of Abraham.

In 1762 Cook was at the recapture of Newfoundland, and afterwards made a survey of the coast. His skill as a map-maker brought him some reputation, and his experience taught him the importance of mathematics as an aid to accurate observation. Therefore, when later, at the instance of his former commanding officer, he was transferred to survey the coasts of Newfoundland and Labrador, it was not surprising that he should arouse attention by his scientific observations of the solar eclipse of August 5, 1766. This paper brought him to the notice of the Admiralty and of the Royal Society. It was to prove the turning point of his life.

A contemporary describes him at this time as a "modest man and rather bashful; of an agreeable, lively conversation, sensible and intelligent. In his temper he was somewhat hasty, but of a disposition the most friendly, benevolent and humane. His person was above six feet high, and though a good-looking man, he was plain both in address and appearance. His head was small; his hair, which was dark brown, he wore tied behind. His face was full of expression, his nose exceedingly well shaped, his eyes were small and of brown cast, were quick and piercing; his eyebrows prominent, which gave his countenance altogether an air of austerity." His portrait, which hangs today in the Painted Hall at Greenwich, bears out this description.

As yet, he had no reputation as an explorer. He was known merely as a competent navigator whose hobby was the study of scientific phenomena and possessing considerable ability as a surveyor and mathematician. These talents the lords of the admiralty proposed to use in connexion with an expedition to the South Seas, which ostensible purpose was to observe the transit of Venus, although it is probable that they were more interested in the prospect of annexing that great South Land, the *Terra Australis* of romantic minded geographers, which had been the quest of so many navigators during the seventeenth and eighteenth centuries. The problem set for Cook by his superiors was to find out whether this continent really existed, and, if so, what was its character and extent.

Looking back to the history of this will-o'-the-wisp of mariners, Cook had not much to guide him. He knew that his predecessors had been lured to the peril of the South Seas by tales of plentiful gold and silver waiting to be taken away. He knew that there was a respectable tradition of Spanish and Portuguese and later Dutch ships which had stumbled on extensive reaches of rocky coast in mid-Pacific, and map-makers on the strength of such yarns deemed every new discovery a part of the fabled continent of the far south.

De Torres, a Spanish navigator, had, in 1605, proved that New Guinea was not a part of the continent by discovering the existence of the straits named after him. However, his discovery remained unknown for a century, and the honour of proving New Guinea an island fell to a rough adventurer, William Dampier, whom the British had commissioned to find the continent. This scallywag sailed down stretches of what is now Western Australia, but reported unfavourably on its forbidding shores and on the demoralized savages who inhabited it. But Dampier had added nothing to the scientific solution of the problem.

The limits of the imaginary continent at last began to shrink considerably when, in 1642, Tasman, a Dutchman, sailed from Batavia on a south-easterly course to find it. Although by discovering both Tasmania and New Zealand he demonstrated to his own satisfaction that the north shores of New Guinea and Australia were not northern peninsulas of the continent, his voyage was a tragic failure. He had actually sailed round Australia without seeing it! When, therefore, on August 25, 1768, Lieutenant Cook and a company of eighty-three men (including a party of scientists, among whom was the great Sir Joseph Banks) set sail in the *Endeavour,* of three hundred and seventy tons register, for a three years' voyage, they had before them the possibility of filling in a substantial area of the globe's surface.

They reached Tahiti in the spring of 1769, and there, on June 3, the transit of Venus was observed. While the astronomical observations were being taken, some of the crew broke into the ship's store and stole a quantity of the large nails which served as money in trading with the islanders. One of the culprits was found with seven of these nails on his person, and Cook, always a stern disciplinarian, sentenced him to two dozen lashes.

Cook now sailed south on his quest for the unknown continent, and skirting the Society Islands, at length reached New Zealand. The excitement of landing after six weeks' confinement to ship was somewhat diminished by the threatening array of tattooed natives who came to meet the crew. Cook greeted these Maori warriors with friendly signs and eventually prevailed on them to lay down their spears in sign of truce. As Cook was to learn, the natives were not always so amiable, and there were occasions when muskets had to be loosed in order to obtain proper respect for His Majesty's uniform. In fact, the general hostility of the Maoris prevented any exploration of the interior.

Cook circumnavigated the North and South Islands and made thoroughly accurate surveys of the coastline, noting especially the straits between them which now bear his name. He landed at Queen Charlotte's Sound, and chose a pleasant clearing in the forest for an impressive ceremony. First a mast was erected, then to the cheers of his men the Union Jack was hoisted. Finally, in a brief statement, he informed the company that he had taken possession of the islands on behalf of His Majesty George the Third.

On leaving New Zealand, the *Endeavour* sailed for nineteen days without sighting land, but at last the look-out man gave the welcome cry, and Cook saw, for the first time, the great island continent of Australia, or as it was then known, New Holland. He sailed down the east coast of Australia, which he also charted with the meticulous care that made his work invaluable.

When Cook anchored, the first of the eager explorers to land was Joseph Banks, the naturalist. During many days he hunted for specimens of ferns and flowers hitherto unknown to science. Happy in his finds, for the district possessed an unexpected variety of plants, he persuaded Cook to call this harbour Botany Bay. Banks, in his enthusiasm, exaggerated his description of the country round about, and nineteen years later seven hundred and seventy convicts were landed to discover that he had described as "meadows" what in reality were swamps.

Proceeding along the east coast, which he named New South Wales, after a fancied resemblance to Glamorgan, Cook reached the headland he called Tribulation, where he passed through the most nerve-racking experience of the whole of his career as a navigator. The *Endeavour* grounded on a reef twenty-four miles from the mainland, and it was only by good fortune and the superhuman labours of his crew, after throwing overboard everything that could be spared, that he managed to steer his boat into the calmer waters of a river. As he wrote later, when explaining the motives of his activity as a discoverer, " such are the vicissitudes attending this kind of service and must always attend an unknown navigation. Was it not for the pleasure which naturally results to a man being the first discoverer, even was it nothing more than sands and shoals, this service would be insupportable, especially in far distant parts like this, short of provisions and almost every other necessity."

Before leaving Australia, Cook once again landed his crew for the solemn duty which he owed King George. The Union Jack was run up amid cheers; in a short speech Cook announced that he had taken possession of the whole of Eastern Australia; three shots were fired, and the ship's gunners fired three rounds in reply. This simple ceremony symbolized the winning for the empire of a vast continent, without the shedding of a single drop of blood. He sailed on to New Guinea by way of the straits which Torres and Dampier had discovered, and proved conclusively the contention that New Guinea and New Holland were " not one continued land." The last stage home was by way of the Cape of Good Hope. By his first voyage, Cook had not settled the problem of the Great South Land, although he had narrowed down the extent of the region within which it was likely to be found. All further doubts he was to settle on his second journey.

He was promoted to the rank of commander, and on July 13, 1772, he once more put out from Plymouth in search of what, owing to his recent discoveries, was now proving to be a mythical continent. He now had under his command two ships, the *Resolution,* of four hundred and sixty-two tons, and the *Adventure,* of three hundred and thirty tons, and a crew of one hundred and ninety-three men. This time he made first for the Cape of Good Hope, and then sailed south-east to the Antarctic Circle. In imminent danger from floating ice, he worked up and down the Southern Pacific, until he had proved the impossibility of the existence of a great southern continent in those seas.

We may picture the expedition making its adventurous way through the reef-strewn seas of the tropics and the ice packs of the Antarctic. Then fog separates the *Resolution* from the *Adventure.*

For four thousand leagues Cook navigates his ship without a sight of land, at last putting in for repairs at Dusky Bay in New Zealand. Then off once more in search of the *Adventure,* finally rejoined at Queen Charlotte's Sound. In warmer climes, Cook steps ashore, bearing an olive branch to interview armed savages who never before had looked on a white man. Now, he is ploughing through seas where hurricanes blow with devastating force. Now his wonder is excited by half-drowned islets crowned with stately palms, clothed with luxuriant vegetation, and inhabited by simple men whose ways are strange and sometimes frightful. And so he threads his way among unheard-of wonders, always the same quiet, methodical scientific explorer.

Turning northwards, Cook determined the exact positions of the Marquesas and the Tonga, or Friendly Islands, and he re-discovered the New Hebrides group. Then followed his wholly new discoveries of New Caledonia, Norfolk Island and the Isle of Pines. Back he went to New Zealand, and from there he once more explored the South Pacific from South Australia to Tierra del Fuego. At last he set sail for home, re-discovered South Georgia, crossed the South Atlantic to the Cape, and sailed along the coast of Africa, reaching Plymouth on July 25, 1775.

In three years Cook had covered sixty thousand miles, with the loss from sickness of only one man. This was a wonderful achievement in the days when the death rate from scurvy at sea was enormous. Years before, Cook had taken part in a naval expedition sent out to attack the French in Canada, in which half the ships were put out of action by the scurvy before the Atlantic had been crossed. Salt pork and biscuit diet caused the complaint: green vegetables and fruit, unobtainable at sea, were the antidote. As a preventive of scurvy Cook used to prescribe what he called "portable broth." It was made from scurvy grass, carrot marmalade, sauerkraut, syrup of lemon, and other vegetable ingredients. In addition to introducing portable broth, he created a revolution in the habits of seamen by insisting on daily baths when in harbour, well-aired bedding and cleanliness of quarters. These simple principles of hygiene caused a sensation when he delivered a paper on them to the Royal Society, which awarded him the Copley Medal for it.

The result of Cook's second voyage was to establish in outline the knowledge of the Pacific as we have it today and to lay beyond recall the ghost of *Terra Australis.* The maps he drew have remained essentially the same, although details have been filled in by later cartographers. The record of his wanderings in the frozen Antarctic were, a century later, to be the inspiration of many of the Polar explorers. His rewards were prompt, but meagre. He was promoted to the rank of post-captain and made a captain in Greenwich Hospital, while the Royal Society elected him a member.

For his third and last expedition, Cook had as his goal one of the great lures that has drawn the most adventurous of sailors and explorers in every country: the quest of a north-west passage, a sea-way across the top of the world from the Atlantic to the Pacific, from the old world through the new. Unlike his predecessors, Cook sailed under orders to make the attempt from the west, taking a passage through the Bering Straits from the Pacific across to the Hudson Strait and so into the North Atlantic. Behind this scientific expedition also lay the idea of claiming and annexing unknown islands in the Pacific, so Cook set off to the North-West Passage by way of the South Seas.

He left the Nore on June 25, 1776, with the *Resolution* and the *Discovery* under his command, and after touching at the Cape of Good Hope, made for the scenes of his former discoveries. He first made land at Tasmania, and thence sailed on to New Zealand, the Tonga Islands and Tahiti, sighting in 1777 the larger members of the Cook Archipelago. And now he set his course northward for the true object of his expedition. This brought him to an important re-discovery of the largest of all the Pacific Islands, the Hawaiian group. Gaetano, a Spanish explorer, had found them in 1555, but their existence had been kept such a close secret in Spain that it had long been forgotten! Cook named them the Sandwich Islands, after his friend, Lord Sandwich, who was at that time at the head of the Admiralty.

The explorer next made for the western coast of America, which he picked up off what is now the State of Oregon, and sailed northwards along it. This intrepid man, fresh from a perilous voyage through the warm Pacific seas which he himself had charted, sailed calmly into the unknown and frozen north. He carefully explored the coastline, surveyed, and sailed right through the Bering Straits and on, until at beyond seventy degrees of latitude at a point which he named Icy Cape, his way was barred by a wall of solid ice standing twelve feet above the waterline. So he turned back, but even in retreat he was still an explorer. He made his way down the coast of north-eastern Siberia, touched at Kamchatka and sailed amongst the Aleutian Islands, learning, charting, and writing all the while. And then, at last, he returned to Hawaii.

His two ships anchored at Kealakekua Bay in January, 1779. The crew were greeted on shore with every mark of welcome. After a fortnight they once more put out to sea, but owing to adverse weather were forced shortly to return to their anchorage. A change was noticeable in the behaviour of the natives. Thievish they had always been, but their robberies were more persistent, and their demeanour was sullen. A native had to be flogged for stealing the armourer's tongs. That night the tongs were again stolen, and the cutter of the *Discovery* disappeared into the bargain. Thereupon Cook went ashore to demand a friendly hostage against future depredations in the person of the king of the tribe. The crowd became menacing; the marines accompanying Cook, in spite of his counter orders, opened fire. This was the signal for a mass attack, from which the marines fled to the boats, leaving Cook unguarded on the shore. He was struck down by one of the natives, another stabbed him in the back, and a third held his head under water. In their fury the savages slashed Cook's body, snatching the dagger out of each other's hands. The confusion in the boats and the pusillanimity of the officer in command, made it impossible for the corpse to be retrieved. It was burnt with rejoicing, but his bones were recovered and buried a few days later. Today, an obelisk marks his tomb, but the map of the Pacific is his best memorial.

Thus ended the career of the man universally acknowledged as the greatest explorer of his age. Stern, strict, yet just and honest, Captain Cook subjected his own body to the discipline he expected and exacted from those under him. Utterly fearless, cheerful under the most depressing circumstances, and constantly occupied with some kind of work, he enjoyed the regard of his own men, and by the native races of the Pacific was held in respect and even veneration.

DAVID LIVINGSTONE

(1813–1873)

The civilization which is Central Africa today is a far cry from the "Darkest Africa" of mid-Victorian times. But it was dark indeed in its obscurity in the year 1841 when a young Scottish missionary from London made his first trip into the interior. When we consider that civilization, let us remember the simple fervour, the courage, the enthusiasm and the self-sacrifice of David Livingstone, not only for his achievements, but also for the inspiration of his life, an inspiration which wielded so mighty an influence in the opening-up of Africa.

IN 1891 the famous explorer, Sir Harry Hamilton Johnson, then Commissioner for Nyasaland and Consul-General for Portuguese East Africa, who had been, in his own words, "the agent in placing 'Livingstone's land' under the protection of the British crown," wrote as follows:

"Beyond the southern extremity of the continent, the Portuguese province of Angola, and a narrow strip of country from Kazembe's town to the lower Zambezi, the interior of South Central Africa from the Bight of Biafra to the Orange River, from Somaliland to Delagoa Bay, was either a mere blank or a bewildering maze of false and nonsensical geography until the Apostle of Africa commenced those explorations which incited others and yet others to explore, and sent forth ever widening circles of knowledge; so that, in less than fifty years from the commencement of Livingstone's career, Central Africa, in its main geographical features, its marvels, its riches, and its horrors, has been completely laid bare to the contemplation of the white man."

In that appreciation of Livingstone's work there lies a claim to undying fame, a claim that is enriched and multiplied a thousandfold by the life story of the great path-finder.

David Livingstone was born on March 19, 1813, at Blantyre, near Glasgow. His father, Neil Livingstone, of Highland descent, was a retail tea dealer by trade and a missionary by nature. If on occasion he devoted more time to the distribution of tracts than to his business, he was content to know that he was acting according to the dictates of his conscience.

His spiritual fervour drove David to mild rebellion, though the latter ever regarded his parent with respect and affection. He forbade the boy to read books of science and travel that attracted him, and directed him to find refreshment in theological works. But the son, who throughout his life was deeply devout and sincerely pious, without the least trace of bigotry and religious ostentation, could not appreciate his father's idea of mental food.

"The difference of opinion between father and son," Livingstone wrote later, "reached the point of open rebellion on my part, and his last application of the rod was on my refusal to peruse Wilberforce's *Practical Christianity*." He goes on to admit that "this dislike to dry, doctrinal reading and to religious reading of any sort, continued for many years to come."

At the age of ten David was sent to work in the local cotton factory, where he toiled for fourteen hours a day, first as a "piecer" and later as a spinner. He was more interested in educating himself than in his work: he even had a book on his spinning-jenny from which he snatched sentences when he could, though Dr. W. G. Blaikie tells us that the "utmost interval" at one time was less than a minute. His fellow workers in the factory thought him "just a sulky, quiet, feckless sort o' boy." The iron will was hidden from them.

Travel and natural history were the subjects which attracted him, and when he read the work of a German missionary named Gützlaff, he resolved to become a missionary himself. Two books by Dr. Thomas Dick confirmed his belief "that religion and science are not hostile, but friendly to each other." By dint of saving and working his education proceeded apace. At twenty-three, with the help of his parents and brother, he entered Glasgow University, where he assiduously applied himself to the study of Greek, medicine and divinity, and in 1837 he was accepted as a probationer by the London Missionary Society.

His failure as a preacher almost ruined his career at the outset. Called upon to occupy the pulpit at Stanford Rivers, near Ongar, Essex, he was overcome with nervousness and fled the building. But he conquered the difficulty of facing a congregation, and threw himself wholeheartedly into his medical work, walked the London hospitals and finally passed his examinations. China was to have been the field of his operations, but the Opium War had broken out. Thus, for a reason all unsought and contrary to his own early ambition, Livingstone was sent to the Dark Continent. Towards the end of 1840 he sailed for South Africa.

After a long voyage, during which the captain of the ship taught him how to take astronomical observations, he landed at Algoa Bay, and then made the seven-hundred-mile trek by ox-wagon to Kuruman, in Bechuanaland, the missionary society's headquarters.

No sooner had Livingstone arrived than he set off on journeys into the interior, looking for a suitable place in which to make a settlement. His first trip was in 1841, and others took place in the two succeeding years. On each journey he made faithful records of his observations in geology, botany and natural history: they were the first chapters of his invaluable journals.

In 1844 he married Mary Moffat, the daughter of Dr. Robert Moffat, who had founded the mission station at Kuruman and settled at Mabotsa, some two hundred miles away, where Livingstone built a house, largely by his own efforts. "She is not romantic," he wrote of his bride, "but a matter-of-fact lady, a little, thick, black-haired girl, sturdy and all I want." She made him a comfortable home in the wastes of Africa, and suffered with patience and fortitude the loneliness and hardships of an explorer's wife.

While at Mabotsa, Livingstone had a terrifying adventure with a lion at which he had fired but only disabled. The wounded beast sprang upon him and pulled him to the ground, where it bit the flesh of his shoulder to the bone. "Growling horribly close to my ear, he shook me as a terrier does a rat." His left arm was partially disabled for the rest of his life.

From Mabotsa, the Livingstones removed to Chonuane, which they were soon compelled to evacuate on account of drought. Thence they journeyed westwards to the River Kolobeng, Sechele, the chief of the Bakwena and his people accompanying them. At the new settlement Livingstone taught the natives how to irrigate their fields, and a prosperous agricultural colony sprang up.

All the while Livingstone was dreaming of the unknown lands to the north, convinced that exploration and the meeting with new tribes were consistent with his work as a missionary, and indeed essential to it. At that time men were trying hard to find the rumoured Lake 'Ngami, and in 1849 Livingstone, accompanied by two English sportsmen, William Oswell and Mungo Murray, set out to search for it. They crossed the inhospitable Kalahari Desert, which had "hitherto presented an insurmountable barrier to Europeans," and then, striking boldly in a north-westerly direction, found the Zouga, then "a glorious river" but now almost a dry watercourse, and, abandoning ox-wagon for canoe, at last came to the lake. 'Ngami was Livingstone's first great discovery: from that moment his life was spent almost continuously in increasing the world's knowledge of unknown Africa.

In the following year Livingstone again started northwards, this time with his wife and children, but the tsetse fly stopped his travelling; his children fell ill with fever, and he was forced to return to Kolobeng. Fever, the tsetse fly—which attacked the cattle and draught animals—and horse sickness, were the three factors which doomed Livingstone's scheme for establishing missions on the Upper Zambezi.

The great River Zambezi was first sighted by Livingstone and Oswell in 1851 at Shesheke, after they had been kindly received at Linyanti by the powerful chief of the Makololo. Livingstone then decided to send his wife and four children to England, and took them down to Capetown. His salary as a missionary was £100 a year, and only the generosity of Oswell enabled him to send his loved ones home.

At Capetown, Livingstone perfected his skill in astronomical observations under the direction of Mr. (later Sir) Thomas Maclear, the Astronomer Royal, and acquired a high degree of accuracy which was to be invaluable.

Then, in June, 1852, he set out on an expedition which was to make his name ring through the world. He made first for Kolobeng, where he found that the Boers had burned the town, killed a number of the natives, carried off the cattle, plundered his house, smashed his precious bottles of medicines, stolen his stores and torn up his books. With a grim shrug of his broad shoulders he proceeded northwards to seek the unknown.

His next halt was at Linyanti, where he was well received by the Makololo, and there he remained for a month making preparations. His first idea was to go up the Upper Zambezi until he had cleared the swampy district, and find suitable places for missions, and with this in view he travelled along the river as far as the confluence of the Kabompo. He found nothing but unhealthy country and the dreaded tsetse fly. Disappointed in his primary object, Livingstone determined to push on in the hope of discovering a practicable route from North Bechuanaland to the west coast.

Sekeletu, chief of the Makololo, provided him with twenty-seven men, and with what must surely have been the most modest outfit of any explorer, Livingstone started on a long trek through unknown country, with Loanda, on the coast of Angola, as his objective.

Livingstone was utterly regardless of comfort, believing with St. Paul that it is worthy to " endure hardness," and it was largely due to indifference that he undermined his constitution. Here is his own description of the simple outfit with which he set out for Loanda:

> "I had three muskets for my people, a rifle and a double-barrelled smooth-bore for myself; and, having seen such great abundance of game in my visit to the Liba (the extreme Upper Zambezi), I imagined that I could easily supply the wants of my party. Wishing also to avoid the discouragement which would naturally be felt on meeting any obstacles if my companions were obliged to carry heavy loads, I took only a few biscuits, a few pounds of tea and sugar, and about twenty of coffee, which, as the Arabs find, though used without milk or sugar, is a most refreshing beverage after fatigue or exposure to the sun. We carried one small tin canister, about fifteen inches square, filled with spare shirting, trousers and shoes, to be used when we reached civilized life, and others in a bag, which were expected to wear out on the way; another of the same size for medicines; and a third for books, my stock being a nautical almanac, Thomson's logarithm tables, and a Bible. A fourth box contained a magic-lantern, which we found of much use. The sextant and artificial horizon thermometer and compasses were carried apart. My ammunition was distributed in portions through the whole luggage, so that, if an accident should befall one part, we could still have others to fall back upon. Our chief hopes for food were upon that, but in case of failure I took about twenty pounds of beads, worth forty shillings, which still remained of the stock I brought from Cape Town; a small gipsy tent, just sufficient to sleep in; a sheepskin mantle as a blanket, and a horse-rug as a bed. . . ."

Livingstone left Linyanti on November 11, 1853. The party travelled by canoe up the Zambezi, passing out of the Makololo country at Libonta. From that time they were in the territories of strange and sometimes hostile chiefs, but the leader's tact and patience smoothed the way. Fever racked him all the time they were going through the unhealthy Barotse Valley, but he pushed on, passed Lake Dilolo in the swampland that gives rise to streams flowing into the Zambezi and the Congo, and entered the Kioko country. He was entranced by his journey through the luxuriant tropical forest, which provided such striking contrast with the sun-baked deserts of Bechuanaland, but so careless was he of his health that he became seriously ill of fever. His Makololo men became discouraged and began to revolt against his orders, but Livingstone, still a very sick man, showed his firmness:

> "Knowing that discipline would be at an end if this mutiny were not quelled, and that our lives depended on vigorously upholding authority, I seized a double-barrelled pistol and darted forth from the domicile, looking, I suppose, so savage as to put them to a precipitate flight. As some remained within hearing, I told them that I must maintain discipline, though at the expense of some of their limbs; so long as we travelled together they must remember that I was master, and not they. There being but little room to doubt my determination, they immediately became very obedient, and never afterwards gave me any trouble, or imagined that they had any right to my property."

Fighting every kind of difficulty the party made its way westwards, found help from outlying Portuguese garrisons in Angola, and at long last, to the astonishment of the Makololo, reached the sea and Livingstone's objective, Sao Paulo de Loanda, on May 31, 1854.

Livingstone refused the offer of a passage to England. He had not finished with exploration. He felt bound to take back his Makololo men to their own country, and he wanted to strike right across Africa and follow the Zambezi eastwards to the sea. "I return," he wrote, "because I feel that the work to which I set myself is only half accomplished."

His departure from Loanda was delayed by attacks of dysentery, but eventually he set out for Pungo Andongo, where he stayed for some months. On New Year's Day, 1855, he started off once more, and following roughly the route by which he had come, riding for the greater part of the journey on an ox which "had a softer back than others but a much more intractable temper," he made the long trek back to Libonta. The Makololo received him and their countrymen with unbounded delight. The journey through the Makololo country was a triumphal procession. Arrived at Linyanti, he found that his wagon had not been shifted by so much as an inch and his goods were exactly as he had left them. The chief gave him a magnificent welcome, and provided him with cattle, goods, provisions and a company of new men for his expedition down the Zambezi.

In the following November Livingstone set out, and after a fortnight's journey discovered the great Victoria Falls, then called the

Falls of Mosioatunya ("Sounding Smoke"). After proceeding through hostile country and living on roots and honey, he reached the little settlement of Tete on March 2, 1856, very much exhausted. Again the Portuguese gave him hospitality, but it was not until May 22, 1856, that he arrived at Quilimane, a "man-killing spot" on a large mudbank.

On his return to England at the end of the year, Livingstone became a national hero. The Royal Geographical Society gave him the Victoria Medal, honorary degrees were conferred on him by the universities of Oxford and Cambridge, and he was presented with the freedom of the cities of Edinburgh and Glasgow. Yet he refused to be elated. "I cannot pretend to a single note of triumph," Livingstone avowed. "A man may boast when he is pulling off his armour, but I am just putting mine on." His lecture at Cambridge was responsible for the foundation of the Universities Mission to Central Africa, but he resigned from the London Missionary Society. He was appointed Consul at Quilimane and leader of an expedition for the exploration of eastern and central Africa.

Livingstone the man stands out clearly in his magnificent reply to one who protested at his "abandoning" the missionary service:

> "Nowhere have I ever appeared as anything else but a servant of God, who has simply followed the leadings of His hand. My views of what is *missionary* duty are not so contracted as those whose ideal is a dumpy sort of man with a Bible under his arm. I have laboured in bricks and mortar, at the forge and carpenter's bench, as well as in preaching and in medical practice. I feel that I am 'not my own.' I am serving Christ when shooting a buffalo for my men, or taking an astronomical observation, or writing to one of His children who forget, during the little moment of penning a note, that charity which is eulogised as 'thinking no evil'; and after having by His help got information which I hope will lead to more abundant blessing being bestowed on Africa than heretofore, am I to hide the light under a bushel merely because some will consider it not sufficiently, or even at all *missionary?"*

For the second Zambezi expedition he was accompanied by his brother, Charles, and Dr. (afterwards Sir) John Kirk. It started in 1858, and was marred throughout by misfortune. Dissension among the officers, the inefficiency of the steam launches and the evil temper of the natives, brought disaster after disaster. Nor was this all, for Mrs. Livingstone died at Shupanga in 1862. "I loved her when I married her," said the bereaved husband, "and the longer I lived with her I loved her the more." When Time's healing finger had softened the blow a little, the energy and enthusiasm of Livingstone welled up anew and led him to new efforts. He revisited the River Shiré, discovered and explored Lake Nyasa, and was within ten days' march of the rumoured Lake Bangweulu, when the government recalled the expedition. The horrors of the Waiyau slave raids and of the inhuman traffic in men and women which was being carried on by native chiefs and half-caste traders burnt into his very soul. It was clear that the Portuguese officials were behind the dreadful traffic, but Livingstone could do nothing as yet. Then came a letter from Earl Russell recalling the expedition by the end of the year. Charles Livingstone and Kirk were both far from well. The expedition did not wait for the end of the year to disband.

In order to dispose of the *Lady Nyasa,* a tiny craft built for lake and river navigation, Livingstone sailed her across the Indian Ocean, a voyage of 2,500 miles, to Bombay, and from that port left for England, which he reached in July, 1864. Back in the homeland, he wrote an account of his Zambezi travels, but before the book was published he had returned to Africa. The object of his new expedition was twofold: to discover the sources of the Nile and to put an end to slavery, the "great open sore of the world," by introducing the benefits of civilization.

With a band of sepoys and mission negroes, Livingstone reached the mouth of the Rovuma from India. His men on this occasion were to prove inefficient rogues.

He made his way up the Rovuma, through the Waiyau country and round the south of Lake Nyasa. Here some of his men deserted and brought word to the coast that Livingstone had been killed. A search expedition was sent out from England immediately, and in 1867, Edward Young, at the head of it, proved conclusively that the story was false. Meanwhile, Livingstone had pushed on northwards and had reached Lake Tanganyika, whose fresh water covers the vast area of twelve thousand seven hundred square miles, and is therefore considerably bigger than Belgium. But a major disaster had occurred on the journey: a Waiyau porter had deserted and taken the explorer's medicine chest. By the time he reached Tanganyika he was seriously ill with fever, and he lay at Pambete suffering from temporary paralysis of the limbs.

Livingstone sent messages to the coast asking for stores to be forwarded to Ujiji, and as soon as he could move turned westwards to visit Lake Mweru. He was travelling slowly and desertions were frequent. After more delays he made southwards, and at last discovered Lake Bangweulu in July, 1868. Although his health went from bad to worse, he still neglected himself, wading through rivers and letting his clothes dry on him, and paying little attention to his food. A party of Arabs travelled with him back to Tanganyika and on to Ujiji, and their kind treatment and nursing pulled him through.

Having rested and recovered something of his strength, Livingstone started for the great Lualaba River, of which he had heard, and, after making west and north, reached its banks at Nyangwe. His return journey was a nightmare. He was suffering from fever and dysentery, and hostile tribes attacked him. To crown his misfortunes he reached Ujiji to find that all the stores that had been sent to him had been stolen and sold.

Desperately ill, "a mere ruckle of bones," saved only from the depths of despair by his sense of humour, he lay at Ujiji. Suddenly help came, and from the most unexpected quarter. H. M. Stanley, at the head of a relief expedition organized by James Gordon Bennett, the proprietor of the *New York Herald,* found the explorer whose silence had alarmed and puzzled the civilized world. "There is a group of the most respectable Arabs," wrote Stanley; "and as I come nearer I see the white face of an old man among them. He has a cap with a gold band around it; his dress is a short jacket of red blanket cloth; and his pants—well, I didn't observe. I am shaking hands with him. We raise our hats, and I say, 'Dr. Livingstone, I presume?' and he says, 'Yes.'" From that moment Livingstone took new heart.

Together, the two explored the northern end of Tanganyika, and then, with Livingstone firmly refusing to leave Africa, they parted. Stanley, who met the official British Livingstone Relief Expedition at Zanzibar, sent a fresh batch of porters up to Livingstone at Unyamwezi. Thence, in August, 1872, the great explorer began his last journey, to what he thought were the sources of the Nile.

He travelled southwards along the swampy shores of Lake Bangweulu, but he was a dying man. He was in constant pain, was losing blood and often fainted away; he had to be carried gently and with frequent halts. He could not even sit up, but lay flat when they travelled in canoes. Still he pushed on, until at last he could no longer stand the pain.

So he came to Ilala. The last entry in his journal was written on April 27. The scrawled message betrays the anguish of the writer: "Knocked up quite, and remain . . . recover . . . sent to buy milch goats. We are on the banks of the Molilamo."

The next day he was too weak to do anything else but wind up his watch. Then, early in the morning of May 1, 1873, he was found kneeling as if in prayer by his bedside—dead.

His native servants, with great courage and defying superstition and physical difficulties, dried his body as best they could in the sun and carried it, together with his papers and instruments, across Africa one thousand one hundred miles to the coast of Zanzibar. Livingstone was buried in Westminster Abbey, but his heart was interred in Africa. Where could it more fittingly rest?

ROBERT FALCON SCOTT

(1868–1912)

Throughout the centuries the British race has produced men who have thrust the name of Britain from the known realm of civilization into the wastes of the unknown. "The outposts of Empire" has so long been a stock phrase that it has become almost a joke: yet it embodied the spirit and ambitions of a people that transformed a small island into a world-power. Britain's explorers have been one of the glories of her history, and none surpasses in fame or courage Robert Falcon Scott, whose story is an epic carved in ice.

"HALF-STARVED lairds who rode a lean horse and were followed by leaner greyhounds; gathered with difficulty a hundred pounds from a hundred tenants; fought duels—cocked their hats—and called themselves gentlemen."

Thus wrote Sir Walter Scott in a letter describing the type of people his ancestors were. Thus also might Captain Scott have described his forbears; he was descended from the same great Border clan—the "Rough Clan" as they were called, for they were always to be found in the thick of any fighting that was afoot.

It was not easy for the descendants of such people to settle down to sedentary pursuits when quieter days came to their country, and for several generations the fighting services claimed the majority of the men-folk of the Scott clan. There was, however, one exception. John Edward Scott, one of five brothers—the eldest of whom was a naval surgeon, the other three officers in the Indian Army—was of delicate health and worked in a family brewery at Plymouth.

This stay-at-home had six children, of whom four were girls.

Robert Falcon Scott, the third child and elder son, and Archibald, two years younger, upheld the family tradition and adopted the profession of arms, one in the Navy and the other in the Army.

Robert Falcon Scott was born near Devonport on June 6, 1868. A governess taught him at home until he was eight, when he was sent to a day school at Stoke Demeral. Later, he went to Stubbington House, Fareham, and from there was entered as a naval cadet on the *Britannia*, being then thirteen years of age. In August, 1883, he went to the *Boadicea* as a midshipman, served two years in her, and then after three months in the *Monarch* was sent to the *Rover,* one of the ships of the training squadron under Commodore Sir Albert Hastings Markham, the Arctic explorer, cousin of Sir Clements Markham, geographer and historian, who, as president of the Geographical Society was afterwards to set on foot the *Discovery* expedition.

The young cadet little guessed that when Sir Clements came to the squadron as the guest of the commodore, he was already looking for a likely man to lead an Antarctic expedition. Not only was this so, but it was then that the choice was made.

In his posthumous book, *The Lands of Silence,* Sir Clements writes: "I had selected the fittest commander in my own mind in 1887 when I was . . . the guest of my cousin Commodore Markham. . . . On the 5th he (Scott) dined with us. He was then eighteen years of age and I was much struck by his intelligence, information and the charm of his manner. My experience taught me that it would be years before an expedition would be ready, and I believed that Scott was the destined man to command it. At Vigo we were thrown together again, when my young friend was torpedo-lieutenant of the *Empress of India,* and I was more than ever impressed by his evident vocation for such a command."

Towards the end of 1888, Scott was transferred to the *Amphion,* then at Esquimault, in British Columbia. It was while on the journey to join his ship that he drew upon himself the notice of people competent to judge men. Owing to the snowing up of the railways he had to take passage on a tramp steamer which was going from San Francisco to Alaska. The ship, overcrowded with passengers, ran into a gale and there was chaos on board. Everybody was sea-sick, including, probably, Scott himself, for like many another famous sailor he never entirely rid himself of that trouble. Stewards could serve no meals. Women and children were lying about on the floor of the little saloon. Scott, young sub-lieutenant of twenty, took the situation in hand and organized the men passengers—rough Californian miners on their way to a new mining camp—into watches to wash, dress, feed and nurse the women and children. They gladly became a disciplined crew obeying his every order—surely a tribute to those qualities which were later to shine forth to the world in all their perfection!

He returned from Esquimault a full lieutenant in 1891, and was posted to the *Vernon*—the naval torpedo school at Portsmouth, for he intended to specialize in torpedo practice. Then came posts in sea-going ships as torpedo-lieutenant, in the *Empress of India,* the *Jupiter,* and finally the *Majestic,* flagship of the Channel Fleet.

In June, 1899, when Scott was spending a short leave in London, he met Sir Clements Markham again. Scott, in the preface to his *The Voyage of the "Discovery,"* thus describes the meeting:

"Chancing one day to walk down Buckingham Palace Road, I espied Sir Clements Markham on the opposite pavement, and naturally crossed, and as naturally turned and accompanied him to his house. That afternoon I learned for the first time that there was such a thing as a prospective Antarctic expedition; two days later I wrote applying to command it."

It was not until a year later that his appointment as prospective leader of the expedition was announced. In June, 1900, he was promoted to the rank of commander. When Sir Clements Markham had prompted him to apply for the leadership, he knew that the expedition would definitely start, for funds had been raised sufficient to finance it. Mr. Llewelyn Longstaff gave twenty-five thousand pounds, and with Mr. Balfour, then First Lord of the Treasury, supporting the appeal, the government gave pound for every pound that was otherwise raised. Thus a total of ninety-two thousand pounds was raised, and the *Discovery* was built.

There was a great deal of work to be done before the expedition could set forth, and Scott was released from his naval routine duties to superintend. Thanks to his insistence, backed by the recommendation of high naval officers, the ship's company, with the exception of the scientific personnel was almost entirely recruited from the Royal Navy. Then he went over to Norway to consult with Dr. Fridtjof Nansen, who put at his service all his experience of polar travel.

In the summer of 1901 the *Discovery* set forth. The expedition surveyed South Victoria Land, the interior of the Antarctic Continent, made the southern record, discovered King Edward VII Land, sounded the Ross Sea, and made an investigation of the nature of the ice barrier. It returned in September, 1904, after an absence of three years and three months. The reception given to Scott was tremendous. He was promoted a captain as from the day of his return. Honours were heaped on him. He was commanded to Balmoral, where he gave a lecture in the presence of the king, the prime minister, and other distinguished personages. Foreign countries and their geographical societies awarded him their medals and decorations. *The Times* of September 10, 1904, in a leading article wrote, in appraisal of the expedition and its results:

"The expedition commanded by Commander Scott has been one of the most successful that ever ventured into the polar regions, north or south. True to the spirit of his instructions, he has done what he was sent out to do, and even more. He has added definitely to the map a long and continuous stretch of the coast of the supposed Antarctic continent. His sledge expeditions, south and west and east, have given us a substantial idea of the character of the interior. The geological collections brought home will enable us to read a part at least of the history of this land of desolation. The life of the sea and such scanty life as is to be found on the land apart from the migrating penguins, has been thoroughly investigated. The observations in meteorology and terrestrial magnetism, extending over about three years, will probably take as long to work out. These are some of the spoils which this great British expedition has brought back. Apart from their immense value to science, it is not improbable that the meteorological and magnetic work will prove to be of considerable practical importance in human affairs. All this has not been obtained without an endurance of hardships by officers and men of which those who have not been in like conditions can have no conception. Yet there was only one death in the expedition, a circumstance probably unparalleled in a similar enterprise. Every member of the little company of fifty who sailed three years ago in the *Discovery*—officers, civilians and men—has done his work efficiently and borne his hardships bravely and cheerfully. Moreover, probably on no previous expedition has there been such unbroken harmony among its members. The example of 'grit' and self-sacrifice in the service of science shown by Commander Scott and his companions, will no doubt serve to keep alive amongst us the spirit which has done so much for England's greatness in the past."

The work of the expedition was not finished with his return. Nine months' leave was granted him for the writing of his record of the expedition. He had already written and sent home in advance from New Zealand his report to the Admiralty. In this and in the subsequent book we read names which were afterwards to become famous—Shackleton, Worsley, Wild, Thomas Crean, William Lashly, Edgar Evans, and a young doctor named Wilson.

The book *The Voyage of the "Discovery"* was finished in August, 1905, but before it was published Scott was appointed to a staff post as Assistant Director of Naval Intelligence at the Admiralty. Then came the command of the *Victorious* and the *Albemarle*. On leaving the latter in August, 1907, he met in London Miss Kathleen

Bruce, a young sculptor, daughter of Canon Lloyd Bruce of York. In January, 1908, he was posted to the battleship *Essex*, and five months later to the *Bulwark*. In September of the same year he married Kathleen Bruce and rejoined his ship after a few days' honeymoon at Etretat.

It was natural that after his marriage his comrades in the Navy should conclude that this meant the end of polar exploration for "Scottie," as he was called in the service, but already in September the plans of a new expedition were made known to the public and an appeal for financial support was launched. The British, Australian, New Zealand and South African governments gave grants, but the expedition was not an official one· To Scott alone belongs the credit for its initiation.

On the day following the announcement, Scott's son was born.

The objects of the expedition were: (1) to reach the South Pole; (2) to further scientific exploration of the Ross Sea area. The second of these was Scott's main interest, and for its attainment he got together the strongest scientific team ever recruited for polar work. Dr. E. A. Wilson, who had been on the *Discovery*, was zoologist, artist and chief of staff. Dr. G. C. Simpson, now Director of the British Meteorological Office, was meteorologist. There were biologists and geologists, a physicist, and one of the naval surgeons, Atkinson, was a parasitologist.

On June 1, 1910, the *Terra Nova*, the whaler chosen, left the Thames, under the command of Lieutenant Evans (later Admiral Lord Mountevans, K.C.B., D.S.O.). Scott went on to the Cape in a mail-boat. The expedition left Capetown under Scott on September 2, and reached Melbourne on October 12. Here Scott received a cable from Amundsen informing him that he, too, was about to make an effort to reach the South Pole. This was a blow, and the apprehension he felt lest the Norwegian arrive at his destination ahead of him haunted him ever afterwards, as may be seen from the many entries in his diary.

The *Terra Nova* finally sailed from Dunedin on Tuesday, November 28, 1910. Mrs. Scott stayed on board until the ship was past the Heads, when a tug took her ashore. Husband and wife never met again.

The intention was to find a landing place at a spot already known to Scott from the earlier expedition—Cape Crozier on Ross Island, but this proved impossible owing to the heavy swell, and Scott sought another place at Hut Point. Stores, horses and dogs were landed in quick time. By January 12, 1911, everything necessary was out of the ship. Captain Oates, of the Inniskilling Dragoons, was in charge of the horses.

All stores for the Pole were first collected at a camp which was named Safety Camp. Scott himself superintended every detail, and prepared to lay depots for his journey.

The *Terra Nova* left for New Zealand before the beginning of the long Antarctic night, but not before Scott learned that the Amundsen party was at the Bay of Whales, sixty miles nearer the Pole than he.

The year that followed was occupied firstly in laying depots and in getting his various parties installed in winter quarters, then in wintering during the long night from April to September. Finally, he set out for the South Pole.

A start was made on November 1, 1911. The journey may be divided into three stages—first the snow plain of the Ice Barrier, then the Glacier, called by Scott the Beardmore Glacier, and then the terrible summit plateau, a dreary waste, apparently endless, of monotonous dry snow. The plan was to transport three units of four men each to the Beardmore Glacier, then two of these as supporting parties could help the polar party to within reasonable distance of their objective.

The first part of the plan was carried out successfully. The two teams that then went forward were led by Captain Scott and Lieutenant Evans respectively. Scott's crew had Dr. Wilson, Captain Oates and Petty-Officer Edgar Evans, while Lieutenant Evans had Lieutenant Bowers, and the two bluejackets, Lashly and Tom Crean.

By January, 1912, they had reached 87° 34′ S. when Lieutenant Evans's party was sent back with the exception of Lieutenant Bowers.

When Scott's team went on alone they were one hundred and fifty miles from the Pole. Signs of tiredness soon appeared in all of them, for they were dragging heavy loads at a height of over ten thousand feet above sea-level. On January 13 they had still sixty miles to go. The next day they covered twenty miles. On the sixteenth they suffered a cruel blow.

They started off in the morning, cold and tired but in high spirits, for they felt certain of reaching their objective next day; but it was not long before they saw a black speck in the distant whiteness. It was a black flag—ominous sign! Then the remains of a camp, with sledge track and the spoor of many dogs!

Amundsen had reached the Pole a month before, had hoisted

the Norwegian flag, and left a small tent enclosing two letters, one to Captain Scott asking him to forward the other one to King Haakon should the Norwegians meet with an accident.

"Great God!" Scott wrote, "this is an awful place and terrible enough for us to have laboured to it without the reward of priority."

His disappointment was acute. The "appalling possibility" of the "Norwegian flag forestalling ours" had become a reality. "It will be a wearisome return," he wrote. Never were truer words penned.

The allowance of food was scanty. Captain Oates and Petty-Officer Evans were early victims of frost-bite. Wilson strained a tendon. Scott himself fell and bruised a shoulder.

Yet on February 8, they said adieu to the terrible summit plateau and reached the ice of the glacier. By then Edgar Evans was very ill. On the seventeenth he died. The four survivors struggled on, though becoming daily weaker. Captain Oates was the most seriously ill, for his feet were black with frost-bite. By the beginning of March things were hopeless, though none would admit it. On the tenth Oates realized that he was hindering the others and asked them what he ought to do. They advised him to march on as long as he could, and Wilson handed to each man enough opium to give a painless death should all hope be lost. On Thursday the fifteenth the Inniskilling dragoon said he could not go on and asked the others to leave him in his sleeping bag. They refused, and persuaded him to struggle along for that afternoon. He slept that night, and next morning a blizzard was blowing. Oates struggled out of his bag.

"I am going outside," he said to Scott, "and may be some time."

They never saw him again.

"We knew," wrote Scott, "that poor Oates was walking to his death, but though we tried to dissuade him we knew it was the act of a brave man and an English gentleman. We all hope to meet the end with a similar spirit, and assuredly the end is not far."

Next day Scott's right foot had gone. Frost-bite had eaten his toes before he knew of it. On the nineteenth they had got within eleven miles of their food depot when a blizzard came up and prevented further marches. On the twenty-first it was agreed that Wilson and Bowers should march on, but the blizzard continued—continued for eleven days.

On March 29, though they can have had no food for a week, all were apparently still alive, for Scott made his last entry in his diary on that day. As usual, his thoughts were of others. *"For God's sake look after our people!"*

* * * * *

For eight months they lay there, their fate unknown to those at home. Then in November searchers found them. Everything was orderly, "taut and shipshape." Dr. Wilson had "died very quietly with his hands folded over his chest." Bowers lay "in the attitude of sleep." Scott lay between them, his left arm over Wilson, his oldest friend. His diaries were under the head of his bag. Letters for his dear ones lay beside him.

The searchers did not disturb the bodies. Dr. Atkinson read the burial service; a cairn was built, surmounted by a cross and there, in the words of a friend, "alone in their greatness they will lie without change or bodily decay, with the most fitting tomb in the world above them."

SOLDIERS AND STATESMEN

ALEXANDER THE GREAT

(356–323 B.C.)

The name of Alexander the Great still lives in the legends of the East, and traces of his swift conquest are still stamped upon the fabric of western Asia. For this genius of victory, who conquered half the known world in thirteen years, who swept aside the mighty armies of the Persian Empire and established his rule as far as the Punjab, was far more than a general and a leader of armies. His colossal victories were followed by sympathetic, understanding administration: he won the loyalty of the defeated, and conquered them again with the culture of Greece. After his death, his mighty empire crumbled and decayed, but the influence of Alexander will last as long as the world itself.

WHEN Bucephalus, the most famous horse in history, was brought for sale to King Philip of Macedon, skilled riders tried in vain to manage him. The boy prince, Alexander, came forward and took the bridle, turned the horse towards the sun so that it should no longer be frightened by its shadow, coaxed and soothed it, and finally mastered the brute.

"My son," cried Philip, "look thee out a kingdom worthy of thyself, for Macedonia is too small for thee." It was a prophetic utterance, for within the space of twenty years the youth who had conquered the horse had conquered Persia and established an immense empire in the East. Plutarch, the Greek historian who records the above incident, also tells us that when Bucephalus died in India, Alexander mourned as at the death of a beloved friend, and founded the city of Bucephalia in memory of his favourite charger. One of the great Macedonian's most likeable characteristics was his recognition of loyal service, and his generosity to those who rendered it.

It is unfortunate that the early historians and biographers of Alexander were so dazzled by the brilliance of his military exploits that they have told us of very little else concerning him. But it is wrong to regard him as being merely a brave and skilful soldier, fired with the lust of conquest. Alexander was much more than this. He was a great statesman, inspired by a mighty vision of world unity. He carried the banner of Greek civilization and culture through the East, and opened up the route to India. During his reign of barely thirteen years the confines of man's knowledge were widened, and great advances were made in the realms of science. Alexander is entitled to a place among the great pioneers of progress.

If ever a man was born to victory, that man was the son of Philip. In 356 B.C. his father had just achieved a brilliant military success when he received from three messengers the news that his great general, Parmenion, had overthrown the Illyrians in battle, that one of his horses had registered a signal triumph at the Olympic Games, and that his wife, Olympias, had given birth to Alexander. The astrologers who told the king his son would be invincible in battle were more fortunate than the majority of prophets.

Among the tutors of the young Alexander was Aristotle, one of the world's greatest thinkers, and his teaching was doubtless a potent factor in moulding the mind of the all-conquering soldier-statesmen. But the youthful heir to the throne, in addition to being taught "to live worthily," also studied with eager ambition the art of war. A well-thumbed copy of the *Iliad* found a place under his pillow at night: its companion was a dagger. He is said to have lamented his father's victories as likely to leave fewer glories for the son to win. As an instance of his pride, it is recorded that when Alexander was asked by his friends if he would compete in the Olympic Games, he replied that he would, if he might have kings to run with him.

He won his spurs in battle when he was a mere boy of sixteen. In the absence of his father, he took the field against the rebellious Mædians, and stormed their principal town. When, in 338 B.C., Philip won the great battle of Chæronea against the Athenians and their Theban allies, the two most powerful states of Greece, his son commanded the Macedonian cavalry, and played a decisive part in the victory.

He was not yet eighteen, and before he was twenty he became king, after Philip had been assassinated. Philip was an able ruler and a skilful captain, but he made the fatal mistake of "filling his house with division and bitterness." He had put Olympias away from him, and married a Macedonian maiden named Cleopatra, who must not be confused with her more famous namesake of Egypt. There was an ugly scene at the wedding feast. Attalos, uncle of the bride, drunk with wine and vainglory, invited the nobles to pray the gods for "a legitimate heir to the throne." Alexander flung a flagon in the face of the man who had thus insulted his mother. Philip, flushed and unsteady, started up and drew his sword on his son. He reeled and fell, and, as he lay prostrate, Alexander contemptuously remarked: "Behold the man who would pass from Europe to Asia, yet trips and falls in passing from one couch to another."

It has been suggested by some writers that Alexander was involved in the murder plot against his father, but there is no evidence to justify this terrible accusation. That his mother was implicated is far more probable. She certainly ordered the unfortunate Cleopatra to commit suicide, and the boy to whom she gave birth was sacrificed to the gods.

When Alexander succeeded Philip on the Macedonian throne in 336 B.C., he was not quite twenty. He was dead before he was thirty-three. But the thirteen intervening years had witnessed such a vast and glittering panorama of conquest that men have been dazzled by it for twenty-three centuries.

On his accession he found himself menaced by a ring of enemies. "The impression which a ruler makes at the beginning of his reign," he said, "remains throughout his life. The death of my father has taken by surprise the rebels as much as myself, and we must seize the opportunity before they rally." There were hostile agitations in Thrace, Thebes, Illyria and Thessaly. Alexander dealt promptly with the situation. He marched against the Thessalians, evaded their army by cutting a new path over Mount Ossa, and won a bloodless victory. He conciliated not only Thessaly but other Greek states, and the Congress of the Confederacy at Corinth elected him supreme general of the Greeks for the invasion of Asia, which had been planned by his father.

It was while at Corinth that he had an historic meeting with the eccentric philosopher, Diogenes. Asked by the young king to name any boon he craved, the philosopher replied: "Stand out of the sun." As he departed, Alexander remarked to his followers: "Were I not Alexander I should like to be Diogenes."

Before he could set out on his Persian campaign the commander-in-chief had to teach a stern lesson to the rebellious Thracians. These hardy mountaineers gathered to the defence of a steep defile known as the Shipka Pass, through which the Macedonians had to make their way. They had hauled up their war-chariots to the top in order to roll them upon the invaders, but Alexander's tactics easily overcame the danger. He commanded the infantry to advance up the defile, opening the ranks when possible to let the chariots pass through the gaps. When that was impossible, the soldiers were directed to fall on their knees and hold their shields locked firmly together, thus forming a roof on which the chariots would fall and roll away. The stratagem was successful and the pass was taken. He drove the Triballi to the Danube—then known as the Ister—and crossing to the northern bank scared the Getæ almost out of their wits so that they fled in terror from the field.

Alexander next overthrew the Illyrians, and then marched on Thebes, where King Darius of Persia had stirred up a revolt against Macedonian rule. Thebes was taken by storm, and six thousand of its inhabitants were put to the sword. The League of Corinth decreed that the city should be levelled to the dust, her territory divided, and her women and children sold into slavery. It was an appalling punishment, and a severe lesson to would-be revolutionists.

The fall of Thebes and the restoration of peace to the Greek states ended Alexander's campaigns in Europe. They had occupied little more than a year, but they had firmly established his reputation as a general. He had given ample evidence of his brilliance in strategy and his boldness of resolution. He had shown those qualities which caused Napoleon to name him first of the world's seven greatest captains—Alexander, Hannibal, Julius Cæsar, Gustavus Adolphus, Turenne, Prince Eugène and Frederick the Great. Now, at last, the young commander was free to turn eastwards. Henceforth his life was spent in Asia, where his camp became not merely a military organization, but a centre of Greek culture, a moving metropolis of the arts and sciences.

Before setting out on his new campaign, Alexander portioned out nearly all the royal estates among his friends. One of them, Perdiccas, asked him:

"What will you have left for yourself?"

"Hope!" replied the king.

"Your soldiers will be your partners in that," said Perdiccas. "We who go forth to fight with you need share nought save your hopes."

The story illustrates the way in which Alexander inspired his followers with enthusiasm and confidence at the outset of his tremendous venture.

He crossed the Hellespont—the Dardanelles of less happy but more recently memory—in 334 B.C., with an army of some thirty thousand infantry and five thousand cavalry. At the River Granicus he was opposed by a strong force of Persians, but crossed the stream with his cavalry under a shower of darts from the foe, and secured a passage for the infantry.

Alexander fought in the van, and, being easily recognized by his shield and the plume of white feathers on either side of his helmet, he was hotly attacked. His friend, Cleitus, came to his rescue at a desperate moment, and saved the Greek commander's life by a shrewd spear thrust. Little did Alexander think that one day he would repay Cleitus by slaying him.

The conqueror now set himself to the task of subduing Asia Minor, but before he renewed his march he sent a vast array of Persian armour to the Parthenon at Athens, "spoil . . . taken from the barbarians of Asia." Cities and fortresses fell swiftly before his onslaught. At Gordium, he cut the famous Gordian knot. "Whoever shall loose the cord which binds this chariot shall rule over Asia," said an ancient oracle. The conqueror wasted no time over the mysteries of the knot. He drew his sword and cut it. The gesture was characteristic of one whose astonishing swiftness of decision gave him always the advantage in all his campaigns, but it illustrates also the headstrong impatience which brought him to death's door at the very moment when he stood in the gateway of Asia, preparing to give battle to the hosts of Darius.

After a long ride under a burning sun he plunged recklessly into the cool waters of the River Cydnus. This brought on a violent fever, and the physicians despaired of his life. But a wise man known as Philip of Acarnania offered to prepare a draught which would cure the king. Even as he was making up the medicine, a messenger arrived with a letter from the veteran Parmenio, one of the Guards of the King's Person. It contained a warning that Darius had bribed Philip to poison Alexander. The physician brought the draught as the king read the letter.

"Read this," said Alexander, taking the cup and swallowing its contents. His confidence was justified. Under Philip's care he made a rapid recovery, and soon took the field against the advancing Persians.

Darius, King of the Persians, called himself the "Great King." He felt he was lord of the known world. He ruled all western Asia and Egypt; but there were Greek cities under his rule, and they, and many other of his subject peoples, hated his yoke and were only too willing to welcome Alexander and his free, cultured civilization.

Darius was a weak king and an incompetent general, but his army was five times as large as that of his enemy. Numbers, however, proved of no avail against skill and discipline. The armies met in the plain of Issus, and the Macedonians won a decisive victory.

Alexander's rival fled ignominiously from the field, leaving his mother, wife and children in the hands of the conqueror.

When the Greek general returned from the pursuit, his first care was to send an assurance to the captive women that Darius lived, and that they would be treated with all the respect and consideration due to their station. This humane and generous attitude astonished Alexander's contemporaries. The captive Queen Stateira, who was reputed to be the most beautiful of women, would undoubtedly have met with very different treatment from most conquerors in those days.

Even then Darius refused the complete submission Alexander demanded. Alexander determined he must be defeated utterly. But before plunging into Persia to overwhelm Darius finally, the invader turned his attention to the conquest of Syria. His hardest task—perhaps the hardest he ever encountered—was to capture Tyre, an important naval station. Alexander's great difficulty was that this island fortress had to be attacked from the mainland. He built a great mole, or causeway, stretching across half a mile of sea. He collected a great fleet of galleys furnished by Sidon, which he had won over to his cause, and finally, after superhuman feats of engineering, he was able to launch a terrific assault and take the stubborn city.

Palestine and Egypt fell before him, and he now took a step which, even had he performed no other notable exploit, would have made his name memorable for ever. For in Egypt he founded the city of Alexandria, and the history of this great port through more than twenty centuries proves the shrewdness and keen foresight of its founder. In Egypt, too, the conqueror visited the temple of Ammon where, it was said, the god recognized him as his son.

In the spring of 331 B.C., the new Lord of Egypt and Syria returned to Tyre and collected his forces for the great march into Persia. Darius, with an army estimated to be a million strong, but more probably half that number, met the Greek invaders, who numbered under fifty thousand men, near Gaugamela (the camel's house), though the battle is now more generally named as Arbela. The Macedonian leader's masterly handling of his cavalry decided the issue. Once again Darius made good his escape, but this time the fate of the Persian Empire, the greatest the world had known, was sealed. Babylon and Susa opened their gates to the victor, and finally Persepolis, the royal capital of Persia, "the richest of all the cities under the sun," fell into the hands of Alexander. Treasure to the value of scores of millions of pounds sterling was his.

Here, according to Plutarch, occurred one of those mad carousals which more than once tempted the new Lord of Asia to dangerous excess. Thaïs, an Athenian courtesan, excited a crowd of drunken revellers to set fire to the palace of Xerxes, who had destroyed the Acropolis at Athens with fire, and Alexander threw the first blazing brand. Within a few moments he repented of his folly, and ordered the flames to be quenched. This incident, so far as the debauchery is concerned, is no longer believed. Competent authorities hold that Alexander gave the instructions solely for moral effect. In any case, no serious damage seems to have been done.

He now set forth to capture the fugitive Darius, but before he came up with him the unfortunate Persian had been stabbed by conspirators, and left for dead. He was found thus by Macedonian soldiers, to whom he murmured a few dying words of gratitude to Alexander for the courtesy he had extended to the royal captives. The Greek king covered the body with his own mantle as a mark of respect.

By 328 B.C., the Macedonian was master of all the Persian Empire. The tolerance he showed to the conquered provinces was generous and wise, but his policy of conciliating the Persians was by no means pleasing to his Macedonian followers, and feelings of discontent burst into sudden explosion in a tragic incident. One night, in the fortress of Samarcand, there was a great festival, and some of the guests sang the praises of Alexander, exalting him to the stature of the gods. His friend Cleitus, flushed with wine, sprang up to denounce the blasphemy, and was carried away into an angry denunciation of the king. It was to the Macedonians, he said, that Alexander owed his victories, and he reminded the conqueror that he—Cleitus—had saved his life at the Granicus. Other banqueters forced Cleitus out of the hall, but he returned to hurl fresh taunts, and Alexander, in a frenzy, struck him down with a spear. It was a mortal blow, and an agony of remorse followed. For a day and night Alexander was inconsolable. He lay in his tent, sleepless and refusing food, cursing himself as a murderer.

The black stain remains as an indelible blot on the record of the great captain. It is pleasanter to contemplate an episode of romance which occurred a few months later. At the capture of the Sogdian Rock the beautiful Roxana was taken prisoner. Alexander had always shown indifference to women, but he was made captive by the tender grace of the daughter of Oxyartes, in whose territory the mountain fortress was situated. He resolved to make her his wife, and on returning to his headquarters at Bactra he divided a loaf with his bride, according to the fashion of the country, and celebrated the nuptials.

In his last years Alexander turned his thoughts to the conquest of India, then almost an unknown land. He crossed the Indus, defeated a rajah named Porus in a desperately contested battle at the passage of the Hydaspes (Jhelum) and took his brave opponent prisoner. When he asked the captive how he would fain be treated, the reply was, "Like a king," and Alexander restored his territory to him as a protected state under Macedonian suzerainty.

An unexpected obstacle held up further advance, when the Hyphasis (Beas) was reached. The war-worn Macedonian veterans absolutely refused to march another step. They had trudged nearly twelve thousand miles and were weary both of fighting and of victory. So their king had to give up his plans for further conquests. It says much for Alexander's magnanimity that some thousands of these men returned home "with rich rewards."

Alexander the Great passed away in the palace at Babylon after a few days illness following a great banquet (323 B.C.). Rumours were afterwards spread that he had been poisoned, but it is more probable that Alexander had "burned himself out." He had crowded into half the normal span a score of lifetimes. The empire he founded passed away, but not before it had played its part in the pageant of progress. As conqueror and colonizer, as explorer and civilizer, Alexander reached "an eminence of human grandeur," to quote Arrian, which has not been equalled.

DEMOSTHENES

(*c.* 383–322 B.C.)

The classical tradition of public speaking, which governs the oratory of today as much as it did that of bygone ages, springs from the works of one of the greatest and the noblest of ancient Greeks, Demosthenes. His style and art have moulded the rhetoric of nations. His own life-work was a fight for the freedom and independence of Athens and Greece against the invasion of Philip of Macedon and his son, Alexander the Great. Demosthenes' failure cannot dim the flaming magnificence of his patriotism, nor can political calumny obscure his transcendent idealism.

THOSE citizens of Athens who were accustomed to walk by the seashore as twilight fell, something over two thousand years ago, were sometimes startled by the sight of a young man declaiming aloud against the competition of waves breaking and surf surging back over the stones. They probably thought he was mad—certainly they would not have believed they had witnessed the rigorous self-training of one of the greatest orators the world has ever known.

Demosthenes was born with a bad impediment in his speech, and in his efforts as a boy to control his words, he contorted his face into quite terrifying grimaces. Tradition tells us how the youthful Demosthenes set out to cure his physical defects. Lemprière, the foster-father of tradition, declaims:

" To correct the stammering of his voice, he spoke with pebbles in his mouth; and he removed the distortion of his features, which accompanied his utterance, by watching the motions of his countenance in a looking-glass. That his pronunciation might be loud and full of emphasis, he frequently ran up the steepest and most uneven walks, where his voice acquired force and energy; and, on the seashore, when the waves were violently agitated, he declaimed aloud, to accustom himself to the noise and tumults of a public assembly. He also retired to the solitude of a subterranean cave, to devote himself more closely to studious pursuits; and to eradicate all desire of appearing in public, he shaved one half of his head. In this silent retirement, by the help of a glimmering lamp, he composed a great part of his orations, which have been the admiration of every age. . . ."

Certainly Demosthenes required his hard-won eloquence early in life. He was born about 383 B.C., at Pæania, a deme of Athens. His father, who was a rich sword manufacturer, died when the orator was seven years old. His money was left in trust for the widow and the boy, but the three guardians plundered the property and made no provision for either.

When Demosthenes was legally of age he brought actions against the guardians. They were men of position and influence, and they used every resource and trick to defeat him. But Demosthenes won in the end, only to find, as is not unusual in cases of this sort, that there was hardly any inheritance left to win.

No sooner had he recovered the residue of the estate, than he was forced to undertake a state "liturgy." This was a public duty discharged at his own expense by a citizen, and Demosthenes spent his money in an eminently practical way by fitting out a trireme (warship) for the service of Athens. Then he settled down to earn his living as a lawyer and writer of speeches.

In his legal practice he only took cases of the highest order, and his political speeches were written on behalf of the Opposition, who consisted of the war party. There was a desultory and long-drawn-out campaign in progress against Philip, the astute and ambitious King of Macedon, and father of Alexander the Great, and the policy which Demosthenes supported was that of strenuously pressing the war against Philip.

It was not even that Demosthenes regarded Philip, or even Macedonia, with any real hatred, but in his burning patriotism he felt that a Greece that was not led by the Athenian state was a lost and degraded country. Therefore, he fought with every ounce in him against the threat of Philip's supremacy.

In 352 B.C., Philip made an unsuccessful attempt to invade southern Greece, and Demosthenes roused Athens by his fighting speech, the First Philippic. It was the first of those great orations against the "pestilential Macedonian," which added a word to the dictionary to denote powerful and fervent invective.

Later in the same year he delivered a notable speech "For the Rhodians," in which he counselled Athens to assist a democratic rising in Rhodes in order to recover some of her lost influence in the affairs of the Ægean.

Meantime, Philip, checked at Thermopylæ, turned northwards and laid siege to Olynthus. The Athenians knew the importance of the position and were making every effort to relieve the town. To distract attention, Philip stirred up a revolt in Euboea. Now Euboea was almost at the gates of Athens—no more than forty miles as the crow flies—and Olynthus was in the northern Chalcidian peninsula, and the government, naturally enough, turned its attention to Euboea first.

In three great speeches known as the Olynthiacs, Demosthenes urged the Athenians to go to the relief of Olynthus. He was overruled. Euboea was saved, while Olynthus was captured by Philip. But the victory was costly, and did more harm than good to the prestige of Athens. They were too exhausted to continue the war, and Demosthenes supported the proposals of peace.

A commission of ten was sent to treat for terms with Philip: it included Philocrates, Aeschines, and Demosthenes. Demosthenes was the only one who was a real match for the wily Philip, and he saw quickly that the Athenians were going to allow themselves to be outwitted.

After long negotiations a treaty was made. In it there was a clause that left each party in possession of what it held at the time of signing the treaty—Philip should keep what he had, Athens and her allies what they had. Here the Athenians were outwitted, for the Athenian allies were not mentioned by name. Now Philip was at war with the state of Halus in Thessaly, and could intervene in a war between Thebes and Phocis. If the Halians and the Phocians had been mentioned by name, Philip would be bound by the treaty to cease warfare—but they hadn't, and Philip went on fighting.

Demosthenes dragged his unwilling colleagues in search of Philip, but the king was wily. Delay after delay prevented the Athenian commissioners from meeting him, and when they did, Philip had won all he had set out to win.

Demosthenes' anger knew no bounds. He refused the diplomatic presents which Philip offered in accordance with custom, stayed away from the official banquet, quarrelled with his colleagues, and returned home alone. As soon as he reached Athens he made a proposal that the crowns usually conferred upon ambassadors should not be awarded to the commission.

Philip was not slow to follow up the advantage he had gained. Within a month he had conquered the Phocians and gained the right to sit on the Amphictyonic Council, which ruled the affairs of that collection of Greek states, a council in which Athens had hitherto held premier place.

The Athenians, outraged at this, demanded that the treaty of peace should be revoked. It was Demosthenes who insisted that, having made the peace, they must abide by it.

In 344 B.C. Demosthenes delivered his second great rhetorical blow against Macedon in the Second Philippic, and three years later, as a prelude to war, came the magnificent patriotic call of the Third Philippic, one of the grandest speeches in any language.

Meanwhile, Demosthenes and others of his party were accusing the members of the commission. Aeschines managed to escape condemnation, but Philocrates fled his trial and was condemned.

War was declared in 340 B.C., and at first the Athenians met with success; but a religious dispute led to the Amphictyonic Council calling upon Philip, and the Macedonian marched into southern Greece and won the crushing victory of Chaeronea in 338 B.C.

Athens prepared for a fight to the death, but Philip was preparing for war with Persia. The party friendly to Macedon at Athens made an easy peace and an alliance with Philip; and then they tried to purge the city of the old war party. Action after action was brought against Demosthenes, but he won them all, and Athens showed her appreciation of his services by choosing him to make the funeral speech on those who had fallen at Chaeronea. That oration has been broadcast in Great Britain many times on Armistice Day.

Macedon had a firm hold on the city, and resistance was impossible. In 336 B.C., when about to lead the main Hellenic army against Persia, Philip was murdered. Plans were made for revolt, but they were too slow. The young Alexander, no more than twenty years of age, took swift action, and Athens repented. Demosthenes went so far as to propose a public thanksgiving for the death of the late king.

A year later it was rumoured that Alexander had been killed in Thrace, and Thebes rebelled again the Macedonian yoke. Demosthenes moved that she should be supported: money was sent, and the army and fleet were being equipped, when Alexander appeared, sacked Thebes and requested the delivery to him of ten Athenian leaders, including Demosthenes. Demades, who had helped to make peace after Chaeronea, pleaded successfully with the king, with the result that of the proscribed leaders only the general Charidemus was condemned.

After this narrow escape Demosthenes grew more cautious, with the result that he fell into disfavour also with the extreme war party that he had once supported, and this gave the Macedonian party an opportunity for making a new attack upon him.

Some years before, a citizen named Ctesiphon had proposed that Demosthenes should be presented with a golden crown, the highest honour awarded in Athens, for his services to the state. In 330 B.C., Aeschines, on behalf of the Macedonian party, indicted Ctesiphon on three counts: that it was illegal to crown an official of the state and at the time of the proposal Demosthenes was holding office; that it was against precedent to award crowns in the theatre, as Ctesiphon had suggested; and thirdly—and this was the real object of the attack—that Demosthenes was a bad citizen and not worthy to be crowned.

Aeschines, who was second only to the defendant as an orator, handled the case in a clever way. He played for the support of the war party by suggesting that Demosthenes had abandoned his cause, and actually accused him of neglecting opportunities to rebel against Alexander. Obviously, the accused could only answer these charges by admitting treason and delivering himself up to the mercy of the Macedonian overlords. In his superb defence, known as the speech "On the Crown," Demosthenes does not answer the charges: he leaves it for his hearers to decide whether he has acted as a true patriot or as a repentant rebel. Aeschines failed to get the legal minimum of a fifth of the votes, and he left Athens in disgrace.

It is quoted as an instance of the generosity of Demosthenes that afterwards, when Aeschines had set up as a schoolmaster in Rhodes and was in difficulties, the great orator helped him with gifts of money.

A new turn to affairs came in 324 B.C., when Harpalus, Alexander's administrator at Babylon, deserted with a fleet and the huge sum of seven hundred and twenty talents (roughly £140,000) and made for Athens. The war party were overjoyed and were in favour of receiving Harpalus and using his resources in a new effort against Alexander, but Demosthenes had learned prudence.

He received Harpalus as a private refugee and insisted on dismissing his fleet. Macedon demanded that Harpalus should be detained and the money stored in the Parthenon on trust. To this Demosthenes agreed.

Then Harpalus escaped, and the Macedonians asked that the money should be counted. More than half of the treasure had disappeared; Demosthenes himself suggested that an investigation should be made to find out what had happened to the rest. After a long delay a report was published naming a list of people guilty of appropriating the funds, though without mentioning what had been done with the money. The name of Demosthenes headed the list. He was put on trial and convicted. The Macedonian party had triumphed at last. Unable to pay the enormous fine of fifty talents (about £10,000), Demosthenes was banished to Troezene.

Less than a year later, in 323 B.C., came the news of the death of Alexander. Demosthenes was recalled, and was received by the people with joy and enthusiasm. Once more the patriot was in command: again he was leading the fight for a free Hellas, for the liberty of the true Greeks unrestrained by the barbarian overlords from Macedon.

He joined hands with Hyperides, who had been a prosecutor at his trial, and together they set out to rouse the whole of the Peloponnese.

Athens began the new campaign brilliantly. After Alexander's death, Macedonia was under the rule of Antipater, who had been one of the great conqueror's generals and had been left behind as governor. He was routed by the Athenians in Thessaly and forced to retire to the town of Lamia, where he was besieged.

But there, Leosthenes, the Athenian commander, was killed, and the tide of fortune turned. The siege was raised. Antipater received reinforcements from Asia, returned to the attack, and decisively defeated the Athenians at Crannon.

This time the Macedonians were making no mistake in dealing with their old enemy. Antipater demanded that Demosthenes and Hyperides, the two great orators who had inflamed the Athenians to their last bid for freedom, should be delivered up to him.

Demosthenes fled to the island of Calauria, where, in October, 322 B.C., he took refuge in the temple of Poseidon. One Archias, who had formerly been an actor, came after him with a guard of Thracian spearmen: he was not the sort of man to stop short of violating the rights of sanctuary, but he hesitated to profane a shrine so sacred as that of the god of the sea. So he spoke to Demosthenes, asking him to leave the temple, and suggested that if he surrendered quietly Antipater would pardon him.

"Archias," the orator replied coldly and contemptuously, "you have never moved me by your acting, and you will not now move me by your promises."

Archias began to bluster and threaten.

"Now you speak like a real Macedonian oracle," said Demosthenes. "Before you were acting. Wait a moment while I write to my friends."

He then retired to the inner part of the temple, where he was still in sight of Archias and the soldiers. He took up the pen and bit the end of it, as if in thought. Then suddenly he flung his cloak over his head.

The spearmen jeered, and Archias went into the temple to persuade the refugee once more to come out. There was no reply. The poison, which had been secreted in the pen, was slowly taking effect.

Demosthenes staggered to his feet.

"Now," he cried, "you can play the part of Creon in the tragedy as soon as you like and cast forth my body unburied. But I, gracious Poseidon, quit thy temple while I yet live. Antipater and his Macedonians have done what they could to pollute it."

He reeled past the altar of the god, and fell dead.

Thus in the bitterness of defeat and suicide Demosthenes ended his long struggle for justice and his country's freedom. He had fought with conviction and with courage against enemies at home and a powerful enemy abroad, and his failure was as glorious as it was inevitable.

His ideal was the great Athens of old, the free city, mistress of an empire, dispenser of justice, guardian of the liberties of Greece. In Philip and the Macedonians he saw ruthless barbarians who would crush beneath their heels the fine flower of freedom that had been the greatest boast of the true Hellene.

To further that ideal he had used his powers as a writer and an orator, powers that have never been surpassed. For Demosthenes has been the model for all the ages that came after him.

Cicero acknowledged him to be the master, and we can trace his influence upon Cicero, upon Burke, upon all those who have swayed the world by their nobility of utterance and their command of rhetoric.

As for his life's work, the Athenians acknowledged the truth in the inscription they placed upon his monument:

Didst thou to wisdom equal strength unite,
Then never Greece had bowed to conquering might.

ASOKA

(*c.* 300–232 B.C.)

Asoka, first of the great rulers of India to emerge, as a historical figure, from the mists of antiquity and legend, left to us an unique series of inscriptions carved upon pillars and rocks throughout the length and breadth of India. They disclose a lover of justice and piety, of gentleness and humanitarianism, of charity and generosity. Asoka stands alone in history as having ruled a great empire successfully with scarcely a resort to force and with an unwavering respect for the sanctity of human life. The first Buddhist ruler, he impregnated his empire with all that is best in that faith and in doing so assured the spread thereof throughout the Eastern world. A man of deep wisdom, compassion and strength of character, he ranks among the great men of the world, not only by reason of what he did but of what he was.

INDIAN history in ancient and medieval times moved in a series of startling ups and downs. Great dynasties arose, held sway over great parts of India, then rapidly collapsed, to be followed by long periods of uncertain anarchy, of which today we know little or nothing. The first of these dynasties was the Maurya, the kings of which ruled from their capital, Pataliputra, in the third and part of the second centuries B.C.; and the most remarkable of these kings was Asoka.

Alexander the Great conquered North-Western India in 327 B.C. and on his death in 323 B.C., that portion of his vast dominions was taken over by one of his generals, Seleucus Nicator. His hold was effective, however, only in the western fringe of what Alexander had conquered, the rest had reverted to the leading Indian kingdom of Magadha, now ruled by Chandragupta, the first of Mauryas. The origins of Asoka's grandfather are obscure, but it is likely that he was the natural son of the King of Magadha by a low caste woman. It is certain, anyway, that soon after Alexander's departure in 324 B.C., Chandragupta overthrew the reigning dynasty and became himself King of Magadha and equally certain that within twenty years he had made himself master of much of and suzerain of all India except the extreme south and south-east. He was succeeded by his son,

Bindusara, who, in a reign of about twenty-five years, held all that his father had left to him.

Tradition ascribes to Bindusara one hundred children and there is a legend that Asoka murdered ninety-nine brothers and sisters in order to ascend his father's throne. The legend is without foundation, but it is probable that there was a war of succession between Asoka and his elder brother, Susima. Probable, but like so much about Asoka, not certain. Of all the early Indian rulers, we can, thanks to the famous rock edicts and to the mass of oral Buddhist tradition, conjecture most about Asoka, but there can be very little certainty, for except for the edicts no written contemporary evidence exists. It is a remarkable fact that when, late in the eighteenth century, Englishmen began to take an interest in India's past, they could find among the Indians of that day no knowledge at all of the Maurya period or of Asoka's existence.

The probable date of Asoka's accession is 273 B.C. and that of his ceremonial coronation is four years later. From the accounts of Megasthenes, Greek envoy at the court of Chandragupta, we know that Asoka inherited a highly centralized form of government at Pataliputra and an empire divided into the viceroyalties of Taxila in the north and Ujjain in central India. Asoka acted himself for a time as viceroy at Taxila. In the outlying portions of the empire there was little interference with local administration, but the royal army, large and well organized, was always available to quell disturbances.

In the first years of his reign, Asoka behaved much as was expected of a ruler in those days. He kept splendid court and ruled as an autocrat, untrammelled by advice or, probably, scruples. His favourite pastimes were hunting, feasting and war. Thousands of beasts were slaughtered daily for the royal kitchens, quite apart from those killed on the frequent occasions when Asoka took part in a royal hunt.

In warfare there was less opportunity, since little of India had been left unconquered by his grandfather, but about the ninth year of his reign he determined to conquer the kingdom of the Kalingas, the centre of which was the modern province of Orissa. He was successful, but the struggle was fierce, and the slaughter that accompanied it and the disease that followed it were appalling. Asoka records in one of the rock edicts that 100,000 were slain and 150,000 taken prisoners.

The effect of this slaughter on Asoka's mind was profound, causing a change of heart only comparable in its suddenness and completeness to that caused in Saul by his vision on the road to Damascus. In the thirteenth Rock Edict he records that: "His majesty feels remorse on account of the conquest of the Kalingas, because during the subjection of a previously unconquered country, slaughter, death and taking of captive people necessarily occur, whereat his majesty feels profound sorrow and regret." Many conquerors may have secretly felt likewise, few have had the courage publicly to acknowledge the fact; but what is beyond all else remarkable about Asoka—Asokavardhana was probably his full name, though in most of the inscriptions he is called Priyadarsin—is the thoroughness with which he acted upon his newly found convictions.

Almost immediately after the Kalinga War he joined the Buddhist community. For two years he was only a lay brother, and at first it seems that he was not over impressed by what he was taught, but early doubts were rapidly dispelled and, after two years, probably in 260 B.C., he became a Buddhist monk, subscribing in full to the vows of the order. Such vows did not preclude him from taking part in the affairs of the world—he could be king as well as monk; simply he swore to obey certain rules and principles of conduct, but actually he went further than that; not only did he obey them himself, he imposed them also upon the whole of his vast empire.

Buddhism, since the days of its founder, Gautama, had existed as a branch of Hinduism, but at the time of the Mauryas it rivalled neither Brahminism nor, in all probability, Jainism in the extent to which it was practised. Almost certainly Asoka was attracted to the faith, in reaction from the Kalinga slaughter, by its absolute insistence on the sanctity of human life, but after he became a monk he embraced with all its implications the Buddhist *dharma,* the law of piety, right living and morality. From the rock edicts we can learn what to him *dharma* meant; perhaps the best summary can be found in an edict inscribed quite soon after his conversion, in which he bade his lieges, commissioners and district officers to proclaim:—

> "The law of piety, to wit, obedience to father and mother is good; liberality to friends, acquaintances, relatives, Brahmins, and ascetics is good; respect for the sacredness of life is good; avoidance of violence and extravagance and violence of language is good."

Noticeable in this summary are the references to the sacredness of life and to Brahmins and ascetics. In place of the enormous provisions of animal flesh allowed to the royal kitchens before the Kalinga War, there was now to be permitted only two peacocks and one deer each day. The rock edict dealing with the sacredness of life states:—

"Formerly in the kitchen of his majesty King Priyadarsin, each day many thousands of living creatures were slain to make curries. At the present moment when this pious edict is being written, only these three living creatures, namely, two peacocks and one deer, are killed daily, and the deer not invariably. Even these creatures shall not be slaughtered in future."

Later he prohibited, not only for himself but for all his subjects, the killing of bats, tortoises, ants, parrots, wild geese, squirrels, porcupines and many others, and of all quadrupeds neither useful nor edible; in fact, there was to be no killing that was not purely for sport. In addition, no fish were to be caught on fifty-six specified days in each year.

The fact that he commanded that there should be liberality to Brahmins and ascetics has caused him to be hailed as a champion of religious toleration. Perhaps he was, but it should be remembered that in Asoka's day every sect subscribed fundamentally to the same philosophy of life; there was no such cleavage as later there was to be between Mohammedan and Hindu or even between Protestant and Catholic. There was nothing in *dharma* that was unacceptable to a Brahmin. Buddhists had not, under the two earlier Mauryas, been persecuted, but the priestly Brahmin class was dominant, and almost certainly at that time proud, aloof and narrow-minded. Asoka's edict was more a command that such an attitude should be discarded than the proclamation of religious toleration that some have thought it to be.

Asoka took practical steps to see that *dharma* was inculcated into the minds of all his people, his most important innovation being the creation of Censors of Piety who should see that everywhere *dharma* was observed.

"Now in all the long ages past, officers known as the Censors of the Law of Piety had never been appointed, whereas in the fourteenth year of my reign Censors of the Law of Piety were appointed by me. They are engaged among people of all sects in promoting the establishment of piety, the progress of piety and the welfare and happiness of the lieges . . . as well as other nations on my borders. . . . They are engaged in the prevention of wrongful imprisonment or chastisement, in the work of removing hindrances and of deliverance, considering cases where a man has a large family, has been smitten by calamity, or is advanced in years."

Some little time earlier in his reign, governors of local districts had been ordered to hold assemblies every five or in some cases three years, in which *dharma* should be discussed and explained. Asoka himself set an example by his charitable gifts, and a special royal almoner's department was set up at Pataliputra to organize their distribution.

Asoka was not content that Buddhist principles should triumph in his dominions alone; he sent forth missionaries far and wide. They went to the independent Cholas and Pandyas in the far south of India, and to Ceylon. Nepal and Kashmir, whether or not they were part of Asoka's empire, adopted the Buddhist faith, and Asoka's emissaries preached *dharma* as far afield as Syria, Egypt and probably Macedonia and Epirus.

> "And this is the chiefest conquest in his majesty's opinion . . . the conquest by the law of piety; this also is that effected by his majesty both in his own dominions and in all the neighbouring realms as far as 600 leagues . . . even to where the Greek king named Antiochus dwells, and beyond that Antiochus to where dwell the four kings severally named Ptolemy, Antigonus, Magas and Alexander."

Where Alexander sent generals to conquer men's bodies, Asoka sent monks to conquer men's minds.

There can be little doubt that after the Kalinga War Asoka determined to govern by kindness rather than by force; even when he dealt with the wild tribes on the borders of his empire he condemned the use of all but strictly necessary force by his subordinates. In one of the rock edicts, found in what had been Kalinga territory, and dealing with the duties of officials to border tribes, he states:—

> "Do your duty, and inspire these folk with trust, so that they may be convinced that the king is unto them even as a father, and that, as he cares for himself, so he cares for them, who are as the king's children."

Having as his aim conversion rather than repression, he realized the importance of a high standard of behaviour among his provincial officers.

> "There are, however, certain dispositions which render success impossible, namely, envy, lack of perseverance, harshness,

impatience, want of application, idleness, indolence. You therefore should desire to be free from such dispositions, inasmuch as the root of all this teaching consists in perseverance and patience in moral guidance."

He expected his subordinates to act upon the same principles as he laid down for himself.

"I have accordingly arranged that at all hours and in all places—whether I am dining or in the ladies' apartments, in my bedroom, or in my closet, in my carriage, or in the palace gardens—the official reporters shall keep me constantly informed of the people's business, which business of the people I am ready to dispose of at any place."

And in another passage of the same edict:—

"Work I must for the public benefit—and for what do I toil? For no other end than this, that I may discharge my debt to animate beings, and that while I make some happy in this world, they may in the next world gain heaven."

Buddhist tradition ascribes to Asoka the habit of making pilgrim tours, in the course of which he visited learned holy men, including Brahmins, and mingled, clad in saffron robe, with the common people. Probably many of the edicts were inscribed on such occasions; certainly he visited Gautama's birthplace, a visit commemorated today by a finely preserved pillar, crowned with the figure of a horse, on which is engraved:—

"His majesty King Priyadarsin in the twenty-first year of his reign, having come in person, did reverence. Because here was born Buddha, the Sakya sage, he had a stone horse made and set up a stone pillar. Because here the Venerable One was born, the village of Lummini has been made revenue free and has partaken of the king's bounty."

Asoka reigned for about forty years, the probable date of his death being in 232 B.C. Apart from the Kalinga War they were years of internal and external peace. There is no record of any attempt at civil war, no hint of trouble with neighbouring states. Indeed, neither to the east nor west was there a ruler who could compare in power with the Maurya emperor. Conditions thus favoured Asoka's great experiment, the rule of the Law of Piety. It is unlikely that it would have stood the test of a war, but in peacetime, backed by the personality and power of the emperor, it took deep hold on large sections of the races of the great Indian peninsula.

Asoka, we have seen, was no mere theorist. Not only did he appoint Censors of Piety, he took practical steps also to put into practice the rules he had laid down for himself: "Work I must for the public benefit." He established a wide system of road communications throughout his empire, planting the sides of the roads with shady banyan trees, and establishing free rest houses at frequent intervals; and it seems likely that he instituted hospitals in many districts.

> "Everywhere on behalf of his majesty King Priyadarsin have two kinds of remedies been disseminated—remedies for men and remedies for beasts. Healing herbs, medicinal for man and medicinal for beast, wherever they were lacking, have everywhere been imported and planted. In like manner roots and fruits, wherever they were lacking, have been imported and planted. On the roads trees have been planted and wells have been dug for the use of man and beast."

It may be imagined how his subjects, seeing that he practised what he preached, were the more willing to pay attention to his preaching, and that Asoka was himself aware of this is proved by another passage from the edicts:—

> "Whatsoever meritorious deeds I have done, these deeds the people have copied and imitated."

Little is known of the emperor's family life, though there is mention in the edicts of a wife, Karuvaki, who is referred to as "the second queen," a son, Tivara, and a grandson, Dasaratha. If the traditional Cingalese story is to be believed, however, by far the most important of his relations was his brother Mahendra. To him is ascribed the peaceful conversion of the then powerful kingdom of Ceylon to the Buddhist faith. His importance in this case can hardly be overstressed, for when Buddhism grew feeble in India it remained and has ever since remained dominant in Ceylon.

Within sixty years of the death of Asoka the Maurya dynasty had crumbled, the empire had split up, and India had re-entered a period of chaotic uncertainty. It has been alleged that this was largely due to Asoka's policy, that though he himself was great enough to carry it out, his successors were not, and that he had blunted for them the only weapon—autocratic force—that would have enabled them to hold the empire together. There is probably some truth in this assertion, but on the other hand the rapid fall of an empire in India has always been the rule rather than the exception. In any event it is hard to blame Asoka for having successors less great than himself.

Rather should we remember the extent of his achievement. The sites of the various pillars and rock inscriptions make it certain that he ruled over all the lands from the Hindu Kush mountains in the west to the Brahmaputra River in the east, from the foothills of the Himalayas in the north to a line drawn west from Madras in the south; and he certainly exercised some sort of control over Kashmir and Tibet. Throughout this vast empire—the size of Europe without Russia—there was peace and it is safe to say, since no single legend or tradition suggests otherwise, prosperity and contentment. Not even Akbar or Aurangzeb controlled so much of India, and it is doubtful whether, eighteen hundred years later, conditions of life were as good as in Asoka's day. Such was his achievement in the non-religious sphere.

But it is as the establisher of Buddhism that he will remain important for all time; in Buddhist eyes he must rank next to Gautama. Buddhists have survived in India only as a comparatively small sect, but Buddhism in the East today has one hundred and fifty million adherents, is the chief religion of Ceylon, Burma and Malaya, and counts as many devotees in China and Japan as Confucianism and Shintoism. Asoka made this possible. Previously Gautama's teachings had not spread beyond the Indian peninsula, or indeed far beyond the valley of the Ganges; henceforth, though Buddhism was to wane in the land of its birth, its message was to be spread throughout the Eastern world by missionaries, who would tell not only of its spiritual value but of the success which had attended Asoka's application of it to practical, everyday affairs and the ruling of an empire. Buddhism today is one of the world's chief faiths. The precepts and commands that Asoka had inscribed on rocks and pillars were as vital to the achievement of this position as was the pen of St. Paul to Christianity.

HANNIBAL

(247–183 B.C.)

During that long period of the world's history in which Rome grew from a tiny settlement to the centre of a mighty empire, only once was her might and destiny seriously threatened. And that threat was conveyed not by the power of her rival, Carthage, but by the patriotism, courage and genius of the Carthaginian general, Hannibal. Greatness has often been claimed for victorious soldiers, but Hannibal, whose ultimate portion was defeat and death, in the glorious battle his genius gave to the power of Rome has a claim, disputed only by Napoleon and Alexander, to be considered the greatest military leader the world has seen.

HAMILCAR BARCA, the great general and virtual dictator of the mighty North African state of Carthage, was going to war. Before he set out to lead his army against the allies of Rome, and to start again that struggle for the mastery of the Mediterranean and of the world, he was making an offering to his gods. Suddenly he turned and ordered the priests and others to leave. He wished to be alone with Hannibal, his nine-year-old son.

"Would you like to come to the war with me?" he asked the boy.

"Yes," came the eager answer.

"Then lay your hand upon this sacrifice, and swear eternal hatred to the Roman name."

The oath bound the young Carthaginian for life. He was the implacable enemy of Rome, and his hatred was fostered by genius. There is no more terrible combination.

Hannibal, son of Hamilcar Barca, was born in 247 B.C. He was born and bred in hatred of the Roman Empire, which always threatened the very life of Carthage.

The Carthaginians were not in reality, or by choice, a nation of soldiers. They were merchants, and they had inherited from their Phœnician ancestors skill as sailors and shipbuilders. But in the wars with Rome they suffered a disadvantage. Their army was largely reinforced with foreign mercenaries, and Hannibal and his father, Hamilcar Barca, were unique in the race in their genius for generalship.

From the day of his oath taken before the altar of Baal-Moloch, the young Hannibal lived in an atmosphere of war. He shared his father's tent and learned the soldier's life and the soldier's needs at first hand. His father took him campaigning in Spain, and realized that in the child he had a worthy successor.

Although slim, he was firmly built. He distinguished himself at sport, was known as a good boxer and runner, and was fearless in the saddle. Thus he hardened himself to the rigours of warfare. He knew how to appreciate food, and how to do without it, how to carry on without sleep; he learned how to work and how to rest his men. Hannibal's military training was the hard school of experience.

Although Livy, the Roman historian, with a prejudice unworthy of his work, paints Hannibal as a cruel and treacherous barbarian, he was in fact a cultured man. He received the finest education that could be given to the noble Phœnicians of the times. An excellent Greek scholar, he could compose State papers in Greek, and wrote books in that language.

At the age of eighteen, he took an active part in warfare. He was fighting at his father's side when Hamilcar Barca met his death, after having added a considerable part of Spain to the possessions of Carthage.

Appointed commander of the Carthaginian cavalry, Hannibal for the next eight years served under his brother-in-law, Hasdrubal, until the latter fell, sword in hand, in 221 B.C. Hannibal, at the age of twenty-five, was chosen by the army to be its supreme commander. He proved himself worthy of the distinction. At the head of a force of mercenaries, he led them through the varying fortunes of a long campaign. Not once did his men turn against him, though they were no more than adventurers, the hired soldiers of various nationalities.

What was the secret of his success?

In the first place, Hannibal had a genius for strategy; he understood the art of warfare as few generals have understood it. His skill in making the disposition of his forces and the efficacy of his tactical movements enabled him to command success, and it was not until the Roman generals, more particularly Scipio Africanus, had profited by his example that Hannibal suffered defeat.

His strategical skill was based on his unique ability to anticipate the enemy's movements. He had an uncanny gift of foreseeing the next move of the game. Yet that was not all. Hannibal was a master of the spy system. He had spies throughout the enemy camps, in the enemy armies and, during the great war with Rome, in the capital itself. The general was not above collecting necessary information himself. Cleverly disguised, he made a number of dangerous expeditions to secure vital knowledge about his foes.

His training and early life with the army had taught him how to handle men, how to nurse their energy, keep up their morale, and stabilize the commissariat. His administrative and organizing skill was later made fully evident at Carthage after the conclusion of the war.

Brilliant leader as he was, Hannibal made two vital mistakes in his conduct of the campaign against Rome. He underestimated the value of sea power and allowed the Romans to maintain their naval supremacy, thus hampering him vitally while fighting on foreign soil. In addition, he left his Spanish troops, which might have turned the war in favour of Carthage at the end of the Italian campaign, in command of his young brother, Hasdrubal, who was too youthful and inexperienced for the task.

The oath he made before the altar of Moloch was constantly in Hannibal's mind. He lost no opportunity of attacking the might of Rome. In 221 B.C., finding himself at the head of a powerful Carthaginian army in Spain, he determined to challenge Rome and the Roman confederation for the leadership of the world. He laid siege to the city of Saguntum, the one city in eastern Spain he had not as yet captured. Now Rome had warned the Carthaginians that should Saguntum be attacked it would mean war. The town fell to Hannibal after a siege of eight months. The might of Rome had been provoked; the Second Punic War began.

Hannibal was at once on the offensive. He raised three large armies, sent one into Africa, left another to look after Spain, and with the third set out for Italy. It was a mad, unbelievable thing. Italy, with its girdle of mountains in the north, was impregnable. There was no way for the invader, save by sea. But Hannibal did the mad, unbelievable thing. He reached the Pyrenees, sent some of his soldiers home, and pressed on with a force of 50,000 infantry and 9,000 cavalry—veterans all. And he had a force of elephants as well.

He crossed the lofty Pyrenees and the Rhône, swept aside the defending Gauls and then marched over the mighty barrier of the Alps.

Hannibal's march across the Alps is considered one of the greatest feats in the world's history. His soldiers were mostly plainsmen, the majority of them accustomed to the burning heat of the north coast of Africa, and these men were heavily equipped. He took, besides his heavy siege engines, a number of elephants to carry or to draw heavy loads. The elephants, of course, were wonderful pack animals, but in the Alps were as great a worry and responsibility as they were an assistance.

Many stories are told of that epic journey; how Hannibal built bridges and roads; how, when he had not time, or could not build bridges, he ordered that the elephants should be made to stand in the swift-flowing Alpine streams and break the force of the current so that men could pass through the icy waters with a greater degree of safety.

It was a tremendous effort against hostile tribes and bitter weather, through rocky passes and along broken roads. Men stumbled and fell on the slippery stones or were almost carried away in the fords of the swollen rivers. Avalanches thundered down on them, and men went mad in the unfamiliar mountain heights. In the dual conflict against men and Nature Hannibal lost heavily; he arrived, it is said, with only 20,000 infantry and 6,000 cavalry, although it is probable that historians have exaggerated the casualties. Hannibal's skill in nursing his army and his subsequent successes point to a much larger force than this.

The Romans were thunderstruck. The Carthaginian was on Italian soil. They sent their armies scurrying north to meet him.

Hannibal rested his men after their great exertion, but not for long. Victory in a cavalry skirmish on the Ticino was no more than a prelude to the campaign. In the December of 218 B.C., Hannibal met a Roman army in the Battle of Trebia, near Placentia and utterly routed it. He crossed another range of mountains, the Apennines, and invaded and ravaged Etruria.

Two mighty battles followed. First he routed the army of the consul Flaminius at Lake Trasimenus in June, 217 B.C. He lured the Romans into a defile by the shore and then closed it behind them. It was a death trap. The men in the defile were cut down; those that remained outside were driven into the lake by the cavalry. Why Hannibal did not immediately push on to Rome is one of those mysteries of which history affords so plentiful a supply.

In the following year at Cannae, the victorious general annihilated the largest Roman army that had ever crossed swords in action. Of the 76,000 Romans who had gone into battle against a Carthaginian army of half that strength, it is said that no fewer than 70,000 were killed.

In this battle Hannibal gave one of his most masterly displays of tactical skill. The Romans had drawn their forces up in the better position, on one of the banks of the River Aufidus. Hannibal was fighting with his back to the sea, and defeat for him meant utter annihilation. He made use of a stratagem which has been copied in all ages, even down to the World War.

He drew up his army in the usual formation of the time, with the infantry in the centre and the cavalry on the wings; but he made his centre thin and weak and kept strong detachments of Libyan infantry on each flank. At the first assault, the Gauls and Spaniards who formed the centre gave before the solid Roman infantry. On and on pressed the Roman centre until they had driven a deep wedge into the Carthaginian army and seemed to be certain of victory. Then Hannibal gave orders for the Libyan infantry to attack from each flank. This movement had the effect of cutting off the flower of the Roman army, and the heavy cavalry completed the victory.

The story goes that Hannibal sent three bushels of gold rings to Carthage; they had been taken from the fingers of Romans slain in the battle. His more human side was shown when he sought out the body of the consul who had been killed and honoured it with a funeral worthy of Rome's dignity. He was always a generous and honourable enemy.

Hannibal was now master of the greater part of Italy. Had he swept on and attacked at once, the might of Rome must have fallen before him. But Hannibal had deeper plans in mind. He wanted something more than a showy victory over the capital. He was hoping to overturn and crumble the whole empire by first winning the Latin allies and the people of Italy to his cause and then crushing the city. So he turned south and made his great effort to break up the Roman confederation. In 212 B.C. he captured Tarentum and made himself master of the south.

Already the Romans had begun a new policy under the generalship of Quintus Fabius Maximus, nicknamed Cunctator, the Delayer. They no longer offered battle to Hannibal: they massed troops in strong, impregnable positions and waited for him; they watched him and followed him, but did not fight. Hannibal was given no chance to show his superiority in open battle. He had to maintain his army in the enemy's country and preserve those cities which had come over to him.

Hannibal was still supreme. Year after year he marched through Italy, but though he reached the walls of Rome he never attacked. Slowly his forces weakened; the wearing-down policy of the Romans was having its effect. Then he must have realized the truth of the remark made to him by Maharbal, the commander of the Numidian cavalry, "You know how to win a victory, Hannibal, but not how to use one."

He sent to Carthage for reinforcements, but there was jealousy amongst the rulers, and he received no adequate support. When Hasdrubal brought soldiers from Spain they were too few, and the enemy defeated him at the River Metaurus before he could effect a junction with Hannibal. His first news of the battle was when the Romans tossed the bleeding head of Hasdrubal into his camp.

Falling back on Bruttium, in the extreme south, Hannibal kept his hold on the "toe" of Italy. For sixteen years he had held his army together, living on the land and giving Rome no peace. Then he was recalled to defend Carthage against Publius Scipio, who had conquered Spain and had carried the war into Africa. The two armies met at Zama in 202 B.C. The Carthaginian displayed all his old masterly touches in the disposition of his troops and in his tactical arrangements in the face of heavy odds; but the Roman pupil had learned from the master; he played for safety, and his superior numbers gained the day. Rome had won the war.

Hannibal left the field on which the flower of his army lay; his veterans had fought to the death. When at length the beaten general returned to his native city of Carthage, it was his first sight of it for thirty-six years.

Rome made peace with Carthage, but not with its most distinguished citizen. For Hannibal was as dangerous and as powerful in peace as he was in war. His mighty personality could stamp a policy and lead a state as ably as it could weld an army into an invincible fighting force.

His moral courage was equal to his physical courage. When in the Carthaginian senate he burst out laughing while the grave elders were bewailing the fate of their country, he was attacked by his jealous enemies, but Hannibal gravely excused himself by saying that one who had spent all his life in the camp could hardly be expected to have the polished manners of a courtier.

In peace, as in war, Hannibal took charge of his country's destiny. He reorganized the state after its humiliation by Rome, and so rapidly did he put affairs in order that in a short time Carthage had paid off the huge sum which Rome had demanded as an indemnity. But he had made the West too small for him. The Romans feared Carthage with Hannibal at the helm of the ship of state, and they accused him of plotting against the peace.

He went into voluntary exile at the court of Antiochus III, King of Syria, then about to wage war against Rome. The great general was in his element, but the monarch distrusted the man who had never betrayed an oath, and disregarded the advice of his genius. Antiochus was crushed by the Romans, who demanded Hannibal as the price of peace. The exile heard of the condition and slipped away to the court of Prusias, King of Bithynia. The Romans were soon on his track. They demanded that Prusias should give him up. Looking out one morning from a window, Hannibal saw that his house was besieged on every side. The agents of Rome had come to take him, alive or dead. He opened the poison casket in a ring which he always wore and swallowed the dose.

"Let us rid the Roman people of its daily worry," he smiled.

It was about 183 B.C.—the exact date is uncertain—when he chose death rather than surrender, still faithful to his childhood oath, hating and fighting the power of Rome.

Scipio, who was known as Hannibal's "conqueror" and was called Africanus after his victory at Zama, admitted that the man whom he had defeated was the finest general the world had seen, and those who fought against him were the first to praise his generosity and his fairness.

A few years later Carthage was destroyed by Rome, and a new city was built that became the imperial centre of government in Africa. It, in turn, was razed to the ground by the Arabs in A.D. 698. Of the once mighty city of Carthage, less remains today than of any ancient civilization.

JULIUS CÆSAR

(102–44 B.C.)

"Why, man, he doth bestride this narrow world, like a Colossus." So Shakespeare made Cassius speak of Julius Cæsar, and in cold fact the Roman did bestride the world. He was the general who thrust northward the power of Rome; he was the dictator who made possible the existence of a Roman Empire. The influence of his achievements has moulded the civilization of Europe in countless ways, and it will last as long as that civilization itself shall last. "Imperial Cæsar, dead and turned to clay," scoffed Hamlet, but despite his mortal clay the achievements of the greatest of the Cæsars have lived on.

To Cæsar it was better to be first in a village than second in Rome. He was destined to become first in Rome, and to receive the proud title of Father of the Fatherland. Had he been less ambitious, the history of Europe and its civilization would have assumed a very different form.

Here was a man who claimed kinship with the gods, who was regarded at the height of his career as if he were a god himself; a man who thrust the boundaries of the Roman Empire north and west, and left a mark on history that has never been effaced. The romance of his career may be seen in this, that, centuries later, missionaries poured out from Rome along the roads on which the legions had marched, and, on the foundations laid by this pagan genius, reared the great structure of Christian Europe.

For generations before his birth—in the year 102 B.C., and in a month that was to change its name to July in his honour—a struggle had been proceeding, now this way, now that, for mastery in the centres of civilization on the shores of the Mediterranean. The Greeks had left their mark on mankind by conquest, by amazing progress in philosophy, literature and the arts. The Carthaginians had risen as a trading nation, ruled by merchants and financiers, eager always for power. Meanwhile, the settlers who had poured into the unpromising land of Italy had begun to assimilate the many things that could be taught them by Greek travellers and traders, and had gradually become a menace to their wealthy neighbours.

Conflict between the Carthaginians and the Latins, who turned to Rome as their centre, had become a grim struggle for survival. Carthage ruled in Spain and along the southern coast of Gaul. The Romans watched them apprehensively, and were defeated when they matched themselves with the forces of Hannibal, the Carthaginian. For Hannibal succeeded in crossing the Alps and ravaging Italy. Still the failure of the Romans did not entail their extinction as a nation. Hannibal lost all that he gained as a result of the brilliant harrying tactics adopted by Rome. In the end full revenge was exacted; Carthage was occupied and destroyed; Rome at last was mistress of the Mediterranean, having subdued the Greeks, whose civilization she had adopted, and having established a strong protectorate in Asia Minor.

The strength of Rome's position lay in this. She had a genius for adaptability, and she knew how to make use of the fruits of conquest. The morale of the average man in Carthage was lower because he was merely a cog in a profit-making machine. The rulers of Greece made the mistake of looking down upon subject nations. But Rome was as ready to borrow ideas as she was to borrow and re-name the Greek gods. And the immigrants her land attracted, or the people over whom she gained power, were treated in such a way that they were induced willingly to offer allegiance. A conquering nation that imposes itself by force upon its defeated enemies is liable to crack in times of adversity. Rome found her strength in the pursuit of other policies, and by cleverness in colonization, the extension of citizenship, and the prosecution of sound plans of government, was able to present a bold front to her attackers.

It is necessary to bear these points in mind when considering the career of Cæsar, who exemplified many of the virtues as well as the vices of his time. He came of a patrician family which traced a legendary descent from Venus and Æneas, an imagined association with the gods that nourished his pride and may have influenced him strongly in later life, when he began to think that his powers were really superhuman.

As a young man he became attached to the popular party led by his aunt's husband, the great general, Gaius Marius, and was rewarded, when it came to power, with the position of priest of Jupiter, the chief god of the Roman people. But success was short-lived, for Marius died shortly after having been elected consul for the seventh time, and his followers were obliged to leave Rome, having lost positions and property. Sulla, who led the party in opposition, returned to Rome in triumph. He was prepared to pardon Cæsar, but wished him to divorce his young wife, the link with the hated democratic party. Cæsar refused, and that refusal placed him in grave danger. Rome was not deemed a safe place for him, and so he travelled east with the legions, gaining his first knowledge of warfare and thus preparing himself for the great role he was later to play in Gaul. When the fortunes of politics had swung once more his way, he returned to Rome to study law, then, as now, regarded as a stepping-stone to high office in the State.

Following a visit to Rhodes to learn oratory under the famous Apollonius Molon, Cæsar was attracted by dissipations that offered a contrast to the discomforts of army life and the concentration of learning. Squandering money on games and banquets, on the expensive pleasures of a man-about-town, he piled debt upon debt, until, it is said, his creditors had claims against him to the amount of £200,000. An opportunity was given for him to exercise a governorship in Spain, but his creditors would not let him go. Luckily, Crassus, the richest man in Rome, came to his aid and paid his debts, to be repaid when Cæsar returned re-established financially, and enjoying the credit due to military success.

With considerable skill, Cæsar reconciled the wealthy Crassus to Pompey, whose brilliant military career had made him the most powerful man in Rome, and in 60 B.C. the three formed the partnership known as the First Triumvirate. Cæsar obtained the consulship, but instead of a military command he was assigned the care of the roads and forests.

Affairs in northern Europe were then attracting a great deal of attention. The German tribes had succeeded in establishing themselves on the left bank of the Rhine, and were able, therefore, to challenge Rome in Gaul. The tendency of Rome in the past had been to drive eastward and around the Mediterranean. Cæsar wanted to drive north and west. His wisdom displayed itself when Europe began to grow into a federation of tribes or nations. Cæsar pressed for the command of the territories beyond the Alps, and rejoiced when it was given him. But he had to deal with major problems. Not only had the German tribes succeeded to such an extent that Rome was prepared to treat with them, but the Helvetii, whom the Germans were driving from what is now called Switzerland, were demanding a passage through territory known as the Province, which had been a Roman possession since 121 B.C., as a means of reaching the Atlantic. His attitude to the second peril offered ample illustration of his genius; for he drove the marchers back, hurriedly collected fresh forces, brought his soldiers to the attack with a minimum of delay, and finally defeated the Helvetii.

As a result of this victory Cæsar was asked to protect the Gallic chieftains against the German king, Ariovistus, whom he summoned to a conference. The only answer was a new invasion of Gaul from across the Rhine. Thereupon Cæsar attacked and pursued the survivors to the Rhine. Later, in 57 B.C., a rising by the Nervii and the Belgæ of northern Gaul was suppressed with greater difficulty. What Cæsar wrote about the valour of the Belgians was recalled with pride in 1914. In the following year he defeated the Veneti of Brittany, and other tribes, and then turned once more to fling the invading Germans back across the Rhine.

Cæsar's victories at this period of his career added not only to the prestige of the Roman Empire but also to his own. But he was not content to be merely a conqueror. He was a ruler, too; and he ruled with vision. By giving a system of government and rights of citizenship to the conquered, he made possible the establishment of the Roman tradition in the greater part of Europe. He strengthened small communities, inspired the building of highways, and created a strong peasantry. On the ideals suggested by these reforms, the solidarity of European civilization was built.

Despite other outbreaks, directed from both sides of the Rhine, Cæsar gained his mastery over the tribes. In 55 B.C. he bridged the Rhine, made a rapid campaign in Germany, destroyed the bridge on his return, and then set out for Britain. It may be said that the invasion was intended more as a demonstration than as a serious attempt at conquest, for some of the tribes had helped the Belgæ, and Cæsar's force was limited to two legions, a legion varying from three thousand to six thousand men. A year later he returned with five legions and a large force of cavalry, marched north to the Thames, which he crossed, and demanded tribute before going back to Gaul. The tribute was not forthcoming, and was never paid. Cæsar's invasion of Britain was the least successful incident in his military career.

For two or three years afterwards Cæsar's attention was devoted to the subjugation of Gaul. The tribes rose and were defeated. Difficult campaigns in various parts of the country had to be instituted. But Cæsar's star was rising. In spite of a defeat by the Gallic leader, Vercingetorix, at Gergovia in 52 B.C., where he met with heavy losses and was compelled to retire, he besieged and captured Alesia (Mont-Auxois) and crushed the united army of Gaul. He made Gaul a province and imposed a yearly tribute; but having secured what he wanted he was careful to placate his victims. Following the Roman tradition, he defeated his enemies as a prelude to turning them, so far as was possible, into friends.

Victorious in Gaul, Cæsar had now to face hostility in Rome. Bribes might accomplish much, but enemies were active against him, and he knew that he had exceeded his authority sufficiently often to be in danger of failure.

The Triumvirate, which had been solemnly renewed in 56 B.C., was drifting apart. Three years later Crassus was killed in Syria. Pompey and Cæsar were two suns in the firmament of power, and there was only place for one.

Pompey sided with the senate. When Cæsar's period of command ended, the senate demanded that he should disband his army. Cæsar's reply was to cross the Rubicon, a small river which marked the Italian frontier, at the head of a legion in arms. "The die is cast," he said, for by that unconstitutional action he had forced the issue of war.

Pompey fled, with Cæsar hotfoot and reinforced on his heels, as far as Brindisi, on the east coast. But there was a Pompeian army in Spain. He would first fight "an army without a general," to use his own words, and then pursue Pompey and fight "a general without an army." After a brief and triumphant campaign in the west he returned to overawe Rome, was elected consul, and set out to pursue his enemy in the east. In 48 B.C., at the battle of Pharsalus, in Thessaly, Cæsar won an overwhelming victory. Pompey fled to Egypt, where he was murdered.

Cæsar, in pursuit of his old enemy, went to Egypt, where he was made captive, it is said, not in warfare, but to the charms of Cleopatra, who was reputed to have borne him a son. But these months of amorous dalliance gave Cæsar's enemies time to collect their forces. Cæsar was forced to return to save his own affairs.

He proceeded to Asia Minor, where he defeated an old ally of Pompey. This was Pharnaces, King of Pontus. They fought at Zela, near the site of the victory of his father, Mithradates the Great. By this victory, Cæsar placed himself once more in a strong position. Incidentally, it was during this campaign that he sent his famous message, beloved by every schoolboy learning Latin: "*Veni, Vidi, Vici*"—"I came, I saw, I conquered."

No sooner had he set foot in Italy once more than he was called upon to quell a mutiny. That done, he was compelled to cross the Mediterranean to wage a campaign in Africa.

Finally, he returned to Italy, the first, not in a village, but in

Rome. He received the dictatorship for ten years, and then for life. His short period of office was distinguished by wise judgment, but marred by the vainglory that brought about his death. Enfranchisement was extended beyond the Alps, tribes in virtual subjection received friendly overtures, the calendar was reformed, the free man received further guarantees of freedom, and colossal public works were put in hand. Yet ambition had intoxicated him. Harking back in his mind to a legendary pedigree, he fancied himself as one so close to the gods that he could enjoy their privileges. His statue he caused to be set up among those who were supposed to have given the greatest glory to Rome; it was inscribed "To the Unconquerable God." His "modesty" when he was offered the dignity of kingship was carefully publicized beforehand, like the modesty of a modern film star. *Imperator,* the title he most loved, is the Latin source of emperor. He ruled from a throne of gold. And yet Rome was a republic!

At the foot of Pompey's statue in the Senate House, on a day of thunder, howling wind and terror, Cæsar fell to the daggers of assassins. It was said that there were more of his friends than of his enemies among those who murdered him. We know his last words, "You, too, Brutus," were spoken by one who saw himself deserted even by his closest companions. Achievement had brought him to defeat.

Cæsar turned the eyes of Rome from the Mediterranean to northern Europe; brought isolated, warring communities within the orbit of Rome's influence; put aside the sword of which he was so consummate a master to pen commentaries which are invaluable as history and literature, and paved the way to the empire which his nephew and successor, Augustus, founded. Lord Tweedsmuir has summed up the character of the man in his fine study:

"The burden of the globe on his shoulders did not impede his lightness of step. War and administration never made him a narrow specialist. His culture was as wide as that of any man of his day; he loved art and poetry and music and philosophy, and would turn gladly to them in the midst of his most critical labours. . . . Combined in him in the highest degree were the realism of the man of action, the sensitiveness of the artist, and the imagination of the creative dreamer—a union not, I think, to be paralleled elsewhere."

ATTILA

(?–c. A.D. 453)

Western civilization has more than once trembled at the onslaught of a destroyer, but rarely has it been so near doom as when the crumbling western empire of Rome faced the attacks of Attila and his horde of Huns. Ruler of the nomad warriors from the Rhine to China, leader of the fastest and most furious fighters the world had seen, this squat, fierce barbarian made the emperors of the East and West quiver at his very name. He was the arch-destroyer, the Scourge of God. Yet he created and held together an empire of nomads. His only other creation was that of fear. But he was responsible for the foundation of Venice—by families who fled before him on his invasion of Italy!

"THERE where I have passed the grass will not grow again." Thus boasted Attila, the Scourge of God.

He came out of the East, followed by his warriors mounted on small wild horses from the Steppes, their only saddle the strips of steaming raw meat that would feed them that day. Behind them rode their women, dank haired, flat chested, as hideous as their men.

For many years Rome and her dependants had trembled at the word Hun; always before them was the knowledge that sooner or later these destroyers must fall upon them, burning, pillaging, and ravaging their lands. Signs and portents gave body to their fears. In the year A.D. 450 western Europe was shaken by earthquakes. A comet appeared on the eastern horizon, the moon was eclipsed; and, it is said, upon Rome one day there fell a rain of blood. And then from the north came the news: Attila and five hundred thousand barbarian warriors had invaded the western empire.

* * * * *

Let us turn back to the beginning of the fifth century. The empire was then the whipping-post of corrupt bureaucrats, adventurers, and intriguers possessing but one common ambition—the amassing of gold. The great legions of the republic and early empire had dwindled in numbers and in worth, and Rome had gradually come to rely more and more upon her paid mercenaries and chieftains of the races on the outskirts of the empire, such as the Visigoths and Franks. She was conscious of the menace constituted by these allies, whose covetous eyes were turned greedily on her, and her policy was to pit one against the other. Thus, although gaining no real security, the empire kept afloat.

In the spring of A.D. 405 a grave crisis arose: a barbarian general, Radagaisius, at the head of an army of Slavs and Germans, attacked the empire. The Roman armies were easily defeated, and the only factor that saved them from utter disaster was the help of the Visigoths. But a victorious defence in which the Visigoths should have played the chief role was as much to be feared as a triumph by Radagaisius. The policy of balance had to be maintained, and therefore, Stilicho, the emperor's minister, engaged a new corps of cavalry from beyond the shores of the Danube. The new cavalry saved Rome.

The city went wild with delight, and prepared to receive her deliverers. Triumphal arches were raised, songs of praise prepared. The populace awaited their new allies with curiosity and excitement.

On the great day, the strangers rode through the gates, and wild acclamations broke forth. But in an instant they were almost drowned by gasps of horror and roars of laughter. The Romans had never seen such grotesque and ferocious hideousness. These barbarians resembled beasts more than men—short, squat, bow-legged, clothed in fur, and armed with quivers bristling with arrows. If their bodies were grotesque, their faces inspired terror and repulsion: the yellow skin was dragged tightly over their noses, their foreheads receded artificially, having been deformed from childhood by leather thongs, and their eyes were small, oblique, and cruel. Their voices were raucous and, if addressed, they seemed to repeat but one sound: "*Ioung.*" The puzzled Romans turned that into "Hun," and so named them for ever.

Nothing was known of the origin of these people, except that they had come out of Asia, and that they roamed the shores of the Danube and the Volga in nomadic tribes. They were reputed to be the descendants of witches and demons, living without gods, but with many strange superstitions.

Thus came the Huns to Rome—the first time.

* * * * *

Attila was born about the beginning of the fifth century in one of the nomadic chariots which formed the only home of the Hun, on the banks of the Danube—a king's son.

His hatred and contempt of Rome began almost with his first

consciousness. It was the custom in those days for barbarian kings and chieftains to send a number of their many sons to Rome. Such visitors were, in practice, part hostages and part pupils of the empire. Attila, at the age of twelve, was already dangerous to his uncles, who had succeeded their brother, Mundzuk, as joint kings of the Huns. What better plan than to dispatch this too-ambitious child to Rome, where luxury and soft living might prove a tempering influence? But Attila was more than a child with ideas—the germs of greatness were in him. The Latin influence neither tamed nor corrupted.

It was during those years in Rome that Attila's great plan took shape. He returned to the Danube with a vision which was to guide him through the rest of his life: his people were a great people and great warriors; at their head he would conquer the world. When he had unified the many tribes of his people under his solitary kingship, he would command the largest army in the Levant or Occident. And so Attila waited.

On the death of the Hun, King Rhuas, Attila succeeded to the leadership of the hordes that ranged from the Caspian to the Danube. His brother, Bleda, was joint king, but after ten years Attila had his ineffectual partner removed by the sword.

Within a few years, Attila had become supreme monarch of the barbarians without the Roman Empire. He spared conquered peoples in order to make them his allies. The Vandals, Ostrogoths, Gepidae and Franks fought under his standard. He extended his empire throughout Germany and Scythia until he held sway from the Rhine to the frontier of China, from the Baltic to the Danube.

Now he turned upon the eastern empire, and swept down upon the territory of the Emperor Theodosius. His armies invaded the whole land between the Black Sea and the Adriatic. Thrace, Macedon and Greece were subdued and seventy cities were captured and sacked.

Theodosius, after a series of defeats, sued Attila for peace, and peace was made on the most humiliating terms for the emperor, who had to cede large areas of land south of the Danube and also to pay tribute to the Huns.

And now, in A.D. 450, Attila was ready to attack the western empire and invade Gaul. The ostensible reason for the expedition was to aid his Frankish allies against the Visigoths, but the power of Rome was the real objective.

Through days and nights, out of Asia and from the shores of the Black Sea, the Huns and their allies rode to the banks of the Danube in answer to Attila's summons. The army was almost entirely composed of cavalry, and was the fastest moving machine of war ever known.

Attila reached the Rhine, where he was joined by some of the Franks. He proclaimed himself the deliverer of the oppressed, and offered a share of the prizes of war to all those who would throw in their lot with his. To those who withstood him he offered torture, rape, burning, massacre. In good or evil, Attila was a man of his word. The German barbarians had received him without hostility. Their towns were untouched, their women and children safe. The Burgundians and Salian Franks resisted him. Worms, Spires and Mayence were razed to the ground. And Basle, Strasbourg, Besançon, Arras, also fell before him.

Deploying his horde from the ocean to the Jura Mountains, Attila laid siege to Metz, a fortified town, governed by its warrior-bishop.

The Huns, who fought like huntsmen, and were invincible in open battle, knew little of the art of siege. After futile attempts at battering down the walls and forcing an entry, Attila, impatient of delay, swept on, leaving the untaken town behind him. A few days later news came to him that one of the walls of the town had suddenly collapsed. The repeated attacks made upon it had not been without effect.

The army turned back, and the citizens of Metz, desperately trying to fill the breach, were fallen upon by fur-clad, stinking demons. It was the night of Easter. Into the churches the destroyers rode, massacring, plundering the altars, giving no quarter. At dawn the Huns were riding on, leaving behind them a burnt city of smouldering ashes.

The news of the atrocities committed at Metz travelled faster than the Huns. They found Rheims deserted, except for a few horsemen who defended their city heroically. Attila forced an entry, and put to the sword the bishop and the handful of men who had dared to check his army. Then he rode up the steps of the cathedral. Behind those doors were gold and riches, the prize of the conqueror. But Attila never passed the threshold. As the doors swung back, a mysterious and terrible voice thundered from the altar, and Attila, the Scourge of God, knew fear for the first time. The Huns fled in superstitious terror from the deserted town, convinced that they had heard the voice of the God of the Christians.

Twenty-three days after the sack of Metz, Attila set siege to Orleans. The city had been strengthened with new fortifications, and the soldiers within fought valiantly against the repeated attacks of the Huns. For two months they held out, and then, as the very walls were cracking beneath the battering-rams of the savage enemy, the Roman standards appeared on the horizon. Aetius, leader of the Roman army, and Theodoric, the ancient king of the Visigoths, were marching against the Huns.

Attila at once raised the siege and withdrew his army to a more convenient battleground. He waited for the Romans and the Visigoths in the plains of Chalons, and there, in the summer of A.D. 451, was fought one of the bloodiest and most decisive battles of the world.

With a wild scream the Hun horsemen swept into the solid, living wall of their enemy. They fought with the fury that has made their name a by-word in history, yet their valour was matched by that of the Visigoths who withstood them. Yet the Huns carried all before them; Theodoric was slain, the army of Aetius crumbled, and it seemed that Attila, king of the barbarians, had mastered the world. And then the Visigoths, led by Thorismund, son of Theodoric, thirsting for revenge for the death of their king, fought their way to the possession of a small hill above the plain, and from there they charged in a new fury upon the Huns. The onslaught was terrific; the conquering Huns were thrust back, and their almost certain victory was turned into a crushing defeat.

Attila fled from the field with the remnant of his host and barricaded himself behind his baggage wagons, determined to fire them and be burned to death rather than be captured alive.

By the valour of the Visigoths the tottering civilization of Rome had been saved. A quarter of a million lay dead on the plains of Chalons, one of the most memorable and most terrible battlegrounds in the history of the world.

Attila waited in vain for the pursuit of the victors. Aetius was playing the old Roman game of playing off one people against another, and he allowed the Huns to retreat.

Attila alone realized the extent of his defeat. To his army, loot and riches meant victory. They returned to the Danube with chariots heaped with golden vessels from the churches, rich stuffs and jewels from the slain. Therefore, they had been victorious. Yet, in defeat, Attila roused his savage hordes. He would begin again.

He had learned much. His army must be disciplined in the Roman manner; those formations that had proved so effective against his cavalry at Chalons must be introduced. Arrows and whips were good offensive arms in battle, but machinery must be acquired if he were to attack the walls of fortified cities. And, another thing: it might be wise to adopt Christianity, and enlist the help of that God whose voice had so terrified him, and whose bishops had so often withstood him. They seemed inspired by some supernatural force that had filled him with a sense of approaching fear, even as his sword had sunk into their throats.

Rome, her glory, and her heroes, obsessed him. All that such men had made, he must destroy, and on the ruins raise his own, Attila's empire.

He began to build a city on the Danube. A Roman officer was hired to train his army.

Less than a year after the Battle of Chalons, Attila called together his sixty sons, his princes and generals, and at the head of his newly disciplined army marched on Italy and Rome.

Aetius, the Emperor Valentinian's general, and Marcian, emperor at Constantinople, prepared the defence.

Meanwhile, Attila attacked Aquilia, the most fortified town on the frontier, the gateway to Italy. It was a city used to sieges, but its defenders looked with dismay at the Huns. This army managing catapults, battering-rams, and executing the "turtle" and the "phalanx," was not the undisciplined horde they had expected.

At the same time, the walls were strong, the granaries full, and there was a natural spring within the town. Thus the siege dragged on, the Huns grew impatient, and famine and disease began their ravages. Attila pondered the advisability of lifting the siege, and marching on. Then one day from one of the walls a stork flew up, driving her brood before her. Birds sense the doom of bricks and mortar, and Attila's superstitious soul believed in bird omens. He determined upon a fierce and immediate attack.

All his engines of war were launched against the walls, and his wild army, raging and athirst for blood, swarmed the ramparts.

A few minutes later, a yellow sea of barbarians overran the proud town that had withstood all sieges.

The massacre was over. Attila rode triumphantly through the streets, among the acclamations of a once more contented army. Two hours of pillage ensued. Then, singing their wild Asiatic war songs, Attila and his men marched on.

A strange campaign followed. Attila was disquietened. He advanced, and no resistance was shown. He found only deserted towns, destroyed crops. Sometimes towns, such as Mantua, received him with honours and festivals. But there was no sign of Aetius and his legions. And the Huns, who could not endure heat, began to suffer from the oppressive summer. Fever broke out, and contaminated water produced another epidemic. The army would soon be useless.

Aetius's plan was to let Italy's summer reduce Attila's army to its lowest ebb, and then to fall upon it and wipe it out for ever. On the other hand, Valentinian, the Roman emperor, would not put complete confidence in Aetius.

At that time Leo was pope in Rome, a wise, cultured and saintly man. Valentinian went to the pope, and begged him to go to Attila and sue for peace.

Meanwhile, despite the condition of his men, Attila prepared to march on Rome. He dare not wait longer.

One day, a scout riding in from the outposts, announced the arrival of an army, and Attila rejoiced. It must be Aetius come at last, prepared to give battle. This time they would crush him, and Italy would be theirs. He swiftly ranged his warriors in battle order along the banks of a formidable river.

But the army advancing towards him was the strangest he had ever seen. It was headed by a snow-bearded patriarch, garbed in white, and followed by men in golden robes. And as it came forward, there was the sound of chanting. A hush of apprehension fell upon the Huns.

The strange array halted near the banks of the stream, and for many minutes the white figure and Attila confronted each other. Then Attila called out violently: "Who are you?" The chanting ceased, and the patriarch's voice was heard: "Leo."

Attila hesitated. Then, fording the stream alone, he climbed the bank and rode up to the pope.

No one has ever known what was said at that interview, but suddenly Attila swerved round, recrossed the river, and cried out a few hoarse commands. The army turned, marched north, and out of Italy.

But Aetius did not share the general enthusiasm at this bloodless triumph. This was but a respite. He knew his great enemy's soul, and that he would repent his weakness and return. He was right, for rumours came again out of the East that Attila was preparing a third invasion. But before that rumour reached Rome, Attila was dead, and emperors could sleep peacefully once more.

Here was the end of one of the greatest destroyers ever known, the man who came near to changing the face of the world:

He returned to find the tribes of the Danube restless and mutinous. His many sons censured their father openly for the evacuation of Italy, and none of his followers possessed his great patience, his ability to start again. Some of his German vassals rebelled, and he dealt mercilessly with them, executing chiefs and their entire families.

On one occasion, as he marched into a vanquished German camp, a girl named Ildico flung herself upon her knees, begging for her father's and brothers' lives. Attila's heart was not softened, and her father, mother and brothers were decapitated before her eyes. But Ildico's beauty saved her life, for Attila reserved her for himself. At the age of sixty, on the eve of his third invasion, he prepared with great ceremony to marry for the four-hundredth time.

Chieftains from all parts of Asia and eastern Europe, loaded with gifts, came to the nuptial feast. All day the revels continued, Attila drinking and eating incessantly, while at his side sat Ildico in frozen silence. When night fell, Attila retired with his bride.

At noon next day his generals went to waken him, but no answer came. After repeated hammering, the doors were broken down.

There was seen, lying on white furs now crimson with his blood, the dead and naked body of Attila. His excesses in eating and drinking had killed him; he had burst a blood vessel.

In a corner, dumb with terror, crouched Ildico.

So died Attila, King of the Huns, at whose name Imperial Cæsars had trembled.

The Huns buried the little yellow man who had made their name great, if only in infamy, with barbaric glory. All day his body lay in his tent, around him the swords of vanquished chieftains, the crowns of kings he had dethroned, the treasures of churches whose sanctity he had violated. At his head lay a bow and arrow.

That night, four of his warriors who had claimed the honour of following their master into death, dug a vast ditch, into which Attila and his treasures were lowered. Then the four rode round the grave in a last parade. When the salute was ended, their throats were cut and their bodies impaled upon their horses at the four corners of the tomb.

Thus was the last watch kept over Attila.

CHARLEMAGNE

(*c.* 742–814)

"The man who led the Franks to victory and so created modern Europe was Charles the Great. In the last resort it is true that national developments are independent of the individual's effort. But without Charles, and the legend of Charles, Europe would have had a different history and a different character. Her civilization would have been more tardily matured, and would have lacked some important elements which it now possesses. Rightly did the cathedral builders of the Middle Ages blazon the exploits of the great emperor upon those buildings which symbolized their highest beliefs and aspirations. Rightly did the Catholic Church inscribe his name in the roll of those who had been foremost in building up the Kingdom of God upon earth. Nor did popular tradition err when it saw in him the originator of the Crusading policy which made Christendom the armed camp of the Church militant; when it traced back to him the beginnings of feudalism, of central power hostile to feudalism, of national no less than of imperial aspirations, of the union between State and Church, of the wise jealousy of the State towards the Church. In his policy all these diverse tendencies were co-ordinated and harmonized."
—Mr. H. W. C. Davis.

When Pepin the Short, King of the Franks, died in 768, his kingdom was divided between his two sons, Charles and Carloman. Charles, the elder, who was twenty-five, took Austrasia and Neustria—roughly the country from Brittany to beyond the Rhine, together with the lands lying between the Loire and the Garonne. Burgundy, Provence, Alsace, Alemannia, and the south-eastern part of Aquitaine fell to Carloman. Thus the Frankish realm, which comprised a heterogeneous collection of states and nations, was partitioned according to custom, and in such a way that the territory of Charles half surrounded that of his younger brother.

From the first it was clear that the two brothers would not reign together in harmony, and it was clear also that the elder was the stronger of the two. The first sign of friction was shown in 769, when Aquitaine revolted. Carloman, whose realm was not affected, refused to go to his brother's help, and although Charles had no difficulty in quelling the outbreak he did not forget Carloman's defection.

After that Charles did everything to isolate Carloman and diminish his power. He concluded an alliance with Didier, King of the Lombards, and in spite of the opposition of the pope, whose feud with Lombardy was long-standing, Charles married Didier's daughter, Desiderata. The marriage did not last long. Desiderata soon fell out of favour, and within a year Charles divorced her and married Hildegarde, a beautiful young Swabian.

Didier soon had an opportunity of avenging the insult. Carloman died suddenly in 771, and his widow, with commendable foresight, fled with her two infant sons to Pavia, where Didier gave her protection. He did more. He marched on Rome and demanded at the point of the sword that the pope should crown the children, and not let the kingdom of Carloman fall into the hands of Charles.

Pope Hadrian sent a legate to Frankland asking for immediate aid, reminding Charles of the oath he had taken as a patrician to defend the Holy See. Charles made careful inquiry into the causes and conditions of the quarrel, and finally decided to intervene on the pope's behalf. A summons was sent out for the army to assemble at Geneva.

An impressive picture of the Frankish host, the very appearance of which was often enough to scare an enemy into flight, is given by Mr. Davis:

> "Every landholder was expected to appear under the banner of his count; and the king's vassals brought with them all their free retainers. Poor men came on foot armed solely with lance, bow and shield; there were also those who, unable to afford even this humble equipment, made shift to furnish themselves with knotted clubs, scythes and flails. The rich were mounted and wore long shirts of mail; in addition to the weapons of the foot-soldier they carried a sword and dagger; their heads were defended by iron skull-caps. This heavy cavalry formed the corps d'elite (scaræ) upon whose impetuous charge the Frankish general relied for victory. The infantry were held in reserve to finish off the enemy when his ranks were broken. The baggage train was a remarkable feature of the host. Each local contingent brought with it a number of wagons covered with leather aprons; they

contained food for three months, arms and clothing for half a year, and such tools as might be needed for siege-works or encampments."

Charles divided the army into two parts, and they crossed the Alps by different passes, united in the plain of Lombardy, swept all before them, and besieged Pavia. In June, 774, the city fell, and from that time Charles took the title of King of the Lombards. He left a few garrisons of Frankish troops, and went on to Rome, where he was cordially received by the pope.

To the Christian Franks, Rome was the centre and the glory of the civilized world. The visit to Rome, his meeting and cordial compact with the pope, left a deep and lasting impression upon Charles. From that time he became the mighty champion of the Church, the Charlemagne who gave his name to legend.

* * * * *

In the summer of 772, a year before the pope had called upon him, Charles undertook a campaign against the Saxons, who had refused to pay the tribute imposed by his father. That campaign was the first in a war which was to continue intermittently for thirty years.

The expedition of 772 ended in the complete submission of the Angrarii, but Charles's Italian engagements gave them and the Westphalians an opportunity for revenge. They invaded Frankland, burning and ravaging the land. They were checked by the sudden reappearance of Charles, whose rapidity of action was his most valuable strategical weapon. And his interview with the pope had made him a new champion: he announced to his council that he was going to give the Saxons a choice between baptism and annihilation.

A successful campaign in 775 ended in the submission of many of the Saxon tribes, and Charles left his missionaries to the work of making them Christians. But a year later both Lombardy and the Saxons were in arms against him.

A swift march with picked troops took Charles into Italy, where he crushed the rebels, and before the summer was out he appeared in the heart of Saxony. The Saxons made no resistance. They submitted to his will, embraced Christianity, and so certain was Charles of the settlement of the country that he began the building of a royal borough at Paderborn.

And to Paderborn, in 777, came three emirs who sought the help of Charlemagne against their hated overlord, the Saracen ruler of Spain. They offered to raise an army in Africa which would unite with his, if he came to their help. The king assented, and in the next year he marched with his host throughout his realm from Saxony to the Pyrenees. He swept into Spain, but the plan of the emirs miscarried, and Charlemagne, unable to take Saragossa, was forced to retire.

On the retreat his rearguard was ambushed at Roncesvalles; Roland, the Warden of the Breton March, was slain, and the story of that fight became the inspiration of song and epic.

Again the old enemy from the east attacked. The Saxons found an inspiring leader in Witikind, and in 778 he headed a new rebellion and led war-bands into Hesse, into Austrasia, and to the very banks of the Rhine.

Charles waited until the next summer to march against him, and won a signal victory at Bocholt. Onwards he went and extended his dominion to the Elbe. He did not colonize the conquered land, but bestowed on the new vassals Frankish titles and powers. Saxony was divided up into mission districts, priests were brought in from the west, and churches rose beside new forts.

Charles was grimly determined to enforce Christianity, and the regulations he issued are remarkable for their severity. Two of the clauses in the Saxon Capitulary run:

> "If any man despise the Lenten fast for contempt of Christianity, let him die the death.
>
> "If any man among the Saxons, being not yet baptized, shall hide himself and refuse to come to baptism, let him die the death."

At the same time Charles caused much property and wealth to be confiscated and applied to the Church.

It was not to be expected that the Saxons would suffer the innovations patiently. As soon as Charlemagne withdrew revolt broke out once more. Charles retaliated by massacring over four thousand Saxon councillors. The result was a war of unparalleled fierceness. Bloody battles and intense heat taxed the Franks to the utmost, but after two years they prevailed, order was restored, and even Witikind consented to be baptized. The conquest and conversion of Saxony was almost complete. Peace reigned for eight years, and although more revolts broke out in 793, 797 and later, by a steady process of colonization and transportation of the Saxons, Charles tightened his grip upon the land and the long period of fighting ended at last in 804. The domination of Saxony by the

Franks was the first unification of the German peoples: its conversion established the German Church.

But the constant battles with the Saxons did not occupy all the king's attention. He was a statesman as well as a fighter, and his wonderful grasp of detail, and his ability to pay attention to the affairs of every part of his wide realm are proofs of the man's greatness.

Tassilo, the Duke of Bavaria, had ceased to acknowledge his vassaldom to Charles, and in 781 the king took his first steps to bring him and his country to heel. Hard pressed as he was, he did not immediately make a show of force, but prevailed on the pope to force Tassilo to renew his oath. But the duke, encouraged by his wife, was bent on defiance. After another forced submission, in 787, he began preparations for war and invited the nomad tribes of the Avars to come to his assistance. Charles heard of his treachery, for Tassilo's own nobles, rather than rely on the support of the heathens, denounced him to the king.

The duke was arrested, tried for treason, and condemned, and Bavaria became part of the Frankish empire. With Bavaria under his rule, Charles's next step was to deal with the Avars, who lived beyond its eastern boundary. They were a confederacy of nomad tribes, of Mongol origin, not unlike the Huns who had swept Europe three centuries before. Against the armoured and disciplined forces of the Franks they had no chance, and Charles drove them before him as far as the Raab. Revolt in Saxony, and a conspiracy in Bavaria prevented him from continuing the campaign, but he left the war to be brought to a successful conclusion by his generals. By the end of the century, the Avars were not only subdued, they were exterminated.

And now the conquering king was once again called upon to espouse the cause of the pope. On the death of Hadrian, in 795, Leo III had been elected to the papacy. Leo had the reputation of being an acute statesman, and according to his enemies he had reputations of other kinds. His enemies in Rome were many—they were mostly of the late Pope Hadrian's family—and they made such attacks upon the character of Leo that Charles's great minister, Alcuin, was sent to Rome to investigate the rumours: they were proved to be false, yet Leo's reputation was still under a cloud.

In April, 799, the pope was attacked while he was leading a religious procession. He was dragged from his horse and beaten into unconsciousness, but he was rescued and carried to a monastery. As soon as he recovered, he made his escape from Rome, and sought the protection of Charles's commissioners at Spoletum: thence he was conveyed to the king's camp at Paderborn, and after an interview Charles had the pope escorted back to Rome by his royal commissioners.

The Romans were frightened and surrendered the leaders of the Hadrian faction: then they waited. But Charles did not come. Leo was neither condemned nor acquitted, and the Christian world wondered to whom to turn. The Emperor Constantine VI was by tradition still emperor, but Constantinople was far away: and then came the news that he had been blinded and deposed by his mother, Irene. Who was now to champion Christendom? The Saracens were in Spain, and men had heard of the great Haroun al Raschid at Baghdad. Supposing the heathens were to sweep into Europe, who would stay them? These were the questions on men's lips, when at last Charles went to Rome.

He held a public trial, and the calumniators of the pope were finally silenced. And two days later, on Christmas Day, 800, Charles was crowned emperor of the Holy Roman Empire. In that impressive moment Charles had his reward for his lifetime of strenuous endeavour, and Christendom had proclaimed its champion.

For the last fourteen years of his life Charles was content to rule and consolidate his mighty empire which stretched from Brittany and the Ebro to the Elbe and the Theiss, from the North Sea to the Mediterranean. The constant wars in defence of its boundaries he left to his sons: he concerned himself with administration and reform.

Charles's reign saw the foundation of the medieval political system: in his last years he was trying to correct the abuses that prevailed. His system of commissioners, who, representing the king, travelled in circuits to supervise and correct resident nobles and bishops, was tightened up and improved, and he also attempted to reform the local law courts. In 802 he caused the national laws to be codified.

Charles was the champion of learning as well as the warrior of the Church. He encouraged scholars to flock to his court, and he delighted in their conversation. Chief of those he gathered about him was Alcuin, an English churchman from Northumbria, who became the king's adviser. Wisdom and piety were the ruling factors of the power Alcuin wielded, and "no personal influence was more widely felt in Francia and in Europe than that of the secluded English scholar."

Alcuin was responsible for the foundations of schools, and although some of the learned men of the court, such as Theodulf and Eginhard, the king's biographer, had knowledge of the classics, the knowledge taught was rudimentary, and mainly theological. But the effort to educate and to enlighten was there, and full credit must be given to the king and his advisers.

Charlemagne himself liked to plague his scholars with questions and argue theology with them. It was a strange scene when the king sat at his table discussing fine points with Alcuin, while his vassals and lords drank themselves under the table.

Charles himself was temperate and a moderate eater: his court was not. Its appetite was immoderate in every direction, and Aachen reproduced many of the features of that court of an earlier Rome.

The king did not allow his daughters to marry, but he ignored their numerous and scandalous love affairs. He himself married four wives in quick succession, and had many mistresses before, between, and during his legal unions.

Charles was a cheerful man of coarse humour, and his morals were those of his ancestors and his age. But his character was moulded and changed during the course of his reign, and the harshness and cruelties of his campaigns, the starkness of his nature in later years are, in part at least, attributable to years of warring against foes without, and jealousy, revolt and conspiracy at home. His piety was real, and his belief in conversion by force was genuine. He was not only the champion, but also the patron of the Church. He built, endowed and gave lavishly: in his will he left three-quarters of his wealth to his churches.

Charles was a giant of a man physically: his presence was worthy of his greatness. He was tall, broad-shouldered, bull-necked, heavily built, and bore himself with magnificent dignity. He was cheerful looking, and wore the long moustaches of the Franks; his eyes were bright and his voice unexpectedly shrill. The poets tell of his strength and hardiness, as well as of his justice: even his enemies, the Saxons, sang: "The best man on earth and the bravest was Charles: Truth and good faith he established and kept."

In 806 he made, according to custom, partition of his domain among his sons, Lewis, Pepin and Charles: in 813 Lewis was crowned emperor at Aachen, and in the following January Charlemagne died, at the age of seventy.

He had reigned forty-seven years, and in that time he had laid the foundations of the German nation, brought into existence the German Church, established a Christian empire, and left his mark indelibly upon the history of the western world.

ALFRED THE GREAT

(*c.* A.D. 849–900)

If ever a king, or a man, deserved to be crowned with the title of the Perfect Knight and be clothed in the glory that has been reserved for the shadowy figures of the Arthurian Legend, that man is Alfred, called the Great, King of the West Saxons in the ninth century A.D. *In a lifetime spent in fighting against the Danes, from whom, after years of defeat and disaster, he freed his country, he found time to foster the spiritual and intellectual wherever he found it. To his people he was all in all; their lawgiver, protector, and educator. A mighty soldier, he reorganized an army to beat the Danes, strengthened the navy to hold them off; a great king, he preserved law and order and organized his state for the benefit of its citizens; a learned scholar, he wrote the first prose works of the English tongue and fostered the education of his people; a pious Christian, he founded monasteries, religious institutions, and gave a large part of his income in charity and good works. He was the model king; in every sense of the words, Alfred the Great.*

ALFRED, King of the Anglo-Saxons, lives in history as having delivered his country from the Danes, with whom he was in conflict during the greater part of his life. Notwithstanding his preoccupation with marches, battles and sieges, with negotiating treaties and enlisting allies, he managed to organize a militia, to inaugurate a navy, to encourage learning and science, to found monasteries and churches, and to write several important works. For these reasons, he has been called "the Great"; and it may be said that he earned the title far more truly than other historical figures whose main claim to it rests on devastated countries, conquered provinces and hecatombs of soldiers.

Alfred was the fourth son of Æthelwulf and his first wife, Osburh, and was born at Wantage in 849. At an early age he took part in the campaigns against the Danes, being the right hand of his brother Æthelred, during the latter's short and troubled reign. Alfred, of course, was the real general, and as early as 866 he had begun his great task of expelling the invaders. The year 870 may be described as Alfred's " year of battles." In the first five months of that eventful year nine pitched engagements were fought. At Reading the Danes were victorious, being reinforced by a host from beyond the seas. A few days afterwards, this victory was turned into defeat at Ashdown, in Berkshire. The Danes were in two bodies, one of which was attacked by Æthelred and the other by Alfred. The enemy was next met at Basing, whither they had hastily retreated, but Alfred could not prevail. He was similarly unlucky at Marton a few weeks later, and a short while after the latter fight, Æthelred died, and Alfred succeeded to the throne.

One of the first events of the new reign was an indecisive battle with the Danes at Wilton; and thereafter for some years there was peace, the invaders being occupied in other parts of Britain. The new king contented himself with reorganizing the army, and keeping a watch on the frontier of his kingdom. The year 876 saw the Danes again on the aggressive. They took Alfred by surprise, and seized Wareham. Later, they besieged and took Exeter; and another Danish army, landing in Devon, besieged Kenwith Castle, which they eventually captured, putting the inhabitants to the sword. In this exploit, their chief, or " king " (as he is called in the chronicles) was slain; and his raven-banner taken.

Some time in 878, Alfred located a Danish army at Chippenham, and resolved to give battle. His star, however, was not in the ascendant, and he was forced to retreat. So far, Alfred had been dogged by bad fortune in his struggle against the Danish hordes. The one bright spot in the tale was the great victory of Ashdown, a few weeks before the death of Æthelred. The patched-up peace which followed Wilton was neither glorious nor lasting. Alfred's unhappy realm seemed permanently under the shadow of the wings of " Odin's bird," the great raven which the Danes took as their symbol.

From Chippenham, Alfred and some of his forces took their way to the Isle of Athelney, in Somerset, where they encamped. But, after years of unsuccessful struggle, Alfred was not giving way to despair. Athelney might have been a camp of refuge—some historians have called it a " hiding-place "—but the king's mind during his sojourn was occupied in the organization of victory. Various legends have clustered around Alfred's stay at Athelney, including the well-known story of the housewife's burnt cakes, but they need not take up our time.

His preparations completed, Alfred marched out of the Isle of Athelney. He added men of Somerset, Wilts and Hants to his forces, while the Danes moved out of Chippenham to meet him. They were more or less taken by surprise at Alfred's proximity, but the king had made forced marches. One authority estimates the speed of his forces at forty miles a day, but this is probably an exaggeration, for it is difficult to see how the shire levies could have moved at this pace. There ensued a great battle at Edington, in Wiltshire, and a decisive victory for Alfred. After tremendous slaughter, during which no quarter was given, the Danes were forced to surrender. A spot near the scene of the battle is called Slaughterford to this day, and on the hillside above the battlefield is the great White Horse which Alfred had cut out to commemorate the victory. Besides killing many Danes, including some of their most important leaders, Alfred seized great stores of provisions and munitions of war, besides large numbers of horses and cattle.

To acknowledge his defeat, Guthrum, King of the Danes, came out to meet Alfred, accompanied by thirty of his most trusted earls. He and they were baptized as Christians; and thereafter Alfred royally entertained his late foes. Alfred was in a position now to dictate his will to the defeated Danes. In consequence, the invaders quitted his kingdom, although much of the east and north of England and London remained in their hands. This result was achieved by the so-called Treaty of Wedmore, which is said to have come into force after the Battle of Edington, and by the terms of which the Danes were to remain east of Watling Street, that ran from London to Chester.

The first part of the weary struggle was over, and for a while the land enjoyed peace. But in 884 Alfred and Guthrum were at war again. This time Alfred gained a swift victory. Another treaty was signed, known as "Alfred's and Guthrum's Peace," and by it Alfred considerably strengthened his position at the expense of the Danes. He had seized London in 885 and now he fortified it strongly. While he was there he received the submission of the leaders of the Angles and Saxons and from several of the princes of Wales: he became, in fact, Overlord of England.

In 892 came a large invasion of Danes, who arrived with the purpose not merely of attacking and plundering, but of seizing the land and settling here. A period of fierce fighting with its inevitable slaughter set in.

Alfred smote the Danes at Farnham in 893, inflicting a severe defeat. Again at Thorney, and again at Benfleet, he out-generalled and outfought them. Then, hearing that a second Danish army was besieging Exeter, he dashed thither at full speed, and drove away the besiegers. In the meantime, Alfred had created a sea force as well as a land force. His captains met the galleys of the invading Danes on the water and beat them.

Later, large bodies of Danes marched up the Thames Valley, and several fierce fights with Alfred's forces took place. More Danes seized Chester and established themselves there. Alfred, a diplomatist as well as a soldier, won over some Welsh chieftains to his side. The Danes remained behind the walls of Chester until the country around was swept bare of everything that could be used for food, and then they retreated again into Essex in 894.

Next year, the Danes, who had fortified themselves on the Thames, twenty miles above London, were attacked. A fierce frontal assault failed; but Alfred obstructed the river so that no galleys could pass to or fro. Seeing this, the Danes decided that it was better not to remain pent up in a fortified place where no help could reach them, so they abandoned it and struck north-west. They went into winter quarters at Bridgnorth; but by this time Alfred had gained such an ascendency that they gave up the contest in 896. King Alfred thus attained the ambition to which he had dedicated his youth, his young manhood, and his maturity, and had driven the Danes out of his kingdom.

The task had taken nearly thirty years. It had involved scores of pitched battles and sieges, and more skirmishes and raids than can be counted. Over and over again had Alfred come to terms with the treacherous foe, only to find them break faith at the most convenient moment thereafter. Dauntless courage, unwavering hope and implacable tenacity, combined with a genius for war, had enabled Alfred the Great to overcome all obstacles and realize his life's dream.

From an early age this great captain was devoted to literature. As a boy, he coveted so much a missal in which he saw his mother reading that in order to gain possession of it he learnt some of it by heart in an astonishingly short space of time. This story is well known, and it cannot be altogether one of those legends which grow up around the early years of kings, for it is related in the contemporary life of Alfred by Asser, the monk whom he brought from Wales to become his friend—and eventually his biographer. Asser was created Bishop of Sherborne.

Alfred would carry a Book of Hours about with him constantly. He also learnt many Anglo-Saxon poems by heart and when he was weary, would delight in having poems or chronicles read to him. Asser was not the only scholar with whom Alfred was eager to associate. Plegmund, Archbishop of Canterbury, and Werferth, Bishop of Worcester, were two among the learned men who were the king's teachers and companions. Werferth was left a considerable sum of money in Alfred's will, though curiously enough the name of Plegmund is not mentioned in the document as entitled to a bequest.

Not only did Alfred consort with notable English scholars, but he was so enthusiastic about learning that he sent to other countries for instructors. From the famous monastery of St. Bertin, in Flanders, came Grimbald, recommended to Alfred by the Archbishop of Rheims. He was of great assistance to the king, and subsequently became abbot of the monastery at Newminster (sometimes called Hyde). John the Saxon was another scholar from overseas whom Alfred delighted to honour.

This combination of soldier and scholar was also an author. He translated into English Boethius's *Consolations of Philosophy* and Gregory's *Pastoral Care,* and he was also the translator of Bede's *Ecclesiastical History of the English People.*

Alfred's works were not mere translations, he remodelled texts to suit his own tongue and people, and his prefaces were remarkable. He was, in fact, the father of English prose, for before that only verse had been written in the native tongue. Alfred's writings are a very real and great contribution to early English literature, and they were conceived with a noble ideal. Alfred set out to be the spiritual father and educator of his people, and he knew that the greatest appeal to men can only be made in their own tongue.

As befits a soldier, Alfred was a keen huntsman. He could instruct verderers and falconers in their own trade, for this many-sided genius was a practical man as well as a scholar and visionary. He could also give advice on their crafts to goldsmiths, jewellers and other workers in metals and precious stones.

Alfred was as pious as he was brave and skilful and learned. From his infancy he was eager to visit holy places, and when only five years old was taken to Rome, when he was confirmed by the pope. He carried relics of the saints about with him, and it is known that he founded at least two monasteries. Of a convent endowed by him at Shaftesbury, his daughter, named Ethelgitha, was the first abbess. His charities were well-nigh boundless. He received and cared for foreigners and strangers coming to his court, and it was said that he allotted one-eighth of his revenue to the poor and needy. He had the sons of his nobles educated along with his own children, and in many other ways showed his generosity.

As an administrator, Alfred would have been notable if for nothing else. He instituted a system of fortified posts (burgs) in various parts of his realm, long before such things became part of the art of war.

He divided the national militia (the fyrd) into two parts, so that each could relieve the other at regular intervals and thus ensure continuity in military operations, and he took measures to provide his kingdom with the continuous service of highly-equipped troops. He built up an English navy from very small beginnings, and he has been called the "Father of the Navy." This is not strictly true, for king's ships existed in the reigns of his father and brothers; but undoubtedly Alfred enlarged and improved the fleet. This policy was more or less forced upon him, because he wished to drive off the increasing numbers of marauding Danes who might have landed on his coasts.

Alfred instilled such a respect for law and order in his kingdom that it was said that a wayfarer might hang a valuable jewel on a bush by the wayside and that nobody would dare to touch it. This poetical exaggeration indicates the high standard of Alfred's administration of peace and justice. We know that he always kept a close and critical watch on all his judicial officers and would threaten to deprive some of their posts unless they learned to read.

This king restored towns ravaged by war and founded new ones, besides constructing beautiful dwellings for his own use. He paid the workmen he employed with liberality. In every way he was a model of what a king should be, besides being pious, chaste and upright as becomes a God-fearing man.

In those days the world outside the limits of a man's own home was a dark and mysterious region; but we have already seen how Alfred sent to the continent of Europe for men who might be useful in various ways, and how he himself journeyed to Rome. He also had correspondence with the Patriarch of Jerusalem; and William of Malmesbury, who wrote in the twelfth century, records with wonder that Alfred dispatched a mission to India. This is hardly probable, and Gibbon suspects that Egypt was meant. The term India was generally used in the ninth century in a very loose and inexact manner.

Of Alfred's domestic relations we are told little by the chroniclers, though we know that he married, in 868, a lady named Ealhswith, daughter of a Kentish nobleman, who survived him. In October, 900, Alfred died, then fifty-one years of age, and was buried at Winchester. Three daughters and two sons are mentioned in his will. One of the daughters, as we have already seen, became abbess at Shaftesbury; another, named Ethelfled, married a Mercian dignitary; of the third, nothing is known.

These words, taken from the writings of Alfred the Great, aptly epitomize his mind:

"Therefore he seems to me a very foolish man, and very wretched, who will not increase his understanding while he is in the world, and even wish and long to reach to endless life, where all shall be made clear."

WILLIAM THE CONQUEROR

(1027–1087)

1066 is the most famous date in the calendar of English history, and deservedly so, for it marks the foundation of the England that we know today. England owes much to the Norman invaders; she owes more to their leader. In spite of his callous ruthlessness, his sudden passions, and his selfishness, William the Conqueror made a great ruler. He was just, firm, prudent, and far-sighted; his moral strength and courage equalled his physical. Against his cruelty and indifference to human suffering may be set the blamelessness of his private life and his abolition of capital punishment: and as for his rule, even an Englishman wrote of "the good peace he made in the land, so that a man might walk from end to end with his bosom full of gold."

"STARK he was to men who withstood him; so harsh and cruel he was that none withstood his will; all men were obliged to be obedient, and to follow his will, if they would have lands or even life."

So runs the monkish record known as the *Anglo-Saxon Chronicle* on William the Bastard, Duke of Normandy, who invaded England and became its king. "Stark he was," and that ruthlessness, wedded to strength, determination, and indomitable courage, made the man the greatest figure of his day and enabled him to create a nation in the land he had won.

For centuries he has been known as William the Conqueror, but the title was not used by him or his contemporaries in the modern sense. Conqueror meant acquirer, or purchaser, and William certainly did not stress the fact that he had won England by the sword, but that he had acquired it in a proper manner after the death of his kinsman Edward the Confessor.

The story of William the Conqueror is that of one long, fearless struggle against disloyal barons, treacherous enemies and scheming friends. Born at Falaise, in Normandy, in 1027, he was the illegitimate child of Robert the Devil, Duke of Normandy, and of Arlette, a tanner's daughter.

Seven years after the birth of his son, Duke Robert decided to go on a pilgrimage, and before setting out he made his subject lords elect William as his successor and swear fealty to him. Within twelve months came the news of Robert's death, and the boy William was Duke of Normandy and Maine.

The removal of the father was the signal for strife and revolt. Despite their oaths, almost every baron was ready to fight for increased power; few were willing to recognize the illegitimate son of Robert as their overlord. An attempt was made to seize William, but his mother's brother Walter saved him and hid him in the house of some poor peasants.

The struggle between the factions went on, but soon William showed his courage and his wisdom in accepting counsel. By the age of fifteen he was strong enough to insist that the Truce of God should be observed in Normandy. Desperate fighting broke out again in 1047, but William, once again evading capture, enlisted the help of Henry I of France and crushed the rebels. In return he assisted the French king in a war against Geoffrey Martel, Count of Anjou. He showed such conspicuous courage in action that Henry asked him to be a little less daring. His answer was to capture Domfont and Alençon.

At Domfont he challenged Geoffrey Martel to personal combat. The challenge was accepted, but the count retreated before a meeting could take place. At Alençon the citizens mocked William by beating hides against the town walls and shouting "Tanner!" As an indication that he was not the type of man to be trifled with, he had the hands and feet cut off from thirty-two of the offenders.

In 1051 William visited the English court. It was on this occasion, so tradition relates, that Edward the Confessor, who was a great-cousin of William, promised that the Norman duke should succeed him on the throne.

Meanwhile, William was trying to make a match of great political advantage with Matilda, daughter of the Count of Flanders. Pope Leo IX had forbidden the marriage in 1049, but it was celebrated in 1053. Malger, Archbishop of Rouen, threatened his nephew with excommunication, but William enlisted the aid of Lanfranc, then Prior of the Abbey of Bec and later to become Archbishop of Canterbury. Eventually, in 1059, Pope Nicholas II granted a dispensation. In return, the duke built the Abbey of St. Stephen at Caen. William's married life was conspicuous in an age of loose living for its chastity and happiness. Throughout his life of battle and turbulence he lived faithfully with Matilda, and he mourned her sincerely on her death in 1083.

The year of his marriage saw William once more plunged into war. William of Arques, an uncle of his and brother to Malger, made a determined effort to seize the duchy, and he was assisted by Henry I of France. William won a sweeping victory, and a year later met another attack in a similar way. Peace came in 1055, and William took advantage of the visit of a papal legate to depose Malger from his archbishopric. This was an indication of the strong ecclesiastical policy he was later to pursue in England.

Within three years Henry and Geoffrey of Anjou were fighting for Normandy again, but always William held the upper hand. In 1060 death took these two inveterate enemies. Philip, the new King of France, and Geoffrey's successor in Anjou, were more peacefully disposed than their immediate predecessors, and William could rest secure awhile in possession of Normandy and Maine.

During a campaign against Brittany, in 1064, William compelled Guy of Ponthieu to deliver up to him Harold, Earl of Wessex, who had been wrecked upon the coast of Ponthieu. Here was an opportunity for exacting a promise that might prove useful. Before the unfortunate Englishman was allowed to depart, he was made to swear on some holy relics that he would support William's claim to the throne on the death of Edward the Confessor.

Two years later came news that changed the history of Europe. William was hunting, his favourite sport, when he heard it. The weak and pious Edward had been gathered to his fathers, and the Witan had elected Harold king. Speechless with rage, William returned to his palace and began preparations for the invasion of England. He dispatched embassies for assistance to the German king, Henry, to Sweyn, King of Denmark, and to Philip of France. He interviewed Tostig, Harold's brother, and persuaded him to invade England. Furthermore, he sent Gilbert, Archdeacon of Lisieux, to Alexander II to ask for the papal blessing on his expedition.

The chief argument used by Gilbert was that William would bring the English Church more closely and firmly beneath the authority of Rome. That was clever diplomacy, and it may have been sincere. Some of the cardinals opposed the giving of a blessing on the grounds that it was not right for the Church to encourage bloodshed, but Hildebrand, later Pope Gregory VII, used his influence in support of William's cause, and Alexander sent the duke a consecrated banner and declared him to be lawful claimant to the English throne.

Meanwhile, William was assembling his forces and collecting a fleet, setting a precedent for Napoleon over seven hundred years later. Adventurers came from all parts of France and Flanders, eager for booty and reward from the spoiling of England. The ships assembled in August, and after over a month's delay, set sail with a favourable wind. On September 28, 1066, William landed in Pevensey Bay with a force of about 25,000 men. They fortified themselves in camp and ravaged the countryside.

Harold was at York. Harold Hardrada, King of Norway, had invaded England at the invitation of Tostig, and Harold had marched day and night from London to York. He had met the invaders at Stamford Bridge on the twenty-fifth and utterly routed them; Hardrada and Tostig were among those killed. Now, while he was celebrating the victory at a great feast in York, came news of William's landing.

Hastening south, Harold was joined by thousands of volunteers. He drew up his army on the hill that has been known ever since by the name Battle. He dug a trench and threw up earthworks around his position and waited for the Normans to begin hostilities.

On the morning of October 14, Duke William received communion, and then disposed his forces. He took command of the centre, at the head of the Norman troops. The French and Flemings were on the right flank, those from Brittany and Maine on the left. With shouts of *"Dieu nous aide,"* the heavy-armed foot and the mounted Norman knights attacked the English position.

The Norman cry was met by stout English ones, "God Almighty" and "Holy Cross," and the assaults of the knights were beaten back by javelin thrusts and the heavy double-headed battle-axe of the English foot soldiers. Wave after wave of the attackers was thrust back from the palisade.

A rumour that the duke had been killed passed along the ranks of the Normans. It reached William when there were evident signs of panic. Tearing off his helmet he roared: "I live, I live, and by God's help I will yet win the day." Mad with anger, he put his horse straight at Harold's royal standard and smashed his way through to the king. Gyrth, the king's brother, killed William's charger, and William, on foot, slew Gyrth with his mace. Of all the deeds of valour done in that memorable battle, none exceeded William's. Three horses were killed under him, yet he fought on where the fight was thickest.

The story of William's stratagem that gave him victory is well-known. When he saw that he could not take the English position, he ordered his men to feign flight, and with the English lured from

The Frankish king, Charlemagne, whom legend has made the champion of Christendom, created what became known as the Holy Roman Empire, and it was his example that Napoleon had in mind when he tried to assure his succession in 1804. On Christmas Day, 800, Charlemagne was crowned Emperor of the West by Pope Leo III in Rome after he had helped the Pope against the latter's enemies (*above*). Julius Caesar (*right*) made the Roman Empire possible by unifying the state after a century of discord, by establishing an autocracy in place of an oligarchy and by pacifying Italy and her provinces. He excelled in war and statesmanship, and his literary works are studied by all schoolboys who learn to appreciate his beautiful and concise Latin.

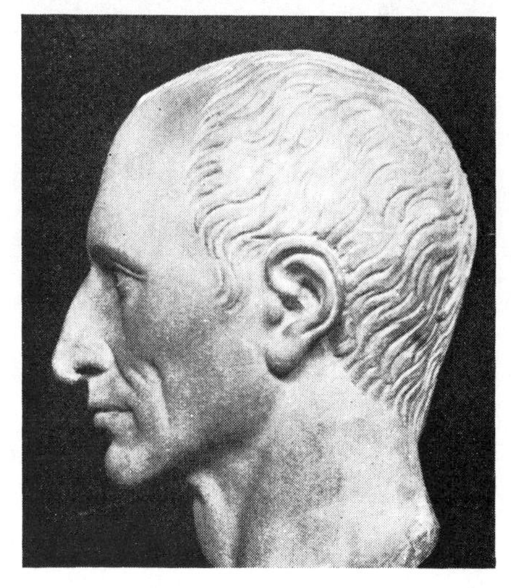

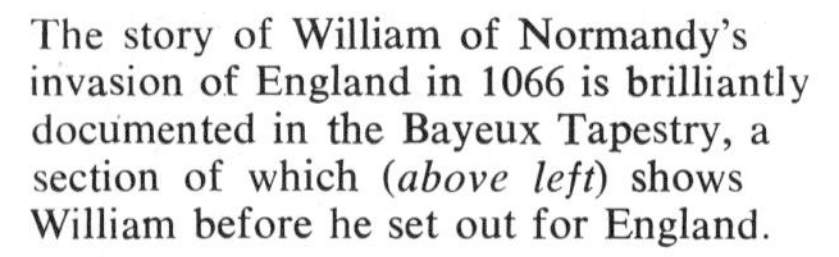

The story of William of Normandy's invasion of England in 1066 is brilliantly documented in the Bayeux Tapestry, a section of which (*above left*) shows William before he set out for England.

(*Above right*) A statue of Niccolò Machiavelli, the Italian author and statesman, who was one of the outstanding figures of the Renaissance. (*Below*) The meeting between Cortes and Montezuma.

the hill in pursuit, the Normans turned and gave battle once more. But the battle was not over. For three hours more the fight ranged round the English standard, and once more the knights of Normandy were beaten back. Then William ordered his archers to shoot into the air, "that the arrows might fall like bolts from heaven." Harold fell, pierced through the eye: the English broke, and William had won the most important battle in the history of England.

A few days later he marched through Canterbury and made for London, which, after he had ravaged the surrounding land, submitted and offered him the crown. The coronation took place at Westminster Abbey on Christmas Day. The ceremony was marked by disaster, for the Norman guards mistook the shouts of the people for signs of an insurrection and set fire to the buildings around the abbey. There was an immediate panic, and William was left with the clergy alone in the abbey.

His first act as king was to make a royal progress through the land. The powerful English earls, Edwin, Morcar, and Waltheof, and lesser landholders, came to make submission to him. Taking them and the natural leaders of the English with him to keep them out of mischief, William then returned to Normandy, leaving England in charge of Odo, his half-brother, and William Fitzosbern.

When he came back to England in December, 1067, he found the country in a state of wild disorder and revolt against the tyranny of his regents. In Wales, in Devon and the West Country and in the north, the English were rising, and Sweyn of Denmark was preparing an invasion. For the next few years William fought savagely for his newly-won kingdom.

When, in 1069, he heard the news that three thousand Normans, the garrison at York, had been killed by the English, he swore "by the splendour and resurrection of God" that he would exact vengeance sixtyfold for everyone of them. He bought off Sweyn's fleet, and then set out with his army to deal with the north. He ravaged the land between the Humber and the Tyne and left it a desert: the people were slain, died of starvation or sold themselves into slavery for food. Then, with the north wasted and subdued, William took Chester and crushed the hopes of the English in the west. Only Hereward the Wake held out in the Isle of Ely, but in 1071 William rooted out this last stronghold of the rebels.

The conquest of England was complete. The land and the power were in the hands of the Conqueror. And he took care to keep them there. He made every baron and landowner to whom he gave territory hold the land directly from the crown, and by this means he consolidated the central power and saved England from some of the worst abuses of the feudal system. In making his grants of land, he saw that the favoured lords should have their holdings in different counties, so that no powerful baron could build up a little kingdom within the kingdom.

In 1086 he caused the famous Domesday Book to be compiled, and in the same year he summoned all the Norman and English landholders to meet him at Salisbury and do homage to him. The administration of the law was also made dependent on the Crown, and thus William ensured strong central government.

His administration of the Church showed equal strength and wisdom. He deposed the English Archbishop of Canterbury, Stigand, and appointed Lanfranc in his place. His aim was to organize the Church as a separate department of the government, under the archbishop as his regent, and he refused to allow the pope to excommunicate or send papal letters to the clergy without his own express consent. But he dealt justly and generously with the Church. William was never guilty of the prevalent crimes of simony or the plundering of livings, and he was responsible for building churches and abbeys.

Strength, wisdom and justice marked the beginning of William's rule. As he grew older he grew greedy and more unscrupulous. His sense of justice was blunted by avarice, he used his ruthlessness more and more for personal gratification. He laid heavy taxes upon the people, and for his own pleasure laid waste thousands of acres in Hampshire to form a deer forest, the New Forest. It is still lovely in its spacious woodlands. "He loved the tall deer like a father," and would blind or mutilate any man who killed a deer. William was callous and always paid little heed to human suffering: he punished savagely, yet only one man in his reign, the Earl Waltheof, was sentenced to death.

His government gave, at length, peace to the land and unity. He encouraged commerce and allowed Flemings and Jews to settle in England. Many of the roots of British greatness lie in the reign of William the Conqueror.

Throughout his reign he was allowed no rest; when England was at peace, war came to him from Normandy. Robert Curthose, William's eldest son, asked for the duchies of Normandy and Maine, but William answered: "Don't think I shall take off my clothes before I go to bed."

So Robert, with the help of France and the barons, began an insurrection, and once more William had to fight for his inheritance.

At the Battle of Gerberoi, in 1079, Robert wounded his father in the hand, and then, recognizing him, leapt from his horse and begged forgiveness.

William kept his clothes on and maintained his grip of Normandy, and Robert later came to England where he built the New Castle on the Tyne.

William had done his great work: and now a joke brought him to his death. The Conqueror was a man of middle height and of great muscular strength, but as he grew older he became very fat. While in Normandy he heard that Philip of France had compared him to a woman in child-bed.

" By the splendour and resurrection of God," shouted William, " I will light a hundred thousand candles when I go to my churching Mass."

And with that he set out to burn and lay waste the border-lands of his enemy. Mantes he burned to the ground, and as he was riding through the ruined town his horse trod on a red-hot cinder, shied, and plunged William violently against the pommel. He suffered so severe internal injury that he had to be carried to Rouen, where he lay in agony for several weeks.

On his death-bed he gave Normandy to his eldest son Robert, England to his son William, who he advised to hurry across the Channel, and to Henry, the youngest son, five thousand pounds of silver. Henry had it carefully weighed before hurrying away from the bedside of the dying king.

There was neither kinsman nor friend present when William died on September 9, 1087. Even his burial was not free from strife, for as the coffin was being lowered into the grave at Caen, a man named Asselin Fitzarthur stepped forward and cried, " This land was my father's and was taken by force by this duke. In God's name I forbid this burial!" The full price of the land was promised to Fitzarthur, and the ceremony went on.

Thus, amidst bitterness and wrangling, they interred the mortal remains of the Conqueror, who had won for himself and his heirs a new land and laid the foundations of a mighty nation.

NICCOLÒ MACHIAVELLI

(1469–1527)

"Unscrupulous schemer; one who practises duplicity in statecraft, whence Machiavellian ..." Thus "The Concise Oxford Dictionary" under the heading "Machiavelli." Niccolò Machiavelli, the Italian who gave two words, a noun and an adjective to the English language and made his name a household word in every civilized country, has been the most widely read, the most abused, and most influential of all writers on the art of politics. He was a keen-sighted analyst of states and statecraft, and his works are the foundations of modern political science. Yet because he believed that political good could be achieved only by expediency without regard to right or morality, this mild-mannered, pleasant, kindly, pleasure-loving man has become, in the popular view, the Devil incarnate.

THE next time that the Prime Minister makes a speech of simple clarity implicit with sibylline subtlety, or when a leading Cabinet Minister introduces a new measure writhing in the involutions of subacute statesmanship; when the front pages of the newspapers are ablaze with the mangled details of an international intrigue or the politer proceeds of diplomacy, think of a slight, dark man writing feverishly in the seclusion of an Italian country villa: his bright eyes gleaming in his small head as he works, and a sarcastic smile playing on his thin, close lips. He is Niccolò Machiavelli, the founder of the science of modern politics.

There is no need to look far for Machiavelli's influence on the world. We commonly use the word Machiavellian to describe the acts of an unscrupulous or cunning schemer. And that gives the key to the reputation which this pioneer of politics has borne through the centuries.

Macaulay, in a famous Essay, opens his remarks on Machiavelli as follows:

"We doubt whether any name in literary history be so generally odious as that of the man whose character and writings we now propose to consider. The terms in which he is commonly described would seem to impart that he was the Tempter, the Evil Principle, the discoverer of ambition and revenge; the original inventor of perjury, and that before the publication of his fatal *The Prince,* there had never been a hypocrite, a tyrant, or a traitor; a simulated virtue, or a convenient crime.

"One writer gravely assures us that Maurice of Saxony learned all his fraudulent policy from that execrable volume. Another remarks that since it was translated into Turkish the Sultans have been more addicted than formerly to the custom of strangling their brothers. . . . Several authors have hinted that the Gunpowder Plot is to be primarily attributed to his doctrines, and seem to think that his effigy ought to be substituted for that of Guy Faux, in those processions by which the ingenuous youth of England annually commemorate the preservation of the Three Estates. The Church of Rome has pronounced his works accursed things.

"Nor have our own countrymen been backward in testifying their opinion of his merits. Out of his surname they have coined an epithet for a knave, and out of his Christian name a synonym for the Devil." And here, in a footnote, the historian quotes a couplet from *Hudibras:*

> "Nick Machiavel had ne'er a trick,
> Though he gave his name to our old Nick"

with the playful rider "But, we believe, there is a schism on this subject among the antiquarians."

The cause of this accumulative outburst, Niccolò Machiavelli, was born at Florence on May 3, 1469. His father, Bernardo, was a jurist, and although not a man of wealth had a small income from landed property in addition to what he obtained by his legal work. A man of culture, his son resembled him in an early fondness for literature. He read deeply of the Latin and Italian classics, and concentrated more especially on Roman history. This early training helped him to write with vigour and conciseness; he said what he wanted to say without frills or ornament. "The result is," says Symonds, "that, without thinking about expression, Machiavelli created Italian prose anew, and was the first to form a monumental modern style."

Italy was the cockpit of Europe. There was almost constant strife between the petty states that constituted the peninsula, between cities, and often enough between factions in those cities. Ambitious individuals established despotisms, with their inevitable sequel of intrigues, assassinations, imprisonments and exiles. Florence had retained her republican institutions, but the powerful Medici family had dominated the government.

Machiavelli entered public life in 1494, a year of crisis in which the Medici were expelled by reason of the craven fear of Pietro de' Medici when Charles VIII of France crossed the Alps to conquer the kingdom of Naples, a project in which he signally failed. Machiavelli started as a clerk in the second chancery of the commune, under his old master, Marcello Virgilio Adriani, a learned man of letters. When the latter became chancellor of the republic in 1498, notable for the burning of the Dominican friar, Savonarola, in Florence, Machiavelli was made second chancellor and secretary, a post which he held for fourteen years. The body to which he was attached, although subordinate to the Signory, was in control of the departments of war and in part of the interior or home affairs. Machiavelli's duties also concerned the organization of embassies and the transaction of business with the Florentine cities.

Machiavelli himself made many journeys on diplomatic missions during the course of his official career, and it was his wide experience of men and affairs in war and peace that helped to shape his political philosophy. The first of his many missions to the petty courts of Italy was in 1499, when he went to arrange the continuance of a loan to Catherine Sforza, Countess of Forlì and Imola, and also to purchase munitions, and again in the following year he was sent to France on a mission to Louis XII, who had now succeeded Charles VIII.

Machiavelli married, in 1502, Marietta Corsini, for whom he seems to have had sincere affection, despite occasional lapses.

In the October of that year, he was sent as an emissary to Cesare Borgia, Duke of Valentinois, in camp in Romagna, with instructions to watch his every action, for he had already threatened Florence. Machiavelli was impressed by the man's combination of audacity and diplomatic prudence; with his clever manipulation of fraud, ruthlessness and cruelty; with his whole-heartedness and disdain of half measures; with his firmness and self-reliance. All these Machiavelli noted: they helped to mould his own political principles.

From his letters to Florence we get intimate glimpses of Machiavelli the man, and of his conduct during his delicate mission. Borgia was a man of action, not words, and conscious of his own practical superiority he overrode Machiavelli in conversation. But the other, although unwilling and unable to make suggestions for immediate action, saw clearly beneath the surface of men and events and analysed them with precision.

Machiavelli was holding a watching brief for the Florentines with considerable skill, but Borgia was always attempting to draw him out, to get some definite statement on the matter of a Florentine alliance.

"Nothing can be settled with these Florentines," Machiavelli quotes him as saying, but the man of action was always trying to play cat and mouse with the subtle politician.

Machiavelli was more than a match for him. His reports were so valuable that Piero Soderini, the *gonfaloniere* or head of the Signoria, and his associates of the Council of Ten would not listen to the repeated requests of their agent for a recall: instead they sent him praise and twenty-five gold ducats towards his expenses. He warned the Government not to regard Cesare Borgia "like the other barons, but as a new Power in Italy, with whom they might conclude treaties and alliances, rather than offer him an appointment as *condottiere*."

To relieve tedium, Machiavelli wrote ribald letters as well as reports to his official colleagues. His witticisms were evidently appreciated, for in one of his replies Ruffini says: "Your letters to Biagio and the others are most grateful to all, and the jests and merry saws contained in them make all crack their jaws with laughter."

Sometimes Machiavelli withdrew to study and meditation. He was constantly writing to his friend Buonaccorsi for books and money and all kinds of assistance.

"We have been searching for Plutarch's *Lives,* but it is not to be bought in Florence. Have patience, for we must write to Venice for it; and to tell you the truth, you are a worry to ask for so many things," wrote Buonaccorsi to him in October, 1502.

While Machiavelli was studying the ancients he was also examining the moderns. In Cesare Borgia he saw the type of ruler which he was later to idealize in *The Prince;* he had his first conceptions of statecraft and the art of ruling exercised without reference to morality.

There were two other points in Borgia's policy which Machiavelli found good. His firm administration of conquered provinces, and his use of troops recruited from his own duchy in place of mercenaries. Unreliable mercenary armies, made up for the most part of adventurers willing to fight for any one who could pay, were the common means of defence adopted by the Italian cities. Cash and not patriotism was the essence of the contract. Machiavelli was quick to see the worthlessness of the *condottieri* system. In 1503 he outlined to Soderini plans for a national militia for Florence, and for three years spent every available minute developing his scheme. It was approved, and a ministry set up with Machiavelli as secretary.

The country districts were divided up into departments, from each of which a levy of infantry was made. Machiavelli worked with feverish energy, delegating little of the work to others and attending to the smallest and apparently least important detail. Unfortunately he wrecked the plan by a blunder. He and his colleague, Soderini, chose the wrong man as commander-in-chief. They selected none other than a Spaniard of notorious cruelty who had served with Cesare Borgia.

The next few years were busy ones for Machiavelli. War was being waged for the recovery of Pisa, the greatest conquest of the republic, and he had to attend camp and raise levies. Yet the urge to write could not be restrained, and in 1504 he began his *Annals of Italy,* a poem on events that had happened during the previous ten years, and wrote a comedy, *Le Maschere*—Masks. Then he proceeded on embassies to Perugia and Sienna, and accompanied the new pope, Julius II, when he entered the province of Emilia to subdue the rebels of the Church. Asked by Michelangelo if he should represent him in a statue with a book in his hand, the militant Pontiff answered, "No, with a sword!"

In 1507 the Emperor Maximilian made arrangements for his coronation in Rome, and, as it was to be a brilliant and costly affair, he demanded subsidies of the cities. The republican Florentines, while not altogether averse to a subscription, frankly thought that he was asking too much, and Machiavelli was sent to treat with the emperor. He went through Switzerland by way of Geneva to Maximilian's court at Botzen. On his way, Machiavelli studied with particular care the Swiss and the Germans and their way of life. He tried, as we gather from his notes, to sum up the political worth of the German nation, and to penetrate the secrets of its strength and weakness. His effort shows the remarkable quality of his political and historical judgment and observation. He pursued the same course with the French when he visited Louis XII at Blois in 1510.

Machiavelli returned from Germany in June, 1508, and it was mainly due to his activities that the war was brought to a successful end by the surrender of Pisa after a twelve years' siege in June, 1509. Three years later, Spanish and papal troops occupied Florence, Soderini was deposed, the Medici returned in triumph, and Machiavelli was exiled. Worse was to follow. In the February of 1513, Machiavelli's name was found on a piece of paper dropped by Pietro Paolo Boscoli, who had initiated a conspiracy against the Government.

Although Machiavelli was innocent, he was seized, imprisoned, and put to torture. Proof of his courage may be found in the fact that while in prison after he had suffered six turns of the rack, he wrote satirical sonnets dedicated to Giuliano de' Medici, the new ruler of the city. In one his biographer, Pasquale Villari, tells us, he describes his jail: "The stench was horrible, the walls 'crawling with vermin so big and swollen that they seem like moths.' On all sides is a noise as of hell. This prisoner is being chained, that one loosened, a third cries that the ropes are hoisting him too far from the ground." In another he sends Giuliano a gift of thrushes, to be given to his enemies to nibble, so that they might cease to gnaw Machiavelli so ferociously. "And if the thrushes are thought lean, I shall answer that I, too, am lean, yet they get good mouthfuls out of me."

He was released on Giovanni de' Medici's election to the papacy shortly afterwards, and writing to Francesco Vettori, ambassador in Rome, of his ordeal, he said that he had borne his affliction with such bravery "that I am really pleased with myself, and think there is more in me than I ever before believed."

On his release he retired to a farm near San Casciano, at no great distance from Florence. Exiled, with no work to employ his mind, the feverishly active Machiavelli sought an outlet in writing. In this period he penned his world-famous political treatises and brilliant comedies. Yet he interspersed these fine and nervously written works with vulgar and obscene correspondence. He relapsed from the friendship of the wise and leaned to the company of drinking companions and casual loves. At one moment he was the keen, far-seeing political philosopher; at another a pot-house rake.

"I rise with the sun in the morning," he tells a correspondent, "and go into one of the woods for a couple of hours to inspect yesterday's work, and to pass some time with the woodcutters, who have always some troubles to tell me, either of their own or their neighbours'. On leaving the wood, I go to a spring, and thence up to my *uccellare* [a place where decoy birds are kept] with a book under my arm, either Dante, Petrarch, or one of the minor poets, such as Tibullus, Ovid. . . . I read their amorous transports, and the history of their loves, recalling my own to my mind, and time passes pleasantly in these meditations. Then I betake myself to the inn by the roadside, chat with passers-by, ask news of the places whence they come, hear various things, and note the varied tastes and diverse fancies of mankind. This carries me on to the dinner hour, when in the company of my brood, I swallow whatever fare this poor little place of mine and my slender patrimony can afford me. Dinner over, I go back to the inn. There I generally find the host, a butcher, a miller, and a couple of brickmakers. I mix with these boors, the whole day, playing at *cricca* and at *tric trac,* which games give rise to a thousand quarrels and much exchange of bad language, and we generally wrangle over farthings, and our shouting can be heard at San Casciano. Steeped in this degradation my wits grow mouldy, and I vent my rage at the malignity of fate, content to let it crush me in this fashion, if only to see whether it will not take shame of its work.

"At nightfall I return home and seek my writing-room, and, divesting myself on its threshold of my rustic garments, stained with mud and mire, I assume courtly attire, and thus suitably clothed, enter within the ancient courts of ancient men, by whom, being cordially welcomed, I am fed with the food that *alone* is mine, and for which I was born, and am not ashamed to hold discourse with them and inquire the motives of their actions; and these men in their humanity reply to me, and for the space of four hours I feel no weariness, remember no trouble, no longer fear poverty, no longer dread death, my whole being is absorbed in them. . . ."

Machiavelli, who had apparently sacrificed so much for so little, withdrew to his pastoral retreat in the March of 1513. Italy, he avowed, was "more enslaved than the Hebrews, more servile than the Persians, more dispersed than the Athenians, without a head, without order, beaten, despoiled, ravaged, overrun, and enduring every kind of ruin." His despondency did not last for long. By the end of the year he had completed his most famous work, *Il Principe*—"The Prince." It was not written for publication, and was dedicated to Lorenzo de' Medici. The treatise remained unprinted until after its author's death.

In his *Discorsi*, a series of comments in the light of his own experience on Livy's Roman history, which he had begun at the same time, he inquires into the origin, being and maintenance of states. In *The Prince* he writes of one branch of this vast and complicated subject. The work is an analysis of the means by which a man may achieve and maintain sovereign power. It is neither entirely philosophical nor wholly an analysis of political abstractions. Machiavelli was inspired by a great ideal. He wanted to see a unified Italy defended by a national army. He put forward "the first logically reasoned aspiration" to the unity and national independence which the Italians eventually achieved in the nineteenth century.

The reason for the general abhorrence of Machiavelli is that he subordinated morals to political expediency. Most people overlook the important fact that he sought to advise a particular individual in particular circumstances, and not every ruler in all circumstances. Moreover, he wrote according to the morals of his own time. The thought of the early sixteenth century was not the advanced thought of today, though it may be held that in some countries Machiavelli's findings are by no means obsolete. He did not attempt to frame a system of ethics.

He quotes cruel and treacherous murders by Cesare Borgia as being justified and praiseworthy for the benefits they conferred upon the state which he ruled, and later goes on: "All depends as to whether cruelties are well done or ill. Those may be said to be well done, if it may be permitted thus to speak of evil deeds, which are done suddenly for the sake of establishing a safe position, and not continued afterwards. Ill done are those which are also carried on afterwards. It is requisite from the first to calculate what cruelties are necessary, execute them at one stroke, and then reassure men's minds, otherwise you are forced to be always sword in hand. Injuries which are suddenly inflicted are less felt, and therefore give less offence, while nevertheless producing all the desired effects; benefits, on the contrary, should be conferred gradually, so that they be better relished."

He scouts all thought of seeking for an ideal prince, "for there is so much difference between how we live and how we ought to live, that he who leaves that which is done for that which ought to be done, studies his ruin rather than his safety; because a man who should profess to be honest in all his dealings would necessarily come to ruin among so many that are dishonest. Whence it behoves every prince, desirous of maintaining his power, to learn how to be dishonest, and to make use or not of this knowledge according to circumstances."

Again: "It would be better, were it possible, to be loved and feared at the same time: but as that is not possible, it is better to be feared, when you have to choose the alternative. Love is maintained by a bond of obligation, which, owing to the wickedness of human nature, is always broken whenever it clashes with private interests; but fear is maintained by a dread of punishment that never abandons you. Men love at their own pleasure, but fear at the pleasure of the prince, who should therefore depend upon that which is his own, not upon that which is of others. Yet he may be feared without being hated if he refrain from touching the property and womankind of his subjects, and if he avoid bloodshed excepting when there is good cause and manifest justification for it; inasmuch as men more easily forget the loss of their father than of their property. Besides which, when you begin to live by others' property, there is no end to it, whereas occasions for bloodshed may seldom arise."

These few quotations give the tone of the much-read and much-criticized *Prince*. While Machiavelli was willing to admit that virtue and honour played their parts in private transactions, he would allow no consideration for them in the conduct of his ideal state, and although he allows that the honest private citizen is the backbone of the state, yet that citizen must become a pawn in the hands of the wise politician—the dictator. Religion is good only so far as it is a powerful instrument in the hands of a wise ruler to sustain the national morale. But he criticizes Christianity for exalting the contemplative virtues rather than vigorous action, and condemns the Church of his time for its corruption. His weakness was that he considered man only as a political animal; he ignored the essential relationships of politics with ethics. Hence Machiavelli the villain.

But it must be remembered that by his abstraction of the essence of political science, by his turning thought to political principles, by his very processes of thought, he established himself as the founder of modern political philosophy. His greatness lies in the fact that he studied man as a whole in history, and drew his conclusions from his knowledge of the nature of men, "ascribing all things to natural causes, or to fortune."

This historical insight is further displayed in the completed part of his *History of Florence,* which he was commissioned to write in 1520. In 1519, Pope Leo X, a son of Lorenzo de' Medici, appealed to Machiavelli, amongst others, for advice on the form of government to be given to Florence. Machiavelli wrote a treatise based on his experience and practical knowledge, and influenced by his political opinions. A year later he produced *The Art of War*. This was also a contribution to his ideal of a unified and strong Italy. The main points of the treatise stress the advantage of native national troops, the inefficiency of fortresses, the comparative uselessness of artillery and the absolute necessity for reliance on infantry. He also wrote the life of Castruccio, in which he sketched again his ideal prince in 1520.

Four years later his comedy *Mandragola* was published in Rome. Its wit, satire and humour in dealing with the decadent manners of the day make this play one of the finest, and certainly the richest, in

Italian literature. He wrote another comedy, the *Clizia,* a novel and a number of minor pieces while in retirement.

In 1526 he was active again. It is quite possible that *The Prince* was written in the hope that he might be called back to service. Indeed, Sir Richard Lodge states that Machiavelli's chapter in which he details Cesare Borgia's cause was due "solely to the curious similarity of his *fortuna* (opportunity or environment) with that of the restored Medici in Florence." Pope Clement VII employed him to inspect the fortifications of Florence, and later we find him undertaking diplomatic missions for Francesco Guicciardini, who, besides being the pope's commissary of war in Lombardy, was a historian hardly inferior to Machiavelli himself.

But there was little more work for Machiavelli: his death came in June, 1527.

In the opinion of Lord Morley, no mean authority, we shall best understand Machiavelli "if we take him as following up the divorce of politics from theology, by a divorce from ethics also. He was laying down certain maxims of government as an art; the end of that art is the security and permanence of the ruling power; and the fundamental principle from which he silently started, without shadow of doubt or misgiving as to its soundness, was that the application of moral standards to this business is as little to the point as it would be in the navigation of a ship. The effect was fatal even for his own purpose, for what he put aside, whether for the sake of argument or because he thought them in substance irrelevant, were nothing less than the living forces by which societies subsist and governments are strong."

HERNANDO CORTES

(1485–1547)

Four hundred years ago America was the New World, a fabled land of wealth and danger and opportunity. The brave adventurers of Europe turned to the West and set out in their little ships to win what they might from that great New World. From Spain went the Conquistadores, who claimed the south of the new continent for their motherland. Greatest of them was Hernando Cortes, whose conquest of Mexico is one of the romances of history. It is a tale of courage and cruelty, of diplomacy and faith: an epic story of a tiny band of men, under a great leader, who set out and succeeded in conquering a mighty nation.

A ROLLING stone that gathered gold for an emperor, a law student who became a soldier, a dissolute adventurer who was the greatest military captain of his time—such was Hernando Cortes. His ambition led him to conquer a new world and made Spain the mistress of the West. Though a soldier, he was also a diplomat who outwitted the subtlest schemes of a race in which cunning was second nature; though a member of the lesser nobility of Spain, he subdued the proud Aztec emperor, Montezuma, and gave to Charles V of Spain a new meaning to his title—Emperor of the West.

Hernando Cortes was born of noble parentage at Medellin, in Spain, in 1485, seven years before Columbus discovered the New World. There was nothing in young Hernando that could have foreshadowed his future greatness. As a child he was delicate and had several severe illnesses which nearly killed him. When he was fourteen years old, he was sent to the University of Salamanca to study law, and there he passed two of the unhappiest years of his life, though it is said that he learned quickly. The dull routine of lectures on rhetoric and civil law was too much for him. All around him he heard tales of the great things that were being done in the world outside the university and beyond the shores of Spain.

The Moors had been driven from Granada, after an occupation of 800 years; Aragon and Castile were now one kingdom; and a new world where the very pebbles were said to be of gold had been discovered. The great Gonsalvo de Cordova had driven the French from Naples and all southern Italy now belonged to Spain. How was it possible, with such things going on, that the restless spirit of Cortes could be content with being shut up in a university or living quietly in the pious atmosphere of his father's house?

The solution of Cortes's problem seemed near at hand. Don Nicolás de Ovando, a friend of the Cortes family, had recently been appointed Governor of Santo Domingo, one of the newly discovered West Indian islands, and it was arranged that young Hernando should accompany this expedition. But his high spirits were often Cortes's undoing and he was not destined to sail with Ovando. One night shortly before the departure of the expedition, Hernando went to pay a clandestine visit to a young woman. The gates of the house were barred, but no obstacles ever deterred Cortes in his desires. As he was clambering over a roof, the wall of a courtyard collapsed and Cortes, fully armed and with breastplate and spurs, clattered to the ground. Instantly the place was alive with men. A young member of the household, thinking the visit was to his wife, ran out, sword in hand, and would have killed Cortes, lying in agony on the ground, had he not been stopped. Cortes's injuries were so bad that fever set in and he was unable to join Ovando in his expedition. So Cortes spent a year as a common soldier leading a life of dissipation, but when he was just nineteen his chance came again and he sailed for Santo Domingo in a merchant ship. By this time he was an accomplished horseman, a skilful swordsman and had, as one of his later companions in arms has said, " what is most important of all, courage and spirit." He was kindly received at Santo Domingo by Governor Ovando, whom he should have followed three years before, and shortly afterwards a rising of natives occurred in which Cortes received his baptism of fire. It was during the quelling of these disturbances that he made the acquaintance of a man who was to play a large part in his life. Don Diego Velasquez was an officer under Ovando and at first he and Cortes were fast friends. But Velasquez was a much older man than Cortes and the insatiable ambition and ultimate success of this young man turned the friendship into enmity. For a time, however, all was well and Cortes went as second in command to Velasquez on an expedition to the island of Cuba. There he showed such ability that Velasquez decided to entrust him with the conquest of the recently discovered Mexico. A former expedition under a lieutenant of Velasquez, Juan Grijalva, had only landed but not attempted to form a settlement.

They reached the island of Cozumel, where they were joined by a strange outcast, black as a negro, but an undoubted Spaniard. He said he was a priest named Aguilar, who seven years earlier had escaped from the cage where he and his shipwrecked comrades were being fattened for a cannibal feast by a native tribe on the mainland. He spoke the Maya language fluently, and henceforth served Cortes as an interpreter.

Reports had been brought back of a wonderful new land where there were houses and temples built of stone and a great town, which, seen from the sea, seemed to be as large as Seville. The people, who were known as the Aztecs, were said to be subject to a great emperor, and, what was much more interesting to the Spaniards, there was gold in abundance. On his way, Cortes called at Macaca, a small part of the island of Cuba, and laid in supplies of food and water. His methods were so high-handed and his behaviour so autocratic that when news of his action reached Velasquez, the latter began to wonder if Cortes were not trying to be greater than his master. Velasquez decided to recall Cortes. But the future conqueror of Mexico was not the man to be stopped from anything he had once begun, and he went on with his voyage. On March 4, 1519, Cortes landed on the coast of Mexico close to the deserted encampment that Grijalva had founded a year before, and the first thing that he did was to burn his fleet so that none of his followers could turn back. His next step was to reassure the natives. He gave them presents, told them that they were now subjects of a great king with all the privileges that went with such allegiance and that they would receive a knowledge of the true religion. This kindly treatment was returned by the natives. They brought bread, honey, fish and fruit to the Spaniards, they pulled down their idols and erected a cross and a statue of the Madonna.

Whenever he could, Cortes tried to conquer by peaceful methods. In this he endeavoured to be faithful to the injunction of Pope Alexander VI, who in his famous Bull dividing the New World between Spain and Portugal, urged both countries to respect the persons of the natives and to remember that black men had equal rights with white men.

On his march to the interior, Cortes subdued many small towns without firing a shot, but there were times when sterner measures had to be taken, and on these occasions he was absolutely ruthless.

When he arrived at the town of Tobasco he met his first opposition. The natives of the place had long been the laughing stock of the other tribes for their supposed cowardice, and it seemed that on this occasion they had been derided into resistance to the Spaniards.

They were armed with javelins tipped with bone or sharp stone, slings, bows and arrows, lances, and a long two-handed sword known as a *maquahuitl*. This had a blade nearly four feet in length, having on each side a groove set with hard obsidian stone whetted to a razor edge. The Spaniards wore steel helmets, but these left their faces exposed; many of them wore steel breastplates or doublets of cotton which were quilted thick enough to stop an arrow but did not reach below the knee. And the natives attacked in hordes, the air was black with their missiles, and these, whenever they struck bare faces or legs, inflicted terrible wounds.

"They came on like mad dogs and surrounded us on all sides and hurled so many arrows, javelins and stones that at the first onslaught they wounded more than seventy of us," wrote Bernal Diaz, one of Cortes's captains, of this first great battle with the natives of Mexico. "They kept on shooting and wounding. With our artillery and muskets and crossbows we fought hard. Mesa, our gunner, killed many of them because they were dense squadrons, but with all the hurts and wounds we gave them we could not drive them away."

It was the cavalry that saved the day. The inhabitants of Mexico had never seen horses before and thought mount and rider were one creature. While the infantry held the natives in front, Cortes and his cavalry charged them in the rear again and again, until the natives, terrified by the strange monsters, broke and fled to the woods, leaving behind eight hundred dead. But the superb courage which the Indians displayed was of no avail against the small Spanish force and the town surrendered to Cortes.

Cortes then made overtures of peace, which were accepted. The natives brought him gold and jewellery and twenty women. One of these, a noble Aztec lady, had been sold as a slave to these Maya natives of the coast. She spoke both Maya and Aztec, the language of the cities of the interior, so with the aid of Aguilar and Marina, as the Spaniards called this woman, Cortes was able to make himself understood henceforth among all the tribes he encountered. He took her as his mistress, and later she bore him a son.

To mark this first victory over the Aztecs, he made three cuts with his sword in the trunk of a large tree in the central square of the city, and shouted that he took possession of the land in the king's name. But by omitting the name of Velasquez from this symbolical act, Cortes definitely ranged himself against his superior. The small losses the Spaniards had suffered caused them to be regarded as gods by the Aztecs; and numerous *caciques,* or petty chieftains, made their submission and sent presents.

Meanwhile, far away in Mexico City, the capital of the ancient and mighty Aztec empire, strange tidings had reached the great Montezuma, Lord of the Aztecs. For many weeks he had been disturbed in spirit by untoward signs and omens. Comets shot through the sky almost nightly, the Temple of Huitzilopochti had caught fire through some unknown cause, a shrine on a hilltop had been struck by a thunderbolt. And now messengers from the coast brought news of huge birds with white wings that skimmed over the waters, carrying men with bearded faces, superhuman beings who rode four-legged monsters and who could deal death from afar among the bravest warriors of the coast.

Might not their leader be the god Quetzalcoatl, who, after teaching Montezuma's ancestors the arts of peace, had departed to the East, promising to return one day in the form of a tall, bearded man of fair complexion? The time for the fulfilment of this old prophecy had arrived, and lo! here were bearded white strangers who wielded thunder and lightning. Tormented by these doubts, Montezuma, who was high priest as well as emperor, feared that the god had come to claim dominion over the land, and that his own throne was doomed. He decided to send gifts to the newcomers and to implore them to leave his territories.

One morning there arrived in Cortes's camp two envoys from the Great King, with a retinue of slaves bearing a wheel of gold as big as a cartwheel, a still larger wheel of silver, a helmet full of grains of gold from Aztec mines, many life-size imitations in gold of ducks, dogs, tigers, lions and monkeys, and countless ornaments adorned with beautiful plumes, loads of cotton cloths worked in patterns, and numerous other presents.

The advance of the Spaniards after the victory of Tobasco is one of the most amazing feats of arms and human endurance in the history of the world. Now drenched by heavy rains, now sweltering in torrid heat, the men struggled onwards under the burden of full armour and weapons, which native porters would have carried, had it not been for Cortes's stern and invariable rule that every man must be ready to fight on the instant. They splashed through swamps alive with alligators and water-snakes, hacked their way through dense bush infested by snarling jaguars and hissing serpents. Scorpions bit them, poisonous ants, spiders and mosquitoes stung their faces into ulcers.

They staggered on until they reached the lower slopes of a great mountain range topped by volcanoes, climbed up steep and slippery ridges to a pass twelve thousand feet high, then descended on the other side to a vast desert plateau, still eight thousand feet above sea level, which took three days to cross. Here the adventurers were almost frozen by tempests of hail and sleet; for many hours they thought they were lost, and stumbled about among the desolate salt marshes and volcanic ashes of that great waste like wandering souls in the inferno. But when the desert ended they found themselves in a lovely valley, yellow with aloe, red with blossoming cactus, and golden with fields of maize, for they had reached the town of Xocotla, where the chief was a loyal vassal to Montezuma. Surlily and grudgingly he gave them a little food. Before one of the temples in the market-place the Spaniards saw a pile of a hundred thousand human skulls. They did not stay long in that place, but hastened on until they came to the frontier of the little independent state of Tlascala, guarded by high mountains from the Aztecs and their subject peoples, who surrounded them on all sides.

A typical example of the suspense Cortes had to endure is shown by the behaviour of the people of Tlascala, a proud and autonomous state which was in revolt against the great Aztec emperor, Montezuma.

This state was a confederacy of four tribes, each subject to its own prince or *cacique*.

When they heard that Cortes was marching on their city, the Tlascalans held a council to decide whether they would support him against Montezuma, whom they hated and feared, or whether they would resist him. The result of the council was a decision which was typical of the character of the people with whom Cortes had to contend. The two first members of the council proposed divergent policies. The one said that as Cortes was clearly the white conqueror, whose coming Aztec legend had foretold would come to reclaim the kingdom of the god Quetzalcoatl, who centuries before had appeared no one knew whence, inaugurated a period of great prosperity and then disappeared none knew whither, he should be allowed to pass and be given every assistance against Montezuma. The second, a blind old man of great influence, spoke against the proposal. If the Spaniards were gods, that fact would appear whatever happened; until it were proven, it would be a sign of weakness for the Tlascalans to let them through.

The third speech was a triumph for the middle way, and was typical of Aztec diplomacy. It suggested the adoption of both proposals. Let friendly messages be sent to the Spaniards welcoming them, but at the same time let an unofficial army, composed for the most part of the Tlascalans's neighbours and friends, the Otomis, be sent to ambush Cortes if he persisted in his advance. If the unofficial army were victorious, it would bring glory to the Tlascalans. If, on the other hand, it were defeated, then the blame could be laid on the Otomis. The army could be repudiated, and Cortes assured that he had the friendship of the Tlascalans.

This counsel won the day, and preparations were made immediately to carry it out. Cortes continued to advance, and as he met with no opposition he supposed the natives would be friendly to him. A great wall nine feet high and twenty feet thick ran from mountain to mountain around Tlascala. Cortes rode ahead and reconnoitred until he found the only entrance, about ten feet wide, which ran in a kind of semicircle between two walls, so that any troops trying to enter would be exposed to a deadly hail of missiles from above on both sides. But the entrance was undefended, and the Spanish army passed through into Tlascala, marched for several miles through deserted countryside, then suddenly, as they emerged from a ravine, found themselves surrounded by thousands of howling natives, who began to close in upon them. Cortes sent messages of peace. The reply was, "We will kill you and eat your flesh." And yelling their war cry, forty thousand natives, armed with slings, bows, javelins and two-handed swords, rushed at the little band of invaders.

The Spaniards had good cause then to be thankful for their armour—a single blow from a long sword on a horse's chest opened it to the entrails—for their six guns, which wrought havoc in the dense throngs, and for their cavalry, which routed the natives in charge after charge. But they were sorely beset, and had to take refuge in a temple that night. Next day another great battle was fought. Before it started, Cortes gave each branch of the service—musketeers, gunners, crossbowmen, cavalry, foot soldiers—careful instructions as to how each squad should take and maintain its place and manage its weapons. Then all day they fought amid a storm of stone, four hundred men, many of them wounded or sick with fever, against forty thousand. But the natives were closely packed, every shot told among them, and their leaders quarrelled and plunged the divisions into confusion, and "above all," reports Bernal Diaz, "the great mercy of God gave the Spaniards the strength to endure." Finally, after the death of many of their captains, the enemy drew off, pursued by the few cavalry as far as their wearied horses would take them.

Fifty Tlascalan envoys now came offering peace. Cortes, shrewdly questioning them, found they were spies, cut off their hands and sent them back. The Tlascalans consulted their priests, who told them that the mysterious white men lost their strange powers after nightfall. So, contrary to all traditions of Mexican warfare, the Tlascalans attempted a night attack. But throughout the long campaign, Cortes saw to it that his army was always prepared for action, and the storming party found to their cost that the Spaniards, in the words of Diaz, " slept ready shod and armed, with the horses saddled and bridled." The attack was repulsed with heavy loss, and Cortes took reprisals by two savage onslaughts by night on nearby towns, where he butchered hundreds of natives and burned their homes.

The Tlascalans soon begged for peace, and when Cortes realized they were sincere, he granted it. They welcomed the Spanish army with festivities into their capital, and henceforth were devoted allies of Cortes, hailing him as their champion against the hated Aztecs.

To rest his men and heal their wounds, Cortes stayed in the city of Tlascala three weeks. It was the biggest town the Spaniards had yet seen on the unknown continent. " It is much larger and stronger than Granada," Cortes wrote to the King of Spain. " It has excellent buildings, and it contains many more people than Granada did at the time of the conquest, and it is better supplied with bread, birds, game, fish, vegetables and other provisions. In the market, every day, there are more than thirty thousand people buying and selling, not to mention several little markets in other parts of the city. In this market all their wares are to be found, not only provisions, but clothes and shoes. There are jewellery shops, as well arranged as in any market-place anywhere; the earthenware and crockery are as good as the best in Spain; there are shops for wood, coals, edible herbs and herbs for drugs. There is a kind of barber's shop where there is shaving and heads are washed; there are baths."

The Tlascalans had assured Cortes that the attack had been carried out by a base and ungrateful people, the Otomis, and that the Tlascalans only wished to be friends with Cortes and to allow him to pass freely.

After occupying Tlascala, Cortes had yet another city to take before the road to Mexico City, or Tenochtitlan as the Aztecs called it, lay open. This was the city of Cholula. And here occurred an event for which Cortes has been unjustly condemned. The Cholulans first of all sent Cortes an embassy of the men of the lowest estate they could find. This was an insult that Cortes well appreciated. He sent the envoys back with the imperious message that he would see none but the Cholulan *caciques* themselves. After this, another typically Indian stratagem was resorted to. They came to Cortes, protested their friendship to him, and then withdrew to their city. But they had seen to it that the road along which Cortes would have to pass was blocked with great tree trunks, and that another road left clear for him had had special pits dug in it, at the bottom of which sharp spears were placed.

Again the instinct of Cortes saved him. He chose the road that had been blocked, cleared away the obstacles, and arrived unexpectedly at Cholula. There he ordered all the *caciques* and their retinue to meet him in conference, and he took them into a small courtyard and addressed them. After telling them how he had taken them into his confidence and had ordered all the Christians in his army to do them no harm, he exposed the plot that had been made against him.

"For this wickedness you shall all die," he said. "You shall pay for your treachery by the destruction of your city, and no memory of it shall remain."

He then ordered some of the *caciques* to be imprisoned, and the rest put to death.

The horrible butchery of these men and the ravaging of the city was not the work of the Spaniards alone. They were helped by Tlascalans, who had allied themselves to him, and other natives.

This massacre cannot be justified, but it must be remembered that Cortes was employing only the methods common in his time, and that he was at the head of a force of no more than five hundred men in a country which was almost entirely hostile to him. He also knew the terrible fate that awaited him and his men if they should be taken prisoners by the Aztecs. Human sacrifice was part of the structure of Aztec civilization, and the torturing of the victim was a necessary part of their ritual.

After these events, Montezuma redoubled his efforts to prevent Cortes reaching Mexico City. Seeing that armed resistance was in vain, he besought him in every possible way not to continue his march. He even said there were not sufficient provisions in the city to maintain the Spaniards. But still Cortes marched on.

At last, on November 8, 1519, Cortes entered Mexico City. There he was kindly and courteously received by Montezuma. The emperor showered presents of gold dust and priceless ornaments on him, and told him at the end of his speech of welcome: "All I possess you shall have, whenever you wish. I leave you now, but I leave you in your country, in your own home," and with tears trickling down his cheeks, the great Montezuma, last ruler of the Aztec Empire, left the audience chamber. Cortes saw that if he was to maintain his precarious hold on Mexico City he must get the emperor into his power. His opportunity came sooner than he expected. News reached Montezuma that a Spanish fleet under Narvaez, a subordinate of Velasquez, had arrived at the coast with a force of 1,400 men and was marching against Cortes. The natives of the coast, probably acting on orders from Montezuma, at once attacked the settlement of Vera Cruz, which Cortes had founded soon after his landing. The surprise assault was successful; the head of a Spaniard was sent to the capital, and the legend of Spanish immortality was finally destroyed.

Cortes acted swiftly. He marched straight to Montezuma's palace with a strong body of men, and took the emperor back to his own quarters as a prisoner. He followed this blow with an even more audacious move.

Leaving half his force behind him to guard Mexico City and his august prisoner, Cortes marched with two hundred and fifty men against Narvaez. He met him at a place not far from Tabasco, and although he was facing an army as well disciplined as his own, and three times its size, he offered battle at once. The swiftness of the attack took Narvaez by surprise, and the expedition, which should have brought back Cortes as a rebel in chains, had ignominiously to surrender. Meanwhile, news reached Cortes that the Mexicans had risen against his men in Mexico City. Again the amazing personality of the man asserted itself. He achieved the apparently impossible by winning over the soldiers of Narvaez, whom he had just defeated, and he began the weary march back.

On his return, he found that the soldiers he had left behind were on the verge of surrendering to the infuriated Mexicans. He relieved them and put to death the principal *caciques* responsible for the rising. But still the trouble continued, and finally Cortes permitted the imprisoned Montezuma to show himself once more to his people so as to restore order. But the Mexicans would have nothing to do with the man whom they considered had betrayed them to the Spaniards; and when he appeared before them, they stoned him. Montezuma's spirit was shattered; and he died more from a broken heart than from the wounds he had received.

After Montezuma's death, his nephew Guatemoczin was elected emperor, and immediately a fresh attack was made on the Spaniards. Cortes was driven out of the capital, and his rearguard was cut off and totally destroyed. But Cortes never knew when he was beaten. With the aid of the Tlascalans—whose treachery caused him as much anxiety as the ferocity of the enemy—he faced overwhelming odds at Otumba on July 7, 1520, and won. He returned to the attack, forced the Aztecs back to the capital, laid siege to the city, pounded its fortifications with his cannon, and finally re-entered it in triumph on August 13, 1521.

Cortes by this time had abandoned his earlier methods of clemency, and after this victory he had the new emperor tortured to reveal where his treasures were concealed. He then had the brave Aztec executed. This action, besides being abominably cruel, was also useless, for the bulk of the Mexican treasures had already passed into Spanish hands, and in any case Cortes had always exaggerated the importance of the person of the emperor. The Mexican system was, above all, tribal, and the allegiance that was paid to the elected emperor was, particularly in times of stress, very loose.

The elimination of an emperor, therefore, was not such a disaster to the Mexicans as it would have been to a European nation.

Cortes was, nevertheless, complete master of the situation, and his power was so great that the Spanish Court became anxious lest he should set himself up as an independent monarch. Commissioners were sent out to control him, his property in Spain was seized, and his dependants imprisoned. He had, therefore, to return to Spain. On his arrival, paradoxically enough, he was received almost with royal honours. The Spanish Crown did not dare to offend the people, by whom Cortes was regarded as a national hero. But his power had to be limited. He was created Marquis del Valle, invested with the Order of Santiago, which, next to the Golden Fleece, was the highest in the gift of the king, and he was given some twenty cities in Mexico and appointed Captain-General of New Spain and the Coasts of the South Sea.

This was the beginning of the end of his power. On his return to Mexico, he was in constant conflict with the civil governor, as he not unnaturally felt that he should have had supreme command of the country he had conquered. He sent many expeditions of exploration, but they were for the most part failures. He was recalled to Spain, and put on trial for many events that had occurred during his conquest of Mexico over which he could have had no possible control. The trial was inconclusive, as it was meant to be.

The Emperor Charles V knew that if Cortes were acquitted, his popularity would have been increased. If he were found guilty, Cortes was still powerful enough to make a dangerous rebel. So he was allowed to experience a worse torment—neglect. He who once had the right to enter the presence of the emperor unannounced was unable to obtain an audience, and it is said that on one occasion

Cortes pushed his way through the crowd to the imperial carriage, put his foot on the step, and tried to speak to the emperor. Charles turned and said, "Who is this man?" "I am the man," stormed Cortes, "who has gained you more provinces than your father left you towns."

Cortes married twice. His first wife was Doña Catalina Juarez, the daughter of a Cuban merchant. It is said that he had compromised her, was forced to marry her, and was even responsible for her death; but the evidence for these allegations is tainted.

After his return as the conqueror of Mexico, he married Doña Juana de Zuñiga, a noble lady whom he so loaded with jewels as even to incur the jealousy of the queen. The bonds of matrimony sat lightly on Cortes, however, and, in common with other military adventurers of his time, his love affairs were many. But his closing years were embittered, and he died suddenly while on a visit to his daughter.

At Seville he fell ill with dysentery, and there he made his will on October 11, 1547. He grew worse, and went to the little town of Castille ja de la Cuesta, where, in the words of his old companion in arms, Bernal Diaz, "It pleased our Lord Jesus Christ to take him from this laborious life on the second day of December, 1547." The same writer continues, "May God pardon his sins and mine, too, and give me a righteous ending, which things are of more concern than the conquests and the victories we had over the Indians."

In 1629 his body was taken to Mexico and re-buried in the city that had been the scene of his triumphs.

HENRY VIII

(1491–1547)

Traduced by film producers, mocked at by moralists, and deplored by historians, the giant figure of Henry VIII still straddles the stage of English history with undiminished greatness. The selfishness and meanness of his motives may be forgotten in the consequences of his actions: his own desires became public policy. He had patriotism as well as passion; he may have been a libertine but he was also a very great statesman. Far from being the coarse, gross vulgarian that he has sometimes been depicted, he was one of the most cultured men in Europe, and to the end of his days delighted in learning, keen wits, fine poetry and good music. He inherited from his father, Henry VII, a land that could be built up strongly into a great power. He did not betray that trust. He left England greater than he found her.

"His Majesty is twenty-nine years old, and extremely handsome. Nature could not have done more for him. He is much handsomer than any other sovereign of Christendom—a good deal handsomer than the King of France—very fair, and his whole frame admirably proportioned. On hearing that Francis I wore a red beard, he allowed his own to grow; and as it is reddish, he has now got a beard that looks like gold. He is very accomplished, a good musician, composes well, is a most capital horseman, a fine punster, speaks good French, Latin and Spanish, is very religious, hears three Masses daily when he hunts, and sometimes five on other days."

The writer is the Venetian Ambassador to England, the year 1519, and the king he describes is Henry VIII.

It is a fair picture, for Henry VIII was a man of learning and accomplishment. When Erasmus visited England in 1498, he met the seven-year-old prince and was struck by the precocity of his intellect and his polished manner; later, the scholar and the scholar prince became friends and correspondents. The strength and beauty of Henry grew with his mind. He excelled at all outdoor sports, wore out ten horses a day at hunting, and played skilfully at the game of games, tennis. It was a royal fellow who became King of England in 1509.

But the seeds of trouble, causes of the mighty events of his reign, had been sown some years before the accession. Henry, who was born at Greenwich in 1491, was the second son of Henry VII, and was being educated for the Church; but in 1502, Arthur, Prince of Wales, died, and a year later it was arranged for Henry to marry Arthur's widow, Catherine of Aragon. Three years later, the young prince protested against the engagement, which had been made in his minority, but this protest was only a device of Henry VII to force Ferdinand to pay the remainder of Catherine's dowry. On April 22, 1509, Henry succeeded his father. On June 11 he was married to Catherine.

The reign began bravely with feasting and sport. The nation, restored to order and peace, was lusty and powerful. The New Learning had come to England, and the enlightened scholars of that country, John Colet, Thomas More and Thomas Linacre, joined with Erasmus to spread the new thought and culture.

Colet, the gentle Dean of St. Paul's, reformed the whole system of education when he founded St. Paul's School in 1510. Thomas More gave men an entirely new conception of democracy and ideal government when, five years later, he published his *Utopia*.

Soon the new king felt the power of his wealth and his country's strength. He was determined to excel in war and diplomacy as he excelled in learning and sport. His Spanish marriage had made him a natural enemy of France, and he believed, as England believed, that he could take up the old English task of conquering France. In alliance with the unreliable Ferdinand, and subsidizing the Emperor Maximilian, Henry attacked the French.

The first attack, launched in 1512, failed owing to a mutiny of the soldiers; but in the same year the French fleet was beaten off Brest, and in 1513 Henry himself landed at Calais, and, with Maximilian serving under him, routed the French at Guinegatte. The French knights fled so precipitately that the engagement has been known ever since as the Battle of Spurs.

France's old ally, Scotland, now invaded England to harry Henry and recall him from France. Queen Catherine sent Thomas Howard, Earl of Surrey, north to meet the Scots, and at Flodden Field, Surrey won a signal victory, annihilating the Scottish army and killing their king, James IV.

But Henry realized that conquest of France was beyond him: his allies had got what they wanted and he could not fight single handed. So a peace was made in 1514, and the old king, Louis XII, married Henry's sister, Mary.

The change to the new policy of war and international diplomacy had demanded new advisers, and Henry had soon picked his helper. He was a keen judge of character, and it was a common saying of the people that "King Henry knew a man when he saw him." The new minister was Thomas Wolsey, and his advance was as rapid as his gifts were exceptional. Henry made him Archbishop of York in 1514. In 1515 the pope made him a cardinal and the king made him his chancellor. When, in 1518, the pope sent Cardinal Campeggio as a legate to England, Henry refused to admit him until Wolsey had been made joint-legate.

The chancellor became the most important man in England and the arbiter of foreign affairs, but the shrewd Henry was always in control, and his were the policies that the cardinal carried out.

Years of diplomatic intrigue followed. Henry was playing off Francis of France against the Emperor Charles V. In 1520 he met Francis in that setting of splendour and pomp which has been named the Field of the Cloth of Gold; in the same year Charles V visited England and made a secret alliance with Henry. Two years later England and France were at war again, and Henry caused national indignation by his efforts to raise a loan, although the blame was successfully shifted on to Wolsey. Peace came in 1525. There was a lull before the great events which were to create a new epoch and make the reign of Henry a turning point in national history.

Henry's marriage with Catherine had begun happily, and in January, 1511, a son had been born. But the boy had died a month later, and the only offspring of the union who lived was Mary, born in 1516.

Now, in 1526, he was attracted by the young Anne Boleyn, who had come to court as a girl of sixteen four years before. Henry wanted a divorce from Catherine.

Although his motive was mainly selfish, there was no doubt that the question of succession influenced the king in this matter. He had only a daughter, and a queen had never sat on the throne of England. As was so often the case with Henry's actions, private desires and public policy combined to form his reasons.

Wolsey, too, had his hand in this intrigue. . . . He desired very greatly to strengthen the English alliance with France, and to break the friendship with Spain. He felt that nothing could do it better than a marriage between Henry and a princess of France.

It was Wolsey, then, who first suggested to Henry that his

marriage with Catherine might be set aside. Henry, for all his bold defiance of the pope, had a superstitious dread of getting on the wrong side of Heaven, and when Wolsey gently hinted that the death of all Catherine's children might be a direct sign that the marriage was not blessed by God, even if sanctioned by the pope, Henry was only too willing to listen.

Wolsey, who admitted himself to be no more than a tool of the king, made one grave mistake. He underestimated the strength of Henry's passion for Anne Boleyn. He went forward with his schemes, even, at one stage, approaching the French king with the subject of the marriage alliance, and regarding with contempt the ambitious Anne Boleyn, who swore to herself that she would be queen or nothing.

So Henry, in 1527, attempted to induce Pope Clement VII to declare his marriage with Catherine null and void. He had induced Wolsey to support his policy, and to further his ends was veering towards the side of France. But the pope was in fear of Charles V, who had sacked Rome, and Charles naturally supported Catherine, with an eye on his cousin Mary's accession. After negotiations between Wolsey and Rome, the pope at last sent Cardinal Campeggio to join Wolsey as legates to consider the case, but took care to reserve the final decision to himself.

The legatine court tried to compromise, but both Henry and Catherine were adamant. The queen's cause was popular, and while Wolsey worked hard, Campeggio delayed, until at last the pope revoked the whole affair to Rome. The impatient, imperious Henry would wait no longer. Sick of the whole affair, he turned on Wolsey. He deprived him of his power, and the great cardinal, broken in health and spirit, died within a year. The great minister died grieving bitterly over his disgrace. "Had I but served God as diligently as I have served the king," he said, "He would not have given me over in my grey hairs."

The wise, witty and gentle humanist, Thomas More, who fascinated Henry by his talk and learning, was made chancellor in Wolsey's place.

But the question of divorce had not been settled. Then came forward Thomas Cranmer, "a divine and a courtier," who suggested an appeal to the learned doctors of the universities. The questions were: "Do the laws of God allow a man to marry his brother's widow?" and whether in this matter Henry need heed the pope.

Henry declared that Cranmer "had got the right sow by the ear," and forthwith delegates were sent to Oxford and Cambridge and to the universities of France and northern Italy to bribe the learned divines to a right decision. In 1531 the decisions of eight great learned corporations, all for Henry, were read out in Parliament. In January, 1533, Henry secretly married Anne Boleyn.

But now that it was impossible to receive the pope's blessing, Henry decided to end the pope's jurisdiction. His advisers were ready. More, foreseeing the trend of affairs, had resigned in 1532, and had been succeeded by Thomas Cromwell, once Wolsey's secretary, and an astute schemer. Cranmer had been made Archbishop of Canterbury. By the Act of Appeals in 1533, and by further enactments in 1534, Henry severed his country from the power of the pope and declared himself Supreme Head of the Church of England.

In 1521 the learned Henry had attacked Luther, the reformer, in a scholarly work that provoked the German to angry retort, and in gratitude Pope Leo had conferred on him the title of Defender of the Faith. And now this same king had delivered a deadly blow at the power of the papacy. Although his motives throughout were grounded mainly in selfishness and the desire to attain his own ends, yet such was Henry's sway, such was his gift of identifying himself with England, that he made men forget the meanness of his motives by directing their minds to the great aim of national independence.

The change was not accomplished without bloodshed. The Friars Observant were suppressed, imprisoned and killed. More and John Fisher, Bishop of Rochester, refused to take the oath of supremacy acknowledging Henry to be head of the Church, and were executed.

The new order now gave Henry opportunity for plunder. He had assumed the power of the pope and the Church, now he would take the wealth.

There were over six hundred religious houses in England, great and small, rich and weak. An attack had actually been made on them in 1523 by Wolsey, who obtained Bulls from the pope authorizing the suppression of forty of the smaller monasteries and applying their incomes to maintain colleges and schools. Now, in 1536, Cromwell brought in a bill to dissolve the smaller monasteries, those with an income of less than £200 a year, and to give their estates to the king. Again Henry acted with plausibility, for, he said, with some truth, that the monasteries had grown corrupt, and that the ideals of their orders had been forgotten in indulgence. In 1539 Henry suppressed the larger monasteries and the whole of their property passed into the hands of himself and his nobles. He made some slight compensation by the creation of half a dozen new bishoprics and a number of clerical appointments.

He had achieved his object. Anne Boleyn was his legal wife and queen—but there was still no son to succeed him! Anne Boleyn's only child was Elizabeth. Three years after the marriage, Henry had her charged with monstrous crimes, and promptly executed. Within ten days he had married Jane Seymour, and an act was passed settling the succession on Jane's children, making both Mary and Elizabeth illegitimate. The next year, 1537, Jane died in giving birth to Edward.

"So much was the king's grief at her death, that he continued a widower two years after." And then Cromwell took a hand in the marriage game. He wanted an alliance with the German Protestants against the Emperor Charles V, and so he suggested an alliance between Henry and Anne of Cleves. Her portrait was sent over to England and Henry made the match: unfortunately, the lady did not live up to her portrait! Henry had no intention of going through life with a woman whom he designated "The Flanders Mare."

He got to work quickly and had the marriage annulled: Anne of Cleves, the luckiest of his wives, was pensioned off. He married again at once. The new wife was Catherine Howard, a niece of the Duke of Norfolk. She lasted two years and then Henry discovered that she was unfaithful, and had been incontinent before her marriage. She was beheaded. Next year, 1543, he took to wife Catherine Parr, widow of Lord Latimer, and she survived him.

The king had grown fat, and illness troubled him. A fistula in his leg gave him great pain, and the handsome young prince had become a bloated and irritable old man.

His last years saw wars and victories against Scotland and France. He had strengthened the English hold on Ireland, and was the first English king to be called King of Ireland. He left his crown by will to his son Edward, with succession, if the boy had no heirs, to Mary and then Elizabeth. On his death-bed almost, he had Henry Howard, Earl of Surrey, executed on a charge of treason; no doubt he had his eye on strengthening the position of Hertford, who was to be the protector of Edward. Surrey's father, Norfolk, was also arrested and was to be executed, but in January, 1547, the king died.

So ended the reign of the most absolute despot who had ever occupied the throne of England.

Wolsey had said of him: "He is a prince of royal courage, and hath a princely heart; and rather than miss any part of his will or pleasure, he will endanger the loss of one half of his realm." And yet in the pursuance of his will or pleasure Henry had managed to identify himself with the aims and aspirations of the new England, the England that was feeling its strength.

His split with Rome established English independence. English versions of the Bible were made by Tyndale and Coverdale in his reign, and the people were encouraged to read it. He had made England a power to be reckoned with and sought after in Europe. He had laid the foundations of English naval supremacy.

Says one historian: "There was never a man more representative of a people than was Henry VIII of the England of his day. In him met the brutal passions of his subjects with their dogged persistency, their love of show and splendour, their intellectual, moral and religious tendencies. Low and high, coarse and cultured, mocking and serious, he had a side for all. He could speak to each rank, to each character, in the name of England, because all England was in himself."

It was not entirely by force of circumstances that the Renaissance flowered so splendidly in England during Henry's reign. He encouraged true learning—he encouraged men to use their brains. He even encouraged men—and this may seem a paradox in so great a despot—to speak the truth.

The gentle Colet, who wrote to his scholars, "Lift up your little white hands for me—for me which prayeth for you to God," was a different being in the pulpit, thundering out his denunciations of the Church. So violent were his attacks that he was charged with heresy. Henry turned a deaf ear to his accusers.

"Let every man have his own doctor," Henry said, "and let every man favour his own, but this man is the doctor for me."

Sir Thomas More, who stood out against the king's imperious commands almost more than any other man dared—and certainly more than Wolsey—kept the king's confidence and affection for longer than any other favourite. He respected More's courage, respected the soundness of his opinion, and would have given More any boon he craved to have had him on his side—but since More would not retract his opinions, the king had him executed!

No man could, in the end, stand out against the king's wishes. He loved men for speaking the truth, but he could not, for long, listen to truth that was unpalatable for him!

By the time Henry had been on the throne twelve years "all sense of loyalty to England, to its freedom, to its institutions had utterly passed away." Green writes: "The one duty which fills the statesman's mind is a duty 'to his prince,' a prince whose personal will and appetite was overriding the highest interests of the State,

The military skill and force of character of Oliver Cromwell are universally recognized. (*Above*) Contemporary print showing Cromwell contemptuously dismissing the Rump Parliament in 1653. A similarly strong character, if superficially more frivolous than Cromwell, was Charles II (*below left*).

As a young man Henry VIII was both accomplished and personable, but as he got older his moral fibre showed a marked deterioration. This portrait of him (*below right*) by Holbein personifies the "Bluff King Hal" that his subjects always loved.

A contemporary print (*above*) shows the "Sun King", Louis XIV, playing an early game of billiards with his courtiers at Versailles.

The great Russian ruler Peter I is shown (*below*) with his son who was tried for plotting against his father and tortured to death.

trampling under foot the wisest councils, and crushing with the blind ingratitude of a Fate the servants who opposed him. But even Wolsey, while he recoiled from the monstrous form which he had created, could hardly have dreamed of the work of destruction which the royal courage, and yet more royal appetite, of his master was to accomplish in the years to come."

Henry was a tyrant, but he was a statesman. He was a despot of unlimited power, but he knew just how far the national temper would allow him to go. He believed in himself, but he believed also in England, and to him we owe the new nation that flowered into greatness under his daughter Elizabeth.

As Professor Pollard says, "He ruled in a ruthless age with a ruthless hand; he dealt with a violent crisis by methods of blood and iron, and his measures were crowned with whatever sanction worldly success can give. He is Machiavelli's *Prince* in action. He took his stand on efficiency rather than principle, and symbolized the prevailing of the gates of hell. The spiritual welfare of England entered into his thoughts, if at all, as a minor consideration; but, for her peace and material comfort it was well that she had as her king, in her hour of need, a man, and a man who counted the cost, who faced the risk, and who did with his might whatsoever he had found to do."

ARMAND JEAN DU PLESSIS DE RICHELIEU

(1585–1642)

The reign of Louis XIII was one of the most important in the whole history of France, for it saw the rise of the country to power and greatness. But the rise was not due to the king, it was engineered by his great minister of state, the Cardinal Richelieu. Cold, just, and unswervingly patriotic, Richelieu established the absolute power of the monarchy by crushing the Huguenots and smashing the power of the nobility, and he worked to assure the diminution of Austria's position in Europe. France owes a heavy debt to the minister she hated, "Monsieur le Cardinal."

For eighteen years there sounded through the corridors of the Louvre and the Palace of St. Germain a rustling of cardinal's silk. The Queen of France and her nobles trembled; heads fell upon the block, and the mighty were exiled and imprisoned like common felons. But during those years France, from being the toy of chambermaids and jumped-up lackeys, grew to be the foremost kingdom of Europe; for Richelieu, the Cardinal, was her Prime Minister.

* * * * *

Armand Jean du Plessis de Richelieu was born a soldier and brought up as a soldier. He came of a noble but impoverished Poitou family. In 1594, at the age of nine, he was sent to Paris to study for a military career at the fashionable Collège de Navarre, and then passed into the Academy of Pluvinel to be turned into a soldier and a courtier. Through the narrow streets of the filthy Paris of the early seventeenth century, he who was to become the greatest man of his time rode as a young cadet. He learned to fence, to dance, and to bear himself with courtly grace. Then when he was seventeen, and showed promise of a brilliant military career, his heart full of glamorous stories of fighting and gay court life, a message came from his widowed mother that was to change his whole career: the bishopric of Lucon, that belonged to his family, was vacant, and he had been chosen from among his brothers to fill the bishop's seat.

Richelieu had no natural leanings towards entering the Church, but it is typical of his nature that, being called upon to do so, he threw his entire interest and energy into theological studies. At the age of twenty-two he was named Bishop of Luçon, "the poorest and dirtiest bishopric in France." His diocese had been ravaged by the late civil wars, his cathedral was in a terrible state of disrepair, the clergy lax, and his palace filthy. This lithe young soldier in bishop's robes applied his inexhaustible energy to improving all things within his reach.

He disciplined and reorganized his clergy, and sought and obtained for the people, through his friends and brothers at court, relief from oppressive taxation; he spent his own money in repairing the cathedral and improving the bishop's palace. In these ways he gained his people's confidence and the respect of the nobles of his see.

But Richelieu's ambitious nature could not be confined to the narrow channel of provincial ecclesiastical affairs. When, in 1610, Henry IV was assassinated by the madman, François Ravaillac, and Marie de' Medici, the mother of the nine-year-old Louis XIII, became Regent of France, Richelieu saw his opportunity. The age of soldiers was at an end; the age of courtiers and clerics was at hand.

For the next four years he remained at Poitou, making rare visits to Paris, but constantly in touch with friends who kept him acquainted with the affairs of the capital. The States General, consisting of representatives of the clergy, nobles and burghers, were convoked in Paris in 1614, and Richelieu, then twenty-eight, was named orator for the clergy. He seized this opportunity to bring himself to the notice of Marie de' Medici, who was greatly impressed by this eloquent young prelate, and offered him the post of Almoner to the future Queen of France, Anne of Austria. Richelieu accepted. From this position at court, in those days of favourites, it needed but one more step to lead him to his ambition: a political career. It is significant that this meeting of the States General was the last to be held until the coming of the revolution in 1789, one hundred and seventy-five years later.

These were days of confusion and degradation for France. Marie de' Medici was a stupid woman, whose love of power was only surpassed by her lack of ability. She studiously kept her young son Louis away from the affairs of State, while her maid, the Florentine hunchback Leonora, and her husband Concini, ruled France and helped to drain the Treasury for their own purposes. They were a strange pair, for Concini was noble by birth and his wife was the daughter of a laundress who had nursed the queen. Richelieu loathed this form of government, but it was the only ladder at hand by which he could climb to the place he coveted, and from which he hoped one day to serve the country he loved. In 1616, a few months after the young king's marriage to Anne of Austria, Concini bestowed on Richelieu the office of Secretary of State for War. He had at last entered politics.

But Louis, now a saturnine youth of sixteen, had tired of being only nominally King of France. He hated the upstart Concini. For many months he and his favourite falconer, Charles l'Albert de Luynes, talked late into the night, and one day, as Concini arrived at the Louvre, he fell under a shower of bullets. Leonora was placed in safe custody in the dreaded prison of the Bastille on a charge of sorcery. The reign of Concini and Marie de' Medici was over. The queen mother was exiled to Blois, and Richelieu followed her. From 1617 to 1624 de Luynes ruled both Louis and France.

During those years, Richelieu contrived by tact, and no doubt duplicity, to serve the interests of the fallen de' Medici and at the same time to keep in close touch with de Luynes. And so, on the death of the latter, four years after the rift between the king and his mother, Richelieu had arranged a reconciliation. The queen mother was back at court, and, because of the deep gratitude she felt for Richelieu (and was later to regret so bitterly), used all her influence to obtain for him the cardinal's hat. This the pope bestowed on him in 1622.

The story of how Richelieu became President of the Council, and thereafter Prime Minister of France, is an amusing illustration of the subtlety of his able mind. On the recommendation of Marie de' Medici, Louis XIII gave Richelieu a seat on his Council. The Council met on April 29, 1624, and all eyes turned towards the slim figure in scarlet, whose cold and haughty mien had already aroused antagonism and suspicious fear in many.

The usher indicated to the cardinal a seat in the third row. Richelieu's cold grey eyes surveyed the hall, and then he deliberately walked to the seat next to the president, the Cardinal de la Rochefoucauld. The indignation that greeted this arrogant gesture was general. But in cold, level tones Richelieu explained his action. He had but taken his rightful place: a cardinal of the Church must take precedence over all other members of the Council—the dignity of his rank demanded it. Cardinal de la Rochefoucauld was an aged prelate who rarely attended the Council, and thus Richelieu became virtually president. The assembly was outraged but helpless. It had no argument with which to confound this arrogant man of thirty-seven.

Louis XIII, although he instinctively disliked Richelieu, perceived in him a great brain that would work for the good of France. Thus it was that, two years later, he dissolved his Council and named Richelieu Prime Minister.

Although the cardinal had climbed to power with the help of Marie de' Medici, no personal loyalties influenced his actions as minister; his duty was to France and to the king. He began his ministry with a fully formed programme, and in its execution became the most hated man in the kingdom.

In his own words, he found, on his accession to power, that " the Huguenots divided the State with the king: the great nobles comported themselves as if they were not his subjects, the governors of provinces as if they had been kings themselves. Foreign alliances were neglected, personal interest preferred to the public good: in one word the dignity of the royal majesty was so besmirched and so different from what it should have been that it was almost impossible to recognize."

Having observed these facts, Richelieu presented Louis XIII with the following programme: " Ruination of the Huguenots' political faction, lowering the power of the nobles, and re-establishment of the external power of France." These ambitions were successfully realized.

Richelieu attacked the Huguenot situation first. This was in no way a religious war, but purely political. The Edict of Nantes, signed by Henry IV, had given the Huguenot party the privilege of an independent army and navy, and the fortified towns of La Rochelle and Mantauban. Thus they constituted " a State within a State " and had formed independent alliances with the Protestant countries of the north, notably England. In 1627, Richelieu launched the attack.

In the character of " Lieutenant-General," armoured and helmeted, he set siege to La Rochelle. The ramparts of the town were strong, and from the sea the English ships could bring help. Richelieu had a dyke, forty thousand feet long, built out at sea to prevent such help reaching the city, and this Herculean work took six months to complete. The English could no longer supply food, but still the city did not surrender. The Mayor of La Rochelle was a worthy opponent of Richelieu, and for a year, under his leadership, the Huguenots fought the cardinal and famine. But surrender was inevitable, and when the king and Richelieu entered the town, the streets were strewn with the corpses of the starved. Of the fifteen thousand who had defended the city, only sixty-four Frenchmen and ninety Englishmen remained.

Richelieu had broken the Huguenot power, and was content to treat his fallen foes with generosity. He merely destroyed their fortifications and published the Pardon of Alais. By the title of this document he plainly showed that it was no case, as in the past, of one power treating with another, but of a king granting mercy to his rebel subjects. The Pardon of Alais took away from the Huguenots all their extraordinary privileges; they were once more French subjects, with the duties and rights common to all Frenchmen. Richelieu kept to the terms of the pardon scrupulously. The Huguenots' liberty of conscience was never denied by him, for, like his counsellor, Father Joseph, he believed that "religion is not sown with blood," and utterly condemned religious coercion.

From the fall of La Rochelle, in 1629, Richelieu remained on good terms with the Huguenots, for both sides kept strictly to their bond.

The second part of his programme was less easily accomplished. His fight against the feudal independence of the great nobles lasted almost until his death, and he had to face many armed revolts and plots. The intrigues revolved chiefly about the figure of Gaston d'Orléans, the king's brother, and for many years heir to the throne. At his side the queen and the queen mother also plotted; they hated Richelieu and his policy, for he would never serve their whims.

But plots and rebellions were dealt with mercilessly. The king's natural brothers, the Vendômes, were arrested, and the Comte de Chalais lost his head in 1626 for plotting against Richelieu. The nobles were aghast; it had always been their privilege to plot with impunity. Such treatment had never been known to them before.

In 1632 the Duke of Montmorency, Governor of Languedoc, tried to raise an insurrection in the cause of Gaston d'Orléans, who was in secret alliance with Spain. The duke was taken prisoner during a fight at Castlenandary, and a few months later all France rang with the terrible news: the Duke of Montmorency, "first Christian and first Baron of the Kingdom," god-son of Henry IV, husband of the king's cousin, had been condemned to death and decapitated at Toulouse. This terrible example gave Richelieu ten years of comparative peace.

But in 1642 another plot was discovered. France and Spain were at war and the French army was besieging Perpignan, at this time a Spanish town. Cinq-Mars, the king's favourite, was plotting the overthrow of Richelieu, and had signed a private treaty with Spain. Like all other important papers in the kingdom, the treaty fell into Richelieu's hands. His army of spies had seen to that. And one grim morning in Lyons the twenty-two-year-old Cinq-Mars and de Thion, whose only crime was that of not having betrayed his friend, were decapitated side by side. The king wept for his favourite, and although Cinq-Mars's father, Richelieu's personal friend, had begged for the lives of these little more than children, Richelieu was merciless; in his code there was but one punishment for treason.

There were many other victims of Richelieu's ruthlessness. Among them there stands out the unhappy figure of the Comte de Montmorency-Bouteville, who defied the edict against duelling on the day after the passing of this law, and in a jesting spirit challenged a friend to fight beneath the walls of the palace. But he learned that Richelieu did not make laws on which one might exercise one's sense of humour, and a few days later a weeping populace watched the comte's execution.

One by one the old feudal castles, with the exception of those on the frontiers, were demolished and their ramparts razed. The king's subjects no doubt needed castles to live in, but not forts that would enable them to withstand their master.

Thus Richelieu fought the nobles, relentlessly and, withal, justly, although in his justice there was not one spark of mercy. But he achieved his object, for on his death there was but one king in France.

We shall not understand the character of the man nor his significance unless we realize that he worked always and only for France, though in addition, by his determination to lessen the power of the House of Austria, which in his time was a menace to the rest of the western world, he affected the future history of Europe.

Through all his years of internal turmoil, he was incessantly engaged, directly or indirectly, in the great Thirty Years War, that lasted from 1618–1648, involving successively all the great powers of Europe. The Protestant princes of Germany were fighting for their religion and their independence, Austria was fighting to annex Germany to her already tremendous empire. Through the early years of this war, Richelieu upheld politically and diplomatically the King of Denmark and the King of Sweden, the successive allies of the German princes and adversaries of the Austrian emperor, but he avoided entering into open warfare until the Swedish king, Gustavus Adolphus, died victoriously at the Battle of Lützen in 1635. Then Richelieu entered the war directly.

The campaign started unsuccessfully for France. Burgundy and Picardy were invaded by the Austrians, who came within leagues of Paris. Then the soldier instinct arose in the cardinal's heart, and at the head of an army organized in a few days, Louis XIII and his fighting cardinal rode forth to meet the enemy. From that moment the fortunes of war changed. The invading armies were repelled, and in the north the French took the town of Arras and occupied the province of Artois. On the Rhine, Richelieu's ally, Bernard de Saxe-Weimar, occupied Alsace. In Italy, the Comte d'Harcourt won successively the battles of Turin, Cassal and Ivrèe, and re-established Louis's vassal, the Duchess of Savoy, on the ducal throne. In the south, Louis XIII took the town of Perpignan and added the province of Rousillon to France.

The war was still raging when Richelieu died, but he had lived long enough to see certain victory ahead. France had already gained two provinces, and Austria's power was declining.

* * * * *

The internal story of the eighteen years of Richelieu's ministry is the story of two sick men. Both Richelieu and Louis were of delicate constitution, and subject to fevers, and yet, without friendship or liking for each other they fought side by side for the one thing they had in common: the love of France.

Many times during these years Richelieu had faced ruin. In 1630, when Louis fell ill and was reported to be dying, Richelieu paced the floor of his palace, booted and spurred, prepared to fly should the news of the king's death reach him. Gaston, the heir to the throne, was no friend of the great minister, and had sworn to achieve his downfall when opportunity served.

Later that year the comedy which has come down in history as the "Day of Dupes" was enacted. Marie de' Medici and Anne of Austria, acting for once in concert, demanded that the "ungrateful" Richelieu should be dismissed. Louis temporized by asking them to wait until the war in Spain had ended, but when the news of the Treaty of Regensburg came through, Marie demanded fulfilment of her claim. The king attended her in her apartments at the Luxembourg, but Richelieu entered also, by the unguarded door of the chapel. After she had recovered from the shock of this impudence, Marie abused the cardinal before the king, and he retired with the feeling that all was lost. The king indeed showed signs of yielding, and actually appointed Marillac, Marie's protégé, as the leader of the army in Italy. Then he left for his shooting-box in Versailles.

The two queens sat in the Louvre receiving congratulations. Messengers were sent out through Europe announcing the fall of the great minister.

But at Versailles the king had met and listened to two of Richelieu's friends, and in the middle of the wild rejoicing at the Louvre there arrived a messenger: Richelieu had seen the king at Versailles, and the king "would defend Richelieu in his office against all opponents." By the following day Richelieu's enemies were either in prison or in exile, and two disconsolate queens went once more in fear of "Monsieur le Cardinal." That was the Day of Dupes, and it ended all hope in Richelieu's enemies that Louis would ever dismiss his minister.

Richelieu did not spend all his days in affairs of State. He had ambitions for literary fame, and such writings of his that were published proved that he could wield a pen as well as a sword. It could be claimed for him that he was one of the earliest French journalists, for he contributed to Renaudot's *Gazettes,* the first weekly domestic journal published in France. The cardinal extended his patronage to literary men—Corneille, the dramatist, in particular had reason to be grateful to him—and he founded the French Academy.

* * * * *

In November, 1642, Richelieu lay dying. His frail body had given all its tremendous energy for France, and was now weary. His work was done. The majesty of the king was respected throughout Europe; the Huguenots had ceased to be a menace. He had re-established the balance of power in Europe, had broken the might of Austria, had given back to France her natural frontiers.

Perhaps it was inevitable that the man who had done all this should have aroused much hatred and little love. Not a spark of humanity seems to have influenced him throughout his career, and in Richelieu one sees a man with a brain and no emotions, just without mercy, relentless without cruelty, scrupulously honest in dealing with the affairs of the people, and yet not despising the riches which were his due. He was a good Christian and Prince of the Church, but one who never allowed religious scruples to interfere with his worldly battles. On his death-bed, having received humbly and reverently the last consolations of his religion, he was asked if he forgave his enemies. He answered with a spark of the old vigour. "My enemies? I had none except those of the State."

On December 3, Louis visited him for the last time. Richelieu was fast losing consciousness, but with a mighty effort he managed to convey his last message, a message for the good of France: "Sire, I have been training a new minister. I recommend Mazarin to your Majesty."

The hated cardinal did not die unmourned. Louis left the Luxembourg with tears in his eyes for the partner of so many difficult years, and Richelieu's own servants wept at the loss of a kind master.

On the day after his death, his body lay in state, and town and country folk, who had understood him so little, filed past to pay him a last homage. They did not know it, but they were saluting him who had been the true King of France.

OLIVER CROMWELL

(1599–1658)

A plain country gentleman, fervent in religion, relentless in battle, brilliant in organization, with a genius for cavalry warfare: such was Oliver Cromwell, who in the great seventeenth century civil war between king and Parliament proved himself also a born leader of men. With a psalm on his lips and a sword in his hand, he led his Ironsides to victory, and then himself became the dictator of his country's fortunes. His stern figure is one of the greatest that has ever dominated the affairs of Britain.

THE scene is a court of justice from which a royal prisoner has just been removed, not too gently. A group of men, soberly dressed, stand round a table on which is a document. Amid dead silence, one after another seats himself and signs the parchment. Some of them write with trembling hand, as though unwillingly, some firmly and with confidence. In the background, looking on, stands a man dressed in ill-fitting clothes. He has a heavy, ruddy-complexioned face, with a prominent, fleshy brow, and sad, penetrating eyes of steely blue. He walks to the table, and as one of the men signs, his attitude changes: he grins, and in a spirit of rough horseplay, smears the writer's face with ink. It is reaction after a terrible mental conflict; neither cruelty nor callousness enters into it.

The document was a death warrant. By its authority, Charles I, King of England, went to the scaffold. The man standing in the Court of Justice at Westminster Hall was Oliver Cromwell.

Cromwell was not a genius, but he was a great man. And he is one of the most amazing characters in history. Profoundly religious, he was sincere even in the exaggerated notions of the Puritanism of that day. He was both kind and harsh, morose and jovial, fond of music and a joke. His religion was based rather on the teaching of the Old Testament than of the New. He was a fine soldier, a good friend and a bad enemy. He could temper justice with mercy and yet descend to heartless cruelty. A strange bundle of contradictions, this man who overthrew the monarchy in England.

Oliver Cromwell was born at Huntingdon in 1599. He came of a group of ancestors, among whom was a sister of the

Thomas Cromwell, who had suddenly amassed wealth on the plunder of the monasteries. A certain brewer of Putney also figured in the pedigree—his name was Morgan Williams, who married the sister of his patron, Thomas Cromwell and adopted the latter's name. On at least two occasions Oliver dropped the Cromwell and used the name of Williams.

Young Oliver was brought up in comparative luxury, for nearby was his uncle's lovely manor of Hinchinbrook, where James I was entertained in lavish splendour. Oliver knew this great mansion as well as his own home. His early life is not clear-cut for us. His schooldays were spent in Huntingdon, and afterwards he was at Sidney Sussex College, Cambridge. He did not seem to care for book-learning, although he emerged as "well read," but from youth, he was a careful student of men, which perhaps served him in better stead. It is possible that he sowed the usual number of wild oats before he was out of his 'teens, but much of his private life up to his marriage is pure conjecture. It is not important, for the strange man's career did not really begin until he was middle-aged.

In 1620 Oliver was married to Elizabeth Bourchier, the pleasant, not uncomely daughter of Sir James Bourchier, a wealthy merchant of Tower Hill, London, with a large estate in Essex. The bridegroom was twenty-one years of age, the bride twenty-two. Cromwell proved himself an affectionate husband, with a deep love towards his children, but his wife's sphere of influence extended no farther than her home.

Cromwell was already married when he became an enthusiastic member of the Puritan cult in opposition to the very High Church and suspected Catholicism of the court. His friends and acquaintances were men who talked an exaggerated Biblical language with a profusion of "yeas" and "nays." Their conduct was based upon their own interpretation of the Bible. Many of them read nothing else. They believed literally in the inspiration of its every word. They saw the direct hand of God in every incident of their daily lives and the cloven hoof of Satan in all that did not conform to their ideas.

In 1628, when he was twenty-eight, Cromwell's fellow-citizens of Huntingdon chose him to represent the borough in Parliament. His public life had begun. Three years earlier, Charles I had come to the throne. Two Parliaments met him and were dissolved. It was the third Parliament that Oliver attended as a member. After two stormy sessions of less than five months in all, the House was dissolved after having taken the first step in the dreary struggle with the king.

Cromwell did little. For the most part he sat in silence, watching with quiet intentness the faces of his friends—of John Hampden, Pym and Sir Francis Barrington. He took a small part in the debates, but appeared to leave no impression. His mind worked slowly.

For more than eleven years no further Parliament was called. Cromwell lived quietly among his own people, quietly, that is to say, but for one brief interval. He was brought up on warrant before the Privy Council for making "disgraceful and unseemly speeches" against a new charter granted to the borough of Huntingdon, apologized and acknowledged that he had spoken "in heat and passion." There the matter ended, but the time was to come when he was to say harsher things without asking forgiveness.

The Short Parliament came and went. Cromwell was returned as the member for Cambridge, but his name does not appear in the proceedings. Charles dismissed this, his fourth Parliament, after a session of twenty-three days. On November 3, 1640, Cromwell took his seat in the fifth Parliament—the famous Long Parliament. He was now nearly forty-two, a leader among the Puritans. His days of peace were ended.

There is a well-known pen-picture by a contemporary of Cromwell haranguing the assembled House. It is "a gentleman speaking, very ordinarily apparelled; for it was a plain cloth suit, that seemed to have been made by an ill country tailor; his linen was plain and not very clean, and I remember a speck or two of blood upon his little band which was not much larger than his collar; his hat without a hat-band; his stature of a good size; his voice sharp and untuneable, his eloquence full of fervour." Sir Philip Warwick adds that Cromwell "was very much hearkened unto."

Small wonder that the speaker makes an impression. He believes that he is in direct communion with God, that his steps are guided by the Divine hand. With such a conviction the iron of his character turns to steel.

In 1641 the first dark shadows of the Civil War began to gather. Cromwell and his Puritans were seething against king and State, and in November the Grand Remonstrance was passed. This was a manifesto setting out to the public the misdemeanours of the monarch and the aims and hopes of Parliament. It was a direct challenge to Charles, and the concluding debate was carried on amidst scenes of wild fury. Members drew their swords on the floor of the House, and bloodshed was only just averted.

"Had the Remonstrance been rejected," said Cromwell, as he

left the House, "I would have sold all I possess next morning and never seen England more."

The storm broke in 1642. In January of that year Cromwell proposed a committee to put the kingdom "in a posture of defence." On the 10th of the same month Charles left Whitehall, never to return a king. In February Cromwell offered £500 towards the defence of the Parliament. In July blood was drawn, and Cromwell raised volunteers in Cambridge.

The great Civil War had begun—a war that was more humane than all the wars which were to follow it. It opened with skirmishes, but there came a time when the army of the king and that of the Parliament met in massed combat, and Cromwell revealed his genius as a soldier. Instinctively he realized that the arm on which the fighting of his day depended was the cavalry, and it was as a cavalry leader that he achieved fame.

The first great battle of the war was at Edgehill. It began in the early twilight of an October afternoon. Dashing Prince Rupert, on the right wing of Charles's army, charged furiously, and scattered the Parliamentary troops under Essex. But as the royal cavalry pursued and hacked their way far from the main battle, thirteen unbroken Parliamentary cavalry troops—one commanded by Captain Cromwell—dashed into the royal infantry and played havoc in their ranks. At that moment Rupert returned and saved the king's army from total rout. Night closed the fight with 4,000 men lying on the bloodstained field, and the advantage to neither side.

Cromwell was quick to learn the lesson of Rupert's lightning strokes. He said to Hampden that it was plain that men of religion were wanted to withstand these gentlemen of honour. "He set out to find 'honest' men, with spirit to carry them 'as far as gentlemen could go'; such men as have the fear of God before them." He returned to the eastern counties to raise them.

Farmers and peasants formed his troops of horsemen. He picked trustworthy men and religious stalwarts. His troops sang psalms and hymns and heard lengthy sermons on the field of battle. Cromwell knew how to sway them; his words carried conviction. But he knew also how to train them and how to organize them into a disciplined force. And because of their discipline and his genius for cavalry warfare, because of their belief in him and his belief in them, they went from victory to victory.

It was at Marston Moor in 1644 that Cromwell, now a lieutenant-general, won his first great victory. The day was dull and thunderous, the two armies faced each other on the moor, glaring at each other hour after hour across the ditch and the hedge which separated them. From time to time the Parliamentarians broke into a chant. Prince Rupert's troops were silent and grim. At seven o'clock in the evening all was silent but for the confused murmur of many voices, audible but indistinct. Then suddenly the army of the Parliament fell on Rupert. The flower of the cavalry of both armies was locked arm to arm, knee to knee, in a deadly grapple. For a time the result was in the balance. Fairfax's infantry on the Parliament right wing were cut to pieces and the Roundheads reeled. Then Cromwell played his master-stroke. Swooping with the bulk of his own cavalry round the rear of the king's army, he fell upon Goring's victorious troopers and routed them. Then he closed round the centre, and the day was over. Cromwell's brilliance had won the field. "God made them as stubble to our swords," wrote Cromwell after the battle. The day's work earned his troops the name of "Ironsides," by which they live in history.

In 1645 the New Model Army was established. It was simply Cromwell's own troop of Bible-warriors enlarged, and at Naseby these troops, under Cromwell, Fairfax and Ireton, won a great victory, though it did not bring the first Civil War to an end. There was much clearing up to be done, and Cromwell and Fairfax rode through England doing the necessary work. Castle after castle, county after county, regiment after regiment, eventually surrendered to them.

The three years which elapsed between the defeat and imprisonment of the king and his death are occupied with triangular clashes between the king, the Parliament and the Army. The chief struggle was between the last two; the main question was Presbyterian orthodoxy or Bible freedom. Parliament wanted to disband the Army, but the Army demanded its pay and refused to be disbanded. Cromwell was sent by Parliament as a negotiator, but he eventually joined the Army. Parliament supported Presbyterianism; the Army, within limits, wanted religious tolerance. Endeavours were made to come to terms with the king. They failed, and Charles, who had sought refuge with the Scots in 1646, was handed over by them to the Parliamentary commissioners early in the following year.

Cromwell swiftly showed his hand. In the early summer of 1647 he suddenly left London for the Army, and on the same day a strong body of horse under Joyce, an insignificant cornet of Fairfax's guard, took the king into custody. Charles was treated with every respect, and Fairfax kissed his hand. Cromwell still kept in the background. A week or so afterwards the Army marched to St. Albans, and openly threatened London and Parliament. It marched on into London. The city was respectful, the Speaker sought refuge, and the House of Commons yielded.

Charles tried to play off the Army against the Presbyterians: he still regarded himself as indispensable. He made an unsuccessful effort to escape from captivity. Then came a Royalist rising in Wales, which Cromwell swiftly suppressed, in time to meet a new invasion of Scottish Presbyterians and Royalists.

This second war was brief but formidable. On August 17, 1648, Cromwell gained a smashing victory at Preston. He quickly broke up the Royalist army, and some 10,000 prisoners were taken. We see Cromwell, tired but victorious, sitting on a camp-stool, perspiration streaming down his red face, while he pens his dispatches. He pauses, thinks, and slowly begins. "It pleased God to enable us to give them a defeat . . ."

On December 6, 1648, a body of soldiers under Colonel Thomas Pride, descended upon Westminster, prevented some members from entering the House, and arrested forty-one others. This was "Pride's Purge." Cromwell played no part in it, although he had agreed that the Army should march on London. The purge came as a surprise to him, and when he was informed what had happened, he agreed with the course events had taken.

Charles's death was now certain. Cromwell, who had endeavoured to negotiate with the king, argued long and deeply with himself before he came to the conclusion that there was no alternative. The Army had passed a resolution "That it is our duty . . . to call Charles Stuart, that man of blood, to an account for that blood he has shed . . ." A revolutionary tribunal, called the High Court of Justice, was appointed to try the king. The death warrant was signed on January 27, 1649, under circumstances already noted, and on the 30th, Charles Stuart went to the scaffold outside the Banqueting House at Whitehall.

That Cromwell played the leading part in this drama there is no doubt, but there is no doubt also that he acted according to the dictates of his own conscience. The charge of hypocrisy against Cromwell fails. The depths of his fanaticism were to be plumbed in his campaign in Ireland. Ireland had rebelled in 1641, and the plans for her reconquest were laid with care. Cromwell landed at Dublin, and immediately made a speech to the people in which he spoke of his purpose as "the great work against the barbarous and blood-thirsty Irish, and all their adherents and confederates, for the propagating of the Gospel of Christ, the establishment of truth and peace, and restoring that bleeding nation to its former happiness and tranquillity."

In September, 1649, he took Drogheda. For two days the town reeked of slaughter. In or near St. Peter's Church, whither they had fled for safety, nearly 1,000 were put to the sword, including priests and friars. Cromwell forbade anyone to be spared who carried arms. He afterwards wrote, as though in half apology, that at the time he was "in the heat of action," but to another correspondent he avowed, "Truly I believe this bitterness will save much blood through the goodness of God." The age-long excuse for terrorism!

Limerick was besieged, and here occurred some of the most horrible cruelties of the campaign. Cromwell had gone home and Ireton was in command. The non-combatants, women, children and old men had been driven from the town. Ireton had them flogged back. Some he hanged in sight of the walls for a moral warning.

To Cromwell, all this killing and maiming was a signal triumph of the truth. "It hath pleased God to bless our endeavours . . ." he wrote. Ireland was subdued—for a time.

Next came the campaign in Scotland, following his appointment as Captain-General and Commander-in-chief of all the forces raised or to be raised within the Commonwealth of England. His sudden advance, fresh from the blood-stained victories of Ireland, struck dismay into the border. Preachers inveighed against him as a blasphemer leading an army of murderers and plunderers. A long series of manifestos followed. Both sides declared, with a vast interlarding of the Scriptures, that God was on their side. It was like a conflict between two large congregations.

Cromwell found it impossible to force the enemy to battle. He made appeals to the Kirk. "Are you sure," he argued, "that this your league with wicked and carnal men is a covenant of God?" and "I pray you read the twenty-eighth of Isaiah, from the fifth to the fifteenth verse." At last came the Battle of Dunbar.

The night before the fight was wet and wild. The English lay in soaking tents, the Scots crouched for shelter in the sodden shocks of corn. Dawn came slowly. The battle was a rout, and the Scottish army fled in confusion.

Gradually the bulk of the southern population grew accustomed to the rule of Cromwell. But in January, 1651, Charles II was crowned king at Scone, and gradually withdrawing himself from the Kirk, he gathered an army of the old Royalist type. This army dashed across the border and Cromwell, leaving a garrison in Perth, hastened after him. Fairfax raised his men in Yorkshire, Colonel

Hutchinson raised his in Nottingham. Finally the armies met at Worcester. A terrible clash ensued, the Scots were totally overthrown, and over 10,000 prisoners were taken. Cromwell's victory was complete, but he wrote that it was "As stiff a contest for four or five hours as ever I have seen."

So, at the age of fifty-two, Cromwell sheathed his sword. His life as a soldier was over. Campaign after campaign had been fought and won, and Cromwell's tactics had proved themselves far superior to those of his rivals. Parliament received the news of this last victory with relief and enthusiasm, and Cromwell was recognized as practically dictator. He was now at the height of his power and prestige.

He returned to London in triumph in September, 1651. He was Captain-General of the Army, and a member of the Council of State. He was given an additional £4,000 a year and the magnificent palace of Hampton Court as a country residence.

The country, of course, was in a state of chaos after the revolution. Twenty-three thousand unheard cases were waiting in Chancery, the nation's finances were in a tangle, and unemployment was rife. The Army had to be reduced, and diseased and wretched prisoners had to be disposed of. And the struggle between Cromwell and the Parliament began.

Cromwell's whole soul rejected the idea of a mere Parliamentary executive. What he wanted was double authority—a person permanently charged with the executive, and a co-ordinate elected legislature. The great issue between himself and the Parliament was one of religion. Cromwell held for entire freedom of worship; the House to Presbyterian orthodoxy.

The great clash came when the House began to press a Bill for a new representation, a plan which was simply a scheme for their own perpetuation. Cromwell was informed that the members were in an ugly mood and that his friends would not be able to suspend proceeding with the Bill, as had been privately arranged. Then occurred one of the most famous scenes in history. He entered the House in plain black clothes and grey worsted stockings. After a fiery speech and much feeling on both sides, Cromwell called in his musketeers, and told the leader to take away the Mace—"this bauble." Then he rounded on the members as they filed out and addressed them in terms of bitter contumely. One he called a drunkard, another a whoremaster, a third a thief, a fourth an adulterer. Finally he seized the Bill, ordered the guard to lock the door, and went away to Whitehall. That ended the Long Parliament.

Scribbled on the door of St. Stephen's, the work of one unknown, were the words, "This House to be let unfurnished."

Cromwell was determined to have his own way. He was resolute that the Government should be a civil government, with an elected legislature, a Parliament to vote taxes and make laws, and an executive bound in legal limits. He chose 150 persons from a number nominated by the independent Churches of England, Scotland and Ireland, called them and made a long and powerful speech, weeping, singing, quoting, sermonizing, calling repeatedly upon the Almighty.

But this assembly, the "Barebones Parliament," was a failure. It resigned, and on December 16, 1653, Cromwell was made Lord Protector of the Commonwealth of England, Scotland and Ireland.

Cromwell was now absolute ruler. In his home policy he was for religious toleration, except for Catholics and prelatists. In actual practice prelatists were little interfered with, and Cromwell himself would have allowed religious freedom to Catholics, but public opinion was against it. His tolerant consideration for Jews and Quakers represented a view much in advance of his age.

He restored the nation to order, built up trade, commerce, fostered learning and schools, and re-established justice, though his attempts to reform the criminal and civil law were hardly successful.

His foreign policy was largely marred through ignorance and inexperience, as when he tried to build up a Protestant League throughout northern Europe. But he settled disputes with Denmark and Portugal, concluded an alliance with Sweden, and then, with Blake as his admiral, restored the supremacy of the seas to England. Blake showed the British might in the Mediterranean and in the West Indies, and once again England dealt deadly blows at Spain. England under the Protectorate was feared and respected in Europe as she had never been since the days of the Tudors.

In 1657 Cromwell was offered the title of king, but with the Army in opposition, he wisely retained that of Protector and continued with his rule. "I cannot undertake this government with this title of king," he said, "and that is mine answer to this great and weighty business."

His bugbear was a fear of assassination, and to this many of his vagaries in policy were due. He had a special lifeguard at double pay, and a double back to his carriage, carrying armed men. The wearing of armour underneath his shirt, and his sudden changing of his bedroom show his abnormal nervousness. Armies of spies helped to protect him and the Protectorate.

Never had his cause stood so firm as in July, 1658. But his end was drawing near. He was stricken with ague, contracted some years before, and had to be conveyed to Whitehall in a carriage. The last scenes show the incredible imagination of the man—imagination that made his sincere superstitions absurd.

A terrific storm had raged in the country, unroofing houses, uprooting trees, spreading wreckage and desolation with it. His wife and the physician and friends were with Cromwell. He shivered and coughed, his face was not so coarse, not so red, his eyes less piercing. Suddenly, the Protector ordered all to withdraw, save his wife and the physician, for God, he declared, had personally revealed to him his approaching recovery. After saying this, he took to his bed, and died on September 3, 1658, the anniversary of his great victories at Dunbar and Worcester.

So passed the man who held England in his hand. The coarse, red-faced soldier, who could weep or smile, torture or fondle, help or deceive, who rose from the countryside to be Britain's first and only dictator.

His whole life was governed by his religion and his love of liberty, as he understood it. Posterity has either hated him as a destroyer or worshipped him as a hero, but history leaves no doubt as to his greatness.

CHARLES II

(1630–1685)

This is not the story of a reign. The history books tell the facts of the English story from 1660 to 1685 and the deeds and misdeeds of the king. This is the account of Charles the man. For his easy life they dubbed him the Merry Monarch, but it is a shallow, meaningless epithet for that keen wit and fine mind. While he toyed with women and fenced with statesmen, he let his taste and sense bring forth the best of England. He restored its social life, he was a patron of the arts, a benefactor of science: he gave it the Royal Society, Greenwich Observatory, and a dozen other stimulants to artistic and intellectual development. Let this be set against the blots of his kingship: he led England towards the fuller life.

IN the great dining hall of Christ's Hospital hangs a great picture by Verrio. The canvas, which occupies most of one side of the hall, depicts a scene at the Court of Charles II of England.

What was that scene which surrounds the seated figure of the Merry Monarch? One conjures up the representation of a gay banquet, a wild debauch of wits in wine, and painted wantons; a Whitehall rout, so beloved of the word-painters of our Merry Monarchy? But it is anything but these.

The court is thronged with grave men of learning, and in the foreground, before the throne, are assembled in solemn array the girls and boys of Christ's Hospital, the latter in their dress of blue coats and yellow stockings which they still wear today. For the painting was done, at the suggestion of Samuel Pepys, to commemorate the foundation of the Royal Mathematical School at Christ's Hospital by Charles II.

An unusual aspect of Charles, perhaps, but not inconsistent with his character; for he was a queer contrast with himself. A debauched seducer, and a patron of the arts; a scientist and a fop; a seeming fool, and a subtle schemer, a charming wit, and an unprincipled egotist; a lazy man who got his own way, a brave figure whom his people loved even when they hated his rule; a king who laughed and loved and died a king: that was Charles II, the first ruler of modern England.

He was born in London, at St. James's Palace, in May, 1630, and his childhood and early youth were spent in happiness. For then he laughed among those pleasant palaces, whose names are music and promises of peace: Windsor, Whitehall, Hampton Court and Greenwich.

Then came the dark days. Civil war, and the execution of his father. The Scots immediately proclaimed Charles II king; but he had to sign the Covenant, guaranteeing the Scots their own religious freedom. He bought his Scottish support drearily, for they preached at him and lectured him, prayed at him and fasted him, until he cried out: "Presbytery is not a religion for a gentleman."

On January 1, 1651, he was crowned at Scone, and in the same year, weary of Edinburgh and sermons, he led an army into England. Cromwell routed him at Worcester, and Charles, who had spent a brave day in the thick of the fight, and had had a horse killed under him, had to fly for his life.

His black, silky hair was hacked off, his fine clothes changed for a peasant's shirt and leather jerkin, and Charles, a fugitive in his own country, went into hiding. How he hid in the oak at Boscobel, while Roundhead troopers searched for him beneath, how he slipped through England and a thousand risks, how loyal men risked their lives for a hunted king, is one of the thrilling romances of history.

And how much truth and how much wit was there in that famous retort, which the disguised Charles made to the blacksmith who was shoeing his horse? For the smith said that the chief rogue, Charles Stuart, had not been captured. "If the rascal is taken, he deserves to be hanged for bringing in the Scots," answered Charles.

But the rascal was not taken, and Charles escaped to the Continent and the long years of exile. That exile gave him an opportunity to show his virtues—his courage, his tact and his good humour, his gust for life and living. And so he wandered from France to Holland, from Cologne to Brussels, until in 1660 the bells of England rang with joy, and the people knelt in the streets to welcome the king into his own again.

The whole nation rejoiced at his restoration to the throne, and the demonstrations at Dover, and from Dover to London, were remarkable, and astonished even the staunchest Royalists. Even then, at the moment of his triumph, Charles could drawl out the ironic jest that he was foolish not to have come home before, since every man in England was protesting that he had always longed for his return.

For all his seeming elegant indifference to affairs of State, Charles felt the pulse of his people fairly accurately. He said himself that he had no desire to go on his travels again, and so in most ways he was prepared to allow Parliament to do as they pleased—provided that they supplied him with money. His complaisant attitude had its limits, however. Not for nothing was the cynical travel-worn Charles the son of the idealistic Charles I who believed in the Divine Right of Kings. Parliaments might do as they would, pass what measures they would, the arrogant Stuart went his own way heedless —but he kept his throne.

The tremendous reaction from the Puritanism of the Protectorate can be traced almost entirely to Charles himself, the man and his tastes. The rudeness of the Roundheads was swept away, and elegance came back to life. For Charles was an intelligent, joyous man, and liked to live elegantly.

He was a patron of the arts, a connoisseur and a collector. In the King's Closet he had rare treasures, old masters, jewels, vases, and cabinets, and since he was also a scientist and a lover of mechanics, he collected models of ships, maps, clocks and watches. He encouraged painters to come to his court: Streater, Cooper, "the rare limner," and Lely were some whom he patronized. As well as painting he was interested in architecture. He supervised in person alterations and improvements to the royal palaces, and in his reign the mighty Wren rebuilt a new London on the blackened ruins of the old, destroyed by the great fire of 1666.

And he had another enthusiasm, for which we of today may thank him: a love of animals and a passion for planting. He re-created the park of St. James, planted there flowers and walks of trees, and stocked the lake with water-fowl, whose progeny we see today. Music, too, he would have with him wherever he went. He gathered round him players and composers; the king's fiddlers played for him while he supped; he had his own guitar. And he founded the office of Master of the King's Musick, which is still an honour.

But most of all he was a scientist, and he gave science a stimulus which brought it from the musty alchemy of the bygone years into that search for truth which has given us the modern world and has not yet ended. Charles had his own laboratory in Whitehall, and had there his own chemists. His eager mind inquired into this and that, he set learned men talking and thinking, too; telescopes and air-pumps became as much a part of fashionable conversation as wine and women. The Royal Society was founded in the years of the Restoration; Charles gave it his Royal Charter in 1661. Boyle, Halley, Newton were the great men of his reign. In 1675, Charles created yet another office: he made John Flamsteed the first Astronomer Royal, and sponsored the foundation of Greenwich Observatory.

So artists of all kinds, astronomers, mathematicians, chemists, physicists, benefited by this king; and yet their interests did not exhaust his.

He patronized the theatre, and brought a new era to the stage. He loved dancing, stately French measures and English country dances. He played a good game of tennis, went hunting, racing, riding, sailing, hawking, beagling, swimming: he loved all sports. And he loved talking. He told funny stories well, and his wit was superb; but he would converse on any subject. Evelyn mentions as some of the topics he had heard Charles discuss, astronomy, smoke abatement, architecture, gardening and bees.

Thus we may see one side of Charles II. It makes an attractive picture; but his life unfolds another; there had been no need for a Clarendon to play "Hyde" to Charles's "Jekyll."

When Charles returned to take his throne he was allowed as much liberty as he wished. The first task, of course, was to settle up old scores. He treated generously enough those who had helped him in the Worcester escape, but he was unable to help most of the royalists who were plaguing him for favours. Still, he managed to deal with some of the men who had condemned his father to an ignominious death. Ten of these were executed, and nineteen others were imprisoned for life; the bodies of Cromwell and Ireton were dragged from their tombs, and hung in chains upon the gallows in public places. The reign of the Merry Monarch had begun.

A letter written to Clarendon, the day after Sir Harry Vane had made a spirited defence at his own trial, gives a glimpse of the new king: "If he [Vane] has given no new occasion to be hanged, certainly he is too dangerous a man to let live, if we can honestly put him out of the way."

The next few years were spent by Charles, or rather by his great minister, Clarendon, in restoring the Church to its old power, and ridding religion of the Cromwellian influence.

But Charles had other amusements.

In July, 1660, Pepys wrote in his diary, "great doings of musique at the next house . . . the King and Duke's there with Madame Palmer, a pretty woman that they had a fancy to."

Pepys was right. The king had taken a fancy to Barbara Palmer. She became the king's mistress, and in the next year her husband was created Earl of Castlemaine, " the reason whereof everybody knows," wrote Pepys.

In May, 1662, Charles was married to Catherine of Braganza. (She brought him a large dowry, which included Bombay.) In June of the same year, Lady Castlemaine bore Charles a son. Charles's married life became a circus and Whitehall a seraglio.

At one party at Somerset House, Charles was present with his queen, his mistress, Castlemaine, and a son he had had by another mistress, Lucy Walter. The king and queen were very merry; he pretended that she was an expectant mother, and she laughed, " You lie!" Then he tried to make her say in English, " Confess and be hanged!" And after this little scene of domestic chaffing, the strange party of wife, mistress, mistress's son and husband, all went home in the same coach.

Charles could not resist women. He took mistress after mistress, and raised their illegitimate children to peerages. Yet few of his women had influence on him in State matters. Charles could keep his head, though he was always losing his heart.

Lady Castlemaine, who afterwards became Duchess of Cleveland, was supreme for the first part of his reign. Her successor was Louise de Querouaille, a Breton woman, whom Charles made his mistress and Duchess of Portsmouth. And a third was that gay, Cockney wit, Mistress Gwynn, whom all London loved and called Nelly. Nell Gwynn stands for all that was generous and gay in the recklessness of the court.

In all his life there was probably only one person whom Charles really loved, and that was his little sister, Henrietta Maria, whom he called Minette.

Minette had shared with him the poverty and humiliation of exile. Together with his mother and the little girl, Charles had trailed wearily from one European court to another—the royal beggar. Even more than he cared for himself (and that for Charles is saying much) he hated to see the little Minette deprived of fine clothes, of luxurious surroundings, of proper attendants, of all the respect and ceremony that should surround a princess of the Royal House of England.

Charles was restored to his throne, and Minette married the Dauphin of France—both came into their own again; but until

Minette's early and tragic death, the tenderest of letters passed between brother and sister, and Charles himself counted it the happiest few weeks of his life when Minette was allowed to come over from France to visit him.

But Charles's pleasures cost money, and money was hard to find. He raised funds by selling himself to the King of France, with whom he made a secret treaty. He was working more and more towards absolute government.

The game went on. No one was paid. England was fighting the Dutch for the supremacy of the seas, but Charles had no money to spare for the sailors' pay. The sailors deserted to the Dutch, and shouted across the river: "We did heretofore fight for tickets; now we fight for dollars."

And while the court danced and sang, the king's own harper died of want, and was buried at the expense of the parish.

Two great national catastrophes plunged the whole country into further gloom and depression. In 1665 the Great Plague suddenly swept over London, and spread with appalling and terrifying swiftness over the countryside.

In six months, a hundred thousand Londoners were dead. The plague carts travelled through the streets collecting their awful burden. People barricaded themselves in their houses if they could not fly—and those who did escape from London too often carried the plague further afield. Every second door carried the dreaded cross with the words, "Lord have mercy on our souls"—and London became a city of the dead.

Even as the plague still raged, the Great Fire of London broke out, which reduced the whole city to a mass of charred ruins. Thirteen hundred houses and ninety churches were destroyed, and nearly all the city merchants were ruined. It was supposed to be Charles himself who in the end ordered that a row of houses should be demolished to make a clear space beyond which the fire could not creep.

But when at last the plague and fire were over, the capital was exhausted with its sufferings. There was no money, and neither ships nor forts had men or provisions. It was then that the Dutch Fleet sailed unchallenged up the Medway, and the people of England heard the thunder of alien guns over her own lands. For the first time since the Norman Conquest, England had suffered invasion by enemy ships. It was the blackest hour. England had to seek a degrading peace.

But Charles was still getting his own way. And though he was unpopular in the country he was still loved as a man—still welcome at Newmarket when he went to sup with the jockeys, still a favourite at cock-fights and plays and races. When Sir Robert Viner, the Lord Mayor of London, got drunk at a Guildhall banquet, and refused to let the king leave until he had taken t'other bottle, Charles laughed and quoted the song:

"He that's drunk is as great as a king,"

and stayed with his host.

A gay companion, but hardly a sturdy friend. In 1678, Titus Oates came out with the story of a popish plot, and Protestant England panicked. Catholics were indicted and promptly executed. And Charles, himself a Catholic, signed the death warrants, although it was well known that most of the charges were false and the victims were innocent.

But this was the same man who founded Chelsea Hospital for old soldiers at a time when he himself was impoverished. That was the man they called the Merry Monarch. There was little of merriment in his appearance, save for the sardonic gleam in his eyes.

"King Charles II," wrote a contemporary historian, "was tall, and well proportioned; his Complexion black, but Manly and Majestical; a certain Goodness of nature and noble Benignity appeared in his Looks; his Mean had in it all the marks of a Royal Ayre, but nothing of a Tyrant; he had experienc'd many Hardships and known the Severities of Fortune, yet was his countenance seldom or never disturb'd, but, like a Prince, sedate and untroubl'd."

Whatever his faults as a king, he was a delightful companion. He would tell stories to his delighted ministers, talk of humanity with Dryden and "manly" Wycherley, of music with Purcell and of architecture with Wren. His commonest small talk was an experience and a joy; his tact and charm endeared him to all who approached him.

Once, when Penn the Quaker kept his hat on in the royal presence, the king removed his own, explaining that it was the custom in that place for only one person at a time to remain covered.

Charles died as he had lived. He was brave, witty and cynical to the last.

On Sunday, February 1, 1685, Evelyn saw the king at Whitehall. "I can never forget," he wrote in his diary, "the inexpressible luxury and profaneness, gaming and all dissoluteness, and, as it were, total forgetfulness of God which . . . I was witness of, the king sitting and toying with his concubines, Portsmouth, Cleveland and

Mazarin, a French boy singing love songs in that glorious gallery, whilst about twenty of the great courtiers and other dissolute persons were at basset round a large table, a bank of at least two thousand in gold before them."

On the next day the king was seized with apoplexy, and lay suffering under the crude treatment of his physicians. By Thursday his case was hopeless. Father Huddleston, a Roman Catholic priest who had saved his life after Worcester, was smuggled into the king's presence.

"Sire," said the Duke of York, soon to be King James II, "here is a man who saved your life, and is now come to save your soul."

"He is very welcome," whispered Charles.

He bore great pain bravely and without complaint. Late at night, the queen came to his bedside, but she was carried fainting from the room. She sent to ask his forgiveness.

"Alas! poor woman! She asks my pardon? I beg hers with all my heart: take her back that answer."

And then in the small hours of Friday morning a flicker of his old wit returned through all the pain: he apologized for taking so long to die. He asked the duke, his brother, to look after Louise and his poor children. "And don't let poor Nelly starve," he added.

By noon on Friday he was dead.

Rochester, that young rake, had earlier written a mock epitaph:

"Here lies our sovereign Lord the King,
Whose word no man relies on,
Who never said a foolish thing,
And never did a wise one."

It was a lie, but it provoked a good-humoured answer: "My words are my own," said Charles, "but my acts are my ministers'."

LOUIS XIV

(1638–1715)

Louis XIV has been compared to the sun; for like the sun he reigned supreme and alone; like the sun he dazzled men by his splendour. And France beneath his rule rose like Icarus to the heights, and fell like Icarus through the blaze of her own sun. At Louis's court gathered elegant women, magnificent artists, great soldiers and statesmen. He ruled like an Eastern despot, and with all the glory of the East about him. And his ambition raised his country to her greatest pitch of power, until Europe, in fear and jealousy, combined against him.

"It must be acknowledged," wrote Saint-Simon in his *Memoirs,* "that Louis XIV possessed many good qualities and a certain greatness, yet it cannot be denied that there was much in him that was bad, and even petty. . . . His natural gifts were not even mediocre; but he had a mind capable of development, or receiving polish, of taking what was best in the minds of others without exactly imitating it; and throughout his life he profited greatly by associating with the ablest and wittiest persons, both men and women, of various stations of society."

It is hardly a flattering description of the Great Monarch, *Le Roi Soleil,* the king who dazzled Europe, whose reign was the Augustan age of French literature and arts, in whom the power of the monarchy reached its zenith, who raised his country to its highest pitch of ascendancy. Yet it was that same king whose despotism deprived his people of political independence, whose extravagance drained his country dry, whose ambition led eventually to defeat in war and the loss of colonies. The great king who brought France to the height of glory, left her on the brink of ruin; the monarch who identified the state with himself, sowed, all unknowing, the seeds of the Revolution.

Louis XIV was born in 1638, and succeeded to the throne at the age of five. His mother, Anne of Austria, was regent during the king's minority, but power was concentrated in the hands of Cardinal Mazarin, who had succeeded Richelieu as chief minister of France. The young king was kept in the background while

Mazarin triumphed over his enemies at home and abroad. In 1660, Louis was married to Maria Theresa, the eldest daughter of the King of Spain, and in the following year Mazarin died. The twenty-three-year-old king took the power in his own hands; he was determined to have no more ministers who could overrule him. From 1661 the reign of Louis was that of a pure despot.

Saint-Simon says maliciously:

"He formed the determination . . . to govern the country himself. Though he was never to realize it, he was unable to carry this out. It was this that he took most pride in, and of this his flatterers took most advantage. But he was never under a greater delusion."

But whatever influence his ministers and his mistresses may have tried to exert, from that time the policy of France in peace and war was governed by the desires and ambitions of Louis alone.

The *Memoirs* give us a more favourable picture of the external Louis:

"The king . . . acquired that air of politeness and gallantry which he retained throughout his life, and which he understood so well how to combine with a kingly dignity. This manner suited him exactly. Among all who surrounded him he was by his handsome appearance, the dignity of his manner, the sound of his voice, as easily distinguished as the queen-bee in her hive. Even if he had been born in an obscure family, he would have shone wherever there were fêtes, amusements and gallantry, and have had many successes in love."

And, lest the prejudice of Saint-Simon has crippled the great king at the outset of this story, let us hear the judgment of Mr. A. H. Johnson:

"Louis XIV was one of the ablest men of his generation. To an excellent memory and a remarkable knowledge of the conditions of Europe, he added an immense capacity for work, great fertility of resource, diplomatic gifts of a high order, and unwearied patience in the pursuit of his policy. He was served at the opening of his reign by Colbert, a master of finance; by Lionne, an acute diplomatist; by Turenne, probably the greatest strategist of his age; by Condé, a brilliant leader of cavalry; and by Vauban, of whom it is said that he never lost a fortress which he defended, or besieged one without taking it."

The first task that faced the young king was that of internal reform, especially of the financial system of the country. Internal dissension and maladministration had brought the country to the verge of ruin. Colbert was entrusted with the task of financial reform, and he fell to it with energy and resource. Individual interests were ignored for the sake of the State's welfare: taxation was reformed, industry encouraged by every means: tariffs were put on imported goods, subsidies were given to home producers, trading corporations were formed, communications were improved, and the navy was revived and strengthened.

Meanwhile Le Tellier and Louvois reorganized the army: the new discipline it received may be judged from the fact that one of the chief officers under the new system was Martinet, whose name has become a household word. Codes of law were drawn up and issued, the judicial administration was centralized, a police system was instituted.

And while reform renovated the country, Louis gilded it with the magnificence of his court. The king surrounded himself with wit and elegance in a setting of luxury. The arts were encouraged by munificent patronage. In 1664 the Academy of Sciences was founded after the example of the British Royal Society, and five years later came the Academy of Music. It was a wonderful start to the reign that boasts Corneille, Racine, Molière, Boileau, Fénelon and Bossuet among its writers and divines.

For a little while the country enjoyed peace and found a new prosperity. But Colbert died in 1683, and Louis now determined to rule his country as an absolute monarch in earnest. Louis had ambitions: he wanted glory. France was great; he would make her greater. And so, with Louvois, "the great and most brutal of clerks" as his Minister of War, and a man of unsuspected force of character, he plunged into the series of wars that were to ruin all Colbert's careful plans for prosperity.

Louis soon found a pretext for war. He had married the eldest daughter of Philip IV of Spain, and on Philip's death, in 1665, he claimed the Spanish Netherlands for her. The war broke out in 1667. Turenne swept into the Netherlands and occupied the frontier fortresses, while Condé marched eastwards and occupied Franche Comté. But the Powers of Europe, which had been quarrelling among themselves, found common cause against the French king. In 1668, England, Holland and Sweden formed the Triple Alliance against him, but anxious to prevent further warfare, advised Spain to let Louis have either his conquests in the Netherlands or Franche Comté. Louis then made an astute move. He concluded a secret treaty with the Emperor Leopold, which provided that Franche Comté and the Spanish Netherlands should be ceded to France on the death of Charles II of Spain, and then offered peace to Spain on condition that he retained the towns he had conquered in the Netherlands. Spain had to agree, and the Peace of Aix-la-Chapelle was signed in May, 1668.

Holland was Louis's next objective, and he took care to isolate her before attacking. Charles II of England was bought off by the secret Treaty of Dover, and the Swedish Council of Regency was also bribed: the neutrality of the German princes almost unanimously secured. Louis seized the Duchy of Lorraine, and then sent his armies under Turenne and Condé down the Rhine and into Holland. The Dutch flooded the country by letting the water through the dykes and sued for peace, but Louis demanded impossible terms.

Once more Europe was alarmed at the strength of the French king, and allies came flocking to the side of Holland. Disaster hit France, for after clearing Alsace of the enemy, Turenne was killed by a chance bullet in 1675, and in the same year Condé had to resign through ill-health. The war dragged on until it was ended by the Peace of Nimeguen, in 1678. By it Louis had once more increased his hold of Europe, for he gained a number of fortresses in the Spanish Netherlands and Franche Comté; and he skilfully used the terms of the treaty to confiscate territory belonging to the Elector Palatine and other portions of the Rhineland.

So Louis gained by diplomacy what he had snatched at by war; but the war had weakened the country. It had cost too much. Yet there was no sign of weakness in the kingdom, and Louis was respected and feared throughout Europe, while the French looked up to him like slaves to an absolute master.

It was not only war which drained the nation of money. Louis was extravagant in every way, and he built magnificent palaces to house his magnificent court. Versailles alone cost twenty-four million pounds. And then there were his mistresses. Saint-Simon says of the king's love affairs:

"All Europe was shocked by them, and in France they created deep and lasting ill effects. . . . The first 'regular' mistress he had was Mlle. de la Vallière. It is regrettable that his other mistresses were not like her. Quiet, modest, and unselfish, she gave herself up to genuine love; she was ashamed of her weakness and its results, the children, who were acknowledged much against her will. At last, after suffering tortures of jealousy, she betook herself from court and devoted her life to pious penitence. Even while Mlle. de la Vallière held sway, the king was attracted by the beauty of Mme. de Montespan. . . . He then outraged public opinion in Europe by appearing at reviews, and even with the army during battles, with two mistresses at once, who were seated in the queen's carriage. The masses, in their simplicity, used to call them the 'three queens' and point to them."

It was Madame de Montespan herself who introduced her rival and successor to the court. Françoise d'Aubigné was born in the West Indies and came to France alone. In Paris she met and married Scarron, the burlesque-writer and poet, but on his death she was in extreme poverty until Madame de Montespan had her put in charge of the king's children, and in spite of the fact that the king hated her, procured for her the estate of Maintenon. So Madame Scarron became Madame de Maintenon. "She was young, beautiful, clever and brilliant." And soon the king who had hated found that he could not do without her. Madame de Maintenon was clever enough: she got rid of Madame de Montespan by reconciling Louis with the queen, and when the queen died, in 1683, she actually persuaded Louis to marry her. In spite of several efforts to have herself declared queen, the marriage was never publicly acknowledged.

But Madame de Maintenon was in power. Under her pious influence—the Jesuits had her ear—the atmosphere of the court changed, and Louis became more than ever rigidly orthodox in his faith. Yet he quarrelled with the pope, insisting on his own temporal power over the Church in France. At the same time he aimed a blow at the Protestants. In 1685 he revoked the Edict of Nantes which made Huguenot opinions illegal.

The result of this act of religious intolerance was disastrous. The Huguenots formed one of the most skilled industrial classes of the country, and their flight—over half a million emigrated—was a severe drain on French prosperity. It was a blow at the great plans Colbert had made for the revival of the nation's trade. England and Holland gained by the invasion of the skilful Huguenot craftsmen, while the Protestant allies of France were repelled and alienated by Louis's action.

The French historian, Michelet, has described the effects of this emigration:

"The Protestants fled from the country," he says. "The police were unable to prevent them. Certificates of confession were required from all travellers, sentence of death was pronounced against anyone who countenanced or assisted others in emigrating. The emigrants had been deprived of seventeen millions of francs in house and land property, the frontier was guarded by numerous troops;

but all these measures were in vain, and in spite of them fifty thousand families left the kingdom, and took refuge in Holland, England, Germany, and Switzerland. They consisted of nobles, tradesmen, and manufacturers. This active, energetic, and enlightened body of men, placed at the service of foreigners their talents, their swords, the secrets of French manufactures, their wealth, and a relentless hatred of the tyrant who had banished them. Their emigration did an irreparable injury to France. They were received everywhere with the greatest kindness; they were even invited to leave their country, and good positions were promised them. One part of London was peopled with silk-weavers and workers in crystal and steel; and England became the leading manufacturing nation. Brandenburg rose from its abasement; Berlin became a town; Prussia was opened up; the influence of the refugees on Frederick William's states was so marked that it is from this time that their greatness and their subsequent weight among European powers may be dated. Amsterdam built a thousand houses for them, William gave them pensions, granted them privileges, and provided them with places of worship; he formed them into a royal guard of six hundred noblemen and two regiments. He made use of their ministers, embittered by hatred, to flood Europe with pamphlets against Louis XIV. Henceforth on every battlefield the French would meet these emigrants filled with a fierce hatred of their country, and, for more than a century afterwards, French soldiers found that their bitterest enemies in Germany were the descendants of these refugees."

In 1684 Louis XIV was at the height of his power, and France was supreme in Europe. But he had gone too far, and Europe was preparing to pull him down. The League of Augsburg, a coalition of Sweden, Spain, Saxony, Bavaria, Savoy and the United Provinces, and secretly supported by the pope, was formed in 1685.

The police was the creation of Louis XIV. In 1687 he appointed a magistrate to oversee the Paris police, Nicholas de la Reynie, who was succeeded in 1697 by the Marquis d'Argenson—these were the first two *lieutenants de police*. They established order, decency, and security in the city. Now commenced the system of public lighting; from November 1 to March 1, lanterns, burning candles, were placed at the ends and in the middle of every street. There were five thousand of these lights in Paris. The watch was augmented and reorganized. Firemen replaced the Capuchins in the fire service. The narrow streets, often cut up and always filthy, were cleaned, widened, and paved; coaches and cabs for the public were introduced; Pascal even devised the omnibuses, which did not succeed at that time. The custom of going about Paris on horseback was no longer kept up except by a few obstinate representatives of the olden times.

A year later Louis claimed the Palatinate for the Duchess of Orleans, and invaded it: in the same year his great enemy, William of Orange, became King of England and James II fled to France. Louis naturally supported James, but the defeats at the Boyne and La Hogue put an end to his hopes of a Jacobean restoration, and William now flung England into the war against France. Louis's armies were holding their own in the field, but his country was desperate with exhaustion. Louis was forced to ask for peace, and at Ryswick in 1697 the terms were made: he had to give up some of his gains, but nevertheless he had advanced his power since the Peace of Nimeguen.

But France was distressed and the people were discontented. That should have been a weightier blow than the set-back of Ryswick, but the king was not thinking of his people: there was a new chance for the glory and the increase of France, another great opportunity for snatching power and land. Ryswick had set his hands free . . . and Charles, the childless King of Spain, was dying. So Louis planned and waited, and the distant thunder of war rumbled as he strolled with his mistress. . . .

"It was strange to see the king and Mme. de Maintenon on their walks in the Marly Gardens, which she took to please him. He would have been infinitely more relaxed in his manner towards the queen, and would not have treated her with anywhere near so much polite attention. . . . She rode in a sedan-chair beside his carriage, and he often went on foot by her side. He would constantly take off his hat, and lean over to speak to her, or answer her if she spoke first; she seldom did this, because he was in the habit of calling her attention to various things. Since she feared fresh air, even in the best weather, she used to open the windows an inch or two and shut them again at once. When they reached the new fountain, or some other spot, her chair was put down and the same thing went on again. Often the dauphin would stand near one pole and join in the conversation, but the window of the chair was never opened. The king would go with Mme. de Maintenon back to the castle, take obsequious leave of her, and continue his walk."

The eyes of Europe had long been on Spain, with its vast colonies in the New World, and its European possessions of the Spanish Netherlands, Milan, Naples and Sicily. Charles II had no children. His elder sister had married Louis XIV, but in doing so she had renounced her claim to the Spanish throne. Louis tried in vain to have the renunciation declared invalid, and he still laid claim to the succession on behalf of his son or grandson: the other two claimants were the Electoral Prince of Bavaria, and the Archduke Charles of Austria.

But the other European powers were not anxious to have Spain under either French or Austrian domination, and in 1698 a treaty of partition was drawn up between France, England and Holland, by which Milan was promised to the Archduke Charles, Naples, Sicily and the Tuscan ports to France, and the rest to the Electoral Prince. This plan was made fruitless by the death of the Electoral Prince in the following year, and a new partition treaty was drawn up. But Spain was not a party to this arbitrary division, and Charles II made a will leaving his crown to Philip, the second son of the dauphin. When Charles died in 1700, all Europe waited to see whether Louis would stand by the treaty of partition. He did not. He accepted the will, and his grandson was declared Philip V of Spain.

England and Holland, to maintain the balance of power and protect their commercial interests, formed the Grand Alliance with the emperor and his German allies. France was once more facing Europe. Louis might still have carried his claims by diplomacy, but he made a bad blunder. In 1701, James II died at St. Germains, and Louis acknowledged the Pretender as King of England. England was roused to fury. In 1702 the War of the Spanish Succession broke out, and the English armies crossed the Channel under the great Marlborough.

The war opened in Italy, where Prince Eugène pushed back the French, while Marlborough established himself in the north. Louis set out to attack Vienna, but the brilliance of Marlborough saved the city by the victory of Blenheim in 1704. In 1706, Eugène drove the French out of northern Italy: then came Marlborough's smashing campaign in the Netherlands, with the hammer blows of Ramillies, Oudenarde and Malplaquet. But the Grand Alliance fell to pieces and Louis was able to make the Peace of Utrecht (1713) on reasonable terms: the war with Austria lasted nearly a year longer.

By the Peace, England gained colonies from Spain and France, and obtained Louis's recognition of the Hanoverian succession. Philip V retained Spain on condition that the crown was never united with that of France. And France, although she could no longer dominate Europe, retained most of the land she had acquired in Louis's wars. But she had paid the price.

Louis's great reign closed in gloom. Once more there was religious persecution, this time against the Jansenists: and Louis was saddened by the death of the dauphin in 1711, and of his grandson and great-grandson in 1712.

He died on September 1, 1715, after a reign of seventy-two years, leaving his kingdom to a weakly great-grandson with the advice: "Do not imitate my love for building and for war, and assuage the misery of my people."

"It had been a royal epoch! Louis XIV had the rôle of a demi-god. His Olympus was only a theatre, his fêtes were only fairy-like scenes and masquerades, but all was on a grandiose scale. Before his time the King of France lived in a strong castle. He was, even after the time of Francis I, a mighty baron shut up behind his battlements, his thick walls, his deep moats. One can see the gloomy shadow of the monarch flitting from window to window in the vast halls of the Château de Bois, isolated, cold, imprisoned, anxious. Spies, guards, armed men; courts where echoed the tread of sentinels, secret staircases where men, charged with dark errands, mounted and descended—all proclaimed a shadowy king watching with his hand upon his sword, spying out all, sharing the fear which he inspired in others. But under Louis XIV all was changed. The staircases widened, air and light circulated in the royal house; fêtes replaced the gloomy official receptions; courtiers succeeded soldiers. This time royalty was sure of victory. It trod on laurels, as half a century later it walked on roses, without dreaming that either the laurel- or the rose-strewn path would lead to the scaffold. On that splendid horizon of the seventeenth century great storm clouds appeared one by one, lightning still unaccompanied by thunder flashed through space; but the eyes of the multitude, blinded by the royal sun, did not perceive these threatening gleams. Intoxicated France abandoned herself to the contemplation of her present glory, without thinking to seize or to understand the true reasons of that glory, and did not realize that she was being dragged to a yawning chasm." Thus the historian, Martin, who continues:

"Never was error more excusable. How resist that seduction which all realized, but which all contributed to exercise? Society is like an immense concert, all of whose parts mingle together to form, by their divers accents, a universal harmony. Every class, every man, gave all that he had to give to the work of common grandeur. The mass of the people, confident in the good intentions of their prince, comforted by the good order of the administration, bore their burden the more lightly, and patiently awaited from the future a still greater relief. The clergy, more worthy and more enlightened than in any other epoch of French history, instructed and guided the society it no longer governed. The nobility, which had gained in discipline not less than in polish what it had lost in independence, furnished the majority of the warriors; the third estate furnished almost all the rest, especially the great administration and the great writers. By means of intellectual and moral energy, of practical sense, of inventive and active force, the French bourgeoisie reached the highest degree of its development—what a bourgeoisie, to have produced within a half-century Colbert, Corneille, Pascal, Molière, Racine, La Fontaine, Boileau, Bossuet, Bourdaloue, Arnauld, Nicole, Domat, Fabert, Poussin, Lesueur, Lorraine, Lebrun, the Perraults, and Puget, without counting those men as powerful and more for evil than for good—Fouquet and Louvois!

"Marvellous assemblage of the most highly developed and complete society that has appeared in the world since ancient times; vast and living picture whose aspect produced on those who regarded it an enduring fascination! All peoples admired and imitated it. The language, the fashions, the ideas of France invaded Europe. Literary styles, like the styles of costume, like the styles of objects of art and of luxury, like the habits of life, formed themselves, at least in the upper classes, and for long, after the French. It was not the breath of a momentary fancy, but it was an atmosphere which enveloped little by little all objects and all beings, a medium outside of which it became impossible for man to live."

JOHN CHURCHILL, FIRST DUKE OF MARLBOROUGH

(1650–1722)

John Churchill, first Duke of Marlborough, was one of the greatest of English soldiers and a general comparable with any the world has seen before or since. He never besieged a fortress he did not take, and never left a field of battle save as the conqueror. His grasp of position and tactical skill were only equalled by his coolness and courage. As a diplomat and politician he was skilled as on the field, although his dealings are marked by an unscrupulous and selfish determination to gain his own ends. As a man he was an inspired leader and handler of men, a loving husband and father, a charming and tactful friend: if his consideration for the welfare of his own soldiers brought him the reward of victories, his mercy and courtesy towards his prisoners were the gratuitous expressions of the man's own character.

On the morning of August 21, 1704, a red-coated horseman galloped into London. He was weary with days of hard riding and begrimed with the dust of long roads as he turned his horse's head to the Palace of St. James. There he delivered his message to Sarah, Duchess of Marlborough. It was no elaborate document, no scroll worthy of the messenger's high rank; only a pencilled scrawl on the back of a tavern bill:—

August 13, 1704.

I have not time to say more but to beg you will give my duty to the queen, and let her know her army has had a glorious victory. Monsieur Tallard and two other generals are in my coach and I am following the rest. The bearer, my aide-de-camp, Colonel Parke, will give Her an account of what has passed. I shall do it in a day or two by another more at large.

Marlborough.

That simple note brought the news to England of the greatest victory of English arms since the Middle Ages, and it proclaimed the rise of Marlborough to the summit of military reputation: for Blenheim was the first of those mighty battles which made

Marlborough the compeer of Alexander and Hannibal and of the Napoleon who was yet to come.

The story of John Churchill, first Duke of Marlborough, is a breathless and dazzling tale of war and diplomacy, business and intrigue, unscrupulous determination and courage—a tale of outstanding ability winning the heights and plumbing the depths of fortune.

John Churchill was born at Ash, in Devonshire, on May 26, 1650, and received his education at St. Paul's School. While he was still there, his sister, Arabella, became mistress to the Duke of York, and young John, with picturesque irony, became a page of honour in the duke's household on leaving school. In September, 1667, he was made an ensign in the foot guards, and during the next few years saw his first service in Tangier, then—but not now—British territory.

John Churchill was, from the beginning of his career, a fine soldier, but in those early days his military skill did less for him than his personal beauty and his charming manners.

By the French he was known as "the handsome Englishman." Lord Chesterfield, who was himself a studiously courteous and polished man, knew Marlborough in his latter days, when the charm of his personality might well have been dissipated by age, but he said of him that "he engrossed the graces."

The return of the handsome young soldier to the court of Charles II resulted in his becoming the lover of the king's mistress, the Duchess of Cleveland, who was nine years his senior. Historians, forgetting the licence of the age, have been shocked by his conduct, and more especially at his receipt of money from the lavish Barbara, though in this particular matter it is difficult to see why their censure has been so particularly severe on young Churchill, unless it be the fact that he invested her gift in an annuity, thereby turning the romantic into the practical. The court was notoriously lax, the duchess was rich and Churchill was poor; perhaps payment would have been condoned had it been spent on drink, but illicit love and insurance have offended. It is not for his early youth that the true moralist will censure Churchill.

Warfare drew John Churchill from Barbara's side, and he set out for the Continent to learn his business. He served under the Duke of Monmouth's command with the French army in the war against the Dutch, and soon made a name for himself. Turenne distinguished "the handsome Englishman" for gallantry at Nimeguen, and at the siege of Maestricht in 1673, Captain Churchill was one of a handful of volunteers who supported Monmouth in a desperate and successful assault. The immortal d'Artagnan of Dumas's *Three Musketeers* was killed in the same action. Churchill's bravery earned him the public thanks of Louis XIV, and Monmouth presented him to Charles II with the words, "I owe my life to his bravery."

When Churchill returned to England he found a new arrival at the court. She was the beautiful and clever Sarah Jennings. Churchill fell in love with her, and she with him: it was a love that lasted a lifetime. In 1677 or 1678—the exact year, date and place are uncertain—despite considerable opposition, they were married, and from that time formed a perfect partnership. In Churchill's rise to power and fame Sarah played a conspicuous and invaluable part.

Churchill was no sentimental idealist, no rash lover. It must have been a strong passion indeed that caused this ambitious, unscrupulous, brilliant opportunist to marry a penniless beauty. Green, the historian, says of Sarah Jennings: "Marlborough's affection for her ran like a thread of gold through the dark web of his career. In the midst of his marches and from the very battlefield he writes to his wife with the same passionate tenderness. The composure which no danger or hatred could ruffle broke down into almost womanish depression at the thought of her coldness or at any burst of her violent humour. He never left her without a pang. 'I did for a great while with a perspective glass look upon the cliffs,' he once wrote to her after setting out on a campaign, 'in hopes that I might have had one sight of you.' It was no wonder that the woman who inspired Marlborough with a love like this bound to her the weak and feeble nature of the Princess Anne. The two friends threw off the restraints of State, and addressed each other as 'Mrs. Freeman' and 'Mrs. Morley.'"

The next few years he spent in following his patron, James, Duke of York. The king's brother was a Catholic, but Churchill remained, as he had always been, a staunch member of the Church of England. He went on diplomatic errands to the Continent, followed James into exile at The Hague and Brussels, and returned with him to Scotland and England and back to Edinburgh and London. In 1682 these services were rewarded by a Scottish barony; in the following year he received his commission as colonel of the newly-raised King's Own Regiment of Dragoons, and his wife was appointed a Lady of the Bedchamber to the newly-married Princess Anne. The clever and vivacious Sarah was the stronger of the two characters, and for many years Anne was under her influence.

The death of Charles II in 1685 and the insurrection of

Monmouth, his illegitimate son, gave Churchill another opportunity to display his military prowess. At Sedgemoor his courage and his coolness were decisive factors in Faversham's victory. " I see plainly," Churchill had written, " that I am to have the trouble, and that the honour will be another's."

When, in 1687, Protestant feeling against James II ran high and communication with William of Orange was taking place, the value of Churchill, with his growing influence in the army and of his wife's influence on Anne, was fully recognized. Churchill, who seems to have been sincerely attached to the person of the king, while hating his policy, interviewed William's envoy, Dykevelt. In May, 1687, Churchill wrote to William telling him that " my places and the king's favour I set at nought, in comparison of being true to my religion. In all things but this the king may command me."

In the next year he was made lieutenant-general, and when William of Orange invaded England, he rode with James to join the royal army at Salisbury. James still trusted him. But five days later, Churchill, with some four hundred officers and men, made off to William. He left behind an eloquent letter explaining his desertion on grounds of religion and conscience.

There is no reason to doubt Churchill's religious devotion, and it may be argued that James's political actions had necessarily turned the young general away from him. But it is impossible to acquit him—despite the plea of Sir Winston Churchill that the decision was " compulsory and inevitable "—of a selfish gamble on the main chance, a charge that is weighted by his subsequent relations with James.

In the first year of the new reign, Churchill, an English baron since 1685, was made Earl of Marlborough. He and Sarah made themselves politically valuable to William, he by voting in the House of Lords that the Prince of Orange and his consort should be joint rulers, and she by persuading Anne to allow the new king to reign for life. The accession of William meant a new and vigorous prosecution of war against the French king, Louis XIV, and 1689 found Marlborough on the Continent commanding the English troops of the Prince of Waldeck's army. In the assault on Walcourt, Marlborough's skilful flank attack flung back the French and was responsible for the victory.

Meanwhile Louis was supporting the cause of James in Ireland, and there Marlborough received his first independent command. He sailed from Portsmouth in the middle of September, 1690, captured Cork and Kinsale, and returned to England in the following

October. As was usual in those days, his army had gone into winter quarters. He had accomplished everything he had set out to do.

The story of the next few years is confused and hotly debated, but the clear result was that the Marlboroughs fell from their proud position.

Again it seems pretty certain that Churchill relied on his wife to influence Anne to desert her father, James II, when he was deposed from his throne; and later still, Sarah had her hand in Churchill's intrigue to depose William and Mary and put Anne herself on the throne. The somewhat stolid William was roused to fury when this plot was unmasked.

"Were I and my Lord Marlborough private persons the sword would have to settle between us," he cried. He stripped Marlborough of his honours and offices and Sarah was forced to leave the Court of St. James.

Anne followed her favourite into exile; and once again the ambitious Churchill began to plot and intrigue. He got into communication with James in exile. How far this Jacobite intrigue, which was indulged in by most of the leading men in the kingdom, was sincere, and what real interest Marlborough had in the restoration of James is a question that cannot be satisfactorily settled, but it appears that the Jacobites were frightened that he would use his influence to place Anne rather than James on the throne.

The faithful Anne still stood by the Marlboroughs, although she was disgraced and humiliated by the king and queen, and she remained on intimate terms with Sarah in her social and political exile.

Still worse was to befall the earl. In May he was implicated in the plot revealed by Robert Young, the purpose of which was to seize William and restore James, and was promptly imprisoned in the Tower. But Young was proved to be an impostor and the plot a forgery, and in June Marlborough was released.

At the end of 1694, Queen Mary died, and Anne became heiress to the throne. The new importance of his friend, the princess, made Marlborough an earnest supporter of William's policy, although it was four years before he was restored to favour.

As the old king felt his end drawing near, he felt he must protect the somewhat stupid Anne by providing her with good advisers and leaders. In Marlborough he saw the ideal man. Despite his treachery, he was the only man fitted to cope with the European situation. Besides, Anne had been a good friend to Marlborough; surely he would stand by her!

Not long after, a fall from his horse proved fatal to William. He lay on his death-bed sorely worried by the situation as he must leave it.

"There was a time when I should have been glad to have been delivered out of my troubles, but I own I see another scene, and could wish to live a little longer." So spoke the dying man, fretting as he lay. But his wish was not granted. Anne ascended the throne, and Marlborough's way to power lay clear. He did not now abuse his high position. As Green says:—

"The temper, indeed, of Marlborough fitted him in an especial way to be the head of a great confederacy. Like William, he owed little of his power to any early training. The trace of his neglected education was seen to the last in his reluctance to write. 'Of all things,' he said to his wife, 'I do not love writing.' To pen a dispatch indeed, was a far greater trouble to him than to plan a campaign. But Nature had given him qualities which in other men spring specially from culture. His capacity for business was immense. During the next ten years he assumed the general direction of the war in Flanders and in Spain. He managed every negotiation with the courts of the allies. He watched over the shifting phases of English politics. He had to cross the Channel to win over Anne to a change in the Cabinet, or to hurry to Berlin to secure the due contingent of Electoral troops from Brandenburg. At the same moment he was reconciling the emperor with the Protestants of Hungary, stirring the Calvinists of the Cevennes into revolt, arranging the affairs of Portugal, and providing for the protection of the Duke of Savoy. But his air showed no trace of fatigue or haste or vexation. He retained to the last the indolent grace of his youth. His natural dignity was never ruffled by an outbreak of temper. Amidst the storm of battle men saw him 'without fear of danger or in the least hurry, giving his orders with all the calmness imaginable.' In the Cabinet he was as cool as on the battlefield. He met with the same equable serenity, the pettiness of the German princes, the phlegm of the Dutch, the ignorant opposition of his officers, the libels of his political opponents. There was a touch of irony in the simple expedients by which he sometimes solved problems which had baffled Cabinets. The King of Prussia was one of the most vexatious among the allies, but all difficulty with him ceased when Marlborough rose at a State banquet and handed to him a napkin. Churchill's composure rested partly, indeed, on a pride which could not stoop to bare the real self within to the eyes of meaner men. In the bitter moments before his fall, he bade Godolphin burn some querulous letters which the persecution of his opponents had wrung from him. 'My desire is that the world may continue in their error of thinking me a happy man, for I think it better to be envied than pitied.' But in great measure it sprang from the purely intellectual temper of his mind. His passion for his wife was the one sentiment which tinged the colourless light in which his understanding moved. In all else he was without love or hate, he knew neither doubt nor regret. In private life he was a humane and compassionate man; but if his position required it he could betray Englishmen to death in his negotiations with St. Germains, or lead his army to a butchery such as that of Malplaquet. Of honour or the finer sentiments of mankind he knew nothing; and he turned without a shock from guiding Europe and winning great victories to heap up a matchless fortune by speculation and greed. He is perhaps the only instance of a man of real greatness who loved money for money's sake. The passions which stirred the men around him, whether noble or ignoble, were to him simply elements in an intellectual problem which had to be solved by patience. 'Patience will overcome all things,' he writes again and again. 'As I think most things are governed by Destiny, having done all things we should submit with patience.'"

So at last he was given back his military rank, put once more on the list of Privy Councillors, and was, moreover, made governor to the young Duke of Gloucester. It is said that on making this last appointment, William exclaimed, "Teach him but to be what you are, and my nephew cannot want for accomplishments."

But soon the war clouds began to gather on the horizon; the question of the Spanish Succession, key to the balance of power, was being decided. At last Louis XIV flung a defiance to Europe and supported his grandson's claim to the Spanish crown.

With the accession of Anne, her friends the Marlboroughs became the greatest in the land. Sarah was appointed Groom of the Stole, Mistress of the Robes, Keeper of the Privy Purse, and Ranger of Windsor Park. John was made a Knight of the Garter, Captain-General of the Forces and Master-General of the Ordnance. With Godolphin he shared the power, if not the name, of Prime Minister. In December, after his first victories in the war, he was created Duke of Marlborough and given £5,000 a year during Anne's life. But the fascination of this period of his career lies not in the power to which he rose, but in his dazzling display of military genius.

In 1702 the Dutch appointed Marlborough commander of their forces, and at the head of the combined armies he began the campaign by reducing the border forts, capturing in rapid succession Kaiserswerth, Venlo and Liége.

Then Bavaria threw in her lot with France, and the combined armies marched on Vienna, while Marlborough was held up in the Netherlands owing to the Dutch indisposition to join an offensive attack. When he realized the danger to Vienna, he immediately determined to go to the assistance of Prince Eugène. This necessitated deceiving not only Villeroy and Tallard, the French generals, but also his cautious Dutch allies, who would not have consented to his plan.

So Marlborough declared that he was going to turn the French position and attack France along the Moselle. But when he reached Coblenz, he struck off to Mainz, which he made by forced marches. Then he made south-eastwards as fast as he could, joined Prince Eugène at Ulm, on the Danube, and flung himself between the Franco-Bavarian army and the Austrian capital. Marlborough determined to attack the French under Marshal Tallard, who had united with those under Marsin and the Elector of Bavaria's troops, before Villeroy could join them.

They met on August 13, 1704. Tallard, who was superior in numbers, had strongly fortified the village of Blenheim on his right flank, but Marlborough, after an assault on the village had been repulsed, flung his main attack at the French centre, pierced it, and forced Tallard's men, other than those who were compelled to surrender in the village, to retire upon Ulm. The Bavarians fled westwards and were pursued by Eugène.

It was a complete and far-reaching triumph. "From that moment Vienna was safe, and France was never again able to take the offensive in Germany."

Blenheim made Marlborough an international hero. England acclaimed him, the nations of the alliance cheered his progress through northern Europe. The queen gave him the royal manor and park of Woodstock, near Oxford, where the magnificent palace of Blenheim was to be built at a cost of £240,000 out of the public purse, and at the same time his Civil List pension of £5,000 was made permanent. The emperor offered to make Marlborough a sovereign prince of the Holy Roman Empire with a vote in the Diet, and although he afterwards repented of his generosity, Marlborough held him to his word, and he was eventually given the principality of Mindelheim, in Swabia.

Prince Eugène returned to continue the north Italian campaign against the French, while Marlborough once more dominated the northern theatre of war. In 1706 he met Villeroy at Ramillies, and by brilliant generalship gained a crushing victory. The French were ultimately forced to evacuate Brussels and fall back from the Netherlands.

Louis XIV was making overtures to the young Charles XII of Sweden, who was fresh from his victories over Peter the Great and Augustus of Saxony, and Marlborough fought another battle, this time in the realms of diplomacy. But he was as good a diplomat as he was a general, and in his interview with Charles, he succeeded in persuading that king to leave the west alone and stick only to his Russian campaigns.

Meanwhile Marshal Vendôme had recaptured Bruges and Ghent and was attacking Oudenarde. Marlborough, joined once again by Prince Eugène, defended the position and defeated and broke the French army. Once more the Netherlands were free of the enemy, and only Mons and Namur stood in the way of an advance into France.

Now, in 1709, the French made a desperate attempt to save Mons. With a new army under Marshal Villars, they fought the allies at Malplaquet. It was the hardest fought and bloodiest battle of the war, but once more victory went to Marlborough—but only just, for the enemy had fewer losses and withdrew in good order.

While John was battling abroad, Sarah at home was having another desperate campaign. She was a supporter of the Whigs, who formed the war party, while the queen, under the rising influence of Mrs. Masham, a cousin of the duchess, was turning to the Tories. Sarah urged her views upon the queen with more vigour than tact, and although Marlborough did valiant political work in the brief intervals he could spare, the balance was going against him. In 1710, Godolphin, Marlborough's lifelong intimate, went out of office and the Tories came in. In January, 1711, Sarah was dismissed from all her offices; in December, the duke, charged with appropriating public money, was dismissed in his command and all other offices which he held.

The charge of corruption was unsubstantiated, and in the early winter of 1712, the general, who had raised his country's arms to their greatest prestige, left England in despair. The next year Sarah joined him. They stayed at Frankfort, visited his Principality of Mindelheim, and remained in exile until the news of Anne's last illness brought them hotfoot home.

They landed at Dover on August 1, 1714, the day of the queen's death. George I received him courteously, and once more

Marlborough was restored to the honours he had held. But his active life was finished, and most of his remaining years were spent in semi-invalidism at the great palace of Blenheim with the duchess who had long loved and fought for him. At the time of his dismissal in 1711 he had said wearily, that "his great age and numerous fatigues in war made him long for repose." But it was not until June 16, 1722, that the rest which death alone can give came to one of the greatest generals that the British nation has produced.

PETER THE GREAT

(1672–1725)

When the barbarian turns reformer—reforms happen. Peter the Great, uncouth, undisciplined young ruler of a mighty empire, set out to study, to acquire learning and make himself fit to build up a mighty state. He came to Europe, saw, and was conquered. Then he returned to Russia and set about the task of Westernizing his ignorant people, who were more Asiatic than European. It is a task that has more than once been attempted but never successfully effected; yet no one has ever worked harder or more furiously for the improvement of Russia. Peter's energy, capability and courage, his willingness to learn and his indomitable determination, mark him as outstanding among the monarchs of the world.

ATTACHED to the magnificent Muscovite Embassy that set out on a visit to the capitals of Europe in 1696, was a certain non-commissioned officer named Peter Mihaïlof. He carried with him a seal bearing the picture of himself as a young carpenter with his shipwright's tools and the inscription, "Myself a pupil; I seek teachers."

In this way Peter the Great, Emperor of Russia, sought to hide his identity and to find out things for himself. At twenty-five he was free for the first time to turn his full attention to his own education. So far he had achieved first-hand knowledge of brutality, drunkenness and debauchery; he had acquired at least the rudiments of shipbuilding, and was moderately experienced in navigation; he had tasted both utter defeat and complete victory on the battlefield. These attributes he felt were scarcely sufficient to enable him to shoulder the responsibilities of a vast and isolated empire. He would like to see what other countries were doing and how they did it. Hence the mission undertaken officially for the purpose of uniting the Christian Powers against Mohammedan Turkey, and unofficially with another object by Peter.

Immediately after his father's death, when he was a boy in his fifth year, Peter had witnessed the persecution and massacre of his mother's relatives. With her he was sent out of the capital to live in retirement at Preobrazhenski, a few miles from Moscow, where he was left very much to his own devices. Then, in 1682, the Czar Feodor died childless. Of his two brothers, Ivan, the elder, was sickly, three parts blind and more than half an idiot. Encouraged by the ambitious Princess Sophia, Peter's half-sister, unlovely of face and of character, the military forces in Moscow demanded that Ivan should be named joint czar with the princess as regent.

So at last it was arranged. Peter was sent back to Preobrazhenski; Ivan was totally disregarded; Sophia had the reins of government securely in her hands. For seven years more Peter remained in exile, learning to navigate the boats that had become his passion, playing at soldiers and indulging in sham fights with an odd collection of friends, and swearing and drinking like the proverbial trooper. His mother, Natalia, seemed little concerned with the life he was leading; but in 1689 she took steps to regulate it by persuading him to marry Eudoxia Lopukhina, the daughter of a prominent noble. Within one year Peter had left his pretty but empty-headed wife to go back to his navigating.

In the same year the tables were turned upon Sophia. Rumours of a plot to murder Peter were sufficient to cause the malcontents in Moscow to desert the regent and rally round the young czar. The numbers of his supporters swelled rapidly until at last, abandoned even by her paramour, the chancellor, Basil Golitsin, Sophia was forced to retire to a convent, where she remained, lonely and forgotten, until her death.

Even after this revolution, and when Ivan had resigned the crown, Peter did not take up full responsibility. He remained for some years engrossed in his sham armies and his ships. Russia at this time had no navy and no disciplined army. Peter determined to supply her with both. Russia had no seaports; Peter planned to remedy the defect. Visits to Archangel, hundreds of miles from the capital, aroused his enthusiasm to fever heat.

In 1695, he made his first attack upon Azov, the key to the River Don and of the Black Sea. He was utterly defeated by the Turks. He renewed the attack in the following year and was entirely successful. He returned in triumph in Moscow and levied large sums to build and maintain a fleet upon the waters he had conquered, to drive the Turks from the Crimea and start a new Crusade. On the medal struck to commemorate the victory, were the words, "We conquer by water and by fire."

In 1697, having already sent a number of Russians to study the arts of civilized life in Holland, Venice, England and Germany, he resolved to follow them himself. Peter soon left the political embassy with which he travelled incognito, to hurry on with three servants to Holland. At Zaandem he established himself at the village inn and afterwards in a cottage, dressed himself up as a boatman, in red waistcoat, short jacket and wide breeches, and worked for a time with terrific energy in the shipyards. " Being of Adam's line," he wrote to the Patriarch Adrian, " we labour."

His interest extended itself to other subjects. In Holland he studied architecture, mechanics, fortification, printing, anatomy, astronomy. He learned to use the compass and even the instruments of the tooth-drawer. He built a frigate; made his own bed, did his own cooking, constructed a Russian bath for his own use; took drawing lessons, learned to engrave on copper and made elaborate notes for future service. He recruited a whole staff of captains, commanders, physicians, sailors and cooks, fitted them out with stores, and sent them off to Moscow to await his return.

From Holland he crossed to England, where, he was told, " the theory and practice of shipbuilding went hand in hand." He had already met William III at Utrecht, and was sure of a courteous welcome. He was at first given apartments in Buckingham Street, London, where he gave his mind to many things likely to be of profit to his country—the Mint, the Observatory, the Royal Society, hospitals, universities, cathedrals and churches were visited and examined. Not unwilling to do a little business, he granted a licence to Lord Carmarthen to import tobacco into Russia, despite the fact that smoking was forbidden by the Orthodox Church. For the privilege he charged the nobleman £20,000 cash in advance.

But his principal purpose was to visit the naval establishments and dockyards. For this reason he later lodged in the house of John Evelyn, at Deptford. Peter toiled at Deptford as an apprentice, dressed to suit the part, and spent his leisure hours in the neighbouring taverns with the mixed company that frequented them. Incidentally, he and his suite ruined the famous diarist's holly hedge, smashed a fair amount of furniture, broke hundreds of panes of glass and did other damage, for which Evelyn was paid compensation —but not by Peter.

In England, as in Holland, the czar recruited numbers of scientists and engineers to work for him in Russia, to all of whom he promised liberal rewards. The deep-drinking, boisterous emperor made a deep impression on William Penn, the Quaker, of all people, and the University of Oxford conferred on him the degree of Doctor of Laws. From England he went to Vienna, intending to visit Venice, but news came from Moscow of military revolt, and he was obliged to abandon his travels and return to the capital. The revolt was settled in the usual summary manner, with hangings, beheadings and burnings.

With the impressions made upon him by his glimpses of Western Europe still sharp and clear in his mind, Peter set about the reform of the persons of his subjects. By no means devoid of a sense of humour, he started by ordering that all beards should be cut off and German suits worn by men instead of long garments as hitherto. He engaged barbers to operate at the gates of the capital upon all offenders, but he afterwards allowed a beard provided the owner attached a disk to it as proof that a permissive tax had been paid.

Meanwhile, with the assistance of the English shipwrights, a large fleet had been built on the Don, and Peter, satisfied with the progress in the south, turned his attention to the northern seaboard. The coasts of the Gulf of Finland and the banks of the River Neva were in the possession of the Swedes. Peter determined to take possession of that coast and to erect there his capital.

In 1700, an alliance was formed between Augustus II of Poland, a boon companion of Peter, Frederick IV of Denmark, and the Czar Peter, against Charles XII of Sweden, then a boy of eighteen. Charles, to the astonishment of his own court and the dismay of his enemies, speedily defeated Frederick.

Peter, having only his maiden campaign of Azov behind him, went boldly forward. In November, 1700, he laid siege to Narva. Nine days later Charles XII fell upon the Russian army during a tremendous snow-storm, routed it and cut to pieces or captured sixty thousand Russians. Peter returned to Moscow quite calmly to raise more men and prepare for further engagements. He would never, throughout his life, admit defeat.

"I know very well," he wrote in his journal, "that the Swedes will have the advantage of us for a considerable time; but they will teach us at length to beat them."

Before the close of 1702, the czar's troops had driven the Swedes from Livonia and the Neva, and had taken possession of Karelia (eastern Finland) and Ingria, where in May, 1703, work was begun on the building of Petersburg (Leningrad). On that terrible swamp land, thousands of wretched workmen, many of them prisoners of war, perished in the first twelve months; but the work went on.

While Charles ravaged Poland and Saxony, Peter added much of what became for a time the states of Estonia and Latvia to his domain. He now felt inclined to treat for a cessation of hostilities, but Charles would only dictate terms at Moscow. The decision proved his downfall. Peter gave orders for the territory through which Charles must pass to be laid waste; the Swedish army, exposed to all kinds of misery in a barren land throughout the winter, perished in thousands. At Pultova, in June, 1709, Peter took full revenge for the defeat at Narva. By 1710, Livonia (Estonia), Courland (Latvia), Viborg, Erensburg, Riga and Reval (Tallinn) had been added to the Russian territories.

In the following year Peter was obliged to march his forces south against the Turks and the Tartars. Crossing the Pruth near Jassy he found himself in the most perilous situation he had ever faced. Hemmed in by Turks and Tartars, cut off from his own dominions by the river, and abandoned by his double-dealing ally, the Hospodar of Wallachia, he seemed to be offered the choice between death or capture. At the last minute a truce was arranged, Peter agreeing to the loss of Azov and the dismantling of its forts and ports.

The period of warlike activity was now almost at an end. After defeating the Swedish ships in the Baltic, Peter returned to his new capital to devote more of his time and energy to the cultivation of peaceful arts.

In 1704, he had taken as his mistress a young Livonian girl, formerly the mistress of his favourite, Menshikof. This girl, whose real name and origin no one seemed to know, was called Catherine. Coarse-looking and unattractive, she possessed a physique as robust and indifferent to fatigue as Peter's own, and a moral temperament better balanced. She has been described as "a typical officer's wife, well able to go on active service, lie on the hard ground, live in a tent and make double or treble stages on horseback."

He had long ago repudiated his wife, Eudoxia, who dragged out a wretched existence in a convent, and now he first secretly, and later publicly, married Catherine. Her influence over him was considerable. She did much to curb his wild and intemperate ways, to calm him in his paroxysms of rage, and comfort him in the sufferings which those outbursts usually brought on.

But his fiery temperament soon precipitated a domestic crisis that nearly cost Catherine her life. She was suspected of an intrigue with the handsome Moens de la Croix, a court chamberlain. Peter set spies to work and discovered evidence that caused him to rage with fury for two hours.

W. K. Kelly describes the conclusion of the drama:

"Moens and his sister were at once arrested. They were both confined in the winter palace, in an apartment to which none had admission except the emperor himself, who carried them their food.

At the same time a report was spread that the brother and sister had been bribed by the enemies of the country, in hopes of bringing the empress to act upon the mind of the czar prejudicially to the interests of Russia. Moens was interrogated by the monarch in presence of General Uschakov; and after having confessed whatever they pleased, he lost his head on the block (November 27). At the same time his sister, who was an accomplice in the crime and a favourite of Catherine, received the knout, and was banished to Siberia; her property was confiscated; her two sons were degraded and were sent to a great distance, on the Persian frontier, as private soldiers.

"Moens walked to meet his fate with manly firmness. He always wore a diamond bracelet, on which was a miniature of Catherine; but, as it was not perceived at the time of his being seized, he found means to conceal it under his garter; and when he was on the scaffold he confided this secret to the Lutheran pastor who accompanied him, and under cover of his cloak slipped the bracelet into his hand to restore it to the empress.

"The czar was a spectator of the punishment of Moens from one of the windows of the senate. The execution being over, he got upon the scaffold, took the head of Moens by the hair, and expressed with brutal energy how delighted he was with the vengeance he had taken. The same day Peter had the cruelty to conduct Catherine in an open carriage round the stake on which was fixed the head of her unfortunate lover. He watched her countenance attentively, but fortunately she had self-command enough not to betray her grief. Repnin adds that, from that dreadful night till his death, Peter never more spoke to the empress except in public, and that, in his dwelling, he always remained separate from her."

So far we have been concerned chiefly with the czar. Let us consider the man. Peter has been described as well-built, over six feet eight inches in height, extremely dark, powerful in frame and majestic in appearance. His hair grew long, thick and curly; his eyes were large and wide open; his cheeks full and round.

The terrors he had been subjected to in childhood left him with a permanent nervous disorder. His temper was wild and impetuous; he would one moment be in the deepest despair and the next full of noisy optimism. His most striking characteristic was the strong vein of buffoonery that he indulged to the full throughout his life.

On one occasion he had the tocsin sounded in the night turning all the people of Petersburg—where fires were frequent and terrible—out of their beds. Rushing distracted to the supposed scene of the disaster, they found a brazier lighted by his orders in the middle of the square, and soldiers on guard who greeted them with cries of "April Fool's Day!"

His energy was boundless, his activities countless. He undertook the highest and the humblest tasks with equal zest. He founded schools, museums, factories; reformed the Church, setting himself at the head in place of the Patriarch; freed the women from the seclusion of the harem and made social assemblies compulsory by law; he attended operations at the hospitals, acted himself as surgeon, dentist and even executioner!

His preference for humble surroundings amounted almost to a mania. He was always happier in a workman's cottage than in the most splendid palace—yet no magnificence was too great for his favourites. In Holland he chose to live in a boatman's cottage. In 1717, when he was on a tour of France accompanied by Catherine, he left the Louvre to stay in an hotel; even there the apartment prepared for him was too fine: he had his camp-bed placed in a closet. He was always careless in dress, often shabby. He delighted in dressing up in outlandish costumes, as in Holland and England, in the clothes of labourers. He had all the vices of a barbarian; he was brutal, coarse, and licentious, and from his youth indulged in terrific drinking bouts. His companions and his amusements were always of the lowest. To Eudoxia and her son Alexis, Peter was unmerciful. Alexis, after a terrible trial for treachery based on trumped-up evidence, and condemnation by his father, died in the torture chamber of a fortress.

Peter's faults were the exaggerated weaknesses of a barbarian glossed by the influences of Western civilization. He eagerly desired to reform his own nature, and to some extent he did reform it. When he first appeared in European courts he was a boor and a savage; but in the few months he spent there his manners were softened. His natural gaiety and sociability made him always a good companion: he was liked, even admired, where at first he had been ridiculed.

In 1720, Peter concluded terms of peace with Sweden, after a war which had lasted for two decades, though open hostility with that country had long since ceased. His last campaign was against the Persians in 1722, when he triumphed and added to his dominions three provinces of the Caspian. To the end he exerted himself to the utmost in improving and beautifying Petersburg, and in carrying out military and social reforms.

His death was of a piece with his turbulent life. In 1724, though in violent pain due to various complications resulting from his life-long excesses, Peter insisted on inspecting the Ladoga Canal, an iron works at Olonetz and a salt factory at Staraya Rus. Utterly regardless of the low state of his health, he slept in a tent on bitter cold nights and traversed half-frozen swamps on horseback during the day. On his return to Petersburg by water in the middle of November he saw a boat aground near Lakhty, and the soldiers on board her in great peril. He at once went to the rescue and plunged up to his waist in the water. The crew was saved. But by the time the czar reached his capital he was in a high fever. He never rose from his bed again, but died in January, 1725, after a period of intense suffering. He left no will: the man who had exhausted himself in his efforts to advance his country made no provision for that country's future.

Peter in a few years had broken the fetters of centuries. As a youth he had realized that Russia, with no sea coast, no organized army or navy, with little communication with the outer world, was powerless to escape from its savagery. With fierce determination he had set himself to provide her with all that she lacked, to compel her to accept civilization. His success was due to a volcanic energy which made him both physically and morally one of the most turbulent men in history.

He had no desire for personal glory, never pretended to be a great general or a great statesman, never wished to parade abroad as the great monarch. He lived only to serve Russia, and he served her whole-heartedly. He proposed to himself the mighty task of converting a semi-Asiatic empire into a powerful European state.

"Let us hope," he said, "that within a few years we shall be able to humiliate neighbouring countries by placing our own on the highest pinnacle of glory."

ROBERT CLIVE

(1725–1774)

Robert Clive was born in 1725. He committed suicide in 1774. In that short lifetime he had established the basis of British power in India and created a supremacy for that country in the East that was to be the source of untold wealth and prestige. His achievements are equalled only by his methods of achieving: he displayed uncanny foresight, sterling courage in the face of tremendous odds, and administrative ability. Had not the sum of his work—the foundation of British India—been so great, his tremendous fight at Arcot and his victory at Plassey would alone have ensured him lasting fame.

THREE incidents from the turbulent career of Robert Clive show forth vividly the character of the man, and give a mental picture of the fearless, ruthless genius who won India for the British Empire.

Here is the first: The sleepy streets of the picturesque old town of Market Drayton in Shropshire are in an unaccustomed commotion. Townsfolk and market women, shopkeepers and slow-spoken farmers are gazing upwards, and talking and shouting in a confused, amazed way. They are staring at the summit of the steeple of their parish church. Away up, silhouetted against the blue sky, astride a gargoyle, is a tiny figure that waves a tiny hand to the congested mass of folk below. That was Robert Clive, the schoolboy.

Here is the second: Nearly twenty years later a young man, covered with blood and dust, stands on the crumbling walls of a tumbledown fortress rallying a handful of mixed European and Indian troops, and waving defiance at a rabble of ten thousand native soldiery laying siege to the little garrison. That was Robert Clive at Arcot, the decisive step of his career, and a turning-point of Indian history.

And the third: Years have rolled by. A man faces his accusers at a Parliamentary inquiry. Hard words have been used. "By God, Mr. Chairman! At this moment I stand astonished at my own moderation." That was Baron Clive of Plassey, not long before his death, defending his character and his actions during his period of administration in the province he had given to the empire.

* * * * *

Clive has been hardly used by his biographers. Many have cast aspersions on his personal character and against the motives which prompted him throughout his amazing career. Some have called him desperado, adventurer, unprincipled and corrupt. Others have sought to gloss over certain phases of his life, or endeavoured to justify or explain away actions which Clive's impetuosity and recklessness had led him to perform.

The truth lies between the two schools. Clive was neither saint nor devil. He was an impulsive, utterly fearless Englishman, born with a magnificent gift of leadership and a ruthless streak in his character which forced him on to gratify his personal ambition, sometimes at heavy cost.

Undoubtedly young Robert was a source of trouble in his early days. At the head of a gang of schoolboys, he terrorized the peaceable inhabitants of sleepy old Market Drayton by levying a toll on shopkeepers for the protection of their windows from stones. Many stories of his turbulent boyhood have been passed down. His schoolmasters' opinions have been preserved. His capacity for fighting was noted when he was only seven, and his rebellious attitude towards authority was notorious.

It was probably with many sighs of relief that his relatives heard, in 1744, that he had secured a post with the East India Company, and would find a fresh and remote sphere for his somewhat embarrassing activities. The story of Clive's experiences after leaving his native country is none too happy. In the first place he was short of money, and as the voyage was long and difficult, he found himself substantially in debt when he arrived at Madras. He had no friends there. The work he was set to do was tedious and dull and he found no outlet for his adventurous spirit. Shortly after his arrival he attempted to put an end to his troubles by shooting himself. The pistol jammed, and the misfire altered the course of history.

Trouble between the French and British in India flared up soon after Clive landed, and Madras was taken by the French. Clive as a prisoner of war had more scope for ingenious devices than he had as office clerk, and making a pretext of the altered terms of his parole, he escaped and travelled across country to the nearest English garrison, which was at Fort St. David. Here he was in his element, and many stories have been preserved of his various escapades during this part of his career.

The long-drawn-out war between France and England at last spread to India, when both countries realized what rich fortunes were at stake.

Since the days of Elizabeth, England had been trading in India, and it was the Virgin Queen who granted the charter which launched the East India Company in their enterprise. But for centuries, the activities of the company had been confined to a comparatively small sphere. There was a station at Madras, one at Bombay and, later on, one at Calcutta.

The company's stations were forts which guarded warehouses and the port where the company's ships swung at anchor, and the fort was manned by sepoys commanded by British officers who were the company's servants.

This rather curious state of affairs explains why Clive, who went out as a clerk in the East India Company's service, found it so easy to lay aside the pen for the sword whenever crisis threatened and soldiers were needed.

He was detailed to the company's station at Madras, and scarcely had he really settled to his position there than Labourdonnais, Governor of the French colony of Mauritius, besieged the fort and later carried the clerks and merchants prisoners to the French station at Pondicherry.

Clive was one of the prisoners, but he managed to escape, and the company were only too glad when he offered to act as a soldier.

The fall of the English fort at Madras had brought matters to a head between the French and the English in India.

Dupleix, France's brilliant governor in India, realized the full possibilities of a French Indian empire, and set himself in far greater earnest to drive out the English.

The death of the last of the great Mogul emperors, Auranzeb, only a few years previously, had meant that once more India fell into a state of disruption and confusion. There was no one great man to hold the vast land together. Small principalities and kingdoms sprang up, and prince fought against prince. The Mahrattas, who were at that time little better than a tribe of bandits, poured down upon the western coast, and filled the hearts of the people there with terror.

Out of this chaos Dupleix intended to win an empire for France. He offered his services to the heir of Auranzeb who sat on the Mogul throne, but without the strength of his great forbears. In the name of the Mogul Emperor, Dupleix made himself master of vast tracts of Central India, and of Hyderabad.

This was the situation when Clive took up arms for the East India Company.

After witnessing his first action at Pondicherry, Clive returned to civilian life once more on the signing of the Treaty of Aix-la-Chapelle, which temporarily stopped hostilities between the British and French in India, though it must have been clear to him that the position there was so tense that war would inevitably break out again. But he had made a friendship which was to mean much to him in after years. Major Lawrence, who was in charge of the garrison at Fort St. David, had recognized in this young clerk something akin to genius. The conduct and bearing of Clive at Pondicherry must have had a good deal to do with this, for there are many stories told of the troublesome ways, amounting almost to insubordination, which Clive exhibited during these days of comparative inactivity.

It was as a full lieutenant that Clive next took the field. This was at Davikota, where there was an engagement made necessary through the troubles following the dethronement of the Rajah of Tanore. With his usual fearless dash, young Clive justified the faith placed in him by Major Lawrence, and we find him well established in a military career, though for lengthy periods his services were of a purely civilian nature.

A troubled peace reigned over India in these years, but it was not to last long. Those were the days when both the French and the British companies had fully realized the immensity of the prize that was at stake. The Indian trade was a consideration so great that neither side could tolerate the thought of the possibility of its loss. Gradually there had grown up side by side rival trade organizations sponsored by the two countries, and backed by Indian princes with their wealth, their influence, and their great armies. Trading concessions were jealously sought and guarded, and it was clear to the most inexpert observer that neither side would be content to allow the position to remain in this decisive condition for long. War on a grand scale was inevitable.

Dupleix, who was the head of the French interests at Pondicherry, was, as has been said, an ambitious man, and a skilled soldier. He was clearly not the type to remain inactive while the British interests grew and flourished. He was also a master of intrigue, and intrigue was being carried on by both sides with considerable skill and patience.

And now a crisis arose over the rulerships of the Deccan and the Carnatic, rich areas for enterprise which were desired ardently by both French and English. For these two key positions there were rival claimants, supported respectively by French and British interests. It was inevitable that a decisive trial of strength should take place. The claimant to the throne of the Carnatic was one Mohammed Ali, a son of the late nawab, and he was being besieged in Trichinopoli by the French nominee, Chundra Sahib, who was a son-in-law of a former nawab.

By this time young Clive had secured his captaincy, and had some voice in the military councils which were being held. It was his inspiration which prompted the brilliant tactical step of raising the siege of Trichinopoli by marching on Arcot, the capital of the Carnatic, an action which would inevitably centre all military operations on that town.

The action at Arcot took place in 1751, when Clive was only twenty-six. Asking that reinforcements should be sent after him from Madras, he set out with a tiny force numbering some five hundred, and after a forced march through terrible weather, descended upon Arcot, only to find that the garrison had deserted. It was said that the Indian troops in the garrison, learning of the fierce energy of the young leader who had brought his troops through flood and thunderstorm, thought they were pitted against some devil, and fled rather than oppose his purpose. Whatever the cause of their flight, Clive had a bloodless victory, and immediately took possession of the ancient fort round which the town of Arcot was built.

Then started one of the most remarkable battles in history, remarkable chiefly on account of the unprofessional nature of the engagement. Clive, comparatively inexperienced, had a force which could by no stretch of imagination be regarded as adequate to defend the fort, which was in a fearful condition of disrepair, almost of ruin, while the town itself was practically impossible to defend. In spite of this, Clive boldly took out parties in pursuit of the fleeing native soldiery, and cleared the surrounding country of the foe. Then he prepared to wait in Arcot for the reinforcements he had been promised, and for the news of the raising of the siege of Trichinopoli.

Gaining courage through the temporary cessation of Clive's raids into the country surrounding Arcot, the Indian forces rallied some distance from the town, and eventually sent out an army of three thousand men to effect its capture and to dislodge the "devil" who had entered it. Hard-pressed, and labouring under severe handicaps, the little force put up a stout resistance and beat off a force ten times its strength.

But this introductory skirmishing was child's play compared with what followed when the great force that had been laying siege to Trichinopoli was diverted to the siege of Arcot. Fully ten thousand troops, including a strong force of French soldiery, marched against the town, and, taking it, proceeded to attack the ancient fort. By a well-nigh incredible feat, Clive managed to maintain the courage and morale of his few hundred men. But the relief force did not arrive, and starvation and disease threatened to wipe out those who were not killed in the furious attacks made upon the crumbling fortress. For fifty days the battle raged, with no sign of relief. Supplies were nearly exhausted, and the courage of the remaining troops was the only bulwark against complete extermination, when, without warning, the huge investing force raised the siege and decamped. Clive's effective force had been reduced to eighty Europeans and one hundred and fifty sepoys! Within a few hours relief arrived, but the work was done, and the greatest blow in history had been struck for British prestige in India.

From Arcot onwards, for fully two years, Clive was in the thick of battles. Trichinopoli, Fort St. David, Vellore, Caveripak, Covelong, Chingleput, at all these places he saw service. He seemed to bear a charmed life, for in all the raids and attacks, fierce encounters and long marches, his reckless daring exposed him to risks of death which would have daunted any other man. Two years of hard campaigning made this young soldier the most feared and most admired man in the whole of India. He defied death with impunity, and seemed to impart his courage to his men. Everywhere he was successful, until at length he realized that his health could stand no more, and he wisely decided to return to England for a rest.

The psychological effect of the Arcot victory was immense in India, in France and at home in England; and the fame of Clive and his exploits was on everyone's lips. When he arrived in England in 1753 with his wife, the reception he was accorded was almost royal in its enthusiasm and gratitude.

Clive had married Margaret Maskelyne, the sister of the friend with whom he escaped from the French shortly after his arrival at Madras. The records do not tell us much of Clive's married life, but there is every reason to believe that it was a happy marriage, and although his life was turbulent and tempestuous throughout its course, it was to his home and his family of boys that he turned again and again for relief from the fearful strain that was imposed upon him.

Clive was a rich man when he returned to England, but he squandered his money with a lavish hand, and made the mistake of trying to buy his way into Parliament via a Cornish seat, an experiment which cost him dear in cash and in nervous strain. Two years of feverish spending and hectic activity in various directions dissipated most of the fortune he had brought home with him, and the time came when the call of the active life of the campaigner, together with the necessity for making money to keep up the rate of expenditure to which he had accustomed himself, led to his acceptance of the post of Lieutenant-Governor of Fort St. David, with the right of succession to the governorship of Madras, and he returned to India with the rank of Lieutenant-Colonel.

He had scarcely settled once more to his old life when there came a call for the tremendous energy and daring for which he had established such a high reputation. News of the massacre of the Black Hole of Calcutta came through, and it was unanimously agreed that Clive was the ideal man for the task of leading a punitive expedition and recapturing Calcutta from the notorious Suraj-ud-Dowlah.

It was in October, 1756, that he set out to revenge that fearful outrage, with a force of some nine hundred British troops and one thousand five hundred sepoys. The campaign was long and exhausting, made more difficult and dangerous by the Judas-like complexity of the intrigues for ever being carried on between the French and Suraj-ud-Dowlah on the one hand, and the English and Meer Jaffir (Suraj-ud-Dowlah's chief of staff) on the other. Clive was driven to distraction by the duplicity and cunning of the men with whom he had to deal, and he had, in addition, an active campaign to prosecute. Actions at Calcutta, Hoogli and Chandernagore were successful, and for a time it seemed that the French and their allies were preparing to admit British supremacy.

It was about this time that the most questionable and most discussed incident of the whole of Clive's career occurred. The defection of Meer Jaffir from Suraj-ud-Dowlah was sought, and protracted negotiations were carried on to ensure that this step could be carried out effectively before a decisive action brought the campaign to a crisis. The intermediary in these negotiations was bilked of his promised bribe by a trick with a faked treaty, and the responsibility was laid at Clive's door. The question of ultimate responsibility for this step formed the basis of the many charges of corruption and graft which later Clive had to face.

The moment for a decisive battle approached, and Clive realized how poorly equipped he was for a big engagement. He had only a thousand British troops, and they were tiring. His Indian troops numbered two thousand, and were untrained. On the other hand, Suraj-ud-Dowlah had a force of fourteen thousand infantry and fifteen thousand cavalry, besides fifty guns.

It was hoped that on the eve of the action Meer Jaffir would desert with his troops to the British, but to the very last moment the matter was in doubt. Meer Jaffir was promised the governorship of Bengal Province if he would come over, and gave his pledge, but as the time drew on there was no sign of his complying. Wily as his master, Meer Jaffir delayed his decision until he saw how the battle went.

It was at Plassey, on June 23, 1757, that the decisive battle of the campaign was fought, and the power of France broken in India. The vast, unwieldy force, outnumbering the British by more than ten to one, was outmanœvred and utterly disorganized. Plassey is one of the great battles of history, and Clive was its hero. Victory belonged to him alone, for Meer Jaffir did not come over with his men until the tide of battle had turned irrevocably against his old master. Suraj-ud-Dowlah fled, but was later captured and put to death by the son of Meer Jaffir. The latter became Governor of Bengal, in name if not in actual fact, for it was said that he was little more than Clive's puppet. Wealth undreamed of flowed into Clive's private coffers. From Meer Jaffir he received more than a quarter of a million sterling, and an income of £27,000 a year.

In 1760, Clive returned to England, and honours and distinctions were showered upon him. He became Baron Clive of Plassey in 1762, and Knight of the Bath two years later. He achieved his old ambition of entering Parliament, returning to his native county of Shropshire, and sitting for Shrewsbury.

Perhaps it was his extravagance, his lavish expenditure, the tendency to overbearing self-will and the gratification of ambition, that caused ill-feeling and jealousy to arise among his former employers, the heads of the East India Company. Whatever the cause, it is certain that bitter animosity was displayed against him by certain of the British "nabobs," and evil rumours were circulated.

It was in the midst of these wordy wars that again a call for Clive's services was received from India, where things had been going badly under Meer Jaffir's misrule. Stories of corruption and graft on a huge scale were in the air, and were found to be only too true.

In 1765, Clive was back at his duty again, unravelling the complicated tangle of deceit and bribery which had grown up in his absence. With masterly foresight and ruthless determination, he cleaned up the fearful confusion into which Indian affairs had slipped, and though he made many enemies in the process, his purge was effective and lasting. Meer Jaffir had died, and from his successor Clive obtained for his company the Lordship of the Province of Bengal. He thus set the seal upon his great work and laid the foundations of British rule in India.

Meer Jaffir had left seventy thousand pounds to Clive, who devoted it to founding a pension fund for invalided European soldiers and their widows. Bengal claimed him for nearly two years, but again his health failed, and he was compelled to return to England.

Clive's third return was not the triumphal affair that his previous visits had been. During his absence his detractors had had ample opportunity of fomenting trouble, with the result that he found himself accused of a host of crimes of the majority of which he was transparently innocent. At length he found it necessary to defend his honour before a Parliamentary commission, and the phrase quoted at the commencement of this brief account has rung through the intervening years as the sincere, forthright reply of a man driven to fury by the persistent yapping of smaller and meaner minds.

The select commission admitted that Clive had benefited financially in his administration, but they acknowledged his great services to his country. In spite of this acquittal, there was to be little happiness for Clive. Ill-health and physical and mental strain had taken their toll. To relieve his suffering he had recourse to opium, and either by accident or with set purpose took an overdose of the narcotic and died on November 22, 1774.

Robert Clive had played an invaluable part in the building of India.

"In the awful close of so much prosperity and glory," writes Macaulay, "the vulgar saw only a confirmation of all their prejudices; and some men of real piety and genius so far forgot the maxims both of religion and of philosophy as confidently to ascribe the mournful event to the just vengeance of God, and to the horrors of an evil conscience. It is with very different feelings that we contemplate the spectacle of a great mind ruined by the weariness of satiety, by the pangs of wounded honour, by fatal diseases, and more fatal remedies.

"Clive committed great faults; but his faults, when weighed against his merits, and viewed in connexion with his temptations, do not appear to us to deprive him of his right to an honourable place in the estimation of posterity. From his first visit to India dates the renown of the English arms in the East. Till he appeared his countrymen were despised as mere pedlars, while the French were revered as a people formed for victory and command. His courage and capacity dissolved the charm. With the defence of Arcot commences the long series of Oriental triumphs which closes with the fall of Ghazni. Nor must we forget that he was only twenty-five years old when he proved himself ripe for military command. This is a rare if not a singular distinction.

"From Clive's second visit to India dates the political ascendancy of the English in that country. His dexterity and resolution realized, in the course of a few months, more than all the gorgeous visions which had floated before the imagination of Dupleix. Such an extent of cultivated territory, such an amount of revenue, such a multitude of subjects, was never added to the dominion of Rome by the most successful proconsul. Nor were such wealthy spoils ever borne under arches of triumph, down the Sacred Way, and through the crowded Forum, to the threshold of Tarpeian Jove. The fame of those who subdued Antiochus and Tigranes grows dim when compared with the splendour of the exploits which the young English adventurer achieved at the head of an army not equal in numbers to one-half of a Roman legion.

"From Clive's third visit to India dates the purity of the administration of our Eastern empire. When he landed in Calcutta in 1765, Bengal was regarded as a place to which Englishmen were sent only to get rich, by any means, in the shortest possible time. He first made dauntless and unsparing war on that gigantic system of oppression, extortion and corruption. In that war he manfully put to hazard his ease, his fame, and his splendid fortune. The same sense of justice which forbids us to conceal or extenuate the faults of his earlier days compels us to admit that those faults were nobly repaired. If the reproach of the company and of its servants has been taken away; if in India the yoke of foreign masters, elsewhere the heaviest of all yokes, has been found lighter than that of any native dynasty; if to that gang of public robbers, which formerly spread terror through the whole Plain of Bengal has succeeded a body of functionaries not more highly distinguished by ability and diligence than by integrity, disinterestedness, and public spirit; if we have seen such men as Munro, Elphinstone, and Metcalfe, after leading victorious armies, after making and deposing kings, return, proud of their honourable poverty, from a land which once held out to every greedy factor the hope of boundless wealth, the praise is in no small measure due to Clive. His name stands high on the roll of conquerors. But it is found in a better list, in the list of those who have done and suffered much for the happiness of mankind. To the warrior, history will assign a place in the same rank with Lucullus and Trajan. Nor will she deny to the reformer a share of that veneration with which France cherishes the memory of Turgot, and with which the latest generations of Hindus will contemplate the statue of Lord William Bentinck who," writes G. M. Trevelyan, "represented in India at a propitious moment the liberal and humanitarian spirit of the new age in Europe."

FREDERICK THE GREAT

(1712–1786)

Of the Great Powers of Europe, England and France have stood as united and powerful states for centuries, whereas the creation of Italy and Germany as national entities has been comparatively recent. In the formation of the German Empire, Prussia took the leadership, and Prussia owed her strength and power to Frederick the Great. Poet, philosopher, dilettante, he became the leader of a mighty military machine, a soldier feared throughout Europe, a ruthless spoiler of land. Yet he ruled humanely, encouraged industry and agriculture and education, and laid the foundation of Prussian prosperity. He was a paradox but a king with the undisputed right to the title of "the Great."

As a youth his father had attempted to strangle him, and as Crown Prince of Prussia he had been threatened with disinheritance. He preferred a silk gown to a military uniform, playing the flute to handling a sword, and reading and writing French verses to conversation in his mother tongue. Moreover, he had a reputation for laziness and effeminacy.

The ingredients did not suggest the making of a king likely to bring either prosperity or happiness to his subjects. Yet he became Frederick the Great, the most respected soldier in Europe. He lifted Prussia from insignificance to might and nearly doubled her area. He laid the foundations of the future German Empire. In all her eventful history, Europe was never more surprised than by this man.

What force enabled him to achieve that greatness which made him pre-eminent? Was he a great military genius? Was he fired by a fanatical patriotism? Or was he one of those born leaders of outstanding character for whom men fight and die almost as a privilege? He had none of these qualities, yet he won the success that attends their possession.

From the moment when Frederick ascended the throne in May, 1740, until he breathed his last forty-six years later, he was an absolute monarch. He was his own minister of finance, of agriculture, of commerce, and his own commander-in-chief. None of his subjects seriously influenced either him or his country's history during his reign. He moulded Prussia with his own hands to a pattern designed by himself. His capacity for work was prodigious, for despite the size and scale of his operations, with much of Europe as his chess board, his mind mastered and dealt with the smallest detail in the day's task. He made many mistakes, but he learnt by them and lived long enough to repair the damage of his errors.

We see him first as a king at the age of twenty-eight amazing and enraging his late father's ministers by taking control completely out of their hands; telling them just what they were to do in all their departments and exactly how they were to do it.

Money he spent carefully; he was only lavish on war material. His father had been a mean man, and like all mean people had spent unwisely when he spent at all: he had squandered a fortune on creating his world-famous Guard Regiment, picking the tallest men from all Europe, regardless of cost. Almost the first action of the new king was to disband the giants. This did not mean that he was going to neglect the army. On the contrary, a strong standing army was Frederick's greatest care during his reign, and under his personal supervision his forces were always being increased in numbers and improved in training. "Who knows," he had stated three years before his father's death, "whether Providence has not reserved for me one day to make a glorious use of these military means and to employ them to realize the plans for which my father's foresight intended them?" His financial policy was always sound, and his wisdom in its manipulation, especially in the period of weakness and recovery after the Seven Years War, was responsible for the industrial expansion and internal concord of Prussia under his rule.

Frederick showed himself to be a broadminded and tolerant ruler. He declared complete religious freedom in Prussia: he himself was an agnostic. "My only God is my duty," he avowed. He liberated newspapers from the ban of censorship and encouraged freedom of speech among his subjects. He abolished torture, save for the graver crimes such as conspiracy and *lèse-majesté,* and the people of Prussia recognized in him a humane ruler.

In his last years as crown prince, when he had reinstated himself with his father by carrying out the duties allotted to him and marrying according to the king's wish, he had occupied his leisure time mainly in writing, and his *Anti-Machiavel,* published in the year of his accession, was a work outlining the duties of sovereigns. "The prince," he asserted, "is not the absolute master, but only the first servant of his people." Frederick ruled Prussia without check from his ministers or heed to their desires, but he never forgot his own maxim. His wife exercised no influence whatever: it was not a love match and there were no children. His mother he held in the greatest respect.

As soon as he was king he fulfilled his youthful ambition to meet Voltaire. The two had corresponded for many years and on Frederick's private life and outlook the great French reformer certainly exercised the greatest influence. But in Frederick's life the part that was private had nothing whatever to do with that which was public. Voltaire may have helped to mould Frederick the man; he had no effect on Frederick the king. He could inspire Frederick's philosophy and his literary style, but, as he himself says, "There was something in Frederick's nature that makes him act wholly in opposition to what he says and what he writes. This is because when he writes and talks he is stimulated by one kind of enthusiasm, and when he acts he is prompted by another." It is hard to see anywhere the touch of Voltaire's hand in the shaping of Prussia under Frederick.

The meeting took Frederick away from Berlin for a time, and his ministers began to hope that his zeal for work and government had been a bubble that Voltaire's arrival had pricked. They were wrong. Frederick astonished every one by returning to Berlin and working himself and every one else as hard as in the first months of his reign. Next he surprised them and all the world by marching off to war within twelve months of getting the throne. Frederick the philosopher and poet and flautist was swept aside by the Frederick who was to be "the Great."

Frederick marched on Breslau; it surrendered without a struggle. But Hanover, whose king was George II of England, and Saxony were preparing to support Austria, whose troops were on the move. On April 10, 1741, Frederick's forces of 30,000 men met them at Mollwitz, and Prussia's army won the day. It was not Frederick who led his country to success at Mollwitz but rather Prussia that led Frederick. Prussia won in spite of him, not because of him. His father's excellent army, under Schwerin, outmatched Austria, but Frederick and his personal cavalry failed conspicuously. At his general's advice he had left the field, and in the hour of victory was sitting, solitary and miserable and on the verge of nervous collapse, in an old mill miles from the scene of victory. Had Frederick been defeated in this his first battle he would have been known to posterity as Frederick the Fool. His army won it for him, and he became "the Great." Yet the taste of glory was bitter. Before Mollwitz he had written: ". . . these are my occupations. I would gladly exchange them for others if it were not for this ghost called glory which appears so often. In truth, it is a great folly, but a folly one cannot forget if one is obsessed with it." After Mollwitz he sat in tears. Fame had come to Frederick, and power and prestige, and he found that he liked them little.

The new king's armies swept all before them and the war had a speedy conclusion. By the Peace of Breslau, which was drawn up on June 11, 1742, Prussia acquired Breslau, the county of Glatz and Upper and Lower Silesia as far as the Oppa. The German expansion was beginning.

Two years later, the death of the Prince of East Friesland gave Frederick the opportunity of annexing that territory also. The same year found him concluding a secret treaty with France.

In 1744 Prussia was again in arms. Frederick invaded Bohemia and captured Prague, but later was forced to retreat. His well-trained armies turned the tide, however, and a series of victorious engagements led to the Peace of Dresden on December 25, 1745, by which the Prussian possession of Silesia was confirmed and assured.

After the Silesian Wars, Frederick gave Europe an opportunity to see him in the role of lawgiver. In 1747 was published the *Codex Fridericianus,* which established the Prussian judicial body. By it he reformed the whole German legal code, speeding up trials and setting a higher value on justice to the individual than on the majesty of the law. Injustice under Frederick did not find justification in the quibbles of lawyers or in the loopholes of legal phraseology. Indeed, his quick sympathy with his subjects sometimes led to his personal interference in cases, and on one occasion he actually dismissed and punished judges whom he thought had been responsible for a wrong decision. Frederick's character shows best of all in the strict laws under which the nobility were restrained from abusing the peasants. He appears to have tolerated the former, despised the latter and detested the bourgeoisie, although he saw to it that they and their industries and banks and markets should prosper. This was less for their sake than for the consequent profit to the State.

Greater than the *Codex Fridericianus* was the great legal code, *Allgemeines Preussisches Landrecht,* which was begun under the patronage of Frederick, although it was not actually finished and put into force until 1794, eight years after his death. The code combines the two systems of German and Roman law, supplemented by the law of Nature.

Frederick was a man without peace of mind. Even the companionship of Voltaire, so long desired, gave no comfort. There was only one happiness left to Frederick—the whole business of soldiering. " This trade," he wrote to a friend, " can go to the devil, but I like it—a proof of the inconsistencies of the human mind." Inevitably the climax came. Hearing that Maria Theresa of Austria was forming new alliances against him, with callous recklessness Prussia challenged the world in 1756 as she did in 1914 and 1939. With the same disregard for neutral territory and human feeling, she set the Continent seething at her frightfulness. France, Austria, Russia, Saxony and Sweden were her enemies; England and the little states of Brunswick and Hesse-Cassel alone were friendly.

The coalition of powers which fought against Prussia in the Seven Years War was formed ostensibly to recapture for Maria Theresa the lost territory of Silesia, but in fact Europe was determined to smash the colossus who was overstriding it—Frederick the Great.

Pitt recognized Frederick's military genius and England's opportunity. He subsidized Frederick so that the Prussians could carry their land campaigns on three fronts while the British fleet was busy seizing French islands in the West Indies and British soldiers were conquering Canada and French territory in India.

From 1756 to 1763, seven weary years, the war went on and on. Nation after nation was worn down by Frederick's admirable army, which still fought well even when exhaustion made it necessary to drive men into battle at the bayonet's point. " All this," Frederick wrote when the conflict was only half over, " has made me so old that you would hardly know me again. On the right side of my head the hair is all grey; my teeth break and fall out; my face is wrinkled and downcast like a monk of La Trappe." Nation after nation revived to attack again. Silesia was lost and won and lost and won again. When the end came at long last, and the charred lands of central Europe were once more quiet, it was not so much because Frederick had conquered as because the alliance against him had crumbled, and just at the moment when he himself was on the point of defeat, Prussia had become a Great Power.

Never did Frederick so well display his genius as a ruler as in the difficult years that followed. He made strenuous and sustained efforts to ensure the recovery of the exhausted nation. Many parts of the kingdom were relieved of taxes for a time to enable industries and agriculture to find their feet once again. The debased coinage was gradually brought back to normal value, and a fillip was given to trade by the foundation of the Bank of Berlin. Only one action of his aroused Prussian resentment and marred his popularity with his own people. He adopted the French excise system of collecting revenue. This led to gross abuses by a horde of petty officials who came to be called " cellar-rats " on account of their extortions.

In 1764 Frederick signed a treaty with Catherine of Russia, and six years later he shared in the shameful partition of Poland: more land had come to the Prussian Crown. In 1778 he engaged in the War of the Bavarian Succession, which acquired for him Franconia.

Frederick was always jealous and fearful of the power of Austria, in spite of the friendly advances that had been made earlier by the young emperor, Joseph II, and in 1785 he organized a defensive League of Princes among the states of Germany. This was the first attempt by Prussia to take the lead in Germany.

To the end of his reign he continued the policy with which he had begun—sound finance and a strong standing army. When he died on August 17, 1786, at the age of seventy-four, he had accumulated an enormous sum in the Treasury, and his troops numbered 200,000.

Carlyle's description of his death reveals vividly the human side of the emperor and the affection in which he was held by his entourage.

"Towards the evening of August 16, the king fell into a soft sleep, with warm perspiration; but on awakening, complained of cold, repeatedly of cold, demanding wrappage after wrappage (*kissen,* soft quilt of the old fashion), and on examining feet and legs, one of the doctors made signs that they were in fact cold, up nearly to the knee. 'What said he of the feet,' murmured the king some time afterwards, the doctor having now stepped out of sight. 'Much the same as before,' answered some attendant. The king shook his head, incredulous.

" He drank once, grasping the goblet with both hands, a draught of fennel-water, his customary drink; and seemed relieved by it—his last refection in this world. Towards nine in the evening, there had come on a continual short cough, and a rattling in the breast, breath more and more difficult. Why continue? Frederick is making exit, on the common terms; you may hear the curtain rustling down. For the most part he was unconscious, never more than half-conscious. As the wall-clock above his head struck eleven, he asked, 'What o'clock?' 'Eleven,' answered they. 'At four,' murmured he, 'I will rise.' One of his dogs sat on its stool near him; about midnight he noticed it shivering for cold. 'Throw a quilt over it,' said or beckoned he; that, I think, was his last completely-conscious utterance. Afterwards, in a severe choking fit, getting, at last, rid of the phlegm, he said, '*La montagne est passée, nous irons mieux*' (We are over the hill, we shall go better now).

"Attendants, Herzberg, Selle and one or two others were in the outer room; none in Friedrick's but Strutzki, his Kammerhussar, one of Three who are his sole valets and nurses; a faithful, ingenious man, as they all seem to be, and excellently chosen for the object. Strutzki, to save the king from hustling down, as he always did, into the corner of his chair, where, with neck and chest bent forward, breathing was impossible—at last took the king on his knee; kneeling on the ground with his other knee for the purpose—the king's right arm round Strutzki's neck, Strutzki's left arm round the king's back, and supporting his other shoulder, in which posture the faithful creature, for above two hours, sat motionless, till the end came. Within doors, all is silence, except this breathing; round it the dark earth silent, above it the silent stars. At twenty minutes past two the breathing paused, wavered, ceased. Friedrick's life-battle is fought out; instead of suffering and sore labour, here is now rest."

He had reigned throughout regarding his power as a trust; if his foreign policy had been brutal and acquisitive, he had fostered education, industry, agriculture in his own land; if he had neglected the German language and German art, he had deepened the national life from which that art was to spring, and he had left little upstart Prussia a powerful nation on which was to be built an empire in the years to come.

MAXIMILIEN FRANÇOIS MARIE ISIDORE DE ROBESPIERRE

(1758–1794)

". . . Some achieve greatness, and some have greatness thrust upon them." Maximilien Robespierre seems to belong to both categories: his fanatical persistence and indomitable devotion to his ideals achieved his ends, the conditions of the times thrust him forward. His integrity earned him the name of " the sea-green incorruptible," but his fanaticism dyed his bilious complexion with blood. At the height of the Revolution, Robespierre held the fate of France in his hands, he was dictator with unlimited power; during his supremacy the Revolution took on a new direction and alienated foreign sympathizers; at his death the Revolution died. Robespierre's brief spell of power decided the future history of the whole of Europe.

IN the hall of the College of Louis le Grand in Paris, a delicate-looking, sombre young scholar stands before the hundreds of his fellow students, before the college authorities and a group of august visitors. His shoes and linen are neat but shabby; but his hair is elegantly curled, his shoulders covered by a fine new coat. He has been chosen out of all the youths assembled there to present to his monarch a complimentary address of welcome and loyalty.

Within a few years those same thin, cynical lips are to pronounce, before the same king, words not of welcome but of doom.

The fine coat that Maximilien de Robespierre wore so proudly on the occasion of that visit of Louis XVI to his college, had been provided for him by the authorities. For, if he was the most industrious and the most successful student of his time, he was also one of the poorest, a state of affairs which caused the lonely boy endless misery in an institution where it was not unusual for the young students to have with them several servants and to live sumptuously.

From his babyhood Robespierre had known nothing but misery. He was born at Arras on May 6, 1758. When he was only six years old his mother died. His father, refusing even to sign the death certificate, threw up his practice as a barrister in Arras, vegetated in idleness for a few months, then set off on aimless wanderings in Europe, abandoning his four children to destitution. The two little girls were eventually cared for by two maiden aunts; Maximilien and and his baby brother, Augustin, went to the home of their maternal grandfather, the brewer Carrault of Arras.

Maximilien soon began to attend the classes of a college where priests, under the direction of the bishop, gave free education to the children of the town. Even at this age the boy showed an obstinate determination to gain the first place. His amusements were few, and far from exhilarating. His sister Charlotte writes that he rarely shared in the games of his fellow students, preferring to be alone, to meditate at ease.

His grandfather intended to apprentice the boy in his own business; but the schoolmasters were indignant at the idea of such a career for their promising pupil. The bishop himself intervened, and obtained for Robespierre a foundation scholarship connected with the University of Paris. In 1769, at the age of eleven, Maximilien left Arras to become a member of the fifth form in the College of Louis le Grand.

His successes there were sufficient indication of his industry. He gained neither the friendship of his schoolfellows nor the confidence of his masters. Always too conscious of his extreme poverty and of his own talents, he habitually held himself aloof from them all. His scholarship gave him the right of staying at Louis le Grand till he had taken a degree in medicine, theology, or jurisprudence. In 1781 he took his degree and was called to the bar of the Parlement of Paris. His brother Augustin inherited his scholarship, and Maximilien, with a final grant of about thirty pounds from the college, returned to Arras.

There life did not prove easy for him. He was entirely without means, and his practice as barrister was only indifferently successful. In 1782 his friend the bishop procured his appointment as judge of the episcopal tribune; but after serving faithfully for a short time he resigned this position, and for a cause all the more surprising in view of his ultimate role.

As Carlyle sarcastically writes: "Behold, one day a culprit comes whose crime merits hanging; and the strict-minded Max must abdicate, for his conscience will not permit the dooming of any son of Adam to die!"

What first struck those who met him was his neatness. Though never rich, he always contrived to dress elegantly—if not fashionably.

His favourite coat was light blue--a garment he put on for the great moments of his life. He was only five feet three inches tall, and spare. His hands and feet were small and delicate. His face was smooth and pale with a small, somewhat feminine, pointed chin. High cheekbones sloped up to pale, hard, grey-green eyes, above which a high forehead receded slightly to his carefully-powdered hair. The slightly pointed nose, the small, thin-lipped mouth betrayed a certain acerbity of mood.

Perhaps his face betrays the strength and weakness of his character. The neatness, the coldness, the pallor—all are words which could be accurately applied to his mind. He was, above all things, emotionally cold. He had one passion in his life. And this was not for any woman—not even any human being—but for an idea. To this idea his cold intensity would sacrifice any human being, from a peasant to the king himself. His emotions never flowered. He loved no woman; he never married. All his life he had few friends —none at all whom he was not prepared to sacrifice to his idea. Pity he never knew—neither for others nor for himself. Joy or sorrow he very rarely expressed. Always he preserved an expression of indifference touched by cynical amusement. Even on the guillotine he was composed.

But if he was undeveloped emotionally, he had compensations in his intellectual life. At the age of twenty-two he had won almost all the prizes for which he tried. As a lawyer he was excellent, and very elusive. As an orator he was very logical, cynical, but rather verbose.

What was this idea which fascinated him, which raised him from ordinary men, which carried him into power in revolutionary France, and for which his head fell?

It was the philosophy of Rousseau. He has been called the man who tried to put Rousseau into practice—and just failed. Rousseau had written many books whose general theme was "Back to Nature." Everything "natural" was good; civilization introduced all evils. Organized religion must go. God and eternity exist only as a Supreme Being who is everywhere, in everything beautiful, especially in the hills and trees. Politically, and here, of course, he most intimately affects Robespierre—politically, Rousseau was a democrat. He says: "As soon as in a democracy the few outstrip the many in the matter of wealth, the State must either perish or cease being a democracy." And again: "No citizen should be rich enough to purchase another or so poor as to be forced to sell himself."

These principles Rousseau elaborated in *The Social Contract,* and popularized in novels such as *Emile,* which is reported to have decided two or three European queens to nurse their infants themselves!

This, briefly, then, was the creed that Robespierre absorbed. For this he killed many, betrayed others and finally lost his own life. He was a political fanatic—whose claims to greatness cannot be denied. He has been well called "Principle in the Flesh."

We shall see how he puts his one great principle into practice.

In Arras his sister Charlotte kept house for him. After some preliminary lean years work came to him—of a kind. For he could not keep his politics out of his law, and he often took on cases for the poor who could pay him little or nothing. But he never worried about money. "A little suffices for him who has no desires," he wrote once. With more truth he might have said "for him who has but *one* desire." At his death his belongings were valued at about thirty pounds.

His one sensational success at the bar after this occurred in 1783, when he triumphantly defended M. de Vissery of Saint-Omer in the matter of his celebrated lightning-conductor, which had been threatened with destruction as a public menace.

An interesting light is thrown on to his character at this time by his literary attempts. He was always anxious for literary fame—poems and speeches were written and re-written with meticulous care. They cost him hours of trouble, but never made it possible for him to be called a "writer." This he himself recognized and so turned to another method of expression—oratory. As a counsel in court, he used his opportunities very effectively. It was here he practised and developed the weapon with which he was going to sway the Convention and the Jacobin Club so vitally.

For four years he struggled in vain to establish himself, keeping few friends on the bar and making many enemies. Then, when his affairs seemed entirely hopeless, political events worked in his favour. It became known that Louis XVI intended to convoke an Assembly of all the provincial states in the kingdom, and that deputies were to be elected. Robespierre at once busied himself in his native town, declaiming against oppression, stirring up the people, drawing up Writs of Grievance, attacking the governor and the States of Artois, urging the electors of the Third Estate to elect men who were incorruptible. In all these activities he was perfectly sincere. Finally he was himself elected fifth deputy for the State of Artois and in this capacity he set off for Versailles, in May, 1789.

The causes of the French Revolution were complex, but mention must be made of the method of the Revolution in so far as it affected Robespierre. The poverty of the State was amazing. The king was at his wit's end for money. In his efforts to obtain it appalling hardships were inflicted, not on the aristocrats, or even the middle classes, but on the peasants. The Church, which owned vast tracts of land, was exempt from taxation. The aristocrats were also exempted. The original move for reform came, not from the powerless peasants (they were too easily kept down by military force), but from the uneasy merchants who said the Government was becoming bankrupt. This middle class wanted a neat little revolution whereby power was slipped out of the king's hands into theirs—but no further.

Where did the peasants come into this programme? The answer is not at all, if the merchants could help it.

But Robespierre thought otherwise. Except for the last month of his life he was always on the extreme left politically. His opponents failed to go far enough, and one by one he defeated them. It is this conflict that accounts for the continuous fall of heads during the Revolution. His own was the last to fall, and with it ended the Revolution.

On May 4, 1789, the States General opened at Versailles. Robespierre, in the black cape of the representative of the Third Estate, was there. But he was unknown by Paris, whose attention was fixed on the burly Mirabeau. To everyone's surprise the Bishop of Nancy delivered a powerful address on the abuses of the old régime—and this in the presence of the king!

On June 17, the Third Estate declared themselves the National Assembly—the Revolution had begun.

The obscure lawyer from Arras made little impression on the members of the Assembly. How could he hope to be noticed? He was poor, small and feeble in physique, shabbily dressed, without experience of parliamentary tactics or of public oratory. Yet he tried again and again to make himself heard, and although his earnest speeches were ignored, he was soon marked as one of the more turbulent spirits.

In July the Bastille was stormed. The Revolution was already going "too far" said some. Robespierre, at Versailles that day, took no part in this historic event. Exhibitions of passion were not for him. It was his violent college friend, Desmoulins, who mounted the café table and hurled passionate words at the people, fanning the violence that already had broken out in various parts of Paris into the blaze that engulfed the Bastille. It was the tall, swarthy

Maillard who led on that crowd of frenzied patriots. All through the night the cry had gone up: "To the Bastille!" On the morning of July 14, the mob seethed towards the Hôtel des Invalides, where nearly thirty thousand muskets were stored. Within an hour that mob was an army—an army on the march to the Bastille.

The demand for surrender meets with refusal—a few ragged musket shots killing one or two patriots. It is the signal for chaos! Din and shouts, blood and powder drive on these fiery spirits into a drunken orgy of brutality. They kill—it is their passion. For five hours they fire at those dark grey walls, manned by a mere hundred soldiers, until a white flag signals surrender. The Bastille is taken! Men and women, mad with victory, surge in—butchered heads appear on pikes carried by blood-stained patriots. It is victory over the oppressor—over the king!

Some days later an unknown deputy stood quietly, coldly inspecting the gloomy prison. He was cheered as he walked through the streets, because he was a deputy of the National Assembly—but no one knew his name. He did not like this violence, but it had to be. So mused Robespierre.

Events crowd on one another now—the juggernaut of the Revolution has broken loose. Woe to those who try to steer it! In October, the maddened, starving women of Paris lead their haggard, grotesque procession to Versailles. Led again by Maillard, ten thousand of them trudge through the rain and mud to Versailles. Their rags soaked, their steaming bodies huddled together for warmth on this chill October day, the women waited outside the palace. A deputation of twelve came into the Assembly with Maillard as their spokesman. Some taunted him and sneered. It was Robespierre who jumped up and replied; he had a familiar task, and his words took effect. His enemies remembered him—but so did the women of Paris. For the first time he glimpsed his goal!

That night the palace was raided by the mob. The dashing, but sleepy Lafayette woke just in time to prevent serious harm coming to the king and queen. Later he conducted these two, surrounded by the enraged mob, back to Paris. The Assembly followed.

Back in Paris, Robespierre looked for cheap lodgings. Eventually he found them in the rue de Saintonge, where he lived with Pierre Villiers. The Assembly used the Salle du Manege as its meeting-place. This long, gloomy hall was to see much of the pain and terror of the Revolution. Much of Robespierre's life was to be played out between this and the Jacobin Club, which met in the refectory of the Dominican monastery in the rue St. Honore. At first the club was moderate in its politics. Gradually, however, the shift towards the left became more apparent. And as this happened, so Robespierre emerged more and more into prominence. This elegant man, with his superior ways, his flowery oratory, and superb, cold sincerity, convinced his fellow men in spite of themselves.

In this same year he joined the Jacobin Club, where his influence grew rapidly. In 1791, he carried his fatal motion that no member of the Constituent Assembly should be elected to the forthcoming Legislative Assembly. His influence was growing beyond the confines of the Jacobin Club. The people of Paris saw in him already their future champion. In September, 1791, they acclaimed Pétion and Robespierre the two "incorruptible patriots."

At the end of that year, accompanied by Pétion, he made a brief, triumphant visit to Arras, then returned to establish himself permanently in Paris, in the home of Duplay, a carpenter. He was now first deputy for Paris, firmly established as the favourite of the people.

He had served for a short time as Public Prosecutor, but he resigned the post, seeming undecided in his aim.

As first deputy for Paris in the Convention, he had as his supporters Marat, Danton, Collot d'Herbois and Billaud Varenne. His adversaries, headed by the famous members of the Gironde, were more numerous and more brilliant. In the Convention he was not yet considered a man to be feared. At the time of the king's trial, he demanded the monarch's death without debate, without inquiry, without defence. "The greatest of all criminals cannot be judged," he said, "he is already condemned." Robespierre had his way: the king died undefended, unheard.

In July, 1793, the Committee of Public Safety was recomposed as an executive body. Robespierre was elected to it, and his influence was supreme. With three powerful instruments in his hands—the Committee of Public Safety, the Revolutionary Tribunal and the Jacobin Club, he was now master of the Convention. But on all sides he saw enemies; enemies to himself and enemies to his country. In September the Revolutionary Tribunal was remodelled and the Law of Suspects passed, enabling local authorities to arrest whom they pleased, and to detain him in prison even when acquitted. The prisons were full, the guillotine working unceasingly.

The leaders of the Opposition were wiped out ruthlessly and methodically. Robespierre was possessed with ideals of purification: the Convention was to be purged of corruption; the State was to be grounded on solid virtue. He took as his guiding precept the formula: "Virtue, without which terror is baneful; terror, without which virtue is powerless." So the Terror continued.

His own private life was, all this time, a model of integrity. He lived quietly with his carpenter friend, on the modest eighteen francs a day allowed to a deputy. He was austere, frugal, and insensible to the pomps and vanities of this world. He worked incessantly and with indefatigable perseverance to attain his ideal.

The Gironde had been first defeated, then obliterated. Hebert and his followers had followed them to the guillotine. Now Danton seemed to threaten, to be leaning towards moderation. From February to March, 1794, Robespierre retired from active work to consider his position. Danton had been his friend and supporter, and Danton had many supporters himself. But the Incorruptible was not to be deterred by considerations of friendship. Danton and his friends—among whom was Camille Desmoulins, a former school-fellow of Robespierre—were arrested on March 30: on April 5 they died.

Robespierre had now reached the pinnacle of his career: he held in the hollow of his hand the Convention, the Jacobins, the Parisian army, the Electoral College, and the Revolutionary Tribunal.

One thing remained for him to carry out. On May 7, he mounted the tribune at the beginning of the sitting and began to read a report. It was a profession of faith in the Supreme Being, and the immortality of the soul. The reign of virtue could only survive if based on a strong religious belief. Religious beliefs had been set at nought by the Revolutionaries: Robespierre intended to establish a natural cult, opposed to Catholicism as much as to atheism. Such was his ascendancy over the Convention that he secured a decree recognizing the existence of the Supreme Being. His speech was read at the Jacobin Club amidst acclamations, and was published in the streets. A date was immediately fixed for the fête of the Supreme Being.

Elaborate preparations were made; the streets were decorated; "Details of the Order to be Observed" were widely circulated, informing all the groups taking part in the procession how to behave. Robespierre himself, dressed in long purplish-blue coat encircled by a wide tricoloured scarf, a waistcoat of pique with points, dimity breeches and parti-coloured stockings, led the procession, and delivered an address.

Robespierre had gone too far. Even as he walked in that procession—which was, to all appearances, an unqualified success—he heard the mutterings of the storm that was to break over his head—

the jibes and abuse of his own colleagues. At that moment not a monarch in Europe could compare with him in power: but a gulf was opening before him, and he was aware of his peril.

On June 10, Couthon, his ally, passed in the Convention the terrible law which changed the Tribunal into a simple court of condemnation. The committee was to be empowered to send whom it chose before the tribunal, and if the jury was satisfied, no time was to be lost with witnesses, written depositions, or arguments. Identification was to be sufficient.

So began the period of the Great Terror. Between June 12 and June 28, 1,285 victims perished. No deputy was safe; Robespierre's great band of supporters—the people—cringed behind closed shutters, turning in panic from the man they had raised to such giddy heights.

Robespierre himself was not seen in the Convention for four weeks; he left his colleagues to control matters while he considered in solitude the next step to be taken. On July 26, he took his place in the tribune and spoke for an hour. The Terror was to be ended, but certain deputies were to be punished—he would not name them then; the Committees of Public Safety and General Security were to be renewed. When pressed to denounce his enemies, and the enemies of the Convention, he would mention only Cambon and Fouché. Having obtained a vote of acceptance of his speech, he was satisfied: but therein he made a mistake. Cambon turned on him with the words: "What paralyses the Republic is the man who has just spoken."

The superb piece of daring turned the Assembly; it recalled its vote and referred the speech to the committee. Robespierre sank upon his seat and was heard to mutter: "I am a lost man."

On the following day, Saint-Just, speaking ardently on behalf of Robespierre and demanding that he should be named Dictator, was violently interrupted, faltered and was heard no more. Robespierre was not allowed to speak: there were cries of "Down with the tyrant!" An unknown deputy moved that Robespierre be arrested; his young brother offered himself up as equally guilty, and several others of his friends were arrested with them.

The fallen dictator still had friends in the city. The troops of the Commune released his friends from jail. Robespierre himself had been refused admittance—and escorted them to the Hôtel de Ville. There Robespierre ultimately joined them. The Convention at once declared the arrested deputies outlaws, and those of the populace who had drawn up before the Hôtel de Ville with the intention of helping the leaders made no move. His friends implored Robespierre to sign a warlike proclamation. He never wrote more than the first two letters of his name.

Bourdon and the gendarmes burst into the room fully armed: the outlaws scattered; Robespierre was shot through the lower jaw, either by his own hand or by one of the gendarmes; most of the others were eventually captured without trouble.

Robespierre lay all that night in agony on a table in the Tuileries where, for hours, people came and stared at him. From the moment when the shot was fired he never spoke.

At ten next morning he was locked in the Conciergerie, in the cell next to Marie Antoinette's.

As he lies there perhaps the agony of his wound wrings from this man of stone some awakening emotion of pity for the headless ghosts that crowd around him, ghosts of his friends, of the innocent, sent to die in their thousands by his word.

At five that afternoon a tumbril drew up outside. Into it was put Maximilien Robespierre, Hanriot, the handsome Saint-Just, the crippled rebel Couthon, and Augustin, Maximilien's brother. Outside Duplays's house the tumbril stopped. Women danced around it with frenzied hatred. One sprinkled with blood the house that had been his home. The mob he had ruled had turned against him. The tumbril moved on. At the guillotine he saw the others, save one, mount and die. He climbed up without assistance. Only when the executioner tore off the bandage round his shattered jaw did he utter a cry. In a few seconds he was tied down, his head adjusted, and the knife screeched down. The principle had killed its flesh.

He rose from obscurity to become the idol of the people; and he died the most hateful character in history. There was more in him than appeared. In his youth he had met Rousseau, had absorbed his works and had taken ardently to heart the precepts they taught. He was elected to the States General in a critical moment, when he was full of bitterness at his own humiliations, full of visions of the ideal social state. He saw his opportunity to act, and from the moment his political career was established and his power began to increase, he worked with the ardour of a fanatic.

He was always a fanatic. His strict mind was ruled by three dogmas: the support of virtue by terror; the sanctity of property, and the existence of God.

He was the enemy of corruption and of war: he fell because he attempted to bar the progress of unbelief, which was the strongest current of the age. His private life was a model of integrity. He handled millions of secret service money, and might have made himself rich as well as powerful. He did not desire wealth, and seemed to have no personal ambition.

This hard, dry man was without imagination, without courage; his constitution was feeble, his temperament sombre. Yet he numbed the Convention by that very coldness, swayed it by the fanatical intensity of his purpose. The stony glance of his short-sighted blue eyes was enough to quell opposition; a few biting words from his thin lips aroused dread in the ranks of the Assembly. His face was remarkable for the tension of the brow, eyes, mouth and facial muscles.

With the death of Robespierre the Reign of Terror came to an abrupt end, and with it the Revolution virtually ended. For Robespierre had already swept before him all the moderate and reactionary elements: now his own party, the extremists, had exceeded the limits of horror and were to be swept away in its turn. France had had its fill of revolution and confusion; there was an immediate return to the principles of constitutional government. And the reaction to Robespierre was to be Napoleon: they had swept away a monarch to set an emperor in his place.

GEORGE WASHINGTON

(1732–1799)

George Washington was a gentleman farmer, with, in his own words, "inferior endowments from nature," little military knowledge, and a distaste for politics. He became the commander of a victorious army, the leader of a nation establishing its independence, and the first President of the United States of America. These achievements were due to his courage, his determination, his self-discipline and his idealism. Washington has been called the first American: he was the first to think of developing the West, and welding the states into the united nation of which he became president, of which he was, in a real sense, the founder.

STRENGTH of character is an essential quality in the builder of a nation. It predominated in the make-up of Washington, whose determination tore the North American colonies from British rule, and whose discipline welded the freed colonies into the United States of America.

The tall, sinewy figure, with the big, square-jawed face, to which set lips and steely eyes gave an expression of sternness, left an impression of coldness, almost of indifference. In reality he was a man of deep feeling and passions, who controlled himself with the same ruthless discipline that he imposed upon others. Gilbert Stuart, the painter of a famous portrait of Washington, asserted that "all his features were indicative of the most ungovernable passions, and had he been born in the forests he would have been the fiercest man among the savage tribes." He was lamentably deficient in humour.

To him America owed victory in the War of Independence, and his triumph was due to wise leadership and a capacity for inspiring loyalty rather than to strategy.

George Washington was born in Virginia in 1732. His father, who was descended from a Northamptonshire family, owned half a dozen large plantations on which he raised cattle and grew tobacco. George, who was the eldest child of a second marriage, spent his youth on the estates, where he picked up a mere smattering of formal education, but learned a great deal about practical farming and surveying.

Washington's father died when the boy was eleven, so he went to live with his half-brother Lawrence, who had married a member of the Fairfax family, the richest landowners in Virginia. When Lord Fairfax came out from England to settle in America, George made his acquaintance and profited greatly from the culture and the library that his lordship imported to his new home.

Fairfax was interested in Washington, and when in 1748 he sent out a party to inspect his six million acres in the Shenandoah Valley, he appointed the boy assistant surveyor. Washington kept a lively but misspelt diary of the journey. He tells us of the discomfort of sleeping under "one thread Bear blanket with double its weight of vermin such as Lice, Fleas, etc.," and of meeting German emigrants who were "as ignorant a set of people as the Indians, they would never speak English but when spoken to speak all Dutch."

The expedition over, Fairfax had him appointed surveyor to Fairfax County in 1749. Two years later George accompanied Lawrence on a voyage to Barbados, in the West Indies, where he caught smallpox, which marked him for life. On their return his half-brother died and left the estates to his daughter, but under George's management, with remainder to George in the event of his daughter's death. Within a few years the daughter did die, and George became a wealthy landowner.

An enthusiastic and intelligent farmer, he devoted himself to experiment and improvement. He had seen the vast, rich lands to the west, and had visions of the great new nation of farmers that would rise to cultivate it.

"The work," writes Mr. Herbert Agar, "that Washington had to leave unfinished at Mount Vernon, each time he was called away by public affairs, was not simply that of a country gentleman administering a large estate. Washington was aiming, by experiment and example, at the reform of American husbandry. He had learned that in the implements used, in the size of crops, and particularly in the size of farm animals, the United States was far behind England. Washington studied the new books, corresponded with men like Arthur Young in England, imported implements, and tried out new methods. This work seemed to him as important as any he could do for the welfare of the agricultural empire that he foresaw in North America; and it was the work that he knew himself best fitted for by training, taste, and character."

Washington bent to his task with energy, and under his direction

Mount Vernon became a model estate. With prosperity Washington increased his holdings until eventually his land totalled eight thousand acres, of which three thousand five hundred acres were in cultivation. The estate was virtually self-contained. Its proprietor's retinue numbered over two hundred slaves, and included artisans who could build and forge, and men skilled in the making of liquor and the grinding of corn. Wool from the sheep which wandered about the broad acres was woven on the master's looms, and not a few of the products were profitably disposed of in markets far and near. "Keep an account book," he advised, "and enter therein every farthing of your receipts and expenditures." On another occasion he avowed, "There is no proverb in the whole catalogue of them more true than 'A penny saved is a penny got.'"

So much for the work on which Washington set his heart. His amusements were those of the spacious Virginia of his time: shooting, fishing, riding to hounds and racing. House parties were frequent at the Washington home; he was fond of dancing and cards, of play-going and afternoon tea and picnics.

Such was the life of the man who was called upon to lead and make the country of his dreams.

In 1752, Washington had been appointed adjutant of one of the military districts of Virginia, and a year later saw him in active military service. He was sent by the Governor of Virginia to order the French to leave disputed territory on the Ohio River: the order was disobeyed, and Washington was sent back to enforce it. According to the historians Parkman and Howitt: A regiment of six hundred men, of which Washington was appointed lieutenant-colonel, marched in the month of April, 1754, into the disputed territory, and, encamping at the Great Meadows, were met by alarming intelligence; the French had driven the Virginians from a fort, which, owing to his own recommendation, they were building at "the Fork," the place where Pittsburg now stands, between the junction of the Monongahela and the Alleghany, the importance of which position he had become aware of on his journey to Venango. This fort the French had now finished, and had called Duquesne, in honour of the governor-general; besides which, a detachment sent against him were encamped at a few miles' distance. Washington proceeded, surprised the enemy, and killed the commander, Jumonville—the first blood shed in this war. French writers claimed that, on catching sight of the English, Jumonville's interpreter at once called out that he had something to say to them; but Washington, who was at the head of his column, declared this absolutely false.

The French claimed also that Jumonville was killed in the act of reading the summons. "There was every reason," says Parkman, "for believing that the designs of the French were hostile; and though by passively waiting the event he would have thrown upon them the responsibility of striking the first blow, Washington would have exposed his small party to capture or destruction. It was inevitable that the killing of Jumonville should be greeted in France by an outcry of real or assumed horror; but the Chevalier de Levis, second in command to Montcalm, probably expressed the true opinion of Frenchmen best fitted to judge when he calls it 'a pretended assassination.' Judge it as we may, this obscure skirmish began the war that set the world on fire" in the Seven Years War.

On his return to the Great Meadows, Washington was joined by troops from New York and South Carolina, and here erected a fort, which he called Fort Necessity. Frye, the colonel, being now dead, the chief command devolved upon Washington, who very shortly set out towards Duquesne, when he was compelled to return and entrench himself within Fort Necessity, owing to the approach of a very superior force under De Villiers, the brother of Jumonville. After a day of hard fighting, the fort itself was surrendered, on condition of the garrison being permitted to retire unmolested. A singular circumstance occurred in this capitulation; Washington, who did not understand French, employed a Dutchman as his interpreter, and he, either from ignorance or treachery, rendered the terms of the capitulation incorrectly; thus Washington signed an acknowledgment of having "assassinated" Jumonville, and engaged not again to appear in arms against the French within twelve months.

Villiers claimed to have made Washington sign this virtual admission that he had assassinated Jumonville. Some time after, Washington wrote to a correspondent who had questioned him on the subject: "That we were wilfully or ignorantly deceived by our interpreter in regard to the word assassination I do aver, and will to my dying moment; so will every officer that was present. The interpreter was a Dutchman little acquainted with the English tongue, therefore might not advert to the tone of the word in English; but, whatever his motives for so doing, certain it is that he called it the 'death' or the 'loss' of the Sieur Jumonville. So we received and so we understood it, until, to our great surprise and mortification, we found it otherwise in a literal translation."

His first taste of battle pleased Washington, whose courage was of the greatest. He wrote to his brother: "I heard the bullets whistle, and, believe me, there is something charming in the sound." On being told of this remark George II, who had fought at Dettingen and never forgotten it, commented, "He would not say so if he had been used to hear many."

Washington was soon called upon to give further proofs of his bravery. He refused to join Major-General Edward Braddock's expedition against the French because officers of any ranking holding a royal commission took precedence over colonial officers, and Washington had already had one quarrel on this ground. But Braddock wanted Washington and offered him an unpaid staff post. Washington accepted, and was present when the French and their Indian allies almost annihilated the British force. The British general had the courage of a lion—he received a mortal wound after four horses had been killed under him—and Washington showed equal gallantry. He was the only mounted officer who was not killed. It has been said that he was responsible for the safe retreat of the remnant of the British and Colonial force, but this is untrue. They got away because the French stayed their hand and did not pursue.

The grim experience did not daunt him. He could still write, "My inclinations are strongly bent to arms." In 1755, after the defeat and death of Braddock at Fort Duquesne, Washington was made a colonel and commander of all the Virginian forces. "The supplicating tears of the women and moving petitions of the men," he said, "melt me into such deadly sorrow that I solemnly declare, if I know my own mind, I could offer myself a willing sacrifice to the butchering enemy, providing that would contribute to the people's ease." Three years later he resigned on account of ill-health, and for the next seventeen years he lived at Mount Vernon and looked after his estates, appearing only in public life as a member of the Virginian House of Burgesses. He married Martha Dandridge Custis, a wealthy widow. She was not his first love, for he had already been twice rejected, and even at the time he was really in love with Sally, the wife of his friend, George Fairfax. But on this, as on many other occasions, Washington suppressed his passions. He married the widow and lived with Martha in contented happiness.

It was in the pursuit of one of his early aims—the development of the West—that Washington first saw fit to disagree with the vagaries of British rule. In 1763 a proclamation was published prohibiting settlers from entering the Indian country beyond the Appalachian Mountains. Washington did not regard this regulation very seriously, for in the same year he sent an agent into the Ohio Valley with orders to buy "some of the most valuable lands in the king's part, which I think may be accomplished after a while, notwithstanding the proclamation that restrains it at present, and prohibits the settling of them at all; for I can never look upon that proclamation in any other light (but this I say between ourselves), than as a temporary expedient to quiet the minds of the Indians." But in 1774, when Washington was already planning a canal between the Ohio and the Potomac, came the Quebec Act, which definitely excluded settlers from the territory between the Ohio and the Mississippi. It was this type of legislation that stung Washington and the landowners of the south and west, while the Stamp Act and the Tea Act had given the restive spirits of the north excuse for rioting and revolt.

When the first Continental Congress was summoned by the colonists in 1774, Washington was one of the Virginian delegates. It met at Philadelphia, lasted for seven weeks, and drew up a Bill of Grievances. In the following year, largely through the influence of John Adams, of Massachusetts, the second Continental Congress appointed Washington commander-in-chief. "It has been a kind of destiny that has thrown me upon this service," he wrote to his wife. He still hoped that there might be no severance of the thirteen colonies and the Motherland.

Adams knew that the southerners would not join in the war which the New Englanders had started unless a southern general were appointed; the New Yorkers also wanted a man of substance to lead the army. "Lastly," writes Mr. Agar, "in addition to being a rich man and a southerner, it was desirable that the general should have had some military experience. Washington had commanded as many as a hundred and fifty men in action; he had been an unofficial member of Braddock's staff; and in boyhood he had received instruction in tactics and swordsmanship from two old soldiers."

But shrewd observers at the congress had found him a man "of solid information and sound judgment," and Washington never belied their estimate. At first, like most of the American upper classes, he did not believe it necessary to break with the British Empire; but once the struggle was really joined, Washington fought for complete independence, the unity of the states, and an American nation.

It has been said earlier that Washington was no heaven-born general, like Clive of India, and it is true that some of his tactical moves were weak and unsound. But Washington's worst enemies were not the British generals, who were experts at leaving each other in the lurch and defeating themselves, but the weakness of his own forces and the jealousy and incompetence of Congress.

His army, sometimes swelled by an erratic militia, was unpaid, ill-armed, ragged, and badly fed. "We eat every kind of horse food but hay," Washington complained. But in spite of every handicap, in spite of defeat and bitter weather, Washington kept an army in the field. His discipline was always strong. It was Washington, and the inspiration of Washington's leadership, that enabled the Americans to win the War of Independence.

The conflict started inauspiciously for Washington. John Knox describes the fall of New York as follows:

Washington had transferred his quarters from Boston to New York (April 13), which he was busy fortifying against the expected foe. Troops from Halifax, under General Howe, joined by British and Hessians under his brother Admiral Howe, and by the discomfited forces of the southern expedition, landed at various times on Staten Island. General Howe found himself at the head of twenty-four thousand of the finest troops of Europe, well-appointed and supplied, while further reinforcements were expected daily, which would swell his numbers to fifty-five thousand. As Washington had supposed, the intention of the British was to gain possession of New York, and, having command of the Hudson River, open communication with Canada, and thus separate the eastern from the middle states and be able to carry the war into the interior; while Long Island, adjacent to New York, which abounded in grain and cattle, would afford subsistence to the army. By the middle of summer the American forces were driven out of Canada and the northern frontier was exposed to attack.

Soon after the landing of the British Army, Admiral Lord Howe sent a letter containing an offer of pardon to all who would submit. This letter was directed to "George Washington, Esq." Washington, however, declined receiving in his private capacity any communications from the enemies of his country; the style of the address was then changed to that of "George Washington, etc., etc., etc.," and it was requested that the offer of pardon contained in the letter might be made known as widely as possible. Congress ordered it to be published in every newspaper throughout the Union, "that everybody might see how Great Britain was insidiously endeavouring to amuse and disarm them," and replied that, "not considering that their opposition to British tyranny was a crime, they therefore could not solicit pardon."

Nothing being gained by this attempt at conciliation, the British now proceeded to the prosecution of the war. Washington, aware that the enemy would advance to New York by way of Long Island, had entrenched a portion of the American Army, nine thousand strong, at Brooklyn. On August 22, the English landed on the southern shore of Long Island, and advanced to within four miles of the American camp. On the twenty-seventh the British silently advanced at night by three several roads towards the American Army. Clinton, proceeding by the eastern road, having seized an important defile, which through carelessness had been left unguarded, descended with the morning light into the plain and within sight of the American camp. General Sullivan, who had hastened out to meet them with a considerable force, had fallen in with Generals Grant and Heister, whilst Clinton, who by this time was safe on the plain, hastened forward and threw himself between Sullivan's corps and the American camp. The Americans attempted a retreat, but it was too late. The English drove them back upon Heister's Hessians, and thus locked in between two hostile armies, some few managed to escape, but the greater number were killed or taken prisoners. It was a disastrous day. The true number of the Americans killed was never ascertained; about a thousand were taken prisoners. The English lost only about four hundred.

But by the end of the next year, 1776, Washington had gathered a force of two thousand four hundred men and surprised Trenton, where he captured a thousand Hessians and large supplies of ammunition and stores. Lord Cornwallis, who had been sent from England with reinforcements, immediately marched on him at the head of an army eight thousand strong, in January 1777, but instead of attacking immediately on arrival, waited overnight to "bag the old fox." The old fox proved too wily. Washington left his camp fires burning and silently withdrew his men from their position: then he marched swiftly round to Cornwallis's rear and attacked Princetown, where the British lost five hundred men.

In 1777, the year of Burgoyne's surrender to the Americans at Saratoga, Washington was badly beaten at Brandywine, and he retired with the remnant of his army to winter quarters at Valley Forge. In the face of cold and hunger, and with Congress plotting to depose him from the command, Washington kept his army together.

His grim tenacity met with reward. The tide turned in favour of the Americans: the French sent them reinforcements on land and sea, entrusting their troops implicitly to Washington's command, and in 1781 Cornwallis was trapped at Yorktown and surrendered.

Two years later Washington handed his accounts of personal expenditure on the war—it amounted to £14,500—to the Controller of the Treasury, resigned his command, and retired to the peace of Mount Vernon. "The first wish of my soul," he wrote to a friend, "is to spend the evening of my days as a private citizen on my farm."

He turned to his schemes of developing the west, and once more applied himself to his projected Ohio-Potomac Canal. He arranged a meeting between representatives of Maryland and Virginia, who came to an agreement about the charges and trading conditions on the river that divided them. That meeting was the forerunner of others between all the states, and from those meetings sprang the Convention of 1787 which established the Constitution of the United States. Washington arrived at the building where the first session was held to the minute; he was the only delegate neither early nor late. Washington was chosen to take the chair, and when the Federal Government was organized he was elected by unanimous vote the first president of the new republic.

Many hoped that the War of Independence and the break with the British Empire would herald a new era of communism or socialism in America. The propertied classes did not share this view. They had regarded with horror the outbursts of the "Sons of Liberty" in the early days of the agitation against Britain, and now the war was over they felt that firm measures must be taken to restore ruined business, deflate money, and establish once more the rights of property. For this a strong central government was needed.

Washington was among those who saw the necessity for a firm Federal power. Before the Constitution Convention was called, he wrote, "Something must be done, or the fabric will fall; it is certainly tottering." The people must decide by their actions "whether the Revolution must ultimately be considered a blessing or a curse."

So Washington became president as a champion of strong conservative Government. He was no traitor to democracy, for he had never been a democrat. "Mankind," he once wrote, "when left to themselves, are unfit for their own government."

Naturally the radicals abused him, and his manner and dignity in his new office irritated them the more. Washington thought that as the head of the State he should not shake hands, should not return calls, and not accept hospitality. He travelled in a white coach with decorated panels and a gilded frame. The outriders wore a livery of scarlet and white.

In his cabinet, Washington tried to combine the two opposing groups. Alexander Hamilton, a pillar of the capitalists, was made Secretary of the Treasury, while Thomas Jefferson, who was working for a democratic and agrarian State, became Secretary of State. The two men clashed; Washington supported Hamilton's policy, and in 1793 Jefferson resigned.

Washington wished to retire at the end of his first term of office, but Hamilton persuaded him to accept a second term. Hamilton, who has been termed the greatest constructive statesman in United States history, among other measures founded a National Bank and set up a system of tariffs to protect American industry. Capitalists, traders and industrialists benefited by these schemes, and when Washington retired from office, in 1797, the Hamiltonian régime was firmly established. Washington refused to serve a third time as president, thereby setting a precedent which obtained until Franklin Roosevelt's time.

Mount Vernon and his estates claimed him once more. "How much more delightful," he wrote to Arthur Young, the great agriculturist, "is the task of making improvements on the earth than all the vain glory which can be acquired from ravaging it by the most uninterrupted career of conquests." With renewed zest he took up again the life he loved, only to lay it down for ever in December, 1799, when he caught a cold and a quinsy developed. Washington knew it was the end. "I die hard," he said, "but I am not afraid to go." The courage that typifies the man was with him to the last.

Major-General Henry Lee was not guilty of rhetorical exaggeration when he proclaimed Washington "First in war, first in peace, first in the hearts of his countrymen."

Two tributes to his greatness may be added as an indication of the Motherland's opinion of Washington. The first is by the Earl of Stanhope:

"It has been justly remarked that of General Washington there are fewer anecdotes to tell than perhaps of any other great man on record. There were none of those checkered hues, none of those warring emotions, in which biography delights. There was no contrast of lights and shades, no flickering of the flame; it was a mild light that seldom dazzled, but that ever cheered and warmed. His contemporaries or his close observers, as Jefferson and Gallatin, assert that he had naturally strong passions, but had attained complete mastery over them. In self-control, indeed, he has never been surpassed. If sometimes on rare occasion, and on strong provocation, there was wrung from him a burst of anger, it was almost instantly quelled by the dominion of his will. He decided surely, though he deliberated slowly; nor could any urgency or peril move him from his serene composure, his calm, clear-headed good sense. Integrity and truth were also ever present in his mind.

"Not a single instance, as I believe, can be found in his whole career when he was impelled by any but an upright motive, or endeavoured to attain an object by any but worthy means. Such are some of the high qualities which have justly earned for General Washington the admiration even of the country he opposed, and not merely the admiration but the gratitude and affection of his own.

"Such was the pure and upright spirit to which, when its toils were over and its earthly course had been run, was offered the unanimous homage of the assembled Congress, all clad in deep mourning for their common loss, as to 'the man first in war, first in peace, and first in the hearts of his fellow citizens.' At this day in the United States the reverence for his character is, as it should be, deep and universal, and not confined, as with nearly all English statesmen, to one party, one province, or one creed. Such reverence for Washington is felt even by those who wander farthest from the paths in which he trod. Thus may it be said of this most virtuous man what in days of old was said of Virtue herself, that even those who depart most widely from her precepts still keep holy and bow down to her name."

Finally, Sir Archibald Alison:

"Modern history has not a more spotless character to commemorate. Invincible in resolution, firm in conduct, incorruptible in integrity, he brought to the helm of a victorious republic the simplicity and innocence of rural life; he was forced into greatness by circumstances rather than led into it by inclination, and prevailed over his enemies rather by the wisdom of his designs and the perseverance of his character than by any extraordinary genius for the art of war. A soldier from necessity and patriotism rather than disposition, he was the first to recommend a return to pacific counsels when the independence of his country was secured; and bequeathed to his countrymen an address on leaving their government to which there are few compositions of uninspired wisdom which can bear a comparison. He was modest, without diffidence; sensible to the voice of fame, without vanity; independent and dignified, without either asperity or pride. He was a friend to liberty, but not to licentiousness—not to the dreams of enthusiasts, but to those practical ideas which America had inherited from her British descent. Accordingly, after having signalized his life by successful resistance

The Emperor Shah Alum delivering to Lord Clive the formal grant conferring in perpetuity the administration of the revenues of Bengal, Behar and Orissa on the East India Company (*above*). Maximilien Robespierre (*below*) has been regarded by some as a ruthless dictator, by others as the idealistic champion of social revolution. The Duke of Marlborough (*right*) was one of the greatest military commanders of history. Besides being a great strategist on the field, he was an astute diplomat.

General Rochambeau and George Washington (*above*) giving their orders for the last assault on Yorktown during the American War of Independence. Abraham Lincoln's famous address at Gettysburg in 1863 (*below left*). (*Below right*) A painting by Gros depicts Napoleon Bonaparte at the Battle of Eylau where he fought the allied Russian and Prussian forces in 1807.

to English oppression, he closed it by the warmest advice to cultivate the friendship of Great Britain, and exerted his whole influence, shortly before his resignation, to effect the conclusion of a treaty of friendly and commercial intercourse between the mother country and its emancipated offspring. He was a Cromwell without his ambition; a Sulla without his crimes; and, after having raised his country, by his exertions, to the rank of an independent state, he closed his career by a voluntary relinquishment of the power which a grateful people had bestowed."

HORATIO NELSON

(1758–1805)

Britain's most celebrated seaman was not only a master tactician but a great leader. Officers and men alike trusted and revered him, indeed the common seamen were his "band of brothers." It is perhaps not too much to say that the British sailor and all that he stands for is as much a memorial to Nelson as his victories at the Nile, Copenhagen and Trafalgar. The man who smashed Napoleon by sea, whose courage and genius have become legendary, was indeed worthy of the sentiment that has made him the greatest of his country's heroes.

"WHAT has poor little Horatio done, who is so weak, that above all the rest he should be sent to rough it at sea? But let him come, and the first time we go into action a cannon ball may knock off his head and so provide for him."

Encouraging words! And they launched the career of England's greatest hero of the sea. Yet Captain Maurice Suckling, Nelson's uncle, who accepted the young Horatio as a midshipman on his own "sixty-four" with those words, could hardly have been expected to recognize a future hero in the pale, puny weakling of a twelve-year-old boy. But the spirit was mightier than the body, and, fortunately for England, that cannon ball did not strike.

Horatio Nelson was the sixth of a family of eleven: he was, as were many of his brothers and sisters, a sickly child. His father was a country parson, his mother was of gentle birth: they were poor. Horatio was born in September, 1758, at Burnham Thorpe, Norfolk. Nine years later his mother died, and at the age of twelve he joined the Navy at a time when brutality, drunkenness, mutiny, flogging and killing were the chief amusements of life at sea.

The stature of Nelson may be gauged, like that of the heroes of ancient mythology, by the number of stories and legends that have grown about him. They start early in his life. There is the classic rebuke to his grandmother, "Fear never came near me." That story is probably pure legend, for it conveys nothing of the true Nelson, who succeeded in overcoming fear as he overcame his bodily weakness, by determination. But there is another picture of the young Nelson which reflects the truth.

He was going to school with his brother William. It was snowing heavily and travelling was dangerous in the roadless wilds of eighteenth-century Norfolk. Their way was a narrow track across a quagmire. William and Horatio set out doubtfully into the snow. They were told to try and get to school, but to turn back if the way became dangerous, and they were put on their honour not to turn back without good reason. When they came to the deep drifts of snow which made the going difficult and not without danger, William saw reason to turn back. But Horatio refused. "We must go on," he said. "Remember, it was left to our honour."

Nelson went to school at North Walsham and was instructed under a stern disciplinarian named "Classic Jones." Classic Jones grew fine pears in his garden, which young Nelson stole and gave to his friends. "I only took them," he remarked, "because every other boy was afraid."

In those two remarks you may find the secrets of Nelson's success.

Nelson's first ship was the *Raisonnable,* but she was paid off soon after he joined her. Captain Suckling was then given the command of the *Triumph* and Nelson followed him to that ship. In order to teach the lad practical seamanship, his uncle sent him on a merchant vessel on a voyage to the West Indies. Soon after his return he was transferred to the *Carcass,* which was about to make an expedition to the Arctic. On this expedition the young sailor gave more proof of his personal courage; for while his ship was jammed in the pack ice, he slipped overboard in the night and made his way across the ice in the hope of shooting a bear.

When Nelson returned from the Arctic, his energy and thirst for adventure were keener than ever. He managed to get appointed to the frigate *Seahorse,* which was proceeding to the East Indies, but after two years his health broke down and he was invalided home. Ill-health bred depression. Nelson became thoroughly dejected. He foresaw failure in his career. And then:—

"A sudden glow of patriotism was kindled within me and presented my king and country as my patron. 'Well, then,' I exclaimed, 'I will be a hero, and confiding in Providence, I will brave every danger.'"

Nelson was favoured in early life by one external circumstance—family influence at the Admiralty. It had procured him service, voyages and initial experience. In 1777 he was made lieutenant, and two years later was promoted to captain. At that time he was in the

West Indies on service against the revolting American colonists and their allies, and it was thought worthy of remark that this young captain was more concerned with honour than with prize money. Fever again laid him low and he was invalided home. Soon, however, he was back at sea. He sailed to Quebec, fell in love with a girl there, and nearly left the service. Then again to the West Indies, where Admiral Hood presented him to the future King William IV as an expert on tactics. Yet he was only twenty-four, and had never been in a fleet action!

Nelson's next triumph was one of moral courage. He insisted on enforcing the Navigation Laws and Admiralty Regulations in the West Indies, in spite of the opposition of a lazy and inefficient admiral and the hostility of the governor and the people. It was a bitter struggle, but Nelson won.

In 1787, while still on the West Indian station, he married Frances Nisbet, a widow. He seems to have been attached to her, to have esteemed and respected her; it is doubtful whether he really loved her.

And now the Nelson saga really starts. In 1793 came the war with France. Nelson was appointed to the command of the *Agamemnon,* a "sixty-four," and sailed for the Mediterranean under Hood. After the surrender of Toulon, the *Agamemnon* was sent to Naples to fetch Neapolitan troops, and there he first met Lady Hamilton, the wife of the British ambassador.

There were skirmishes and land actions in Corsica during the next year, and in one of these, at Calvi, Nelson was wounded and lost the sight of his right eye.

In 1797 he was with Jervis at the Battle of Cape St. Vincent, and by his initiative and daring was largely responsible for the crushing defeat of the Spaniards.

His promotion came automatically now, according to seniority. As a rear-admiral he was sent to the Canaries, and he made an unsuccessful attack on Santa Cruz. This action was his only failure, and it cost him the loss of his right arm.

Then he was sent back to the Mediterranean, to find and chase the French fleet. And find them at length he did in Aboukir Bay, where, on August 1, 1798, he fought the Battle of the Nile, a triumph of skill and a glorious victory.

Nelson found that the French were prepared only for an attack from the seaward side, so he manœuvred his ships between them and the shore, and trapped them so thoroughly that only two frigates escaped.

The victory of the Nile was a smashing blow at the power of

Napoleon. England rejoiced. Nelson was made a baron, and every court in Europe bestowed awards and decorations upon him.

After the Nile, Nelson sailed to Naples. The whole city was waiting to greet him. A procession of boats came out to meet his battered ship, headed by the King of Naples in his barge. After him came Sir William and Lady Hamilton, with a band playing "Rule Britannia." Lady Hamilton climbed to the quarter-deck to see the man she had met five years before. In the place of the slim, young captain, stood a feeble, pale wreck, one eye blinded, one arm hacked off, a fresh wound healing on his forehead: a man aged and worn by the stress of grim fighting.

"Oh God, is it possible!" she cried, and fell in a faint.

But they had met again, Nelson and the woman who was to be the only love of his life.

Emma, Lady Hamilton, was a remarkable woman. She started life as a servant girl, but her beauty attracted men. She was seduced by a naval officer and abandoned, but after some adventures became the mistress of Charles Greville, son of Lord Warwick. Her beauty attracted Romney, who painted her, and her charm fascinated all who met her. And then Greville, whom she loved, sold her to his uncle, Sir William Hamilton. The old man treated her well, educated her, brought her out, and married her. She became an intimate friend of the Queen of Naples. And Nelson fell in love with her.

He had seen little of his wife since their marriage, and there had been nothing in their courtship to suggest passion. But now Nelson knew passion. He became Lady Hamilton's lover and lived with her in Sir William's household. Despite the irregularity of the association, and of the situation, Nelson seemed to be unconscious of any wrong. He regarded Lady Hamilton as his wife in his own eyes and "in the sight of God."

While Nelson was away in Leghorn, the French, assisted by the rebellious Neapolitan Jacobins, captured Naples. Ruffo, the leader of the royal forces, had agreed to a capitulation by the rebels, but Nelson, returning in 1799, would have none of it. He demanded the surrender of all the Jacobins, court-martialled and hanged Caracciolo, who had deserted from the Neapolitan navy, and by firm measures restored the civil power and order in the kingdom of Naples. For his services he was made Duke of Bronte, in Sicily.

In 1800 Nelson returned home to England. He travelled with the Hamiltons, but in England he went to live with his wife. They soon parted, and from that time until his death Nelson was under the domination of his Emma. There was, of course, scandal, but it was an age of scandals; and in the eyes of the people of England Nelson could do no wrong.

In 1801 Lady Hamilton bore Nelson a daughter, who was named Horatia after him. In the same year he settled her, and her husband, in Merton Place, but the third member of the household, Sir William —he shared the expenses with Nelson—died in 1802.

Lord Minto gives a picture of life at Merton:—

"I went to Lord Nelson's on Saturday to dinner. The whole establishment and way of life are such as to make me angry as well as melancholy, but I cannot alter it, and I do not think myself obliged or at liberty to quarrel with him for his weakness, though nothing shall ever induce me to give the smallest countenance to Lady Hamilton. She looks ultimately to the chance of marriage, as Sir William will not be long in the way, and she probably indulges a hope that she may survive Lady Nelson; in the meanwhile she and Sir William and the whole set of them are living with him at his expense. She is in high looks but more immense than ever. The love she makes to Nelson is not only ridiculous, but disgusting; not only the rooms but the whole house, staircase and all, are covered with nothing but pictures of her and him, of all sizes and sorts, representations of his naval actions, coats-of-arms, pieces of plate in his honour, the flagstaff of *L'Orient,* etc, an excess of vanity which counteracts its own purpose."

Yet Nelson, on the night he left Merton for the last time, on his way to Portsmouth and Trafalgar, wrote in his private diary:—

"At half past ten drove away from dear, dear Merton, where I left all which I hold dear in this world, to go to serve my king and country." And he concludes the entry with a prayer: ". . . relying that He will protect those so dear to me that I may leave behind. His will be done. Amen, Amen, Amen."

In 1801 came the Baltic expedition. Denmark, Sweden and Russia were arming in a League of Neutrality against Britain who, in the prosecution of the French war, interfered with their trade. Sir Hyde Parker was sent out to dissolve this league, and Nelson was under him. It led to the famous Battle of Copenhagen.

The fight with the Danish fleet was furious. The Danes fought stubbornly and well, the British vessels were raked with shot. Nelson stood calmly on the quarter-deck, inspiring his men by his courage in the face of death. Then Parker flew the signal to withdraw. Nelson ordered that the signal should not be repeated to his squadron, but asked, "Is No. 16 (Engage the enemy more closely) still hoisted?" and ordered it to be kept flying. "Leave off action, damn me if I do," he said, and, turning to Captain Foley, went on, "You know, Foley, I have only one eye. I have a right to be blind sometimes." Then he raised his telescope to his blind eye and said, "I really do not see the signal."

Thanks to Nelson's heroism and determination, the Danes were defeated, and Nelson added another to the list of victories inspired by him.

Now he had a short rest at home; a little peace. There is time to take stock of him. The frail boy had become an admiral; he had served in the hard school of experience, and had come out on top; but he had not been hardened. He was still warm and generous. Sailors were pleased to serve under him: he never forgot the hardships of middies; he inspired his junior officers. He never forgot his friends, never omitted to do a kindness, if he had the opportunity. And, above all, he was inspired by a glowing patriotism, an unfailing determination to give of his best for England, and he supported that inspiration with a fund of moral and physical courage which has been unsurpassed in any man.

In 1803 the country once more called on Nelson. He was given the Mediterranean command. He hoisted his flag on the *Victory* at Portsmouth on May 18, and set out on his last campaign to undying glory.

He blockaded Toulon from 1803 to 1805, and then Villeneuve, the French admiral, gave him the slip. Nelson gave chase to the West Indies and back, and at last the two fleets met in battle off Cape Trafalgar.

Before the battle Nelson had drawn up his famous Memorandum, which contained his plan of action. He was determined to engage the enemy in two lines. The stronger, under Collingwood, was to attack the enemy's rear, while Nelson, with the other line, would prevent the van from going to assistance.

The action took place on October 21, 1805. As the two British lines sailed into battle, Nelson conceived the last and greatest of the "Nelson touches." He hoisted the signal, "England expects that every man will do his duty." A tremendous burst of cheering rang through the fleet, and the British went on to victory.

Collingwood played his part well. He set up an attack on the French and Spanish fleets' rear and went into action so that he could give them the benefit of our broadsides. Meanwhile, Nelson in the *Victory* went straight for the head of the enemy's line. Villeneuve, the French admiral, was puzzled and forced to wait for Nelson to declare his intentions. Nelson appeared as if he were going to sail across the head of the French van, and to prevent this they drew away from the rear that Collingwood was already engaging. Then Nelson turned down along the French line until he found a gap. The *Victory* went through, and dealt out heavy damage to the two French vessels on each side. Nelson's line now followed his example, cutting through the gaps and engaging. By this means the French van was left out of the action, and by the time they had come round to help, Nelson had turned his inferior numbers to advantage, for his twelve ships had cut off and overwhelmed seven of the enemy before the others could come to the rescue. Meanwhile, Collingwood had nobly carried out his part. The battle was a triumph. Twenty of the enemy's ships were captured or sunk, and 12,000 prisoners were taken, yet Nelson had gone into action with only twenty-six ships against the thirty-three of the enemy.

The triumph of Trafalgar was the greatest naval victory in British history. That of the Nile was more smashing, but there the French were in a confined position. At Trafalgar they were in the open sea, with a friendly port behind them. By his daring plan, a mixture of unorthodoxy and traditional warfare, Nelson had prevented the French from slipping out of his clutches and had utterly routed Napoleon's sea power.

The flagship *Victory* was in the thickest of the fight. Nelson himself was shot in the hour of triumph. A bullet fired from the mizzen-top of the *Redoubtable* laid him low. He was carried down to the cockpit, and the surgeon hurried to him. But Nelson knew that it was his last hour.

"I am gone," he said. "I have to leave Lady Hamilton and my daughter Horatia as a legacy to my country."

While he lay dying the battle raged on. Nelson was told that twelve of the enemy's ships had struck their colours. Again and again he exclaimed, "God be praised, I have done my duty."

Captain Hardy came down and told him that fifteen ships had struck. "That is well, but I bargained for twenty," answered Nelson.

He was sinking fast.

"Don't throw me overboard, Hardy," he moaned. "Take care of my dear Lady Hamilton, Hardy; take care of poor Lady Hamilton. Kiss me, Hardy."

The captain kissed him, and Nelson was heard to murmur, "Now I am satisfied. Thank God I have done my duty."

He murmured some prayers with Dr. Scott, referred again to Lady Hamilton and Horatia. He died with his creed on his lips. He breathed out his soul with the words, "God and my country."

NAPOLEON BONAPARTE

(1769–1821)

Perhaps no man captured the imagination of his own and following times as did Napoleon Bonaparte. The little corporal, who by his force of personality, clear thinking, military genius, and dominating ambition, made himself Emperor of France and defied the united forces of the Powers of Europe, must always dazzle us. But the glamour and success of his campaigns have obscured the more worthy and lasting products of his genius as a ruler and lawgiver.

"SOLDIERS, you are ill-fed and almost naked. The Government owes you much but can do nothing for you. Your patience, your courage do you honour, but bring you neither advantage nor glory. I am about to lead you into the most fruitful plains in the world. Rich provinces, great cities will be in your power. There you will find honour, and fame, and wealth. Soldiers of the Army of Italy, will you be found wanting in courage?" With these words addressed to a ragged and half-starved French army of which he had just taken command, Napoleon Bonaparte, the son of a happy-go-lucky Corsican lawyer, raised the curtain on a drama which has held mankind spellbound for more than a century.

"*Sauve qui peut. . . .*" "Save yourself who can," the cry that rose as he fled from Waterloo, rang down the curtain. The play was over. Critics and others have been discussing and analysing it ever since.

In the crowded years in which he was the principal actor on the stage of history, Napoleon won brilliant victories and met with terrible reverses. But always, in victory or defeat, his was the dominating figure. It is unfortunate that his overmastering genius as a warrior so dazzled his contemporaries and successors that his genius as a thinker, a statesman and an educationist has been underestimated. Yet he was a ruler as well as a general, and while his military career ended in disaster, much of his work as an administrator endures to this day.

When, in 1796, General Bonaparte launched his campaign against the Austrians in Italy he was twenty-seven. His rise had been meteoric. Born at Ajaccio, the capital of Corsica, in 1769, he received a military education as a humble pensioner of the King of France, and by 1792 was a captain of artillery. His republican sympathies and his brilliance in his first fight with the English at the siege of Toulon in 1793, the year in which his royal patron was guillotined, won him rapid promotion. Within three years he had been given his command as general. And so now he was the head of an army, or rather the remains of an army which had achieved nothing, young, ardent, ambitious and passionately in love. On the eve of his departure from Paris he had married the charming Creole widow, Josephine de Beauharnais, whose first husband had perished during the Reign of Terror. In the midst of the brilliant victories which he won with his tattered heroes at Montenotte and Lodi, Arcola and Rivoli, battles which established his fame, he wrote burning letters to his capricious bride. "Away from thee there is no more joy. . . You have robbed me of more than my soul; you are the one thought of my life. . . . I feel passion strangling me." In after years, an exiled prisoner on the lonely rock of St. Helena, he spoke of Josephine as the only woman with whom he had ever been in love —a little.

But the lover was swiftly transformed to the man of action. Lodi had fired "the spark of great ambition." Napoleon returned from his Italian triumphs to launch new schemes of conquest. He would conquer Egypt, turn the British out of India, and crush the power of Turkey on his way back. His Egyptian expedition of 1797–98, a daring but reckless enterprise, was defeated by the English fleet. It was a fatal weakness of Napoleon that he always underestimated the strength of England and the importance of sea power. His victories in Egypt were nullified by Nelson's destruction of the French fleet in Aboukir Bay—the Battle of the Nile—and after an unsuccessful siege of Acre, "the key of Constantinople or of India" as he told a companion, Napoleon hastened back to France. It was a hazardous undertaking, but by great good fortune the two frigates which carried him and his officers escaped the vigilance of the British.

He arrived at an opportune moment. The currents of the Revolution needed direction. Anarchy threatened, and a second coalition had been formed by the enemies of France, whose armies had many able captains but lacked a master mind. Bonaparte, assisted by his grenadiers, seized the reins of civil power, became First Consul and made his home in the magnificent palace of the Tuileries. The little corporal found the quarters more to his liking than a certain cell he had once occupied on account of conduct regarded as suspicious. Not that there was time for ease, luxurious or otherwise. Crossing the Alps with an army of forty thousand to fifty thousand men, he launched a lightning stroke against the Austrians, who were making headway in Italy, and overthrew them in June, 1800, at Marengo.

It was a dramatic victory. Melas, the Austrian commander, attacked the French in force, drove them back, and retired from the field. But now arrived the cavalry division of Desaix. A decisive charge, in which Desaix was killed, routed the over-confident Austrians, and Bonaparte returned to Paris to be acclaimed as a conquering hero.

In this moment of triumph the man who is often regarded as the scourge of Europe paused to devote himself to the internal affairs of France. By the Treaty of Lunéville peace was restored to the Continent; the Treaty of Amiens secured a cessation of hostilities with England, and by the Concordat the Christian faith, which the Revolution had rejected, was re-established in the republic. With amazing energy Napoleon sought to revive social life and commerce, inaugurated public works, attended to a thousand and one administrative details, and, as though these exertions were not sufficient, set himself to the codification of French law and to planning far-reaching reforms in education and public services.

"The Code Napoléon," says Professor Holland Rose, "with the accompanying Codes of Civil and Criminal Procedure, Penal Law, and Commerce, presented a reasoned and harmonious body of statutes such as had not appeared since the days of Justinian. It did more. For the first time in human society the poor and unlettered had the chance of knowing what the laws were; for Napoleon brought to bear on legal phraseology his own habits of clear thinking, with the result that he who ran might read and understand nearly all the articles of the Code . . . an ideal not yet fully attained by any branch of the practical English race." This is indeed a notable tribute from so eminent an English historian. He strengthens it by adding: "Contrasted with the gloom and chaos pervading the laws and feudal customs of Germany and Italy, the Code appeared like a social gospel. Well might the emperor say at St. Helena that his glory consisted not in having won forty battles, but in the deliberations of the Council of State and in the Code Napoléon. None of his works bears so markedly the imprint of his forceful personality."

Bonaparte's interest in education and also his extraordinary power of concentration, are illustrated by an incident of one of his campaigns. On the eve of his great victory at Austerlitz, he detailed his plan of operations to his generals, and immediately turned aside to dictate a scheme for the organization of a girls' boarding school at St. Denis. The battle was won on the morrow. The school was conducted for many years on the lines laid down by Bonaparte in that brief hour before a day of conflict.

He inspired municipal and national developments for the benefit of the people of France. "I wish to do something both great and useful for Paris," he said, and while he ruled as first consul and as emperor the capital was enriched and beautified. He planned and constructed four bridges over the Seine, ordered the paving of many streets and brought about a much needed improvement in the water supply of the city. Under his rule there was an immense development of the canal system of the country. The construction and improvement of roads was another outstanding feature of his administration, though in this matter both military and civil interests were served. It is well to ponder these facts before we return to the consideration of his military career.

The curtain rises on the second act of the drama. The first consul, elected for life, plunged into the war with England which contributed so much to his ruin. From 1805 to 1814 he led the armies of France in a series of campaigns in which he displayed the supreme genius of the soldier, and hurried through blood-stained fields to St. Helena.

He became Emperor of the French in 1804, after the short-lived peace had been broken. England had retained Malta, the half-way house of the Mediterranean, because French troops had been kept in the Batavian Republic (Holland) and Switzerland, whose independence France had guaranteed. Napoleon's aggressive policy had alarmed the rulers of Europe, for he had annexed territory and established control in northern Italy. Again he had to face a European coalition backed by Britain with ships, money and men.

His plans for an invasion of England were wiped out by the victory of Nelson over a combined French and Spanish fleet at Trafalgar, in 1805. Napoleon broke up his camp at Boulogne, where immense preparations had been made for crossing to "perfidious Albion," and marched against England's allies, Austria and Russia. In this swift campaign the master of strategy was seen at his best. His forces out-marched and out-manœuvred their foes in such a manner that the Austrian commander, Mack, was compelled to surrender at Ulm with some seventy thousand men. The losses of Napoleon's army were insignificant. At Austerlitz, in 1805, the emperor faced the forces of Russia and the remnant of the Austrian army, and won a victory which caused William Pitt to say, "Roll up that map of Europe. It will not be wanted for ten years."

But Europe was in arms against the conqueror. Prussia mobilized for war, and paid for it dearly. Her armies were overwhelmed at Jena and Auerstädt in 1806, and Napoleon entered Berlin in triumph as he had entered Vienna. Next he defeated the stubborn Russians at Friedland, and concluded the Treaty of Tilsit, which reduced Prussia to the position of a conquered state. No detailed analysis of these campaigns is necessary in a brief sketch of Napoleon's life. Let us quote, rather, some of the great captain's epigrams on the art of war:

"Courage is like love: it feeds on hope.

"At the beginning of a campaign thought should be expended as to whether an advance should be made or not, but when once the offensive has been assumed it should be maintained to the last extremity.

"Men must be led by an iron hand in a velvet glove."

In that last saying the spirit of Italian dictatorship and diplomacy is crystallized. Napoleon was an Italian, despite his French citizenship. But he possessed, above all, the art of inspiring the confidence, the admiration, the burning love of his men. He possessed what, for want of a better term, we call a magnetic personality.

In the earlier days during the French Revolution, when he was in imminent danger of being sent from Antibes to Paris as a suspect friend of the Robespierres, who had just perished on the scaffold, two soldiers planned to kill his guards and carry him over the border to safety. These two soldiers afterwards became famous as Marshals Marmont and Junot. Describing the influence on him of the young Napoleon in those wild days of 1794, Marmont said: "He had so much future in his mind."

This faculty of inspiring the confidence of his men, added to his mastery of strategy and tactics, placed Napoleon in the forefront of the world's great captains, yet could not save him from disaster. After the Treaty of Tilsit, he set himself to use all Europe as a sword wherewith to smite England. The sword turned in his hand!

His fatal effort was his attack on Spain. He captured Madrid, then left his brother Joseph to rule as king, and Marshal Soult to drive the English army from Corunna, where Sir John Moore died a hero's death. But "the Spanish ulcer" was to eat away the military power of the despot in the south while his mightiest army floundered to ruin in the north.

In 1809, Austria collected her forces for another blow at the conquering Corsican. She was fighting "for liberty and nationality" under the leadership of her ablest general, the Archduke Charles, but Napoleon triumphed once more, though only after desperate and costly battles. His victory at Wagram was followed by his divorce of Josephine and his marriage with the Austrian Archduchess Marie Louise in March, 1810. The bride was in her eighteenth year, the bridegroom in his forty-first. Though a political marriage, it was not altogether without affection. Napoleon desired a son, and in March, 1811, amidst great rejoicings, the little King of Rome was born.

We come now to the last tragic act of the drama. In 1811, Napoleon was at the zenith of his power. So long as Russia remained his ally he was virtually master of Europe, though the grim and tenacious Wellington was maintaining a stubborn defensive in Portugal. But the "Continental System" by which Napoleon sought to close every European port against the goods of his relentless enemy, Britain, now began to break down. The Czar Alexander broke away from this economic bondage and thus brought about the fatal rupture which ended in the great invasion of Russia in 1812. As a result of that disastrous campaign the greatest army that had ever been led by a European general was engulfed in the land of snows. The flames that consumed Moscow set fire to the funeral pyre of Napoleon's insensate ambition.

The more cautious of his ministers frowned dubiously on the invasion project, but the emperor paid no heed. "He will ruin us all," Admiral Decrès confided to a friend, "many as we are, and everything will end in a frightful catastrophe." He had gathered together a mighty host, more than four hundred thousand strong, and he set forth resolved on the conquest of Russia. "The states of Europe," he said to Fouché, "must be melted into one nation, and Paris must be its capital." The Russian plan of campaign was to yield ground to the invaders, suffering them to plunge further and further into a deliberately wasted country with the object of exhausting their resources and energies. The snows of the coming winter, it was argued, would complete the discomfiture of the French. The one great battle of the invasion was fought at Borodino. It was a costly and inconclusive struggle, but the Russians were again forced to fall back, and Napoleon's troops marched on to Moscow.

Here a surprise awaited them. The home of a quarter of a million people was practically deserted, and the few Russians who remained were there for a sinister purpose. At midnight the soldiers were roused by the alarm of fire. This outbreak, which occurred near the emperor's quarters, was hurriedly quenched, but more and more fires followed, and it became evident that they were the result of a preconcerted plan. Supplies were falling short, and nearly four-fifths of the city had been laid in ruins by the flames. Napoleon waited for weeks, expecting Alexander to make overtures for peace. He did nothing of the kind. Reluctantly the emperor decided to retreat. He had left it too late. The French army, perpetually harassed by the pursuing Cossacks, was caught and crushed in the iron grip of winter, and it suffered heavily in the severely contested crossing of the Beresina. One hundred thousand emaciated scarecrows emerged from the Russian wilderness; three hundred thousand remained behind, a few as fugitives, some as prisoners, most as dead. It is said that the heroic Marshal Ney, ragged, dirty, bloodstained and disillusioned, staggered into the town hall of a border town, and, being asked who he was by the astonished mayor, gave the terrible reply, "I am the Grand Army!"

This ruinous campaign gave heart to the allies. It was followed by a revival of the coalition against Napoleon. Austria, Prussia and Sweden joined forces with the Russians. Overtures for peace were made, but the emperor would not listen. The French were defeated at Leipzig, the "Battle of the Nations," in 1813, and after the emperor had fought a series of brilliant but unavailing actions on the soil of France, the Allies entered Paris, and in the spring of 1814 Napoleon was forced to abdicate.

Napoleon slipped quietly away on the British cruiser *Undaunted,* and was installed as sovereign of Elba. This face-saving expedient, the substitution of dominion over a Mediterranean island, nineteen miles by six, instead of most of Europe, was due very largely to the chivalrous intervention of the Czar of Russia, who had played a large part in the emperor's downfall.

One day at the end of February, 1815, a swarthy, much-moustached fisherman left a tall-masted felucca and trudged uphill to Napoleon's palace. He carried lobsters to the ex-emperor's kitchen, but, having arrived there and deposited his basket, he suddenly disappeared. A valet was startled to find him in animated converse with his master in the study.

For a week there was bustle on Elba, fortunately without the damping audience of the Allied Commissioner, who had gone for a few days to the Italian mainland. The island kingdom boasted a tiny fleet. Its brig was disguised to look like an English warship. Carriages, plate and bullion were stowed aboard. The veterans polished their arms and accepted a new issue of shoes. On the night of February 26, the brig *Inconstant* and six smaller vessels set sail for France, with Corsica's hills to port and Italy's to starboard. A thousand men devoted to one leader had set forth to win back an empire.

On the afternoon of the third day after they left their island they saw the peaks of the Maritime Alps draw closer and closer. Napoleon came on deck in his emperor's dress. A scarlet flag was cut into tiny pieces and a liberal investiture with the Legion of Honour took place there and then. Off the fishing village of Golfe Juan, not two leagues from teeming Juan les Pins of the *Côte d'Azur* of our time, the brig with her convoy cast anchor. Longboats took the invading army ashore; the men in greatcoats and bearskins, a few horses swimming behind them. The emperor had returned once more.

Meanwhile, news of his escape and enterprise was on its way to Paris. It was on its way to Vienna, too, where the repartition of Europe was still in progress. Men galloped all day with the alarm, but even so it took a week to reach the Congress and burst like a bomb among the assembled royalty and statesmen. Prince Metternich was the recipient of the dispatch. The Emperor of Austria, the King of Prussia and the Czar, Talleyrand of France and the Duke of Wellington, held a hasty council of war. It was of war that they spoke, although, for all they knew, Napoleon had no other troops than those he had brought with him. They must have thought that he could be certain of strong support, in spite of the past defeats and loss to his country, for instead of an expedition to capture a rebel it was war against all France that was immediately discussed. They would send their armies at once. Austrians, Russians, Germans, and British, more than seven hundred thousand men, were assembled, ready to move towards the French frontier. Thus began the famous Hundred Days that was to end on June 18 at Waterloo. A gamble that had nearly won.

"It has been a damned serious business," Wellington told Mr. Creevey on Monday morning, "the nearest-run thing you ever saw in your life!"

On Tuesday the news of the defeat came to Paris. Fouché, Napoleon's former Minister of Police, was not altogether surprised. He was ready and waiting for Napoleon to arrive, which he did at eight o'clock on Wednesday morning. The emperor was nearly dead with exhaustion and strain, but still indomitable. He had hardly limped from his carriage before he was talking of raising more men, more armaments. That fool Ney had spoilt things by his useless cavalry charge. He met his council at ten and suggested placing eighty thousand men to stop the Allies at Laon before they could get to Paris.

The Chamber had been convened. Fouché played his part. Word presently came to Napoleon that now the Chamber, and no longer himself, was in charge of France's destiny. Davout, the Minister of War, declared no action could be taken without the people's consent, and the people had had enough of fighting. Napoleon gave in. He offered to abdicate. He was weary to death, and he could do nothing now unless he called on his own following and began a civil war.

Next day they asked for a formal abdication in favour of his son. The allied armies in a vast crescent were on their way. At one o'clock on June 22, Napoleon ceased to be emperor. It was expedient, and he saw also the immediate necessity of leaving France. Blücher's troopers might see fit to hang him if they caught him in Paris.

He went into retirement at Malmaison, the house where he had lived with his first empress, Josephine. There he stayed with his stepdaughter Hortense, hoping to be able to leave very soon for America. But no ship was put at his disposal. He had no powers. Only on June 29 was he given formal permission to depart by Fouché. One more wild moment there was, when he heard a marching roar, "*Vive l'Empereur!*" He sprang to his feet and swore that the Prussians should never overrun his France.

Fouché, however, was adamant. Napoleon must go, or France would receive short shrift from the advancing Allies. The glorious, tremendous Hundred Days were ended. The little man who had been emperor departed from Paris, first of all to Rochefort, while his fate was decided finally by his conquerors. This time they chose St. Helena for him, that desolate African island, whence they made it their business to see that he never returned.

For six years he lingered there, a caged eagle, before he died of cancer. He was then fifty-two.

It is unfortunate that the stormy splendour of Napoleon's campaigns has caused both admirers and detractors to regard him mainly as a great soldier—a dark angel of destruction. His greatest and most enduring achievements were, as he himself admitted, his constructive and administrative work as ruler and lawgiver. The Code Napoléon is a more impressive monument than any triumphal arch or statue of victory, and it may be more enduring.

ABRAHAM LINCOLN

(1809–1865)

That famous phrase " From log cabin to White House" sums up the career of Abraham Lincoln, but his true greatness lies not in the story of his rise, but in his work for his country and for humanity. By his firmness and his courageous determination he defeated the Secessionists and piloted the nation through the agony of a civil war. And in 1865 he carried the Thirteenth Amendment to the Constitution of the United States, by which he abolished slavery. The simple, sincere, country lawyer that was Abraham Lincoln was indeed worthy of the respect that America has given him as her national hero.

"I have done nothing to make any human being remember that I have lived. Yet what I wish to live for is to connect my name with the events of my day and generation, to link my name with something which will be of interest to my fellow men."

THUS wrote a young man whose thirty-two years of life had had more disappointments than joys, at a time when hope and ambition were beginning to revive after a fit of depression which had brought him even to the contemplation of suicide. No one could have had his wish more amply granted, for the writer, the son of a poor man, born in a log cabin, in turn woodman, flatboat-man, surveyor, village postmaster, legislator, country lawyer, member of Congress, and finally president, was Abraham Lincoln, the man whose story, read aright, is the epic of the United States of America, which owe to him today their existence as a nation of united states.

He was born on February 12, 1809, on the Big South Fork of Nolin Creek, three miles from Hodgensville, Hardin (now La Rue) County, Kentucky. Thomas Lincoln, his father, was a shiftless individual who worked as a carpenter when he could, and whose guiding principle in life seemed to be " faraway hills are greenest." When the boy Abraham was four years old, the family moved to Knob Creek, eleven miles further north, where the soil was rich and the woods were full of game. In 1816, Thomas Lincoln, still restless, abandoned his clearing and went to Indiana, where he staked a claim on Pigeon Creek, near Gentryville, Spencer County. For a year the family lived here in a " half-faced camp " of unhewn logs, floorless, enclosed on three sides only, the open front protected only by the pelts of the animals, the shooting of which the father preferred to his trade of carpentering. In course of time Thomas Lincoln built a cabin, but the life was hard, the region marshy, horses and cattle did not thrive and the human beings fell victims to malaria. Young Abe, already strong of frame, had to lend a hand both to his father out of doors and to his mother in the house.

Two years after their arrival, Abraham's mother fell ill of a mysterious disease called the " milk sick." The nearest doctor lived thirty-five miles away, and after a week, Mrs. Lincoln, thin and ill-nourished, and apparently lacking the will to live, died.

A year after her death the widower set out on a journey, and did not return until one evening in December, 1819, when he drove up to his cabin in a four-horse wagon, laden with boxes and baskets, " a walnut bureau valued at fifty dollars," a wardrobe, and real beds —the first that young Abe and his sister Sarah had ever seen. Three children were peeping out from under the wagon cover, and there stepped to the ground a strong, bright-looking, talkative woman with curly hair and a friendly face. It was the new stepmother, Sarah Bush Johnson, a widow, and former sweetheart of Tom Lincoln. With her were her three children, John, Sarah, and Matilda.

A new life began. Thomas Lincoln's second wife had what the first had lacked, robust health and energy, and soon Tom Lincoln had laid a new floor, doors were mended, and the chinks between the logs filled in with clay. Until the arrival of his stepmother, young Abe had had little or no chance to learn anything of books. His father disapproved of them, but the new Mrs. Lincoln insisted that all the children should go to school. Between her and her young stepson there grew a love which lasted all his life. She declared that he was the best son woman ever had.

Abe went to school by fits and starts, hardly a year in all, but he learned to read and write, and to cipher " to the rule of three." He knew enough to correct the spelling and pronunciation of the family name, which was known as Linkern or Linkhorn.

From this time onward he read everything that came his way. At nineteen he had grown to be an ungainly figure strong enough to " lift and bear a pair of logs." He was " six feet two inches tall, weighing one hundred and fifty pounds—with long arms and legs, a slender body and small head." His father's description of him was: "He looked as if he had been rough-hewn with an axe and needed smoothing with a jackplane." He became known in the neighbourhood as an eccentric, but the country people listened to him willingly as he talked, for he was of a humorous turn, and as a mimic of the local preachers and stump orators he had no equal.

In 1828 he was offered his first chance to see something of the outside world when he was hired to take a flatboat of farm produce to New Orleans. Here for the first time he saw slavery in operation.

The turning-point in his existence came when he was again hired to take a boat load of produce to New Orleans. This time he stayed there a month, and he had more opportunity to study the conditions of the negro slaves. He vowed then that if ever the chance came his way he would hit slavery, and "hit it hard."

On his return, Offutt, the owner of the produce he had sold, engaged him as manager of a store he intended to open in New Salem. Here he occupied himself, while the store was being built, as clerk of the polls at an election, thus being introduced into local politics. As store manager Lincoln, for the first time in his life, had real time for reading. The local inhabitants had probably never met with such a strange storekeeper. With a bolt of calico print for a pillow, he would lie full-length on the counter, book in hand, and roll off only when a rare customer came in.

Being the "scholar" of the district, he was naturally a participator in the local political debates, and James Rutledge, who kept the local tavern, suggested to him a career in politics. At Rutledge's house he met the daughter, Ann, a slim, good-looking girl with auburn hair, who was betrothed to a young New Yorker who called himself McNeil. Lincoln at once fell in love, but felt it impossible in the circumstances to declare himself.

His political ambitions were interrupted about this time by the Black Hawk War—the last Indian uprising in Illinois. Abraham was among the first to volunteer for service. He was elected captain of his company, "a success," he wrote later, "which gave me more pleasure than any I have had since." But he saw no fighting, and returned to New Salem in July, 1832, to canvass the county as candidate for the Illinois legislature. He was defeated.

Meanwhile Offutt went bankrupt, and Lincoln, with a man named Berry, ventured in a store. This failed, for Berry drank the whisky he should have sold while Abraham was deep in books.

After a short term as postmaster of New Salem, when he carried the letters in his hat, and read all the newspapers before delivering them, Lincoln became assistant surveyor for the district. In 1834 he was again candidate for the legislature, and this time he was elected at the head of the poll. At the state capital the library was his only relaxation from his legislative duties.

It was while he was attending to these that it was learned that the pretty Ann Rutledge had been jilted by McNeil, whose real name was found to be McNamar. She sickened and died in 1834. Towards the end she sent for Lincoln, and at the last he was alone with her—the woman who was the first and greatest love of his life.

The capital of Illinois had meanwhile been moved to Springfield, and Lincoln decided to take up his abode there, having finished his law studies and been admitted to the bar. He arrived in Springfield with all his possessions in his saddle-bags.

By this time he had become engaged to a certain Mary Owens, who in size, according to Lincoln himself, "appeared a fair match for Falstaff," and in age was approaching the "old maid" stage. The engagement ended after Lincoln had made it clear to the lady that she could not look forward to a life of leisured ease as his wife.

He entered into partnership with his friend, John T. Stuart, but as both men were thinking more of politics than of law, the practice did not prosper. In 1838 he was again elected to the legislature, and once more in 1840.

During this period he met Stephen A. Douglas, who for a quarter of a century was to be his rival in politics, and was in those early days his rival in love as well, for both aspired to the hand of Mary Todd, a Kentucky girl and a member of the local aristocracy. It would be crediting her with more perspicacity than she apparently possessed to say that she saw in the plebeian, ill-clad, lanky lawyer a future President of the United States, but, whatever the reason, she chose him in preference to the dashing, brilliant Douglas. She was a buxom type, vivacious when speaking, but with a hard expression when silent, and she was vain in a degree which many years later was to bring her almost to the verge of insanity.

The course of the engagement was not to run smoothly. Mary Todd was snobbish, domineering, and madly jealous. Quarrels were an everyday occurrence. The date of the marriage was, however, fixed. Lincoln did not turn up. After this came the illness during which Lincoln contemplated suicide. Shortly after his recovery, Mary Todd and he came together again, and in spite of the misgivings which still beset him they were married on November 4, 1842.

The following year Lincoln formed a law partnership with William H. Herndon, later his biographer, which endured until his death, in spite of the antipathy shown on every possible occasion by Mrs. Lincoln. She was determined that her husband should not stagnate in Springfield, and she pushed him forward towards the higher goal of Congress. In 1846 he was nominated, and went to Washington in 1847 to take his seat.

He had not been long there before he became known as "the champion story-teller of the Capitol," but he took his mission seriously none the less. The question of slavery was ever at the back of his mind, and during the second session he introduced a bill for the abolition of slavery in the District of Columbia. It was rejected, and Lincoln returned to Springfield a disappointed and disillusioned man. At the end of the term he was not re-nominated. He resumed his law practice, and was daily to be seen dressed in black wearing a high hat into which most of his legal documents were stuffed, with one of his children usually tugging at his coat tails.

He became famous on the Illinois circuit, and was employed on the most notable cases of the time. He was losing his interest in politics when, in 1854, the question of slavery aroused him again. "This nation," he declared, "cannot exist half slave and half free." Douglas, his former rival in love, now a Senator, was the principal object of his attack. That autumn Lincoln was elected to the legislature against his will, but he resigned and became candidate for the United States Senate. He was defeated.

Then came years of fighting. The question of the secession from the Union of the southern slave-owning states was becoming acute. Senator Douglas was now the leader of the Democrat Party, and Lincoln, whose antipathy towards him was personal as well as political, conducted a vigorous campaign against him. The Republican Party sprang into being within a year, and in 1858 the Illinois members of it met, and declared that "Hon. Abraham Lincoln is our first and only choice for United States Senator." It was, however, not yet to be. Senator Douglas was re-elected.

Lincoln was disappointed, but he could joke about it. He felt "like the boy who stumped his toe—it hurt too bad to laugh and he was too big to cry." He was not, however, to disappear from view. An address he gave in New York gained for him a national reputation. People were beginning to ask who was this uncouth Western lawyer who could so sway his audiences.

The National Convention of the Republican Party met in Chicago in May, 1860, and nominated him as candidate for the presidency. When the news came to him he was in Springfield playing a game of handball. He looked at the telegram a moment, and said: "I reckon there's a little short woman down on Eighth

Street who will be glad to hear this news." He ran off to tell her —one of the few really happy homecomings of their married life!

When he had written the formal acceptance of the nomination, he who had drafted thousands of letters and legal documents took it to the superintendent of education "to see if it was all right."

"I wouldn't like to have any mistakes in it," he declared.

The other looked at it. He had one change to suggest.

"You have," he said, "written, 'it shall be my care to not violate it or disregard it in any part'; you should have written 'not to violate.' Never split an infinitive is the rule."

Lincoln looked at the phrase for a moment with a puzzled air.

"So you think I better put those two little fellows end to end?" he said, and made the alteration without more ado.

Between his nomination and the election in November, Lincoln remained in Springfield. The Democrat Press attacks on him were savage. He was a "third-rate country lawyer," "a nullity," "a maker of coarse and clumsy jokes," he "could not speak good grammar," he "sat in his shirt sleeves and tilted his chair," he was not a gentleman, and he resembled a gorilla!

During the campaign the hatred of the South for the North flared up. The slave-owning aristocrats despised the "greasy mechanics, filthy operatives, small-fisted farmers, and moon-struck theorists" of the northern states.

Lincoln was elected. Four days later the South began to fulfil its secession threats. The *Charleston Mercury* published the result of the election under the headline "Foreign News." South Carolina began by firing on the ship entering Charleston Harbour with supplies for the garrison of Fort Sumter.

In February, 1861, Lincoln went to Washington, and on March 4 his inauguration took place. The fear of assassination was already abroad, and the crowd was small. Lincoln, in new clothes, was embarrassed, and stood awkwardly holding in one hand his hat, and in the other his cane. Douglas, his old adversary, stepped forward, gracefully relieved him of them, and held them till the ceremony was over. Lincoln's address disavowed any intention to interfere with slavery, but was firm in its insistence on the inviolability of the Union.

On April 12, the South Carolinians bombarded Fort Sumter, where the garrison was at the end of its rations, and the Civil War had begun. Lincoln, who, in spite of his hatred of slavery, would not have sacrificed a single life for its abolition, felt obliged to call for men to defend the integrity of the Union. The effect of the fall of Fort Sumter was immediate. The South had been the aggressors. The North rose as one man.

Lincoln, sad at heart, worked hard to prevent the secession of other states, watched over events, consulted with officers, encouraged the men; while Mary, his wife, furious that the war prevented her from giving full scope to her vain social aspirations as "first lady of the land," nagged and sulked by turns.

The defeat of the Northern troops at Bull Run was a terrible blow to Lincoln, but it sobered and steadied the North, which had been inclined to take the war with less seriousness than it merited. As president, Lincoln was commander-in-chief of the armies, but he soon found that the professional generals were more difficult to deal with than children—all except one, Ulysses S. Grant, whose idea of a soldier's duty was that he should fight. Others urged Lincoln to remove Grant. "He fights," Lincoln protested. "He drinks," they said. "Do you know what brand of whisky?" he asked. "I'd like to send a barrel to each of my other generals."

Lincoln's difficulties were increased at this time by a diplomatic incident which might well have caused war with England. On November 8, 1861, the warship *San Jacinto* stopped the Royal Mail Packet *Trent* on the high seas by a shot across her bows, and took from her Mason and Slidell, commissioners of the Confederates, who were on their way to Europe. Lord Palmerston demanded their surrender and an apology. In the teeth of inflamed public opinion, Lincoln complied, and war was averted.

In Washington, Lincoln was having trouble with members of his Cabinet, some of whom were under the delusion that they could "run him," and they had to be taught that he was master. Amid all his public troubles, his private affairs were a source of trial. His wife was for ever making scenes both in public and in private. His sons, Willie and Tad, were ill with typhoid, and the death of Willie almost prostrated him.

While ostensibly the war was being fought for the maintenance of the Union, everybody knew that the slavery question was at the bottom of it. Even among Lincoln's advisers there was no unanimity on the matter, though public opinion was growing in favour of abolition. The president at first suggested gradual emancipation of slaves, but finally he signed a proclamation of complete emancipation.

Lincoln's term of office was drawing to a close, but he was nominated again and re-elected. His famous inaugural speech, which ranks with his other speech at the dedication of the burial ground at Gettysburg as a superb piece of oratory, was that of a man tired of the fraticidal war which seemed to have no end, but it was full of his conviction of a Divine Purpose in all things—even in the continuance of bloodshed.

For yet a year the fight was to go on. Longing for peace, Lincoln, nevertheless, was firm. "The war," he said in his message to Congress, "will cease on the part of the Government whenever it shall have ceased on the part of those who began it." Meanwhile, in 1865, he succeeded in having passed the Thirteenth Amendment to the Constitution of the United States, which ended slavery for ever.

Lincoln had met Confederate peace delegates at Hampton Roads, but he would make no agreement with people in arms against the State. At last the end came. General Lee surrendered. "Let them down easy!" Lincoln instructed his generals.

The Union flag was raised again over Fort Sumter, and on April 14 its guns thundered once more, but this time the charges were blank. Washington was *en fête*. Lincoln sat at his desk in the White House. In front of him was a picture of General Lee. He studied it. "It is a good face," he said then, "the face of a noble, brave man. I am glad the war is over at last."

Mrs. Lincoln, delighted to be free from the restrictions of war time, had arranged a theatre party for that evening. They were to go to Ford's Theatre to see Laura Keene play in *Our American Cousin,* and everything was made ready for a gala performance. Lincoln had been warned to be on his guard, but he only smiled. Who would wish to kill him, now that an era of peace had been inaugurated?

Let us watch the scene.

The play has already begun, when the president's party enters the theatre. The acting is interrupted by a mighty cheer which greets the careworn father of his country. Lincoln bows, and sits down in his stage box. The play is resumed. Does he listen to what the actors are saying? Who knows? Two hours pass. It is nearly ten o'clock. Softly a figure nears the door of the box, produces a card, and tells the attendant that he bears important news. He is admitted. There, close to the door, sits the president, beside him his wife, and to the right a young army major and his bride. Before anyone has time to turn round, the visitor puts a pistol to Lincoln's ear and pulls the trigger. He sees the major springing at him, but he has a dagger, and uses it. Then, with a leap, he is over the parapet of the box and on the stage. A woman's voice screams: "He has shot the president!"

The man brandishes his dagger, as he has often done before on that stage, and cries theatrically: "*Sic semper tyrannis!*" Then, brushing the frightened actors aside, he disappears.

Lincoln is taken to a house opposite the theatre, but he never recovers consciousness, and at seven o'clock on the following morning, Stanton, the Secretary of War, stands erect as if in salute. "Now he belongs to the ages," he says.

The murderer, one John Wilkes Booth, an actor and a fanatic in the Southern cause, had had a horse waiting for him outside the stage door, and had ridden off to Maryland. But long before the wonderful funeral procession from Washington to Springfield had ended, he was run to earth in a barn and shot down amid the flames which consumed his hiding place.

Lincoln's character and ideals are well expressed in the following tribute by his close friend and associate, John C. Nicolay:

"The Declaration of Independence was his political chart and inspiration. He acknowledged a universal equality of human rights. He had unchanging faith in self-government. Yielding and accommodating in non-essentials, he was inflexibly firm in principle or position deliberately taken. 'Let us have faith that right makes might,' he said, 'and in that faith let us to the end dare to do our duty as we understand it.' Benevolence and forgiveness were the very basis of his character; his world-wide humanity is aptly embodied in a phrase of his second inaugural: 'With malice toward none, with charity for all.' His nature was deeply religious, but he belonged to no denomination; he had faith in the eternal justice and boundless mercy of Providence, and made the golden rule of Christ his practical creed. History must accord him a rare sagacity in guiding a great people through the perils of a mighty revolution, and admirable singleness of aim, a skilful discernment, and courageous seizure of the golden moment to free his nation from the incubus of slavery, faithful adherence to law, and conscientious moderation in the use of power, a shining personal example of honesty and purity, and finally the possession of that subtle and indefinable magnetism by which he subordinated and directed dangerously disturbed and perverted moral and political forces to the restoration of peace and constitutional authority to his country, and the gift of liberty to four millions of human beings. Architect of his own fortunes, rising with every opportunity, mastering every emergency, fulfilling every duty, he not only proved himself preeminently the man of the hour, but the signal benefactor of posterity. As statesman, ruler, and liberator, civilization will hold his name in perpetual honour."

BENJAMIN DISRAELI

(1804–1881)

A new star to blaze in the firmament of British politics, Disraeli was received coldly by the English country gentlemen of whom he wished to become one. Time taught him wisdom—taught him that the strain of the Orient in him, even more than his Jewish blood, must keep him a man apart. Those very attributes which at first were stumbling blocks to him, proved to be powerful factors later in his rise to success. His astuteness, his opportunism, above all his sympathy for the East, which made him realize the vast potentialities there when other statesmen seemed blind, combined to make him one of the greatest men of the latter half of the nineteenth century.

THE House of Commons was in an uproar. Derisive shouts and bursts of laughter interrupted the Member who was trying to make himself heard. "I am not at all surprised, sir," said the speaker, "at the reception which I have received." Renewed guffaws followed this remark. "I have begun several times many things, and I have often succeeded at last. I will sit down now, but the time will come when you will hear me!" So ended the maiden speech of Benjamin Disraeli.

He was born at what is now 22 Theobald's Road, London, on December 21, 1804. His grandmother came of old Jewish families, proud of her traditions. His father, Isaac D'Israeli, as the name was then spelt, became a man of letters who played with the idea of many professions. He was until 1813 a strict member of the synagogue, but in that year he had a violent quarrel with the officials, with the result that both he and his family renounced the Jewish faith.

Benjamin, four years later, was baptized into the Church of England at St. Andrew's, Holborn. By such a curious chance was he enabled to follow his later career; for it was not until late in the nineteenth century that Jews and Catholics were allowed to take their seats in Parliament.

The Law, which had been selected as his profession, did not suit his romantic and flamboyant temperament, and he left it. A short experience in dabbling with stocks and shares proved that he had no genius for speculation. A short-lived attempt to found a daily paper called *The Representative* satisfied the publisher, if not Disraeli, that the latter was scarcely suited to the rough and tumble of journalism. The rolling stone having proved his disability in three directions, turned to literature, and was more successful.

His first book, *Vivian Grey,* published anonymously in 1826, became the talk of the town. The public discerned that a novelist of some magnitude had arrived. The author's philosophy of life is revealed in a single telling sentence: "Man is not the creature of circumstances. Circumstances are the creatures of men." That Disraeli was thinking in terms of himself when he wrote the following is obvious: "It was one of the first principles of Mr. Vivian Grey that everything was possible. Men did fail in life, to be sure, and, after all, very little was done by generality; but still all these failures and all this inefficiency might be traced to a want of physical and moral courage. Now Vivian Grey was conscious that there was at least one person in the world who was no craven either in body or mind, and so had long come to the comfortable conclusion that it was impossible that his career could be anything but the most brilliant."

With the proceeds of *The Young Duke,* Disraeli went on a tour of the Near East. The strain of Orientalism in him was strong. In everything but his religion, which he had not himself chosen, Disraeli was Hebrew and Oriental. During the journey, which included Constantinople, Egypt, Syria and Jerusalem, he collected experiences that later were to figure in his books and colour his life. They affected his foreign policy and his attitude to Britain's Eastern possessions, which of all the empire were nearest his heart.

His companion on this tour was William Meredith, who was engaged to his sister Sarah. Disraeli gave full vent to his passion for florid dress, for he wore "red cap, red slippers, broad blue-striped jacket and trousers," and he fitted his belt with a strange assortment of firearms and armoury generally. But his intelligence was keen and his powers of observation really remarkable. His letters home to his sister told of his experiences and adventures.

He attempted to get into the Mosque of Omar at Jerusalem which stands on the site of the Jewish temple. He was caught in a fanatical mob, and escaped with difficulty.

He had an interview with Mehemet Ali, the great pasha, when he was in Cairo, and discussed politics with this man who probably was the greatest authority on affairs in the Near East.

When he returned home, he had material for yet more novels;

but not only was he saddened by the death of William Meredith, but his book *Contarini Fleming* was not altogether a success.

Not altogether forswearing literature, Disraeli now decided on a political career. In this, his fifth attempt to find himself, his mode of address and exaggerated courtesy did him disservice. His clothes, in which Orientalism was aggravated by youthful foppishness, made him a laughing stock. Throughout his career he never quite gave up being theatrical. He once went to a party dressed in green velvet trousers and a black satin shirt. But in later life he realized the necessity for curbing this tendency, which exasperated rather than impressed Englishmen. In literary matters his sense of the dramatic and of his own importance was evident. Thus he prefaced his *Revolutionary Epick* with these words: " It was on the Plains of Troy that I first conceived the idea of the work." He goes on to refer to the *Iliad*, the *Æneid*, Dante and Milton, and adds: "And the spirit of my time, shall it be uncelebrated? . . . For me remains the Revolutionary Epick."

After several unsuccessful attempts to secure election, Disraeli was returned as Tory Member for Maidstone in 1837, only to be laughed down in his Parliamentary début. Yet he was not dismayed. He never for one moment doubted that he would shine in politics.

In 1840 he married. His wife was the widow of Wyndham Lewis, his fellow Member for Maidstone. She was middle-aged, had a house in Park Lane, and £4,000 a year. Between Disraeli and the lady of his choice there grew up a love and tenderness that nothing could shake. To him she was " the perfect wife," a solace in his hours of disappointment, and a spur to encourage him on the road to success. Thirty years later he avowed that she had never given him a dull moment.

He used to be fond of telling her in public that he had married her for her money, to which she would reply: "Ah, but if you had to do it again, you would do it for love." " Dizzy "—her pet name for him—always agreed.

Parliament soon began to notice the flamboyant newcomer, who had bought an estate at Hughenden in Buckinghamshire, and become a country gentleman. The House learned that his eloquence was not to be despised, and that his biting sarcasm was something to be feared. Peel squirmed when Disraeli called Conservatism " an organized hypocrisy " because of its attitude towards the Corn Laws.

The cautious conservatism of Peel was not to the taste of Disraeli. The latter disliked the new industrial magnates and middle classes who had come to power with the Reform Act of 1832, and was evolving a policy of "Altar, Throne and Cottage" that he wished the Conservative Party to follow. He wanted a strong monarchy—a fact to be remembered when considering his later relations with the queen—the Church strong as a social institution, and fair play for the labouring classes. The "Young England" Party, a coterie inside the Tory Party, of which Disraeli became the inspiring genius, inclined to a romantic feudalism, with the landed aristocracy, aided and abetted by the Church, as the main supports. To all intents and purposes this remained his political philosophy.

Although Disraeli was officially of Peel's party he was Peel's worst enemy politically. Frankly the two men did not agree. After his marriage to Mrs. Wyndham Lewis, Disraeli considered himself eligible socially and financially for higher rank. He wrote to Peel asking for a seat in the Government, and received in reply a curt refusal.

In 1844 and 1845 his political novels *Coningsby* and *Sybil* were published. Both dealt with the conditions of the agricultural and industrial workers, and did much to rouse the country to a realization of the evils of the day. They were, too, a reflection on Peel and his ministry. With the appearance of *Tancred,* in 1847, Disraeli bade farewell to novel writing for a quarter of a century, and devoted himself exclusively to politics.

In 1845 the agitation of the repeal of the Corn Laws was reaching its height. Peel was in a predicament. His party was pledged to maintain tariffs, yet he himself was increasingly convinced of the necessity of abolishing them.

Disraeli already saw the plight that Peel was in when he said of him that "he had caught the Whigs bathing and walked away with their clothes."

In the autumn of 1845, blight attacked the potato crop in Ireland and the situation was made doubly worse by the failure of the English harvest which suffered badly owing to incessant rain in the late summer. Peel, in order to get cheap food into the country, was forced to come forward as an out and out Free Trader.

It was Disraeli's chance! It was he who during the stormy debates in the House lashed Peel with his tongue. At one time in the debate, Peel flung into Disraeli's face the taunt that he had asked for office under him. Disraeli denied it flatly. His opposers have said that it was the lie direct, his supporters maintain that he honestly forgot.

Despite the opposition of Disraeli—and indeed most of Peel's one-time supporters, the Bill for the repeal of the Corn Laws was passed. But the same night Peel was defeated on another motion, and his Cabinet fell.

His golden opportunity came in 1852, when, on the death of Lord George Bentinck, he was chosen as leader of the party in the House of Commons, Lord Derby, his chief, being in the Lords. For years the Conservative Party had been disintegrating, and the repeal of the Corn Laws, which Disraeli had opposed whole-heartedly, was a staggering blow. The country gentry, the backbone of the Tories, had been bitterly opposed to this Free Trade measure, and the unity of the party had gone to pieces. Disraeli set himself to rebuild the party, and succeeded. The task was no easy one, since it was essential to wean the Tories from Protection to which, despite its unpopularity, they were bound both by tradition and interest. Guizot, the French statesman, remarked to Disraeli, "I think your being leader of the Tory Party is the greatest triumph that Liberalism has yet achieved."

Disraeli first held office in 1852, when he became Chancellor of the Exchequer in the second Derby government. Though the prospects of the ministry were poor, Disraeli felt "just like a girl going to her first ball." The House rejected Disraeli's Reform Bill, the event being made notable by the first real clash between Disraeli and Gladstone. Gladstone dealt the Government its death-blow in an impassioned speech that was a taste of things to come. For the next thirty years the two personalities mentioned were to fill the political stage. In Disraeli's private correspondence, A.V. (arch-villain) identified Gladstone.

In 1866 Disraeli became Chancellor of the Exchequer in Lord Derby's third government. A year later he put through a Bill giving the franchise to all ratepayers. This was the famous Bill which "dished the Whigs" by outdoing even their reforms.

Not until 1868, when Lord Derby resigned, did Disraeli realize his life's ambition and become Prime Minister. He had, to use his own expression, "climbed to the top of the greasy pole," but he did not stay there long, for he was defeated in the same year.

Disraeli's peculiar relations with the queen have been the subject of much writing. From the first Disraeli had always been popular with Victoria. Middle-aged and a widow, she still mourned the death of her beloved husband. The latter had been her mentor and guide, and in this respect Disraeli set himself to take his place.

Unquestionably he flattered her, often, as he admitted, "laying it on with a trowel." He referred to her as "the Faery" and "Gloriana," paid her courtly attention and succeeded in gaining an ascendancy over her mind. It is easy to condemn his attitude as one of deceitful self-seeking, but there was much more to it than that. The personality of the queen, both as a monarch and as a woman, appealed to him. His devotion was genuine. In addition, he was a fervent believer in the monarchy, and would have liked to increase the power of the Crown. He certainly succeeded in raising its prestige.

Disraeli would amuse the queen with anecdotes, though her sense of humour was not too evident. Describing a drive to her, he said: "We came upon a real feudal castle with a donjon keep high in the air. It turned out to be the new city prison in Camden Road, but it deserves a visit; I mean externally." The thread of irony which runs through life fascinated him. Of her opinion of Disraeli the queen made no secret. When he died she referred to his passing as a "national calamity."

In 1870 he published *Lothair,* which dealt mainly with the religious problems of the moment. Two years later he suffered the greatest blow of his life. His wife, who had been created Viscountess Beaconsfield in 1868, on her husband declining a peerage, died. For thirty-three years they had lived a life of delicate romance and tenderness, and Disraeli on her death said he felt "like a man without a home."

In 1874 he became Prime Minister again, but the strain of leading his party in the House of Commons was beginning to tell on him, and in 1876 he asked the queen for permission to retire to the Upper House. He was created Earl of Beaconsfield. In the same year, and at her own suggestion, Parliament proclaimed her Majesty as Empress of India.

He took his seat in the House of Lords, still as Prime Minister, on February 8, 1877. A friend asked him what he thought of the change. "Dead," he said, "dead—but in the Elysian fields."

But before the change of scene, Disraeli had accomplished his master-stroke, one that conferred lasting benefit on his country.

In 1875 he obtained for Great Britain control of the Suez Canal. The manner in which he did it was typical of the man—swift, colourful and dramatic—and, as Disraeli would himself have chosen, it was connected with the East. This is the story of it:

The Khedive of Egypt, Ismail Pasha, having accumulated in a comparatively short time a huge stock of debts, found himself faced with the necessity of selling his shares in the Suez Canal.

When Disraeli heard that the Khedive was negotiating privately with French financiers, he realized his opportunity and made a great stroke.

(*Above*) Horatio Nelson's death aboard the *Victory* at the hour of his defeat of the French at the battle of Trafalgar, 1805. Benjamin Disraeli (*below left*) is generally regarded as the founder of the modern Conservative Party because he strengthened the Tory Party with his twofold policy of democracy and imperialism. Kemal Ataturk (*right*) whose genius rebuilt a Turkey shattered by the First World War.

(*Above*) Lloyd George and his wife with Winston Churchill on Budget Day, 1910, when Lloyd George was Chancellor of the Exchequer and Churchill was President of the Board of Trade.

(*Below left*) Franklin D. Roosevelt's three terms in office proved him to be one of the greatest of American presidents. (*Below right*) A portrait of Sir Winston Churchill by Karsh.

Four millions of money were required immediately, and Parliament was not sitting. Moreover, the matter had to be kept a complete secret.

Disraeli dispatched his secretary, Corry, to Baron Lionel de Rothschild to ask for four million pounds "tomorrow." Rothschild, who was at luncheon, swallowed a grape and said, "What's your security?"

"The British Government," was the reply

"You shall have it," said Rothschild.

Within a week the transaction was completed and Britain had control of the Suez Canal, and with it the vital sea-way to India. A statesman, as Disraeli himself said, is one who is wise before the event.

Disraeli's final triumph came in the last few months of his political life. In 1878 Russia had fought and defeated Turkey. The Treaty of San Stefano, which ended the war, gave Russia more than Britain was willing to let her have. Particularly was she opposed to the creation of a state under Russian control stretching from the Danube to the Ægean Sea.

Disraeli, accompanied by Lord Salisbury, crossed to Berlin to attend a conference on the subject. To obtain the conference the Prime Minister had gone so far as to order a British fleet to the Dardanelles and to move Indian troops to Malta, an action that aroused much comment at home as provocative of war.

At the conference Disraeli was successful. He returned to England, and was acclaimed by the populace amid cries of "peace with honour."

Both his political career and his life were now drawing to a close. In the next two years the Zulu War, economic troubles, and discontent combined to weaken the prestige of the Government. Gladstone took his opportunity. He toured the country amid scenes of terrific enthusiasm. In the elections of 1880 the Tories lost one hundred and ten seats. On April 21, Disraeli resigned, leaving the queen no alternative but to ask Gladstone to form a ministry.

The Earl returned to Hughenden to write *Endymion* and to end his days in the peace and quiet of the countryside.

In March, 1881, he was taken ill. The flame burnt lower and lower, and on April 19 flickered out.

DAVID LLOYD GEORGE

(1863–1945)

David Lloyd George will be remembered for two services to Britain—his battle for social reforms and his leadership during the last years of the First World War. Throughout his long Parliamentary career he was a fighter, rousing, like Franklin Roosevelt, the hatred of his opponents and the love of his supporters. He was a masterly Chancellor of the Exchequer, and it was in this capacity that he introduced the National Insurance Bill of 1911. During the blackest years of the 1914-18 war he asserted his powers to bring about full unity of control in the Allied Command and thus ensured victory. At Versailles in 1919, he supported President Wilson's proposals for the setting-up of the League of Nations.

In the little Welsh village of Llanystumdwy, near Criccieth, within sight of Snowdon, there stands a sturdy stone cottage, once the home of Richard Lloyd, the village shoemaker. In that cottage David Lloyd George spent his boyhood. His father, William George, a schoolmaster who came of Pembrokeshire farming stock, had married Richard Lloyd's sister when teaching at Pwllheli. David was born on January 17, 1863, in the back street of a Manchester suburb where his father was holding a temporary post. William George died seventeen months later on a Pembrokeshire smallholding to which he had retired, and Richard Lloyd brought his widowed sister and her young family to Llanystumdwy.

The Welsh peasants among whom David grew up were sturdy Nonconformists. His uncle was unpaid minister to a little church of Disciples of Christ—a branch of the Baptists—at Criccieth. Llanystumdwy had, too, a proud tradition of Welsh literary culture, so the boy breathed in Welsh nationalism as well as stubborn antagonism alike to the Established Church and to the local Tory landowners with their alien English ways. In school he organized revolt against the teaching of the catechism, and out of school he and his allies played at poaching in the landlord's woods and salmon river.

In his subsequent career he was instinctively on the side of the poor, the peasant, the little nation, and an unfaltering champion of the under-dog.

Even as a youngster he was brilliantly clever, and his uncle resolved to give him a profession. He liked preaching, but as a Dissenter he could not take orders in the Established Church. Medicine did not attract him and the training for it was long and costly. Their choice fell on the law. But to pass his preliminary law examination he had to know French and Latin, and the village school taught neither. His uncle Richard got the books and valiantly set to work to learn both languages in order to coach his nephew. The shoemaking no doubt suffered, but young David passed his examination and was articled to a firm of solicitors in Portmadoc.

He worked hard at his law studies, and at the age of twenty-one was admitted to the roll of solicitors. The firm to which he had been articled offered him a good position, but he preferred to venture on his own, and soon built up a busy practice. He was much in demand by any tenant farmers, poachers, Dissenters or quarrymen who were in trouble with the higher powers, and won local fame by his defiant handling of the landowning Justices of the Peace. One affair in particular, the Llanfrothen Burial Case, brought him renown all over Wales. The local parson had refused to allow an old quarryman to be buried beside his daughter by the Methodist minister, and on Lloyd George's advice the people broke open the churchyard and carried out the funeral. The rector sued them, but on appeal Lloyd George won their case, the judge severely censuring both parson and magistrate.

So popular had Lloyd George become that the Liberals of the Caernarvon Boroughs chose him for their candidate. In 1890, the sitting member—a Tory—died suddenly and a by-election was held. The squire of Llanystumdwy, Ellis Nanney, stood for the Tories, and Lloyd George, the village lad who as a boy had headed revolt against the squire, as his opponent. It was a dramatic contest with an exciting finish. The first count put Nanney in, but one of Lloyd George's tellers found some misplaced votes and on a recount the village lad won by eighteen votes. Caernarvon Boroughs was far from being a safe Liberal seat, and at nearly every later election Lloyd George had to fight, but to the end of his life he was always returned.

He quickly established his reputation as a powerful orator in the country and a skilful debater in Parliament, who could oppose Tory measures even more adroitly than the Irish members with their reputation as obstructionists. At first more a Welsh Nationalist than a Liberal, he worked hard during his first ten years in Parliament to get Welsh Liberals to unite and demand Home Rule for Wales. But North and South Welsh would not hold together, and his defeat in Wales broadened his political horizon and objectives.

In 1899 the Boer War broke out. Lloyd George was not a pacifist, but as a member of a small nation he instinctively sympathized with the Boers and felt that the war had been unjustly forced on them by Britain, so he opposed it with passionate conviction. In consequence he was nearly ruined and nearly killed. He addressed meetings up and down the country denouncing the war and demanding a fair settlement. He was frequently mobbed. His meetings were broken up. At Bangor in his own constituency he was hit on the head with a bludgeon, and when he held a meeting in Birmingham Town Hall a frantic mob attacked the place and wanted to kill him. The police smuggled him away in a policeman's uniform. But though he was for a time the most execrated figure in the country, his fearless courage, complete sincerity and brilliant oratory won him an outstanding position.

He added to his renown in the following years by the skill with which he led the campaign in Parliament, and later in Wales, against Balfour's 1902 Education Bill; and when Chamberlain launched his Tariff Reform programme, Lloyd George and Winston Churchill—who crossed the House from the Tory to the Liberal side on this issue—were effective speakers against it all over the country. The "Welsh Wizard" was indeed the supreme orator of his time, and could hold even a hostile audience spellbound.

In the 1906 election the Liberals swept the country and Lloyd George became President of the Board of Trade. The fiery rebel now won a new reputation as a skilful statesman who not only pushed through many practical reforms but brought to a high level the art of consulting in advance the interests concerned and getting them to support his schemes. He set up the Port of London Authority, carried the Merchant Shipping Act to protect seamen, established the Road Fund to improve the country's roads and the Development Commissioners to raise the level of its agriculture. As a Celt, he profoundly believed in education and had little sympathy with the Anglo-Saxon fondness for "muddling through." He liked to put trained and qualified men where they could see that things were done efficiently. He later started the Medical Research Council to watch over the nation's health and the Department of Scientific and Industrial Research to carry on the same service for its industry.

Lloyd George was the real driving force behind the social reform programme which the Liberals carried through between 1906 and 1914. In 1908 he succeeded Asquith as Chancellor of the Exchequer and had the satisfaction of piloting through the scheme of Old Age Pensions for which he had fought ever since he concerned himself with politics. But pensions had to be paid for, so he devised a scheme of taxes on land values, on increment values created by public improvements, on maturing leaseholds and on mining royalties. These he incorporated in his 1909 Budget. The land-owning interests in the country were furious, and the House of Lords took the unprecedented step of throwing out the Budget. Lloyd George had hoped for this. The Lords had been rejecting one Liberal Bill after another, and while their power of veto remained he had no hope of carrying Irish Home Rule or Disestablishment of the Welsh Church. There were two general elections in 1910, both won by the Liberals. After the first, the Budget went through the Lords. After the second, they agreed to the Parliament Act, limiting their powers of veto. Irish Home Rule and Welsh Disestablishment started their journey to the Statute Book.

In 1911, Lloyd George carried his National Insurance scheme for Health and Unemployment Insurance. It has been added to and expanded since, as he hoped and intended, but at the time it was bitterly opposed. Then he started a Land Enquiry with a view to restoring British agriculture and clearing away slums and bad housing.

He was interrupted in 1914 by the First World War. Intent on his plans for domestic reform, he was not at first eager for Britain to join in the war; but when the Germans invaded Belgium as a means of attacking France, he hesitated no longer. For Belgium was a small nation.

Britain declared war on August 4, 1914, and Lloyd George, as Chancellor of the Exchequer, took such skilful steps by moratorium and temporary bank holidays to deal with the financial crisis resulting from the outbreak that City men who had been his bitterest foes declared he ought to be made a Duke! Then he turned his keen mind and alertly warlike spirit to the problems of the war itself. Apart from young Churchill and the elderly Kitchener, whom Asquith had brought in as War Minister, none of the Cabinet was a soldier; and with the further exception of Lloyd George, none was a real fighter. They could debate but they could not act. Lloyd George was a fighter and a doer. He flung his whole energies into the job of winning the war. He started arrangements on his own initiative to get arms from America; and when reports of the appalling shortage of shells for the troops in France, and Churchill's quarrel with Admiral Fisher about the Dardanelles expedition resulted in the formation of a Coalition Government, he agreed to give up his post as Chancellor of the Exchequer—the highest post after that of Premier—in order to organize a new Ministry of Munitions. Once again he risked his whole political future to do what he felt must be done. In a few months he had worked a revolution in the country's industry and swung it over to war production. Shells, heavy artillery, machine guns and munitions of all kinds were soon streaming out to Britain's armies.

But his Cabinet colleagues still fumbled and debated vaguely about burning problems in so irresolute a fashion that towards the end of 1916 they had nearly lost the war. Lloyd George insisted that there must be decision, not talk, and when Asquith rejected his proposals for Cabinet reorganization, he resigned. This brought down the Government, and after the Tory leader, Bonar Law, had declined to become Prime Minister, the King sent for Lloyd George. He formed the Second Coalition, and at once reorganized the machinery of wartime administration, setting up Ministries of Shipping, Food, Air, Health, Transport, National Service, and inducing the reluctant Admiralty to adopt the convoy system to counter the submarine menace.

When the Russian revolution led to the collapse of the Eastern Front and the Germans were able in the spring of 1918 to throw their whole force against the British and French, Lloyd George persuaded the Americans, who by now were in the war, to rush their armies to Europe, and he mobilized British shipping to convey them. He extracted the unwilling consent of the Army chiefs for unity of command on the Western Front under General Foch, and had his reward when in the summer the tide turned and the German forces were driven back across France. In the darkest days his courage and confidence and fertility of resource had heartened and inspired the nation, and when in the autumn the Germans collapsed and an armistice brought the fighting to an end, he was hailed by everyone, not only in Britain but all over the world, as "the man who won the war."

Lloyd George hurried over to Paris to prepare for the Peace Conference, while a General Election was being held to elect a new Parliament, which was already two years overdue. His Government was a coalition of Conservatives, Labour and that part of the Liberal Party which had not followed Asquith into opposition at the end of 1916. The Labour Party now withdrew from the Government, and the Coalition Whips gave "coupons" to those candidates whom they approved as pledged supporters of the Lloyd George Government. In the circumstances, most of these went to Tories and war profiteers, and both wings of the Coalition raised funds from this latter class, many of whom hoped for titles and honours in recognition of their services to the national war effort.

The resulting Parliament was a hard-faced, reactionary body, which despite pledges of support sent threats to Lloyd George when it thought he was being too tender to the Germans in the peace terms he was framing at Paris with Wilson, the American President, and Clemenceau, the French Premier. In view of the passions that ruled at the time, the Treaty of Versailles was an extraordinarily fair and reasonable settlement of the tangled wreckage of postwar Europe; but its reparation clauses were left indefinite because the victors' claims far exceeded Germany's capacity to pay. Lloyd George doubted if any large reparation payments could successfully be extracted, and later history proved that he was right.

During both his wartime and postwar administrations, he pressed on with the social reforms that were his lifelong interest. Women's suffrage, Welsh Disestablishment, the Fisher Education Act, Housing, Town Planning, Small Holdings Acts and measures to relieve unemployment were carried during these years and a peace treaty negotiated with Ireland. The Tories who formed his Parliamentary majority grew restive, and when trouble blew up with Turkey in 1922 over the peace settlement between her and Greece, a number of them broke away and the Government fell.

Lloyd George never again held office, but in the years that followed he played an active and at times a dominant part in national affairs. The Liberal Party had been broken in two in 1916, and the Asquithian wing never forgave Lloyd George, though an uneasy peace was presently patched up. Leadership of the left wing of politics passed to the Labour Party. Lloyd George devoted himself to working out programmes of the reforms which he regarded as urgent for the country: land policy to restore agriculture and the countryside; housing and town planning policy; industrial reconstruction. When unemployment on a large scale became constant he called experts together and prepared schemes to provide work, setting out the plans in a booklet, *We Can Conquer Unemployment*, which he used as the Liberal programme in the 1929 election. In this election and in the work of planning and trying to revive the Liberal Party he used up most of the Coalition Liberal share of the funds raised for the Coalition campaign in 1918.

The Liberal Party did not revive. Labour came out on top in the election, and took office in time to face the economic crisis resulting from the 1929 slump in the U.S.A. In 1931, while Lloyd George was undergoing a major operation, the Labour premier, Ramsay MacDonald, threw over his party and formed a National Government with the Tories and Liberals. In the dismal years that followed, Lloyd George strove unsuccessfully to induce the Government to adopt a bold programme of national reconstruction and to stand by the League of Nations. When his proposals were flouted, he organized a Council of Action to press this programme on Parliamentary candidates.

At last the irresolute National Government drifted into the Second World War. Lloyd George's last outstanding public act was to rise in Parliament when the Premier, Neville Chamberlain, was heading the nation for defeat, and denounce him so effectively that he was compelled to resign and Winston Churchill took his place. The plans which Lloyd George had improvised for the First World War—Ministries of Food, Shipping, Munition Supply—were revived successfully; and though now too old to accept office, he had the satisfaction of knowing that the work he had done was a second time helping to save the country.

Towards the end he settled again in Llanystumdwy among his own Welsh people, who recognized him to be the greatest of all Welsh princes. Shortly before his death the King made him Earl Lloyd George of Dwyfor—the river in which as a boy he had paddled and poached salmon; but no title could fully express the greatness of his services to his country and his fellows, every phase of whose life from birth to old age shows benefits devised and achieved by him. The victorious end of the Second World War was already in sight when, on March 26, 1945, he passed quietly away and was laid to rest, as he had always wished, in a sheltered spot beside the Dwyfor. His tomb has already become a shrine for the Welsh nation.

KEMAL ATATURK

(1880–1938)

Kemal Ataturk fought his way through rivers of blood to become Dictator of Turkey. He put down, stamped out and eliminated all who opposed him. Yet he alone was strong enough to save Turkey from extinction both during and after the First World War. He alone braved the might of the Allies and outwitted them by his cunning. He alone had the genius to rebuild his shattered country on new and enduring foundations.

REBELLION against every form of authority was the breath of life to young Mustapha Kemal. Born at Salonika in 1880, he came of hardy peasant stock from the Macedonian uplands—home of the fieriest revolutionaries in eastern Europe. When eleven years old, he proved so unmanageable at his first school, refusing to study or play games, assaulting in a fury of flying fists and boots not only boys but any master who interfered with him, that he had to be withdrawn.

He was sent to the Military Cadet School at Salonika. Morose and contemptuous, he spurned all attempts to win his friendship. Nor would he brook any rival in his struggle to become "top dog." He made life a misery for any youngster who tried to beat him in mathematics or military strategy or to cut a better figure on parade. He was hated, feared—and respected. At seventeen, when he left Salonika for the Military School at Monastir, he was hardened to almost every vice.

After two years at Monastir, he was gazetted as a sub-lieutenant and sent to the Imperial Staff College at Constantinople. For several months he abandoned himself to debauchery in the vilest capital of Europe. Then he turned to politics, and found a mission that was to make him one of the greatest men of his day—the creation of a new Turkish Empire.

A group of young officers in the Staff College had founded a secret revolutionary society called the *Vatan*—Fatherland—to resist Abdul's senile despotism and rid Turkey of foreign intrigue. Kemal became its leader. One of the sultan's agents won his way into the inner circle. He waited until a meeting of all the members was held, then informed the police. Closed vans rushed to a hovel in the slums, scores of police forced an entry, and the plotters were immediately hustled away to the Red Prison.

But the sultan, Abdul Hamid II, hesitated. His prisoners were the future staff-officers and generals of the army. Their mass execution might cause a revolt. No doubt they would become good and loyal servants after this outbreak of youthful folly. They had had a terrifying lesson. He sent for Ismail Haki Pasha, Director-General of Military Training, and ordered him to suppress rigorously any future attempts to revive the *Vatan*. Then he announced that by his gracious clemency he had decided to release the prisoners.

Kemal was cautioned never to incur the suspicion of the Secret Police again. He was posted to a cavalry regiment south of Damascus and took part in a fierce campaign against the Druses—the wild hill tribes of that rocky and barren country. On his return to Damascus, he immediately formed a new branch of the stringently forbidden *Vatan*.

Hearing that an open revolt was being planned against the sultan in Macedonia, Kemal resolved to return secretly to Salonika. He obtained a few days' leave, went to Jaffa, bought false papers, disguised himself as a merchant, and took passage on a ship to Egypt, crossing from there to Athens, and then to Salonika.

Scarcely had he arrived when he was detected by the sultan's agents. His capture would have meant death. Kemal dashed into Greece and took a passage back to Jaffa. But orders from Constantinople for his arrest had reached Jaffa before him.

The commandant at Jaffa, Ahmed Bey, was a member of the *Vatan*. He boarded the ship with Kemal's uniform and papers, and smuggled him out of the town and down to Gaza, where the Turks were fighting native tribes. Then Ahmed Bey reported to Constantinople that Kemal had been fighting on the Gaza front and had never once left Syria.

Kemal had failed for the moment—though he had learnt enough to realize that Salonika would be the headquarters of the first big rising against Abdul Hamid. Now he worked incessantly for a transfer to the town of his birth. And at last, in 1908, he was appointed to the staff of the 3rd Army Corps at Salonika.

Here a revolutionary society called the Committee of Union and Progress had been formed two years earlier under the leadership of Enver, a romantic visionary, a man of brilliant inspirations which proved too grandiose for achievement—the exact opposite in character to the grim and sardonic realist, Mustapha Kemal, who was to become his biggest rival for power.

Kemal had no sooner joined the committee than he found himself at odds with all its leaders—Enver, the irresolute dreamer; Jemal, a crafty Asiatic; Niazi, a hot-headed Albanian; Talat, a dull-witted clerk; Javid, a Jew who had become a Moslem. Unlike himself, burning with passion for a new and vigorous Turkish Empire for the Turks alone, they seemed imbued with all kinds of queer international theories. And they, in turn, detested his acid sarcasm and blunt contempt for all their magnificent plans to unite all the races and creeds of the Near East under one great suzerainty.

In 1908, Niazi suddenly justified Kemal's suspicions that he was completely lacking in common sense. Without consulting his colleagues, without any plan of action, and at the head of only a few hundred men, the tempestuous Albanian marched into the mountains of Macedonia and defied the Turkish Government.

But fortune smiled upon his fantastic daring. The sultan's punitive expedition deserted to Niazi. Throughout Turkey, groaning under long servitude and poverty, arose shouts of revolt. Entire regiments went over to the committee. Enver, at the head of a large army, was about to march on Constantinople when the wily old sultan announced a Constitution and declared himself in favour of many of the reforms demanded by the revolutionaries.

To wildly cheering crowds massed in thousands before the Olympus Palace Hotel, in Salonika, Enver, now the idol of all Turkey, proclaimed the triumphs he had won. Behind him on the balcony, white and trembling with jealous rage, stood Mustapha Kemal—a nobody.

Hundreds of exiled politicians flocked back to Constantinople at the tidings of a new régime. Swiftly they seized the reins of power and elbowed the inexperienced committee leaders out of the scene. Niazi was murdered on his way back to Albania. Enver was sent on a military mission to Berlin, Kemal posted to Tripoli.

Abdul Hamid, the Red Fox, made a cunning bid to regain his tyranny. His agents bribed the army in Constantinople, spread widespread reports that the empire was breaking up under the rule of these new liberal politicians with their foreign ideas, and sent out priests to warn the people that Jewish and Christian agitators were planning to destroy Islam and the Caliphate.

The army in Constantinople mutinied and killed their officers. At the head of a great throng of citizens, it proclaimed its loyalty to Islam, the sultan and the caliph.

Enver returned post-haste from Berlin, crushed the counter-revolution, hanged scores of its leaders, deposed Abdul Hamid, and placed his doddering cousin on the throne as a figurehead, while the committee itself held supreme power.

For two years Kemal plotted and schemed to overthrow Enver. Then Italy's seizure of Tripoli interrupted his plans. Kemal was promoted to major and given command of the section of the Turkish army facing Derna. His headquarters were in Ain-al-Mansur, where Enver had established himself as commander-in-chief.

In 1912, Montenegro, Serbia, Bulgaria and Greece attacked Turkey, drove her out of Europe, and would have crushed her altogether had not Enver rallied the Government to a successful defence. And the next year again it was Enver who saved Turkey's last stronghold in Europe by capturing and holding Adrianople while Bulgaria, Rumania, Serbia and Greece were snarling over the division of the Turkish spoils.

Hailed almost as a god by the Turkish people, Enver rode into an Adrianople decked with flags. Far in the rear of this triumphant conqueror came Mustapha Kemal—just an unknown officer at the head of his column.

Enver now revived his ambitious dream of creating a vast Ottoman Empire which should unite all Turkish-speaking peoples. But first he decided to reorganize the army, and called in a German general, Liman von Sanders, to perform this task.

Kemal flew into a fury, held public meetings to protest against "this insult to the Turkish nation" and emphasized the perils he saw ahead if Turkey drifted into an alliance with Germany. Enver lost his temper and "banished" Kemal by sending him as Military Attaché to Sofia.

But the First World War suddenly reversed the fortunes of these implacable rivals. In 1915, Enver devised a brilliant plan to outflank the attacking Russians, smash their line of retreat, and drive them back across the Caucasus. He forgot only one thing—the winter. The Turkish columns were trapped in the snow-swept defiles of the mountain range; 88,000 out of 100,000 were frozen to death.

Kemal, on the other hand, won one of the most sensational victories of the war. The British were trying to capture Constantinople by forcing the Dardanelles, and had planned to land a force of eighty thousand men on the Gallipoli Peninsula. Kemal had taken over a command on Gallipoli under General Liman von Sanders.

When, on April 25, 1915, the Anzacs landed at Ari Burnu in what appeared at first only a small force, Liman von Sanders thought this was the feint he had expected. Kemal's superb instinct of generalship told him, however, that it was really the spearhead of the main attack. Ignoring von Sanders's orders, he launched a counter-attack and threw in all his reserves to the last man. The Anzacs outnumbered the Turks by two to one, but Kemal held them back until reinforcements arrived. Later, in August, his furious onslaught at Suvla won back the key position of Chanak Bay, pinned the British to the coast, and eventually forced them to abandon the entire Gallipoli expedition as an utter failure.

Kemal returned to Constantinople to be fêted as the "saviour of the Dardanelles" and Turkey's greatest general. Enraged by his success, Enver sent him to the Caucasus front, where the vast armies of Grand Duke Nicholas threatened what seemed certain defeat for the Turks. But luck had turned at last for Kemal—the Russian revolution of 1917 suddenly threw the grand duke's forces into such confusion that the hero of the Dardanelles won fresh laurels.

Enver now strained every nerve to get his dangerous but popular enemy out of the way. Kemal was posted to Syria under General von Falkenhayn—with whom he quarrelled fiercely and resigned his command—then attached to the staff of Vaheddin, Crown Prince of Turkey, on an official mission to Berlin. Next, he was again sent to the Syrian front under Liman von Sanders. The English smashed the Turkish army there on August 19, 1918; Kemal strove like a demon to check the rout, but failed.

As the war drew to its close, Enver fled into exile, the Committee of Union and Progress disappeared, and the Allied Armies were in control of Constantinople under the senile Vaheddin, who had become sultan on the death of his father.

Meanwhile, Kemal was toiling night and day to organize a national movement of resistance to the Allies. His followers called themselves the Kemalists. He established a National Government at Ankara, and defied the feeble sultan's Government in Constantinople, whose policy was to truckle to the English. In 1920, the Allies announced in the Treaty of Sèvres their terms of peace for Turkey. These were so stringent that the entire country united in protest. Kemal raised an army and set out to attack Constantinople.

The Allies had disbanded most of their troops and were sick of war. Yet it would be necessary to fight if the harsh terms of the Sèvres Treaty were to be enforced.

In this dilemma, the Prime Minister of Greece, Venizelos, put forward a tempting plan to the Allied statesmen in Paris. Venizelos wanted to create a Greek Empire in Turkey. For several months he had been assembling a large army of invasion, equipped with guns and ammunition, arms and military stores, bought from the disbanding Allied armies. Venizelos offered to smash the Kemalists, who were irregular troops with no artillery. His offer was accepted.

A year later, all Turkey in Europe had been captured by the Greeks. Moreover, they had landed a huge force at Smyrna and advanced on Ankara to wipe out the Kemalists. Eventually, they entrenched between two villages, Eska Shehir and Afion. Eska Shehir was a railway junction and the key to Ankara. It was held by one of Kemal's best commanders, Ismet.

In a stone house in the village of Chan Kaya, a few miles from Ankara, Mustapha Kemal pored over maps and plans, and awaited the Greek onslaught. He had reached the biggest crisis of his life. If he failed to withstand the Greeks, both he and Turkey were doomed. He had only a few regular troops; the rest of his army consisted of roving bands of tribesmen. Food and equipment were scarce; he had neither artillery nor transport. And facing him was an enemy far superior in numbers, well-conditioned, and trained and equipped to a high degree of efficiency.

In the first week of July, 1921, the Greeks swept forward, took Afion, and menaced Eska Shehir. The Kemalists were suffering heavy losses in a hard-fought battle. Kemal decided to fall back two hundred miles to the last natural line of defence before Ankara—the Sakaria River.

And here, on August 24, began one of the bloodiest and most decisive battles of modern history. After a heavy artillery bombardment by the Greeks, the two armies came to death-grips. Centuries of hatred between Greek and Turk, Christian and Moslem, fused into the white-hot fury of fourteen days' indescribable carnage.

When at last the Greeks were slowly driven back from a battlefield that had become a shambles, and retreated to Eska Shehir, the Turks were too shattered by the victory to pursue them.

Kemal recruited and equipped a new army. Russia lent him money; France, in a secret treaty, enabled him to leave the Syrian front almost unguarded, thus releasing 80,000 men. He organized his forces until August, 1922. This time there must be no failure.

At dawn on the 26th, before the Greek position at Afion, he issued the order to his troops: "Forward! Your goal is the Mediterranean!"

Amid a terrific barrage of artillery from both sides, the Turks rushed forward, and by nightfall had cut the Greek army in two and severed its communications with Smyrna. The Greeks broke and fled in disorder the next day, leaving most of their artillery, equipment and stores behind them in their panic-stricken dash for the sea.

Kemal had no ships to pursue the enemy at sea. Between him and the Greeks in Thrace were the British forces, strongly entrenched at Chanak. Would they allow him to cross the Dardanelles?

Britain, he decided, was tired of war. If he acted boldly and swiftly, he might win the success he craved. He ordered his troops to advance to the English lines with arms reversed. They were to be friendly and peaceful, but must not stop until they had passed through to the straits. The English troops in their trenches were completely bewildered by Kemal's astute move. They had orders to hold up the Turks, but not to fire on them. It was a moment fraught with peril. One shot fired on either side, a single outbreak of temper—and England would have been at war with Turkey. The Turks had advanced to the barbed wire; they had begun to clamber through, the English were advancing threateningly—when suddenly orders came to both sides to stand fast. An armistice had been arranged.

At the conference of Mudania that followed, the Allies agreed to evacuate the Greeks from Thrace and promised that they themselves would leave Constantinople soon afterwards. Kemal accepted. He had won another great victory—this time without the loss of a single man. He had saved the independence of Turkey, made it a free and sovereign state again, and got rid of foreign influence within its boundaries.

A few weeks later he took control of the Constantinople Government by a *coup d'état*. The terrified old Sultan Vaheddin hurried out of a back door of his palace to the safety of a British warship. His nephew, Abdul Mejid, became caliph in his place, but Kemal would not allow him to be made sultan or to hold any power over the Government.

During the following year, Kemal formed his People's Party. By a clever political intrigue, he created a long Parliamentary crisis. The old Government was dissolved, and the wrangling deputies could not unite to form a new one.

At the height of the crisis, a leading member of the People's Party, Kemalledin, proposed in Parliament that Kemal should be sent for to form a Government. When Kemal arrived, he staggered the deputies by bluntly declaring he would take office only on condition that Turkey became a republic, with himself as its first president.

The political chaos was so extreme that they had no choice but to accept. Kemal then instantly began to create a dictatorship.

His People's Party had already obtained a strong hold on every town and village. He was Commander-in-Chief of the Army. He ruled all departments of State. But the biggest threat to his power had yet to be challenged—religion. Unless Islam, with its age-old customs strangling all progress in Turkey, were abolished, he would never realize his dream of making his country a modern Power.

Kemal began a propaganda campaign against Islam in the Government newspapers. The opposition press was drastically censored. Like wildfire a movement of revolt spread through Turkey. Dervishes and religious leaders denounced Mustapha Kemal in every mosque and market-place. They declared he had broken every law of religion and even of common decency. He had forced the women of Ankara to unveil. He had brought the accursed modern dances to the land.

Kemal replied by accusing the caliph, leader of all the Faithful, of intriguing with England to destroy Turkey. Then he began to act—savagely. A deputy who attacked his anti-religious campaign was murdered. Finally, in March, 1924, Kemal presented a Bill to Parliament to abolish the caliphate and make Turkey a secular nation, unhindered by outworn laws based on religion and ancient formulas.

Most of the deputies rose in a storm of protest. Kemal silenced them with an ominous hint of violence if they did not vote in favour. The Bill passed without further demur.

Kemal's old associates of the Committee of Union and Progress began to conspire against him. Led by Javid, the Jew of Salonika, they formed secret societies in all the big towns and borrowed money from foreign financiers for a new revolution. Kemal countered by honeycombing the land with spies and *agents-provocateurs* until he obtained the evidence he needed. Then he had the leaders suddenly arrested. He gave a magnificent ball to the Diplomatic Corps, and while the ambassadors and foreign ministers were beginning the first dance, the rebel chiefs were hanged a few miles away.

Kemal was now absolute ruler. But he was still far from satisfied. His aim was to transform the entire life of his people from Oriental to modern European—a colossal task of centuries which he determined to accomplish in a few short years. The Turk must renounce everything that distinguished him as a Turk—his ancient customs, beliefs, habits, dress, even the intimacies of his family life. His very mind must be changed, his entire outlook upon the world.

First, Kemal banned the fez, which every Turk wore proudly as the badge of an Ottoman and Moslem. Riots broke out, officials were stoned when the police went round towns and villages tearing fezzes from Moslem heads. Kemal sent forth his troops. They hanged and tortured hundreds of Turks. A few weeks later every Turk wore a hat, any and every sort of hat with a brim or peak; there had been a wild scramble for ancient bowlers, dilapidated straw hats, and even women's hats with ribbons and artificial flowers.

Next, he replaced the old Islamic laws by legal codes based on those of Switzerland, Germany and Italy. These forbade polygamy and the harem, destroyed the right of husbands to own women like chattels, and gave every adult the vote.

He cleaned up the Civil Service, for over a hundred years the most corrupt in Europe, made bribery a heavily punishable offence, and established a "code of honour" in all State departments.

The long, flowing draperies, the picturesque yashmaks and veils vanished from Turkish dress. Women attired themselves like their counterparts in Birmingham or Chicago, men learnt to take a pride in ready-made suits.

One of Kemal's most difficult reforms was to make his countrymen write their language in the Latin characters used by Western nations instead of the old Arabic script. Aged Turks had literally to begin learning their ABC all over again. Kemal went through the streets himself with a blackboard and chalk teaching the crowds.

He reorganized the Turkish army and made it one of the most efficient and well-equipped in the world. He also created a small but reliable air force and navy.

He died in November, 1938. History will record him as a ruthless dictator, but also as the greatest figure in modern Turkish history, a man second to none in love of his country, a general and diplomat of genius, and, above all, as the saviour of a land that had fallen into ruin. The new Turkey is his monument.

FRANKLIN D. ROOSEVELT

(1882–1945)

Franklin Delano Roosevelt came to power as President of the United States in the year 1932, when his country was still shaken by the slump and the mass unemployment that followed. He was a vigorous reformer and an eminently practical man, and his scheme of rehabilitation, carried out under the Works Progress Administration, did much to set the country on the road to prosperity again. Roosevelt always realized that the United States had a full part to play in world affairs, and, though he met with opposition from isolationists in his own and the Republican Parties, he was able, when the Second World War broke out, to give the utmost aid, short of armed support, to the Allied cause. He takes his place with Washington and Lincoln as one of the most single-hearted leaders in the fight for his country's greatness.

In 1613, Claes Martenzen of Roosevelt, a village in Holland, sailed across the Atlantic to the Dutch settlement of New Amsterdam. He started a farm in Manhattan where his son, Nicholas, and his two grandsons, John and James, were born. By their time New Amsterdam had become New York and a part of New England; but John van Roosevelt and his sons after him stuck by their Dutch breed and intermarried mainly with Knickerbocker stock. The descendants of James, on the contrary, turned to their English neighbours and blended with the families of the Pilgrim Fathers. The fifth generation from John brought forth Theodore Roosevelt, U.S. President from 1901 to 1909. The fifth generation from James produced Franklin Delano Roosevelt, President from 1932 to 1945.

Franklin was born on January 30, 1882. Despite his Dutch name he was mainly English by blood, with several Pilgrim Fathers among his ancestors. His mother, Sara Delano, was descended from a Flemish settler who joined the Pilgrims at Plymouth, Massachusetts, in 1621 and whose son married a daughter of one of the signers of the Compact.

From the start, Franklin seemed destined to be one of Fortune's darlings. Son of a wealthy family of the untitled aristocracy of New England, in the topmost circle of American society, he grew up a tall, strikingly handsome young man, sporting, athletic, and with easy and charming manners. He had a passion for the sea and wanted to enter the navy, but his fond parents decided otherwise and sent him to Groton and Harvard—the Eton and Oxford of the U.S.A. His father, who was president or vice-president of various railway lines, owned a large estate, Hyde Park, beside the Hudson, sixty miles from New York, where he interested himself in cattle-breeding and lived the life of a country gentleman. He died in December, 1900, just after Franklin entered Harvard.

At school and university, Franklin showed no special scholastic ability. His biggest achievement was to get on to the staff of the college magazine by scooping an interview with the college president. He decided to go in for the law, and while still a student he married in 1905 his distant cousin, Anna Eleanor Roosevelt, who belonged to the senior line of the family. He had fallen in love with her when she was a gawky schoolgirl, and he chose well, for she developed into a most remarkably able woman.

The junior Roosevelts were Democrats in politics. The senior branch had been Democrat, too, till the American Civil War, when, because the South was Democrat, they turned Republican. The two American political parties have not the clear-cut differences of, for example, the British Conservative and Labour Parties. They each contain reactionaries, liberals and labour supporters. They are alternate groupings—the Ins and Outs. But politics are traditionally looked on in the U.S.A. as a rather undignified game, and Franklin originally had no intention of dabbling in them. After studying at the Columbia Law School in New York, he was admitted to the bar in 1907 and joined a firm of New York lawyers. At his country mansion of Hyde Park he was a genial squire and host. A life of ease, elegance and affluence lay before him.

But the Democratic Party bosses of New York State were in difficulties and looked round for a respectable young man to improve their shop window. In 1910 they invited Roosevelt to run for the New York State Senate in a hopelessly Republican constituency up the Hudson River. He accepted, went round making friends with the farmers, and amazingly won the election! He promptly moved with his wife and three children to Albany, where the Senate House stood, and devoted himself to politics.

In 1912 came a Presidential election. Thanks mainly to

Franklin's adroit political tactics at the Democratic Convention, Woodrow Wilson became Democratic candidate. He was elected President, and Franklin got the post of Under-Secretary of the Navy—a post held sixteen years earlier by his fifth cousin, Theodore Roosevelt. He moved again, to Washington.

As a boy, he had wished to enter the navy. Now he had the task of watching over it, and threw himself into his work with the utmost energy and fertile resource. The efficiency of the U.S.A. fleet in the closing phases of the First World War was largely due to him. In the summer of 1918 he visited England and the European battle zones to concert Allied naval strategy with the British and French.

In the Presidential Election of 1920 the Democrats nominated Governor Cox as their candidate, with Franklin Roosevelt for Vice-President. Roosevelt campaigned all over the States, making the League of Nations his main election plank. But the tide had turned in favour of the Republicans, and their nominee, Harding, was returned to the White House.

Roosevelt's career, up to 1920, had been one of constant and seemingly easy success. He had of course worked hard and cleverly; good luck alone will not bring a man the Vice-Presidential nomination at the early age of thirty-eight. But if he worked, he had not to struggle, for by birth and natural gifts he started high up on the ladder. He had a warm sympathy with his fellows, but little actual experience of their woes and tragedies to sharpen his genuine zeal for reform. His ability had been proved, but not his grit.

Now fortune—or a higher and wiser power—turned and thrust upon him a supremely bitter test. He bathed one hot day in the chill waters of the Bay of Fundy and was smitten down with infantile paralysis. From the waist down he became a helpless cripple. His career, it seemed, was ended, though he was not yet forty, and had appeared just before this attack to have the world at his feet.

His devoted and strong-willed mother did not perhaps look on it as unmixed tragedy, for she at once planned to have him back at Hyde Park and to cosset him through the years of helplessness that lay ahead. But Franklin, stripped to the bedrock of his character by the blow, showed that his courage was great, and his will a thing of iron. He refused to accept defeat. Whatever doctors might say, he was resolved by sheer force of determination to regain the use of his legs. His wife backed him loyally; and she, too, had a Roosevelt will.

He held on to his post in a New York office. Within a year he could get there on crutches. In 1924, still on crutches, he attended the Democratic Convention to nominate Alfred Smith as Presidential candidate in a brilliant speech. He also began that autumn to try the effects of bathing in Warm Springs, Georgia, and found the treatment highly beneficial. In a couple more years he could walk with the aid of leg-irons. He later bought the springs and with two-thirds of his private fortune developed them as a non-profit-making institution for the treatment of infantile paralysis.

In 1928, Al Smith tried to persuade him to stand for the governorship of New York State, with a view to improving Smith's own chances in the Presidential election. He refused repeatedly, wanting to complete his cure; but was at last told that he would be nominated anyway. He was elected by a handsome majority. Two years later, the majority by which he was re-elected smashed all records!

His four years as Governor of New York covered the period of the 1929 stock exchange collapse which started the world-wide economic depression. It was his experience of this grim affair which led him to plan for a fairer treatment of what in a great speech on April 7, 1932, he described as "the forgotten man at the bottom of the economic pyramid." That speech bitterly incensed the right wing of his party, but so moved the progressive elements that less than three months later he was nominated as Democratic candidate for the Presidency. He broke with tradition by flying from New York to Chicago to accept nomination in person, and in his speech of acceptance he said: "I pledge you, I pledge myself, to a New Deal for the American people!" Economic laws, he asserted, were made not by nature but by man, and while theorists prated men and women were starving. He called for a campaign to restore prosperity.

He at once gathered a group of advisers who became known as the "Brains Trust"—the first of its kind, and by no means a comic debating society—to plan measures for lifting America out of the slump into which she was daily sinking deeper. This group furnished the raw material for his campaign speeches in the Presidential election, which he won against the Republican President, Hoover, with a majority of more than seven million.

It might well have amazed an onlooker that the American nation should have chosen a crippled man to take charge at this moment; for the prospect was one to dismay the strongest. When Roosevelt was formally inaugurated in March, 1933, the banks in thirty-eight states were closed. An enormous number of people, estimated as between twelve and seventeen million, were out of work. Mortgages were being foreclosed and farms and businesses sold up all over the country and starving bread queues stretched along the city streets. Almost more ominous in some respects was the national corruption which had resulted from the enactment in 1919 of prohibition of the manufacture and sale of alcoholic drink. Since a large section of the nation did not accept prohibition, illicit bootlegging had sprung up and become a vast industry, breeding a crew of gangsters and racketeers who battened on the public and defied all the forces of law and order.

Franklin Roosevelt set to work on this horrible mess with instant energy and fearless originality. He repealed prohibition, restored the banks, went off the gold standard and set the jobless men working for the Government. In his first hundred days he carried through the bulk of his New Deal legislation, setting up the Public Works Administration, the National Recovery Administration, Agricultural Adjustment Administration and a number of other organizations to relieve distressed mortgagors and get people to work. Perhaps his most spectacular scheme was the Tennessee Valley Authority with its vast programme of reclamation and development. When he stood for a second term in 1936, all but two States gave him their support.

By his resolute measures he pulled America out of the mire and set her on her feet. He was not afraid to make mistakes, or to put them right. In the international field he gradually led the U.S.A. away from the policy of isolation which it had adopted after the First World War and taught it that it must shoulder its share of responsibility for world affairs. If war came, he declared on October 5, 1937, "let no one imagine that the United States will escape!" He made public appeals for disarmament and banned the export of munitions. In October, 1937, he advocated putting the aggressor States in quarantine, and in 1938 he stopped the sale of helium to Germany for her airships. In the following April he asked Hitler and Mussolini to give pledges of non-aggression, in return for which he would seek to promote world disarmament. They laughed his offer to scorn.

The Second World War broke out on September 1, 1939, when Hitler invaded Poland. In November, Roosevelt revised the Neutrality Act to allow Britain and France to buy arms on the "cash and carry" system. After Dunkirk, he stepped up the supply of weapons to Britain, where the Home Guard was soon equipped with American rifles and ammunition. In August, 1940, he gave

Britain fifty destroyers in exchange for a lease of bases for his navy's use. In his speeches he made it clear that, while America was for the time non-belligerent, she was by no means neutral, and regarded the Western Democracies as the bulwark of defence for her own freedom.

A fresh Presidential election was due. From George Washington's time it had been a firm American tradition that no President should serve more than two terms consecutively, and Roosevelt did not ask for re-nomination. But the Democrats realized he was their only possible choice and put him forward. He made it clear that he had no time for the isolationists—still a large body in America; but for all that he was re-elected by a five-million majority for a third term, and forthwith proclaimed that America was to be the arsenal of Democracy. In January, 1941, he asked Congress to pass a Lend-Lease Bill, and announced his doctrine of the Four Freedoms—Free Speech, Free Worship, Freedom from Want, Freedom from Fear.

The Lend-Lease Bill was passed in March, 1941, and Roosevelt declared that the British needed and would get ships, planes, food, tanks, guns, ammunition and supplies of all kinds. He was as good as his word and a steady flow of desperately needed supplies came across the Atlantic. When in June Hitler attacked Russia, Roosevelt extended similar aid to her. American troops were sent to Iceland to enable the American Navy to keep the northern seaway clear of German raiders. In August, 1941, Roosevelt met Churchill on a warship in mid-Atlantic and signed with him the Atlantic Charter, setting out the basis for world democracy. The fact was that under Roosevelt the U.S.A. was already lined up in all but name with Britain in her war against the Axis Powers. "We will not accept a Hitler-dominated world!" said Roosevelt on May 27, 1941.

At the eastern end of the Axis, Japan was demanding a free hand to develop a world empire. Roosevelt firmly vetoed it. The Jap envoys came to discuss the matter; and on December 7, 1941, while they were blandly negotiating, Japanese aircraft struck the American Navy at Pearl Harbour, and America found herself flung into war. Roosevelt promptly took a decision which was vitally important for early victory, though by no means universally popular in the States—the decision to concentrate the main American strength against Germany and finish her off before settling with Japan.

On November 7, 1942, the Americans landed in North Africa, and in January, 1943, the President flew over to Casablanca in Morocco for a war conference with Churchill. There they decided to demand unconditional surrender from the Axis Powers: there would be no inconclusive finish to this fight. He flew on to Cairo to consult with the Chinese leader, Chiang Kai-Shek, and then to Teheran in Persia for a conference with Stalin. Physically handicapped he might be, but his mind and will were of giant proportions and he strained them unsparingly in the task of planning victory.

Next summer brought the invasion of France from north and south. The struggle was reaching its final climax in the autumn, and it was unthinkable that Roosevelt should withdraw from the direction of the U.S.A. effort. He agreed to stand for a fourth term, and was again elected. But the strain was telling on him, and it was a visibly frailer man who went in February, 1945, to Yalta in the Crimea for a final conference with his allies, Churchill and Stalin. A month later, American troops forced their way across the Rhine, and the end of the war in Europe was clearly imminent.

He did not live to see it. On April 12 his strenuous work brought on a cerebral hæmorrhage and he passed away. But his great task was done. He had taken charge of the U.S.A. in its darkest moment of ruin and disintegration, had pulled it together and restored its prosperity and sanity. He had brought its might, the might of New World democracy, into the struggle—to use his own noble words—"between human slavery and human freedom; between pagan brutality and the Christian ideal." Greatly gifted, he spent his gifts and wealth in the service of his fellows. But after ages may reckon that the basis of his greatness, the key to his service and his success, was his brotherly sympathy with the little fellow, the forgotten man.

Britain showed her own deep gratitude to this great American when, by Act of Parliament, his memorial statue was erected on the lawns of Grosvenor Square, and was unveiled by Eleanor Roosevelt on the third anniversary of his death.

SIR WINSTON CHURCHILL

(1874–1965)

All of Sir Winston Churchill's remarkable and energetic career is overshadowed by his assumption of power as Prime Minister of Great Britain during the years 1940–45. This was the great climax to forty years' service in the House of Commons, during which time he had twice changed his views and, consequently, his support of the Conservatives and Liberals. His political acumen, his practical knowledge of men and affairs, and his oratorical powers would make him an outstanding statesman in any age, but it was during the years of the Second World War that his steadfast and courageous leadership in the hour of his country's greatest peril captured the heart and imagination of the people, and gave him his place among the very greatest of Englishmen.

A RED-HEADED schoolboy was playing with toy soldiers on the nursery floor; manœuvring a large force against an opposing army of native troops handled by his younger brother. Their father, Lord Randolph Churchill, watched them for twenty minutes, and wondered at the skill and initiative shown by the red-head. For young Winston was a problem to him; a dunce at school, undisciplined, naughty and perverse, clearly incapable of passing his examinations for the bar, to which Lord Randolph had designed to send him. But here he was showing real keenness, and intelligence. "Would you like to go into the Army?" said the father. There was nothing the boy would like better! It was settled on the spot.

His choice was not surprising. The first Winston Churchill, ten generations earlier, a Cavalier squire of Dorset, had fought for King Charles I. His son was the great Duke of Marlborough, the foremost soldier of his day. Winston's father, Lord Randolph Churchill, third son of the seventh Duke, was an active fighter in politics, where, as founder and leader of the Tory Democrats, he grappled not only with the Opposition but with the crusted Blimps of his own side. His mother was the daughter of an American, Leonard Jerome, a lively adventurer in the financial battlefield of New York, where he made and lost several fortunes, owned and edited the *New York*

Times, and armed his staff with rifles and artillery when his office was menaced by a hostile mob. An ancestry in which the military genius of Marlborough was blended with the lively pugnacity of Jerome was not unlikely to produce a natural fighter.

Winston Leonard Spencer Churchill was born at Blenheim Palace on November 30, 1874. How he got into Harrow is a mystery, for he showed no scholastic ability beyond a remarkable capacity for learning poetry by heart. He never mastered Latin and never rose above the Junior School. After two failures he was squeezed by a coach into Sandhurst. There the wilful and unteachable boy suddenly matured. Not only did he do brilliantly in his military studies, but he also began to take a keen and intelligent interest in his father's political career, his schemes of social reform and efforts to turn the Tories into a progressive party. But Lord Randolph died before father and son had established a real understanding.

Leaving Sandhurst at Christmas, 1894, Winston was gazetted to the 4th Hussars. He wanted, however, not only to be a soldier, but to fight. So in the summer of 1895 he spent his leave in Cuba, joining in the Spanish Government's war with its Cuban rebels. He paid part of his expenses by writing descriptive letters to the *Daily Graphic*.

In 1896 he went out with his regiment to India. There he developed into a brilliant polo player. Next year there was a small affair on the frontier, the Malakand Pass Expedition. Failing to get into it as a soldier, he went as war correspondent for the *Daily Telegraph* and the *Allahabad Pioneer*. He got mixed up in a fighting reconnaissance and narrowly escaped slaughter. He wrote a book about the campaign which was a great success with the public and brought him both money and reputation. But it angered the military authorities, whom he criticized frankly for their mismanagement. Already he showed that confident assurance of knowing better than anyone else which has characterized him all through his career.

In 1898, Kitchener set out on his Sudan expedition to crush the rebel Dervishes. Here was a chance of some real fighting, and Churchill determined to join the expedition. Kitchener would not have him on any account—this young sprig of the nobility who wrote to the papers criticizing his superiors! But Churchill won. When even the Prime Minister could not move Kitchener, Churchill got in by the back door, attached to the 21st Lancers by Sir Evelyn Wood, on condition of paying his own expenses.

He settled the expenses problem by getting the *Morning Post* to appoint him its war correspondent. Then he hurried to Egypt and caught up with the Lancers in time to be the first man to sight the Khalifa's army. Next day, September 2, 1898, was fought the Battle of Omdurman, where the 21st Lancers made the last classic cavalry charge in British warfare. Churchill was in the middle of it. It ended in a concealed nullah packed with Dervishes, where nearly a quarter of the regiment were cut to pieces. But Churchill shot his way through, and gathered the survivors of his troop. "Did you enjoy yourself?" he asked a sergeant. His own enjoyment of the fray was immense.

Back in England he wrote the tale of the "River War" in two volumes, which won high praise and profit. He decided to give up the Army and enter politics, relying on his pen for a living. It was earning him far more than his Army pay. In 1899 he fought and lost a by-election at Oldham. The Boer War started in the autumn and he dashed off to it as chief war correspondent of the *Morning Post*. He joined a trip in an armoured train venturing out into Boer territory. The train was ambushed and he was taken, a prisoner, to Pretoria.

The prison did not hold him long. One dark night he climbed out, and, after a series of hairsbreadth escapes, got to Portuguese East Africa and thence to Durban. The Boers had offered a reward of £25 for his capture, dead or alive.

He now joined Byng's South African Light Horse, known as the Cockyoli Birds, and was the first to enter Ladysmith. He rode through Johannesburg on a bicycle while the Boers still held it, and led the Army into Pretoria. Then he came back to England and turned again to politics.

In the 1900 election he was returned for Oldham, and soon made his mark in Parliament as a brilliant speaker. In politics he was a progressive Tory Democrat and Free Trader; so when in 1903 Joseph Chamberlain started his Tariff Reform campaign, Winston opposed him in Parliament and the country. Finally he crossed the floor of the House to join his friend Lloyd George in the Liberal Party.

The Tariff Reform controversy split the Tory Party and by the end of 1905 the Government resigned. The Liberals swept the country in the 1906 General Election. Churchill was returned as Liberal Member for North-West Manchester. He became Under-Secretary for the Colonies, and piloted through the Commons the scheme for giving the Transvaal self-government. In 1908 he moved on to the Board of Trade, following Lloyd George, who had become Chancellor. Facing re-election, he lost his seat at Manchester but got in for Dundee. More than this; he met Miss Clementine Hozier, a granddaughter of the Countess of Airlie, who lived in his new constituency. The two fell in love and got married; and, in Winston's own words, they lived happily ever afterwards.

In 1910, Churchill became Home Secretary. He brought in the Coal Mines Act to improve safety provisions and set up pit head baths at the mines. He also carried through the unemployment insurance sections of Lloyd George's national insurance scheme. In 1911 he got the chance to smell powder again, when an anarchist gangster, Peter the Painter, and his party of gunmen were cornered in Sydney Street after shooting several policemen. The Scots Guards were summoned to the siege and Winston dashed to the spot to superintend the fight.

In November, 1911, he took over the Admiralty from McKenna, and with the aid of Admiral Fisher he set to work to equip the country with battleships. Scenting danger, Churchill in the summer of 1914 arranged a big naval rally and then kept the fleet on an active service footing without Cabinet authority. When the First World War came, the British Navy, thanks to Churchill, was ready. In the first few months the oceans were swept clear of German vessels and every hostile warship was either sunk or bottled up in enemy harbours.

War was Churchill's native air, and he plunged joyously into the struggle. He organized the Royal Naval Air Service to defend Britain's coasts, and directed the unsuccessful defence of Antwerp which checked the Germans advancing towards the French Channel ports. Then he planned an amphibious attack on Turkey through the Dardanelles, but Kitchener would not spare the men and the Navy had to bear the brunt of the attack. Their attempt failed and Churchill got the blame. When the first Coalition Government was set up in May, 1915, the Tories insisted on driving Churchill from the Admiralty into the ineffective post of Chancellor of the Duchy of Lancaster.

He soon resigned and applied for a command in the Expeditionary Force. On arrival in France he was sent to the Grenadier Guards, who looked on him as a "damned politician" and gave him a chilling reception. One general summoned him to a rendezvous in order to enjoy being saluted by a cabinet minister. While Churchill was keeping his appointment, his empty dugout was obliterated by a shell!

Presently he was made colonel of the 6th Royal Scots Fusiliers, and enjoyed himself in the front line, where he had various hairs-breadth escapes. But in May his battalion was fused with another and he was without a job; so he returned to Westminster.

When at the end of 1916 Lloyd George became Premier, he wanted to bring Churchill in, but at first the Tories would not hear of it. In July, 1917, however, Lloyd George made Churchill Minister of Munitions. At the end of the war, he took over the War Office to superintend demobilization. He also used this position to support the White Russian forces in Russia against the Bolsheviks, which made him as unpopular with the left wing of politicians as he already was with the right!

The Coalition fell in October, 1922, and in the election that followed, Churchill lost his seat. He failed to get back in the 1923 election, and was furious when the Liberal Party supported the Labour Party and put it in office. Although a social reformer, he was always violently anti-Socialist, and he now swung back towards the Tories. He unsuccessfully fought a by-election at Westminster in February, 1924, as a Constitutionalist, and was returned at the General Election in the autumn at Epping as a supporter of the Tory Party. The Tories won the election, and Churchill became Chancellor of the Exchequer.

In the following year he unwisely restored the Gold Standard. An early result was the coal stoppage and the general strike of 1926. Churchill rather enjoyed this affair, for he ran the *British Gazette*, and sat in state in the editor's chair of the *Morning Post*—the paper for which he had once been a war reporter.

At the 1929 election the Government fell and Labour again took office. Churchill did not attempt to conceal his poor opinion of Ramsay MacDonald, and he also quarrelled with Baldwin about the Round Table Conference which was discussing Indian self-government. So when under stress of the financial crisis of 1931 the National Government was set up, he was left out. He spent his unwelcome leisure in writing books, building walls and painting pictures. He was a master craftsman in all three fields. His history of the First World War and his life of Marlborough are treasured by the reading public. His paintings, signed "Charles Morin," were exhibited in Paris and fetched good prices.

During those dismal years of "appeasement" which followed, Churchill spoke repeatedly in Parliament and in the country, appealing for genuine support of the League of Nations and for maintenance of Britain's military strength in readiness to resist aggression. His pleas and warnings fell on deaf ears. When in February, 1938, Chamberlain drove Eden from the Foreign Office, Winston declared: "I predict that the day will come . . . when you will have to make a stand, and I pray God that when that day comes we may not . . . have to make that stand *alone*!"

In September, 1939, his prediction was fulfilled and Britain had to make a stand. Chamberlain at once reconstructed his government, and to the delight of the public put Churchill back at the Admiralty. During the first six months of the war, the Navy did the only real fighting. The Air Force was dropping, not bombs, but pamphlets, and the Army waited in French trenches for the Germans to attack. But at sea the U-boats were hunted down, the *Graf Spee* was sunk, and the prison ship *Altmark* raided in a Norwegian fiord, where the British captives aboard her heard the welcome shout: "The Navy is here!"

Chamberlain was not a fighter, and when the Germans invaded Denmark and Norway, his nerveless and hesitant handling of the situation dismayed the country. Many of his own supporters turned on him in Parliament, and when the news came that the Germans had invaded Holland and Belgium, he resigned and on May 11, 1940, Winston Churchill became Prime Minister.

He inherited an appalling situation. The British and French forces advancing to the aid of the Belgians and Dutch were split in two by a massive German thrust across the Ardennes. Holland surrendered in four days, and Belgium a fortnight later. In his first speech to the House, Churchill declared: "I have nothing to offer but blood, tears, toil and sweat!" But he spoke to the heart of the nation, which welcomed his tone of grim, unyielding defiance.

Before the end of the month, the British Expeditionary Force was penned against Dunkirk, and its destruction seemed inevitable. But there followed the "miracle of Dunkirk," in which nearly nine-tenths of the Army was rescued by a fleet of small craft. France crumbled, and although, in a last desperate effort to rally her leaders, Churchill offered them a union with Britain, they surrendered by mid-June. Churchill voiced the nation's spirit in a broadcast address that registered her unconquerable determination:

> "We shall fight on the beaches, we shall fight on the landing-grounds, we shall fight in the fields and in the streets; and even if, which I do not for a moment believe, this island or a large part of it were subjugated and starving, then our Empire beyond the seas, armed and guarded by the British Fleet, would carry on the struggle until in God's good time the New World, with all

its power and might, steps forth to the rescue and liberation of the Old!"

Britain at this stage stood all alone, for Mussolini had brought Italy in on Germany's side, and the whole resources of Western Europe were at Hitler's disposal. Now came the Battle of Britain, when the Nazi aircraft swarmed across to prepare the way for a German invasion. They were brought down in hundreds by the far smaller R.A.F. fighter force. "Never in the field of human conflict," said Churchill in one of those living phrases he had the gift of coining, "was so much owed by so many to so few!"

With far-sighted strategy he took the risk of sending all the tanks and guns he could muster to Egypt to save the Suez Canal from falling into Hitler's grip, though Britain herself was threatened with invasion. When in June, 1941, Hitler turned on Russia, Churchill laid aside his long antagonism to Bolshevism and promised full support for the Soviet. He met President Roosevelt in mid-Atlantic to sign with him the Atlantic Charter, setting out the democratic basis for the world's future. Before the end of the year, the Japanese attacked Pearl Harbour and the United States found herself drawn into the war. Thenceforward, Churchill and Roosevelt met constantly and together planned their strategy.

In August, 1942, Churchill placed Alexander and Montgomery in charge of the North African campaign. October brought the victory of El Alamein, the turning point of the war. Rommel and his Italo-German forces were sent flying, and on November 8 an Anglo-American expedition landed in North Africa. From this time the enemy were almost continually in retreat till the end.

Churchill steadily resisted the clamour for a "Second Front" until his elaborate plans were ready. On June 6, 1944, the blow fell where the Germans did not expect it, on an open Normandy beach, which was turned overnight into an artificial harbour. British and American troops streamed across, and after some months of bitter fighting, broke the German resistance in the north, while another landing, watched by Churchill, was made near Marseilles. In April, 1945, the German armies were surrendering one after the other, and by May 8 the war in Europe was over and wildly enthusiastic crowds were cheering Churchill as their hero leader in the conflict.

This was the supreme moment in his career. The Tory Party's organizers, knowing that he thought of retiring when peace came, persuaded him to hold a General Election before the war with Japan was ended, hoping the magic of his reputation might win them a victory. But the country had not forgiven the Tories for the shameful record of the National Government, and Churchill's election broadcasts describing the horrors of Socialism seemed a dismal anti-climax to his heroic wartime utterances. Labour won with a big majority, and Clement Attlee became Premier. For Churchill's great services King George VI proposed to honour him by conferring a knighthood, but this Mr. Churchill took the unusual course of declining, since it might have been interpreted as marking an end to his political aspirations.

For over six years Churchill led the parliamentary Opposition to two Labour governments, receiving his reward when his party was returned to power in 1951 and he became once more Prime Minister.

In 1953, when Mr. Churchill was yet Prime Minister, he received at the hands of Queen Elizabeth II that honour which her father had proposed and became a Knight of the Garter.

But the stress of the war years and the political struggle which followed had taken their toll of his health, and he resigned office in 1955, a few months after his eightieth birthday celebrations. He remained in Parliament, much the elder statesman, until the election of 1964; only then did he take his full farewell of public life.

Whatever his vicissitudes as Party leader in domestic politics, Britain has known no greater leader in time of war. Sir Winston Churchill will go down in history as a soldier-citizen whose courage and eloquence sustained and inspired the people in their darkest hour, and whose many-sided genius brought them through to victory.

Churchill the writer would have claimed immortality even if Churchill the leader had not. He received the Nobel Prize for Literature in 1953, the year before the sixth and final volume of *The Second World War* appeared. His four-volume *A History of the English-Speaking Peoples* was published during the years of retirement. And if both authorship and statesmanship should fail him in the eyes of posterity, he has left a noble monument in his foundation of Churchill College, Cambridge.

Churchill died in January, 1965, in his ninety-first year. For three days he lay in state at Westminster, while the people came, passing endlessly by, in silent homage. On the fourth day, his funeral procession, in all its majesty of a nation's sorrow, was one of the most deeply moving spectacles of our age.

INDEX